per Tibor W

con tanto piacere di vederlo
in sede

Sett. 1986

[illegible]

NORTH CAROLINA STUDIES IN THE
ROMANCE LANGUAGES AND LITERATURES

ESSAYS; TEXTS, TEXTUAL STUDIES
AND TRANSLATIONS; SYMPOSIA

Other publications of the Department: *Estudios de Hispanófila, Hispanófila Romance Notes*

Distributed by:

INTERNATIONAL SCHOLARLY BOOK SERVICE, INC.
P. O. BOX 4347
Portland, Oregon 97208
U. S. A.

Francis Petrarch, six centuries later.
(North Carolina studies in the Romance languages and literatures. Symposia ; 3)
English, French, or Italian.
Includes bibliographical references.
1. Petrarca, Francesco, 1304-1374—Congresses.
I. Scaglione, Aldo D. II. Series.
PQ4504.F74 851'.1 [B] 75-6983
ISBN 0-88438-953-7

NORTH CAROLINA STUDIES IN THE ROMANCE LANGUAGES AND LITERATURES: SYMPOSIA, 3

FRANCIS PETRARCH, SIX CENTURIES LATER

A SYMPOSIUM

FRANCIS PETRARCH, SIX CENTURIES LATER
A SYMPOSIUM

Edited by ALDO SCAGLIONE

NORTH CAROLINA STUDIES IN THE ROMANCE LANGUAGES AND LITERATURES: SYMPOSIA, 3

DEPARTMENT OF ROMANCE LANGUAGES
UNIVERSITY OF NORTH CAROLINA
CHAPEL HILL
and THE NEWBERRY LIBRARY
CHICAGO
1975

Printed by The Seeman Printery
A Division of Fisher-Harrison Corporation
Durham, North Carolina
United States of America

TABLE OF CONTENTS

ILLUSTRATIONS

FOREWORD

Four of the essays in this miscellany, namely, together with my own, those by Professors Chiappelli, Kohl, and Picchio Simonelli, were read in abridged form at the annual Renaissance Conference held at the Newberry Library on May 4, 1974.

The present volume is jointly sponsored by the Newberry Library and the Department of Romance Languages of the University of North Carolina at Chapel Hill.

I had thought it appropriate that the Newberry, as the outstanding research collection in the area of the Continental Renaissance and history of Humanism, should honor the sixth centennial of the death of "the prince of Humanists" by dedicating to him its annual Conference along with a special exhibit. The Librarian, Dr. Lawrence W. Towner, as well as his associates John A. Tedeschi and James H. Wells, promptly responded to my suggestion and asked me to organize and chair such a program. This publication is an outgrowth of that idea.

Concomitantly, the Chairman of the Department of Romance Languages of U.N.C., Professor Jacques Hardré, agreed to include the volume in our departmental Series as part of our Department's celebration of the Bard of Arezzo, which has comprised a public program held on March 19, 1974 on the U.N.C. campus. The program was flanked by a special exhibit of manuscripts and rare books from the holdings of the Wilson Library of U.N.C. and the Duke University Library, organized under the aegis of the Curator of our Rare Book Collection, Dr. Lawrence F. London.

A. S.

I

PETRARCA 1974: A SKETCH FOR A PORTRAIT*

by Aldo Scaglione
University of North Carolina (Chapel Hill)

1. Petrarch's as an immediate success story; 2. The hero of literature and the diplomat of letters; 3. "The first modern man"; 4. The discovery of the dialectic of the psyche; 5. Relativism and subjectivism; 6. Our global view of the man and his work; 7. "Sincerity" and literariness; 8. Unsystematic yet intellectual; 9. Literature as a way of life; 10. Individualism and independence; 11. An example of the *literatus* as a good man; 12. Petrarch's deep presence.

1. We are somewhat tired of centennials, yet here we are about to celebrate another, one which, of course, seems especially justified. We are celebrating the middle term in the close succession of the "Three Florentine Crowns," and although the centennial of the first Crown, Dante's in '65, is still very close by in our memories, we must make haste to be ready for Boccaccio's next year.

Should anyone ask in this year of our Lord 1974 what makes Francis Petrarch so especially deserving of our remembrance, the answer appears easy enough, though by no means simple.

One month after Petrarch's death, Salutati wrote his famous letter to Roberto Guidi, Count of Battifolle, in which he outdid any literary eulogy on record by extolling Petrarch above all the literary geniuses of antiquity put together. Petrarch was, he said, greater than Virgil because he was not only at least as excellent as he in poetry, but also great in eloquence (prose), where Virgil had left no mark. Therefore he was also greater than Homer, Hesiod, and Theocritus put together because Quintilian, who knew, had found Virgil greater than those "three princes of Greek poetry" (*Inst. orat.* X,I). And he was also greater than Cicero, who had failed in poetry, and Seneca, who was better than any Greek moralist. Thus Petrarch combined in himself the peaks of poetry,

* An abridged version of this introductory paper was also read at the joint annual meeting of the Renaissance Society of America and the Columbia University Seminar on the Renaissance, held on February 2, 1974 at Columbia University's Casa Italiana.

eloquence, and moral philosophy. Add to all this his excellence in his mother tongue, in which he surpassed even Dante. Petrarch was a whole Parnassus unto himself. Nor is this all, for even as a man he had no equal for his virtues among the living or the dead.

This panegyric, in which, with forebodings of many a product of humanistic verbal intemperance, Coluccio seemed determined to outdo the ancient topos of "outdoing," owed to Petrarch the worshipful trust in the power and right of eloquence or rhetoric.[1] One senses, however, a new departure in this tone of exaggeration, one that has left Petrarch behind, or has, so soon, betrayed his heritage and his highest lesson. For Petrarch, even in his rhetorically-bent exercises, very seldom left that exquisite middle tone, that measure of common sense and inner modesty, that was the best of his stylistic, literary and moral lesson. This divergence is especially surprising in a letter which, like this one by Salutati, is thoroughly textured on the example of Petrarch.[2]

The advantageous comparison of Petrarch to all preceding writers on the basis of his broad versatility and, specifically, his equal excellence in prose and verse and in all genres, returned in Bruni's *Dialogi,* in the mouth of Niccoli, and once again in Bruni's own *Life of Petrarch.*[3]

But Petrarch's fortune among the humanists had another, and opposite side too, exemplified at best, or at worst, by Niccoli, who in the words of Bruni's dialogue wanted Petrarch "set to slave labor" for not keeping his touted promises by not completing the *Africa.*[4] One is reminded of Ben Jonson's pronouncement "that Donne for not keeping of accent deserved hanging." These are, of course, cases of severity to the point of injustice, yet Niccoli had perhaps a better point than Jonson. Petrarch did leave behind a large number of incomplete works, and this is characteristic of his career.

What is missed in Niccoli's approach is something he could not have grasped, because only recent criticism has done justice to it, namely a

1. On the topos of outdoing see, above all, E. R. Curtius, *European Literature and the Latin Middle Ages,* trans. W. H. Trask (New York: Pantheon Books for The Bollingen Foundation, 1953), pp. 162-165 of Harper Torchbooks ed. (New York: Harper and Row, 1963).

2. Cf. Salutati, *Epistolario,* III, 15, ed. F. Novati, I (Rome, 1891), 176-187. See the consolatory arguments at the beginning and in the later part and compare them step by step with Petrarch's celebrated and moving *consolatoria* to Philippus Cavallicensis episcopus, *Fam.* II, 1.

3. *Dial.* II, toward end: see D. Thompson and A. F. Nagel, *The Three Crowns of Florence* (Harper paperback, 1972), p. 49; and A. Solerti, *Le vite di Dante, Petrarca e Boccaccio scritte fino al secolo XVI* (Rome, 1904): see transl. in Thompson and Nagel, *The Three Crowns of Florence,* pp. 78-79.

4. Thompson-Nagel, p. 37: Book I of Bruni's *Dialogues.*

full appreciation of Petrarch's peculiar method of work, his open-ended composition, his sense of the artifact as perfectible *ad infinitum*. His difficulty in completing his works is a symptom of a new emphasis on perfection, conceived as gradually-achieved mastery of the subject by total control of the emotions to be expressed, "distancing" from their urgency, and exploitation of all the means afforded by art. This is Petrarch's poetics, a new "classicism" which again made him a master of a particular kind of literature for centuries to come.

2. But I am anticipating. What kind of a man, we might ask, was this who so soon after his death, indeed during his own lifetime, became a legend by persuading his audience of his unique, unprecedented greatness? In what senses was his fame deserved? The first point that imposes itself to our attention has already been introduced by the preceding remarks. Petrarch was a hero of literature, in a sense the greatest "hero" in the literary annals.

Now every age has its heroes, and so has every type of society. But before Petrarch there had never been a time when public attention was seriously focussed on literature as such, in a central way. Even ancient Greece does not afford such precedents. Homer had become the paradigm of all greatness to the Greeks, who hinged their *paideia* upon him and started their children's elementary education with the reading of the *Iliad*. But Homer was for them, rather than a poet as we see him, a master of all wisdom, and, indeed, science, a teacher of moral and political values as well as of all naturalistic and even professional knowledge. When ideals of *paideia* became diversified and controversial, there was a clash between education for public oratory (literature as legal and political training, i.e. rhetoric with the Sophists, who won the competition for organizing the school curricula) and education as a search for truth (philosophy with the Socratic school, which essentially lost). As to the Romans, more than in literature they were of course interested in law, administration, engineering, and warfare. In the Middle Ages the writer and the artist, when not anonymous, were clearly overshadowed by the saint, who replaced in popular imagination the philosopher, the orator, or the political and military leader of antiquity. But Renaissance Italy became the land of the artist and of the man of letters. After having been relegated to the collective ranks of the manual professions, the representatives of the once "mechanical" arts were made so bold by their successes that they could naturally deal with popes and emperors as equals, as Michelangelo and even an Aretino did. But first came Petrarch. Of course he had been preceded by Dante, yet that overpowering genius could not even manage to persuade his government to drop some trumped-up charges and recall him with honor by virtue of his never-before and never-again surpassed poem. Furthermore, his peers insisted on praising him as some sort of poetic philosopher or, more specifically, *poeta-theologus.*

With Petrarch it was a new, and rather clear situation, and it was he who brought it about, since he alone could perform the miracle. One saw a whole society, throughout Italy and Europe, hang from the lips of this writer-poet. He was their hero, meaning that they thought that he, because he was the greatest man of letters, was by definition and by necessity the best, best-equipped and most appropriate man for anything. Even for politics and diplomacy. Popes, though chided by him as unworthy and corrupt; emperors, though rebuked by him as was Charles IV of Bohemia, who could not get him to inscribe his *De viris illustribus* to him because Petrarch thought he was not, in 1354, illustrious enough for that;[5] governments, though spurned by him as his own legitimate government was, Florence, who could not persuade him to show himself a good citizen by taking up residence there when invited: all potentates vied with one another to secure his allegiance and his services. Most times he politely but firmly declined in order to preserve his independence and his sacred privacy—his cherished *solitudo*—, but when he accepted, it mattered not whether his diplomatic services practically ended in failure, as in the peace mission from Genoa to Venice. He was still wanted and sought, unconditionally. If *he* failed, who could succeed? The time would come when, in the midst of most destructive wars of politics and religion, of economic and spiritual turmoil, the Italians became so manifestly engrossed with their *literati* that they would fight, maim and kill just as easily for a dispute on how to gloss a mediocre poem as for any most serious cause practical or moral, as when armed bands on both sides of the quarrel between Caro and Castelvetro or some such writer roamed the streets.

The man who had so placed the *literatus* at the center of his society was none other than Petrarch. Of course Italy was ready for it, or it could not have happened, but it did happen only because Petrarch came along. One of the devoted Petrarch scholars of our time has said that Petrarch "was (and I mean the phrase in no disparaging way) the best salesman of literature that the world has yet seen."[6] I would rather say

5. See *Fam.* XIX, 3, § 13, text in Th. Mommsen, *Medieval and Renaissance studies* (Ithaca, 1959), p. 137, and the whole letter translated in M. Bishop, *Letters from Petrarch* (Bloomington-London, 1966), p. 157.

6. T. G. Bergin, *Petrarch* (New York: Twayne, 1970), p. 191.

that he was the greatest "diplomat of the republic of letters." "Diplomat" because his salesmanship was due in large part to his unique personal charm—and this marked another difference with Dante, who of course was right in scolding the whole world but who made no visible effort to persuade them nicely that they deserved being scolded. "Of the republic of letters" I have said because he was the main force in bringing about precisely that, a movement that crossed social, political, and even national boundaries and brought all European men of literary learning together in the belief that civilization rested on culture, and that culture was nourished by reading and studying all good books of antiquity and of Christianity. It was the cosmopolitan ideal of Humanism, invented, in that form and as a widely successful venture, by Petrarch.

Thus Petrarch was not only a superb salesman of literature, he was a master of self-advertisement, who managed to turn his person into a true object of cult. As a telling anecdote among many, remember the visit to his fan, Enrico Capra, who had insistently begged for the honor of having the great poet in his house in Bergamo. The visit became a street pageant and a triumph worthy of a victorious Roman general, with officials and a throng of admiring public paying homage to him on his way to and from the house. In the meantime, as he describes the scene, he appears to have moved about as graciously and discreetly as a god honored by his awed devotees.[7]

Over the succeeding centuries Europe witnessed one of the widest, subtlest, most enduring cases of personal influence in the history of literature. The impact of Petrarch is comparable only to that of Cicero and Virgil, and clearly second only to that of Plato in another sense. Indeed the story of Petrarch's impact goes beyond Petrarchism, since his actual "presence" is broader, deeper, and more varied than his influence through overt imitation.[8] Even though he moved in the wake of the Provençal troubadours, both for form and content, it is with him that begins the history of modern lyrical poetry not only in Italy but in Spain, in France, in Germany, even in England.

3. Ever since the early nineteenth century Petrarch has been repeatedly hailed as "the first modern man." Modern for his curiosity toward

7. *Fam.* XXI, 11, also available in the Ricciardi ed. of Petrarch's *Prose* (Milan, 1955), p. 1000.

8. Bergin's monograph already cited has an excellent conclusive chapter on "The Enduring Petrarch," pp. 180-191. Other scholars, like Leonard Forster, *The Icy Fire: Five studies in European Petrarchism* (Cambridge, Engl.: The University Press, 1969) have also laid stress on the peculiarities of Petrarch's discovery of a particular kind of chivalry. See my discussion in § 12 below.

the world and all peoples, since he did not only travel for practical reasons and to seek out forgotten codices, but while travelling he kept his observing eyes well open on things and men. Modern for his individualism, which made him seek personal glory even to the extent of arranging for his coronation on the Roman Capitol. Modern for his secularism, whereby he could even turn religious imagery to secular uses (see, e.g., sonnet 16). If the excessive lines in this "romantic" portrait of the man have been challenged and corrected by recent criticism, they nevertheless remain valid in substance. True, he did not climb Mount Ventoux for the sheer enjoyment of the uplifting experience of altitude, as a modern alpinist, but to contemplate the world from a distance and from a moral elevation. Yet he did climb it and produced the first record of such a feat achieved for non-practical reasons. Furthermore, the ascetic meditations on Augustine's text once on the summit were largely an afterthought, since that part of his text stems from later revision and elaboration. As to his "modern" feeling for nature, Bosco, for one, has questioned the notion that Petrarch might have truly enjoyed Vaucluse in a romantic way, for its horrid beauty.[9] Perhaps it would be more cautious to suggest that he was unable to represent that horrid beauty in his writings because his representation of the place leans on literary precedents, like all his production, and no such feeling for sheer nature could be found recorded in preceding literature. As to his own personal reaction to the site, he must have enjoyed it for what it actually is, or else he would have chosen a very different place. Anyone who has seen Vaucluse must have difficulty in believing that Petrarch could see it as a classical landscape, and that anybody but Petrarch could have discovered and loved such an unusual site.

The most important part of his "modernity" lies, however, in his unpredecented concentration on the psyche. Augustine had produced in his *Confessions* a total analysis of the self, which taught Petrarch much, but that discovery of the individual soul was aimed at the finding of God in the man, not at extolling individuality as such—what else could this have been but precisely that sin of pride the book was aimed to expose and eradicate? Petrarch, on the other hand, makes it a life-long career to concentrate his and his audience's attention on his individual self. Nothing else really matters to him as a deserving subject. Even the study of other *viri illustres* from antiquity is, in the end, aimed at providing patterns and models of personal, moral greatness for him and his readers, since the ancient earthly virtues are understood as foundation of all greatness, even Christian.

9. U. Bosco, *Petrarca* (Bari, 1946, 1961[2]), p. 210.

Petrarch is one of the great egotists of all times, ranking with Cellini, Montaigne, Alfieri, Rousseau, and Proust, whose long distinguished line he chronologically opens. We can pick one of his letters as a gem of the "fine art of egotism," namely the one where he congratulates Guido Gonzaga for his true love for Petrarch because he had written to an emissary in Avignon to inquire not about affairs of state, but about Petrarch's personal condition. Of course, he admits, he does deserve so much homage, even if, looking for reassurance, he slyly and diplomatically demurs: "How can I presume to be liked, I who can hardly please myself?"[10] And as usual he surrounds this historical episode of true friendship with literary reminiscences, for inspiration and support. Thus did Augustus behave toward Virgil and Horace, giving a sublime example of that love which keeps the cosmos from chaos and makes the unequal equal. For once he does not hesitate to echo Dante's *amor ch'a nullo amato amar perdona* with *amantem fideliter vix patitur non amari* (l. 15) and, again, *ut amanti vicem referas, amor cogit* (l. 20). Guido can then feel reassured that his true love is not wasted.

In this making of himself a center of attention for the whole world he was, again, successful even with posterity. His method of recording the minutest details of his life and literary activity, even to the extent of dating with place, day and hour, some revisions of single words in his manuscripts, is responsible for our being so well informed on him, whereas for many a first rate author of even centuries later we know little more than name and birthplace—think of Cervantes and Shakespeare, for example. This is another typical Italian achievement, since we are dealing with a consistent national tradition of paying attention to, and keeping accurate records of, the doings of important literary figures, starting at least with Dante. Yet for centuries Petrarch will stand out for the uniqueness of intensity and breadth in this method of leaving records.

4. Finally, the human condition that is thus discovered by Petrarch's unending, unrelenting, merciless search is "modern" because it embodies the principle of dialectics, or to put it with Freud, the principle that the psyche ignores the rule of non-contradiction. The human condition is inherently ambiguous, ambivalent, wavering, dramatic, conflicting, and conflict must not only be comprehended but accepted. Much has been said on this Petrarchan discovery and acceptance of the "conflict." Bosco's penetrating analysis of the question concludes with the char-

10. *Fam.* III, 11; Rossi I, pp. 127-128: "Quomodo enim sperem me aliis placiturum, qui mihi ipse non placeo?"

acterization of Petrarch's predicament as a conflict between his aspiration toward the absolute and his ever-resurgent awareness of the relative.[11] Bosco has also shrewdly pointed out the "secular," non-medieval nature of this conflict, in the sense that it is only another side of that inborn feeling of the ephemeral quality of all things (*il sentimento della caducità o labilità universale*) which, far from deriving either from an involvement in serious religious meditation or from the experience of his love for Laura, pre-dates both, since, as his youthful *Familiaris* I, 3 reveals, it was with him from his youth. Rather than finding its roots in his religion or his unhappy enamorment, it invests both of itself and conditions them.[12] It may seem strange that this sense of the instability of things (everything, not only the object of our desires, but our desires themselves), which returned in a new context in the *Zeitgeist* of the Baroque, has not been invoked as a conspicuous Petrarchan heritage by the students of Petrarchism. And yet the particular direction which this sense takes in Petrarch applies well to the Baroque: while Dante moved from the eternal to the ephemeral (*al caduco dall'eterno,* in Bosco's words), Petrarch moved from the ephemeral to the eternal.[13] Dante's love for Beatrice was directly inspired by God, whereas Petrarch's feelings for Laura have no other root than in the defective heart of man; and God represents here the other term of the contrast, the enemy, as it were, whose inescapable presence is disquieting and forbidding.[14] One is reminded of Croce's perceptive analysis: " 'First modern poet,' then, in the sense that one first witnesses in him the aspiration to an unattainable happiness through the love of a creature . . . ; happiness pursued in sentiment and passion, that is in the particular unredeemed into the universal but, instead, itself erected to the status of a universal; with the despair and the melancholy that this entails, and with the constant sense of caducity and death and decay."[15]

11. U. Bosco, *Petrarca,* op. cit., all of Part One, and most explicitly p. 86: "il poeta non conquista né l'umano né il divino; come non l'appaga quello, con la riconosciuta sua caducità e vanità, cosí questo non lo placa compiutamente, in quanto importa un'eroica rinunzia, che il poeta non sa consumare." ". . . l'oscura coscienza . . . di non potersi contentare mai, effettivamente, di Dio."

12. See Bosco, op. cit., ch. on "Il senso della labilità." Cf., also, *Fam.* XXIV, 1.

13. Bosco, p. 63.

14. Bosco, p. 30.

15. B. Croce, *Poesia popolare e poesia d'arte* (Bari, 1933), p. 71: " 'Primo poeta moderno,' dunque, in questo senso che in lui pel primo si vede l'aspirazione a un'inconseguibile beatitudine nell'amore di una creatura . . .: la felicità ricercata nel sentimento e nella passione, ossia nel particolare non redento nell'universale ma posto esso come l'universale; con la disperazione e la malinconia che a ciò segue o s'accompagna, col senso continuo della caducità e della morte e del disfacimento." Quoted by Bosco, p. 57.

This state of mind gave Petrarch a Heraclitean view of the world. Indeed he himself, always the best analyst and commentator of himself, referred to Heraclitus' notion of reality as a state of warfare, *pólemos:* "illud Heracliti: omnia secundum litem fieri" (*De remediis,* preface to Book II). In his 1924 doctoral dissertation Antonio Viscardi found that Petrarch had discovered in the *Secretum* that the war originated within him, and that if interior peace could be attained, external peace would also follow. But the latter was not forthcoming because the former was not. Thus the material of the *Canzoniere* was already in the *Secretum.*[16] Both in the *Secretum* and in the *Canzoniere* the inescapable contradictions of man's existential predicament are laid bare, analyzed, and practically accepted due to the author's inability to settle them by a choice, since his personal make-up is frankly recognized as lacking in will-power.

When he echoes Augustine's *Inquietum est cor nostrum, donec requiescat in te*—'our heart is restless, longing to rest in you, O Lord'— in his *Est inexpletum quoddam in praecordiis meis semper*—'there is something ever unfulfilled deep in my heart'—, we immediately perceive that it is no longer the same thing, because Petrarch is modern in that his religion is without faith, and in this he is so unlike Augustine. He longs after God and discovers this longing for the infinite as the secret of the human condition, yet he never attains God and remains merely human because his longing is by definition *inexpletum,* an unfulfilled *Sehnsucht.* We are compelled to use this German romantic term because this is, even more than the modern, the romantic side of Petrarch, which in fact appealed to his nineteenth-century readers, like, foremost among them, Leopardi. It is also the secret of his deep, inexhaustible appeal to the Renaissance and Baroque generations of Petrarchists. If he towers so high above his followers it is because even while they were utterly conquered by his myth, the convention he consecrated and canonized, of the necessity for a noble passion to remain frustrated in order to remain noble, they could not reproduce the deep message of that love story. Because of this redeeming quality underlying a sinful love, his was the dream of a love that survives the demise of passion.[17]

5. Petrarch's correspondence is as celebrated as it is little read. It goes without saying that it is a rich mine of revelations on his psycho-

16. See Viscardi, *Petrarca e Petrarchismo,* lectures for the academic year 1965-66 (Milan: La Goliardica, 1966), pp. 135-138.

17. Cf. Croce's beautiful essay "Il sogno dell'amore sopravvivente alla passione," *Poesia antica e moderna* (Bari, 1941), pp. 162-165, a masterly commentary on the sonnet *Tutta la mia fiorita e verde etade.*

logical and intellectual make-up. A point I wish to stress is that it presents insights which suggestively move in the direction of the most admired master of introspection of the whole Renaissance, that is Montaigne, and I shall provide an example.

Fam. II, 2 (Rossi I, pp. 62-6) proposes to console the recipient for the death of a dear friend, and since the grief is reported to linger most bitterly on the circumstance of an unburied death in the waters of the Egyptian sea, Petrarch proceeds to offer an attempt to dispel this prejudice, as he sees it, by a critique of our veneration for one burial rite rather than another. It is wrong and unphilosophical, he claims, to judge situations by the force of popular custom rather than by reason. Let us think of Arthemisia queen of Caria, who thought of expressing her extreme love for her dead husband by giving him no other tomb than her own body: she did so by dissolving his ashes in her beverages little by little. Some tribes are wont to feed their dead to animals, especially dogs. Even if we remain within the boundaries of Italy, our own land, we will do well to remember that the ancients first practiced inhumation, then cremation. The Christians restored the former, but who is to say which is better? (§ 19.) Such practices are nothing but customs, and make no objective difference. Remember "Lambas de Auria," captain of the Genoese fleet in the first battle with Venice, who congratulated his son, dead in that battle, for having the best possible burial, and threw him into the sea with his own hands. Briefly, *plus usum posse quam rationem* is a fact of life, but it is the wrong criterion for our judgment (§ 11, p. 64, citing Cicero). *Nimirum decursu temporis mutati mores opiniones hominum alternant* (§ 18, p. 66). Then, in terms reminiscent of the logical thrust of the previous letter, the magnificent *consolatoria* to the bishop Philippe de Cavaillon for the death of his brother: "quicquid in hac vita patimur molesti, non tam ex ipsa rerum natura, quam ex nostre mentis imbecillitate sive, ut eorum [i.e. illustrium philosophorum] utar verbis, ex opinionum perversitate procedere" (§ 6, p. 63)—to say it with Shakespeare, "There is nothing either good or bad but thinking makes it so" (*Hamlet* II, ii).

Petrarch's deep and obsessive sense of the ephemeral nature of things and events makes of him, rather than a skeptic, a sort of relativist and subjectivist *avant-la-lettre*. Yet, in a significant dialectical turn, when all is said and done, the need for objectivism makes a final appearance where the author concludes with the admonition: "veritatem rerum non vulgi rumoribus, sed insita ratione quesieris . . ." (§ 20, p. 66). We can thus say that Petrarch's world remains objective in a transcendental sense. There is a firm, stable truth, but it is above the phenomena of this world and of our history, it is in God. If in the course of the discussion our mind has time and again been prompted to move ahead to Montaigne "On Cannibals," we also know, now, what separates the two authors. And since critics keep proposing the great master of the *Essais* as the initiator of the techniques of self-analysis which anticipate the great novelists of the twentieth century, especially Proust and Joyce, we ought to feel bound to admit that on a broader scale (and in a less direct line) Petrarch has a high priority to that claim.[18] Petrarch manages to display his "mentalism" even further in the following letter, where he resumes the subject and adds: "As a matter of fact even in all other kinds of fears and apprehensions you will find that no one is unhappy except him who makes himself so; thus it is greed, not scarcity of things, which makes the poor; thus in death, which is most like exile, what harms us is more our apprehension and distortion of opinion than the true hardship of the thing in itself."[19]

6. Morally, Petrarch's Weltanschauung is no longer medieval, as we have seen. Yet is does not belong *tout court* to the Renaissance. It could be more appropriately placed in the waning of the Middle Ages, as Huizinga has portrayed that spiritual climate. The poet is painfully aware of the vanity and the errors of the world. Yet, in his congenital acedia, he clings to this world without true hope of liberation. Although traditional criticism has been aware of these moral characteristics of Petrarch the man, it tended to relegate them to the Latin writer. Furthermore, since the *Canzoniere* so prominently held the center as Petrarch's only truly poetic work, his other writings were occasionally used, but mainly as tools subordinated to the lyrics. At variance with this tradition, the new criticism (say, after Croce) aims at the whole Petrarch, this being seen as the only way to understand properly even the *Canzoniere*. Thus the part is seen through the whole rather than the other way around. Croce still belonged to the prehistory, so to speak, of the new Petrarch scholarship because he still reduced Petrarch's poetry to the love element.[20] Now, instead, we tend to see the story of his love rather as an instance, almost a symbol of the broader cultural and aesthetic predicament that was Petrarch's. Laura is the relative that

18. Cf. R. A. Sayce, *The Essays of Montaigne: A critical exploration* (Evanston: Northwestern Univ. Press, 1973).

19. "Nam et in ceteris formidatarum rerum generibus invenies neminem esse miserum nisi qui se miserum fecit; sic pauperem non rerum paucitas sed cupiditas facit; sic in morte, que exilio simillima est, non tam rei ipsius asperitas, quam trepidatio et opinionis perversitas nocet. . . ." *Fam.* II, 3, § 3, ll. 17-21; Rossi I, p. 67.

20. See, e.g., Bosco's judgment to this effect, op. cit., p. 57. Cf. also p. 22.

awakes the awareness of the absolute; Laura and God are on opposite sides in front of the poet, and the love for Laura, as Augustine unequivocally puts it in the *Secretum,* is on the same level as the love for glory and for literature. Petrarch cannot make a choice because he feels as though he had discovered, as a law of the psyche, that good and bad cannot be sharply divided.

If we apply the "global" view in our approach to Petrarch and his work we find that this position of his not only conditions the *Canzoniere* and the *Secretum,* but even helps him, for instance, to approach and solve some of the thorniest problems of historiography in a more modern way than had ever been seen. Think only of his cautious and enlightened treatment of the figure of Caesar and his historical role, in the *De vita Caesaris.* It had been theretofore incumbent upon any observer of the Roman dictator's career to take a position for the founder of the divinely ordained and providentially willed Roman Empire or against the dictator who abrogated freedom in Rome. The former was basically the Orosius-Augustinian view of history shared as a matter of course by Dante, while the latter view corresponded to the republican libertarian tradition still firmly adhered to by Machiavelli and his Oricellari friends. Having briefed himself carefully on the accessible documents, and especially on the Ciceronian correspondence for what it revealed of the day-by-day crisis as seen from close, Petrarch no longer sees the situation as black or white, and cannot take a clear-cut position on a man who, he avers, was forced by circumstances to overcome or be destroyed by his equally unlibertarian enemies.

7. Petrarch's concern with the possibility of analyzing himself with absolute clarity and precision raises the historically interesting question of his "sincerity." The romantic readers felt disappointed by Petrarch's "lack of sincerity" at the same time that they were attracted by his pitiless uncovering of the disturbing depths of the psyche. Thus begins a modern, utterly "un-Petrarchan" way of looking at literature and art, ending in a new myth under which many of us are still laboring on several levels. The fact is that the romantic notion of sincerity simply makes little sense when applied to Petrarch. For the literary conventions which inform all his production, lyrical and other, and which he transmitted to posterity as the formal essence of "Petrarchism," do not constitute an attempt to cover up or disguise his true self. They are, rather, his way of keeping control of a troublesome personal subject matter by creating a safe, dignified distance between the observer as subject and the overwhelming passion, his own, as object. Never for

a moment is he trying to hide something unpleasant or unflattering in order to embellish his own image. He does not even need to do this, convinced as he is, and quite rightly so, that his personality is uniquely interesting and important.

He will therefore see to it that no relevant aspect of his personality is left unrecorded for posterity. He can speak quite candidly of his virtues and of his vices as well. He can reveal that he has contemplated suicide out of despondency—only to reject it because he is afraid of Hell (son. 36). He can frankly recall his genuine sense of shame at the thought of the "errors" that have made him ridiculous in the eyes of the people (son. 1). He is not only unhappy and melancholy and addicted to frequent crying, he is downright "afraid of himself" ("tal paura ho di ritrovarmi solo," "tal cordoglio e paura ho di me stesso"). With a pervasive sense of guilt he agrees with Augustine that we can only be unhappy by our own fault: "sine peccato nemo fit miser" (*Secretum*). He can go so far as to reveal that he has had to abandon several literary projects because they turned out to be above his forces—his genius is rather agile than strong ("Fuit enim mihi, ut corpus, sic ingenium magis pollens dexteritate quam viribus. Itaque multa mihi facilia cogitatu que executione difficilia pretermisi"—*Ep. posteritati*). Rather agile than strong. Since the abandoned or unfinished projects include, above all, the ones where he was following on the footsteps of the strong as well as agile mind of Dante, his redoubted predecessor and envied rival (we are entitled to think in this context of the *Trionfi,* where the attempt to frame a lyric within a powerful metaphysical structure ended in failure), it is clear how unsavory such an admission must have been to Petrarch. Yet he did not withhold it from his readers.

8. The question of mental strength deserves further elaboration. It has been remarked that Petrarchism, in and out of Italy, found its conditioning in the addition, among other ingredients, of something that Petrarch lacked, to wit a conspicuous reflexive aptitude.[21] This includes the specific neo-platonic framework which added a metaphysical dimension and turned Petrarch's imagery into a sort of loose but recognizable "system" of conceits. The poet of Laura had shied away from such superstructures and had even avoided the few but distinctive philosophico-scientific elements which the Stil Nuovo poets had introduced, such as the paraphernalia of "spirits," humors, and Aristotelian distinctions of mental faculties or functions. This was part

21. Cf. Contini, Introduction to the "N.U.E." edition of the *Canzoniere* (Torino: Einaudi, 1964), p. xxxiv: "le condizioni di questa fortuna . . . sono: quello che mancava a Petrarca, una notevole capacità riflessiva. . . ."

of Petrarch's methodical avoidance of concrete references to objects and events in order to build up an "abstractly" universal, timeless and spaceless ambiance. One can thus speak of the "elusiveness" (again Contini's word) of his language and imagery. His symbolic allusions were, by and large, taken more literally by his imitators, so that they lost some of their subtle charm even while they became more immediately recognizable and transmissible.

What makes Petrarch's language, style, and mental modes so characteristic is also, seen from another angle, a sign of an "organic weakness in methodical thinking," an attitude which contributed to Petrarch's lack of any appreciation for medieval scholastic.[22] Petrarch's rich personality escapes easy definition also because he was, after all, a "man without a center," as Bosco has put it, that is to say without a solid, articulate, complex system of rational principles. The *Trionfi* are a failure insofar as the planning of the Dante-oriented allegory necessitated a robust ideological framework, whereas the author of the *Secretum* bends down on moral self-analysis because he cannot solve his problems by drawing upon a set of objective beliefs outside himself.

Yet, once these necessary strictures have been clearly registered, one must go on to recognize Petrarch's *forma mentis,* of both the man and the author, as eminently intellectual, and this is the correct approach to a proper understanding of his poetics. He is the very opposite of the "romantic" kind of writer who sets value on the "expressive" function of poetry, and tries to keep his writings as close as possible to a "natural," "spontaneous," "sincere" representation of his states of mind as they occur within him. Feeling and emotion, even outright passion are the material of his writing, but art to him lies in the act of revision, abstraction, and ultimate control, to wit in a prolonged, methodical intervention of the intellect. He firmly believed, and his constant practice shows it, that revision should be enacted over a period of time at some remove from the first inspiration because, he used to say, intellectual control can best take place when the emotion is later remembered rather than while it is experienced or too soon thereafter. The material should be handed over to our mind by *memoria* rather than being acted on at the time of perception or close to it. It is the opposite of what Dante would seem to indicate to a romantic reader (but did not actually mean) when he defined his "new" poetics

22. Cf. G. Billanovich, *Petrarca letterato I: Lo scrittoio del Petrarca* (Rome, 1947), "Da Padova all'Europa," pp. 414-415: "debolezza organica per il pensiero metodico."

with the lines: "I' mi son un che quando / Amor mi spira, noto, ed a quel modo / che ditta dentro vo significando" (*Purg.* 24).

It is also in this light that one realizes how Petrarch's constant clinging to literary sources and filtering everything through literature does not in any real way detract from his sincerity or the authenticity of his feelings. Even in writing his autobiography it is natural and imperative for him to lean on Augustine's example, not to alter and distort the truth about himself but to make sure that he follows a meaningful, authoritatively tested pattern and does not stray into irrelevant trivialities. See the passage where he derives the testimony on his chastity from Augustine's *Confessions,* toward the beginning of the *Posteritati.*

While stressing his inherent intellectuality, I have said nothing yet about Petrarch as a "philosopher." It would be a long discourse, perhaps to be prefaced with a disquisition and consequent *prise de position* on the question, raised by several scholars and, negatively though authoritatively, by Gilson, on whether it is legitimate to place such literati as Petrarch, Salutati, Valla, Politian, and even Ficino and Pico, in short all of Humanism, within the history of philosophy proper. I shall only say that in his Invective against the Venetian Aristotelians (*De sui ipsius et multorum ignorantia*) Petrarch had suddenly and influentially broadened the philosophical horizon of the incipient Renaissance by admonishing that it is illegitimate to identify philosophy with Aristotle, that he was only one in a tradition of Greek thought which flowed richly before and after him, and that both his predecessors and successors must be read, were it only because Aristotle himself cannot be understood without them.

The history of philosophy would not be what it is, no matter how we look at it, without the introduction of a philological reading of Aristotle by such humanists as Bruni and Poliziano and many others, and more importantly without the introduction of Plato, in his genuine text, by humanists, starting in the grammar school of Manuel Chrysoloras at Florence. More significant still, it was the humanists who, precisely in the wake of Petrarch and his polemic against the dialecticians and the philosophers of nature, denied ultimate value to the scholastics not only because they were ignorant of letters and eloquence, but because in their striving to read all human problems in a nominalistic logical key, they necessarily lost sight of the complex concreteness of human values, and specifically of the ethical and political angle. It was in this manner that Petrarch's heritage worked powerfully toward the reinstatement of that crucial portion of both Aristotle's and Plato's writings, namely the ethical and political works. The Plato of the Renaissance will no longer be the Plato of the *Timaeus,* the physicist of medieval memory, but that of the *Phaedo* and *Phaedrus* and *Convivium,* and that of the *Republic* first translated by Chrysoloras. Likewise it was no longer the Aristotle of the *Organon* but that of the *Nicomachean ethics,* which passed from hand to hand from Bruni to Manetti, Acciaiuoli, and Ficino, and that of the *Poetics,* from Poliziano to Robortello and beyond.[23]

Furthermore, how can we avoid thinking of the heritage of Petrarch when we contemplate the Florentine circles' commitment to an ideal of *pia philosophia,* a harmony of antiquity and Christianity, a conciliation of Platonic mysticism and modern devotion? The ideal, in short, of Ficino, Pico, and Erasmus. Even on the level of aesthetic speculation, it was perhaps Boccaccio, Petrarch's most illustrious collaborator, who first underlined the "religious" meaning of poetry when he asserted that the first poets had been the first theologians, Homer preceding Plato and Aristotle in a way both chronological and logical.

9. Bosco has written some very fine pages on the literary substratum of all of Petrarch's work. One should not hesitate to say that literature is the substance of Petrarch's personality and life. He lives with books and through books, and never expresses anything that he has not found in literature. This constitutes one aspect of his "classicism" which the romantic-oriented reader finds hard to accept. The problem lies in the use we make of literature. Petrarch uses literature not as a substitute for experience, like someone who finds nothing to say within himself and has to borrow some subject matter from elsewhere. He uses it as part of the selective and controlling process which his method of composition demands. He used to say that imitation rightly practiced implies assimilating the authors' thoughts, never their words. But the thoughts were taken over by him only when they corresponded to his own, and thus confirmed the validity and worthiness of his own. Rediscovering your thoughts in a worthy author means that those particular thoughts have passed the test that discriminates between what is important and what is trivial, unworthy of being expressed. It is part of the selective process which makes our life meaningful and saves it from the chaos and anarchy of a formless multiplicity of experience.

23. See, on all this, the illuminating assessment by E. Garin, "Cultura filosofica toscana e veneta nel Quattrocento," in V. Branca, ed., *Umanesimo europeo e umanesimo veneziano.* Fondazione Giorgio Cini: Civiltà europea e civiltà veneziana, aspetti e problemi, 2 (Florence: Sansoni, 1963), pp. 11-30, esp. 19-20 and 23.

It is in this way that, beyond and above being such a peerless salesman of literature, Petrarch became the greatest example of the serious, integrated, necessary use of literature in order to produce new literature. Paradoxically, it was his emphasis on "literary literature" which, once deprived of its deep functionalism, became a most decisive impulse in moving Italian writers toward that empty literariness and academic quality which made them so inherently "unpopular" especially in the 250-odd years between Bembo and Muratori. On the other hand, and on a positive level, it also made Italy the land of literature *par excellence*.

Far from issuing from a bookish disposition, commerce with the *auctores* is to Petrarch a most vital experience. The letters to the ancients of *Fam.* XXIV are the most eloquent manifestation of this attitude, which remains eminently "human" and "real" because, for all the enthusiasm and awe which the ancients inspire in their newly found correspondent, he never forfeits the independence of his critical judgment. Thus in conversing with Cicero Petrarch praises and scolds (see the two sides of his attitude in the two letters to Cicero in *Fam.* XXIV), in a way that, while it throws light on Petrarch's idea of the necessary aloofness of the sage, also points up an interpretation of Cicero which may have had a decisive influence on the history of his image in western criticism. The traditional idea that Cicero was miscast as a politician, due to an indecisive, unpragmatic personality, does some injustice to the unfavorable circumstances of his career at the time of the direct clash between Caesar and Pompey, and may be in part a consequence of Petrarch's self-serving intervention. This way of establishing a live rapport with dead authors was certainly inspired in Petrarch by Cicero, if we only recall such passages as Cicero's *ad Fam.* IX, 1 (Cicero to M. T. Varro, 46 B.C., during his enforced retirement from public life):

> Know then that I have reconciled myself with my old friends, that is our books, although I had lost touch with them not out of disdain, but of a sense of shame for not having obeyed their teachings well enough when I, confiding in faithless partners, threw myself into the midst of great public troubles. Yet they forgive me, they call me back into our pristine habits, and they declare to me that you have been wiser than I for never departing from those habits.[24]

24. "Scito enim me . . . redisse cum veteribus amicis, id est cum libris nostris, in gratiam; etsi non idcirco eorum usum dimiseram, quod iis suscenserem, sed quod eorum me subpudebat; videbar enim mihi, cum me in res turbulentissimas infidelissimis sociis demisissem, praeceptis illorum non satis paruisse. Ignoscunt mihi [scil. *libri*], revocant in consuetudinem pristinam, teque, quod in ea permanseris, sapientiorem quam me dicunt fuisse."

Certainly Petrarch had such texts in mind when he wrote his *Epistola metrica* I, 6, 178-226, or *Fam.* III, 8, ll. 14-24 to Joannes Anchiseus on his passion for books: "... the pleasure derived from books reaches to the marrow of our bones, since they converse with us, advise us and mingle with us with a certain live and pointed familiarity. . . ."[25] Or, in the preface to *De remediis utriusque fortunae:* "How grateful, pray, must we be to the celebrated and tested writers who, although they lived in this world many centuries before us, still live, cohabit, and converse with us by the fruits of their divine minds and sacred achievements?"[26] Or, more explicitly still, his *Fam.* XV, 3: "Meanwhile in my mind I establish here (i.e. in Vaucluse) my own Rome, my Athens, my fatherland: I often gather together into this tiny valley from all places and all ages, all the friends I have or have had, and not only those contemporaries of mine I have tested through familiar association, but those who died many centuries before me, known to me only by benefit of letters, whose deeds and mind or life and character or style and wit I admire; and I converse with them with greater eagerness than I do with those who seem alive only to themselves."[27]

The humanists' intense cult for books stems directly from Petrarch's example. True enough, as just noted, by and large Petrarch's successors failed to carry out the master's lesson of making life out of literature and learning. Certainly an obdurate bookishness characterizes much of the humanistic tradition. But Petrarch's presence extends beyond the circles of his direct followers. Machiavelli should serve as an eloquent example. Think of the famous passage where, in his letter to Francesco Vettori of December 10, 1513, he describes how he converses with the ancient historians, who courteously answer all his questions, while he, fittingly dressed in his best clothes, sits with them, that is with their books before him, in his study, passing with them the best hours of his day.

25. "... libri medullitus delectant, colloquuntur, consulunt et viva quadam nobis atque arguta familiaritate iunguntur . . . ."

26. "Quanta, oro te, gratia claris et probatis scriptoribus est habenda qui multis ante nos seculis in terram versi, divinis ingeniis institutisque sanctissimis nobiscum vivunt, cohabitant, colloquuntur?"

27. "Interea equidem hic mihi Romam, hic Athenas, hic patriam ipsam mente constituo: hic omnes quos habeo amicos vel quos habui, nec tantum familiari convictu probatos et qui mecum vixerunt, sed qui multis ante me seculis abierunt, solo mihi cognitos beneficio literarum, quorum sive res gestas atque animum sive mores vitamque sive linguam et ingenium miror, ex omnibus locis atque omni evo in hanc exiguam vallem sepe contraho cupidiusque cum illis versor quam cum his qui sibi vivere videntur." *Fam.* XV, 3; Rossi III, p. 139. Cf. P. De Nolhac, *Pétrarque et l'humanisme,* esp. p. cited in B. T. Sozzi, *Petrarca,* p. 201.

10. While dealing above with Petrarch as a diplomat of the republic of letters I alluded to his personal talents for winning sympathy and getting along with people. There are traits in the moral portrait of this man that immediately strike the observer, and others that puzzle him and keep him wondering. We are easily convinced of the charismatic impact of his person, who won his contemporaries by his talents as well as by his charms, especially impressive when we inevitably contrast them with his "rival" Dante, then dead yet ever present in a very real sense, and present with the forbiddingly stern, unbending prosecutorial vigor of his "undiplomatic" personality. Petrarch was clearly of another mold, soft, mild, and in a sense even weak. But not weak in upholding his personal rights, as when he resigned himself to charges of "treason," in Boccaccio's words to him, for not yielding to the Florentine government's entreaties to take up residence in his "native" city and support her republican freedoms, rather than accept the corrupting hospitality of the Milanese Visconti, Florence's irreconcilable enemies and Italy's most fearsome tyrants. He loftily held his ground in spite of such pressures, which he could not quite understand because he felt he was serving no tyrant except on his own terms, in complete, genuine independence. So secure did he feel, hence so undeserving of the Florentines' accusations, that he could not get angry about Boccaccio's strong recriminations. His equanimity had the best of the situation in the end, since they remained the best of friends. But no one could fairly think of accusing Petrarch of hypocrisy when he alluded to this independence toward the powerful. His *Epistolae sine nomine* attack the Avignon popes and the Curia without any fear of possible reprisals, and he was straightforward enough to make a courageous defense of Cola di Rienzo even when the latter was a humbled prisoner in the hands of his enemies, abandoned by all his former partisans.

On a more general level, Bosco has underlined Petrarch's "incapacity to hate," as exemplified especially in the political sphere.[28] But it must be added that in that sphere his individualistic and tendentially ascetic personality found little of direct interest, so that his most basic political message (as in the canzone *Italia mia*) was contained in the rather vague, though at times stirringly eloquent, appeal to the ideal of peace and brotherhood (on the classic, Augustan pattern of the *pax romana*). One must therefore qualify Bosco's assessment, for in the cultural sphere he *was* capable of anger and hatred, as his *Invectives* amply prove. Indeed we might see here a reflection of what was to become a

28. See Bosco, *Petrarca* (1961), p. 181.

traditional aspect of the Italian cultural heritage, whether or not Petrarch had a direct influence on it (he probably had), namely the bad custom of violent manners in literary relations, even while intellectuals and others were willing to accept practically any abuse in their social and political environment. When we think of the interminable list of humanists' polemics we are bound to conclude that Italians have traditionally been prone to ignore literary offences least of all.

11. Despite the apparently contradictory character of some of his moral attitudes when we shift from one sphere of activity to another, a fundamental, instinctive generosity remains Petrarch's most attractive feature. He was in a very true sense a "good" man. The best, concise documentation of this trait can be found in an exemplary study of *Petrarch's Testament* by the late Theodor E. Mommsen, accompanying a semi-critical edition of the text and the first English translation.[29] This will (of 1370) constitutes a most remarkable and revealing document, displaying an unsurpassed degree of thoughtfulness, humaneness, and, to say it with Pascal in a different context, *esprit de finesse*. The Socratic lesson of culture as ethical paideia became an exemplary reality not only in Petrarch's writings but in his person. And in his professed union of *sapientia* and *eloquentia* Quintilian's ideal of the *vir bonus dicendi peritus* was never taken more seriously than by this medieval poet who, unable to be a saint, wanted to be an example of the learned man as a good Christian.

See for example his manner of caring for the needs of his brother Gerardo, a Carthusian monk. The last addendum to the will stipulated that Gerardo would "choose whether he wishes one hundred florins [at once] or five or ten florins annually, as he may please," but, in his customary discretion, he did not notify his brother of this provision until about three years later, when, around 1373, he wrote to him that he had left him a legacy three times as large as he had requested, that he would have sent him money before had he not known that a sum he had once sent him had not reached him, presumably because of the severe monastic rule, but that if it was now possible for him to receive money he would be glad to transmit at least part of his legacy immediately, "for both to you and to myself will be more welcome what I shall have done personally than what my heir will do."[30]

To his servants he was a kindly master. His property at Vaucluse had been in the hands of a caretaker called Monet, whom he cher-

29. *Petrarch's Testament,* edited and translated, with an introduction, by Theodor E. Mommsen (Ithaca, N.Y.: Cornell University Press, 1957).

30. Mommsen, op. cit., pp. 38f.

ished as a paragon of devotion and faithfulness. Eighteen years after Monet's death he remembered him in his will by bequeathing his land at Vaucluse to his two sons or, should these die, his grandsons. In leaving twenty ducats to the simple Pancaldo, one of his current household servants, he showed his paternal solicitude by admonishing him: "May he not use them for gambling."[31] A legacy of fifty gold ducats went to his Paduan friend Giovanni Dondi dall'Orologio, a prominent physician and creator of a famous astronomical clock. Now Giovanni was a wealthy man, so Petrarch asked him to buy with that sum "a small finger-ring to be worn in my memory." The case of Boccaccio was different, since he was relatively poor. So the fifty gold florins reserved to him were to be used for a utilitarian purpose, such as the suggested purchase of "a winter garment to be worn by him while he works through the night hours." It was a worthy gift, yet Petrarch apologized that he was "ashamed by such a trifling legacy for so great a man." Mommsen admirably notes that "in full knowledge of the straightened circumstances under which Boccaccio lived, Petrarch with great tact avoided embarrassing him with an outright monetary present, but gave to his bequest a nicely intimate and personal note."[32]

The considerate benefactor strove to tread softly and delicately on his friends' feelings even when they were not people of prominence. Indeed the gem of the will as the document of a considerate disposition can be seen in the handling of a sizable debt from Donato degli Albanzani, a teacher of grammar who, unable to repay a loan, had long felt uneasy about appearing "to have gained material advantages from their friendship."[33] Now Petrarch was an ideal friend, ever ready to help and do so graciously. So he had done his best to put Donato at ease by feigning that he owned him perhaps nothing or, if anything, less than he thought. He had called Donato's worries "laughable" and written to him that he doubted "whether you have made a mistake in regard to the state of our accounts." At any rate, between friends there should be no question of mine and yours. So in his will he remitted to him "Whatever he owes me on loan," and "at the same time depreciated very tactfully that gift by adding" (Mommsen): "how much it is I do not know, but in any case it is little." It is probably one of the nicest white lies on record.[34]

12. We have been returning step by step to our points of departure

31. Ibid., p. 36.
32. Ibid., pp. 32f.
33. Ibid., p. 31.
34. Ibid., pp. 31f.

in this sketch for a portrait. Another point was the significant distinction between the well known (but not entirely understood) superficial presence of Petrarch in the Europe-wide and centuries-long phenomenon of Petrarchism, on the one hand, and, on the other, his less known but equally important deep presence in western culture, in literature and beyond. This field is fraught with possibilities of surprising discoveries. A couple of the most intriguing ones to see the light in recent years are contained in a rewarding study by a Germanist and comparatist, Leonard Forster's *The Icy Fire*.[35] It shows in what subtle yet powerful ways Petrarch's presence can be felt in most unexpected quarters, and how the realization of this fact can afford an adequate reading of such phenomena—which may not even be primarily literary in nature, but aspects of European taste, manners, and social and political attitudes.

Forster demonstrates that the success of Elizabeth I against so many unfavorable odds was due in part to her conscious casting of herself on the public stage of the court and of the nation in the role of a petrarchistic idol, as the worshipped but unattainable virgin of all virtue set up on a stylized pedestal of refined conventions and emblematic systems. The trick worked admirably and conquered not only England but Europe.

This triumph is especially remarkable when set against the factual background of the relative unpopularity of Petrarch and Petrarchism in a literal sense in Elizabethan England. This contrasting picture is now sketched by George Watson in a statistical census of direct derivations and translations from the *Canzoniere*.[36] Between 1530, the approximate date of Wyatt's introduction of the Petrarchan sonnet into England, and 1625, Watson reminds us that only about 50 poems from the 366 of the *Canzoniere* were translated into English, so that around 1600, in the full flowering of the Elizabethan summer, the system of poetic conventions inherited from Petrarch and his Italian and French imitators sounded decidedly out of fashion. The English were rather inclined to draw their amorous conventions from Castiglione's *Cortegiano,* translated in 1561 by Hoby. This situation, in turn, contrasts with that of France, where the sonnet had been introduced around the same time but by 1600 almost all of Petrarch's sonnets had been translated (and many of these French versions, rather than the orig-

35. Cf. fn. 8 above.

36. Watson, *The English Petrarchans: A critical bibliography of the* CANZONIERE. Warburg Institute Surveys, ed. by E. H. Gombrich and J. B. Trapp, 3 (London: The Warburg Institute—University of London, 1967).

inals, served the Elizabethans). Of the more than 200 printed editions of the *Canzoniere* which appeared in Europe before 1600, none was published in England. Indeed the *Canzoniere* was never printed in any language there, and a complete English version was never to be realized by anyone until the 1850's. In the England of the Renaissance Petrarch was, then, "a name rather than a book"; "but if it was a name, it was a name beyond all others" (Watson, p. 3), as Forster's interpretation of Elizabeth's policies shows.

Forster goes on to offer a reading of the famous reception of Helen in Goethe's *Faust,* Second Part.[37] The ceremony is carefully staged in a way that creates the illusion of improvisation. When Helen enters the hall the court seems to be unprepared for her arrival, and then Faust enters leading his guardian Lynkeus in chains for having failed in his duty to announce such an extolled guest. But it is all a play within the play in the form of an elaborate Elizabethan masque, with a highly literate script designed to cast Helen in the role of a Laura made omnipotent by her virtue and beauty, who literally and figuratively blinds her adoring subjects, including the lynx-eyed Lynkeus, as a new sun more powerful than the physical one, and takes the whole castle by storm by vanquishing all its occupants with her Cupid's arrows. The full arsenal of Petrarchist symbols and conventions is at work, given new life by the genius of a new poet, with the unsuspecting reader paying the price of having at his peril become oblivious of the master from Arezzo's heritage.

But we should not be too surprised. We only have to remember that, of all the things we owe Francis Petrarch, there is also this one, the crystallization for western culture of the chivalric cult of womanhood. He did not invent this cult, the twelfth-century Provençal poets did, thus introducing into human history one of the very few basic psychological changes recorded by man. But if the troubadours were the effective harbingers of this pervasive revolution of manners, Petrarch was its great consolidator, and it is especially him whom we must thank for its permanence.

Civilization may be only skin deep, yet we can hardly exist as self-respecting humans without this epidermic patina, and we shudder every time we realize how many dangers beset its continuance. No century has seen civilization in crisis as often and as seriously as ours, and instead of feeling that civilization begins with Henry Ford we begin to be thankful if it did not end with him. Despite the arrogance of technology we feel more and more respect for the achievements of

37. Forster, op. cit., ch. "Lynkeus' masque in Goethe's *Faust II.*"

the distant past, and the more we study them the more impressed we are with their subtle ways of enduring to our day. The enduring Petrarch is one of these identifiable elements, and for this he surely deserves some degree of celebration.

When we endeavor to take stock of all his legacies to a centuries-long posterity, we feel embarrassed by such riches and hesitate to propose a clear plan to order all those ingredients into a coherent, unified whole. Perhaps his most profound message, his most worthy lesson, beyond all the scintillating paraphernalia of "petrarchistic" memory, is that obsessive idea which indeed made him the "prince of humanists," namely that civilization is epitomized in good literature and grounded in it, but that what makes literature good must be sought, socratically, in something of ethical value, something that makes man better, individually and collectively as well. A simple idea, all told, simple of the simplicity of Socrates, the first creator of humanism and constant inspirer of its renewals.

II

THE PRESENT STATUS OF PETRARCHAN STUDIES*

by Joseph G. Fucilla
Northwestern University (Emeritus)

Carlo Calcaterra opens his long chapter on "Il Petrarca e il petrarchismo" in *Questioni e correnti di storia letteraria* (Milano, 1949) with these words: "Nodo intricatissimo negli studi sul Trecento sono l'animo, l'ingegno, le opere di Francesco Petrarca, per la complessità dell'uomo e dell'artista, per la vivezza dei sentimenti e dei pensieri contrastanti, per gli aspetti multiformi della vita esteriore e di quella intima,

* The three best sources for the description and analysis of critical studies on Petrarch are Ettore Bonora's "Lineamenti della storia della critica petrarchesca," *I classici italiani nella storia della critica,* I (Firenze, 1954), 97-168; B. T. Sozzi's *Petrarca* (Palermo, 1963), 11-133; and Pietro Mazzamuto's *Rassegna bibliografico-critica della letteratura italiana* (2d ed., Firenze, 1970), 84-119, coverage restriction through 1949. Being considerably more complete in the information they include, they should be consulted to supplement the material I offer. Except for the first part of my paper my arrangement differs from theirs. Naturally, as in all bibliographies covering all or a part of the same period, duplications are inevitable. I am indebted to my three colleagues not so much for titles, which I have collected independently, as for some of the ideas these authors express. In my section on the Novecento, with particular reference to studies that have appeared since 1960, it is I who is the supplementer.

Bibliographical sources that can be utilized are the *Cornell Catalogue of the Petrarch Collection . . .* (New York, 1916; reprinted New York, 1971). It is a rich special library, but, unfortunately, it has been surrounded by a kind of myth which has led scholars to believe that virtually everything on Petrarch can be found there. This is far from true for the pre-1916 catalogued material and even less so with reference to publications acquired from then on. Nevertheless, Cornell is the first place to go for information on any important Petrarch project. Prezzolini in his *Repertorio bibliografico* has fallen victim to the myth and hence begins his Petrarch section as of the date of the *Catalogue*. It goes on until 1942. As for periodical items he and his assistants have taken most of them from the "Cronaca" in *Giornale storico,* which is not always complete. Its usefulness applies, of course, to the whole range of Italian literature except Dante, which it omits. Since 1942 the best bibliographical sources are "Literature of the Renaissance: Italian" up to 1968 in *Studies in Philology,* and the *MLA International Bibliography* from 1957 to the present time. I have compiled a virtually complete bibliography from 1916 to 1973, which I hope will be printed in Italy sometime next year.

A complete list of the Cornell Library holdings to date has just been published: *Catalogue of the Petrarch Collection in Cornell University Library* (Millwood, N. Y.: Kraus-Thomson Organization, 1974).

per l'accento lirico dei canti latini e volgari, in cui egli raffigura se stesso, il suo amore, il suo peregrinare inquieto da Arezzo all'ultima sosta" (p. 168). For six centuries scholars have been attempting to untie this knot with varying success.

Criticism of Petrarch was started by Petrarch himself in the autobiographical and self-critical passages in his works, notably the *Epistle to Posterity,* and by Boccaccio in his encomiastic *De vita et moribus Francisci Petrarchae de Florentia* (1348-49), the two primary sources and models utilized by a half dozen biographers in the Quattrocento, the best known of whom is the great Humanist Leonardo Bruni. After Bruni the enthusiasm for Petrarch's Latinity gradually began to wane, due to unfavorable comparisons between it and the Latin of Cicero and Horace. Petrarch's personal admission of failure as an epic poet must also have been a factor in his loss of prestige.[1] Only four single editions of his Latin works were printed in Italy during the last three decades of the century: *De remediis* in 1492, *Familiares* in 1492, *De vita solitaria* in 1498, and, in translation, Albanzani's version of *De viris illustribus.* It was from beyond the Alps, in Basel in 1496, that we have the first collective edition of his Latin works. On the other hand, the same period produced at least thirty-four editions of the *Rime* attesting to a decisive shift in interest. The earliest was issued by Vindelino de Spira in 1470.[2] The Valdezocco edition of 1472 deserves mention as the first publication based on Petrarch's famous autograph, Vat. Lat. 3195. The first commentator of the *Trionfi* is Illicino, 1472,[3] while the first comment on the *Canzoniere,* 1475, though sometimes attributed to Antonio Da Tempo, was very likely done by Filelfo.[4]

In the Cinquecento, according to Ferrazzi, there were one hundred sixty-seven editions of the *Rime,* evidence of the phenomenal vogue of these poems. Much of this is to be credited to Cardinal Bembo's cult of Petrarch. It was he who set up Petrarch's language as the language of poetry in the vernacular in his *Prose della volgar lingua* (1525), and by his example in the *Asolani* (1505) and *Rime* (1530) as the exclusive model to be imitated in amorous composi-

1. See R. P. Oliver, "Petrarch's Prestige as a Humanist," *Classical Studies in Honor of William Abbott Oldfather* (Urbana, Ill., 1943), 140-41.

2. On this edition see Sariette, "Il primo libro stampato in Italia: *Canzoniere.* Venezia. Vindelino de Spira, 1470," *Primato,* III (1942), 88.

3. For further discussion see D. D. Carnicelli, "Bernardo Illicino and the Renaissance Commentaries of Petrarch's *Trionfi,*" *Romance Philology,* XXIII (1969), 56-64.

4. On Filelfo see E. Raimondi, "Francesco Filelfo interprete del *Canzoniere,*" *Studi petrarcheschi,* III (1950), 143-61.

tions, which resulted in the predominance of the Petrarchistic school not only in Italy but also in other countries in Western Europe.[5] Among the annotated editions the four best were prepared by Vellutello, Daniello, Gesualdo, and Castelvetro.[6] Outstripping the other three in popularity was the Vellutello commentary, which went through twenty printings from 1525 to 1584. The first three adopt a biographical-psychological approach. Vellutello gives us a novelized biography; Daniello prefers to dwell on the lyrical motifs in the collection, pays more attention than Vellutello to the quality of its poetry, and makes interesting observations on the poet's variants; Gesualdo submits previous interpretations to a minute critical examination and pays considerable attention to questions of language, style and content. Castelvetro is the most acute and erudite of the four. He copiously analyzes and comments on verbal expressiveness in the *Canzoniere*. For him Petrarch is not so much a poet as he is an artist. The de-romanticized picture he draws of the Trecentista could be called anti-petrarchistic. Though many of his statements are controversial and unacceptable, his commentary has been highly rated.

The most outstanding biography of the time, based directly on Petrarch's Latin and Italian works, was written by Lodovico Beccadelli in 1559. We are all indebted to him as the collector of the author's autograph manuscripts, among them the *Rime* contained in the universally prized Vat. Lat. 3195 and 3196. He is also among the first to recognize the importance of the *Rime disperse*.

The number of editions or reprints of the *Rime* in the Seicento is seventeen according to Ferrazzi, which, compared to the number noted for the Cinquecento, reveals a drastic decline in Petrarch's vogue. It may also be noted that, while editions of his Latin works were printed in France, Switzerland, and Holland, none appeared in Italy. Tassoni's *Considerazioni* (1609) aim their barbs more at the Petrarchists than at Petrarch who, nevertheless, does not miss receiving his share. The Seicentista's remarks are rhetorical in character with hardly any psychological

5. See V. Cian, "Pietro Bembo postillatore del *Canzoniere* petrarchesco," *Giornale storico della letteratura italiana,* XCVIII (1931), 255-90, XCIX (1932), 227-64, and L. Baldacci, "Pietro Bembo: Dal *De imitatione* alle *Prose,*" *Il petrarchismo italiano nel Cinquecento* (Milano, 1957), 1-8.

6. On the four commentators mentioned see Baldacci, op. cit., 59-66, 165-77. On these and others see also B. Weinberg, "The *Sposizione* of Petrarch in the Early Cinquecento," *Romance Philology,* XIII (1960), 374-86. On Daniello alone see E. Raimondi, "Bernardino Daniello e le varianti petrarchesche," *Studi petrarcheschi,* V (1952), 95-130; on Castelvetro alone Raimondi, "Gli scrupoli di un filologo: Lodovico Castelvetro e il Petrarca," *Studi petrarcheschi,* V (1952), 131-210, and *Rinascimento inquieto* (Palermo, 1965), 76-174.

analysis. Galileo's *Postille* (c. 1610) have come to light only recently.[7] The century's two most important contributions are the publication in 1642 of Vat. Lat. 3196 by F. Ubaldini and F. Tommasini's *Petrarca redivivus* (1630). The latter examines a considerable mass of material relating to Petrarch until then virtually unknown; it furnishes us with precious information on the libraries the poet had assembled at Valchiusa and other places, as well as an index of Petrarch's works in the Vatican Library.

The Settecento is the age of the Arcadia, guided by the canon of imitation as a means of achieving poetic immortality through the use of Petrarch, Pindar and Anacreon as models. Muratori is the critical voice of the school. In his *Osservazioni* (Modena, 1711), he wants his readers to be able to perceive "quello che noi chiamiamo buon gusto poetico," but at the same time points out what he considers to be deficiences in the *Canzoniere*. Here and in the *Perfetta poesia* he stresses the idea of the "bello," which for him is verisimilitude enhanced by perfect expression and imagination.[8] Gravina is the first to give us the equation Laura-lauro. De Sade's *Mémoires pour la vie de François Pétrarque* (1764-67) were a great sensation which aroused a widespread interest in our poet throughout Europe. The work is centered on the identification with Petrarch's Laura of a distant member of the author's family, Laura de Noves, married to Hugues de Sade. The legend had already started in the Quattrocento. Though the so-called original documents published by the Marquis to prove his case have never been found, the reading public has continued to believe to this day that she is the woman whom the poet loved. G. B. Baldelli's monograph *Del Petrarca e delle sue opere* (Firenze, 1797), was for

7. See N. Vianello, "Le *Postille* al Petrarca di Galileo Galilei," *Studi di filologia italiana,* XIV (1956), 211-433; Id., "Preoccupazioni stilistiche di Galileo lettore del Petrarca," *La Critica stilistica e il barocco letterario. Atti del congresso internazionale di studi italiani* (Firenze, 1957), 377-43. A note has been added by G. Ottone, "Postille e considerazioni galileiane: *Postille* al Petrarca," *Aevum,* XLVI (1972), 313-15.

8. Studies largely devoted to Muratori are by F. Forti, "L. A. Muratori e il petrarchismo," *Studi petrarcheschi,* IV (1951), 91-128, and by M. Fubini, "Le *Osservazioni* del Muratori al Petrarca e la critica letteraria" published in *Civiltà moderna,* V-VI (1933-34), and later incorporated in *Dal Muratori al Baretti* (Bari, 1946), 9-124, in the 3rd edition, 1968, 55-176. Muratori shares space with Tassoni in A. Tortoreto, "Il *Canzoniere* nelle *Considerazioni* del Tassoni e del Muratori," *Parma a Francesco Petrarca* (Parma, 1934), 257-64; " 'Lo stil più raro' nei più antichi commenti al *Canzoniere*," *Annali della Cattedra petrarchesca,* IV (1933), 161-71, and F. Forti, "Gusto tassoniano e gusto muratoriano," *Studi petrarcheschi,* V (1952), 211-35. Consult also, on these two and others, E. Sala Di Felice, *Petrarca e l'Arcadia* (Palermo, 1959).

many years considered the best biography on the Aretino. Ferrazzi lists forty-six editions of the *Canzoniere*, almost double those of the previous century.

Romantic stress on biographical criticism and on imagination, feeling, and sensibility as prime poetic perquisites combined to bring Petrarch into a new focus. Interest in him and his works acquired an extraordinary intensity which since then has never ebbed. The endless list of names and facts presented by C. Naselli in her 569-page book, *Il Petrarca nell'Ottocento* (Napoli, 1923), is a most impressive testimonial on the meaning of Petrarch for the men of the nineteenth century. She has limited herself to Italy.

Foscolo through his *Essays on Petrarch* (1820-23) is not only the first really significant name in the criticism of our author, he also set the pattern for subsequent criticism from De Sanctis to Croce and beyond. His approach is primarily a blend of the psychological and the aesthetic. The two best of his four essays are the second and fourth: "An Essay on the Poetry of Petrarch" and "A Parallel Between Dante and Petrarch."

With reference to the variants of the *Rime* on Petrarch's work sheets Foscolo notes that the poet always adopts those words which combine at once most harmony, elegance, and energy. When the force of his passion has subsided, the man of genius, Petrarch, "retains for a longer period the recollection of what it has been, and can more easily imagine himself under its influence." . . . "What we call the power of imagination is chiefly the combination of strong feelings and re-collection." Foscolo anticipates one of the most salient aspects of Petrarch where he observes that his dominant thoughts and emotions are not restricted to any one work but to many of them. This theme has been notably developed by Bosco and others.

> By an attentive perusal of all the writings of Petrarch, it may be reduced almost to a certainty—that by dwelling perpetually on the same ideas, and by allowing his mind to prey incessantly on itself, the whole train of his feelings and reflections acquired one strong character and tone: and if he was able to suppress them for a time, they returned to him with increased violence—that, to tranquilize this agitated state of mind, he, in the first instance, communicated in a free and loose manner all that he felt, in his correspondence with his intimate friends—that he afterwards reduced these narratives with more order and discretion into Latin verse—and that he lastly, perfected them with a greater profusion of imagery and more art, in his Italian poetry.
>
> We may thus understand the perfect concord which prevails in Petrarch's poetry between nature and art, between the accuracy of fact and the magic

of invention, between depth and perspicuity; between devouring passion and calm meditation. . . .

The power of preserving and at the same time diversifying his rhythm belongs to him alone—his melody is perpetual and never wearies the ear. . . . [His aim is] to produce a constant musical flow in strains inspired by the sweetest of human passions.[9]

Leopardi's edition of the *Rime* (1826) contains what he terms an "interpretazione," that is, an *explanatio* designed to help the general public to understand and appreciate its poems. Its numerous reprintings which extend into the twentieth century reveal it as the foremost vulgarization of the *Canzoniere*. De Sanctis has called it "un lavoro perfettamente riuscito; vi si ammira la sobrietà e la precisione di una mente superiore." Critical opinions on Petrarch are absent in the "interpretazione," but they do appear in the form of brief comments in the *Zibaldone*. Leopardi saw in himself a kindred spirit of Petrarch, which is revealed in the echoes and imitations from the masterpiece in not a few of his poems.[10]

De Sanctis' studies on Petrarch went through five phases, commencing with his Naples lectures, 1939-48. The fourth phase is represented by the *Saggio sul Petrarca* (1869). It consists of eleven chapters, the best of which is the one entitled "Forma del Petrarca." The fifth phase is the chapter on the *Canzoniere* in his *Storia della letteratura italiana* (1870). Since it is a synthesis of the other four, I have found it convenient to use it in my summary.

The critic dwells on the "sentimento delle belle forme," which is "così connaturato in lui che penetra ne' minimi particolari dell'elocuzione della lingua e del verso. . . .L'obiettivo della sua poesia non è la cosa ma l'immagine, il modo di rappresentarla. Ma questa bella forma non è un puro artificio tecnico e meccanico, una vuota sonorità; anzi vien fuori da un'immaginazione appassionata e che ha il suo riposo, il suo ultimo fine in sé stessa." In commenting on Petrarch's *dissidio* De Sanctis says: "il *Canzoniere* in vita di Laura è la storia delle sue contraddizioni. . . . Il disaccordo interno è appunto questo: nell'im-

9. No analysis of the subject has come as yet anywhere near surpassing D. Bianchi's "Studi del Foscolo sul Petrarca," *Studi sul Foscolo, a cura dell'Università di Pavia nel primo centenario della morte del poeta* (Torino, 1927), 451-524.

10. Cf. G. Berzero, "L'interpretazione del Leopardi alle Rime del Petrarca," *Annali della Cattedra petrarchesca*, IV (1933), 179-212, and *Nuove pagine di critica* (Chiavari, 1933), 57-84; E. Pasquini, "Leopardi lettore dei poeti antichi italiani: Commento alle *Rime* del Petrarca," *Giornale storico*, CXLVI (1969), 77-92. A. Chiari in "Il Petrarca ai bambini," *Indagini e letture*, ser. III (1961), 352-56, makes a strong defence of Leopardi's commentary.

maginazione che costruisce e nella riflessione che distrugge." Not being able to deal with reality the poet is satisfied with its image. "Onde nasce un sentimento elegiaco dolce-amaro: la malinconia . . . . Questa malinconia è la verità della sua ispirazione, è il suo genio. . . ." This constitutes its modernity. Whatever unity there is in the collection is in its *fragmenta.* Interpretations like these and others have become a basic part of Petrarch criticism and guidelines in subsequent studies up to the present time.[11]

Fracassetti edited the *Epistolae de rebus familiaribus et variae,* 3 vols. (Firenze, 1859-63). In them he corrects the older texts, replaces apocryphal passages and adds letters from miscellaneous sources. It was followed by a five volume translation of the *Familiares* and the *Variae* (Firenze, 1863-67), and a two volume translation of the *Seniles* (Firenze, 1869-70). They have served to acquaint a half dozen generations with precious details on the intimate side of Petrarch. The translations are still cited and even re-translated into English and other languages.

Much more important than the sections on Petrarch in Carducci's *Discorsi* is his edition of the *Rime.* Though first partially published in 1876, the definitive edition was printed in 1899, with the collaboration of Severino Ferrari. The notes involve chronology, biography, exegesis, borrowings from Latin writers and Fathers of the Church, comparisons of Petrarch's language with that of Dante and Boccaccio. Reliance is placed on the notes and interpretations of more than forty-five commentators, which are supplemented and discussed wherever it has seemed necessary. A long preface provides brief analyses and appraisals of the works utilized, an account of the *fortuna* of the variants in Petrarch's autographs, in this last instance constituting the first important discussion of the subject. The edition has been frequently reprinted, the latest in 1965 with the "Presentazione" of G. Contini. Calcaterra in the chapter of *Questioni e correnti di storia letteraria,* op. cit., 212, tells us that it has been the "matrice di tutti i commenti successivi, per un vaglio e ripensamento disciplinato e potente di tutte le indagini antecedenti, riprese da capo sia sotto l'aspetto filologico sia sotto l'aspetto estetico."

On Petrarch and Humanism studies had appeared before P. De Nolhac's *Pétrarque et l'Humanisme* (Paris, 1892, 1907), such as

11. Two out of a score of evaluations are V. Titone, "Il Petrarca e la critica del De Sanctis," *Critica vecchia e nuova* (Firenze, 1932), I, 1-84, and C. Trabalza, "Burckhardt e De Sanctis nella critica petrarchesca," *Dipanature critiche* (Bologna, 1920), 7-38.

Voigt's (1859) and Burckhardt's (1860), but no one before or since has brought Petrarch closer to the Roman world than the French erudite through the abundance of information he furnishes, especially on the impact of classical authors on Petrarch. In the second revised edition of 1907 De Nolhac added a new chapter on the poet's knowledge of the Church Fathers. Striking as the various chapters of this book are, they yield in attraction to its introduction in which, taking as his theme the Renan epithet, "Petrarch the First Modern Man," the author demonstrates why his fellow countryman was right in making this designation. The different genres cultivated by the Humanists, we are told, derive from Petrarch—the epic, familiar letters, allegorical bucolics; the epistle in prose was revived by the *Familiares* and the *Seniles*; he introduced the concept of history as a series of portraits and anecdotes in the *Rerum memorandarum* and introduced history as biography in *De viris illustribus; De sui ipsius et multorum ignorantia* is "le premier type de la grande discussion philosophique"; his *Invective contra medicum, Apologia contra cuiusdam Galli calumnias, Sine nomine,* became models for the invectives of the Humanists; to him is due the great revival of the Classics and the stimulus to make translations from the Greek available; his Latin works mark him as "le premier 'styliste' des temps modernes." "Ce qui l'a séduit dans la littérature antique, c'est le caractère de l'oeuvre d'art. Pour la première fois depuis des siècles, on n'en peut douter, la perfection de la forme a décidé des préférences d'un esprit. Cette recherche du beau pour lui–même et cette distinction établie entre les productions qui le révèlent inégalement sont une des plus fécondes initiatives de Pétrarque; en même temps elles instituent de nouveau à la fin de ce Moyen Âge qui ne l'a point connue, la critique littéraire." He attacked ideas that were entrenched in the Middle Ages, pseudo-sciences, astrology, alchemy, scholasticism, Averroism, and brought Platonism into prominence as a rival of Aristotelianism. By implication De Nolhac comes to these conclusions by the contrast between mediaevalism as it existed in Petrarch's time and the cultural world that was modernized through his influence. For the most part they have been accepted by students of Humanism.[12]

In 1886 De Nolhac and, independently, also Pakscher, made one of the most precious literary finds of modern times. This is the text that has continued to be reproduced from Carducci to the present,

12. A Sorbonne dissertation has been written on the Frenchman, G. Zuchelli, *Pierre de Nolhac. Contribution à l'histoire intellectuelle et morale de l'enfant, de l'humaniste et du poète* (Paris, 1970).

Vat. Lat. 3195. The find has led to renewed interest in 3196, which represents an earlier and very important phase in the elaboration of the *Rime,* and on which there have already been a number of studies.

It would be superfluous to point out that in the years before the opening of the Novecento a large group of scholars had already become adept in the use of aesthetic, psychological, and historical criticism and that, as a result, they were much better equipped than heretofore to produce fruitful and estimable studies. Many were able to carry their investigations into the new century and either directly trained the younger generation or transmitted to it their effective new methods. For instance, we know that Mazzoni, Albini, Foresti, Lipparini, Carrara, Chiorboli and Serra were disciples of Carducci. All of them were to become good Petrarchologists. External facts, too, helped to intensify interest. In the Ottocento the fifth centenary of Petrarch's death brought forward scores of commemorative lectures and studies. During the Novecento there has already been one major centenary, the sixth of Petrarch's birth,[13] and several minor centenaries of Petrarch's enamorment, the Coronation, and Laura's death, all of them together resulting in at least another half hundred lectures, articles, and monographs. Two annuals have been devoted to Petrarch, nine volumes of the *Annali della cattedra petrarchesca* (1930-41), three of them composed of papers given at *Convegni* in 1928 and 1931, and the *Studi petrarcheschi* (1948-61) consisting of seven volumes, the last containing the papers delivered at the Aix-en-Provence congress in 1959 on the general topic "Petrarca e il petrarchismo." In short, so great has been the interest in the illustrious Trecentista that the amount of material dealing with him from 1900 to date is in excess of the sum total of all the other centuries. In view of such a plethora of printed information the only alternative left to anyone writing on the "Present Status of Petrarchan Studies" is to limit himself to mentions and discussions of only a few of the most relevant studies.

But before undertaking to take notice of publications of recent vintage, I shall indicate my procedure in dealing with them, which has been dictated by my feeling that a classified approach is the quickest means for readers to find what concerns them. This will consist simply of a grouping of my materials under the following categories. 1. Biographies and comprehensive or collective studies; 2. Latin works; 3.

13. For a long list of publications and analysis of their contents see A. Della Torre, "Il sesto centenario della nascita di Francesco Petrarca," *Archivio storico italiano,* XXXV (1905), 104-89.

Petrarch, Classical Antiquity and Humanism; 4. The *Canzoniere, Trionfi,* and *Rime disperse;* 5. Petrarchism; 6. Petrarch, the figurative arts and music.

1. *Biographies and comprehensive or collective studies:*

Deserving mention if only because it furnished English readers for many years with their main source of information on Petrarch's life, is H. Hollway-Calthrop's *Petrarch* (New York, 1907, reprint, New York, 1972). In his preface the author makes it clear that his book is a popularization. Though his narrative is, as he states, substantially taken from his subject's writings, and this has a positive value, it suffers grievously from his failure to utilize much of research published within a period of thirty or more years prior to the appearance of his book.

E. H. R. Tatham in his lengthy two-volume study *Francesco Petrarca, the First Modern Man of Letters. His Life and Letters. A Study of the Early Fourteenth Century (1304-1347)* (London, 1925-26), aims to present Petrarch as exemplified by his writings and the times in which he lived. More than one fourth of the text is given to history, the Church, universities, classical studies, much of which is not as integrated as it should be with Petrarch's activities. Possibly the most useful service performed by the Rev. Tatham is in the form of copiously scattered translations from the *Epistolario* and other works.

The miscellany by A. Foresti, *Aneddoti della vita di Francesco Petrarca* (Brescia, 1928), constitutes a notable contribution toward the biography of Petrarch, particularly on the chronology of certain episodes, the identification of individuals alluded to in his *Rime* and letters, and historical interpretations of the *Epistolae metricae.* His materials have been and are still widely used.

F. Rizzi's *Francesco Petrarca e il decennio parmense (1341-1351)* (Torino, 1934), traces in minute detail Petrarch's wandering from year to year and his numerous contacts with friends and notables of the time. A flood of new light is shed on the decennium.

The story of the inner Petrarch is excellently portrayed by L. Tonelli in his *Petrarca* (Milano, 1930). It is the most extensive treatment of the subject up to the date of its publication. While Calcaterra in *Giornale storico della letteratura italiana,* XCVI (1930), 94-100, sees weaknesses in the book, he praises the sections dealing with the Coronation, *Africa, Trionfi,* the "equilibrio energico e sereno" of Petrarch's last years. Its value is summed up in the following words: "Il senso nuovo del libro sta proprio in questa più viva comprensione di tutta la spiritualità petrarchesca. Come tale l'opera del Tonelli non deve essere giudicata soltanto una rievocazione dei suoi scritti . . . ma una valutazione di tutti gli aspetti della sua anima. . . . Perciò si potrebbe dire che i primi sei capitoli non sono che un'assidua e speciale preparazione a cinque paragrafi sintetici del capitolo ultimo, a cui Tonelli converge per tutte le vie percorse mirando a raffigurar oggettivamente e nitidamente l'uomo, il pensatore, il letterato, il patriota e il poeta."

It is safe to say that no one has ever kept more assiduously abreast of Petrarch studies than C. Calcaterra. His most active period as a reviewer was 1928-30, when he wrote *rassegne petrarchesche* for the *Giornale storico,* XCI (1928), 92-169, XCIV (1929), 279-355, XCVI (1930), 88-103. In *Convivium,* II (1930), 3-29 he printed "Sugli studi petrarcheschi." For a proficient sizing up of the virtues and faults of the Petrarchiana published at approximately these dates it would be wise to rely on him. His main contribution, however, is the collection of studies *Nella selva del Petrarca* (Bologna, 1942), in which he confronts a number of thorny problems that had been plaguing Petrarchan scholars for a long time. The essays that stand out most are three, "La prima ispirazione dei *Trionfi*," a superior piece of historical and aesthetic analysis, which, incidentally, includes an excursus exonerating Petrarch of any envy towards Dante, a much repeated condemnation made over a period of five centuries;[14] a long discussion on "Sant'Agostino nelle opere di Dante e del Petrarca," stressing that the influence of the saint is not limited to the *Secretum* but permeates almost all of his major works; and "Giovene donna sotto un verde lauro," a masterful performance. Calcaterra scrutinizes the *Parnasia laurus* myth, the identification of Laura with Dafne, that is, poetry, its incidence in the *Rime* and other writings, its coalescence with the motif of the *dì sesto d'aprile,* day of Christ's passion, which he makes coincide with his enamorment of her and the day of her death. The myth is replaced in the *rime in morte* by the concept of Laura, *guida al cielo.*[15] The sixth of April date is also

14. A. S. Bernardo in his discussion on the subject, "Petrarch's Attitude Towards Dante," *Publications of the Modern Language Assoc.,* LXX (1955), 488-519, takes a middle stand. He does not entirely exonerate Petrarch nor does he make him envious. Instead he makes his opposition stem from a difference between his and Dante's poetics or poetic principles.

15. In another essay, "Dante, Petrarch and Boccaccio," *Italian Poets and English Critics, 1755-1859,* edited by B. Corrigan (Chicago, 1969), Bernardo reexamines this myth. Calcaterra had used only Wilkins' article on the "Pre-Chigi Form of the *Canzoniere,*" *Modern Philology,* XXIII (1926), claimed to be the first form. The other forms discussed by Wilkins in the chapter, "The Making of the *Canzoniere,*" which furnishes the main part of the title of his book (Roma,

given separate treatment in a short chapter, "Feria sexta aprilis." Some of the *Nella selva* matter re-appears in condensed form in "Petrarca e il petrarchismo . . . ," op. cit. 167-273, a good orientative study based upon his intimate knowledge of the "complete" Petrarch.

It is Bosco who in his *Francesco Petrarca* (Torino, 1946, 4th ed. Bari, 1968), has made the most important contribution of a comprehensive character in our century. The book is abridged in *I maggiori* (Milano, 1956). In his Preface Bosco prepares us for what we may expect in the main part of his study. He notes that it is impossible to construct an external biography because he, Petrarch, "è senza storia se lo si considera come si deve nel concreto di tutta l'opera sua." What we have are the writings of a mature man starting in 1338 or thereabouts. Before then we do not know how he thought and felt. Furthermore, the fact that he made two and sometimes three redactions of almost all of his compositions helps only to determine "il prima e il poi della sua cultura, il modo di attuarsi del suo gusto letterario, esse non ci permettono di dire: il Petrarca era un uomo così e poi cambiò in questo modo e per queste ragioni. . . . Che cosa concludere dunque se non che non abbiamo, si può dire, una pagina che rispecchi con sicurezza un determinato preciso momento della vita di lui?" "Tutte," i.e. his major works, "rispecchiano tutto il Petrarca; immobile nella sua perplessità dal principio alla fine." For this reason the only remaining solution is "affrontare decisamente il problema unico dell'uomo e del poeta, tentare di sciogliere l'unico nodo dal quale dipendono tutte le fila della sua azione, del suo pensiero, della sua poesia." The *nodo* is Petrarch's obsessive sense of the transitoriness of all earthly things which pervades all of his writings. This could be proven by making any of his major works the center for this discussion, but Bosco logically chooses to center it in the *Canzoniere*. Here he finds that the *dissidio* about which so much has been written is not due to any conflict between love and religion, or between Christianity and paganism, but to his perennial, gloomy dissatisfaction with himself, what he sees and what he has learned. The protagonist of the *Canzoniere* is not Laura, who merely serves as a vehicle for the externalization of Petrarch's prepossession. Bosco further points out that the expression of the poet's introspection is basically elegiac, and on this matter quotes De Sanctis. Yet the *dissidio* is finally reconciled, and this takes place shortly before he dies, as is evident in the *Trionfi*. Other chapters, some of which are only marginally linked with his main thesis, such as "Letteratura e vita,"

1951), appeared some years later than *Nella selva*. Bernardo ingeniously and interestingly tests Calcaterra's formula in the light of Wilkins' data and finds that it breaks down on reaching the fifth form of the *Canzoniere*.

"Cristianesimo e Umanesimo," "Letteratura e politica," offer many more, perceptive observations.[16]

Wilkins started his main biographical contributions on Petrarch with a long chapter, "Petrarch in Provence, 1351-1353," *Studies in the Life and Works of Petrarch* (Chicago, 1955), 81-181. He continued in *Petrarch's Eight Years in Milan* (Chicago, 1957),[17] and *Petrarch's Later Years* (Chicago, 1959). In these, using largely data in Petrarch's letters, he tells us what the man thought and did from month to month, from day to day and often at a specified hour, all of which has the effect of giving him an intense humanness. The three titles mentioned and many other investigations gave him an exceptionally thorough background which he utilized for his *Life of Petrarch* (Chicago, 1961),[18] in part a condensation of matter in his previous studies in terms of the salient facts of his biography. His purpose in this volume was to reach a wide reading audience. He provides us with an objective account adopting the role of a faithful recorder who notes only what he has read in his subject's writings. He reserves his own personal judgment for the brilliant synthesis which makes up his closing chapter: "Portrait of Petrarch." It is our first really scientific biography on the great man. It is not likely to be replaced as our fundamental factual source on his life.

The importance of Wilkins is acknowledged by M. Bishop in a note of his *Petrarch and His World* (Bloomington, Ind., 1963), 377. "I must record my constant debt to the ten books and many articles by Ernest H. Wilkins. His *Life of Petrarch* has been a sure and unfailing guide." In his Preface, the new biographer makes clear that: "This book is intended for those who may have some interest in Petrarch, but little presumably in the quarrels of critics and interpreters." In other words, it is a popularization. Bishop continues: "Therefore though many of my outright statements are, in fact, disputable, I have generally accepted what has seemed best to me and gone on." As its title implies, its author is interested not only in Petrarch but also in the world that surrounds him, following Tatham in this connection. It is a lively, an extremely well-written and, on the whole, an enjoyable narrative. What makes the volume different from Wilkins is

16. Among the more than a dozen reviews the most detailed information and comment can be found in N. Aurigemma, *Nuova antologia,* CCCCXL (1948), 312-17. See also E. Bonora in *Giornale storico,* CXXVII (1961), 297-302.

17. A partially supplemental study has very recently been published by U. Dotti, *Petrarca a Milano. Documenti milanesi,* 1353-54 (Milano, 1972).

18. This book can be read in Italian in the *Vita del Petrarca e formazione del* Canzoniere, trans. and ed. R. Ceserani (Milano, 1964).

Bishop's personal interpretations of the facts of Petrarch's life, but it is precisely this that has made it vulnerable to the shafts of his critics, T. C. Chubb, *Speculum,* XXXIX (1964), 310-11, N. Iliescu, *Modern Language Notes,* LXXX (1965), 100-05, and G. Billanovich, *Romance Philology,* XX (1966), 130-31. The most severe of them is Chubb. He re-acts to Bishop's treatment of Laura: "The Laura story is told almost as if for a tabloid or for a magazine of true confessions," he writes, and then comes forth with a coup de grace that I don't think is really justified. "When I had finished Mr. Bishop's book—and even with the last chapter to assist me—I not only did not have a clear concept of what Petrarch was, but I was not convinced that Mr. Bishop did either."

The last English biographical-critical book on the famous Italian is T. G. Bergin's *Petrarch* (New York, 1970). It is a semi-popular volume, midway between Wilkins and Bishop, towards both of whom the author expresses special indebtedness. It is equally divided between a biographical account and a description and analysis of his works. As he himself states in his Foreword: "As for critical opinions here expressed they represent my own conclusions," conclusions that, I may add, are those of a sound, very well-grounded and discerning judge. Bergin has translated a number of Petrarch's sonnets (Edinburgh-London, 1956), and has just published a translation of the *Bucolicum carmen* (New Haven, 1974).

R. Amaturo in his *Petrarca* (Bari, 1971), has had the original idea of presenting the inner Petrarch through a commentary on the key passages in all of his works.

2. *Latin works:*

For most of Petrarch's works, which comprise by far the largest group of his writings, we do not have any critical editions. The first of them, of the *Liber sine nomine,* is P. Piur's *Buch ohne Namen und die päpstliche Kurie* (Halle, 1925). The first printed under the auspices of the Commissione nazionale per l'edizione critica delle opere del Petrarca is the rather faulty edition of the *Africa* by N. Festa (Firenze, 1926).[19] It has been followed by three very exemplary editions: V. Rossi's *Familiares* in four volumes (Firenze, 1933-42), the fourth edited by U. Bosco; G. Billanovich's *Rerum memorandarum* (Firenze, 1945); G. Martellotti's *De viris illustribus* (Firenze, 1964), that is, twenty three lives and the last preface. Critical editions of

19. The most searching of the reviews on it has been made by A. Gandiglio, "Appunti sull'*Africa* edita da Nicola Festa," *Giornale storico,* XC (1927), 289-308.

minor works have been made by E. Carrara for the *Epistola posteritati, Studi petrarcheschi* (Torino, 1959); P. G. Ricci, *Invectiva contra quendam magni status hominem sed nullius scientie aut virtutis* (Roma, 1949), and *Invectiva contra medicum* (Roma, 1950). The two Ricciardi volumes, *Rime, Trionfi e poesie latine* (Milano-Napoli, 1951), and *Prose* (1955), with the full and partial texts all of them prepared by leading scholars of our day, provide us in their originals and translations with a big segment of Petrarch's Latin works, much of which would otherwise be hard to obtain. They, of course, are only a partial answer to our need for complete, reliable texts.

Where critical editions are available there has been a gradually growing output of appreciative and analytic studies, but where they are not we find ourselves limited for the most part to studies and notes bearing on dating, chronology, arrangement, texts, discovery of new manuscripts, historical and philological contributions—the sort of information that will eventually be incorporated into critical editions.[20] I shall refer mostly to material of the first two types, namely, appreciative and analytical studies.

No extended collective discussion of the Latin work has yet taken place. For orientative purposes Bergin in his book provides a series of competent accounts. F. Piggioli's *Il pensiero religioso del Petrarca* (Roma, 1951) covers the correspondence, *Secretum, Vita solitaria,* and, somewhat briefly, the *Canzoniere.* Stylistic studies have been undertaken by G. A. Levi, "Sullo stile latino del Petrarca agli inizi dell'Umanesimo," *Atene e Roma,* XL (1938), 121-30, and U. A. Paoli, "Il latino del Petrarca e gli inizi dell'Umanesimo," *Pensée humaniste et tradition chrétienne aux XIVe et XVe siècles. Colloques internationaux du centre de la recherche scientifique. Paris: 26 au 30 oct. (1948),* 57-67. The only study on language until Martellotti has been P. Hazard's "La latinité de Pétrarque. Étude sur la latinité de Pétrarque d'après le livre XXIV des *Epistolae familiares,*" *Mélanges d'archéologie et d'histoire publiés par l'École française de Rome,* XXXIV (1904), 219-46. Martellotti's contributions are "Clausole e ritmi nella prosa narrativa del Petrarca," *Studi petrarcheschi,* IV (1951), 35-46; "Noterelle di sintassi petrarchesca," idem., VI (1956), 195-200, which draws from *De viris,* and "La latinità del Petrarca," in *Petrarca e il petrarchismo, Studi petrarcheschi,* VII (1961), 219-30.

20. Some idea of the arduous task in making critical editions of the works of Petrarch can be gained from N. Mann's article, "The Manuscripts of Petrarch's *De remediis:* A Checklist," *Italia medioevale e umanistica,* XIV (1971), 57-90. Mann specifies 149 complete and 51 partial manuscripts, and though the problem is smaller for other works everyone of them represents a formidable challenge.

In passing on to Petrarch's single works I shall, with one or two exceptions, list them in chronological order, starting with the *De viris illustribus*. The most penetrating study so far is, in my opinion, the one made by Calcaterra in "La concezione storica del Petrarca," *Nella selva,* op. cit., 415-43. Other good discussions are by P. P. Gerosa, "L'opera parallela dello storico: *De viris illustribus,*" in *Umanesimo cristiano del Petrarca* (Torino, 1966), and A. Viscardi, "Francesco Petrarca storiografo," *Cultura,* II (1923), 491-99.

N. Festa's *Saggio sull'*Africa (Palermo, 1926), is rather uneven. He does not exploit all of the possibilities of his interpretation, as C. Foligno has observed in *Modern Language Review,* XXII (1927), 346-50. On the other hand, what he has to say about the lacunae in the epic has received favorable comment. Tonelli in his *Petrarca,* op. cit., 85-112 views it as a "poema storico e mediterraneo," while G. Mazzoni, "La vittoria di Roma su l'Africa nel poema del Petrarca," *Annali della Cattedra petrarchesca,* VII (1937), 29-57 connects it with the cycle of the Crusades. E. Cappa, "Il sentimento della romanità nel Petrarca," *Annali . . .* ,VII (1937), 95-126, makes worthwhile observations on its expression in the poem. E. Raimondi's "Ritrattistica petrarchesca," *Dai dettatori al Novecento* (Torino, 1953), 74-86 and *Metafora e storia* (Torino, 1970), 163-88, dwells on the portraiture of Sophonisba in the fifth Book. The mediocrity of H. de Ziegler's *Pétrarque* (Neuchâtel, 1940) is partially redeemed by a good discussion on the epic. A. S. Bernardo's *Petrarch, Scipio and the* Africa: *The Birth of Humanism's Dream* (Baltimore, 1962), is an admirable study. The task he has assigned to himself has been to analyze and define the thought of Scipio Africanus in Petrarch's life and works. Though Scipio occupies a place in other works, it is in the *Africa* that he finds his most complete definition. Perhaps the most interesting chapter in the book is "Scipio vs. Laura. From Leaves to Garlands" which brings out the persistent link and fusion of the names of Laura and Scipio in the Latin and Italian writings of Petrarch with particular reference to the symbolism with which the poet has endowed them, Glory-Virtue. The chapter on the *fortuna* of the *Africa* is useful for an evaluation of studies from Zumbini to date.[21]

The massive essay by H. Baron, "Petrarch's *Secretum:* Was it Revised, and Why? The Draft of 1342-43 and Later Changes," *Bibliothèque d'Humanisme et Renaissance,* XXV (1963), 489-530, and reprinted in

21. W. F. Mustard's article, "Petrarch's *Africa,*" *American Journal of Philology,* XLII (1921), 197-221, is virtually a summary of the epic from the first to the last page. For those needing a knowledge of its contents only it can conveniently serve as a time-saver.

From Petrarch to Leonardo Bruni (Chicago, 1968), 51-101, furnishes basic discussion for an eventual critical edition. He agrees with others that it was composed in 1342-43, but asserts that it was recast and finally finished in 1358. A. Viscardi has two chapters on the autobiography in *Petrarca e il medioevo* (Napoli, 1925), "Petrarca e il *Secretum*," 15-36, and "La psicologia del *Secretum*," 53-64. He emphasizes the power of the spiritual drama in Petrarch in connection with mediaeval thought and doctrine on truth and reality, which form the principal theme of the critic's book. P. P. Gerosa writes on "Le confessioni del Petrarca" in *Umanesimo cristiano del Petrarca,* op. cit., 82-98 and P. Da Prati on "Il conflitto spirituale nel *Secretum*" in *Il dissidio nell'arte e nell'anima del Petrarca* (San Remo, 1963), 29-40. K. Heitmann in "L'insegnamento agostiniano nel *Secretum* del Petrarca," *Petrarca e il petrarchismo,* op. cit., 188-94, brings out the points where Petrarch strays from Augustinian orthodoxy. The Trecentista's *accidia* is discussed in S. Wenzel, "Petrarch's *Accidia,*" *Studies in the Renaissance,* VIII (1962), 36-48, as well as in Wilkins, "On Petrarch's *Accidia* and the Adamantine Chains," *Speculum,* XXXVII (1962), 589-94. A. Castelli's "Suggerimenti di una lettura del *Secretum* di Francesco Petrarca," *Rassegna delle scienze filosofiche,* XXII (1969), 109-33 injects some fresh observation on the book. He accepts Boccaccio's characterization of the Christian character of Petrarch and sets out to prove it in the *Secretum.* For him it is a confession of the sins. The author contrasts it with the *Confessions* and, at the same time interprets the Saint's role in it. F. Tateo has chosen to discuss the special topic: *Dialogo interiore e polemica ideologica nel Secretum del Petrarca* (Firenze, 1966). He looks at its contents as an attempt to give the problem of existence a moral solution. A. Noferi's "Alle soglie del *Secretum*" in *L'esperienza poetica del Petrarca* (Firenze, 1962), closely links it with the *Canzoniere,* while N. Iliescu's chapter on "Il *Secretum* e le *Rime,*" in *Il* Canzoniere *petrarchesco e Sant'Agostino* (Roma, 1962), 55-66 reveals its contents through its title.

The only recent study on the *Psalmi poenitentiales* is by M. Casali, "Imitazione e ispirazione dei *Salmi penitenziali,*" *Petrarca e petrarchismo,* op. cit., 151-70 and *Humanitas,* XIII (1958), 367-81. Casali finds the seventh psalm most representative of Petrarch's spirituality, and suggests further study in terms of reciprocal rapports between it and other works.

The *Bucolicum carmen* has not received much comment. For good discussions we still need to resort to E. Carrara's in *La poesia pastorale* (Milano, 1909), 87-111, and his "Aridulum rus," *Scritti in onore di*

R. Renier (Torino, 1912), 271-88. S. Benfenati in "Le egloghe del dolore nel *Bucolicum carmen,*" *Convivium,* raccolta nuova (1948), 86-95, comments on IX, X, XI, which deal with Petrarch's sorrow on the death of friends, Laura, and the passing away of earthly beings. G. Mazzoni in "Daedelus del Petrarca," *Studi francescani,* XII (1926), 405-11 and C. Calcaterra, "Daedelus del Petrarca," *Giornale storico,* CXVII (1941), 1-23 attempt to identify the person behind the veiled mythical name. In "Petrarch's Seventh Eclogue," *Mediaevalia et Humanistica,* VIII (1954), 22-31, Wilkins attempts to establish the identity of the cardinals referred to in it. With the sixth eclogue it is a violent attack on the corruption of the papal court in Avignon under Clement VI. G. Ponte's "La decima egloga e la composizione dei *Trionfi,*" *Rassegna della letteratura italiana,* LXIX, (1965), 519-29, has a self-explanatory title.

N. Sapegno's chapter on "Le lettere di Francesco Petrarca," *Pagine di storia letteraria* (Palermo, 1960), 63-114, should be required reading for those interested in the *Epistolario.* The real Petrarch is revealed in the collection as P. Da Prati tries to show in "Il vero Petrarca nell'*Epistolario,*" *Il dissidio nell'arte e nell'anima di Francesco Petrarca,* op. cit., 13-28. P. P. Gerosa had previously touched on the same topic in "La quotidiana ricerca di sé attraverso l'*Epistolario,*" op. cit., 99-111. Two studies by Bernardo: "Dramatic Dialogue and Monologue in Petrarch's *Prose Letters,*" *Symposium,* V (1951), 302-16 and "Dramatic Dialogue and Monologue in Petrarch's Works," *Symposium,* VII (1953), 92-111, stress the great importance of these devices in Petrarch's prose style.[22] English readers will enjoy two elegant translations of Petrarch's letters. One of them has been done by Wilkins: *Petrarch at Vaucluse* (Chicago, 1958), and the other by Bishop (Bloomington, Ind., 1968). They replace the selections in Robinson-Rolfe (New York, 2nd ed. 1914).

R. Argenio has written eight articles on various aspects of the *Metricae.* These have been printed in the *Rivista di studi classici e medievali, Convivium,* and *Studi romani* between 1954 and 1970. They deal with questions of interpretation, variants, favorite authors, Rome as seen in the poems. U. Dotti has made three studies on the collection "Aspetti della tematica petrarchesca, I: Umanesimo e poesia in Petrarca," *Letterature moderne,* IX (1959), 582-90, suggesting that on account of its mythology it has a place in Petrarch's Humanism; "Le *Metriche,*" *Convivium,* XXXV (1967), 153-73, pointing out a close link

22. B. Headstrom's "Historical Significance of Petrarch's Letters," *Open Court,* XI (1926), 1-13 is not a study, it is a panegyric.

between the Latin verse and the *Rime*; "Le *Epistole metriche*," *Belfagor,* XIII (1968), 532-64, arguing that they should be considered youthful poems, a "prima minuta" culminating in the prose letters and the *Rime*. Their Horatianism is stressed in G. Ponte's "Poetica e poesia nelle *Metrice* del Petrarca," *Rassegna della letteratura italiana,* LXXII (1968), 209-19. Indispensable as a tool is Wilkins, *The* Epistolae metricae *of Petrarch. A Manual* (Roma, 1956).

Bernardo's doctoral dissertation (Harvard, 1950) is on the subject of the *Artistic Procedures Followed by Petrarch in Making the Collection of the Familiares.* It laid the groundwork for his "Letter Splitting in Petrarch's *Familiares*," *Speculum,* XXXIII (1958), 236-41, in which he finds that this procedure was motivated by artistic considerations, and "The Selection of Letters in Petrarch's *Familiares,*" *Speculum,* XXXV (1960), 280-88, an attempt to determine some of the criteria used in deciding what letters should be included in the collection. Dealing with special topics are E. Carrara, "Le *Antiquis illustrioribus,*" *Studi petrarcheschi,* I (1948), 63-96 (on Book XXIV), and in his *Studi petrarcheschi* (Torino, 1959), 129-70; U. Dotti, "L'ottavo libro delle *Famigliari:* contributo per una storia dell'Umanesimo petrarchesco," *Belfagor,* XXVIII (1973), 271-94. Dozens of essays and articles have been written on *Fam.* IV, 1, describing the famous ascent of Mt. Ventoux. A thorough discussion can be read in P. Guiton's "Pétrarque et la nature," *Annali della Cattedra petrarchesca,* VI (1935-36), 48-82. Its author also furnishes a complete bibliography up to 1935, pp. 49-50. The latest contribution has been made by B. Martinelli: "L'ascensione al Monte Ventoux," *Studi in onore di Alberto Chiari* (Brescia, 1973), 767-834. See also "The Chronology of the *Familiares* and the *Seniles*" in Wilkins, *The Making of the* Canzoniere . . . (Roma, 1951), 369-77.

Aside from two letters, VII, 3 and XIV, 1, the *Seniles* have received virtually no attention. On the first, containing the famous Latinized version of the Griselda story in the *Decameron* best known to English readers through Chaucer's "The Clerkes Tale," evidence of its wide diffusion can be found in E. Golenistscheff-Koutouszoff, *L'histoire de Griseldis en France au XIVᵉ et au XVᵉ siècle* (Paris, 1933). On the second we have A. Steiner, "Petrarch's Optimus Princeps," *Romanic Review,* XXV (1934), 99-111 and A. Amatucci, "La teoria dell'azione politica nel 'De republica optime administranda' di Francesco Petrarca," *Scriptoria* (Arezzo, 1968-69), 132-64. For an erudite discussion see Wilkins, "The Collection of the *Seniles*," in *Petrarch's Later Years* (Chicago, 1959), 303-14.

Off-hand one would assume that the 70-page introduction in J.

Zeitlin's translation of *De vita solitaria, Life of Solitude* (Urbana, Ill., 1924), would furnish us with some useful information. This is not true. Its best part is the marginal discussion on the history of solitude before Petrarch's time. Nor has the translation much value. See two reviews: D. Bigongiari, *Romanic Review,* XVI (1925), 89-95 and G. Shephard, *Journal of English and Germanic Philology,* XXIV (1925), 560-74. Gerosa, as usual, makes pertinent observations in "Il teorico della vita interiore," *Umanesimo cristiano del Petrarca,* op. cit., 137-55. There is a monograph on the work which I have not been able to see: Francesco Serpagli's *Prolegomeni al* De vita solitaria (Parma, 1967). A. Castelli in "Sul *De vita solitaria,*" *Rassegna di scienze filosofiche,* XXII (1969), 349-68, views the treatise as a document of genuine religious experience. T. E. Mommsen in "Petrarch and the Story of the Choice of Hercules," *Journal of the Warburg and Courtauld Institutes,* XV (1954), 178-92 and *Medieval and Renaissance Studies* (Ithaca, N. Y., 1959), 175-96, takes notice of the close relationship and interdependence between *virtus* and *gloria,* one of Petrarch's favorite ideas.

I can only cite one critical study on *De otio religioso:* C. Calcaterra, "Haec maximus," *Nella selva,* op. cit., 375-88.

The *De remediis utriusque fortunae* deserves more consideration than has been given to it. Based directly on the work is K. Heitmann, *Fortuna und Virtus. Eine Studie zu Petrarcas Lebensweisheit* (Köln-Graz, 1959). His theme, as the title suggests, is the conflict between *Fortuna* and *Virtus.* In an earlier study, "La genesi del *De Remediis utriusque fortunae,*" *Convivium,* XXV (1957), 9-30, he arrives at his conclusions on the dating of the treatise from the happenings and persons mentioned in it. Of special interest is the section "Il titolo del *De Remediis,*" pp. 25-30. E. Raimondi in "Alcune pagine del Petrarca sulla dignità umana," *Convivium,* XIX (1947), 376-93, primarily refers to Chapter XCIII, a "breviario della dignità umana," as he calls it. There is some discussion in the article on parts related to St. Augustine and the Church Fathers. C. H. Rawski's "Petrarch's Dialogue on Music," *Speculum,* XLVI (1971), 302-17 is based on chapter XVIII. Relevant observations have been made by E. P. Rice in his chapter on "Active and contemplative ideas of Wisdom in Italian Humanism," *The Renaissance Idea of Wisdom* (Cambridge, Mass., 1958), 30-36. On the moral influence exerted by the work see N. Mann's "Petrarch's role as a Moralist in Fifteenth Century France," *Humanism in France at the End of the Middle Ages and the Early Renaissance* (New York-Manchester, Eng., 1970), 6-28. No list of titles would be complete without mention of the influence of the *De remediis* on two Spanish masterpieces, the *Coplas* of Jorge Manrique and the *Celestina.* J. Vinci in "The Petrarchan Source of Jorge Manrique's 'Las coplas,' " *Italica,* XLIV (1968), 314-28 brings out that *De remediis* is its leading source. A. D. Deyermond, *The Petrarchan Sources of* La Celestina (Oxford, 1961), after citing the impressive total of ninety-nine borrowings, the bulk of them coming from this Latin treatise, later generalizes by saying that "most of the work can be called Petrarchan," the most glorious single triumph Petrarch had in Spain.

R. Realfonso Dell'Aera, "Uno dei primi messaggi dell'Umanesimo," *Italica,* XXIX (1952), 77-95 claims that the *Invectivae contra medicum* mark the climax in the struggle against the philosophical naturalism that had been popularized by the Arabs.

We are glad to take notice of N. P. Zacour's translation, *The Book Without a Name* (Toronto, 1973), especially since the *Sine nomine* do not appear in the *Prose,* op. cit. It is based upon Piur's critical edition and supercedes the hard-to-come-by translations of Develay (1885) and D'Uva (1895), who, moreover, were dependent on defective texts. U. Dotti has just given us an Italian translation: *Sine nomine. Lettere polemiche e politiche* (Bari, 1974). There are very few discussions bearing on the collection, among them A. Foresti's "Sognando la riforma del governo di Roma" and "Super flumina Babylonis," *Aneddoti,* op. cit., 251-62; Gerosa's "Apologia del cristianesimo," *Umanesimo cristiano del Petrarca,* op. cit., 350-84, and, on a novelletta in letter XVIII, Raimondi's "Un esercizio del Petrarca," *Studi petrarcheschi,* VI (1956), 43-54, and *Metafora e storia,* op. cit., 189-98.

The fundamental discussion for *Epistola posteritati* is E. Carrara, "*Epistola posteritati,*" in his *Studi petrarcheschi* (Torino, 1959), 273-342. See also E. H. R. Tatham in *Francesco Petrarca,* op. cit., Vol. II, and Wilkins, "On the Evolution of Petrarch's *Letter to Posterity,*" *Speculum,* XXXIX (1964), 304-08.

Wilkins and Billanovich bring together for the first time eighteen letters in "The Miscellaneous Letters of Petrarch," *Speculum,* XXXVII (1962), 226-43. They are a supplement to Fracassetti's edition (Firenze, 1863).

I shall close with the *Testamento,* Petrarch's most personal document. It has been edited and translated with an introduction by T. E. Mommsen (Ithaca, 1957) and reprinted under the title "The Last Will: a Personal Document of Petrarch's Old Age" in his *Mediaeval and Renaissance Studies* (Ithaca, 1959), 197-235.

3. *Petrarch, Classical Antiquity and Humanism:*

The term Humanism has already been mentioned a number of times in the foregoing titles and discussions. Since it is closely associated with Petrarch's Latin works, the books he owned, read and annotated, the influence of the Ancients on his life and thought and upon those who were inspired by him, it will be appropriate to take up the topic at this point. Of course, De Nolhac's *Pétrarque et l'humanisme* is an absolutely basic source. The person who has done most to continue the Frenchman's investigations is the indefatigable and enormously learned G. Billanovich. In his *Petrarca letterato. I. Lo scrittoio del Petrarca* (Roma, 1947), he deals with the collections of Petrarch's correspondence, his relations with Boccaccio, that occupy the bulk of his book, pp. 57-294, and the early *fortuna* of the works of Petrarch. The second volume, which is to be an inventory of Petrarch's library, has not appeared. It will presumably, at least in part, be composed of material in more than a dozen articles on manuscripts owned and annotated by "the first modern man," which Billanovich has published in various periodicals and homage volumes between 1951 and 1965. We now know many of the books owned by Petrarch. See B. L. Ullman, "Petrarch's Favorite Books," *Transactions of the American Philological Society,* LIV (1923), 21-38, reprinted in his *Studies in the Renaissance* (Roma, 1953), 117-38, and E. Pellégrin, "Nouveaux manuscrits annotés par Pétrarque à la Bibliothèque Nationale de Paris," *Scriptorium,* V (1951), 265-78. A. Noferi has discussed in "Letture del Petrarca," *Esperienza poetica,* op. cit., 97-11, some of the authors read by him and cites illustrations. Studies on the presence of individual classical writers in Petrarch are many. I shall limit myself to ten, each title bearing on one of the Classics. G. Billanovich, "Petrarch and the Textual Tradition of Livy," *Journal of the Warburg and Courtauld Institutes,* XIX (1951), 137-308; A. Bobbio, "Seneca e la formazione spirituale e culturale del Petrarca," *Bibliofilia,* XLII (1941), 224-91; E. Fraenkel, "Lucan als Mittler des antiken Pathos. Nachwirkungen auf Dante, besonders aus die Renaissance (Petrarca)," *Vorträge der Bibliothek Warburg* (Leipzig), XXVII (1924), 229-57; M. Françon, "Petrarch Disciple of Heraclitus," *Speculum,* XI (1938), 265-71; see also G. Post, "Petrarch and Heraclitus Once More," *Speculum,* XII (1938), 343-50; G. Gasparotto, "Il Petrarca conosceva direttamente Lucrezio. Le fonti dell'Egloga IX: Querulus del *Bucolicum carmen," Atti e memorie dell'Accademia di scienze, lettere ed arti in Padova,* LXXX (1967-68), 309-55; F. Klingner, "Cicero und Petrarca. Vom Ursprung des humanistischen Geistes," *Römische Geistwelt* (München, 1956), 600-18; G. Martellotti, "Petrarca e Marziale,"

Rivista di cultura classica e medievale, II (1960), 388-93; S. Prete, "Plautus und Terenz in den Schriften des Francesco Petrarca," *Gymnasium* (Heidelberg), LVII (1950), 219-75 and in Italian, *Studi petrarcheschi,* V (1952), 85-91; D. R. Stuart, "Petrarch's Indebtedness to the *Libellus* of Catullus," *Transactions and Proceedings of the American Philological Assoc.,* XLVIII (1917), 85-91; V. Zabughin, *Virgilio nel Rinascimento italiano. Da Dante a Torquato Tasso* (Bologna, 1921), 21-39.

St. Augustine's influence also comes up frequently in philosophical and religious discussions. Three extensive treatments are C. Calcaterra, already mentioned, P. Courcelle, "Un humaniste épris de Pétrarque," *Les Confessions de Saint Augustin dans la tradition littéraire* (Paris, 1963), 329-50; P. P. Gerosa in *Didaskaleion,* III-VII (1925-29). Speaking of philosophy, it will suffice for me to cite G. Gentile, "Gli inizi dell'Umanesimo e Francesco Petrarca," *Storia dei generi letterari: La filosofia* (Milano, n.d.), 146-96 and his chapters in *Studi sul Rinascimento* (Firenze, 1936, 1968); and G. Toffanin, "La filosofia del Petrarca," *Grande antologia filosofica,* VI (1964), 492-525.

A fine evaluation of the *studia humanitatis* of Petrarch is contained in E. Garin, *L'umanesimo italiano* (Bari, 1954), 25-35, and G. Martellotti, "Linee di sviluppo dell'Umanesimo petrarchesco," *Studi petrarcheschi,* II (1949), 51-80. Of especial concern to D. Aguzzi Barbagli has been the topic of eloquence in "L'ideale classico dell'eleganza agli albori del movimento umanistico," *Rinascimento,* ser. II, 1 (1962), where twelve pages are devoted to Petrarch. Important even though controversial are G. Toffanin's treatments in *Storia dell'Umanesimo* (Napoli, 1933), 69-126, and J. H. Whitfield's *Petrarch and the Renaissance* (Oxford, 1943).

As to whether Petrarch belongs to the Middle Ages or the Renaissance or whether there was in him a pagan-Christian dualism, there has been a difference of opinion for a long time. These opinions from Foscolo to Bosco are conveniently discussed by P. Mazzamuto in the section on Petrarch in *Rassegna bibliografica e critica della letteratura italiana* (Firenze, 3rd ed. 1970), 83-96. There will be no need to go further into it here.

What the Humanists thought of Petrarch and his writings can be learned from D. Thompson and A. F. Nagel, *Three Crowns of Florence: Humanist Assessments of Dante, Petrarch, and Boccaccio* (New York, 1972). Just as important is W. Handschin, *Francesco Petrarca als Gestalt der Historiographie. Seine Beurteilung in der Geschichtesschreibung von Frühhumanismus bis zu Jacob Burckhardt* (Basel, 1964).

Handschin makes use of biographies on Petrarch, commentaries and introductions to the commentaries.

4. *Canzoniere, Trionfi, Rime disperse:*

In the face of approximately eight hundred studies on the *Canzoniere* since the opening of the century it is virtually impossible to present a satisfactory picture on this subject. It can be said, however, that most of the aesthetic criticism still follows the general pattern of De Sanctis and through him of Croce. The latter does not bring anything essentially new on Petrarch, but refines the three chief aspects which the Neapolitan sees in the *Rime:* 1) "la centralità del *Canzoniere* rispetto alle altre opere del Petrarca, e la centralità di Laura nel *Canzoniere*," 2) "la superiorità della poesia 'in morte di Laura' su quella 'in vita,' " 3) "la discriminazione tra poesia e letteratura nell'opera del Petrarca" (Sozzi, op. cit., 120). Croce's major essay on Petrarchan criticism is "La poesia del Petrarca," which can be read in *Poesia popolare e poesia d'arte* (Bari, 1933), 65-80. Nevertheless, it is through his critical method more than from what he has to say here that his influence has been felt. Of course, all the newer critical methods have also been applied. Some general treatments bearing the names of some of the most distinguished critics of Italian literature of our time are: G. Bertoni, "Il *Canzoniere* del Petrarca," *Lingua e poesia* (Firenze, 1937), 77-101; U. Bosco, *La lirica del Petrarca,* Facoltà di magistero dell'Univ. di Roma (Roma, 1966); A. Chiari, *Pagine di storia e di critica sul Canzoniere e sui Trionfi del Petrarca* (Milano, 1957-58); G. De Robertis, *Corso di letteratura italiana,* Anno accademico 1942-43 (Firenze, 1943); "Il valore del Petrarca," *Letteratura,* VIII, 2 (1943), 9-18 and *Studi* (Firenze, 1944), 32-37, "Petrarca e la magia dell'invenzione," *Primi studi manzoniani e altre cose* (Firenze, 1949), 119-35; E. M. Fusco, *La lirica,* "Storia dei generi letterari italiani" (Milano, 1950), esp. 92-121; H. Hauvette, *Les poésies lyriques de Pétrarque* (Paris, 1931); A. Momigliano, *Antologia della letteratura italiana,* nine editions and many reprintings; "L'elegia politica del Petrarca," *Introduzione ai poeti* (Milano, 1946), "Intorno al *Canzoniere*," *Elzeviri* (Firenze, 1945, 65-71); L. Montano, " 'Voi ch'ascoltate,' " *Pégaso,* I (1929), 566-75, more extensive than its title indicates; G. Papini, "'Francesco Petrarca: *Le rime*," *Pagine scelte* (Milano, 1962), 278-84 and "Il Petrarca nel *Canzoniere*," *Ritratti italiani: 1904-1931* (Firenze, 1932), 33-71; L. Russo, *Il* Canzoniere *del Petrarca,* Anno accademico 1948-49 dell'Univ. di Pisa (Pisa, 1949); N. Sapegno, *La poesia del Petrarca* (Roma, 1965). See also *Il Trecento,* 2d ed. (Milano, 1966), 165-266; L.

Tonelli, *Petrarca* (Milano, 1930), 53-68, 141-56, 209-23.[23] Naturally, very worthwhile essays are to be found in some of the editions of the *Rime*—Chiorboli (1930), Sapegno (1951), Romanò (1958), Muscetta (1958), Baldacci (1962), Bigi (1963), Contini (1964).

There are a number of special *Canzoniere* studies of some relevance. I shall start with N. Iliescu's *Il* Canzoniere *petrarchesco e Sant'Agostino* (Roma, 1962). The author goes into various contacts between Petrarch and Augustine, the saint's presence during his spiritual conflicts as well as in his theme of solitude, and a possible influence on Petrarch's style. One of the significant points made by Iliescu concerns the ordering of the poems as to sonnets 2-4 and nos. 363-65. Petrarch's initial attempt to submit his poems to an arranged pattern in which artistic variety is subordinated to a Christian-moral experience, as Iliescu notices, coincides with the year of the first draft of the *Secretum*. Three studies that involve Dante are F. Neri, "Il Petrarca e le rime dantesche della Pietra," *La Cultura,* VIII (1929), 389-404, *Letteratura e leggende* (Torino 1951), 32-72, and *Saggi* (Milano, 1964), 155-74; M. Santagata, "Presenza di Dante comico nel *Canzoniere* del Petrarca," *Giornale storico,* CXLVI (1969), 163-211; E. Di Poppa Volture, "Dante e Petrarca," *Il padre e i figli: Dante nei maggiori poeti italiani dal Petrarca a D'Annunzio* (Napoli, 1970), 133-53. Others are J. Basile, "Premesse a uno studio dei simboli e delle allegorie del *Canzoniere*," *Fama simbolica ed allegoria nei* Rerum vulgarium fragmenta *ed altre cose* (Assisi-Roma, 1971), 49-133; G. Caione: *Il sentimento del tempo nel* Canzoniere *del Petrarca* (Lecce, 1969); U. Dotti, "Petrarca: il mito dafneo," *Convivium,* XXXVII (1969), 9-23; K. Foster, "Beatrice or Medusa: The Penitential Element in Petrarch's *Canzoniere*," *Italian Studies Presented to E. R. Vincent* (Cambridge, 1962), 31-46; R. Giani, *L'amore nel* Canzoniere *di Francesco Petrarca* (Torino, 1917); R. V. Merrill, "Platonism in Petrarch's *Canzoniere*," *Modern Philology,* XXVII (1929), 161-74; M. M. Rossi, "Laura morta e la concezione petrarchesca dell'aldilà," *Petrarca e petrarchismo,* op. cit., 201-22; C. Sgroi, "Petrarca e la natura," *Saggi e problemi di critica letteraria* (Catania, 1932), 3-81; G. Ungaretti, "Il poeta dell'oblio," *Primato: lettere ed arti d'Italia,* IV (1943), 165-68.

Numerous studies relate either to an individual poem or to a small group. The following will supply a good sampling: P. Antonetti, "Poésie et littérature dans la canzone: 'Di pensier in pensier' (Pétrarque: *Can-*

23. Besides comments on Foscolo, De Sanctis, Croce, and Montano, A. Viscardi in *Petrarca e il petrarchismo,* Univ. degli studi di Milano, Anno accademico 1965-66 (Milano, 1965), discusses "L'interpretazione critica del *Canzoniere* di N. Sapegno," 79-93.

zoniere CXXIX)," *Annales de la faculté des lettres d'Aix,* XXVIII (1964), 195-204, and "Aspects de la poésie de Pétrarque (Pétrarque sans pétrarquisme)," idem, XLI (1967), 214-38; R. Bacchelli, "Chiose petrarchesche," *Approdo,* I, VII, N. 16 (1961), 45-98 and *Saggi critici* (Milano, 1962), 789-841; A. S. Bernardo, "The Importance of the Non-Love Poems of Petrarch's *Canzoniere,*" *Italica,* XXVII (1950), 302-12; A. Bertoldi, "L'ultima canzone di Francesco Petrarca," *Esempi di analisi letteraria,* I (Torino, 1926), 348-62; various poems in R. Brambati, *Avviamento all'analisi letteraria e alla critica* (Roma, 1936); E. Chiorboli, "I sonetti introduttivi delle *Rime sparse,*" *Studi petrarcheschi. Omaggio di Arezzo al suo poeta* (Arezzo, 1928), 64-78; H. Hauvette, "Notes pour le commentaire de Pétrarque: La canzone 'O aspettata in ciel,' " *Mélanges de philologie et d'histoire offerts à Joseph Vianey* (Paris, 1934), 85-92; W. von Koppenfels, "Dantes 'Al poco giorno' und Petrarcas 'Giovene donna': Ein Interpretationsvergleich zweier Sestinen," *Deutsches Dante Jahrbuch,* XLIV-XLV (1967), 150-89; G. Lipparini, " 'Chiare, fresche e dolci acque,' " *Annali della Cattedra petrarchesca,* II (1931), 71-92; F. Maggini, "La canzone delle visioni," *Studi petrarcheschi,* I (1948), 37-50; M. Marcazzan, " 'Chiare, fresche e dolci acque,' " *Didimo Chierico ed altri saggi* (Milano, 1930), 179-219; A. Pézard, "Les sonnets de l'inconstance et de la fidelité: I. 'Io sono stato con amore insieme' (Dante) 2. 'Movesi il vecchierel canuto e bianco' (Pétrarque)," *Revue des études italiennes,* I (1936), 397-415; L. Pietrobono, " 'Vergine bella che di sol vestita,' " *Annali della Cattedra petrarchesca,* II (1931), 135-62; E. Williamson, "A Consideration of 'Vergine bella,' " *Italica,* XXIX (1952), 215-28. For some other studies, see below.

A. Noferi has attracted considerable notice through her essays in periodicals now collected in *L'esperienza poetica del Petrarca* (Firenze, 1962). As she informs us her aim is to "illuminare la qualità e l'essenza dell'esperienza poetica del Petrarca," an experience in which all of the poet's works as well as his readings play an important role. She herself calls her method stylistic, but it is obvious that she has worked on a much broader scale than other stylistic critics, who almost exclusively draw their conclusions from the definitive text of the *Canzoniere,* its variants, or both—an approach that like hers has unlimited possibilities. It has become an increasingly popular trend. Though the studies thus far published tend to show us the artistic rather than the poetic side of Petrarch, there are some exceptions, one of them being the rehabilitation of the poetic value of some of the poet's précieux compositions, a value which has been denied to them by Tassoni,

Muratori, Foscolo, De Sanctis, and which is still frequently echoed. See statements by Bosco on Petrarch's antitheses and the Laura-lauro pun in his *Francesco Petrarca*, and conclusions by Bigi and Le Mollé in the articles cited below.

Continuing with my citation of stylistic titles I shall begin with three general contributions: G. Bertoni, "La lingua della lirica del Petrarca," *Annali della Cattedra petrarchesca,* IX (1935-36), 135-50, and U. Bosco, "Il linguaggio lirico nel Petrarca tra Dante e il Bembo," *Petrarca e petrarchismo,* op. cit. 121-32 and *Francesco Petrarca* (Bari, 1961), 156-85, and *La lirica del Petrarca,* Facoltà di magistero dell'Univ. di Roma (Roma, 1966). Metrical studies that should be mentioned are G. A. Levi, "Analisi metrica della prima canzone del Petrarca," *Giornale storico,* XCIX (1932), 62-73 and in *Da Dante a Machiavelli* (Firenze, 1935), 118-30 and "Commento metrico a tre canzoni del Petrarca," *Convegno petrarchesco* (1928), 31-35 and *Da Dante a Machiavelli,* 130-40; D. Bianchi, "Di alcuni caratteri della verseggiatura petrarchesca," *Studi petrarcheschi,* VI (1956), 81-122; M. Fubini, "La metrica del Petrarca," and "La sestina," *Metrica e poesia* (Milano, 1962), 236-327, 328-46. Investigations that involve structure and technique are: D. Alonso, "Función estructural de las pluralidades. I. En el soneto (de Petrarca a Góngora)," *Estudios y ensayos gongorinos* (Madrid, 1955), 174-207, and "La poesia del Petrarca e il petrarchismo (mondo estetico della pluralità)," *Petrarca e il petrarchismo,* op. cit., 73-120 and in *La correlazione dal Petrarca ai petrarchisti. Pluralità e correlazione in poesia* (Bari, 1971), 144-79; E. Bigi, "Alcuni aspetti dello stile del *Canzoniere* del Petrarca," *Lingua nostra,* XIII (1952), 17-22 and *Dal Petrarca al Leopardi* (Milano-Napoli, 1954), 1-22, which includes a "Nota sulla sintassi petrarchesca;" F. Chiappelli, "La canzone delle visioni e il sostrato tematico della 'fabula inexpleta,'" *Giornale storico,* CXLI (1964), 321-35, "Dall'intenzione all'invenzione: una lettura petrarchesca (*Rime,* CXCIV)," *Giornale storico,* CXLIV (1967), 161-69; "La canzone petrarchesca delle visioni," *Yearbook of Italian Studies* (Montreal), I, 1971, 235-48; *Studi sul linguaggio del Petrarca. La canzone delle visioni* (Firenze, 1972); D. Diani, "Pétrarque: *Canzoniere* 132," *Revue des études italiennes,* XVIII (1972), 111-67; G. Di Pino, "Poesia e tecnica formale nel *Canzoniere* petrarchesco," *Stile e umanità* (Messina-Firenze, 1956), 33-63; R. W. Durling, "'Giovene donna sotto un verde lauro,'" *Modern Language Notes,* LXXXVI (1971), 1-20; F. Figurelli, "L'architettura del sonetto in F. Petrarca," *Petrarca e petrarchismo,* op. cit. 179-86 (I give only the latest of several articles by F.); G. Herczeg, "Struttura e antitesi nel *Canzoniere* petrarchesco," *Petrarca e petrarchismo,* op. cit. 195-208 and *Saggi linguistici e stilistici* (Firenze, 1972), 106-20; T. Labande-Jeanroy, "La technique de la chanson dans Pétrarque," *Etudes italiennes,* IX (1927), 143-214; R. Le Mollé, "Analyse des structures du sonnet de Pétrarque: 'Pace non trovo e non ho da far guerra,' " *Annali della scuola superiore normale di Pisa,* XXXIX (1970), 452-68; E. J. Rivers, "Hacia la síntesis del soneto," *Studia philologica: Homenaje ofrecido a Dámaso Alonso . . .* (Madrid, 1963), Vol. III, 225-33; G. E. Sansone, "Assaggio di simmetrie petrarchesche," *Lingua e stile,* VI (1971), 223-40.

A. Schiaffini, "Il lavorio della forma in Francesco Petrarca," *Momenti di storia della lingua italiana* (Bari, 1950), 57-70, has provided a fine study of the variants and notes in Vat. Lat. 3196. Even more brilliant have been the investigations of G. Contini. They are conveniently included in *Varianti e altra linguistica. Una raccolta di saggi* (Torino, 1970). Contini draws on Wilkins' fundamental studies relating to the different phases in Petrarch's reconstruction of the masterpiece from its first form in 1336-38 to its last in 1373-74, which constitute nine chapters in Wilkins' *The Making of the Canzoniere and Other Petrarchan Studies* (Roma, 1951). They are a magnificent piece of scientific analysis.

This leads us logically to the problem of arrangement and chronology which has also concerned Wilkins. Needless to say, they have been debated and discussed for centuries. Mazzamuto, op. cit., 99-101, cites fifteen scholars who have expressed their opinions on the subject from 1887 to 1951. The latest to write on it is A. Jenni, "Un sistema del Petrarca nell'ordinamento del *Canzoniere,*" *Studi in onore di Alberto Chiari* (Brescia, 1973), 711-30. The *sistema* is presumably variety in thematic and formal grouping, based on the principle of harmony and alternation.

A word must be said about Laura. With the exception of a very few disbelievers, for example, A. Lipari in "Laura di Petrarca," and "Il gabbo semiserio del poeta," *Italica,* XXVI-XXVII (1948-49), 121-30, 196-201, there is no longer any doubt that Petrarch loved a woman he has called Laura. Most people also know that finding out who she really was is likely to remain an insolvable mystery. As many as ten candidates have been proposed at various times with Laura de Noves, who married a De Sade, being the person generally favored. See Calcaterra, "La questione di Laura" in *Questioni e correnti,* op. cit., 211-25, for a list of studies. E. Davin goes into the subject at greater length in "Les différentes Laures de Pétrarque," *Bulletin de l'association G. Budé,* XV

(1956), 83-94. We agree with H. Hauvette in "Ce que nous savons de Laure," *Etudes italiennes,* IX (1927), 10-25, that on her we shall have to accept only what Petrarch tells us, which is pitiably little. E. Carrara in *La leggenda di Laura* (Torino), 1934, traces the figure of this woman as conceived by the Petrarchologists of the Renaissance.

There is a need for a new critical text of the *Trionfi* to replace Appel's edition, which should take in consideration the whole of the manuscript tradition. Until now the Chiorboli edition has been considered the best. An important discovery of a new manuscript has been made by R. Weiss, *Un inedito petrarchesco, la redazione sconosciuta di un capitolo del 'Trionfo della fama'* (Roma, 1950). See the long Martellotti review in *Rinascimento,* I (1950), 157-70. Wilkins, who is also the translator of the *Trionfi* (Chicago, 1962), in his chapter on "The Chronology of the *Triumphs,*" *Studies in the Life and Works of Petrarch* (Boston, 1955), 254-72, thoroughly examines the manuscript evidence provided by Petrarch's work sheets, and in the course of the examination agrees or disagrees with discussions by others. It includes the first of C. F. Goffis' studies, *L'originalità dei Trionfi* (Firenze, 1951), but not his articles in *Rassegna della letteratura italiana,* XLI (1955), 254-72, and *Belfagor,* XIX (1964), 330-40, both of them largely a defence against Raimondi's strictures in *Convivium,* XXV (1957), 475-79. See also Wilkins, "On Petrarch's Re-writing of the 'Triumph of Fame,'" *Speculum,* XXIX (1964), 440-34. Though obviously faulty, R. Serra's 1904 dissertation printed in *Romagna* in 1927, and in Bologna as a monograph two years later, still ranks high as an important study for the chapters in which he brings out that, in the *Trionfi* more than in the *Canzoniere,* Petrarch modelled his language and syntax on the Latin classics. There is, in addition, a chapter on the *Trionfi* and the *Commedia* and another on the *Trionfi* and the *Amorosa visione.*[24] Two studies no one will want to miss are U. Bosco's "La gara del volgare sul latino. Riposato porto," *Francesco Petrarca,* op. cit., 200-72, and C. Calcaterra's "La prima ispirazione dei *Trionfi,*" *Nella selva,* op. cit., 145-208. In this chapter, incidentally, Calcaterra believes that Petrarch's model is the *Divina commedia* against the contention of V. Branca, "Per la genesi dei *Trionfi,*" *Rinascita,* IV (1941), 681-709, who attempts to prove that it was inspired by the *Amorosa visione.* Without explicitly negating the others, L. Spitzer in

24. For a more extended analysis of the study, see C. Calcaterra in *Giornale storico,* XCIV (1929), 319-24, and G. De Robertis, *Pégaso,* I, parte 2 (1929), 628-30, later incorporated in his "Coscienza letteraria di Renato Serra," *Saggi* (Firenze, 1939), 135-39.

"Zum Aufbau von Petrarcas *Trionfi*," *Neuphilologische Mitteilungen,* XLVII (1946), and *Romanische Literatur-Studien 1936-56* (Tübingen, 1959), 614-23, sets up a third source which affects the structure rather than the contents of the poem. Here, as we know, death triumphs over life, fame over death, and eternity over time. This progressive displacement of one event (or of one thing) by another is a commonplace device that, as the critic observes, goes back to Oriental literature. He does not cite any direct model that might have been used by Petrarch.

The lack of authenticated texts has inhibited critics from writing on the *Rime disperse*. D. Bianchi produced a series of articles preparatory to a critical edition, which has never materialized. On the problems involved, see E. G. Parodi, "Rime note o poco note di Francesco Petrarca" in *Poeti antichi e moderni* (Firenze, 1922), 142-53, and *Lingua e letteratura* (Venezia, 1957), 453-61. For critical discussions, see E. Carrara's "Gli improvvisi del Petrarca," *Studi petrarcheschi,* II (1949), 181-203, and M. Fubini, "Petrarca artefice," *Studi sulla letteratura del Rinascimento* (Firenze, 1947), 1-12.

A most valuable tool of unlimited usefulness either for investigations on Petrarch or on Petrarchism is the new *Concordanze del* Canzoniere *di Francesco Petrarca* (Firenze, 1971), 2 vols. For absolute accuracy it should be preferred to K. McKenzie's *Concordanza delle* Rime *di Francesco Petrarca* (Oxford-New Haven, 1912, reprint Torino, 1969).

The only book-length study on the subject of Petrarch and the figurative arts, a very fine one, is Prince d'Essling and E. Müntz, *Pétrarque: ses études d'art, son influence sur les artistes, ses portraits et ceux de Laure, l'illustration de ses écrits* (Paris, 1902). C. Naselli in her chapter "Petrarca e le arti figurative," *Petrarca e l'Ottocento* (Napoli, 1923), 538-48 provides some supplementary material, and so does M. Fowler in *Catalogue of the Petrarch Collection in Cornell University* (New York, 1916), 497-508. There are enough scattered discussions printed during the past half century to warrant bringing them together as part of a new monograph.

The fullest treatment on the topic of Petrarch and music is M. Canitz' dissertation, *Petrarca in der Geschichte der Musik* (Freiburg i. B., 1969). Among the few other music studies relating to Petrarch are A. Bonaventura, "Il Petrarca e la musica," *Annali della Cattedra petrarchesca* III (1932), 23-43; L. Frati, "Petrarca e la musica," *Rivista musicale italiana,* XXXI (1924), 52-68; and U. Sesini, "Modi petrarcheschi in poesie musicate del Trecento," *Studi petrarcheschi,* I (1948), 213-23.

5. *Petrarchism:*

Studies on Petrarchism in various languages have been numerous during this century.

There is no history of Italian Petrarchism. L. Baldacci, *Il petrarchismo italiano nel Cinquecento* (Milano-Napoli, 1957), is largely limited to Bembo, Della Casa and the Cinquecento commentators on the *Rime*. F. Rizzi's chapters on Petrarchism in *L'anima del Cinquecento e la lirica volgare* (Milano, 1928), 23-122, goes too far in trying to prove the sincerity of the movement but otherwise makes many worthwhile observations. For England we have J. E. Scott's *Les sonnets élizabétains* (Paris, 1929). For France nothing has yet superseded Vianey's detailed survey, *Le pétrarquisme en France au XVᵉ siècle* (Montpellier, 1909; Genève, 1969). D. Cecchetti in his university lectures *Il petrarchismo in Francia* (Torino, 1970), while he brings in material on the Latin Petrarch, does not go beyond Ronsard. A. Meozzi, *Il petrarchismo europeo* (Pisa, 1934), though he draws considerably on other studies, especially Vianey, often gives us his own analysis. For Germany there is L. Pacini's *Petrarca in der deutschen Dichtungslehre vom Barock bis zur Romantik* (Köln, 1936). It is supplemented by Raimondi's review in *Studi petrarcheschi,* II (1949), 286-318. For Spanish Petrarchism see my book, *Estudios sobre el petrarquismo en España* (Madrid, 1960). G. C. Rossi's "La poesia del Petrarca in Portogallo," *Cultura neo-latina,* III (1945), 175-70, marks only the barest beginning. It has been reprinted in Coimbra in 1946. With respect to other languages, Wilkins, "A General Survey of Renaissance Petrarchism," *Comparative Literature,* II (1950), 327-42, and *Studies in the Life and Works of Petrarch,* op. cit., 280-99 provides brief comments and bibliographical data. To be added at this point is A. Scaglione's "Cinquecento Mannerism and the Uses of Petrarch," in O. B. Hardison, ed., *Medieval and Renaissance Studies,* 5 (Chapel Hill, 1971), 122-51, with some very refreshing insights on the vogue of structural patterns: antitheses, parallelisms, conceits.

A. Graf's rather disorganized "Petrarchismo e anti-petrarchismo" in his *Attraverso il Cinquecento* (2d ed. Torino, 1926), 3-386 still has some usefulness.

Lastly, H. Vaganay's massive bibliography, *Le sonnet en Italie et en France* (Lyon, 1907), has frequently been consulted in the past and will continue to be. Most of his collection, which forms the bulk of the catalog, is now located in the Yale University Library.

For a critical analysis of some very recent titles, mostly concerning Petrarch's impact in several literatures, see A. Scaglione's "Rassegna di studi petrarcheschi," *RPh,* XXVII (August 1974), 61-75.

III

EPISTOLA METRICA II, 1, AD JOHANNEM BARRILEM
AN ANNOTATED TRANSLATION

by Thomas G. Bergin
Yale University (Emeritus)

Quid mea fata michi toto speciosius evo,
dulcius aut animo poterant melius ve tulisse,
quam si forte tuis capiti nova laurea nostro
pressa foret manibus! Fateor, tunc alma sororum
ex Helicone sacram veniens huc turba choream
duxisset; cytharam melius sonuisset Apollo
serta gerens, adamata sibi Peneia primum,
post longum dilecta michi; spectasset ab astris
letus honoratam, placato numine, frondem
Iupiter, et rapidi posuisset fulminis iras;
denique nulla dies fulsisset lumine tanto
his oculis, cuntos nec fulserat ulla per annos.
Obstituit heu votis semper michi dura paratum
imminuens Fortuna decus, tantoque favori
invidit; tibi, me propter, multa viarum
aspera, tot laquei: soli michi nempe tetendit
insidias; desiste queri: mea tota querela est.
Agnosco expertus fraudem, moresque malignos,
mortales quibus illa ferox intercipit actus,
omnia permiscens. Proh sacra licentia monstri!
Quin alium michi tunc eadem Fortuna parabat,
nequicquam preventa, dolum: ne nobilis Ursus
scilicet ipse meo presens foret auctor honori.
Vix tridui spatium restabat, ut omne senatus
tempore ius hausto flueret, breviorque potestas
que quondam sine fine fuit. Deus ipse nocenti
occurrens direxit iter, vix fine sub ipso

What fairer thing in all my span of life,
What sweeter, happier guerdon could my fate
Have granted had it but conceded me
The joy of seeing you place on my brow
The crown of laurel that but recently
I have received? Then, truly, I believe
The fostering sisterhood of Muses, all
Together would have left high Helicon,
Hither descending to initiate
Their sacred dance; more sweetly than his wont
Apollo, temples circled with the wreath
Peneian, first beloved of him and now—
After so long—so dear to me, would surely
Have plucked his lyre, while, from the skies above
Jove, all benign, marking the honored frondage
Would have put down his wrath and fiery dart.
Certes no day would have been to my eyes
So splendid, none in all my years, I know,
Has shone with such effulgence. But, alas,
Harsh Fortune, ever eager to demean
My honors, moved to envy of the prize
Bestowed upon me, thwarted my desire.
And thus it was because of me you suffered
Such trials and such obstructions in your path;
For me alone she set her traps: complain
No more; complaint is my prerogative.
I know by proof the ways of guileful chance,
The wicked practices her savage will
Employs to frustrate the activities
Of mortals, turning them from their true goals.
Oh, cursed privileges of that monster! Nay,
That foe whose thrusts none can forestall had planned
Another stroke, attempting to detain
The noble Orso,[1] who had first conceived
The ceremony in my honor, so
He too might be unable to attend.
A scant three days remained of the fixed term
Wherein the Senate's privileges endured
And its authority, which in old times
Knew no such limits.[2] Happily God Himself
Took up my cause against my enemy

temporis, immense perventum ad limina Rome.
Obvius intranti fueras comitemque ducemque
pollicitus: vetuit quoniam sors, esse nequisti.
Torqueor, et cuntas qui lustret nuntius oras
mittitur. Ille autem Campanis fessus in arvis,
teque non invento rediens, spem sustulit omnem.
Ultima iamque dies aderat, nec postera tempus
lux dabat; urgebat consumpti terminus anni.
Me quoque magnanimus Comes accelerare monebat
iam gravidus curis, peperit quas fortibus actis.
Post modo, nosti hominem, expedior; subitumque vocati
Romulei proceres coeunt, Capitolia leto
murmure complentur; muros tectumque vetustum
congaudere putes; cecinerunt classica: vulgus
agmina certatim glomerat, cupidumque videndi
obstrepit. Ipse etiam lacrimas, ni fallor, amicis
compressis pietate animis, in pectora vidi.
Ascendo. Siluere tube, murmurque resedit.
Una quidem nostri vox primum oblata Maronis
principium dedit oranti, nec multa profatus;
nam neque mos vatum patitur, nec iura sacrarum
Pyeridum violasse leve est; de vertice Cirre
avulsas paulum mediis habitare coegi
urbibus ac populis. Post facundissimus Ursus
subsequitur fando. Tandem michi delphica serta
imposuit, populo circumplaudente Quiritum.

And Orso, guided by His hand, approached
The walls of spacious Rome, even as the time
Allotted to the Senate neared its end.
You were to meet him as he entered in
The City, you had promised you would be
His comrade and his guide. But Fate decreed
It should not come to pass. You were not there.
I was distraught. A messenger was sent
To search the countryside but he returned
Weary from treading the Campagna's heath
Without a sight of you. Our hopes were dashed.
The last day was upon us. On the morrow
Our rites could not take place. The limitation
Fixed for the annual mandate spurred us on.
The high-souled Count himself, though sore beset
By other cares, the fruits of his exploits
Of valor, urged me to make haste. And soon
Thereafter—well you know me—I so did.
Straightway the leading citizens of Rome
Are summoned. As they congregate, the sound
Of cheerful voices fills the Capitol.
The ancient edifice,[3] the very walls,
You would have said, rejoiced. The trumpets blared.
Vying for place, the throng of folk pressed close,
Chattering and boisterous, eager to look on.
Methinks—if I err not—I can detect
Tears welling in the hearts of all my friends
Whose breasts are compact with emotion. Then
I mount the hill. The trumpet notes are stilled
And all the tumult ceases. With a verse
Of gentle Maro[4] springing to my lips
Unbidden, I then open my discourse.
I spoke not long for such is not the way
Of poets and it is no slight offense
To infringe the sacred principles laid down
By the Piërides whom I had brought
From Cirra's lofty summit to abide
A short while in the town amidst the throng.
With eloquence then Orso followed me
And placed upon my head the Delphic garland
While all around the folk of Rome applauded.

Hinc Stephanus, quo fata virum iam tempore nostro
maiorem non Roma tulit, me laudibus amplis
accumulat. Rubor ora michi mentemque premebat;
indignum tales onerabant pectus honores,
mulcebantque simul: Siculo nempe omnia regi
nil michi: nam quis ego? veruntamen illius alto
iudicio dignatus eram. Tum regia festo
vestis honesta die me circumfusa tegebat,
et dominum referens, et tanti testis amoris,
quam, lateri exemptam proprio, regum ille supremus
rex dederat gestare suo. Solusque loquentis
iste animo ingenium, labiis mulcentia verba
sufficiebat honos: coram michi namque videbar
eloquii spectare ducem regemque serenum,
vellere qui primum se continuisset in illo:
impetus hinc, spesque alta nimis, fiduciaque ingens
ceu presens is ferret opem. Descendimus una
omnibus explicitis, atque hinc ad limina Petri
pergimus, et sacras mea laurea pendet ad aras,
primitiis gaudente Deo. Sua numina testor,
hec inter tota leta, oculis tu solus, amice,
tu deeras, votis quotiens precibusque petitus,
mente tamen memorique animo tua dulcis imago
certe aderat, semperque aderit, nec tempore sedes
deseret acceptas: sic illam pectore in alto
sculpsit amor, fixamque adeo vetitamque moveri
maximus artificum vivoque adamante peregit.
Hunc verbis (quia iam vereor ne longius equo
carmen eat) finem statuo. Tuque, optime, regi

Next Stefano, than whom eternal Rome,
Which had already given her response,
Has brought forth in our time no son more great,
Exalted me with generous words of praise.[5]
A crimson blush suffused my face, my spirit
Was overcome by shame. Such undeserved
Honors weighed heavily upon my heart.
And yet they pleased me too for all pertained
To the Sicilian King and not to me.
For who am I, in truth? Yet was I judged
By his high verdict worthy. And I wore
On that triumphant day his royal robe,[6]
Which made me mindful of my sovereign
And bore clear witness to his gracious favor.
For he, the loftiest of kings, had stripped
That mantle from his back and given it me
To wear, for like it, I am also his.
This privilege alone lent to my wit
The virtue needed and persuasive words
To my poor lips. I seemed to see before me
That prince of eloquence, the king serene
Who first had worn that garment. So from that
I drew my inspiration and my hopes
And my assurance, firm as if he were
Standing beside me, eager to give aid.
Then all together, when the ceremony
Was ended, we came down and turned our steps,
Leaving the Capitol, towards Peter's shrine,
And there before the altar hangs my crown,
For God is pleased with offerings of first fruits.
And let him bear me witness, dearest friend,
When I affirm that in that happy hour
I felt your absence, longed for only you
With every oft-repeated wish and prayer,
Albeit deep within my grateful heart
Your image dwelt and shall forever dwell
Nor ever leave, so well has love engraved
It there, so firmly has the unsurpassed
Craftsman there fixed it, as in adamant.
Thus I shall end for I begin to fear
My letter grows immoderately long.

dum vacuum invenies curarum meque fidemque
commendare meam placido sermone memento.
Sum suus ex merito, sibi me meaque omnia soli
devovi: ingenium, calamum, linguamque manumque,
et si quid superest aliud. Michi carior ipse
sum, postquam dedit esse suum; dominoque superbit
mens mea. Nunc autem, quoniam sibi reddere maius
nil valeo pro tot magnis, sub nomine crescit
Africa nostra suo, tenuis nisi gloria sordet:
parva quidem, at grandi studio longoque labore
invigilanda michi. Iamque ipsa superbior ardet
ad sacros properare pedes, noctemque diemque
orat iter comitemque vie. Vocat eminus ambos
inclita Parthenope: sed adhuc nos Gallia vinclis
nostra tenet blandis; tandem tamen ibimus, et nos
limine suscipies pariter, pariterque videbis.
Vive, vale, nostrique memor lege, dulcis amice,
hec calamo properante brevi que scripsimus hora.

Do you, dear friend, remember, when the King
Turns from his cares, with soft and gentle words
Commend me to him with my full devotion.
By merit I am his; to him alone
I've consecrated everything: myself,
My talent and my pen, my tongue, my hand
And all else there may be that's mine to give.
Since he has suffered me to call me his
I have grown dearer to myself; my spirit
Takes glory in its lord. And inasmuch
As I cannot reciprocate his favors
With aught of greater worth, my *Africa*
Will grow, an offering to him if he
Be pleased with such slight glory. 'T is a work,
In truth, of small account yet one to which
I must devote much care and hours of labor.
The little book itself, now growing bold,
Burns with desire to haste and cast itself
Before those sacred feet, and day and night
Pleads for release and would have me as well
A comrade on its journey. We both hear
Noble Parthenope that from afar
Bids us return but still with flattering bonds
Our Gaul detains us.[8] Some day we shall come
And you shall see us both and give us shelter
Within your dwelling. Live well, dearest friend,
And think of me the while you read these lines
Composed in brief time with a hasty pen.[9]

NOTES

In his exhaustive article, "The Coronation of Petrarch" (*The Making of the* Canzoniere *and Other Petrarchan Studies,* Rome, 1951, pp. 9-70) E. H. Wilkins speaks of this letter as "the main account of the ceremony" of the poet's coronation (p. 63). It was sent, along with a prose letter, *Var.* 57, in which Petrarch mentions the haste in which the lines were composed, to his friend Giovanni Barrili, a high-placed official in the Court of Naples, later to become Seneschal of the Realm. The prose letter is dated "propere ult. Ianuari" [1342].

1. This is Orso, Count of Anguillara and, at the time of the coronation, a Roman Senator. Orso's wife was Agnese Colonna, sister of Petrarch's patron, Cardinal Giovanni Colonna, and daughter of Stefano the Elder, also a Roman Senator, mentioned later in the letter.

2. This is a somewhat puzzling passage. Petrarch's statement would indicate that the term of the Senators in office was about to expire and that their successors

would not be empowered to carry out the planned ceremony. As to the latter implication, it seems most unlikely that, given the high sponsorship of the King of Naples, a new Senate would hesitate to approve a ceremony decreed by its predecessor. But the first part of the statement is even more difficult to accept. Wilkins (art. cit. p. 63) says only that "Count Orso was then one of the two Senators of Rome but April 8 was the last day of his term of service"—and of course as Petrarch's sponsor he was eager to bestow the crown with his own hand. But Tatham's comment (which Wilkins does not discuss) is of interest; he writes:

> There is a . . . difficulty about the Senatorship of Count Orso, which in his verses to Barili (*sic*) Petrarch represents as expiring on the day of his crowning, alleging this fact as a reason for not waiting for his friend. Yet in a Papal letter cited by Gregorovius (Vol. VI, Part i [Eng. trans.], p. 201, n.) we find the same Senators in office as late as July 23 following. Petrarch's expression cannot be taken literally; for the usual term of the Senatorial office was not a year, as with the ancient consuls (though he may have thought it to be so), but six months, unless for special reasons it was prolonged. We do not know exactly when this senatorship began, but in any case it must have lasted longer than six months and March 1 (not Easter Day) was the usual date for vacating the office. It was necessary for the Pope to confirm all such elections, though he did not usually nominate, unless expressly requested to do so; and the only solution I can offer is that the Senators had been elected for a second term (the first having expired), but that the Pope's confirmation had not arrived, and that in this difficulty the Council had by resolution prolonged their office until Easter. (*Francesco Petrarca: Life and Correspondence,* London, 1926, vol. II, pp. 134-5.)

One may suspect that it was at least as much the urgencies of two prominent and busy men as any legal limitation of time that imposed the necessity of expediting the ceremony. As Petrarch notes, Orso had many other obligations and in fact it was he who pressed on the poet the need for haste. Such a hypothesis would explain the tone of Petrarch's letter, which has, in part, the air of being an apology for proceeding without the presence of his dear friend (who was also the official delegate of the King of Naples); the poet dwells rather excessively on his regret for his friend's absence and his detailed account of the time limitation is suggestively circumstantial—if inaccurate.

3. The ancient edifice: probably the Senatorial audience chamber which Petrarch thought to be much older than it was.

4. "Sed me Parnasi deserta per ardua dulcis/ raptat amor." *Georgics* III, 291-2.

5. Tatham (op. cit., pp. 145-6) summarizes Stefano's speech, which concluded by granting Petrarch Roman citizenship and all the rights pertaining thereto.

6. "No scholar, I believe, has noted the fact this gift of one of the King's own robes was not a unique gift but conformed to the Oriental practice of the giving by rulers of robes called 'robes of honor.' Such gifts are always made by a sovereign, consist of garments that have been worn by the sovereign, indicate that the donor includes the recipient within his own *person* through the medium of his wardrobe, and if accepted constitute evidence that the recipient is a vassal of the sovereign." Wilkins, op. cit., p. 49; quotation from F. W. Buckler, "The Oriental Despot" in *Anglican Theological Review,* X (1928), 197-199 and 240-5.

7. "In this highly Christian act, whether consciously or not, P. was reproducing a feature of the triumph of an 'Imperator' who, on reaching the Temple, laid his wreath in the lap of Jupiter's image." Tatham, op. cit., p. 139.

8. Gaul: Cisalpine Gaul, i.e. Northern Italy. Petrarch writes from Parma where he is the guest of Azzo da Correggio. The "vinclis . . . blandis" of lines 96-7 are an echo of the phrase in the accompanying prose letter: "sed catena multiplicis obligationis, qua domino Azoni sum constrictus."

9. It may be useful to add here by way of appendix a translation of the letter (*Fam.* IV, 8) written shortly after the coronation to Barbato da Sulmona. It is a brief account of the events covered in the Metrical Letter; it could have served as a draft of that letter. It reads as follows:

> On the Ides of April in the year of the last era 1341, on the Roman Capitoline there was effected what the King had decreed for me in Naples a few days earlier. The Senator and Count of Anguillara, Orso, a personage of rare intellect, decorated me with the laurel wreath. The hand of the King was absent but his majesty was visible as if present not only to me but to everyone. Absent too were your eyes and ears but not your spirit, which is ever with me. The magnanimous John, who, while on his way, dispatched by the King, fell into an ambush of the Hernici this side of Anagni, was also absent; thank God he escaped but, awaited in vain, failed to arrive on time. For the rest, all went well—beyond hope and expectation.
>
> However, in order that I might have evident proof of how untoward events always go hand in hand with happy ones, I myself, having just come forth from the walls of Rome with the companions who had followed me by land and sea, ran afoul of a band of armed robbers. How we managed to escape them and were constrained to reenter Rome, to what pitch the people were aroused by this, how on the following day, with a good escort of men-at-arms we sallied forth again and what other chances befell us on our journey—all this I could not tell you without spinning too long a tale. Be pleased to hear all about it from the bearer of the present tidings. Farewell. From Pisa. April 29 (1341).

In this letter Petrarch's dating of his coronation as of "the Ides" (April 13) is strange for he cannot have forgotten that it was Easter, April 8; as Tatham puts it (op. cit., p. 134, n. 5) ". . . it is impossible to suppose that P., however careless as to dates, could have forgotten such a red-letter day." Fracassetti (*Lettere di Francesco Petrarca,* Florence, 1892, vol. I, pp. 520-521) discusses the possibilities of error in transcription, Petrarch's faulty memory, etc. Rossi suspects an "approssimazione voluta per motivo retorico" (*Familiari,* Florence, vol. I, 1933, p. 174).

The Hernici were a tribe in ancient Latium, enemies and later allies of the Romans; Livy (II 40. 41) tells of the pact made between the adversaries. Macrobius (*Sat.* V, 12) speaks of Anagni as their *nobilissima civitas.*

* * * * *

Texts: For the Metrical Letter I have reproduced and followed the text printed in *Francesco Petrarca: Opere* a cura di Giovanni Ponte (Milan, 1968), pp. 378-382. In translating *Fam.* IV, 8 I have followed the text of Rossi (op. cit., loc. cit., pp. 174-5); for *Var.* 57 I have had at hand the text of Fracassetti's edition of the *Epistolae* (Florence, 1863), vol. III, pp. 465-6.

IV

STRUTTURE FONICHE NEI *RERUM VULGARIUM FRAGMENTA*

by Maria Picchio Simonelli
Boston College

Scopo di questo studio è di richiamare l'attenzione dei lettori su alcune strutture formali che caratterizzano i *Rerum vulgarium fragmenta,* ma che ancora non sono state messe in adeguato rilievo. Ho incentrato la mia ricerca sopra l'allitterazione, le assonanze e le consonanze, tenendo sempre d'occhio il rapporto consonanza/assonanza-rima, dato che la rima segna il naturale punto limite di ogni assonanza e consonanza.

Il primo dato abbastanza sicuro, offerto da una lettura sperimentale di questo tipo, condotto sul *Canzoniere* completo, è la costatazione che organizzazioni stilistico-foniche, rette dall'allitterazione, dall'assonanza e dalla consonanza, ricorrono con frequenza e funzioni disuguali. Il che sembra indicare una scelta cosciente, o un cosciente rifiuto da parte dell'autore, quasi che il contenuto o il tono poetico delle varie liriche consentissero o no l'uso di questi mezzi formali. Gran parte delle Rime politiche (e si prenda come esempio *Spirto gentil,* cioè la Rima LIII), o certe Rime di corrispondenza o d'occasione o certi sonetti morali (ed ho in mente Rime come la VII, XXIV, XXV, XXVI, XXVII, XXXI, XXXIX, XL, LXVII, CXX, CXXXVII, CLXXIX) presentano una elaborazione stilistica diversa dalle Rime d'amore. Di solito le Rime non d'amore sono costruite su trame di semantica sintattica, non accompagnata o sottolineata da particolari ricerche di effetti fonici. Perfino l'uso della allitterazione, che è senza dubbio il mezzo espressivo-fonico più comune e diffuso, è qui limitatissimo. Qualche eccezione non manca, come la *Canzone all'Italia* (CXXVIII), o il sonetto *Vincitore Alexandro* (CCXXXII), o *Vergine bella* (CCCLXVI): le tre liriche presentano una elaborazione fonica assai più complessa di quanto il loro contenuto potrebbe far supporre. Se la canzone all'Italia si può considerare composta tra il 1344 e il '45,[1] la locazione cronologica delle altre due liriche è molto più incerta. Dando per vero che la CCXXXII fu suggerita al Petrarca da un moto d'ira, violento quanto passeggero, di

1. E. H. Wilkins, *Vita del Petrarca e La formazione del "Canzoniere"*, a cura di R. Ceserani (Milano, 1964), pp. 73 sgg.

Jacopo da Carrara contro i nipoti, come ebbe a dire lo Squarciafico,[2] la lirica sarebbe da porre tra il 1349 (prima visita del Petrarca a Padova) e la fine del 1350, prima cioè dell'assassinio di Jacopo. Il che coinciderebbe con la ipotesi dello Wilkins che "quasi tutti i componimenti che si trovano nella prima parte della raccolta finale erano già stati composti prima del 1351".[3] Problema anche più difficile è datare la canzone alla Vergine. L'idea di chiudere la raccolta con tale poesia risale agli anni 1369-71;[4] ma questo vale soltanto come termine *ante quem*. Io non sarei aliena dal considerare gli anni tra il 1350 e il 1351 o '52 come quelli più probabili per la composizione di *Vergine bella*. Mi sembra infatti che siano chiare le relazioni tematiche con i sonetti CCLXXII, CCLXXIII, CCLXXIV,[5] databili a quel medesimo

2. La notizia è riportata dal Carducci, *Le Rime di Francesco Petrarca* di su gli originali commentate da G. Carducci e S. Ferrari (Firenze, 1899), p. 325.

3. E. H. Wilkins, *o.c.*, p. 341.

4. E. H. Wilkins, *o.c.*, pp. 365 sgg.

5. I tre sonetti fanno parte di un gruppo di 21 componimenti "che piangono tutti la morte di Laura: in uno di essi, il n. 287, c'è anche il lamento per la morte di Sennuccio" (cf. Wilkins, *o.c.*, p. 346), che morì nell'autunno del 1349. I motivi-base dei tre sonetti (la vita che fugge, il poeta che si trova "sconsigliato" in mezzo a un mare in tempesta combattuto dalla memoria degli affanni passati, dall'angoscia del presente e dall'incertezza del futuro -CCLXXII -, il desiderio di volgere il proprio pensiero a Dio, lamentando la pace che Laura gli toglie anche da morta cosí come gliela aveva tolta da viva - CCLXXIII -, l'incolpare di ogni suo guaio il cuore che si lascia invischiare negli "errori" - CCLXXIV) costituiscono gli elementi autobiografici che s'intrecciano nella lode alla Vergine della Canzone CCCLXVI. Al v. 2 del CCLXXII (*et la morte vien dietro a gran giornate*) corrispondono i vv. 87-91 della Canzone (*Vergine sacra et alma, / non tardar, ch'i' son forse a l'ultimo anno. / I dí miei più correnti che saetta / fra miserie et peccati / sonsen andati, et sol Morte n'aspetta*). Ai vv. 3-4 sempre del CCLXXII (*et le cose presenti et le passate / mi dànno guerra*) corrispondono i vv. 78-86 della Canzone (*Vergine, quante lagrime ò già sparte, / quante lusinghe et quanti preghi indarno, / pur per mia pena et per mio grave danno! / Da poi ch'i' nacqui in su la riva d'Arno, / cercando or questa et or quel'altra parte, / non è stata mia vita altro ch'affanno. / Mortal bellezza, atti et parole m'ànno / tutta ingombrata l'alma*). Il paragone di se stesso con la nave in gran tempesta ricorre più volte lungo il *Canzoniere*, come ha notato anche il Chiórboli (Francesco Petrarca, *Le rime sparse* commentate da E. Chiórboli, Milano, 1926), che richiamava a commento dei vv. 69-70 della Canzone i sonetti CXXXII,11 e CLXXXIX,3 (p. 869); ma forse i vv. 10-13 del CCLXXII (. . . *et poi da l'altra parte / veggio al mio navigar turbati i vènti; / veggio fortuna in porto, et stanco omai / il mio nocchier, et rotte arbore et sarte* . . .), sfuggiti alla pur attentissima osservazione del Chiórboli, sembrano i più vicini ai vv. 66-71 della Canzone (*Vergine chiara et stabile in eterno, / di questo tempestoso mare stella, / d'ogni fedel nocchier fidata guida, / pon' mente in che terribile procella / i' mi ritrovo sol, senza governo, / et ò già da vicin l'ultime strida*). Che i vv. 92-93 della Canzone riecheggino (o lo anticipano?) il sonetto CCLXXIII è cosa già stata notata dal Chiórboli (*o.c.*, p. 871); e altrettanto per i vv. 111-115 della Canzone sempre il Chiórboli richiamava il sonetto CCLXXIV (*o.c.*, p. 873). Tuttavia mi sembra

scorcio di anni. Inoltre, per quello che risulta dalle mie richerche, le complicanze stilistiche di ordine fonico si riscontrano più frequenti e insistite nel numeroso gruppo di liriche composte tra il 1345 e il 1355. Sembra quasi che il Petrarca, partito da una ricerca di adeguazione contenutistica, per cui soltanto alcuni temi poetici erano da arricchire con sottolineature foniche, giunga a un particolare sviluppo del suo gusto scrittorio, per cui, in un determinato periodo della sua vita, allitterazioni assonanze e consonanze diventano parte integrante del suo linguaggio poetico, al di là dei limiti contenutistici che sembravano averlo guidato nel periodo precedente.

Un'altra osservazione di ordine generale che mi sembra di poter suggerire, è che nei componimenti in cui il Petrarca giuoca sulle violente opposizioni semantiche l'insistenza dei richiami fonici si attenua o viene ottenuta per mezzo del parallelismo sintattico o la ripetizione di una data parola. Si veda, a titolo d'esempio, il sonetto CXXXII dove l'ipotetica *se* apre ben cinque versi delle quartine e ciascun verso è una interrogativa in sé conclusa, e l'ipotetica iniziale una opposizione dialettica all'interrogativa:

> *S'a*mor non è, che dunque è quel ch'io sento?
> Ma *s*'egli è amor, perdio, che cosa e quale?
> *Se* bona, onde l'effecto aspro mortale?
> *Se* ria, onde sí dolce ogni tormento?
> *S'a mi*a voglia ardo, onde 'l pianto e *lamento*?
> *S'a mio* mal grado, il *lamentar* che vale?

Ai vv. 7-8 la struttura sintattica viene capovolta, al fine, mi sembra, di legare le quartine alle terzine, ripetendo la stessa frase in funzione prima negativa e poi affermativa:

> O viva morte, o dilectoso male,
> come puoi tanto in me, *s'io nol consento*?
> *Et s'io 'l consento,* a gran torto mi doglio.

Oppure il CXXXIII, i cui primi tre versi si reggono sulla ripetizione di *come:*

> Amor m'à posto *come* segno a strale,
> *come* al sol neve, *come* cera al foco,
> et *come* nebbia al vento . . . ;

e in cui l'allitterazione divide il primo verso in due parti ben distinte

---

interessante notare che ogni accenno alla vita personale reperibile nella Canzone CCCLXVI è motivo comune con questi tre sonetti che il Petrarca ordinò senza soluzione di continuità, quasi a formare un insieme.

(*am*or *m*'à posto / *s*egno a *s*trale) con al centro, isolata fonicamente, la parola *come*.

Oppure il CL con il seguito di interrogative rette da *che:*

Che fai, alma? *che* pensi? . . .
Che fia di noi. . . .
Che pro . . .
(vv. 1-3-5);

o il CLIII con il reiterato *Ite* all'inizio delle quartine:

Ite, caldi sospiri . . .
Ite, dolci pensieri. . . .

La "misura" dell'armonia fonica non è mai oltrepassata dal Petrarca, mai ci troviamo di fronte al "troppo" fonico o all'ossessivo. Se prendiamo per esempio il sonetto XVIII, le cui rime potevano condurre a una eccessiva musicalità, dato che si tratta di parole-rima usate in *equivocatio* (*parte* e *luce* nelle quartine, *morte desio sole* nelle terzine) vediamo bene che perfino l'uso della allitterazione è limitato al verso di chiusura di ciascun periodo ritmico (vv. 4,8,11,14):

(v. 4) che m'*arde* et s*trugg*e *dent*ro *a parte a parte.*
(v. 8) che non *s*a ov*e* *s*i *v*ada et *pur* *s*i *par*te
(v. 11) *meco* n*on* *ve*n*ga* *come* *ven*ir sol*e*.
(v. 14) che *le* *la*gri*me* *mie* *s*i *s*pargan *s*ol*e*.

Ed è da osservare che il giuoco allitterativo lega in unità foniche i vv. 4 e 11, mentre divide in due parti distinte i vv. 8 e 14, in modo da ottenere in chiusa ritmica una musicalità franta, non monotona e neppur casuale, dato l'ordine alterno. Sempre in questo sonetto si nota una delle parole-rima delle quartine in consonanza con una delle tre parole-rima delle terzine (pa*r*t*e* / mo*r*t*e*), mentre due delle tre parole-rima delle terzine sono in assonanza fra di loro (m*o*rt*e* / s*o*l*e*); la parola-rima *morte* si trova cosí in consonanza e in assonanza con altre due parole-rima, una delle quartine e una delle terzine.

Si potrebbe anzi dire che il bisogno di congiungere fonicamente il ritmo delle quartine con quello delle terzine fu sentito, con notevole frequenza, fin dall'iniziatore del sonetto: in Iacopo da Lentini, infatti, su una ventina di sonetti pervenutici, 14 presentano un qualche legamento fonico tra le rime delle quartine e le rime delle terzine; in 9 casi il legamento è dato dalla consonanza[6] e in 5 dalla assonanza di una o

6. Mi servo dell'edizione di M. Vitale, *Poeti della prima scuola* (Arona, 1951). I casi di consonanza corrispondono alle rime XIV (*-unta/-unto*), XVI (*-are/-ore*), XIX (*-ento/-anto*), XXI (*-ore/-aro*), XXII (*-ente/-anti*), XXIII (*-are/-ire*), XXVII (*-ire/-are*), XXX (*-ore/-are*), XXXVI (*-ente/-anti*).

più delle rime in terzina con una delle rime delle quartine;[7] in un solo caso si ha in terzina la ripetizione di una delle rime delle quartine.[8] La stessa percentuale rimane, grosso modo, in Guittone, il quale, tuttavia, sembra gustare, assai più di Iacopo, le assonanze, che appaiono quasi nella stessa misura delle consonanze, e la ripresa in terzina di una delle rime delle quartine.[9] La percentuale dei legamenti fonici

7. I casi di assonanza corrispondono nell'edizione Vitale alle rime XV (*-artte /-are*), XXIV (*-ore/-ortte*), XXXI (*-ata/-ana*), XXXII (*-ere/-ese*), XXXIII (*-one/-ore*).

8. Cf. ed. Vitale n. XVIII.

9. Mi servo di L. Valeriani, *Rime di Fra Guittone d'Arezzo* (Firenze, 1828). I sonetti che presentano legamento fonico tra le quartine e le terzine si possono cosí raggruppare:
per rima ripetuta: XXX, XXXIX, XLIX, LII, LXI, LXXVII, LXXXIII, LXXXIX, CVI, CXI, CXVI, CXLVII, CLXXVIII, CLXXXIX, CXCIII, CXCV, CXCIX, CCI, CCXVIII, CCXX, CCXXIII, CCXXX;
per assonanza: XXIX (*-ente/-ete*), XXXIII (*-ate/-asse*), XLVII (*-ace/-are*), LI (*-ee/-ente*), LIII (*-ato/-aggio*), LIV (con una rima in assonanza: *-ello/-ento* e una in consonanza: *-osa/-oso*), LVI (*-ede/-ente*), LIX (con doppia assonanza: *-are/-ale* e *-io/-ico*), LXVIII (*-ento/-egno*), LXXI (*-ato/-aggio*), XCVIII (*-ene/-ente*), XCIX (*-anto/-ando*), CI (*-ente/-ede*), CIII (*-ore/-one*), CXIV (con una rima in assonanza: *-are/-ave* e una in consonanza: *-are/-ire*), CXVI (*-ore/-one* più la rima *-ore* ripetuta), CXVIII (*-ato/-ano*), CXIX (*-oso/-omo*), CXX (*-ono/-omo*), CXXVIII (*-ore/-olle*), CXXXI (*-orto/-omo*), CXXXIV (*-ate/-are*), CXLI (con una rima in assonanza: *-ate/-ace* e una in consonanza: *-oni/-ono*), CXLIV (*-ore/-one*), CXLVI (con doppia assonanza: *-ene/-ente/-esse*), CXLIX (con una rima in assonanza: *-erto/-ento* e una in consonanza: *-aro/-are*), CLVI (*-ato/-anto*), CLVII (*-ee/-ene*), CLXIII (*-anta/-aglia*), CLXIV (*-ato/* rima ripetuta in terzina tutta assonanzata: *-anto*), CLXVIII (*-ore/-one*), CLXXIV (*-one/-ore*), CXC (*-ato/-anno*), CXCVIII (*-ene/-ente*), CCIII (*-oso/-onto*), CCX (*-eri/-essi*), CCXI (*-orte/-ore*), CCXVI (*-elo/-eso*), CCXXIII (*-ene/-ente* con la rima *-ato* ripetuta in terzina), CCXXIV (*-ede/-ente*), CCXXV (*-ene/-ente*), CCXXXI (*-ene/-ente/-ere*), CCXXXVII (*-enta/-ena*);
per consonanza: XXXII (*-ato/-ate*), XXXV (*-oso/-osa*), XL (*-ore/-ere*), XLI (sonetto tutto consonanzato: *-ore/-ere/-are/-ire*), XLV (*-ante/-ente*), LXIII (con una rima in consonanza: *-ore/-are* e una in assonanza: *-ele/-ente*), LXIV (*-aggio/-agio*), LXVII (*-ore/-are*), LXX (*-are/-ire*), LXXIV (*-are/-ere*), LXXVIII (*-one/-ana*), LXXXII (*-anto/-ente*), LXXXVI (*-ore/-ire*), LXXXVIII (*-aro/-ara*), XC (*-ire/-ore*), XCI (*-ento/-ente*), CII (*-ata/-ate*), CIX (*-ore/-aro*), CXII (*-ore/-are*), CXIII (*-oco/-ico*), CXXI (con una rima in consonanza: *-one/-ena* e una in assonanza *-ale/-are*), CXXII (*-ato/-utti*), CXXIII (*-ore/-ari*), CXXXII (*-ire/-aro*), CXXXVI (*-ore/-oro*), CXXXVII (*-ana/-ono*), CXXXVIII (*-ade/-ude*), CLXIII (*-ore/-ora*), CLVIII (con una rima in consonanza: *-ore/-are* e una in assonanza: *-ore/-one*), CLXII (con una rima in consonanza: *-ere/-ire* e una in assonanza: *-ate/-ace*), CLXXI (con le rime tutte in consonanza: *-ere/-ore/-are*), CLXXII (*-ato/-uta*), CLXXXI (doppia consonanza: *-ere/-era* e *-one/-ano*), CLXXXIII (*-aro/-are*), CLXXXV (*-ore/-ire*), CXCI (*-are/-ire*), CXCVII (*-ere/-are*), CCII (*-are/-ira/-ore*), CCV (*-ato/-ate*), CCXII (con una rima in consonanza: *-ire/-ore* e una in assonanza: *-ono/-olto*), CCXV (*-etto/-ita*), CCXVII (*-ente/-onte*), CCXXI (con una rima in consonanza: *-ato/-ate* e una in assonanza: *-esse/-ente*), CCXXXII (con una rima in consonanza: *-ono/-ano* e una in assonanza: *-ono/*

tra quartine e terzine non cambia nel Guinizzelli, il quale, anzi, rimane aderente alla norma lentiniana e usa di solito la consonanza.[10] E' con il Cavalcanti che i due periodi ritmici del sonetto appaiono, di preferenza, disgiunti sia tematicamente che fonicamente. L'abito scrittorio del Cavalcanti lo portava a conchiudere nelle due quartine il momento lirico, e a usare le terzine come commento o ripensamento. E cosí, su 36 sonetti, soltanto 16 mostrano un legamento fonico tra le quartine e le terzine: 10 per mezzo della assonanza e 6 per mezzo della consonanza,[11] con un certo avvicinamento alla lezione guittoniana. Ma esempi di ripresa rimica dalle quartine nelle terzine mancano sia in Guinizzelli che in Cavalcanti. Anche Dante, nei 34 sonetti di attribuzione sicura, rifiuta la ripresa rimica dalle quartine in terzina; solo un sonetto di dubbia attribuzione è tutto birimico (*-uzza / -uzzo*)[12] e di sapore guittoniano. In quanto al legamento fonico tra quartine e terzine, Dante rientra nel quadro tradizionale con 20 sonetti a legamento fonico su 34, di cui 11 per consonanza[13] e 9 per assonanza.[14] Nei 21 sonetti dubbi la percentuale cambia: infatti soltanto 9 hanno il legamento fonico: 2 per assonanza[15] e 7 per consonanza.[16] Il che conferma il generale dubbio attributivo. Anche un bilancio a riguardo dei 73 sonet-

---

-orto), CCXXXIII (*-ate/-uto/-ato*), CCXXXIV (*-ore/-are*), CCXXXV (*-ente/ -ante*).

10. Mi servo dell'edizione a cura di G. Contini, *Poeti del Duecento* (Milano-Napoli, 1960), vol. II, pp. 447-485. I sonetti con una rima delle terzine in consonanza con una rima delle quartine sono: VII (*-ore/-iri*), VIII (*-oro/-ore*), IX (*-are/-ore*), XII (con doppia consonanza: *-ore/-era* e *-ata/-ate*), XIII (*-era/ -ere*), XIV (*-ura/-ire*), XV (*-ita/-ato*), XIX[b] (*-ura/-ire*). Il sonetto XVII presenta il legamento per assonanza (*-ozzo/-oco*).

11. Mi servo della edizione a cura di G. Favati, Guido Cavalcanti, *Rime* (Milano-Napoli, 1957). Sonetti con legamento per consonanza: II (*-ura/-ere/ -ore*), XII (*-enti/-ente*), XXII (*-ore/-ire*), XXXIII (*-ero/-ura/-iro*), XLV (*-ena/ -ina*), LII (*-ura/-are*). Sonetti con legamento per assonanza: VI (*-ite/-ire*), VII (*-ita/-ia*), XIII (*-ore/-osse*), XVI (*-eggio/-egno*), XXVIII (*-are/-ave*), XXIX (*-ia/-itta*), XXXVI (*-endo/-ento*), XL (*-endo/-ento*), XLII (*-esto/-erso*), XLVIII[a] (*-ia/-ina*).

12. Si tratta della rima 73 in Dante Alighieri, *Rime*, a cura di G. Contini (Torino, 1965; I ed. 1946). Mi servo di questa edizione ora e in seguito.

13. Cf. Dante, *Rime*, ed. Contini, 1[a] (*-one/-ene* ma la rima in *-one* è anche assonanzata con la rima *-ore* delle terzine), 9 (*-ento/-enta*), 13 (*-ira/-orre*), 15 (*-are/-ore*), 18 (*-are/-ore*), 22 (*-ato/-ute*), 24 (*-ate/-atto*), 33 (*-ore/-are*), 36 (*-etta/-ita*), 39[a] (*-ato/-etta*) 40[a] (*-ardo/-erde*), 52 (*-ito/-ate*).

14. Cf. Dante, *Rime*, ed. Contini, 2[a] (*-anto/-aggio*), 3[a] (*-arla/-ama* e consonanza di *-omo/-ama*), 14 (*-ore/-one*), 19 (*-ia/-ita*), 25 (*-eco/-ero/-ello*), 27 (*-arne/-arte*), 31 (*-ete/-ente*), 32 (*-ora/-ostra*), 54 (*-ente/-ede*).

15. Cf. Dante, *Rime*, ed. Contini, 62 (*-etra/-eggia*), 65 (*-ina/-ita*).

16. Cf. Dante, *Rime*, ed. Contini, 55 (*-are/-ore*), 66 (*-ore/-iri*), 67 (*-ore/ -ira*), 68 (*-ore/-iri*), 75 (*-ire/-ore*), 78 (*-ice/-uce*), 79 (*-ore/-ura*).

ti di Cino, raccolti dal Carducci,[17] ci porta all'incirca alle stesse conclusioni: 38 sonetti hanno il legamento fonico tra quartine e terzine; 22 per consonanza,[18] 14 per assonanza[19] e 2 per ripresa rimica.[20] Quest'ultima tecnica strutturale farebbe ritenere che Cino, più di Guinizzelli, di Cavalcanti e di Dante, era attento alla tradizione "antica" rappresentata dal Notaro e dal grande Guittone.

Non credo necessario continuare questo spoglio statistico delle Rime antiche per giustificare il comportamento petrarchesco di fronte alla struttura rimica del sonetto: dei 297 sonetti raccolti nei *Rerum vulgarium fragmenta* soltanto 120 presentano un legamento fonico tra quartine e terzine; e di questi, 80 per assonanza,[21] 37 per consonanza,[22]

17. G. Carducci, *Rime di M. Cino da Pistoia e d'altri del secolo XIV,* ordinate da G. C. (Firenze, 1928), vol. I.

18. Cf. ed. Carducci, IX (*-ente/-ento*), XI (*-ore/-are*), XIV (*-are/-ura* complicata dall'assonanza *-are/-ate*), XVI (*-aro/-ore*), XX (*-ore/-iri*), XXVII (*-ate/-ita*), XLII (*-ura/-ora*), XLIII (*-ore/-iri*), XLV (*-are/-ore*), XLVII (*-osa/-esse*), LI (*-uta/-ate*), LII (*-ura/-ore* e assonanza: *-ina/-ita*), LV (*-ore/-ira*), LVI (*-ore/-iri*), LIX (*-iri/-ire*), LXI (*-are/-iri*), LXX (*-ira/-oro*), XCIV (*-ardo/-erde*), XCVI (*-ito/-ate*), CI (*-iri/-uri*), CIII (*-uro/-iri*).

19. Cf. ed. Carducci, V (*-ente/-ere*), X (*-iti/-ili*), XXVIII (*-ise/-ite*), XXXIV (*-ia/-ita*), XXXVIII (*-ore/-ole*), XLVIII (*-osta/-orta*), LVII (*-orta/-ogna*), LX (*-ata/-ana*), LXII (*-ita/-ia*), LXXII (*-anno/-ato*), LXXVI (*-ate/-are*), LXXIX (*-ella/-etra*), CV (*-onte/-ore*), CXIV (*-eggi/-esi*).

20. Cf. ed. Carducci, XXXIX, LXXIII.

21. Uso l'edizione critica Francesco Petrarca, *Canzoniere.* Testo critico e introduzione di Gianfranco Contini. Annotazioni di Daniele Ponchiroli (Torino, 1964). I sonetti con legamento tra quartine e terzine per assonanza corrispondono a: I (*-orno/-ogno*), III (*-aro/-ato*), IV (*-arte/-acque*), VI (*-olta/-orta*), VII (*-ita/-ia*), VIII (*-esta/-ena*), IX (*-orna/-olga*), X (*-oggia/-ombra*), XXVI (*-inta/-ima*), XXXII (*-eve/-ente*), XLI (*-ano/-ato*), XLII (*-ano/-ato*), XLIII (*-ano/-ato*), XLIV (*-iglia/-ira*), XLVIII (*-oggia/-orda*), LIV (*-esta/-eta*), LXVIII (*-ostra/-oltra*), LXIX (*-iglio/-ino*), LXXXI (*-ico/-ino*), LXXXII (*-ancho/-acio*), XCIV (*-are/-arte*), CXXIII (*-iso/-ico*), CXXXII (*-ento/-erno*), CXL (*-egna/-ema*), CXLIII (*-ente/-ede*), CXLVII (*-egge/-eme*), CL (*-erna/-eta*), CLI (*-ero/-eggo*), CLVII (*-orno/-olto*), CLXI (*-ore/-ose*), CLXV (*-ove/-ole*), CLXIX (*-olo/-oso*), CLXXVI (*-arme/-acque*), CLXXVIII (*-ena/-enta*), CLXXXVII (*-ombra/-ora*), CLXXXVIII (*-orno/-oco*), CXC (*-oro/-orno*), CXCI (*-ice/-ive*), CXCVI (*-emme/-ente*), CXCVIII (*-eso/-endo*), CXCIX (*-ore/-ose*), CC (*-este/-erle*), CCIV (*-ensi/-egni*), CCV (*-eso/-empo*), CCXII (*-ento/-erco*), CCXX (*-ena/-era*), CCXXIII (*-una/-ulla*), CCXXV (*-asse/-ale*), CCXXVII (*-oro/-orgo*), CCXXX (*-ena/-ela*), CCXXXIV (*-orto/-oso/-olo*), CCXL (doppia assonanza: *-ego/-egno* e *-ena/-ella*), CCXLIV (*-eggio/-egno*), CCXLVI (*-ove/-ole*), CCLIV (*-ica/-ita*), CCLV (*-anti/-ami*), CCLIX (*-ita/-ica*), CCLXI (*-aglia/-ama*), CCLXIII (doppia assonanza: *-eti/-egi* e *-ale/-are*), CCLXV (*-oglia/-ova*), CCLXXI (doppia assonanza: *-ora/-olta* e *-eso/-egno*), CCLXXII (*-ate/-arte*), CCLXXIV (*-orte/-ore*), CCLXXXIII (*-olto/-orso*), CCLXXXIV (*-oce/-ore*), CCCXIX (*-ervo/-elo*), CCCXX (*-acque/-ante*), CCCXXIX (*-ento/-elo*), CCCXXXVIII (*-erme/-ebbe*), CCCXXXIX (*-erse/-ende*), CCCXLII (*-onda/-orta*), CCCXLIII (*-ora/-ota*), CCCXLVIII (*-elli/-eri*), CCCXLIX (*-esso/*

3 per assonanza e consonanza congiunte.[23] Anche Petrarca rifiuta la ripresa rimica. Il poeta più vicino a Petrarca nel modo di strutturare il sonetto è dunque Cavalcanti: fatto, questo, che non ci sorprende e che è confermato da non pochi richiami tematico-contenutistici, ma che, in ogni caso, è interessante mettere in luce per mezzo di dati statistici assolutamente oggettivi.

Ultima considerazione di ordine generale è che le strutture foniche reperibili nei sonetti petrarcheschi non sono della stessa natura o dello stesso tipo di quelle reperibili nelle canzoni. Il sonetto per la sua struttura isometrica abbisognava, almeno per quanto mi pare di capire, di essere movimentato, arricchito, franto e ricomposto, per mezzo di strutture foniche complicatissime; la canzone, dal ritmo più ampio e certo più complesso e libero al contempo, con le maggiori possibilità di giuoco rimico offerte dall'eterometria, necessitava di minori ricercatezze fonico-espressive: in molti casi bastava la rima, appena accentuata da qualche assonanza o consonanza, e qualche sottolineatura allitterativa.

Dovendo, in qualche modo, ordinare per me stessa e per il lettore il materiale che ho radunato, cercherò prima di mostrare il valore delle assonanze e consonanze nei sonetti e nelle canzoni, e passerò in un secondo momento allo studio delle allitterazioni.

Il linguaggio soavissimo, levigato e terso del Petrarca è sostenuto in gran parte dalla assonanza. Sono gruppi di parole, accoppiamenti di nome-aggettivo, nome-verbo, verbo-verbo, avverbio-verbo, avverbio-nome, che vengono ordinati e posti uno vicino all'altro perché assonanti fra di loro; cosí che la musicalità di una data parola si allarga ad eco e si prolunga nella parola successiva. Gli esempi sono estremamente

---

/*-eno*), CCCL (*-ate*/*-ante*), CCCLII (*-ole*/*-ore*), CCCLIV (*-egno*/*-esto*), CCCLV (*-ali*/*-ai*), CCCLXI (*-orza*/*-ola*), CCCLXII (*-oro*/*-olto*).

22. Cf. *Canzoniere,* ed. Contini, XIII (*-ora*/*-ero*), LIII (*-ente*/*-ento*), LXXV (*-isa*/*-ese*), LXXXIV (*-ore*/*-ari*), C (*-ona*/*-anno*), CI (*-ona*/*-anno*), CIII (*-ura*/*-ora*), CXX (*-etto*/*-itto*), CXXX (*-ede*/*-idia*), CXXXI (*-iri*/*-orio*), CXXXIII (*-ale*/*-ole*), CLXVII (*-ina*/*-ena*), CLXVIII (*-ero*/*-aria*), CLXXXII (*-elo*/*-ale*), CLXXXV (*-ile*/*-ela*/*-ola*), CLXXXVI (*-isto*/*-esto*), CCI (*-unto*/*-ante*), CCXVI (*-ali*/*-ole*), CCXVIII (*-elle*/*-ole*), CCXXIV (*-ese*/*-esso*), CCXXXIII (*-uno*/*-enne*), CCXLI (*-ale*/*-illa*), CCLXVII (*-ero*/*-ire*), CCLXXVI (*-ena*/*-ano*), CCXC (*-ento*/*-ente*), CCXCII (*-ente*/*-anto*), CCXCIII (*-are*/*-era*/*-ore*), CCCIV (*-ermi*/*-armo*), CCCXVII (*-esta*/*-osto*), CCCXXII (*-utte*/*-eta*), CCCXXVI (*-ore*/*-oria*), CCCXXVII (*-ita*/*-etti*), CCCXXVIII (*-eve*/*-ove*), CCCXLVI (*-ate*/*-etti*), CCCLI (*-ate*/*-ita*), CCCLVI (*-ento*/*-inta*), CCCLVII (*-anni*/*-ena*).

23. Cf. *Canzoniere,* ed. Contini, XXXIII (*-one*/*-olle* e *-ella*/*-olle*), CCCXXXVI (*-ita*/*-ima* e *-otto*/*-ata*), CCCLIII (*-ai*/*-ari* e *-ato*/*-ita*).

numerosi. Prendiamo il gruppo nome-aggettivo:[24]

tanta baldanza (XII,9); *destro sentero* (XIII,13); *luoghi tenebrosi - occhi lagrimosi* (XIX,11 e 12); *sotterra in secca verga* (XXII,37: dove l'allitterazione rafforza l'assonanza); *e quella fera bella* (XXIII, 149); *prime olive* (XXIV,8); *affetti acerbi* (XXV,3); *fortunato fiancho* (XXIX,44 con complicanza allitterativa); *obstinato affanno* (L,52); *ventura tutta ignuda - pastorella alpestra - leggiadretto velo* (LII,2-4-5); *donne lagrimose - e i neri fraticelli* (LIII,57-60); *freddo tempo* (LV,2); *a più belle imprese* (LXII,6); *dolce honore* (LXIII,14); *a' preghi honesti et degni* (LXIV,4); *cieco legno - piena vela - dubbiosi scogli - acceso legno* (LXXX,13-29-31-35); *amoroso intoppo* (LXXXVIII,8); *dolci nodi* (XC,2); *L'orsa, rabbiosa* (CIII,5); *de le parole accorte* (CIX,10); *la fera bella et mansueta* (CXXVI, 29 con richiamo al XXIII,149); *mansuete gregge* (CXXVIII,40); *a la tranquilla vita - odorifero laureto* (CXXIX,3-70); *d'amaro pianto - fredda ella - spenta facella - a quella fredda* (CXXXV,21-62-63-68); *leggiadri rami - invescati rami - amati rami - altri rami* (CXLII,7-29-33-39); *guerra eterna* (CL,2); *O passi sparsi - o dolce errore* (CLXI,1 con complicanza allitterativa e 7); *schietti arboscelli* (CLXII,5); *pensero aperto* (CLXIII,1, con l'allitterazione); *carro stellato* (CLXIV,3); *l'erba fresca* (CLXV,1); *vaghi raggi* (CLXXV,10); *boschi inhospiti* (CLXXVI,1); *gli atti vaghi* (CLXXX,13); *vane speranze* (CLXXXIV,14 e cf. I,6); *ombroso bosco* (CXCIV,2); *inescati hami - invescati rami - l'alta piaga* (CXCV,2-3-8; per 3 cf. l'aggettivazione di *rami* alla CXLII); *chiome bionde* (CXCVII,9); *intellecto offeso* (CXCVIII,13); *caro guanto* (CXCIX,9); *amoroso scorno* (CCI,8); *cieca facella* (CCVI,14); *de l'amate piante - d'etterno albergo - stancho coraggio* (CCIV,8-11-12); *tanti affanni - giovenil fallir* (CCVII,10-13); *alpestra vena - dolce sole* (CCVIII,1-9); *I dolci colli - dal lato manco* (CCIX,1-12); *lito vermiglio* (CCX,3); *ombroso bosco* (CCXIV,33 cf. CXCIV,2); *rugiadosi li occhi suoi* (CCXXII,14); *aurato carro* (CCXXIII, 1); *santi atti* (CCXXV,10); *rive fiorite* (CCXXVI,13); *lato manco - dolce humore - preghiere honeste* (CCXXVIII,1-6-13; per 1 cf. CCIX,12); *tranquilla oliva* (CCXXX,12); in *tanti affanni* (CCXXXIV,6 e cf. CCVII,10); *lagrimosa pioggia et feri venti - infiniti sospiri* (CCXXXV,9-10); *tanti affanni* (CCXXXVII,10 e cf. CCXXXIV,6 e CCVII,10); *chiara alma* (CCXXXVIII,2); *novi fiori amorose note* (CCXXXIX,30-33); *l'ingegno offeso* (CCXLVIII,13); *li occhi tuoi molli* (CCL,10); *chiome bionde - amorosa froda - dolcezza honesta* (CCLIII,3-7-11; per il v. 3 cf. CXCVII, 9); *corti riposi* (CCLIV,10); *vive faville - duri costumi* (CCLVIII,1-8); *colli foschi* (CCLIX,7); *danno aspro - orbo mondo - sempiterna bellezza - in vesta negra* (CCLXVIII,13-20-44-82); *prova / meravigliosa et nova - strada manca - dorati strali - capei crespi - amorosa voglia - d'alma villana* (CCLXX,2/3 in cui la rima esalta l'assonanza-26-50-57-66-83); *tanto affanno* (CCLXXVIII,11); *per luoghi ombrosi et foschi* - l'*erba fresca*

24. L'esemplificazione offerta non ha alcuna pretesa di completezza. Ragioni di spazio e di "misura" mi obbligano a sfrondare e a scegliere. Indico in numero romano la Rima a cui mi riferisco e in arabo il verso. La forma grafica è quella stabilita dall'edizione Contini, *o.c.*

(CCLXXXI,6-12 cf. CLXXVI,1); *'n la terza spera* - *quella schiera* (CCLXXXVII,9-11); *pena acerba* (CCLXXXVIII,14); *effetti degni* (CCLXXXIX,12); *secca è la vena* (CCXCII,13); *alma sí vaga* (CCXCVI,10); *dava a l'alma stanca* (CCXCIX,10); *fere selvestre* (CCCI,3); *lieti pensieri* (CCCV,4); *note sí pietose et scorte* (CCCXI,4); *allegre fere et snelle* - *fresche novelle* - *chiare fontane* (CCCXII,4-5-7); *al tempo lieto* - *amici più fidi* (CCCXIV,2-12); *mie pene acerbe* (CCCXV,8); *in sí poche hore* (CCCXVII,8); *et poche hore* (CCCXIX,3; cf. CCCXVII,8); *i dolci colli* (CCCXX,1; cf. CCIX,1); *i rami santi* - *mia vita è trista* - *chiara fontana* - *per la selva altera* (CCCXXIII,25 per il quale conviene confrontare tutta l'aggettivazione a *rami* in CXLII,7-29-33-39 e in CXCV,3); *primo sospiro* - *nel mezzo un seggio altero* - *al mondo sordo* (CCCXXV,18-25-89); *in poca fossa* (CCCXXVI,4); *vista fiorita* (CCCXXVII,2); *speranze sparte* - *grave carne* (CCCXXXI,46 con allitterazione -57); *tempo lieto* - *penseri electi* (CCCXXXII,27 e cf. CCCXIV,2-47); *di penseri electi* - *alma pianta* (CCCXXXVII,9-10 e cf. CCCXXXII,47); *bellezze inferme* (CCCXXXVIII,3); *bei piedi snelli* (CCCXLVIII,7); *deserti paesi* - *ladri rapaci* (CCCLX,46-47); *alma disviata* (CCCLXV,7); *superno regno* - *sante piaghe* (CCCLXVI,38-51).

L'esemplificazione non è certo completa, ma è sufficiente a documentare un gusto che permane costante lungo tutto il *Canzoniere*. Ed è questa una ricerca fonica tra le più semplici, priva quasi di sofisticazione. A questo stesso tipo di assonanza semplice si possono aggiungere le coppie di aggettivi, di verbi, o verbo-sostantivo, avverbio-nome ecc., di cui darò soltanto qualche esempio stralciato qua e là:

solo e pensoso (XXXV,1); *m'à concio 'l foco* (L,77); *la luce che da lunge* (LI,2 con allitterazione); *honesti et belli* (LIX,13); *onde parole et opre* (LXXI,94); *come a morte corre* (XCI,12); *honesta altera* (CXV,1); *bianchi et gialli* (CCXXVII,81); *trapasso sospirando* - *torno, trovo* - *l'alma s'appaga* - *sereno e lieto* (CXXIX,24-30-37-67); *e temo et spero* (CXXXIV,2); *accende et spegne*-*racceso et spento*-*occulta et bruna* (CXXXV, 64-74-85); *ornata et calda* - *fondata et salda* - *mi specchio et tergo* (CXLVI,1-4-6); *non pinto, ma vivo* (CLI,11); *Ove ch'i' posi gli occhi* (CLVIII,1); *terso et crespo* (CLX,14); *ombre et polve* (CLXI,13); *vegghio, penso, ardo, piango* (CLXIV,5); *chiama et scaccia* (CLXXVIII,3); *poggia con orza* - *superbo altero* (CLXXX,5-9); *alberga et regna* (CLXXXIV,2); *leggiadre et care* (CXCIII,10); *di diamanti et di topazi* (CXC,10); *in perle e'n gemme* (CXCVI,7); *tosto è colto* - *s'i' dritto extimo* - *me stesso reprendo* (CCVII,36-87-94); *infermo et lento* (CCXII,8); *rafredda et vela* (CCXVII,5); *m'unge et punge* (CCXXI,12 addirittura in rima); *cercondi et movi* (CCXXVII,2); *santa, saggia, leggiadra, honesta et bella* (CCXLVII,4 dove l'assonanza divide il verso alla cesura); *mi danno assalto* (CCXLIX,14); *experta et vera* (CCL,13); *or piango or canto* - *et temo et spero* (CCLII,1-2); *sordi et loschi* (CCLIX,3); *vaghezza acqueta* - *crescendo meco* (CCLXIV,52-64); *divento et spero* - *sí presso al vero* (CCLXVIII,54-55); *et rotto 'l nodo e'l foco* (CCLXXI,13); *descritti et depinti* (CCLXXIII,6); *doglioso et solo* (CCLXXXVII,1); *cercando in-*

vano (CCLXXXVIII,7); *or veggio et sento* (CCXC,2); *aurato et raro* (CCXCVI,7); *vaghi solitarii et lassi* (CCCVI,6); *sí soave piagne* (CCCXI, 1); *che ferro o vento - per trunco o per muro - rami mai* (CCCXVIII,2-8-11); *et lieto ardendo - al loco torno - honoro et colo* (CCXXI,7-10-11); *riposto, ombroso et fosco* (CCCXXIII,40); *a le pungenti ardenti - piagne et parte - fresca et superba - chiaro mostrando al mondo sordo - acerba et rea* (CCCXXV, 31 in rima -39 -84 - 89 anche qui, come al CCXLVII,4, la doppia assonanza sottolinea la scansione del verso -111); *Or, lasso, alzo la mano - spero et pavento* - non *moria mia vita* (CCCXXXI,7-21-44); *canto et piango - o dite in rime* (CCCXXXII,60 e cf. CCLIII,1,-68); *honesta et bella* (CCCXXXVI,5); *bella e honesta - ascolta et nota* (CCCXLIII,6-10); *grave et frale - volando tanto* (CCCXLIX,11-13); *me stesso riprendo* (CCCLV,4 e cf. CCVII,94); *prendo ardimento* (CCCLVI,2); *pentito et tristo* (CCCLXIV,9); *in guerra et in tempesta* (CCCLV,9); *ingombrata l'alma - sacra et alma - possi et vogli* (CCCLXVI,86-87-106).

Accanto a queste assonanze, che rappresentano particolari insistenze su una musicalità vocalica ripetuta, se ne trovano altre di ben altra complicanza. Abbiamo già visto, al CCLXXIV,4 e al CCCXXV,89, come il modificarsi del timbro assonantico segni la pausa ritmica del verso, e vedremo in seguito quanto Petrarca amasse l'assonanza in cesura, amasse cioè assonanzare la parola in cesura con quella in chiusa di verso. Ma non è tutto: Petrarca, in molti casi, orchestra in un sottile giuoco armonico la musica delle parole, alternandone i suoni o richiamandoli a eco. Ho già sottolineato la coppia assonanzata di aggettivi che apre il sonetto XXXV: *Solo et pensoso*; al v. 2 abbiamo un'altra coppia assonanzata: *passi tardi.* Vediamo adesso l'orchestrazione completa di questi due versi:

> Solo et pensoso i più deserti campi
> vo mesurando a passi tardi et lenti. . . .

Anche a prescindere dall'allitterazione (basata sulla *s p r* e la nasale) che fa del distico una unità inscindibile, si noti come *passi tardi* sia assonanzato con *campi* mentre *et lenti* ripete ad eco la musica di *deserti.* Di modo che *Solo et pensoso* e *vo mesurando* rimangono enucleati in un giuoco fonico che li stacca dalla parte descrittiva, la quale, a sua volta, ha la sua propria misura fonica. E non si tratta soltanto di una sottolineatura sonora del valore semantico della frase, ma anche di una sottolineatura ritmica. Infatti sia *Solo et pensoso* come *vo mesurando* segnano la prima parte del verso con cesura dopo l'accento di quarta: i richiami fonici indicano cioè la possibilità di una lettura verticale ritmica a struttura sintattica diretta: "Solo et pensoso / vo mesurando / i più deserti campi / a passi tardi et lenti". La scomposizione dell'ordine sintattico, senza perdita di chiarezza espressiva, può avvenire proprio tramite l'orchestrazione armonica della frase.

Questo non è un caso limite, ma solo uno dei tanti. Spesso l'assonanza alterna delle parole, oltre a creare un'armonia franta che evita il pericolo del monotonico, sottolinea l'unità semantica. Se ne vedano alcuni esempi, scelti asistematicamente attraverso il *Canzoniere:*

coll'altre schiere travagliate e 'nferme (LIII, 61: si noti l'alternanza vocalica: *a e e e a e e e* delle assonanze[25]); *gli atti suoi dolci soavi* (XCI,4); *un sasso trar più scarso* (CXXXV,27; da notare l'allitterazione che aiuta l'assonanza); *fra quelle vaghe nove forme honeste* (CC,6); *chiaro polito et vivo ghiaccio* (CCII,1); *quelle chiome bionde et crespe* (CCXXVII,1); *per lo dolce silentio de la notte* (CCXXXVII,28); *fermi eran li occhi desiosi e 'ntensi* (CCLVII,2); *un leggiadro disdegno aspro et severo* (CCLXIV, 96); *viver lieto et gire altero* (CCLXIX,6); *mirando dal suo eterno alto ricetto* (CCLXXXV,6); *fere selvestre, vaghi augelli et pesci* (CCCI,3); *l'aria et l'acqua et la terra è d'amor piena - e'n belle donne honeste atti soavi* (CCCX,7-13; in entrambi i versi una parola è fuori del giuoco fonico: *amor* al v. 7 e *donne* al 13; non mi pare dubbio che questo sia un modo per sottolinearne il valore semantico); *l'aura mia antica e i dolci colli* (CCCXX, 1; anche in questo caso *l'aura* è la parola da metter in evidenza e quindi fuori dai richiami fonici); *sola sedea la bella donna* (CCCXXV,26); *vago, dolce, caro, honesto sguardo* (CCCXXX,1); *Solea da la fontana di mia vita* (CCCXXXI,1; con *Solea* isolato); *voglio morire et viver solo* (CCCXLV, 11); *Tu che vedi i miei mali indegni et empi* (CCCLXV,5; con *Tu* isolato e *i miei mali* fuori assonanza, ma con valore di unità fonica a parte, tramite l'allitterazione e l'insistenza sulla *i*).

Ho già accennato al pericolo del monotonico o del 'troppo' fonico che Petrarca ha sempre cura di evitare. Molte volte infatti, egli intercala una parola libera, o la parte centrale del verso, tra due parole assonanzate. Anzi il verso che si apre e si chiude con parole in assonanza o allitteranti fra loro è particolarmente caro al Petrarca.[26] Vediamo qualche

25. Per ognuno degli esempi addotti, potrei, e forse dovrei, sottolineare i giuochi fonici con descrizione e commento. Ancora ragioni di "misura" mi costringono a lasciare al lettore questo compito non spiacevole.

26. Mi permetto di rimandare il lettore a un mio precedente articolo ("La sestina dantesca fra Arnaut Daniel e il Petrarca", *Dante Studies,* XC, 1973, 131-144), in cui cerco di indicare i modelli e le cause della ricerca fonica del Petrarca. In particolare, per i versi 'a cornice', cf. p. 142. Petrarca non fu l'inventore di questo segnale fonico. Anche trascurando gli esempi provenzali, versi di questo tipo si riscontrano in Cavalcanti: ed. Favati, IX, *Io non sperava che lo cor giammai,* v. 4: "*mo*strando per lo viso agli occhi *morte*"; XI,1: *"Poi che* di doglia *co*r *co*nven *ch*'i' *po*rti"; XV, *Se Mercé fosse amica a' miei desiri,* v. 4: "*m*ostrasse la vertute a' *m*iei *m*artiri"; XXII,I: *V*eder poteste, quando *v*'inscontrai"; XXXI, *Gli occhi di quella gentil foresetta,* v. 11: "*I*' *s*ento pianger for li mie*i* *s*ospiri"; XXXIII, *Io temo che la mia disaventura,* v. 3: "*per*ò ch'i' sento nel cor un *pen*sero"; XXXIV, *La forte e nova mia disaventura,* v. 25: "*Par*ol*e* mie disfatt'e *pa*uros*e*," che è forse l'esempio più bello e l'unico in cui alla allittera-

esempio. Il sonetto LVIII si apre e si chiude con due versi di questo particolare tipo fonico: *La guancia che fu già piangendo stanca* (v. 1) —*se la preghiera mia non è superba* (v. 14). Assai spesso gli inizi e le chiuse sono particolarmente curati, ma si veda il bellissimo v. 2 del LXVII: "d*ove* r*otte* dal vento piangon l'*onde*" che riscatta il v. 1 (*Del mar Tirreno a la sinistra riva*) in cui l'assonanza di aggettivo-nome e l'insistenza sulla *r* non erano state sufficienti a liberarlo da una certa andatura pedestre. Il XCVII inizia: "*Ahi* bella libertà, come tu m'*ài*"; il CVI: "N*ova* angeletta s*ovra* l'ale acc*orta*"; mentre il CXII si chiude con "n*octe* et dí tiemmi il signor nostro Am*ore*" e il CXXXII con "e tr*emo* a mezza state, ard*endo* il v*erno*". Tutta la prima quartina del CXLI è costruita con versi di questo tipo; la *variatio* è ottenuta sia con il cambiare assonanza in corrispondenza con il cambiare della rima al v. 2 (il ritmo rimico è *abba*), sia con l'usare l'allitterazione al posto dell'assonanza al v. 3. Si ha cosí l'intero periodo ritmico circolarmente conchiuso, come imponeva, del resto, la struttura semantica diretta, essendo, infatti questi quattro versi il primo termine d'un paragone:

> C*ome* talora al caldo tempo s*ole*
> sempli*cetta* farfalla al lume av*vezza*,
> *v*olar negli occhi altrui, per sua *v*aghezza,
> *onde* aven ch'ella m*ore*, altri si d*ole*. . . .

Al v. 4 il richiamo fonico è insistito in cesura dopo l'accento di sesta, in corrispondenza con la pausa logica.

zione si aggiunge l'assonanza. Gli esempi citati e qualche altro di pura allitterazione, non assommano a più di una diecina in tutta la lirica cavalcantiana. In Dante gli esempi sono più numerosi (circa una ventina), e, oltre ai casi di pura allitterazione (come: *Rime,* ed. Contini, 7, *La dispietata mente,* vv. 27-28: "*S*e dir voleste, dolce mia *s*peranza/ *d*i *d*are in*d*ugio a quel ch'io vi *d*omando"; 12,1: "*D*eh Violetta, che in ombra *d*'Amore"; 13, *Volgete li occhi,* v. 6: "*p*regatel che mi laghi venir *p*ui"; 33, *Due donne in cima de la mente mia,* dopo l'inizio con assonanza in cesura, il v. 14: "*e p*uossi amar virtù *p*er o*p*erare"; 37, *Amor che movi,* v. 15: "*né d*ar *d*iletto *di* color *né d*'arte"; 45, *Amor tu vedi ben,* v. 15: "*p*orto nascosto il col*po* de la *p*etra", e pochi altri), abbiamo casi di apertura e chiusura di verso in assonanza, due dei quali si riscontrano negli inizi; cf. *Rime,* ed. Contini, 20: "E' m'incr*esce* di me sí duram*ente*; 23: "*Onde* venite voi cosí pens*ose*". Altri tre esempi di verso con questa medesima struttura fonica si leggono alla 43, *Io son venuto al punto de la rota,* v. 65: "la m*orte* de' passare ogni altro d*olce*", dove d*olce*, ripetuto dal verso precedente, incornicia la parola m*orte*; vv. 67-68: "d*olce* tempo novello, quando pi*ove* / am*ore* . . .", in cui l'assonanza regge l'enjambement; v. 70 "am*ore* è solo in me, e non altr*ove*". Né Cavalcanti, né Dante offrivano esempio costante di ricercatezza fonica; essi presentavano, tuttavia, qua e là, modelli di strutture foniche che avrebbero potuto dare spunto al Petrarca, il quale, partecipe di un diverso gusto e di altro atteggiamento estetico, le ha riprese, sviluppate e fin quasi esasperate.

Il sonetto CLX si chiude con "tessendo un cerchio a l'oro terso et crespo"; e similmente il CLXI: "deh ristate a veder quale è'l mio male". Nel CLXXXVIII è l'inizio delle due quartine che viene strutturato secondo questo particolare accorgimento: "Almo Sol, quella fronde ch'io sola amo" (v. 1), "Stiamo a mirarla: i' ti pur prego et chiamo" (v. 5). L'inizio del CCXXIII - tutto il sonetto è fonicamente complesso - legge: "Quando 'l sol bagna in mar l'aurato carro"; e la chiusa del CCXLIX è: "mi danno assalto, et piaccia a Dio che 'nvano." Il CCCLV presenta i primi 2 versi del tipo che stiamo esaminando, il v. 3 con appena un'allitterazione interna e il v. 4 con l'assonanza in cesura dopo l'accento di quarta, corrispondente alla pausa logica; le rime si distribuiscono secondo lo schema: *abba*. La struttura completa della prima quartina ricorda dunque da vicino il CLXI:

O tempo, o ciel volubil, che fuggendo
inganni i ciechi et miseri mortali,
o dí veloci più che vento et strali,
ora ab esperto vostre frodi intendo.

Il CCCLVI si chiude con "sciolta dal sonno a se stessa ritorna".

Se questo particolare uso della assonanza è più frequente in apertura o chiusura dei sonetti,[27] ciò non significa che non possa riscontrarsi in altre posizioni, qualora l'armonia della struttura fonica lo richieda.

Un altro tipo strutturale di verso è quello con l'assonanza in cesura. Anche in questo caso la maggioranza degli esempi (più del 75%) si riscontra nei sonetti ed è usato in grande prevalenza per chiudere o aprire un ritmo. I versi che più spesso hanno l'assonanza in cesura sono il 4, l'8, l'11 e il 14; meno frequentemente l'1, il 5, il 9, il 12. Allorché un verso mediano del ritmo ha l'assonanza in cesura difficilmente si trova isolato, ma di regola è fonicamente legato al seguente o al precedente. Vediamo alcuni esempi di assonanza in cesura, utilizzati a chiusura di ritmo:

che quanto piace al mondo // è breve sogno (I,14); *ch'ogni altra voglia // d'entr'al cor mi sgombra* (XI,4); *che vede il caro // padre venir manco* (XVI,4); *vedrà Bologna, // et poi la nobil Roma* (XXVII,8); *si va strug-*

27. L'esemplificazione è come sempre incompleta. Potrei aggiungere l'analisi dei vv. 1-2 del CXI o del v. 1 del CXCVII in cui *L'aura ... lauro* hanno un giuoco fonico-semantico ben più complesso della semplice assonanza o allitterazione. Le consuete ragioni di misura pongono i limiti. Del resto lo scopo di questa ricerca è soprattutto quello di indicare certe tipologie foniche ricorrenti e non certo quello di presentare una analisi fonico-formale dei *Rerum vulgarium fragmenta;* compito, quest'ultimo, che supererebbe di gran lunga la misura di un articolo.

gendo; // onde noi pace avremo (XXXII,8); *de la mia vita, // et posto in su la cima* (LXV,4); *perch'io di lor parlando // non mi stanco* (LXXV, 14); *con sue saette // velenose et empie* (LXXXIII,8); *lodar si possa // in carte altra persona* (XCVII,14); *se brama honore, // e'l suo contrario abhorre* (XCVIII,4); *et d'un dolce saluto // inseme agiunto* (CX,14); *or mansueta, // or disdegnosa et fera* (CXII,8); *danno a me pianto, // et a' pie' lassi affanno* (CXVII,14); *ivi s'asconde, // et non appar più fore* (CXL, 11); *libero spirto, // od a'suoi membri affisso* (CXLV,11); *ch'Appennin parte, // e'l mar circonda et l'Alpe* (CXLVI,14); *che'n un punto arde, agghiaccia, // arrossa e 'nbianca* (CLII,11); *onde Amor l'arco // non tendeva in fallo* (CLVII,11); *col suo candido seno // un verde cespo* (CLX,11 - ed è il sonetto già citato in cui il v. 14 suona: *tessendo un cerchio // a l'oro terso e crespo*); *come a lui piace, // et calcitrar non vale* (CLXI,11); *mai come or presto // a quel ch'io bramo et spero* (CLXVIII,4); *che pensar nol poría // chi non l'à udita* (CXCIII,11); *piena di rose // et di dolci parole* (CC,11); *che de li occhi mi trahe // lagrime tante* (CCI,14); *quel caro peso // ch'Amor m'à commesso* (CCIX,4); *del fiorir queste // innanzi tempo tempie* (CCX,14); *o sacro, aventuroso // et dolce loco* (CCXLIII, 14); *Mantova et Smirna, // et l'una et l'altra lira* (CCXLVII,11); *come chi teme, // et altro mal non sente - e'l riso e'l canto // e'l parlar dolce humano - mi danno assalto, // et piaccia a Dio che'nvano* (CCXLIX,8,11,14); *sí 'l cor tema // et speranza mi puntella - tôrre a la terra // e'n ciel farne una stella* (CCLIV,4,8); *la rividi più bella // et meno altera* (CCCII,4); *con tante note // sí pietose et scorte - come nulla // qua giù diletta et dura* (CCCXI,4,14); *vede, son certo, // et duolsene anchor meco* (CCCXVI, 14); *non è in tua forza; // abbiti ignude l'ossa* (CCXXVI,8); *per far mia vita // subito più trista* (CCCXXIX,14).

Accanto a questo tipo di chiusura di ritmo, ve ne sono altri più complessi, anche se giuocati sempre sull'assonanza. Si veda, per empio, l'ultima terzina del sonetto CXC, che già si apriva con "Una candida cerv*a* // sopra l'erb*a*":

> Et era 'l sol già volt*o* // al mezzo gior*no*,
> gli occhi miei st*a*nch*i* // di mirar non s*a*z*i*,
> quand'io c*a*dd*i* // ne l'acqua, et ella sparve.

Mentre la prima parte del v. 14 è fonicamente legata al v. 13, le parole di chiusura rimangono libere a sottolineare lo svanire improvviso della immagine. Fonicamente sofisticata è anche la chiusa del sonetto CCXXVI:

> S*o*l*o* al m*o*nd*o* paese almo fel*ice*,
> verdi r*ive* fior*ite*, ombrose piagge,
> voi possed*ete* // et io piango il mio b*ene*.

Il v. 12 si apre con due parole assonanzate seguite da due libere, il verso si chiude con il *felice*, la cui armonia viene ripetuta al verso successivo fino alla cesura. La seconda parte del v. 13 è libera, per quanto libera possa essere una parte in rima. Il v. 14 presenta l'assonanza in cesura, ma, a guardar bene, il verso ha doppia pausa: dopo *possedete* (cesura dopo accento di quarta), e dopo *pianga*; *piango* è nella stessa posizione ritmica e assonanzato con *almo* del v. 12. Direi che le assonanze aiutano la lettura, come forse Petrarca la sentiva:

> Solo al mondo /paese almo / felice/
> verdi rive fiorite/ ombrose piagge/
> voi possedete/ et io piango/ il mio bene/

con scansione alterna, ternaria e binaria.

Il sonetto CCLXXIII ha le due quartine in rime assonanzate (*-ardi/-ai*); si apre con un verso ad inizio-fine in assonanza ("Che f*ai?* che pensi? che pur dietro gu*a*rd*i*"- già c'è qui l'armonia che dominerà le quartine). Dopo il v. 1, la prima quartina è strutturata su funzioni allitterative. Il v. 5 ripropone l'andamento fonico del v. 1: "Le so*avi* parole e i dolci sgu*a*rd*i*"; il v. 6 è fonicamente distinto e legato agli altri solo per mezzo della rima ("ch'ad un ad un descritti et depinti ài"- e mi pare inutile sottolineare le due parti del verso stesso, mentre è da notare che tale verso, libero in confronto degli altri e fonicamente conchiuso in se stesso, è semanticamente un inciso); i vv. 7 e 8 tornano a insistere sulla assonanza *a i,* con la quale il componimento si era iniziato:

> son lev*ati* de terra; et è, ben s*ai,*
> qui ricerc*a*rl*i* // intempestivo et t*a*rd*i*.

Gli inizii di ritmo con assonanza in cesura sono meno frequenti, ma non rari. Ne porto qualche esempio:

*Più di me li*eta // *non si vede a t*erra (XXVI,1); *quando mia sp*eme // *già condutta al v*erde (XXXIII,9); *Poi che vostro ved*ere // *in me rispl*ende (XCV, 9); *Piangete donne* // *et con voi pianga Am*ore (XCII,1); *Lasso, quant*e *fiat*e // *Amor m'ass*ale (CIX,1); *Pien di qu*ella // *ineffabile dolc*ezza (CXVI,1); *Né mortal vis*ta // *mai luce divin*a (CLI,5); *O bel viso* ove // *Amor inseme po*se (CLXI,9, in cui anche il v. 11, già citato, presenta la medesima struttura); *Di queste pene è m*ia // *propia la prim*a (CLXXXII, 9); *che la mia nobil pred*a // *non più strett*a (CCI,9 - il v. 14, già citato, ha la medesima struttura); *e'l sol vagheggio,* // *sí ch'elli à già spento - Cieco et stanco* // *ad ogni* altro *ch'al mio d*anno (CCXII,5,9; il v. 12 presenta consonanza in cesura: *Cosí venti anni* // *grave et lungo aff*anno); *L'alma, nudrita s*empre // *in doglia e'n p*ene (CCLVIII,9); *In dubbio di mio stato,* // *or piang*o *or cant*o (CCLII,1); *O nostra v*ita // *ch'è sí bella in vis*ta (CCLXIX,12; e il v. 4: *dal borrea a l'aus*tro, // *o dal mar indo al mauro*); *Or in forma di nimph*a // *o d'altra d*iva (CCLXXXI, 9).

Alcuni inizi sono particolarmente elaborati, oppure la medesima struttura si prolunga almeno al secondo verso, come nella ballata LII:

> Non al suo am*a*nt*e* // più Diana pi*a*cqu*e*
> quando per tal vent*ura* // tutta ign*uda*. . . .

Il sonetto CLXXXI insiste l'assonanza in cesura del v. 1 per i due versi successivi, in modo che la cesura si oppone alle rime. Infatti il ritmo *abba,* seguendo le cesure diviene *aa'ba'ba*:

> Amor fra l'*e*rb*e* // una leggiadra r*e*t*e*
> d'oro et di p*e*rl*e* // t*e*s*e* sott'un ramo
> dell'arbor s*e*mpr*e* verd*e* // ch'i' tant'amo . . . .

Altrettanto complessi sono i primi tre versi del sonetto CCXXII:

> Liete et pens*o*s*e*, // accompagnate et s*o*l*e*,
> d*o*nn*e*,/ che ragionando ite per v*ia*,
> ov'è la v*i*t*a* // *o*v*e* la m*o*rt*e* m*ia*?

Dopo l'assonanza in cesura del primo verso, prolungata dall'inizio del v. 2, il cambiamento di rima (*abba*) impone il diverso timbro vocalico dell'assonanza in cesura del v. 3, in cui la parte centrale del verso, che in tali casi è di solito fonicamente libera, ripete il timbro vocalico dell'assonanza del v. 1.

E' evidente che l'endecasillabo si presta più di qualsiasi altro metro a questi richiami fonici (assonanza fra inizio e fine di verso - assonanza in cesura); ed è questa una delle ragioni per cui gli esempi sono più frequenti nei sonetti che nelle canzoni. Tuttavia, nella misura che anche le canzoni contengono endecasillabi, i due tipi di struttura vi si riscontrano. Nella canzone XXIII (*Nel dolce tempo de la prima etade*) abbiamo sia versi come "Non son mio, no. S'io m*o*r*o* // il danno è v*o*str*o*" (v. 100), in cui l'assonanza in cesura diviene anche assonanza al mezzo, dato che il verso precedente è in rima con questo verso; sia come "*o*mbr*a* di lei, né pur de' suoi piedi *o*rm*a*" (v. 109). La LXXII (*Gentil mia donna, i' veggio*) si chiude con un complesso impasto fonico. Innanzitutto la prima rima del Congedo è assonanzata con l'ultima rima della sirma della strofe precedente (-anti /-anzi), e questo è un mezzo di legamento. Il Congedo di tre versi a rima *abb* dice:

> (v. 91) Canzon, l'una sorella è poco in*a*nz*i*,
> (v. 92) e l'altra s*e*nt*o* // in quel med*e*sm*o* alb*e*rg*o*
> (v. 93) apparecchi*a*rs*i*; // ond'io più carta v*e*rg*o*.

Le due cesure sono assonanzate in modo che quella del v. 92 si lega e con la fine del verso stesso e con la fine del v. 93 (dato che i vv. 92-93 sono in rima); mentre la cesura del v. 93 richiama la rima libera del v. 91. Molto spesso, cioè, nelle canzoni, l'assonanza in cesura vale nel contempo da assonanza al mezzo. Si possono trovare esempi di assoluta semplicità, come la chiusa dell'ultima stanza della LXXIII (*Poi che per mio destino*):

. . . . et sonmi accorto
che questo è'l colpo // di che Amor m'à morto;

o qualche ripresa della CXXIX (*Di pensier in pensier, di monte in monte*):

(v. 14) Per alti monti et per selve aspre trovo
(v. 15) qualche riposo: ogni habitato loco . . . ,

dove l'assonanza delle rime accentua il richiamo fonico al mezzo e in cesura. Nella stessa canzone si leggono i versi seguenti:

(v. 27) *Ove* porge ombra un pino // alto od un colle
(v. 28) talor m'arresto, // et pur nel primo sasso
(v. 29) disegno co la mente il suo bel viso. . . .
(v. 32) dove se' giunto! et onde se' diviso!
(v. 33) Ma mentre tener fiso
(v. 34) posso al primo //pensier la mente vaga. . . .

Il v. 27 è del tipo assonanzato inizio-fine, ma la cesura anticipa il timbro vocalico della rima *-iso* che appare al v. 29; mentre la cesura del v. 28 annuncia il timbro vocalico dell'apertura del v. 29. D'altra parte l'ultimo verso della stanza in cui appare la rima *-iso* (v. 33) viene riecheggiato in cesura dal v. 34. Le canzoni cioè ci introducono a un nuovo tipo di assonanza: l'assonanza al mezzo.

Nei sonetti l'assonanza al mezzo è spesso usata come una controrima quasi a frangere il metro troppo solido e stabile del sonetto. Questo mi sembra confermato dal fatto che non poche volte alla semplice assonanza viene addirittura sostituita la rima. La prima terzina del sonetto I apre questo tipo di esempi:

Ma ben *veggio* / or sí come al popol tutto
favola fui gran tempo, // onde sovente
di me medesmo / meco / mi vergogno.

Pausa o cesura vengono sottolineate dall'assonanza, creando cosí una armonia totalmente staccata da quella delle rime. L'allitterazione del v. 11 (*me* medes*mo* *me*co *mi*) enuclea e accentua l'unica parola libera: *vergogno*.

Caso anche più interessante mi sembra la seconda quartina del sonetto III:

> Tempo non mi parea da far riparo
> contra colpi d'Am*or*:// però m'andai
> secur, senza sospetto; onde i miei guai
> nel commune dol*or* // s'incominciaro.

I quattro versi appaiono legati da una rima esterna (*abba*) e da una interna, opposta a quella esterna (-c-c). L'allitterazione poi unisce tutto il verso 5 (Tem*p*o non mi *pare*a da f*ar* r*iparo*), mentre ha poco giuoco nel v. 6 (soltanto: c*ontra* c*olpi*); acquista nuovo rilievo al v. 7 (*s*ecur *s*en*z*a *s*o*s*petto) in cui accentua la pausa logica; lega principio e fine del v. 8 (nel *com*mune . . . s'in*com*inciaro).

Anche l'inizio del VII appare giuocato sul valore rimico (*abba*) e il controcanto interno della monoassonanza:

> La gola e'l s*o*mn*o* // et l'otiose piume
> ànno dal m*o*nd*o* // ogni vertù sbandita
> ond'è dal c*o*rs*o* // suo quasi smarrita. . . .

Il sonetto XV, che già si apre con un'assonanza al mezzo alla rima del v. 1 ("Io mi rivolgo indietro a ciascun p*a*ss*o* / col corpo st*a*nc*o* // ch'a gran pena porto"), presenta una raffinata complicanza fonica ai vv. 9, 10,11,12 (la prima terzina, cioè, e l'inizio della seconda):

> Talor m'ass*a*l*e* // in mezzo a' tristi pianti
> un dubbio: come posson queste membra
> da lo spirito l*or* // viver lont*a*n*e*?
> Ma rispondemi Am*or*: // Non ti rimembra. . . .

Le rime delle terzine (*cdedce*) s'intrecciano con l'assonanza in cesura del v. 9 con la rima *e* (l'unica che resta in posizione fissa) e con le rime interne dei vv. 11 e 12, che legano in unità espressiva la prima terzina alla seconda. Tale unità è ribadita dalla rima ricca (*membra* / *rimembra*). Indubitabile è il valore semantico delle sottolineature foniche: infatti *assale* e *lontane* sono entrambe parole-chiavi nell'espressione del sentimento e della causa che lo provoca; mentre la rima interna sembra intesa a mostrare l'unicità del soggetto, scisso in *spirito* e *Amore* per la dialettica della forma poetica.

La prima terzina del sonetto XLIII torna a proporre la monoassonanza delle cesure contro il variare della rima (*cdc*):

E cosí tr*isto* // standosi in disparte,
tornar non vide il *viso,* // che laudato
sarà s'io *vivo* // in più di mille carte.

Se poi consideriamo anche l'allitterazione, vediamo bene che, mentre l'assonanza sottolinea la struttura logico-grammaticale, l'allitterazione serve a dare unità al verso; e il v. 9 è l'esempio più chiaro, tutto allitterato com'è sulla sibilante. I vv. 10 e 11 sono quasi liberi dalla allitterazione; vi si nota soltanto *vide il viso* e *sarà s'io.*

Non sempre l'assonanza delle cesure si oppone all'ordine delle rime, talvolta vi si accompagna. La prima quartina, per esempio, del sonetto LXXXI presenta due cesure monoassonanzate in corrispondenza delle due rime uguali. Essendo le rime poste nell'ordine *abba,* i versi con la rima *b* hanno anche l'assonanza interna, mentre i versi con la rima *a* sono legati in unità foniche dalla allitterazione, che manca negli altri due:

*Io s*on *sí st*an*co s*otto'l f*as*ci*o* ant*ico*
de le mie c*o*lp*e* // et de l'usanza ria
ch'i' temo f*o*rt*e* // di mancar tra via,
et di cader i*n man* del *mio nemico.*

Las cesura dei vv. 1 e 4 non è assonanzata, ma in entrambi i casi troviamo una *a* + nasale sotto accento (di quarta nel v. 1, di sesta al 4). Il che senza dubbio aumenta il valore armonico dell'insieme.

La prima quartina del sonetto XC è invece ancora strutturata con le assonanze al mezzo ai vv. 2 e 4, mentre la rima è del tipo *abba.* Le cesure assonanzate corrispondono dunque una volta alla rima *b* e una volta alla rima *a,* interrompemdo l'andatura rimica. E anche in questo esempio i versi hanno ciascuno una propria entità fonica dovuta all'allitterazione, più forte e insistita ai vv. 1 e 3 (liberi dall'assonanza di cesura):

E*ran*o i capei d'*o*r*o* a l'au*ra* sp*ar*si
che'n mi*ll*e d*olci* n*o*d*i* // gli avo*l*gea,
e'*l* vago lume o*l*tre misu*ra ar*dea
di quei begli *o*cch*i*, // ch'or ne *s*on *sí s*car*s*i.

Spesso l'assonanza delle cesure serve, non in opposizione alla rima, per insistere sullo stesso timbro vocalico e prolungarlo oltre le possibilità rimiche. Si vedano i versi 5,6,7,8 del sonetto XCI:

(v. 5) Tempo è da ricovrare ambe le chiavi
(v. 6) del tuo cor, ch'ella possedeva in v*ita,*

(v. 7) et seguir lei per v*ia* // dr*itta* exped*ita*:
(v. 8) peso terren non s*ia* // più che t'aggravi.

E' evidente che la rima in cesura tra i vv. 7 e 8 non è altro che un insistere e un prolungare il timbro vocalico della rima esterna in *-ita.*

Il sonetto C, con le quartine dalla consueta struttura rimica *abba,* nella seconda quartina insiste tanto sul timbro vocalico della rima *b,* che tale rima diviene fonicamente dominante: sarà quella che verrà ripresa in consonanza nelle terzine:

e'l sasso ove a' gran dí pens*osa* siede
mad*onna,* et s*ola* // seco si rag*iona,*
con quanti luoghi sua bella pers*ona*
coprí mai d'*o*mbr*a,* // o disegnò col piede.

L'allitterazione dà unità fonica ai vv. 5 e 6 limitando, e quasi annullando, la frattura dell'enjambement.

Nel sonetto CLI, l'assonanza delle cesure ai vv. 2 e 3, rinforzata dal parallelismo vocalico che precede la parola in cesura, sembra usata per sottolineare il paragone:

(v. 1) Non d'atra et tempestosa onda marina
(v. 2) fugg*ïo* in p*o*rt*o* // già mai stanco nocchiero,
(v. 3) com'*io* dal f*o*sc*o* // et torbido pensero
(v. 4) fuggo ove'l gran desio mi sprona e'nchina.

Invece la coppia di rime interne ai vv. 13-14 del sonetto CLVI direi che rientra nel gusto petrarchesco della sofisticata cura fonica delle chiuse:

(v. 12) ed era il cielo a l'armonia sí intento
(v. 13) che non se ved*ea* // in ramo mover foglia,
(v. 14) tanta doc*ezza* av*ea* // pien l'aere e'l vento.

Un bell'esempio di prolungamento fonico delle rime in opposizione alla struttura *abba* lo troviamo nella prima quartina del sonetto CLXXVIII:

Amor mi spr*ona* // in un tempo et affr*ena,*
assecura et spav*enta,* // arde et agghi*accia,*
gradisce et sd*egna,* // a sé mi chi*ama* et sc*accia,*
or me tene in sper*anza* // et or in p*ena.*

Oltre all'insistito timbro vocalico della rima *a,* che anticipa la ripresa della rima assonanzata in terzina, è da notare la consonanza in cesura del v. 1, l'eco in cesura al v. 4 della rima *b*, e il complicato giuoco allitterativo per cui i vv. 1 e 2 si aprono e si chiudono con parole che iniziano con *a* (*A*mor . . . *a*ffrena; *a*ssecura . . . *a*gghiaccia), mentre il v. 3 è diviso in due parti ben distinte proprio per mezzo della allitterazione (gra*disce* et *sdegna*; *chiama* et s*caccia*), e il v. 4 è diviso in due parti per mezzo del parallelismo sintattico retto da *or* . . . *or.*

In periodi rimici del tipo *aba,* la ripresa del timbro vocalico di *a* alla cesura di *b* è un mezzo efficace per dare unità fonica ai tre versi. Petrarca usa questo mezzo con una qualche frequenza. Si veda la prima terzina del sonetto CCIV:

> Or con sí chiara luce, e con tai s*e*gn*i*
> errar non d*ê*s*i* // in quel breve viaggio
> che ne po' far d'etterno albergo d*e*gn*i*;

oppure i tre versi di chiusura del CCLXXIX:

> Di me non pianger tu, ché' miei dí f*e*rs*i*
> morendo et*e*rn*i*, // et ne l'interno lume
> quando mostrai de chiuder, gli occhi ap*e*rs*i*;

oppure gli ultimi tre versi del CCCXLV:

> ché più bella che mai con l'occhio int*e*rn*o*
> con li angeli la v*e*ggi*o* // alzata a volo
> a pie' del suo et mio Signore et*e*rn*o*,

in cui l'opposizione-richiamo tra rima e assonanza è accresciuta dall'uso della rima ricca (*interno / eterno*). Nel sonetto CCCLV è la prima terzina che presenta questa particolare struttura:

> Et sarebbe ora, et è passata om*ai,*
> di rivolt*a*rl*i* // in più secura parte,
> et poner fine a li'nfiniti gu*ai*;

mentre nel CCCLVII è ancora una volta la terzina di chiusura:

> et or novellamente in ogni v*e*n*a*
> intrò di lei che m'*era* // data in sorte,
> e non turbò la sua fronte ser*e*n*a.*

Quando le terzine sono organizzate su tre rime libere ripetute, le assonanze di cesura possono dar rilievo a una delle rime, come accade nella prima terzina del sonetto CCXIII:

> et que' belli *o*cch*i* // che i cor' fanno smalti,
> possenti a rischiarar abisso et n*o*tt*i*
> et tôrre l'alme a' c*o*rp*i* // et darle altrui.

Una tecnica in certo qual modo simile a questa, ma variata tanto da poter essere applicata a una quartina del tipo rimico *abba,* la troviamo nel CCXVI:

(v. 1) Tutto 'l dí pi*a*ng*o*; // et poi la notte qu*a*nd*o*
(v. 2) prendon riposo i miseri mortali,
(v. 3) trovomi in pi*a*nt*o*, // et raddoppiarsi i mali:
(v. 4) cosí spendo il mio tempo lagrim*a*nd*o*.

Oltre alle due cesure assonanzate fra loro e con la rima *a* e in ordine scambiato rispetto alle rime, il finissimo giuoco fonico di questi quattro versi si appoggia anche alla assonanza in cesura del v. 1, alla allitterazione che divide in due parti distinte, sempre alla cesura, il v. 2. Il v. 3, che torna a proporre l'assonanza con il v. 1 (cesura e fine di verso) e con la rima del v. 4, è calcato fonicamente sul v. 1 fino alla cesura. Non c'è soltanto la parola assonanzata e per di piú derivativa, ma le stesse vocali che precedono l'assonanza vengono ripetute e anche la stessa consonante iniziale: "*T*utt*o* *i*l d*í* *piango*" - "*t*rov*o*m*i* *i*n *pianto*". Il v. 4 ha la parte centrale chiusa dall'assonanza interna "sp*endo* il mio t*em*p*o*", in modo che *cosí* e *lagrimando* acquistano rilievo semantico. Del resto anche la seconda parte del v. 3 era legata dall'assonanza interna: "raddoppi*a*rs*i* *i* m*a*l*i*". Seguendo dunque il giuoco fonico, i quattro versi vengono divisi in unità semantico-foniche, che aiutano e sottolineano la retta comprensione del testo. A un inizio cosí elaborato non poteva non corrispondere una chiusa altrettanto sofisticata:

(v. 12) Più l'altrui fallo che'l mi' mal mi dole:
(v. 13) ché Pietà v*i*v*a*, // e'l mio fido socc*o*rs*o*,
(v. 14) védem'arder nel f*o*c*o*, // et non m'a*i*t*a*.

Il v. 12 è strutturato sulla allitterazione, mentre i vv. 13 e 14 hanno le assonanze in cesura incrociate con le rispettive rime.

Il giuoco fonico risponde, sí, a certe tipologie essenziali che io cerco di ridurre ad esempi, ma è cosí lato e libero che ogni componimento può rinnovarlo o complicarlo. Si prenda, ad esempio, il sonetto CCXXIII: dopo un'assonanza, al mezzo ai vv. 3 e 4, che rientrerebbe nel tipo di assonanze che chiudono i periodi ritmici, le successive assonanze al mezzo o in pausa sono regolarmente usate al fine di legare ciascun periodo ritmico al successivo. Cosí la rima del v. 4 è assonanzata con la pausa logica del v. 5. Ma siccome le quartine hanno l'ordine rimico del tipo *abba,* l'inizio della seconda quartina (il v. 5) presenta ancora la rima in *a,* come il v. 4, accade cosí che la pausa logica del v. 5 è assonanzata anche con la rima dello stesso verso: il v. 5 cioè rientra nella categoria dei versi con pausa-fine assonanzate. Il valore del legamento fonico fra i due versi è confermato dall'uso della rima ricca, falso-derivativa (*innarro /narro*). La rima del v. 8 (ultimo delle quartine) è assonanzata con la cesura del v. 9 (primo delle terzine). Poi avviene un cambiamento nel giuoco delle assonanze, che sottolinea il mutarsi del periodo ritmico: ora è la cesura del v. 11 (ultimo della prima terzina) che è assonanzata con la rima del v. 12, in modo da legare la prima alla seconda terzina. L'ordine rimico delle terzine è: *cdedce*; quindi la cesura del v. 11 si trova in assonanza anche con la rima *d* del v. 10. Come nel caso dei vv. 4 e 5, anche adesso il richiamo fonico è accentuato dall'uso della rima ricca derivativa (*alba/inalba*):

(v. 3) col cielo et co le stelle et co la l*una*
(v. 4) un'angosciosa et d*ura* // notte inn*arro*.
(v. 5) Poi, l*asso*, / a tal che non m'ascolta n*arro* . . .
(v. 8) con Amor, con madonna et meco g*arro*.
(v. 9) Il sonno è 'n b*a*nd*o*, // et del riposo è nulla;
(v. 10) ma sospiri et lamenti infin a l'*a*lb*a*,
(v. 11) et lagrime che l'*a*lm*a* // a li occhi invia.
(v. 12) Vien poi l'aurora, et l'aura fosca in*a*lb*a*. . . .

Questo sonetto CCXXIII è anche uno dei tanti che lega le quartine alle terzine per mezzo della ripresa di una rima delle quartine assonanzata con una delle terzine (*-una/-ulla*); quindi il richiamo fonico fra i vv. 3 e 4 serve anche a dar rilievo al timbro vocalico che verrà ripetuto in terzina.

Anche nel sonetto CCXXX una rima delle quartine viene ripresa in assonanza nelle terzine (*-ela/-ena*), e anche questa volta il Petrarca trova modo d'insistere sopra tale timbro vocalico. Ma in maniera affatto diversa. La prima quartina del sonetto si affida, direi, al semantismo diretto; poche perfino le allitterazioni. Le complicanze foniche cominciano con la seconda quartina. Qui abbiamo tre versi rimati alle cesure, che veramente funzionano come controcanto alle rime (*abba*). La prima terzina ha i versi che portano la rima in *-ena,* assonanzata con la rima in *-ela* delle quartine, con assonanza in cesura, e quindi le due cesure vengono a trovarsi assonanzate fra loro; ed è un modo per rilevare l'importanza del timbro vocalico. La seconda terzina ha i primi due versi con le cesure assonanzate fra loro, in controcanto alle rime (le rime delle terzine sono ordinate sul tipo *cdcdcd*). Il verso di chiusura è assolutamente libero, cosí come libera era stata la prima quartina:

onde e' suol tr*ar* // di lagrime tal fiume,
per accorci*ar* // del mio viver la t*ela*,

che non pur ponte // o guado o remi o *vela*,
ma scamp*ar* // non potienmi ali né piume.
Sí profondo *era* // et di sí larga *vena*
il pianger mio et sí lunge la riva,
ch'i' v'aggiung*eva* // col penser a *pena*.
Non lauro o p*alma*, // ma tranquilla oliva
Pietà mi m*anda*, // e'l tempo rasserena,
e'l pianto asciuga, et vuol anchor ch'i' viva. (vv. 5-14)

La rima interna dà movimento al ritmo assai più delle assonanze: il parallelismo sintattico può originare la rima interna, come nel sonetto CCLXII dove il consueto giuoco rimico *abba* è franto dalla rima interna al v. 2 (*b*) prima, e poi al v. 4 (*a*); cosí che il vero ordine rimico è *ac'bbc'a* (segno con apostrofe la rima interna):

(v. 1) -Cara la *vita*, // et dopo lei mi pare
(v. 2) *vera honestà*, // che'n bella donna *sia*.
(v. 3) -L'ordine volgi: e' non fur, madre m*ia*,
(v. 4) *senza honestà* // mai cose belle o care.

La cesura del v. 1 già richiamava l'attenzione sul timbro vocalico della rima *b*; tale timbro vocalico, per mezzo di assonanze in cesura o fuori cesura dominerà tutta la seconda quartina:

et qual si lascia di suo honor privare,
né donna è più né v*iva*; // et se qual pr*ia*
appare in v*ista*, // è tal v*ita* aspra et r*ia*
via più che morte, et di più pene amare.

Ma il più chiaro esempio di uso di rima interna, con la funzione musicale di basso che ritmi il canto, è il sonetto CCLXV. Le rime sono: *abba abba cde cde*. Niente di più normale e quasi scontato. La rima *d* è in assonanza con la *a*. L'aggiunta di una rima *f* a versi alterni lungo tutto il sonetto rinnova l'andamento ritmico:

Aspro c*or*e et selvaggio, et cruda voglia
in dolce, humile, angelica figura,
se l'impreso rigor // gran tempo dura,
avran di me poco honorata spoglia;
ché quando nasce et m*or* // fior, herba et foglia,
quando è'l dí chiaro, et quando è notte oscura,
piango ad ogn*or*: // ben ò di mia ventura,
di madonna et d'Am*or*e // onde mi doglia.
Vivo sol di speranza, rimembr*ando*
che poco hum*or* // già per continua prova

consumar vidi marmi et pietre salde.
Non è sí duro *cor* // che, lagrim*ando,*
preg*ando,* am*ando,* // talor non si smova,
né sí freddo voler, // che non si scalde.

Il v. 1 anticipa la rima in cesura con *core,* ma la parola, posta sotto accento di terza, quasi sfugge all'attenzione del lettore; se non ché rimane l'eco fonico, e quando si giunge al *rigor* del v. 3 in cesura sotto accento di sesta, *core* riacquista tutto il valore fonico e significante. Al v. 5 la rima in cesura è ripetuta sotto accento di sesta. Al v. 7 la cesura in rima si trova sotto accento di quarta. Le quartine si chiudono con la ripetizione ancora della rima interna su accento di sesta. Il giuoco rimico delle quartine è dunque: *f'abf'baf'bf'a,* e potrebbe essere la fronte di una stanza di canzone. Nelle terzine la rima interna perdura alla cesura su accento di quarta al v. 10, su accento di sesta al v. 12. La chiusa del componimento richiede che anche il ritmo rimico trovi soluzione: ed ecco l'insistere sulla rima gerundiva di verbi della prima già usata al v. 9, in apertura delle terzine che ora appare anche alla cesura (e prima della cesura) del v. 13. L'ultimo verso è libero, ma in cesura appare, non più la rima *f'*, ma una consonanza: *voler.* Le rime delle terzine potrebbero essere rappresentate in questo ordine: *cf'def' cc'e.* Anche l'ordine degli accenti sotto cui è posta la rima interna può essere interessante: 3/6/6/4/6/4/6/4 e l'ultimo verso ha la cesura consonanzata alla rima *f'*, ancora sotto accento di sesta. Se dal puro valore fonico passiamo al valore fonico-semantico di queste rime interne in *-or,* vediamo che si aprono e si chiudono con la parola *cor* (*core* al v. 1); poi abbiamo e dall'alto e dal basso due parole che, staccate dal contesto, sono quasi neutre di significato (*rigor* e *humor*), ma al centro rimangono *mor, ognor, Amore,* chiavi tematiche non di questo sonetto soltanto, ma di gran parte del *Canzoniere.* Se consideriamo infine la faticosa rielaborazione a cui questo sonetto è stato sottoposto da parte del Petrarca,[28] non sussistono dubbi che gli effetti fonici e semantici che ho via via messo in rilievo sono frutto di cosciente e studiatissima fatica.

Altro notevole esempio di elaboratissime strutture foniche, ottenute per mezzo delle assonanze, consonanze e rime interne, è il sonetto

28. Tanto il Carducci, *Le Rime di Francesco Petrarca, o.c.,* p. 364, che il Chiórboli, *Le rime sparse, o.c.,* p. 603, riportano nel commento le varianti trasmesse dal codice casanatense riguardo alla prima terzina di questo sonetto. Senza la parola *umor,* che è conquista di un secondo momento di stesura a ribadire l'equilibrio della rima interna, tutto l'artificio fonico perdeva di evidenza. Scritto, come dice il Chiórboli, *o.c.,* p. 604, il 21 settembre 1350 e trascritto nel 1356, il sonetto appartiene dunque al periodo in cui, secondo quello che mi sembra di aver notato, più forte era nel Petrarca la tendenza a soluzioni foniche.

CCXCII. La struttura rimica è semplice: *abba abba cdc dcd*. La rima *d* è consonanzata con la rima *a* (quindi il sonetto si apre e si chiude con rime in consonanza). Senza considerare i giuochi allitterativi o le assonanze in apertura e chiusura di verso (come al v. 5: "le cr*e*sp*e* chiome d'or puro luc*e*nt*e*"), vorrei richiamare l'attenzione sulle cesure:

Gli occhi di ch'io parl*ai* // sí caldamente,
et le braccia et le m*ani* // e i piedi e'l viso,
che m'ave*a*n s*í* // da me stesso diviso,
et fatto singul*ar* // da l'altra gente;
le crespe chiome d'*or* // puro lucente
e'l lampeggi*ar* // de l'angelico riso,
che solean f*are* // in terra un paradiso,
poca polvere s*on* // che nulla sente.
Ed io pur *vivo*, // onde mi doglio et sdegno,
rimaso senza'l l*ume* // ch'amai tanto,
in gran fort*una* // e'n disarmato legno.
Or sia qui fi*ne* // al mio amoroso canto:
secca è la *vena* // de l'usato ingegno,
et la cetera mia rivolta in pianto.

Gli accenti di cesura seguono quest'ordine: 6646 6446 464 446. Ma l'ultimo verso è fonicamente libero e del resto è una libera traduzione da *Giobbe*, XXX,33, come è ben noto. Le cesure dei vv. 1 e 2 sono assonanzate; e il v. 3 ripete l'assonanza, ma in maniera meno chiara, dato il *sí* accentato e non enclitico e lo spostamento di accento di cesura. Con il v. 4 la cesura apre una serie di rime che legano il v. 4 ai vv. 6 e 7. Il v. 5 ha la cesura in consonanza con la serie rimica e in assonanza con la cesura del v. 8. Del resto la cesura del v. 8 apre la serie consonanzata delle cesure, che caratterizza le terzine. Sia dunque il v. 4 che il v. 8 anticipano il motivo fonico interno del periodo ritmico successivo. Il v. 9, d'altra parte, ha la cesura assonanzata con la rima *b* delle quartine: cosí che il sonetto presenta un doppio legame tra quartine e terzine: la consonanza di una rima (*-ente* / *-anto*) e l'assonanza della rima *b* con la cesura del primo verso delle terzine (*-iso*/*-ivo*). I vv. 10 e 11 hanno le cesure quasi rimiche (*-ume*/*-una e:* dove la a finale di *fortuna* viene elisa per ragioni metriche). I vv. 12 e 13 hanno le cesure consonanzate fra di loro e con la cesura del v. 11. Le tre consonanze (vv. 11, 12 e 13) sono marcate dalla uguaglianza di accento di cesura. Se dalla pura analisi fonica passiamo all'analisi semantica, vediamo che la seconda parte di ogni verso, la parte rimica cioè, ha quasi sempre valore di ornato o allargamento retorico; ma alle parti del verso precedenti la cesura è affidato il messaggio, la cosa da dire: "Gli occhi di ch'io parlai / et le braccia et le mani, / che m'avean sí / (et)fatto singular / le crespe chiome d'or / e'l lampeggiar / che solean fare, /poca polvere son. / Et io pur vivo, / rimaso senza'l lume / in gran fortuna. / Or sia qui fine: / secca è la vena / et la cetera mia rivolta in pianto." Da questo si può dedurre che se le cesure avevano funzione di controcanto fonico, rispetto alle rime, le parti rimiche avevano funzione di controcanto semantico rispetto alle cesure. L'unico verso indivisible è il v. 14 ed è indivisibile sia dal punto di vista fonico che semantico.

Potrei allungare l'esemplificazione a volontà, ma ritengo che gli esempi addotti siano sufficienti a mettere sull'avviso i futuri commentatori dei *Rerum vulgarium fragmenta:* un'analisi delle strutture foniche può dare grande aiuto all'interpretazione e, soprattutto, condurre l'utente della poesia a scoprire i segreti di laboratorio del produttore di poesia.

Un'altra funzione delle assonanze è quella di dare unità fonica ai versi in enjambement. Gli esempi sono numerosissimi, mi limiterò a segnalarne qualcuno:

XIV, vv. 1-2 (ballata): *Occhi miei lassi, mentre ch'io vi giro / nel bel viso di quella che v'à morti*
XXVII, vv. 1-2 (sonetto): *Il successor di Karlo, che la chioma / co la corona del suo antiquo adorna*
XXIX (canzone), vv. 48-49: *ove non spira folgore, né indegno / vento mai che l'aggrave*
L (canzone), vv. 32-34: *drizzasi in piedi, et co l'usata verga, / lassando l'erba e le fontane e i faggi, / move la schiera sua soavemente* . . . (ed è da notare come le parti del verso dopo la cesura assonanzata siano legate dalla allitterazione); vv. 65-66: *gli tenni nel bel viso / per iscolpirlo*
LXXII (canzone), vv. 40-41: *come sparisce et fugge / ogni altro lume*
LXXIII (canzone), vv. 27-28: *Mostrimi almen ch'io dica / Amor in guisa*
LXXXII (sonetto), vv. 6-7: *che'l vostro nome a mio danno si scriva / in alcun marmo*
LXXXV (sonetto), vv. 2-3: *et son per amar più di giorno in giorno / quel dolce loco, ove piangendo torno*
CXI (sonetto), vv. 3-4: *et io per farle honore / mossi con fronte reverente et smorta*
CXIV (sonetto), vv. 7-8: *seco parlando, et a tempi migliori / sempre pensando*
CXXXIII (sonetto), vv. 7-8: *et parvi un gioco / il sole e'l foco*
CXXXVIII (sonetto), vv. 12-13: *ne le mal nate / richezze tante?*
CXLVIII (sonetto), vv. 10-11: *ove conven ch'armato viva / la vita*
CL (sonetto), vv. 5-6: *ella ne face / di state un ghiaccio*
CLXVIII (sonetto), vv. 9-10: *In questa passa'l tempo et ne lo specchio / mi veggio andar ver la stagion contraria*

CLXX (sonetto), vv. 12-13: *E veggi'or ben che caritate accesa / lega la lingua altrui*
CCVI (canzone), vv. 10-11: *Amor l'aurate sue quadrella / spenda in me tutte*
CCVII (canzone), vv. 37-38: *cosí dal suo bel volto / l'involo or uno et or un altro sguardo*
CCIX (sonetto), vv. 6-7: *et non son anchor mosso / dal bel giogo più volte indarno scosso*
CCXXIX (sonetto), vv. 3-4: *ch'a la cagion, non a l'effetto, intesi / son i miei sensi vaghi pur d'altezza*
CCLXI (sonetto), vv. 3-4; *miri fiso nelli occhi a quella mia / nemica*
CCLXIV (canzone), vv. 115-116: *ma variarsi il pelo / veggio, et dentro cangiarsi ogni desire*
CCLXVIII (canzone), vv. 15-16: *perch'ad uno scoglio / avem rotto la nave*; vv. 23-24; *Caduta è la tua gloria, et tu nol vedi / né degno eri*; vv. 37-41: *l'invisibil sua forma è in paradiso / disciolta di quel velo / che qui fece ombra al fior degli anni suoi, / per rivestirsen poi / un'altra volta, et mai più non spogliarsi*
CCLXX (canzone), vv. 76-77: *onde l'accese / saette uscivan*
CCLXXIX (sonetto), vv. 3-4: *o roco mormorar di lucide onde / s'ode* (oltre alla assonanza abbiamo qui anche l'allitterazione che colma lo iato dell'enjambement); vv. 12-13; *ché' miei dí fersi / morendo eterni*
CCXC (sonetto), vv. 10-11: *ch'andar per viva / forza mi convenia*
CCXCVI (sonetto), vv. 5-8: *Invide Parche, si repente il fuso / troncaste, ch'attorcea soave et chiaro / stame al mio laccio, et quello aurato et raro / strale, onde morte piacque oltra nostro uso!*
CCXCIX (sonetto), vv. 1-2: *Ov'è la fronte, che con picciol cenno / volgea il mio core*
CCCI (sonetto), vv. 12-13: *Quinci vedea 'l mio bene; et per queste orme / torno a vedere*
CCCIV (sonetto), vv. 7-8: *ma l'ingegno et le rime erano scarse / in quella etate*
CCCXVI (sonetto), vv. 1-2: *Tempo era omai da trovar pace o triegua / di tanta guerra*; vv. 13-14 *ch'or dal cielo / vede son certo, et duolsene ancor meco*
CCCXXI (sonetto), vv. 1-2: *E' questo'l nido in che la mia fenice / mise*
CCCXXIII (canzone), vv. 28-29: *uscian sí dolci canti / vari augelli*
CCCXXXVII (sonetto), vv. 5-6: *ove habitar solea / ogni bellezza*
CCCXLI (sonetto), vv. 1-2: *Deh qual pietà, qual angel fu sí presto / a portar sopra'l cielo* (l'allitterazione di *presto portar* aiuta a sentire uniti i due versi)
CCCXLIX (sonetto), vv. 9-10: *del terreno / carcere uscendo*
CCCLIII (sonetto), vv. 7-8: *verresti in grembo a questo sconsolato / a partir seco i dolorosi guai*
CCCLX (canzone), vv. 12-13: *et tanti et sí diversi / tormenti ivi soffersi*
CCCLXV (sonetto), vv. 10-11: *et se la stanza / fu vana*
CCCLXVI (canzone), vv. 9-11: *Vergine, s'a mercede / miseria extrema de l'humane cose / già mai ti volse* (dove il primo enjambement è sorretto dalla allitterazione e il secondo dalla assonanza).

Già molte volte, nel corso di questo studio, ho avuto occasione di mettere in evidenza come la funzione allitterativa si associasse a quella della assonanza o della consonanza. Direi che Petrarca usa l'allitterazione a scopi ben precisi, di cui due più squisitamente fonici e due più squisitamente semantici. Scopi più propriamente fonici mi sembrano quelli di dare unità fonica al verso, al di là del valore significante, o di usare l'allitterazione come segnale di apertura e chiusura del verso stesso. Definirei più propriamente semantico l'uso dell'allitterazione allorché essa serve a segnalare le differenti parti del verso rispondenti a diverse strutture grammaticali, o a enucleare parole particolarmente importanti dal tessuto fonico del verso stesso, oppure allorché viene usata a ricomporre l'unità semantica della frase, rotta dall'enjambement. Mi pare cioè di poter affermare che l'allitterazione ha nel Petrarca funzioni assai simili a quelle dell'assonanza, tanto da poter essere usata sia in alternanza con l'assonanza stessa, sia come appoggio suppletivo alle medesime funzioni per cui viene usata l'assonanza.

Ho già segnalato l'accoppiamento nominale assonanzato; altrettanto facile è reperire l'accoppiamento nominale in allitterazione. Stralcio qualche esempio:

secura strada (VI,6); *in pace passavam* (VIII,5); *poetando et poggia* (X,8); *fin farsi* (XII,5); *sbigottito et smorto* (XV,7); *sa star sol* (XXI,11); *trita terra* (XXII,27); *vive voci* (XXIII,98); *vero valor* (XXV,14); *spada scinta* (XXVI,7); *beata et bella - a Dio dilecta* (XXVIII,1-5); *vede vertù - del mio cor chiave* (XXIX,54-56); *schiera di sospiri - so s'io mi speri* (XXXVI, 68-107); *sospira et suda* (XLI,3); *morto il marito - mille morti* (XLIV,3-12); *provo per lo petto et per li fianchi* (XLVI,4); *voler le voglie* (XLVIII, 8); *vulgo avaro* (LI,11); *fiorir faceva* (LX,3); *conven che si converta* (LXVI,3); *fatto infermo* (LXX,47); *vaghe faville - solicito studio* (LXXII,37-69); *Amor m'à morto* (LXXIII,90); *il cor conquiso* (LXXVII, 4); *bello et bianco* (LXXXII,5); *al destinato dí* (XCVIII,10); *vittorïosa sua ventura* (CIII,2); *spenga la sete sua - rete tal tende - di duo fonti un fiume - 'l fianco ferito* (CV,15-47-67-87); *tanto tranquille* (CIX,7); *i dolci dí* (CXXIV,9); *foco et fiamma - né in fior, né'n foglia - fresco fiorito* (CXXV,13-18-74); *sacro sereno - volga la vista* (CXXVI,10-32); *del mio mal meco - il dí si dole - le vïolette e'l verde - Amor armato* (CXXVII,5-26-32-34); *il cor condenso* (CXXIX,58); *ma miglior mastro* (CXXX,11); *man manca* (CXXXIX,9); *se stessa si sdegna* (CXL,8); *freddo foco* (CXLVII, 12; *vergogna il vela* (CLI,10); *morte o mercé* (CLIII,4); *di doglia et di desire* (CLV,7); *famose fronti* (CLXI,5); *fiori et felici* (CLXII,1); *stanca si scompagna* (CLXXIII,3); *prendi a diletto i dolor* (CLXXIV,9); *e'l vento et la vela* (CLXXX,8); *collo candido* (CLXXXV,2); *turbato et tristo - sembiante stella* (CLXXXVI,5-10); *candida colomba* (CLXXXVII,5); *schietti soavi* (CXCIX,7); *Meco di me mi meraviglio* (CCIX,5); *tal piacer precipitava* (CCXIV,11); *soavemente et sporgi* (CCXXVII,3); *dal voler vinta*

(CCXL,7); *pietate à presa* - *foco et fiamma* - *'l dolor distilla* (CCXLI,7-9-10); *partecipe et presago* (CCXLII,8); *nel sommo seggio* (CCXLIV,8); *soavemente sospirando* (CCXLVI,2); *dura dipartita* (CCLIV,11); *'l vento ne portava le parole* (CCLXVII,14); *capei crespi* (CCLXX,57); *si sbigottisce et si sconforta* (CCLXXVII,5); *dispietata et dura* (CCC,12); *lunge da' laghi* (CCCVI,14); *cangiavano i costumi* (CCCXVI,10); *torbida tempesta* - *vertù veste* - *vivendo veniasi* (CCCXVII,2-4-9); *subito svelse* (CCCXXIII, 35); *speranze sparse* (CCCXXXI,46); *i soavi sospiri* - *desir sí dolce* (CCCXXXII,3-19); *thesoro in terra* (CCCXXXIII,2); *amor pò meritar mercede* - *vedea 'l volto* (CCXXXIV, 1-8); *in sé raccolta et sí romita* (CCCXXXVI,6); *misero et mesto* (CCCCXLI,5); *precïoso pegno* (CCCXL, 1); *spirto sciolto* (CCCXLIV,11); *cittadine del cielo* (CCCXLVI,2); *lo stile stancho* (CCCLIV,2); *nel foco affina* (CCCLX,5); *in pace et in porto* (CCCLXV,10).

Il gusto di aprire e chiudere il verso con un segnale di richiamo è caratteristico del Petrarca. Ai numerosi casi in cui il segnale è rappresentato dalla assonanza fra la prima e l'ultima parola del verso, come già abbiamo visto nella esemplificazione che ne ho data, bisogna aggiungere i casi in cui il segnale è invece affidato alla allitterazione: il verso si apre cioè e si chiude con parole allitteranti fra loro. Presento una serie di esempi:

al camin lungo et al mio viver corto (XV,6); *vidivi di pietate ornare il volto* (XI,7); *poi rimase la voce in mezzo 'l pecto* (XX,10); *ver' cui poco già mai mi valse o vale* - *il mio sperar che tropp'alto montava* (XXIII,36-53); *perdendo tanto amata cosa propia* (XXIV,11); *fine non pongo al mio obstinato affanno* - *et duolmi ch'ogni giorno arroge al danno* (L,52-53: il v. 53 oppone al segnale di apertura e chiusura sulla dentale la parte centrale allitterata sulla palatale); *vidi assai periglioso il mio vïaggio* (LIV,9); *sol rimembrando anchor l'anima spoglia* (LIX,10); *perché sparger al ciel sí spessi preghi* - *finir anzi 'l mio fine* - *Ma più, quand'io dirò senza mentire* (LXX,4-6-19); *Con queste alzato vengo a dire or cose* (LXXI,14); *rivolta d'occhi, ond'ogni mio riposo* (LXXII,35); *cose cercando, e 'l più bel fior ne colse* - *sol di lor vista al mio stato soccorro* - *sono il mio segno e'l mio conforto solo* (LXXIII,36-45-51: ai vv. 45 e 51 abbiamo e l'allitterazione e l'assonanza unite); *perdendo inutilmente tanti passi* (LXXIV, 11); *fui in lor forza; et or con gran fatica* (LXXVI,6); *Amor, con cui pensier mai non amezzo* (LXXIX,5); *su per l'onde fallaci et per gli scogli* - *però sarebbe da ritrarsi in porto* - *se non gliel tolse o tempestate o scogli* - *vid'io le'nsegne di quell'altra vita* - *S'io esca vivo de' dubbiosi scogli* (LXXX,2-5-21-23-31); *Se 'n altro modo cerca d'esser sacio* (LXXXII,12); *Sí tosto come aven che l'arco scocchi* - *Misero amante, a che vaghezza il mena?* (LXXXVII,1-10); *volgete i passi; et voi ch'Amore avampa* (LXXXVIII,10); *piangete, amanti, per ciascun paese* - *Pianga Pistoia, e i citadin perversi* (XCII,2-12); *Poi che voi et io più volte abbiam provato* (XCIX,1); *sí dolce lume uscia degli occhi suoi* (CVI,8); *venni fuggendo la tempesta e'l vento* (CXIII,3); *forse tal m'arde et fugge* - *men gli occhi ad ognor molli* (CXXV, 4-10); *sempre è presente, ond'io tutto mi struggo*

(CXXVII,95: dove le due parti logiche sono distinte per mezzo della assonanza: sempre / presente -tutto mi struggo); che se l'error durasse, altro non cheggio - loco mi trovo e'n più deserto lido (CXXIX,39-47); accende, et spegne qual trovasse accesa - simil già mai né sol vide né stella - se nol temprassen dolorosi stridi (CXXXV,64-70-83); volar negli occhi altrui per sua vaghezza (CXLI,3); Se'n breve non m'accoglie o non mi smorsa - Fuggendo spera i suoi dolor finire (CLII,5-12); del bel diamante, ond'ell'à il cor sí duro (CLXXI,10); Raro un silentio, un solitario horrore (CLXXVI,12); Cosí caddi a la rete, et qui m'àn colto (CLXXXI,12); doppia dolcezza in un volto delibo - visibilmente quanto in questa vita (CXCIII,8-13); ch'altri che morte, od ella, sani 'l colpo (CXCV,13); L'aura celeste che 'n quel verde lauro - là've il sol perde, non pur l'ombra o l'auro - ma li occhi ànno vertù di farne marmo (CXCVII,1-8-14); Basciale 'l piede, o la man bella et bianca (CCVIII,12); pianta avrebbe uopo, et sana d'ogni parte (CCXIV,27); frutto senile in sul giovenil fiore (CCXV,3); s'aver altrui più caro che se stesso - se sospirare et lagrimar maisempre (CCXXIV,9-10); ch'or me 'l par ritrovar, et or m'accorgo - ch'i' ne son lunge, or mi sollievo or caggio (CCXXVII,9-10); l'addornâr sí, ch'al ciel n'andò l'odore (CCXXVIII,7); Vincitore Alexandro l'ira vinse (CCXXXII,1); sono importuno assai più ch'i' non soglio (CCXXXV,4); non senta il suon de l'amorose note (CCXXXIX,33); Vedrà, s'arriva a tempo, ogni vertute (CCXLVIII,9); miri fiso nelli occhi a quella mia (CCLXI, 3); perch'a me troppo, et a se stessa piacque - vo ripensando ov'io lassai 'l vïaggio (CCLXIV,108-120); Di speranza m'empieste et di desire (CCLXVII,12); vedel colei ch'è or sí presso al vero (CCLXVIII,55); veggio al mio navigar turbati i venti (CCLXXII,11); veggio, et odo, et intendo ch'anchor viva (CCLXXIX,7); Sennuccio mio, benché doglioso et solo (CCLXXXVII,1); né di sé m'à lasciato altro che'l nome (CCXCI,14); Pietà s'appressa, et del tardar si pente (CCXCV,3); Ch'al suon de' detti sí pietosi et casti (CCCII,13); Ridono i prati, e'l ciel si rasserena (CCCX,5); Tempo era omai da trovar pace o triegua - Poco avev'a 'ndugiar, ché gli anni e'l pelo (CCCXVI,1-9); cangiati i volti, et l'una et l'altra coma (CCCXVII,14); contrario effetto la mia lingua al core - parte da' orecchi a queste mie parole - l'aere et la terra s'allegrava et l'acque - parea chiusa in òr fin candida perla (CCCXXV,2-60-70-80); Vinca 'l cor vostro, in sua tanta victoria (CCCXXVI,12); conven per forza rallentare il corso (CCCXXXI, 14); porto de le miserie et fin del pianto (CCCXXXII, 70); Pieno era il mondo de' suoi honor' perfecti - la si ritolse: et cosa era da lui (CCCXXXVII, 12-14); spento il primo valor, qual fia il secondo? (CCCXXXVIII,8); m'asciuga li occhi, et col suo dir m'apporta (CCCXLII,10); Poiché 'l dí chiaro par che la percota (CCCXLIII,12); la mia lingua avïata a lamentarsi (CCCXLV,2); piene di meraviglia et di pietate (CCCXLVI,4); che madonna mi mande a sé chiamando - cosí dentro et di for mi vo cangiando (CCCXLIX,2-3); Sol per piacere a le sue luci sante (CCCL,14); piene di casto amore et di pietate (CCCLI,2); Vago augelletto che cantando vai -se, come i tuoi gravosi affanni sai (CCCLIII,1-5); con quel suo dolce ragionare accorto - passano al cielo, et turban la mia pace - Ch'or fuss'io spento al latte et a la culla (CCCLIX,4-17-36); perch'à i costumi varïati, e 'l pelo

(CCCLXII,8); Vergine bella, che di sol vestita - fecero in tua verginità feconda - pon mente in che terribile procella - Da poi ch'i' nacqui in su la riva d'Arno - Mortal bellezza, atti et parole m'ànno - lagrime et pïe adempi 'l meo cor lasso - Che se poca mortal terra caduca (CCCLXVI,1-58-69-82-85-114-121).

Gli esempi di unità fonica di un verso, raggiunta tramite l'allitterazione, e al di là di ogni legamento semantico del verso dato con i precedenti o i seguenti, sono estremamente numerosi. Inoltre, rappresentando questo particolare mezzo fonico-retorico, una figura tipica, ben nota alla tradizione di studio delle *artes dictandi,* è anche l'unico che già sia stato messo in evidenza fin dai commentatori del XVI secolo, magari per stigmatizzarlo o denunziarlo come troppo scoperto. In questo caso, dunque, limiterò ancor più la mia documentazione, avendo in mente piuttosto di mostrare in pratica la figura retorica a cui alludo, che di offrire una vera e propria esemplificazione dell'uso fattone dal Petrarca. Avrò cura soltanto di prendere i miei esempi lungo tutti i *Rerum vulgarium fragmenta:*

primavera per me pur non è mai (IX,14); Ma io sarò sotterra in secca selva (XXII,37); et fal perché 'l peccar più si pavente (XXIII,129); ch'io provo per lo petto et per li fianchi (XLVI,4); Se col cieco desir che'l cor distrugge (LVI,1); Padre del ciel, dopo i perduti giorni (LXII,1); perché sparger al ciel sí spessi preghi (LXX,4); se non gliel tolse o tempestate o scogli (LXXX,21); Io son sí stanco sotto'l fascio antico (LXXXI,1); ma già ti raggiuns'io mentre fuggivi (XCIII,8); ne portan gli anni, et non ricevo inganno (CI,10); Amor armato, sí ch'anchor mi sforza (CXXVII,34); furando'l cor che fu già cosa dura (CXXXV, 25); et di far frutto, non pur fior' et frondi (CXLII, 36); facean piangendo un più dolce concento (CLVI,10); di sospir', di speranze et di desio (CLXXXIX,8); ove soavemente il cor s'invesca (CCXI,11); non senta il suon de l'amorose note (CCXXXIX,33); et veggio 'l meglio, et al peggior m'appiglio (CCLXIV, 136); di madonna et d'Amore onde mi doglia (CCLXV,8); menami a morte, ch'i' non me n'aveggio (CCLXVI,6); or se'tu disarmato; i'son securo (CCLXX,90); et per altrui sí rado si diserra (CCC,8); o vaghi habitator' de' verdi boschi (CCCIII,9); Amor vien' meco, et mostrimi ond'io vada (CCCVI,11): sí seco seppe quella seppellire (CCCXII,10); e'l vostro per farv'ira vuol che 'nvecchi (CCCXXX,14); pensando a la sua piaga aspra et profonda (CCCXLII,4); che madonna mi mande a sé chiamando (CCCXLIX,2); sovra miei spirti; et non sonò mai squilla (CCCLX,66).

Di gran lunga più interessante, ai fini della ricerca che sto svolgendo, è l'uso della allitterazione in enjambement. Cosí come abbiamo visto per l'assonanza, Petrarca usa l'allitterazione per ovviare la frattura dello enjambement: spesso, anzi, il giuoco fonico enuclea, per contrasto, le parole che, semanticamente, sono da collegare con quelle del verso successivo, in modo che la struttura logica venga pienamente sottolineata dalla struttura fonica. Se ne vedano gli esempi più significativi: *Benigne stelle che compagne fersi / al fortunato fianco* (XXIX,42-43); *et ch'avete gli schermi sempre accorti / contra l'arco d'Amor che'ndarno tira* (XLIV,10-11: dove il suono velare è cornice del v. 10 e nello stesso tempo sottolinea l'unità logica dell'enjambement; mentre la seconda parte del v. 11 è dominata dalla dentale sonora. Abbiamo cioè tre segmenti fonici con suono dominante: il suono velare per la cornice del v. 10 e l'enjambement; sibilante per la parte centrale del v. 10; dentale sonora per la seconda parte del v. 11); *Fuggendo la pregione ove Amor m'ebbe / mol-t'anni a far di me quel c'a lui parve* (LXXXIX,1-2); *Ma 'l bel viso leggiadro che depinto / porto nel petto, et veggio ove ch'io miri* (XCVI,5-6); *Però mi dice il cor ch'io in carte scriva / cosa, onde . . .* (CIV,5-6); *ch'i le mi strinsi a' piedi / per più dolcezza trar degli occhi suoi* (CXIX,32-33); *poi tornai indietro, perch'io vidi scripto / di sopra 'l limitar...* (CXX,9-10); *né in più tranquilla fossa / fuggir la carne travagliata... - Così carco d'oblio / il divin portamento...* (CXXVI,25-26; 56-57); *Se candide rose con vermiglie / in vasel d'oro vider gli occhi miei* (CXXVII, 71-72); *ne l'acqua chiara et sopra l'erba verde / veduto viva, et nel troncon d'un faggio* (CXXIX,41-42); *ch'è 'l mio sol s'allontana, et triste et sole / son le mie luci, et notte oscura è loro... - ma con più larga vena / veggiam, quando col Tauro...* (CXXXV,55-56; 87-88); *Per le camere tue fanciulle et vecchi / vanno trescando...* (CXXXVI,9-10); *Come talora al caldo tempo sole / semplicetta farfalla al lume avvezza / volar negli occhi altrui . . .* (CXLI,1-3); *. . . ove conven ch'armato viva / la vita che trapassa a sí gran salti* (CXLVIII,10-11); *Né mortal vista mai luce divina / vinse, come la mia quel raggio...* (CLI,5-6); *per quel ch'io sento al cor gir fra le vene / dolce veneno..* (CLII,7-8); *vegghio, penso, ardo, piango; et chi mi sface / sempre m'è inanzi...* (CLXIV,5-6); *e i vaghi spirti in un sospiro accoglie / co le sue mani... - Così mi vivo, et così avolge et spiega / lo stame de la vita...* (CXLVII,2-3; 12-13); *... che sí chiara tromba / trovasti...* (CLXXXVII,3-4); *... il voi veder, felice / fa in questo breve et fraile viver mio* (CXCI,3-4); *la bella bocca angelica, di perle / piena et di rose...* (CC,10-11); *Così avess'io i primi anni / preso lo stil... - ...or a l'estremo famme / et Fortuna et Amor... - ...che devea torcer li occhi / dal troppo lume . . .* (CCVII,11-12; 44-45; 81-82: in 81-82 parlerei di una specie di allitterazione composta, in quanto le due parti dello enjambement ripetono la stessa serie consonantica *d t l*); *col ferro avvelenato dentr'al fianco / fugge...* (CCIX,10-11);[29] *... che 'n un punto / pò far chiara la notte...* (CCXV,12-13); *... et son fra li animali / l'ultimo...* (CCXVI,6-7); *Laurëa mia con suoi santi atti schifi / sedersi in parte...* (CCXXV,10-11); *... col bel vivo raggio / rimanti;...* (CCXXVII, 12-13; *Amor co la man dextra il lato manco / m'aperse...* (CCXXVIII, 1-2); *. . . ond'io mai non mi pento / de le mie pene . . .* (CCXXXI,5-6);

29. Considerata la struttura fonica, tornerei alla punteggiatura proposta dal Carducci, senza la virgola, cioè, dopo *fianco*. Chiórboli prima e poi Contini hanno la virgola.

... che 'l suo possessore / spesso a vergogna... (CCXXXII,13-14); *et pur com'intellecto avesse et penne / passò, quasi una stella che 'n ciel vole;* (CCXXXIII,12-13);[30] *ché spesso nel suo volto veder parme / vera pietà con grave dolor mista* (CCL,5-6); *... che'nnanzi tempo spenta / sia l'alma luce ...*(CCLI,2-3); *de l'imagine sua quand'ella corse / al cor ...; con faticosa et dilectevol salma / sedendosi entro l'alma; e'l lume de' begli occhi che mi strugge / soavemente al suo caldo sereno* (CCLXIV,42-43; 56-57; 78-79); *... ch'ogni aspro ingegno et fero / facevi humile...* (CCLXVII,3-4); *Qual ingegno a parole / poria aguagliare il mio doglioso stato?; et di sue belle spoglie / seco sorride ...* (CCLXVIII,17-18; 71-72); *... né già mai tal peso / provai* (CCLXXI,3-4, con complicanza rimica); *cosí leve, expedita et lieta l'alma / la segua...* (CCLXXVIII,10-111); *né donna accesa al suo sposo dilecto / die'* (CCLXXXV,2-3); *... ch'avendo in mano / meo cor...* (CCLXXXVIII,3-4); *che mai rebellion l'anima santa / non sentí ...* (CCXCVII,3-4); *et ebbi ardir cantando di dolermi / d'Amor ...* (CCCIV,5-6); *... in pochi sassi / chiuse'l mio lume ...* (CCCVI,3-4); *e'n belle donne honeste atti soavi / sono un deserto...* (CCCX,13-14); *... che mia fera ventura / vuol che vivendo...* (CCCXI,13-14); *... una colonna / cristallina ...; et mia viva figura / far sentia...* (CCCXXV,27-28; 48-49); *... ver' te'l mio core in terra / tal fu...* (CCCXLVII,9-10); *... et le mie notti il sonno / sbandiro ...; et sí dolce ydioma / le diedi...* (CCCLX,62-63; 101-102); *poi che madonna e'l mio cor seco inseme / saliro al ciel...* (CCCLXIV,3-4); *Vergine, s'a mercede / miseria extrema...; ne le cui sante piaghe / prego ch'appaghe ...*(CCCLXVI,9-10; 51-52).

Già da questa parziale documentazione è ben chiaro che il Petrarca lavorava continuamente su due piani: quello puramente fonico, alla ricerca di un'armonia che potesse sostituire l'accompagnamento musicale vero e proprio; e quello fonico-semantico, per cui la musica delle parole diviene interpretativa del senso, aiutando la lettura e imponendo le pause logiche del discorso. L'allitterazione, come l'assonanza, serve bene anche a questo secondo fine non soltanto in enjambement, ma all'interno di un medesimo verso. La documentazione potrebbe essere larghissima; la limito, come di consueto, agli esempi che mi cadono sotto mano: *Era il giorno ch'al sol si scoloraro* (III,1). Il verso è fonicamente strutturato a cornice consonante (*era / aro*); ma entro questa cornice si distinguono nettamente due parti foniche corrispondenti ai due nuclei significanti: *era il giorno* (in cui la vibrante è dominante), *al sol si scoloraro* (con forte allitterazione sulla *s*). Nello stesso sonetto al v. 7 la pausa logica è nettamente segnata dal cambiamento

30. Il Carducci e il Contini mettono una virgola dopo *penne* che a me pare di troppo. Il Carducci, tuttavia, metteva una virgola anche dopo *passò,* virgola che il Contini ha sentito di troppo. Il Chiórboli aveva proposto una punteggiatura sovraccarica: "E pur com'intelletto avesse, e penne, / Passò quasi una stella". A mio avviso, considerata la struttura fonica, io metterei una sola virgola dopo *passò.*

fonico: *secur, senza sospetto; onde i miei guai* (con la prima parte tutta legata dalla allitterazione di *s*). La stessa struttura fonica è ben chiara in:

ma dentro dove già mai non s'aggiorna (IX,7); col corpo stanco ch'a gran pena porto (XV,2); che non sa ove si vada et pur si parte (XVIII,8: in cui l'insistenza fonica sulla *s*, ripetuta lungo tutto il verso, dà unità alle due parti); L'arbor gentil che forte amai molt'anni (LX,1); or quinci or quindi, come Amor m'informa (LXXIII,53); sí crescer sento 'l mio ardente desiro (LXXIX,4); ch'almen da lunge m'apparisse il porto (LXXX,18); di quei begli occhi ch'or ne son sí scarsi (XC,4); i miei pensier', come nel cor gli chiudo (XCV,2); De la tua mente Amor, che prima aprilla (CXIX, 54); vola un augel che sol senza consorte / di volontaria morte... (CXXXV,6-7); nido di tradimenti, in cui si cova (CXXXVI,5); Ché bel fin fa chi ben amando more (CXL,14); si specchia e'l sol ch'altrove par non trova (CLIV,4); che sol se stessa, et nulla altra, simiglia (CLX,4); il meglio è ch'io mi mora amando, et taccia (CLXXI,4); ch'i' mora a fatto, e 'n ciò segue suo stile (CLXXXIV,4); siede'l signore, anzi'l nimico mio (CLXXXIX,4); ... sopra l'erba / verde m'apparve, con duo corna d'oro (CXC,1-2; in cui la vibrante sorregge l'unità fonica di tutta l'immagine che si protrae per i primi tre versi del sonetto); et io, pien di paura, tremo et taccio (CCII,8); ov'Amor me, te sol Natura, mena (CCVIII,4);[31] ... sí ch'elli à già spento / col suo splendor la mia vertù visiva (CCXII,5-6); lagrime l'altra che'l dolor distilla (CCXLI,10); tu te n'andasti, e'si rimase seco (CCXLII,13); ma'l vento ne portava le parole (CCLXVII,14); Amor m'assale, ond'io mi discoloro (CCXCI,3); come nulla qua giù diletta et dura (CCCXI,14); ma lasciato m'à ben la penna e'l pianto (CCCXIII,4); perder parte, non tutto, al dipartirme (CCCXXIX,7); spira sí spesso, ch'i' prendo ardimento / di dirle il mal ch'i'ò sentito et sento (CCCLVI,2-3).

Dopo aver tentato di catalogare e caratterizzare in tipologie ricorrenti le strutture foniche del *Canzoniere* petrarchesco, vorrei adesso sintetizzare quanto son venuta dicendo, analizzando un ultimo sonetto. Scelgo il CXCVI, sia perché grosso modo rientra nel periodo cronologico in cui Petrarca più si compiaceva di tali ricerche foniche (il CXCVI è databile fra il 1342 e il 1345); sia perché ne possediamo la prima stesura autografa alla c. 2r del Vaticano Latino 3196. Le stesse varianti dunque fanno certi di una precisa volontà di ricerca.

L'aura serena che fra verdi fronde
mormorando a ferIR nel volto viemme,
fammi risovenIR quand'Amor diemme
le prime piaghe, sí dolci profonde;

31. Anche in questo caso, contro il parere concorde del Carducci, del Chiórboli e del Contini che avevano punteggiato: "ov'Amor me, te sol Natura mena", mi sembra che la punteggiatura debba rispettare la sottolineatura offerta dal giuoco fonico: "ov'Amor me, te sol Natura, mena".

e'l bel *v*iso *v*edER, ch'*a*ltri m'*a*sconde,
che sdeg*no* o ge*lo*sia ce*la*to tiemme;
et le chi*ome* or avOLTE in perl*e* e'n gemm*e*,
allora sciOLTE, et *sovra* *or* te*rso* bi*onde*:
le quali *ella* spargEA sí dolcemente,
et raccogliEA con sí leggiadri nodi,
che ripensando anchOR tre*m*a la *m*ente;
*t*orsele il *t*em*po* *po*i in *p*iú sal*di* no*di*,
et *s*trin*s*e'l cOR d'un laccio *sí* po*ss*ente,
che Morte sola fia ch'i*ndi* lo s*nodi*.

I vv. 1, 3 e 4 erano nati al Petrarca di getto e restano quasi intatti nella redazione definitiva. Soltanto due correzioni: *verdi* al posto di *verde*, al v. 1, e *dolci* al posto di d*olce*, al v. 4. In entrambi i casi credo che si tratti piuttosto di una scelta fonica che di una preferenza morfologica. Infatti il femminile plurale in *-e* per gli aggettivi derivati dalla terza declinazione latina era abbastanza frequente negli antichi testi volgari.[32] Petrarca aveva dunque una scelta fra le due forme. Il rifiuto di *verde* e *dolce* è un rifiuto di troppo fonico: infatti *verde* avrebbe ripetuto la finale di *fronde* e *dolce* era assonanzato con *profonde*; e i vv. 1 e 4 erano già legati dal giuoco allitterativo. Si trattava di trovare la giusta misura. Faticato, nella prima quartina, è il v. 2. Petrarca aveva scritto: *va mormorando e per la fronte viemme*; ma a una rilettura non ne è soddisfatto, cancella *va* e *e per la fronte* e scrive sopra il rigo *a ferir nel volto*. La prima quartina aveva raggiunto cosí la sua forma definitiva con il doppio giuoco rimico, esterno (*abba*) e interno (*-cc-*) in cesura sotto accento di sesta. Difficile era senza dubbio l'attacco della seconda quartina, volendo in qualche modo mantenere il legamento e non cadere nel ripetitivo. Infatti i vv. 5 e 6 sono lente conquiste; specie il v. 5 che presenta tutta una serie di varianti: partito da *e veggia quel che o gelosia m'asconde / o disdegno amoroso chiuso tiemme,* in margine Petrarca tenta differenti soluzioni: *a veder quel che talor mi s'asconde,* poi cancella *talor* e lo cambia con *spesso,* e quindi, sopra *spesso,* scrive *altri m'asconde*. Infine cancella tutto e giunge al *el bel viso veder ch'altri m'asconde*. La soluzione è trovata: la consonanza della cesura, sempre sotto accento di sesta, con le rime interne della prima quartina era il legamento fonico cercato, e il verso con le due allitterazioni (sul *v* nella prima parte, sulla *a* nella seconda) aveva la sua dignità armonica. La correzione del v. 6 pare avvenuta di getto dopo aver trovato la soluzione

32. Cf. G. Rohlfs, *Grammatica storica della lingua italiana e dei suoi dialetti. Morfologia,* Traduzione di T. Franceschi (Torino, 1967), p. 77.

per il 5. Infatti nel margine estremo dopo tutte le cancellature e le correzioni per il v. 5, leggiamo: *che sdegno o gelosia celato tiemme.* Un verso cioè ancora basato sulla allitterazione: palatale dominante (*gn ge ce*), ripetizione a eco della liquida dopo la palatale (ge*l*osia / ce*l*ato), e il suono insistito della dentale in fine di verso (cela*to ti*emme). I vv. 7 e 8 erano stati concepiti ab initio con la rima interna in cesura sotto accento di sesta per il v. 7 e di quarta per il v. 8: *e le chiome oggi accolte*[33] *in perle e in gemme / allor disciolte, e sovra or terso bionde.* Nel 3196 vediamo la correzione di *accolte* in *avolte* e di *allor disciolte* in *allora sciolte.* La correzione di *oggi* in *or* come appare nel Vat. 3195 appartiene, evidentemente, a uno stadio successivo. Ma la struttura fonica, basata questa volta sulle assonanze (*chiome avolte sciolte bionde:* che sottolineano e nel contempo attenuano la rima interna, e *perle gemme*) era già quella definitiva. In questi due versi l'allitterazione viene usata soltanto nelle parole libere dalla assonanza: *et sovra or terso.* Il Vat. 3196 ci è di ben poco aiuto per le due terzine, come appaiono nella redazione definitiva. Soltanto l'inizio del v. 9 *le quali ella spargeva* (corretto in: *quando ella le spargea*) viene ripreso nella stesura definitiva. Il resto è completamente cambiato e nel contenuto e nella struttura fonica: neppure le rime o l'ordine rimico viene ripreso. Infatti alle *-ali, -esca, -ardo,* ordinate secondo l'ordine *cdeced,* Petrarca sostituì le rime *-ente* e *-odi* nell'ordine *cdcdcd.* Già il cambiamento delle rime suggerisce l'idea di una maggiore ricerca fonica: la rima in *-ente* è infatti assonanzata con la rima *b* delle quartine (*abba*) in *-emme* e quasi in consonanza con la rima *a* in *-onde;* mentre le rime primamente scelte non avevano nessun legamento fonico con le rime delle quartine. Nella redazione finale abbiamo ancora nelle terzine la rima interna: alle cesure dei vv. 9 e 10 (ancora con accento spostato come nei vv. 7-8) e alle cesure (ancora di sesta e poi di quarta) ai vv. 11 e 13. I versi liberi dalla rima interna sono legati in vari modi dalla allitterazione. Il valore semantico delle coppie di rime all'interno del verso risiede nell'accentuare il valore del giuoco della memoria: il *ferir* dell'aura serena conduce al *risovenir* dell'immagine di Laura: a il bel viso *veder*, a ricordare le *chiome avolte* o *sciolte* che ella *spargea et raccogliea.* A questo punto il tono cambia, cosí come cambia il ritmo della rima interna: è il tremore, la paura, il presentimento di una prigionia d'amore da cui solo la morte può liberare. La tranquilla serenità primaverile, apportatrice di im-

33. La parola non è chiaramente leggibile, dato che Petrarca l'ha pesantemente cancellata con un tratto di penna. Credo tuttavia che si debba leggere *accolte* piuttosto che *raccolte,* come dice il Chiórboli, *o.c.,* p. 466, dato che la *e* prima di *chiome* è chiarissima. Il Chiórboli per leggere *raccolte* e non far scrivere al Petrarca un verso ipermetro ha dovuto tralasciare la *e* iniziale.

magini dilette, si è perduta per il tormento interno che le stesse immagini avevano risvegliato. La struttura fonica aiuta e impone l'interpretazione.

"C'est en particulier quand on compare les variantes existantes d'un poème que l'on peut se rendre compte de la pertinence pour l'auteur du cadre phonématique, morphologique et syntaxique" ha scritto R. Jakobson[34] quasi in risposta a chi si domandi se "les mécanismes dégagés par l'analyse linguistique ont été visés délibérément et rationellement dans le travail créateur du poète".[35] Ancora con Jakobson vorrei affermare che "toute composition poétique significative . . . implique un choix orienté du matériel verbal". L'analisi delle varianti è dunque una riprova e una conferma.

Concludendo: la ricerca mi ha condotto a riconoscere nel Petrarca alcune ricorrenti tipologie di strutture foniche basate sull'assonanza e sull'allitterazione. Tali mezzi fonico-espressivi vennero usati a fini specifici, talora in comune alle due tecniche.

Possiamo riscontrare l'uso sia dell'assonanza che dell'allitterazione:

1) nelle coppie nominali,
2) come segnale di apertura e chiusura di verso,
3) per ovviare la frattura provocata dall'enjambement.

L'assonanza è usata per arricchire la musicalità rimica sia:

1) in cesura

sia:

2) al mezzo.

L'allitterazione è usata specificamente:

1) per dare unità sonora al verso, senza considerazione del valore semantico diretto;
2) per accentuare il semantismo diretto con il richiamo fonico.

34. R. Jakobson, *Questions de poétique* (Paris, 1973), p. 280. Lo studio era apparso precedentemente sotto il titolo "Subliminal verbal patterning in poetry" in *Studies in General and Oriental Linguistics Presented to Shirô Hattori* (Tokyo, 1970), pp. 302-308.

35. R. Jakobson, *o.c., ibid.*

V

AN ANALYSIS OF STRUCTURATION IN PETRARCH'S POETRY

by Fredi Chiappelli
University of California at Los Angeles

"e le cose presenti e le passate mi danno guerra" (272, 3-4)

per Gianfranco Contini

"We have to fight against Fortune in two ways, somehow, and both carry equal danger. But usually men recognize only one side of them, the one which is called adversity."[1] This passage belongs to the Prologue of the interesting, although indeed rather protracted, treatise that Petrarch wrote between around 1356 and October 1366 about the *Remedies against both Fortunes*.[2] Luck and unluck are equally abounding in human events and each is equally suspect to the moralist who blends stoical, neoplatonic, and Christian traditions of thinking.[3] To the poet, the two polarized worlds of happiness in luck and unhappiness in unluck are a matter of engrossing concern inasmuch as they converge on a sensitive subject, whose crisis from rapture to despair opens a deep field of inspiration.

A beautiful example of a poetic unfolding of variations on this theme can be verified in the composition of canzone 323, the six stanzas of which revolve on one identical basic motif, the disappearance of Laura.[4]

This common axis invariably includes a description of the wonderful appearance of the beloved, the intervention of a destructive force which suppresses the marvelous being, and the lament expressing the terror and

1. "Duplex enim est nobis duellum cum Fortuna, et utrobique quodam modo par discrimen. Cuius nisi partem unicam vulgus novit, eam scilicet, quae vocatur adversitas." In the elegant translation by Giovanni da San Miniato, "Noi abbiamo colla fortuna due battaglie, e nell'una e nell'altra, per certo modo, è uguale pericolo; ma gli omini volgari non conoscono se non l'una, cioè quella che si chiama adversitade" (a cura di Don Casimiro Stolfi, Bologna, Romagnoli, Collez. di Op. ined. o rare etc., 1867, p. 49).

2. Agostino Pertusi, *Leonzio Pilato* etc. (Venice-Rome, 1964), p. 385.

3. Charles Trinkhaus, *"In our Image and Likeness": Humanity and Divinity in Italian Humanist Thought* (London and Chicago, 1970).

4. For the text, and the analysis of the inner growth of the canzone in its variants, see *Studi sul linguaggio del Petrarca* (Florence: Olschki, 1972), quoted here as *SLP*.

the pain of the witness. The two narrative nuclei presenting the miracle of the earthly existence of Laura and the disaster of her premature death are varied on the figurative surface by a successive change of symbols: Laura is first represented as a "fera" with a human face, then as an ivory and ebony ship, as a young laurel, as a clear fountain, as a phoenix, as a white-clad feminine apparition. In coordinated metaphors, the destructive force is represented as the chasing hounds which kill the *fera,* the storm which sinks the ship, the lightning which strikes the laurel, the earthquake which engulfs the fountain, the snake which stings the woman; in the case of the phoenix, the suicidal despair as a synthesis of the previous material disasters.

This last chain of symbols corresponds in substance, if not in order of succession, to the cluster of conditions threatening human fragility as it appears not only in the *Remedies,* but e.g. in the *Secretum.* In whatever order, the *belluarum furor* (fury of the beasts), the *magnarum edium ruine* (ruins of the great buildings), the *sinistro sidere motus aerei* (the stormy jolts of lightning), the *tot terre marisque discrimina* (all the dangers of earth and sea) lead to a common mood, a fundamental meditation on death. The irreducible concept sets a line of unisonant responses in each strophe.

The order of succession is important in the series of the six opening symbols, where the wonder of Laura's worldly existence is depicted. These are prominent components of the *Canzoniere,* gathered from different epochs and ordered in a long belaboured retrospective poem. The reader can measure a first degree of depth in the properly figurative layer by recognizing in the canzone an aggregate of distinct, successive moments of Laura's determinant impact; each of them revived in its splendour, and in turn submerged in the awareness of its perishing.

The emblems of the *fera* and of the ship seem introductory as they compound initial impressions of the physical reality and inner wealth of the creature. They are both synthetic and synoptic, involving a fabulous feeling of exceptional intensity of nature (*fera*), of mythologically transcended humanity (*con fronte umana da far arder Giove*), of extraordinary build (the elaborate ship), of admirable outward features (the silken mast-stays, the sails of gold, the ivory, the ebony). In addition, they express an atmosphere of marvel (vv. 2-3) and a delusion of perfect immunity: the sea is quiet, the breeze is sweet, the sky as it is when no clouds veil it off.

Both the images of *fera* and of *nave* are known material over the whole cycle of the *Canzoniere,* and deserve closer scrutiny. *Fera* as a noun in the *Canzoniere* appears 13 times in this form, 5 times in the plural *fere,* 4 times in the plural *fiere.*[5] In the plural the word is always used in the proper sense, and never related to Laura. In the singular, it is constantly used in the ornate non-diphthongized form; 3 cases only do not relate metaphorically to Laura, otherwise the emblem is directly applied to her. It carries evolving qualifications: in early poems, the ideas of beauty and cruelty are dominant (*quella fera bella e cruda,* 23,149) with development of the cruelty connotation (the simile *sì aspra fera,* 22,20; *una fera che mi strugge,* 50,40; *dentro dal mio ovil qual fera rugge?,* 56,7). This first group belongs to the years 1326-1335 of the book,[6] and thereafter, for some years the image ceases to occur. It appears again around 1337-1341,[7] in the canzone *Chiare fresche e dolci acque;* tracing a dreamy projection of the future the poet imagines that the cruelty has been blended with tameness: "Tempo verrà anchor forse / ch'a l'usato soggiorno / torni la fera bella e mansueta" (126, 29). A second group of instances opens here suggesting a new image of the woman. The poet further complicates the contrast beauty / cruelty by endowing the quality of tameness against the indelible wild connotation of *fera.* In examples like: " 'l bel viso santo / et gli occhi vaghi fien cagion ch'io pèra / *di questa fera angelica innocente*" (135, 45) or "Questa *humil* fera, un cor di tigre o d'orsa, / che *'n vista humana e 'n forma d'angel vène*" (152,1), the position of the attributes shows that the perception of the beloved woman has shifted to a deeper antithetic nucleus, with the notion of beauty as a whole. The allusion to Giove seems to provide a proof of the link between our strophe and that particular epoch of the *Canzoniere*; in 111,6-8, Laura's new attitude is expressed as follows: "A me si volse in sì novo colore / ch' avrebbe *a Giove* nel maggior furore / tolto l'arme di mano. . . ." The *novo colore* and the mythological hyperboles stress the physiognomical evidence of the change, precisely as in our passage of the *"fronte humana* da far arder Giove." The first group corresponds approximately to the years 1326-1336,[8] the second approximately to 1337-1347.[9] It introduces the third

5. As an adjective, 12 occurrences of *fera,* 2 of *fere,* 2 of *feri,* 8 of *fero,* 1 of *fier,* 2 of *fieri,* 6 of *fiero.* Frequence materials are from the *Concordanze del Canzoniere di Francesco Petrarca* (Florence: Accademia della Crusca, 1971).

6. E. H. Wilkins, *The making of the Canzoniere* (Rome: Ed. di Storia e Letteratura, 1951), p. 350.

7. Wilkins, "first residence at Vaucluse, June-July 1337-Feb. 16, 1341" (p. 350).

8. Wilkins, p. 350.

9. For 135, Wilkins, p. 352, "late 1345—20 nov. 1347"; for 152, Ruth S. Phelps, *The earlier and later forms of Petrarch's Canzoniere* (Chicago: Univ. of Chicago Press, 1925), p. 182, "1342-47." Closer connections of the *fronte humana* image to 1341-1343 in *SLP,* 47 and 213.

and last, composed by the *vaga fera* of 304,3, and the strophe that we are studying, both belonging to the period *in morte*. As for *nave, navicella, navigare,* most of the occurrences relate the metaphor to the person of the poet himself, and specifically to his faring in the difficult "waters" of his spiritual adventure.[10] The dantesque parallel of the image, probably not casual, stresses the overall meaningfulness of the narration.[11] The linking to Laura is therefore implicit, by general identification, as in "Ditele ch'i' son già di viver lasso, / del navigar per queste horribili onde" (333,6), and even by integrating the metaphor with a concealed allusion to the inner riches of the beloved: "Né mai saggio nocchier guardò da scoglio / *nave* di merci prezïose carcha, / quant'io sempre la debile mia *barcha* / da le percosse del suo duro orgoglio" (235,6).

In both cases of *fera* and *nave,* the writer aims at stressing the compendious value of the images, in which he sums up the epitome of his story. The dyptich involving *fera* and *nave* affords an integrated view of the whole, and indications of its essential features: the nature of the woman, the duration of the poet's spiritual course, its central significance. It is probably accurate, therefore, to consider the two first emblems as prefatory: hinged together, they introduce, summarizing the main motifs, the iconography displayed in the following parts of the poem.[12]

Quite differently, the other four strophes seem to identify distinct laurean epochs and traits. The laurel elicits the recollection of young Laura's appearance; the fountain evokes the speaking Laura, whose voice is one of the rare physical impacts registered from her throughout the *Canzoniere*; the phoenix, her prodigious capacity of renewing herself as source of inspiration; the Euridice-like myth calls forth the compelling impression of the real reclaim from extinction operated by the poet after Laura's death in the plague of 1348.[13] The "youth" motif is much more clearly defined and articulated than it has been usually observed: when Petrarch states "parmi vedere in quella etate

10. Occurrences: *nave* 8; *navi* 1; *navicella* 1; *naviganti* 1; *navigar* 3; *barca* 2; *barcha* 1; *barchette* 2.

11. Dante, *Comedia, Par.*, II, 1-15; cf. particularly the early Petrarchan instances, as "et non s'aspira al glorïoso regno certo in più salva nave" (29,42). The metaphor occurs at the very beginning of the treatise of the *Remedies,* where the noble philosophers appear as "industrious and expert sailors, and stars shining and fixed in the sky of truth, and sweet prosperous winds showing the harbour of peace in the storm of our soul etc."

12. Other arguments leading to this conclusion can be found in *SLP*. The hinge connecting the two opening figurations can be stylistically indicated in the modal-temporal junction *Indi*; a type of interstrophal junction which will no longer be allowed in the poem.

13. Exactly twenty years before the canzone was completed and transcribed: *SLP,* 15-17.

acerba / la bella giovenetta, ch' ora è donna" (127,21-22), he views through the present image of the woman a preserved state, the *giovinetta.* The self-contained period of the *etate acerba,* a consistent unit as the season of spring, lies entirely visible beyond the inevitable outward changes of an aging body. But the *fiore* does not dissolve in the *frutto* in the exceptional life cycle of the *Canzoniere:* in its world the destiny of deterioration is overcome and the poet will be able to discern the "*frutto* senile in sul giovenil *fiore*" (215,3). This fundamental character is naturally reserved to the motif of Laura: the *età,* when referred to the poet or other beings, constantly implies its normal physical impermanence:[14] only Laura's *etate acerba* lasts as a vivid acquisition in the lapsing of ephemeral phenomena. Towards the end of the *Canzoniere* it is still an intact entity: "Qual io la vidi in su *l'età fiorita,* / tutta accesa de' raggi di sua stella" (336,3-4).[15]

The "voice" motif preserves one of the few bodily traits of Laura which have been admitted in Petrarch's lyrical world. It appears in striking connection with *fera:* "Ahi crudo Amor, ma tu allor più mi 'informe / a seguir d'una fera che mi strugge, / *la voce* e i passi e l'orme" (50,39-41). It becomes progressively defined in its attributes: "La fraile vita ch'ancor meco alberga / fu de' begli occhi vostri aperto dono; et de *la voce angelica soave*" (63,5-7); "le parole / sonavan *altro, che pur voce humana*" (90,10-11); "Con voce allor *di sì mirabil tempre*" (119,43); "oltra la vista agli orecchi orna e 'nfinge / sue *voci vive* et suoi sancti sospiri" (158,7-8); "sì dolce in vista et *sì soave in voce*" (284,8); towards the end of the *Canzoniere* it is brought back in all its qualities and its effects: "Quella *angelica modesta / voce* che *m' adolciva, et* or *m'accora*" (343,3-4).

The "renewal" motif, as the "Euridice" one, are major, all-pervading themes of the book. Let it suffice here to indicate the radiating energy of the idea of renewal. It propagates towards the conception of time, as if the renewal of Spring itself would proceed from Laura's impulse: "Come 'l candido piè per l'erba fresca / i dolci passi honestamente muove, / vertù che 'ntorno i fiori apra et *rinove,* / de le tenere piante sue par ch'esca" (165, 1-4);[16] and towards the metaphorical paradox of love: "et s'io l'occido più forte *rinasce*" (264, 62).

14. 16,2; 23,1; 55,2; 53,58; 119,23; 145,8; 206,38; 304,8; 313,3; 360,80.

15. The link with the Spring is provided by the attribute *acerba:* "Qual dolcezza è ne la stagione acerba / vederla ir sola coi pensier' suoi inseme!" (160,12-13); "Una candida cerva sopra l'erba / verde m'apparve, . . . / levando 'l sole a la stagione acerba" (190,1-4).

16. Cf. "L'aura amorosa che *rinova* il tempo" (142,5); "L'aura gentil, che *rasserena* i poggi" (194,1).

All these emblems carry the same note of illusory immunity; the visions of the laurel, the fountain, etc. are so wonderful that any premonition of their mortal fate seems excluded. The sequence of ecstatic illuminations glowing at the beginning of each strophe charts a graph of high tones, in polarized correspondence with the funeral unisonant tone established by the series of the destruction symbols. The polarization identifies the inner structure of each strophe; by examining this level, a further degree of depth can be measured. It is possible to discern in this canzone how the poet differs in elaborating an occurrence from the philosopher and the moralist. A banal case of contagion destroys the miraculous being: the reality and the continuance of the whole metaphysical world built on Laura is in question. The philosopher dwells on the recognition of earthly frailty, and deduces a wisdom which is applicable to future experience; the moralist enters the orbit of contemplation, contrasts the myth of mortal delusions with the unfailing religious values and seeks spiritual determination and even consolation. The poet's pursuit expands in different areas. To him the moments formed by the past in self-contained entities are not eliminated by the occurrence of death; on the contrary they acquire a new element of importance. The plague has killed the single complete whole of Laura *giovinetta,* has killed the whole complex centered around the voice, has killed each of these figurative units selected for the composition of the canzone. But the turning back to each of them in succession does not aim at repeating a philosophical and moralistic act of recognition. The strophes cannot be compared to a string of altars in front of which the same meditative ceremony is reiterated. The poet is moved to revive his inner crisis, and express its modes; the more he had enjoyed the marvelous feeling of invulnerability in the images of the laurel, the voice, the phoenix, the more tragical is the sudden revelation of their inherent finiteness. His "error," the failure in perceiving the fatal break that each of those ecstatic states was carrying in itself, was total in each case; however, the crisis appeared to become greater in intensity and extent according to the progressive degree of his engagement, apprehension and understanding. The variable is thus to be sought not in the illustrative component of the six isomorphic stanzas, but in the intrinsic increase of the spiritual crisis.

It is our contention that the six figurations of the canzone are graduated to constitute a structure of progression.

In the first strophe the descriptive moment is extremely reduced: the beauty of the *fera* finds expression only in a learned allusion, the atmosphere of mystery and supernatural enrapture is established by factors external to the witness, such as mythological elements and the allegory of the hounds. The idea of the danger incumbent on the woman is not obliterated by the enchantment emanating from her, since the hunt was in progress prior to the vision: and if its predictable effect produces pain, it does not yet convey the utter despair of the ecstasy broken by the unexpected. The first stanza seems to encompass in a sweeping prelude the material data which are going to be developed singularly and in progressive complication. The symbol is here both inhuman and human: the "fera" has a beautiful woman's face. Such syncretism has appeared "unnatural" to the critics;[17] but it must be observed that the strophe deposits the embryo of Laura's identification in all aspects of nature; it even includes the idea of the actual grave of Laura (*sasso,* line 10 of the first stanza) which, out of an introductory structure, would be just as incongruous with the idea of the hunted animal as its human face.

In the second strophe the description of the beauty is more detailed. It is still treated allegorically, but against a natural background, where early, indirect tokens of the witness's participation begin to appear: "l'aura era *soave*" implies a subjective individual perception. The unreal riggings of the ship (silk, gold, ivory, ebony) are depicted with concrete delight; the notion of danger regresses as if blunted by the glamour of the ship, and the storm sternly dispels the serenity of the initial image. In the "contrast" diagram, at this point, the catastrophe moment follows historically the epiphany moment: the transition is not effected through the witness, whose participation will increase in the following stanzas until it reaches its full rational and sentimental level in the last one.

In the "lauro" strophe the witness is identified as a sensitive center. Visual and auditive signals are sent forth by the laurel which is brought (after painstaking elaboration) to be the subject of the scene:[18] its independent vitality appears in the blooming of its branches and in singing of birds issuing from its denseness. The text stresses that the *lauro* is not the object of the seeing and hearing of the witness, that both effects would take place even if the witness were absent. The involvement of the witness consists in being totally transported by his reception of sensorial releases from the *lauro.* He finds himself "dal mondo . . . *tutto* diviso": the ecstatic transport is no longer compared with other pleasures, as it was in early variants,[19] it reaches the planes

17. Cf. Francesco Maggini, "La canzone delle visioni," *Studi Petrarcheschi,* I (1948), 37-50.
18. *SLP,* 53 ff.
19. *SLP,* 62.

of the absolute with the idea of total detachment from the world. The moment of the crisis is centered on him: "Et mirandol io fiso." The catastrophe occurs as the witness is swept in a state of profound absorption. The historical junction occurs in the time and mode of *his* experience.

The figuration of the catastrophe invites a short digression. The manuscript which preserves the elaboration of this strophe shows that Petrarch contemplated two possible figurative solutions. One was allegorical: an old woman of fearful appearance, *con ardente compagna,* who arrives on the scene and uproots the happy bush. The other was naturalistic: a dark cloud covers the sky and a lightning destroys the laurel. It's a dramatic moment of choice between a medieval and a modern solution; while it is noteworthy that he contemplated the first, medieval one, it is clear that a page of literary style was turned when Petrarch chose the second. The *lauro* is destroyed and the sweet singing of the birds is extinguished. In the uncanny silence filling the forest, the vision of the mysterious fountain and its murmur express, by multiple means, a further increase of the witness's engagement. Visual and acoustic data, enumerated as adjacent values in the *lauro* stanza, are represented as intrinsically combined and strongly permeated by the consciousness of a supernatural atmosphere;[20] the state of ecstasy is brought to a higher degree of

20. *SLP,* 95-99 and 203-204 argues that the eerie stillness which envelops the scene and expresses the transcending nature of the experience is established by means of a negative image: the shepherds forbear from approaching the fountain. This image goes back to Ovid, *Met.* III, 407, as Chiorboli pointed out in his commentary: but it does not go back to the classical precedent without implying refusal of more recent examples. The fountain which comes into focus towards the end of the *Roman de la Rose* is allegorized without any discernment for the uncanny awe inherent in the wonder: ". . . tous biens puisent/ A meïsmes une fontaine,/ Qui tant est precieuse e saine/ E bele e clere e nete e pure,/ Qui toute arouse la closture,/ *De cui ruissel les bestes beivent/* Qui la veulent entrer e deivent,/ Quant des neires sont dessevrees,/ Que, puis qu'eus en sont abevrees,/ Jamais seif aveir ne pourront,/ E vivront tant come eus vourront/ Senz estre malades ne mortes" (20386-20397, ed. Langlois, Paris, Champion, 1924). Much closer in time to *Standomi un giorno* is the description of the *Fonteinne amoureuse* by Guillaume de Machaut, even if we take with due caution Hoepffner's dating ("1360-1361": in *Oeuvres de Guillaume de Machaut,* Paris, Champion, 1921, III, xxviii-xxix). Here the poet does resume the Ovidian "forbear" theme, but he needs to justify it with material factors: "Si me mena par la main nue/ Parmi l'erbe pognant et drue/ Sus une trop bele fonteinne/ Qui chëoit, douce, clere et seinne,/ En un vaissel de marbre bis./ *Mais il n'est moutons ne brebis,/ Bische ne serf ne beste bise/ Qui y beüst en nulle guise,/* Car sus un grant pilier d'ivoire/ Estoit assisë, ou l'istoire/ De Narcissus fu entaillie/ Et si soutieument esmaillie/ Que par ma foy! y m'estoit vis,/ Quant je la vi, qu'il estoit vis" (1229-1312). Such materialization of the scene (animals, not men;

intimacy;[21] the disaster scene is extended in duration (first the chasm opens, and then, after a frightful instant of suspension, the engulfing befalls), it implies the perception of total disappearance, not only of the symbol, but of its whole setting, and therefore construes a greater flaring of distress;[22] the final lament moves toward the expression of a detachment from the material circumstance, of a pain of absolute nature, unchangeable because it operates in the memory, and therefore cannot be soothed by time.[23]

The phoenix appears on the scene of the two previous disasters, and it is because of them that the bird commits suicide. The legendary symbol is here largely evocative because of its wide medieval literary tradition[24] which connected it with love[25] and stressed uniqueness, beauty, rebirth of passion, self-purification. In this stanza the consciousness of the enchantment and the sensorial ecstasy reach the area of rational participation. The intellect intervenes from the first line, by appraising the vision in the attribute *strania,* charged with the allusion to the amorous cycle of self-destruction and rebirth.[26] It is reason that calculates its immortality: in lines 3-5 of the stanza, the poet employs *vedere* for the vision itself, and then again for its projection in the thought (*pensai*). It is reason that introduces an explanation for the suicide: *quasi sdegnando*; and the sacrifice is introduced by a sad philosophical proposition: *Ogni cosa al fin vola.*[27]

Finally, the Euridice stanza attains the degree of the highest episodic intensity and of the deepest testimonial participation. The symbol is now human, the engagement of the witness is concomitantly sensorial, intellectual, and sentimental. Note that the initial colors of ivory and gold, allegorized in the ship image, take there the reflected form of the simile: "sì *candida* gonna / sì texta ch' *oro* e *neve parea* inseme." The

causality expressed) is avoided in the Canzone 323: as does the "lauro" strophe, the "fountain" strophe contains evidence, in subtler and deeper manner, of Petrarch's attitude (1368) towards "medieval" solutions.

21. *SLP,* 100.

22. *SLP,* 103-104.

23. *SLP,* 104-105.

24. There are innumerable allusions, but no systematic and comprehensive study of the phoenix motif for the middle ages. Some bibliographical references in the chapter "Le phénix" in Marc-René Jung, *Etudes sur le poème allégorique en France au moyen âge,* "Romanica Elvetica, 82" (Bern: Francke, 1971), pp. 220-226.

25. J. Hubaux and M. Leroy, *Le mythe du phénix dans les littératures grècque et latine,* Bibl. Fac. Phil. et Lettres Univ. Liège, 82 (Liège and Paris, 1939), p. 115, n. 1.

26. *SLP,* 126-129.

27. *SLP,* 135 and 205.

subjective element of anxiety is diffused throughout the ecstatic moment of the vision: the *bella donna* appears *pensosa,* the *trembling* of the observer is mixed with his *ardere*; in an even subtler way, the idea of the dangerous snake is present among the flowers and grass of the scene, just as the idea of non-durability is inherent in the nature of the snow. In the catastrophe, the detail of the *snake in the flowers* underlines the sense of absurdity, which is cruel for the feelings, while reason measures the contrast between the magnitude of the loss and the smallness of its cause. The ultimate pain of the poet combines the individual, instinctive outcry (*Ahi!*) and the universal aphorism which is really conclusive: "Ahi, nulla altro che pianto al mondo dura."[28] The death of the woman is expressed by *si dipartìo,* which, in the language of the *Canzoniere,* is associated with the ascension to Heaven.[29]

Each of the metaphoric variations of the symbol is characterized by a multiplied participation of the poet, increasingly present in the scene: from the periphery and limited to sensorial perceptions in the *lauro* scene, until the central rapport of interaction established in the last episode where both actors are human figures. The dynamics of the symbol are equally evolutive. The *lauro,* motionless, bound to the slow rising of the vegetable growth is struck on the surface of the earth. The fountain, made vivid in its pouring and flowing, is swallowed in a downward abysmal course. The phoenix evokes the image of flight and prepares the culminating phase of the supernatural ascension to Heaven.[30]

The evolutional structure of the canzone, which discredits the usual juxtapositive interpretation, shows that the death of Laura is only part of its thematics; the part which, as the treatise would say, men recognize in Fortune and call adversity. The miracle of Laura's existence, the happy side of Fortune, is equally only part of its thematic. The structural core should be identified in the experience of precipitating from happiness to unhappiness, measured in different views of Laura. It can be one aspect of her sweetness that at a given point appears particularly pungent in the pattern of her disappearance, or an aspect of her youthfulness, or of her inner wealth. The distant images are gradually propagated one into another, so that as the young woman expires when Laura dies, the older woman also expires in her, and the experience is investigated in each phase and in their progressive coalescence.

If now we focus on the conclusive line (*Ahi, nulla altro che pianto al mondo dura*) a yet further dimension can be postulated. We are

28. Detailed analysis of all these and other related points in *SLP,* chapter VI.

29. *SLP,* 178-181.

30. *SLP,* 208.

brought back from the depths of inspiration to a paramount vision of life, and to the conception of a ladderlike sequence of values which the poet develops didactically in his *Trionfi*. Word connections confirm the relationship between this late canzone and the *Trionfi:* we leave to historians of literary chronology to grapple with the question. Here the impetuous maxim culminates in the notion of continuance beyond despair, with the final word *dura*. It is necessary therefore to interpret *pianto:* the meaning of this term might reveal a kind of dark enthusiasm which ranges swiftly across the majestic course of the maxim, neutralizing and ultimately abolishing the utter desolation of its statement. A suggestion by Daniel Sellstrom[31] tentatively identifies *pianto* with the actual practice of writing poetry. A nomenclatory checking of the *Canzoniere* confirms such an equivalence and allows an interesting distinction. "Laughing" and "crying" are the modes which are selected to represent the two sides of Fortune in relation to Love: *"Amore, per cui si ride et piagne"* (28,114); "Amor mi strugge 'l cor, Fortuna il priva / d' ogni conforto, onde la mente stolta / s' adira *et piange*" (124,5-7); "Et come Amor l'envita / or ride, *or piange,* or teme, or s' assecura" (129,8). The mixture of the two states expresses the poet's secret conflict: "Pascomi di dolor, *piangendo rido*" (134,12); "De' passati miei danni *piango et rido*" (105,76); " 'l caro nodo . . . che l'amor mi fe' dolce, e 'l *pianger gioco*" (175,2-4).

The identification of the poetic endeavour with the notion of *pianto* occurs in the very introduction of the *Canzoniere*. The fifth line of *Voi ch' ascoltate* carries the plain endyade "del vario stile in ch'io *piango et ragiono* / spero trovar pietà, nonché perdono" (I,5-6). It is confirmed throughout the book, in a variety of modulations which would deserve an apposite monograph; at the very end of the *Canzoniere* it seems to stress the connection with the first sonnet, by forming the opening of a fully retrospective composition: "I' vo *piangendo* i miei passati tempi / i quai posi in amar cosa mortale" (365,1-2).

The main modulations of the key metaphor include a descriptive bias. The poet is represented as a man who thinks and cries and writes: "lì medesmo assido / me freddo, pietra morta in pietra viva, / in guisa d'uom che pensi et *pianga* et scriva" (122,50-52), where *pianga* identifies the creative moment.

In another view, the sequence of the states enumerates the wake, the thinking, the burning in passion, and finally the present moment where crying and writing coincide: "vegghio, penso, ardo, *piango*; et

31. Presented in the discussion of this paper at the University of Texas at Austin, on March 22, 1974.

chi mi sface / sempre m'è inanzi per mia dolce pena" (164, 5-6). The moment is frequently associated with the night, again as a subsequent to a thinking phase: "Consumando mi vo di piaggia in piaggia / el dì pensoso, poi *piango* la notte" (237,19-20); in concurrence with the information of the Latin marginalia, which refer to poetical work accomplished in the night.

In the last third of the *Canzoniere piangere* is coupled with *cantare*. The first instance of the combination seems to establish a distinction in chronology: "*Cantai,* or *piango,* et non men di dolcezza / del pianger prendo che del canto presi" (229,1-2). The following sonnet, however, stresses that the distinction is rather a disposition of style: "I' *piansi,* or *canto,* ché 'l celeste lume / quel vivo sole alli occhi miei non cela" (230, 1-2). When the poet looks back at the whole of his production, he sees it distributed between the two epochs or styles of the *cantare* and of the *piangere:* he wishes to be taken by Death, to join "colei ch'i' *canto et piango* in rime" (332,60). The equivalence of the two terms appears also in the figures of chiasmas occurring in 252,1ff., where two opposite but coordinated actions, cry and sing, followed by a similar combination, fear and hope, intersect connecting to sighing and rhyming: "In dubbio di mio stato, or piango or canto, / et temo et spero; et in sospiri e 'n rime/ sfogo il mio incarco" (252,1-3); here the binomium *et temo et spero* leads to *sospiri,* the binomium *or piango or canto* to *rime*. Towards the end of the book the two actions are circumscribed as the only ones which can express the lyrical production: "Piansi et cantai: non so più mutar verso" (344,12).

If *pianto* is poetry, lyrical endeavour, the line *Ahi nulla altro che pianto al mondo dura* acquires a totally new meaning. The negation is negated, and the stress on the final word, *dura,* 'lasts,' is accounted for. A fear-reaching vision of the lasting nature of art replaces the commonplace of a protracted moaning over a dead woman, and prefigures the theme that Foscolo's *Sepolcri* or the *Ode on a Grecian Urn* would bring to central focus in Romantic times.

In the poem as a whole, the sub-structures of its various motifs corroborate this vision, dominating over the individual "visions."

The canzone thus offers an opportunity of sharply focussing the different ways followed by the moralist, the philosopher, and the poet on a given major theme: and by analyzing it, the reader acquires an awareness of the connections between the late *Canzoniere* and the *Trionfi,* of the complex interrelations binding all of Petrarch's Italian compositions, as well as an insight into the depth of his poetry.

VI

PETRARCH AS VISIONARY: THE IMPORT OF CANZONE 323

by Julia Conaway Bondanella
Indiana University, Bloomington

Many of the studies written on the influence of Petrarch's lyrics in Europe are historical or primarily concerned with the more introspective and psychologically profound poems.[1] A few have concentrated upon the stylistic aspects of Petrarchism or upon families of sonnets derived from particular poems.[2] The *canzone* "Standomi un giorno solo a la fenestra," which appears to stand apart from the other *Rime* because of its medieval flavor, initiated one such group or family. Composed some twenty years after the death of Laura, Petrarch's *canzone* presents a series of six symbolic visions in which the poet experiences six unforeseen catastrophes. Its finely wrought images furnished inspiration for artists in other media as well, including the creator of the first emblem book in England. More recently the images have been discussed at some length, in metaphorical terms as medallions on a neck-

1. Works such as J. Vianey's *Le Pétrarquisme en France au seizième siècle* (Montpellier: Coulet, 1909); Henri Hauvette's *Les Poésies lyriques de Pétrarque* (Paris: Malfère, 1931); J. Scott-Espiner's *Les Sonnets elisabéthains: Les Sources et l'Apport personnel* (Paris: Champion, 1929); and George Watson's *The English Petrarchans: A Critical Bibliography of the Canzoniere,* Warburg Institute Surveys, III (London: Univ. of London Press, 1967), furnish valuable information on the sources of various Petrarchan poets. Other studies, including L. C. John's *The Elizabethan Sonnet Sequences: Studies in Conventional Conceits* (New York: Columbia Univ. Press, 1938); J. W. Lever's *The Elizabethan Love Sonnet* (London: Methuen, 1956); David Kalstone's *Sidney's Poetry: Contexts and Interpretations* (Cambridge: Harvard Univ. Press, 1965); Donald Stone's *Ronsard's Sonnet Cycles: A Study in Tone and Vision* (New Haven: Yale Univ. Press, 1966); and Donald Guss's *John Donne, Petrarchist: Italianate Conceits and Love Theory in the "Songs and Sonets"* (Detroit: Wayne State Univ. Press, 1966), treat the influence of Petrarchism, particularly that of the *Canzoniere,* on various European love poets.

2. Studies of certain families of poems include Joseph Fucilla, "Superbi colli: Notas sobre la boga del tema en España," in *Superbi colli e altri saggi* (Rome: Carucci Editore, 1963), pp. 7-43; R. O. Jones, "Renaissance Butterfly, Mannerist Flea: Tradition and Change in Renaissance Poetry," *MLN,* 80 (1965), 166-84; and Joseph Fucilla, "Materials for the History of a Popular Classical Theme," in his *Studies and Notes (Literary and Historical)* (Naples: Istituto Editoriale del Mezzogiorno, n.d.), pp. 99-126.

lace,[3] or as metamorphoses,[4] emblems,[5] or examples of *ekphrasis*.[6] Each of these analyses purports to classify the poet's technique, but none of these descriptions, in its strictest sense, definitively characterizes the poetry of "Standomi un giorno." Because of its notable technique and because of its influence, it has seemed worthwhile to re-explore the poem in order better to understand its formal characteristics, its individual unity, its place in Petrarch's works, and its unique contribution to Petrarchism in the Renaissance.

A lesser known facet of Petrarch's enormous influence is his stance as a visionary which finds its most intricate expression in "Standomi un giorno."[7] The poem supposedly treats an occasion when the poet, reflecting on the death of Laura and what it meant to him, was granted a six-fold vision which offered him graphic symbolic illustrations of his sorrow. In his "Coronation Oration," Petrarch describes the task of the poet who sets forth psychological, moral, and historical truths under the veil of fiction.[8] Accordingly, he develops a suitable fiction for this remembrance of Laura's passing by imagining that he is standing and observing a succession of events from a window:

3. Fredi Chiappelli, "La canzone delle visioni e il sostrato tematico della 'fabula inexpleta,' " *GSLI,* 141 (1964), 321.

4. Robert Durling, *The Figure of the Poet in the Renaissance Epic* (Cambridge: Harvard Univ. Press, 1965), p. 83.

5. Mario Praz, *Studies in Seventeenth-Century Imagery* (Rome: Edizioni di storia e letteratura, 1964), p. 13, and "Petrarca e gli emblematisti," in *Ricerche anglo-italiane* (Rome: Istituto grafico Tiberino, 1944), p. 305.

6. Praz, *Ricerche anglo-italiane,* p. 305.

7. We find other instances of Petrarch's use of dreams and visions in the *Trionfi,* the *Bucolicum Carmen* (Eclogue X), and in the *Canzoniere* as well. The dream element appears in "Qual paura ho, quando mi torna a mente" (249), and in "O misera et orribil visione" (251), where the poet explains how his dreams have engendered a feeling of foreboding in him, a fear that Laura has died. In "Quante fiate al mio dolce ricetto" (281) and "Se lamentar augelli, o verdi fronde" (279), the poet's presence in nature reminds him of Laura and he envisions her, as he so often had while she was alive, among the grass and flowers. These episodes resemble the appearance of the lady in the sixth stanza of *canzone* 323. However, in these sonnets, as in "Levommi il mio penser in parte ov'era" (302), he imagines that Laura comforts him, addressing him in the tender terms she had never used in life. In "Quando il soave mio fido conforto" (359), Laura appears to him and displays some displeasure over his continual lamenting. All these poems have to do with Petrarch's memory of Laura and explain some aspect of the lover's behavior, but none are composed of a series of images bound together within a visionary framework. In addition, Mario Praz (*Ricerche anglo-italiane,* pp. 306-307) sees a resemblance in technique between the *canzoni* "Nel dolce tempo" (23) and "Qual piú diversa e nova" (135) and this visionary poem because all three present emblematic images which undergo some form of change.

8. Petrarch defines the nature and function of poetry in "The Coronation Oration," translated by Ernest Hatch Wilkins in his *Studies in the Life and Works of Petrarch* (Cambridge, Mass.: Mediaeval Academy of America, 1955), p. 307.

Standomi un giorno solo a la fenestra,
Onde cose vedea tante e sí nove
Ch'era sol di mirar quasi già stanco . . . .[9]
(lines 1-3)

In the fashion of other medieval dream narratives, Petrarch enhances the immediacy of his vision by his pretense that these are real events recorded from memory. In the ensuing stanzas, the occasional repetition of verbs of sight and an allusion to memory preserve the semblance of reality. Only in the *congedo* is this fiction dispelled so that we may freely ponder the meaning of the vision:

Canzon, tu puoi ben dire:
—Queste sei visïoni al signor mio
Han fatto un dolce di morir desio.—
(lines 73-75)

Although the visionary aspect of *canzone* 323 is almost unique in the *Canzoniere,* it brings to a climax the general dream motif prominent in the second portion of the cycle, and it easily conforms to Petrarch's habitual mode of thought which is pictorial and analogical. The small pageant of figures which passes before the visionary's eyes calls to mind the elaborate pageantry of the *Trionfi.* If at first the six scenes with their images of differing origins seem disconnected, we soon recognize the associational organization common to the processions of vivid images in dreams. Although they are not technically dreams, these visions evince several phantasmagoric traits such as free, undeterminable, unlocalized settings. The background for each vision is vague and generalized because Petrarch mentions only briefly a direction or a place: "un boschetto novo," "quel medesmo bosco," "da man destra," "la selva," "alto mar." While the witness at the window surveys the visionary landscape, each situation arising evokes an appropriate setting which is vividly present for one moment and then abruptly and mysteriously disappears. The poem resembles a dream also in its freedom from the limitations of time and space and in the suppression of explanatory narrative.

United structurally by the fiction of the spectator at the window, the *canzone* is apportioned into six stanzas plus a *congedo.* Each stanza of twelve lines contains one precipitous and dramatic event: the poet

9. All quotations from the *Canzoniere* are taken from Giosuè Carducci and Severino Ferrari, eds., *Le Rime di Francesco Petrarca* (Florence: Sansoni, 1899), and will henceforth be indicated in the text proper by poem number and lines. All italics are my own.

depicts a beautiful image, subsequently dealt a mortal blow in full view of the visionary who is moved to express his grief. These reversals are of the highest seriousness in the *Canzoniere* and relate to the consequences of Laura's death, the nature of human frailty and the universal principle of change. There is, moreover, a minimum of self-analysis in this poem; instead of trying to make us understand his emotions with subtle comparisons, or conceits, the poet tries to make us see and experience firsthand the source of his sorrow. Because the beast, the ship, the fountain, the laurel, the phoenix, and the lady are the most exquisite presences in the milieu of the *Canzoniere,* where they are endowed with mythical significance, the emotional force of their destruction is such that they dominate our initial perception of the poetry.

It is therefore understandable that these images have elicited the varying descriptions of their style. Fredi Chiappelli observes that the work is a variation on the theme of mutability with a "struttura a collana di medaglioni,"[10] suggesting a rapprochement between the poet's and the engraver's craft as well as the underlying unity of the disparate images. Mario Praz classifies Petrarch's poetry as an instance of *ekphrasis,* although "Standomi un giorno" is not really the poetic description of a work of art, despite its apparent similarities to this genre.[11] Perhaps Praz's association of the poem with emblematics is more justifiable historically since the visions were in fact incorporated into an emblem book.[12] Robert Durling calls the cycle of events in each stanza a metamorphosis.[13] However, not change from one physical state to another but catastrophe and grief are the theme of the poem. The comparison of Petrarch's technique in this poem with engraving, metamorphosis, *ekphrasis,* and emblematics is prompted by the history of the poem's influence as well as by its graphic liveliness, a notable illustration of the Horatian dictum *ut pictura poesis.* Further, this draws attention to that dimension of Petrarch's language which enables it to create form and substance in our minds. Petrarch never goes to the extent of creating poetic metaphors out of the terminology of sculpture and painting

10. "La canzone delle visioni e il sostrato tematico della 'fabula inexpleta'," 321.

11. *Ricerche anglo-italiane,* p. 305.

12. *Studies in Seventeenth-Century Imagery,* pp. 10-13. Praz draws a very fine distinction between conceits and emblems, which he calls "fruits of the same tree." He believes Petrarch's images in "Standomi un giorno" to be potential emblems because they are both sensuous and revelatory, each needing only a figure to become an emblem proper.

13. *The Figure of the Poet,* p. 83. Durling states that "Standomi un giorno" further develops the theme of metamorphosis found in *canzone* 23 although it is death as metamorphosis in the later poem.

as Michelangelo later does,[14] but we cannot entirely dismiss the poem's affinities with the visual arts.

Because of the visionary framework, the concreteness and formal beauty of the central images are requisite. However, the physical delineation of the six images is not specific in the modern sense. Motivated by the criteria of decorum and significance, the medieval and Renaissance poet believed that art should find the intelligible in the visible.[15] A vision is intrinsically concrete, but it is also revelatory just as dreams may be. Petrarch's images fulfill both the requirements of sensuousness and utility: the descriptive words are sufficiently colorful while, at the same time, they point to the essential worth of the thing described. The poem is a metaphoric recreation of Petrarch's love affair, specifically of his enchantment with Laura's beauty and of his anguish at her death. And the images, which are metaphors for Laura, are set forth as the treasures of his poetic experience.

Petrarch's images derive from classical sources and appear frequently in the *Rime*. Yet, within this vision, Petrarch reuses them in an original way, recording always the uniqueness of his lady and his experience. This *fera* is still the elusive creature slightly beyond his reach, but here the barrier is death, the final separation. Other vessels in the *Rime* stand as metaphors for the poet's tormented soul; this *nave* is transformed into an extravagant image of Laura whose destruction marks the loss of the poet's most cherished treasure. The last four images are classical or mythical, but even their legends are modified. The pastoral harmony and idyllic beauty of the laurel and the fountain cannot withstand the rigors of the finite world. An unanticipated cataclysm swallows up the fountain, a classical *locus amoenus* which recalls the exquisite creations of Ovid and Horace.[16] The plant traditionally immune to lightning, the laurel, is without warning uprooted by a flash

14. This technique is discussed by C. B. Beall in "The Literary Figure of Michelangelo," *Italica,* 41 (1964), 235-51, and by Glauco Cambon in "Sculptural Form as Metaphysical Conceit in Michelangelo's Verse," *SR,* 70 (1962), 155-63.

15. For a discussion of the criteria of decorum and significance to which this commentary is indebted, see Rosemund Tuve, *Elizabethan and Metaphysical Imagery: Renaissance Poetic and Twentieth-Century Critics* (Chicago: Univ. of Chicago Press, 1947), esp. chps. 2, 7, and 9.

16. Francesco Maggini, in "La canzone delle visioni," *Studi Petrarcheschi* (1948), 44-45, compares Petrarch's fountain with those of Horace and Ovid, noting that the language in this stanza has great polish and is therefore quite classical. Pierre de Nolhac points out in *Pétrarque et l'humanisme* (Paris: Champion, 1907), I, 11: "Ce qui l'a séduit dans la littérature antique c'est le caractère d'oeuvre d'art."

from the heavens.[17] At the climax of the poem, the immortal phoenix, beholding the destruction of the laurel and the fountain, without the usual cycle of burning and regeneration, fells himself with his own beak. When the latter-day Euridice of the final vision is stricken on the heel, not on the ankle, by a small snake, there remains no possibility for her poet-lover to retrieve her from the realm of the dead. In each stanza, the modification reiterates the unexpectedness and the finality of Laura's transition from this life to the next.

Traditionally, these six visions have been interpreted allegorically and the early commentators sought references to Laura in every descriptive element. Sometimes their insistence on the meaning of certain details offends logic or moderation; however, more often it reveals how readers of their time would have understood the poem and the personal nature of the vision. On the whole, Petrarch's method is to make us associate each image with the Laura of the other poems, and thus perceive metaphors of which one term is only implied. The complex of detail in each vision speaks of much more than Laura's death; it also reveals something of her beauty, her life, and her spirituality. Evoking the figure of a woman with such adjectives as *umana,* Petrarch alludes to a burial with the phrase "chiusa in un sasso," and more directly to the plague in which Laura died, a "tempesta orïental." The careful framing of the individual images and their constant association with Laura heightens the emotional impact of their ruin. Modifiers such as *bella, giovenetto, schietto, oro, porpora, ebeno,* and *neve* suggest her physical grace, her beauty, and its value to her lover. Other modifiers pertain more especially to her spiritual qualities (*onesta, lieta, felice, santi, celeste*) and bring to mind the *stilnovisti* and the *donna angelicata* (*bella donna, pietate, gentil, leggiadra, merce*).

Petrarch's attentive reworking of the poem shows his devotion to his poetic vocation and his emulation of the classical attitude toward style, while belying a thoroughly medieval outlook. Such attention to detail presumably motivated De Sanctis' judgment of the world of the *Rime* as a "bel mondo plastico," a judgment which seems to ignore literary history.[18] Maggini notes that this *canzone* is one of the most

17. Petrarch explains the traditional qualities attributed to the laurel in "The Coronation Oration" (*Studies in the Life and Works of Petrarch,* p. 312). On another occasion, the laurel is destroyed by lightning in Eclogue X of the *Bucolicum Carmen,* which is entitled "Laurea Occidens." Of course, this could be interpreted symbolically. Often the laurel is associated with Petrarch's poetic inspiration, which he claims has been dissipated by his loss.

18. Francesco De Sanctis, *Saggio critico sul Petrarca* (Naples: A. Morano, 1932), p. 253.

corrected in the manuscripts and concludes that Petrarch's critical, self-conscious search for perfection of form and style looks toward the "classicism" of the Renaissance.[19] The variety of "Standomi un giorno" is the goal of every element of the poem. This extraordinary workmanship is Chiappelli's real subject, and he attempts to show that each word and sound is motivated by Petrarch's consciousness of the musical possibilities of verse.[20] On the linguistic level, the poet constantly prunes away prosaic phrases and insignificant repetitions. On the syntactic level, the poem is a combination of classical periods and paratactic phrases which set the crucial portions of each vision into relief. In general, Petrarch develops his images within a longer, more complex sentence, while the onlooker's commentary is most often put forth in shorter, simpler phrases. All refinements in style show how Petrarch enriches and makes the things lost splendid and precious, shining and invaluable. Petrarch's craftsmanship is never simply art for art's sake. It is, of course, more than praise of Laura's remarkable fairness; it is his statement of how dear Laura and now her memory are to him.

Elsewhere Petrarch is more analytic in his approach, exploring the lover's psyche and appealing more to our intellect. In "Standomi un giorno," Petrarch wants us to exalt in his lady's inspirational beauty and to grieve with him at her death. The spectacle, always presented in a sympathetic manner, elicits awe, respect, and appreciation as well as moral judgment. The things destroyed have a special nobility ("la fera gentil"), moral superiority ("ricca merce onesta"), youthful purity ("un lauro giovenetto e schietto"), exquisite beauty and even divinity ("forma celeste et immortale"). The visionary, overcome by the beauty and harmony of the sights, is lulled into a kind of religious rapture. Yet, each time his almost mystical experience ends not in the sublime but in the harsh world of reality and mutability. With each catastrophe, the visionary's expectations are disappointed and in the course of each vision, he moves abruptly from bliss to shock. He can do no more than vent his distress in the little maxims which punctuate each stanza, the stylized and greatly controlled reactions to loss and suffering characteristic of the man who became the symbol of literary and moral civility in the Renaissance.

19. Maggini, pp. 45-50.

20. See Fredi Chiappelli, *Studi sul linguaggio del Petrarca: La canzone delle visioni* (Florence: Olschki, 1971) and "La canzone petrarchesca delle visioni: Costanti e variazioni interstrofiche della struttura metrica," in *Yearbook of Italian Studies,* 1 (1971), 235-47, as well as E. H. Wilkins, *The Making of the "Canzoniere" and Other Petrarchan Studies* (Rome: Edizioni di storia e letteratura, 1951), and Ruth S. Phelps, *The Earlier and Later Forms of Petrarch's Canzoniere* (Chicago: Univ. of Chicago Press, 1925).

Petrarch makes us feel the power of Laura's influence in his life, even after her death, both by means of his images and by means of the onlooker's behavior. Praz writes that Petrarch conceals autobiographical facts behind the images in "Standomi un giorno" and that the central images first engage our attention, giving the poem its dramatic force.[21] On the other hand, Chiappelli states that the poet is less concerned with his configuration of Laura's death than with his own emotional reaction. He contends that it is really the spectator who is most revealed in his sudden fall from ecstasy to dismay and that it is his reaction which gives the poem its essential energy.[22] The witness at the window is an integral part of the vision, but Petrarch's attention to the lover's psychology is less keen in this poem than in certain others, where his mental states are probed at some length. In this series of little dramas, spectator and spectacle are closely intertwined.

Of course, the deliberate shading of the expressions of sorrow betrays the poet's interest in the characterization of the visionary. Chiappelli finds a new movement in the poetry after the first two stanzas because the sensory awareness of the onlooker expands to both sight and sound, and because the objective viewpoint he supposedly maintains in the first two stanzas gives way to a realization of personal involvement.[23] However, the visionary makes his involvement in the catastrophes personal when he first places himself at the window, and he stresses this intimacy throughout the poem with common linguistic devices, verbs in the first person, possessive adjectives, emphatic pronouns, and the pronominal construction. Even the sententious refrains which sum up the spectator's feelings reflect this personal involvement. Some of the outbursts express his grief directly; others do so only implicitly. The death of the *fera* makes him weep over its harsh fate ("E *mi* fe' sospirar sua dura sorte"); the destruction of the laurel makes his life sad ("onde *mia* vita è trista"). In the last stanzas, Petrarch reverses the usual order of things and elaborates commonplaces about earthly mutability to define his own bereavement. The proverbial tone of "Ogni cosa al fin vola" or "Ahi, nulla altro che pianto al mondo dura!" conveys his realization that his grief is part of a larger scheme, the inexorable cycle of life and death, a realization with which Petrarch struggles throughout the series of sonnets preceding "Standomi un giorno." As he had in "Chi vuol veder" (248), where he determines that "Cosa bella

21. *Ricerche anglo-italiane,* p. 309.
22. *Studi sul linguaggio del Petrarca,* p. 29.
23. Ibid., pp. 202-203. Maggini, p. 39, on the other hand, sees no development of concepts but only a constant return to the theme of Laura's death.

mortal passa e non dura," Petrarch suggests here that Laura must die because envious death steals away all the sooner that which is most beautiful. Hence, his images progress from the *fera* to the *bella donna,* a most explicit metaphor for Laura, or perhaps, as Maggini suggests, even Laura herself, who was in a sense Petrarch's own Euridice.[24]

Once the poet has tentatively resolved the question of Laura's death, he turns to his own fate, expressing a wish for his own passing. Petrarch, a modern Orpheus, loses his lady to death, but not her memory which continually inspires him. Although the poet's grief is intense, his artistic self-control allows him to sustain an attitude toward death which for the moment lacks bitterness. In Petrarch's works in general, there is neither excessive love of life nor excessive fear of death, neither fanatical denunciation of the flesh nor complete absorption in spiritual matters. Conflict always gives Petrarch's poetry its form and substance, but the balance in tone and diction prefigures that classical equilibrium which became a goal of the Renaissance. Death permeates the latter portion of the *Canzoniere,* yet it is never in itself horrible or ugly but somehow, at times, even desirable. It holds an attraction for the virtuous lady in the sixth stanza of "Standomi un giorno" because she perceives that it is the pathway to spiritual satisfaction. Dying, she is *lieta* and *secura,* consistent with the picture of the womanly Laura-Beatrice that Thomas G. Bergin finds in the last poems.[25] Her posture reassures the poet who, seeking for relief, would in following her partake of her tranquillity and happiness. This expression of the *Liebestod* is epitomized in the antithetic and bittersweet "dolce di morir desio" which the poet voices in conclusion.

Not the emotion of a moment, this desire is the consequence of an act of memory (line 48). Recreating a moment of his emotional life, this time the most painful one, the poet presents it with fascination, with wonder (*novo, estranio*), with surprise (*subito, breve ora, in un punto*), with a sense of past and present, and by externalizing what is inward, like Dante with his pilgrim. It is his old inner treasure that is so rich a *merce* and an inspiration for his patient and passionate description of it. The loss itself has become as much a part of the complex of emotion in the *Rime* as the discovery of love itself, and his despair is something he has grown accustomed to; it is inseparable from the total phenomenon, and is a "dolce di morir desio." Through the power

24. Maggini, p. 47.

25. *Petrarch* (New York: Twayne, 1970), pp. 163-65. Bergin's view is based upon a distinction made by Carlo Calcaterra, *Nella selva del Petrarca* (Bologna: Cappelli, 1942), chps. 2 and 7.

of memory, the past becomes present, and the whole experience is reviewed with freshness and taste.

"Standomi un giorno" finds the poet a spectator, but that which has become spectacle is complex, despite images which tend to simplify it all. The poet attempts to suggest the magnitude of his deprivation through this series of catastrophes which befall metaphorical images of Laura's perfection. Laura alive was an inestimable and unattainable treasure, his sorrow at her death was sharp and deep, but this sad experience has retreated into the past and the memory serves as an inexhaustible source of poetry, a present and attainable treasure. The sorrow is now muted and the lament has become song. Laura's beauty is now generalized, more noble, almost superhuman, and expressed not as a girl remembered, but as an abstraction lodged in an impersonal metaphor. Recapturing the moment of Laura's death and imparting the poet's present state of mind, "Standomi un giorno" is both the climax of a long series of sonnets treating of Petrarch's anger, frustration, loneliness and yearning, and a transitional poem leading to the sorrowful and reluctant acceptance expressed in the last poems.

Belonging to the long tradition of visionary literature and recalling the medieval meditations on death, "Standomi un giorno" is somewhat on the margin of the main current of sixteenth-century Petrarchism, and is somewhat atypical of the *Rime*. Petrarch breathes new life into the visionary framework with elaborate metaphors, classical craftsmanship, and his awareness of the passage of time, the importance of the individual and the power of memory. The striking central images reflect the general prominence of imagery in the rest of the *Canzoniere,* but the modicum of introspection, the visionary structure, the symbolic tableaux and the resultant distancing make it much akin to the *Trionfi* and the Latin writings, and teach us that Petrarch was not so completely emancipated from his fourteenth-century milieu, even at the very end of his career when he composed this poem. The terrible plague of 1348, in which Laura died, influences Petrarch's whole outlook on life; it is the subject of several letters, the inspiration for the tenth eclogue, and one of the major events commemorated in the poetry of the *Trionfi* and the *Canzoniere,* including "Standomi un giorno," where its force is poignantly renewed.

"Standomi un giorno" initiated the growth of one major family of poems which flourished for several decades during the sixteenth century, yet did not participate in the ascendance of Petrarch as a poet of love. The general nature of the poem's history abroad does not differ radically from that of the other *Rime* but precedes it. Indeed, the influence of the visions bridges the two later waves of Petrarchism in Europe, the impact of the *Trionfi* and that of the *Canzoniere*.[26] After its direct introduction into French literature, through the translation by Clément Marot, the *canzone* had a considerable development for a poem regarded as one of the lesser works. Joachim Du Bellay wrote a series of sonnets entitled *Songe* in imitation of *canzone* 323; Jan van der Noot translated it into Dutch, including it in an emblem book; Edmund Spenser translated and imitated all of this vision poetry in his book of *Complaints*. Francesco Maggini, undoubtedly echoing De Sanctis, claims that it is "una poesia del Petrarca che non è delle più alte."[27] But it is precisely the modern sensibility which produces this judgment; the poets and the reading public of the early Renaissance evidently read and took pleasure in this poetic mode. It inspired Du Bellay and Spenser who found its form imitable and its matter adaptable to their own themes, the decline of Rome and the paradox of power. These visions inspired the publication of Jan van der Noot's moralistic *Theatre for Worldlings*, including separate editions in English, Dutch, French, and German.

Had they not profited by the initial vogue of the emblem books, the visions might have been eclipsed even sooner. This type of poetry could not arouse the interest to sustain it in the developing Renaissance. "Standomi un giorno," although it is one of the love lyrics, falls outside the mainstream of the influence of the *Canzoniere*, and therefore represents a specialized form of Petrarchism. The last transformation of the *canzone* was a "Canción fúnebre," composed by Quevedo on the death of Luis Carillo in 1610.[28] By this time, however, the simplistic visionary method seemed less appropriate to the complexities dealt with either by religious poets or by love poets. Another aspect of Petrarchism came to be the primary influence on Renaissance poets, and it was no longer fashionable to view Petrarch either as a moralist or as a love poet in the manner of Dante. Both poets and emblematists began to shift from moralistic subjects with an outmoded manner of presentation to the more courtly or to the more philosophical concerns of love. With this perceptible change in tastes, the visions finally grew wearisome and died.

26. For a treatment of the three waves of Petrarch's influence, see E. H. Wilkins, "A General Survey of Renaissance Petrarchism," in his *Studies in the Life and Works of Petrarch*, pp. 280-99.

27. Maggini, p. 47.

28. *Obras completas de Don Francisco de Quevedo Villegas*, ed. Luis A. Marín (Madrid: Aguilar, 1932), II, 461-63.

VII

ILLUSION DISABUSED: A NOVEL MODE IN PETRARCH'S CANZONIERE

by Oscar Büdel

University of Michigan (Ann Arbor)

Amare et sapere vix deo conceditur.
Publilius Syrus

The ritual of love in all its phases was first conceived by the Greek and Roman elegists, it was then taken up again by the troubadours, and it was eventually perfected to a tenuous and finely honed procedure in stilnovistic poetry. There was the awe-inspiring perception of beauty, its overwhelming experience, imploration and hope of requital, unrequited love, lament and grief at the unapproachable, imprecations, sighs and tears, the endeavor of unlikely escape, suffering, deathwish, paleness, despondence. Thus, indeed, Dante, "in the *Vita Nuova,* had given a seemingly autobiographical (but actually ontological) account of the development and course of the feeling of love."[1]

When Petrarch, after quoting incipits from Arnaut, Cavalcanti, Dante, and Cino da Pistoia in *Lasso me* (LXX), at last turned to his own canzone *Nel dolce tempo de la prima etade* (XXIII), he put himself consciously within that tradition. Indeed, that canzone of his is an account, in the guise of consecutive metamorphoses, of the various phases of love as experienced by the poet. *Lasso me, ch'i' non so in qual parte pieghi,* which in its opening line appropriately expresses a state of perplexity, is thus the natural continuation of the contingencies ex-

1. Leo Spitzer, "Note on the Poetic and the Empirical 'I' in Medieval Authors," *Traditio,* IV (1946), p. 416.

References to Petrarch's works indicated in the text will be taken from the following editions: *Canzoniere:* Testo critico e introduzione di Gianfranco Contini; Annotazioni di Daniele Ponchiroli (Torino, 1966); *Secretum:* a cura di Enrico Carrara, in the volume: Francesco Petrarca, *Prose,* a cura di G. Martellotti *et al.,* La Letteratura Italiana: Storia e Testi, VII (Milano, 1955); Letters: *Le familiari,* Edizione critica per cura di Vittorio Rossi, four vols. (Firenze, 1933-42); *Epistolae metricae:* Francesco Petrarca, *Trionfi, Rime varie e una scelta di versi latini,* a cura di Carlo Muscetta e Daniele Ponchiroli (Torino, 1958). References to the Roman elegists will be taken from the respective editions in the Loeb Classical Library.

pressed in that earlier *Nel dolce tempo.* As if in justification of his self-plagiarism, the poet then hints at a further mode which before him had not been considered a feasible alternative in the situations of the ritual of love. Petrarch is alluding to a step he will be willing to take at a later time. This is to acknowledge illusion and consciously live by it—even though he clearly perceives it as self-deception, but also as his only means to preserve his inner balance and, indeed, ensure his survival.[2]

It is through the power of his imagination, then, that the poet arrives at this new mode of existence. The reader familiar with the tradition will no doubt be tempted to recall parallels to such a *modus vivendi* in stilnovistic poetry, and on the surface it seems indeed as if there were existing correspondences. Yet stilnovistic practice from the very outset opposes to the unapproachability of the beloved the power of the imagination and definitely withdraws to the inner self. For the stilnovistic poets the woman created in the mind surpassed in meaning the one in the flesh. It is for this reason that Dante—at the very moment he is evoking the Beatrice of reality—refers to her as "la gloriosa donna de la mia mente"(*Vita nuova,* I). Most telling in this respect is the paradigmatic conclusion of Frescobaldi's canzone *Morte avversara* which goes so far as to conceive of death as the only means of achieving that final state of the pure idea, of complete spiritualization.[3] There is indeed no need for the continual real appearance of the woman, as she will be only a hindrance to that freely creating power of the imagination. Revealing with regard to that final sublimation of beauty is Cavalcanti's ballata *Veggio negli occhi de la donna mia,* where in a sequence of three stages from the initial perception of beauty, going through an abstract image of it, the final stage of sublimation is reached, that "bellezza nova," which ultimately removes the "woman of the mind" from any definite link with her living "prototype." It is a thinking in figural dimensions: the image of the real woman only serves as an

2. This is a feature which before Petrarch is not developed in its full implications. Acknowledgment should be given here to Hugo Friedrich and his identification of the aspect as a significant departure from earlier positions: "Im Wahnthema dieser Art geschieht die wohl wichtigste ideelle Wendung, welche die Lyrik Petrarcas gegenüber dem dolce stil novo vollzogen hat." *Epochen der italienischen Lyrik* (Frankfurt am Main, 1964), p. 215. See also his discussion of "innere Phasen" in connection with Petrarch's poetry.

3. Compare with this the rather different conviction of Petrarch's as it is expressed in one of the early sonnets that also touches upon the issue of suicide: "S'io credesse per morte essere scarco / del pensiero amoroso che m'atterra, / colle mie mani avrei già posto in terra / queste membra noiose, et quello incarco" (XXXVI, 1-4).

umbra futurorum, as it were, it is only there to accomplish its own interpretation in terms of something new and definitive. Thus the final sublimation of terrestrial beauty serves only the purpose of a definite withdrawal and dissociation from any link with the real existence of the beloved.

With Petrarch, however, when the beloved is perceived in the illusion, it is indeed not a separation that is being sought, but precisely the opposite, and the woman of the illusion is continuously measured against that of the flesh (although, in the last analysis, he will stay aloof and distant).[4] In *Lasso me,* Petrarch thus takes a first step in the direction of a final sanction of an illusion of the beloved, which—though consciously perceived as such—is with the same measure consciously retained. Ultimately, this represents a new dimension in that age-old ritual of the different states and stages in the love for a woman.

In the sequence of these stages, *Nel dolce tempo* had arrived at that final impasse of flight:

> et in un cervo solitario et vago
> di selva in selva ratto mi trasformo:
> et anchor de' miei can' fuggo lo stormo. (158-160)

This possibility of flight is taken up repeatedly and regarded as an alternative to the impasse of the poet's predicament. Yet in the end it will only result in a frame of mind which lent itself to that typical Petrarchan conceit that was to become one of the hallowed *emblemata amatoria:*[5]

> I' chiedrei a scampar, non l'arme, anzi ali;
> ma perir mi dà 'l ciel per questa luce,
> ché da lunge mi struggo et da presso ardo. (CXCIV, 12-14)

4. Evidence of this aspect is readily available even in the second part, as in sonnet *Che fai? che pensi?* (CCLXXIII), or in connection with Laura's dream visits where this measuring against the woman of the flesh comes through repeatedly. Thus in *Alma felice che sovente torni* (CCLXXXII) where this aspect is stressed in the second tercet with an *endecasillabo a maiore* in a polysyndetic arrangement: "Sol un riposo trovo in molti affanni, / che, quando torni, te conosco e 'ntendo / a l'andar, a la voce, al volto, a' panni." In *Quando il soave mio fido conforto* (CCCLIX), the same tendency breaks through: whereas Laura in a dramatic exchange admonishes the poet to think of his salvation, she is immediately answered with a battery of rhetorical questions which evoke once more her physical, terrestrial existence: " 'Son questi i capei biondi, et l'aureo nodo / —dich'io—ch'ancor mi stringe, et quei belli occhi / che fur mio sol?' " (56-58).

5. Cf. Daniel Heinsius, *Emblemata amatoria* (Leyden, 1613), no. 4. On Petrarch's impact on emblem literature, see Mario Praz, *Studi sul concettismo* (Firenze, 1946); also: *Emblemata. Handbuch zur Sinnbildkunst des XVI. und XVII. Jahrhunderts,* eds. Arthur Henkel and Albrecht Schöne (Stuttgart, 1967).

In the search for remedies to the poet's predicament, there was, in the *Secretum,* Augustine's suggestion to follow that Ciceronian advice, "veterem amorem novo amore tanquam clavum clavo eiciendum," which he compounded with a most self-explanatory Ovidian dictum: "successore novo vincitur omnis amor." Such a suggestion is of course rejected out of hand by Petrarch, whose ensuing request to put in a word of his own, however, is more interesting with respect to our problem than that rejection itself, which was to be expected, for he says: "Pateris ne, medico perorante, *egrum morbi sui conscium* aliquid interloqui?" (III, p. 162; italics mine). It is this, as we shall see later, one of the several instances in the *Secretum* where awareness, consciousness of his own situation is clearly stated by Petrarch. And it is this frame of mind which is going to be decisive for the position he eventually will take with respect to illusion.

For Augustine, then, the next solution that offered itself was to be seen in flight: "Potes ne igitur, in animum inducere fugam exilium ve, et notorum locorum caruisse conspectu?" Indeed, only such a radical separation seems to him to promise a sure measure of success: "Si hoc potes salvus eris!" (III, p. 164). Yet, although Petrarch seems to agree ("fugamque iam meditor," p. 172), he is as yet undecided where to turn, and it is at this point that Augustine proposes Italy.[6] After the long paragraph, however, in which Augustine sets forth his reasons, Petrarch still asks for further advice ("Siquid autem alterius remedii

6. The entire *peregrinationes* paragraph in the *Secretum* has been closely examined by Hans Baron in his article: "Petrarch's *Secretum:* Was it Revised—and Why? The Draft of 1342-43 and the Later Changes," *BHR,* XXV (1963), 489-530. Basing himself on external as well as stylistic evidence, Baron came to the conclusion that the paragraph as it stands now (pp. 164-174 in the Carrara edition) must be a later insertion. His final verdict on the whole paragraph concerning the *amor* discussion could also be upheld by internal evidence, namely that Petrarch was not willing to stop at portraying his amorous experience with the stage he had arrived at in canzone XXIII: *Nel dolce tempo de la prima etade,* but that he intended to give a full picture of the phases of his love. Baron concludes: "Eventually, therefore, in revising the *Secretum*—presumably not before '47 and in part not until '49—he used successive experiences for rounding out and dramatizing the dialogue; he turned it into a composite picture of all the motivations that at one time or another had driven him away from the Provence" (p. 524). Baron's question "Does the paragraph in which he is advised to flee from the Provence form a logical and integral part of the argument?" may be answered, perhaps, in part by Petrarch's procedure to combine events of his real life (such as his potential move to Italy, which eventually did come to pass) with aspects of his interior psychological development he may have found to be indispensable in the story of his love. A similar admixture of fact and fiction occurs in *Metr.* I, 6, to Giacomo Colonna, where Petrarch transformed some of his previous travel experiences in such a fashion that some of his students were led completely astray as to the realities involved, and assumed a continuation of his journey northward upon his return from Rome in 1337 (cf. Baron, p. 514).

habes," p. 174), and Augustine then proceeds to the last group of alternative solutions to the predicament of his interlocutor. Of the three Ciceronian remedies that he finally cites as turning the mind away from love, "satietas, pudor, cogitatio," only the latter seems to promise a measure of success, and a host of considerations to be pondered by Petrarch is then presented by Augustine: nobility of mind, fragility of the body, brevity of life, fleeting of time, death, the loathsomeness of the female body, and that notorious "in vulgi fabulam esse."

As a final solution, however, distance was of no avail to Petrarch. Its uses had already been thoroughly analyzed in that *metrica* to Giacomo Colonna (I, 6), of 1338, where Petrarch predicated the absolute futility of such an option. After relating all his peregrinations, his account ended with that rhetorical question, "Quid mihi restabat . . . ?" (82), which then paraded the most out-of-the-way places, implying their uselessness as a palliative. His final conclusion, then, was that indeed all distance had been of little help, and that neither his first trip to Germany, Flanders, and France (1333), nor the second one to Rome (1336) had produced any change. A third attempt would certainly not bring about that much desired state of oblivion:

> . . . Nunquid ego admittam quo tertia demum
> irato facienda deo sint irrita vota? (115-116)

As a consequence, there was implied then in the *Secretum* that final rationale of Petrarch's situation whence any future remedial attempt must depart: "Fugi enim sed malum meum ubique circumferens" (III, p. 164). To stress its inexorable aspect, it was accompanied by that Vergilian simile of the fleeing hind that carries in its flank the lethal arrow, and which became another classic among the *emblemata amatoria:* "heret lateri letalis harundo."[7]

When flight is thus obviated as a possible remedy, the basic obstacle to any recovery is no doubt presented by solitude and its implied hold upon imagination. Small wonder, then, that Augustine in the discussion in the *Secretum* sought to foreclose any possibility of isolation. Solitude in the *Secretum* is being considered, therefore, from an angle quite different than in the later *De vita solitaria.*[8] It is conceived as conducive

7. Cf. Hadriani Ivnii Medici *Emblemata* (Antverpiae, MDLXXXV), nr. 47: "HINC DOLOR; INDE FUGA GRAUIS."

8. The treatment of *solitudo* versus city-life in the paragraphs on *avaritia* and *accidia* is equally examined in Baron's article. As far as our discussion here is concerned, the particular attitude on the part of Augustine is explained by the relation of solitude to Laura in which it is seen whenever it is brought up. Thus, already before the *amor* paragraph begins, Laura is seen as an instrumental agent in preparing the conditions of solitude: "Fr. Et iubes illam oblivisci vel parcius amare,

to a relapse into the poet's former ways and must be avoided at all cost. Thus, on the occasion of recalling to Petrarch some of the earlier stages of his amorous experience, Augustine pointedly speaks of that "tristis et amor solitudinis atque hominum fuga" (III, p. 156), and later on states outright: "Tam diu cavendam tibi solitudinem scito" (p. 172). The two protagonists thus conceive of solitude in a different manner: Augustine warns of it because of its evocative power, and Petrarch will consciously revert to it eventually as to his haven, because in the end it appears to him as the only means to reach the unreachable.

Such a mode of living is not yet mentioned *expressis verbis* in the *Secretum,* but there are several instances where such a frame of mind is implied and hinted at. Thus there is already in the opening paragraphs of the first book that basic pronouncement of Augustine's which singles out the human penchant for dissimulation:

> Atqui omnibus ex conditionibus vestris, o mortales, nullam magis admiror, nullam magis exhorreo, quam quod miseriis vestris ex industria favetis, et impendens periculum dissimulatis agnoscere, considerationemque illam, si ingeratur, excluditis. (I, p. 28)

There is, further, the later characterization of Petrarch as "ingeniosus in perniciem propriam" (I, p. 30), the already mentioned description of himself as "egrum morbi sui conscium" (III, p. 162), and with specific reference to that imaginative power of lovers, Augustine will say: "Ubicunque fueris, quocunque te verteris, relicte vultum et verba contemplaberis et, quod est amantum infame privilegium, illam absentem absens audies et videbis" (III, p. 166).

It is this, however, the solution that Petrarch has in mind: "cum ratione insaniare," as Augustine somewhat cunningly implies with a quotation from Terence. Yet Petrarch makes it clear that he is not about to change his mind when Augustine recalls to him that he is so taken by the beauty of his two "cathene," *amor et gloria,* that he considers them treasures instead. He will merely restate his position by asserting that man in general tenaciously clings to his old opinions and will abandon them only with difficulty. Thereafter ensues the most significant change concerning our subject:

> *Aug.* Inveteratum mendacium pro veritate ducere, noviterque compertam veritatem extimare mendacium, ut omnis rerum autoritas in tempore sita sit, dementia summa est.

---

que me a vulgi consortio segregavit" (III, p. 144). Cf. also CCXCII, 1-4: "Gli occhi di ch'io parlai sí caldamente, / et le braccia et le mani e i piedi e 'l viso, / che m'avean sí da me stesso diviso, / et fatto singular da l'altra gente."

Fr. Perdis operam; nulli crediturus sum; succurritque tullianum illud: "Si in hoc erro, libenter erro, neque hunc errorem auferri michi volo, dum vivo." (III, p. 134)

This position, precisely, serves as a point of departure for a gradually emerging attitude that conceives of illusion as a means of adapting to a dilemma for which there is no solution. For this reason, the *Secretum* has always been considered somewhat of a testimonial to a stalemate *sans issue*—short of renouncing one of the two "cathene" altogether. If there were any way out of this dilemma, it could only be achieved through a conscious and voluntary acceptance of self-deception. This mode is gradually emerging in the *Canzoniere* and represents a definite departure from earlier attempts at grappling with the problem presented by illusion, which, with Petrarch, can no longer be neatly separated from its object.

It is not without significance that *Nel dolce tempo,* the canzone representative of the transitions and phases in the story of the poet's love, is one of the most revised compositions of the *Canzoniere*. Its design must have occupied Petrarch for some twenty years,[9] and when he transcribed it in its final form in 1356, he took care, in his note in Cod. Vat. 3196, to record that this happened "post multos et multos annos."[10] Yet *Nel dolce tempo* had stopped with that alternative of flight which had turned out to be inexpedient. Thus, after this presentation of the different transitions of his amorous experience, there will then gradually emerge, in the *Canzoniere,* the issue of imagination and illusion. It will be approached ever more manifestly, until in *Lasso me* the indication of a definite turn toward a conscious espousing of the mode of self-deception and illusion is discernible and recognized in all of its implications.

Thus, we encounter situations in the *Canzoniere* where the poet is represented as being separated from his beloved, and whose mode of expression, in that early stage, merely seems to result in imparting an acute sense of (topographical) distance. Such appears to be the case with the canzone *Sí è debile il filo* (XXXVII), a typical composition on the theme of *amor de lonh*. Yet, although the treatment of the theme is psychologically far advanced beyond those same and more mechanistically conceived aspects in stilnovistic poetry, distance is still seen as

9. See Ernest Hatch Wilkins, *The Making of the "Canzoniere" and Other Petrarchan Studies* (Roma, 1951), p. 90, where he concludes "that the transcription of the *canzone* probably took place within the period February 13—Nov. 15, 1337."

10. Cf. Cod. Vat. 3196, f. 11r.: "transcripta in ordine post multos et multos annos. quibusdam mutatis 1356. Jovis in vesperis. 10. novembris. mediolani."

a mere topographical hindrance rather than in an evocative function:

> Quante montagne et acque,
> quanto mar, quanti fiumi
> m'ascondon que' duo lumi. (41-43)

When then, in the fronte of the last stanza, all the physical qualities of the beloved are enumerated in a polysyndetic tour de force, they are again merely set against topography to heighten the sense of distance.

Beyond, and beside, such situations of mere statement of distance however eloquent, there may be observed, then, in similar situations, the gradual emerging of the concept of imagination and illusion, pure and simple, which does not as yet betray a conscious acceptance. This does not happen in a precise and well defined linear progression but in accordance with the prelusive manner of composition prevailing in the *Canzoniere,* in a resumptive and widely modulating approach that is merely suggestive of a final outcome and situation. Thus, there begins to appear in the vocabulary a semantically close-knit word group which, in its various configurations, points in the direction of imagination and illusion, such as *adombrare, contemplare, depingere, disegnare, figurare, imaginare, imagine, pensare, pensiero, ritrarre.* It is indicative that almost all of them, in the usage in question here, appear in the first part of the *Canzoniere,* whereas—under similar circumstances, but with a different poet—one might rather expect the opposite. The Laura *in vita,* thus, is indeed farther removed than the one *in morte.*[11]

A first indication of a shift in the poet's conception towards imagination in a creative, illusive function is a passage in the canzone *Ne la stagion* (L). It may be significant as to the importance accorded it that it does not occur in one of the narrative sections of the canzone, but in the last of those five variations which compare in the first person the restless state of the poet with that of a contented and peaceful world. It is the poet's own state of mind that is of overriding importance here, and that fifth and last comparison will then indeed turn exclusively to the poet's inner situation. To do so, it will invert the initial ratio of distribution between narrative and monological portions, beginning its monologue only after three initial narrative verses on the outer world:

> Misero me, che volli
> quando primier sí fiso

11. It is indeed in the second part of the *Canzoniere* that Laura takes on more tangible aspects, such as in her dream visits to the poet where she is presented as speaking, sitting by his bedside, etc. Cf. CCCXLI, 12-13; CCCXLII, 8, 12-14; CCCLIX, 3.

gli tenni nel bel viso
per iscolpirlo imaginando in parte
onde mai né per forza né per arte
mosso sarà, fin ch'i' sia dato in preda
a chi tutto diparte!
Né so ben ancho che di lei mi creda. (63-70)

Introduced as it is by that earlier metaphoric reference to Laura as "L'idolo mio scolpito in vivo lauro" (XXX, 27), this passage represents a first acknowledgment—within the poet's own experience—of the existence and of the power of imagination, but it stops short of conclusions. Yet, if its composition, by virtue of its own *terminus ad quem* which it supplies (v. 55), can credibly be assigned to 1336-37, its first broaching the vagaries of imagination within the web of the *Canzoniere* would coincide with the incipient interest of its poet in Augustine, and would reliably place it in a line with those reflections on kindred problems which were to form the basis for the dialogues of the *Secretum*.[12]

As the effects of imagination are seen here in their bearing upon the within, they are paralleled by other passages which, conversely, display a projection of the beloved into, and onto, the outer world of reality, a projection that will become a common feature in the *Canzoniere,* and from there a model theme for Western poetry to come. Thus, the sestina *L'aere gravato* (LXVI) alludes for the first time to this projection of the beloved into the world of reality as engendered by the imagination: the poet becomes "tal ch'i' depinsi poi per mille valli / l'ombra ov'io fui" (34-35). It will then find its major expression in *Chiare, fresche et dolci acque* (CXXVI), when the mode of conscious illusion, of voluntary self-deception, will have been fully developed. There are earlier examples of the poet's involvement in nature in the Roman elegists, but nature there is essentially invoked as a witness to the lover's grief, rather than being conceived of as an active agent, an accomplice, as it were, in that impromptu of make-believe.[13] Petrarch's

12. On the early aspects of Petrarch's acquaintance with St. Augustine see Pierre Courcelle, "Pétrarque, lecteur des *Confessions,*" *RCCM,* I (1959), pp. 26-43. A parallel to the *Secretum* appears in St. Augustine's *Confessiones,* VII, I, 1, where the issue of "phantasmata" is brought up that beleaguer his mind: "Clamabat violenter cor meum adversus omnia phantasmata mea. . . ." In the same way the Augustine of the *Secretum* will derogatorily speak of illusions and phantasies: "Hinc pestis illa fantasmatum vestros discerpens laceransque cogitatus . . ." (I, p. 64); "Siquidem fantasmatibus suis obrutus, . . . animus fragilis oppressus, . . . examinare non potest" (I, p. 66).

13. Cf. Propertius, I, XVIII: "Si modo sola queant saxa tenere fidem" (4); "Vos eritis testes, si quos habet arbor amores" (19); "Sed qualiscumque es resonent mihi 'Cynthia' silvae, / nec deserta tuo nomine saxa vacent" (31-32). Also

uses of nature include this aspect too,[14] but it is rather one of transition as far as our situation is concerned, and it leads to a direct involvement of nature.

References to such illusive, factitious situations of both types mentioned above may be found throughout the first part of the *Canzoniere* (as, of course, recurrences of phases such as those recounted earlier in *Nel dolce tempo* are not unusual). There will be, on the one hand, imaginative situations within the mind of the poet which recall the image of the beloved, as there is, on the other, the vivid outer projection of her into nature. Both may be referred to in one and the same composition as in XCVI (5-7): "Ma 'l bel viso leggiadro che depinto / porto nel petto, et veggio ove ch'io miri, / mi sforza." Such illusive situations may also be represented as almost compulsive and under a spell as in CXXV, where the heart is viewed as harboring "un che madonna sempre / depinge" (34-35), or, on the other hand, in an active and creative fashion as in CXVI, where four of the earlier mentioned key words appear in one and the same sonnet together with both features of inner imagination as well as outer projection:

> Ivi non donne, ma fontane et sassi,
> et l'imagine trovo di quel giorno
> che 'l pensier mio figura ovunque io sguardo. (12-14)

Needless to say, these situations most often present the beloved in an agreeable, amiable, and obliging manner, as if she were the exact image of the poet's wishful thinking ("tanto piú bella il mio pensier l'adombra," CXXIX, 48), and not "quella fera bella et cruda" (XXIII, 149), although such most agreeable situations often alternate with compositions in which the beloved appears in precisely the opposite demeanour.[15] It is this aspect of the *as if,* accepted without questioning, that clearly separates these situations from the mode of conscious illusion

---

Vergil's *Eclogues,* X, 52-54: "Certum est in silvis, . . . / malle pati tenerisque meos incidere amores / arboribus." Petrarch, however, actively engages the landscape, anthropomorphizes it, as it were. Cf. CXXIX, 40 ff.: "I' l'ò piú volte . . . / veduto viva, et nel tronchon d'un faggio, / e 'n bianca nube." On this aspect see also Hugo Friedrich's remarks on "lyrische Landschaften," *Epochen,* p. 210.

14. It appears particularly in *Solo e pensoso* (XXXV, 9-11): "Sí ch'io mi credo omai che monti e piagge / et fiumi et selve sappian di che tempre / sia la mia vita, ch'è celata altrui." A further example in *Perché la vita è breve* (LXXI, 37-38): "O poggi, o valli, o fiumi, o selve, o campi, / o testimon' de la mia grave vita."

15. For a discussion of this aspect, see this author's earlier *Francesco Petrarca und der Literaturbarock.* Schriften und Vorträge des Petrarca-Instituts Köln, XVII (Krefeld, 1963), pp. 22 ff.

which, although aware that all is a pious distortion of the facts, nevertheless upholds this tenuous contingency since it has been found to be a viable means of carrying on a human existence that is not at any moment exposed to potential failure in securing such a state of obliging relations.

The transition from such a mode of mere illusion and wishful thinking to a recognition of it for what it is, and to a willing acceptance of this *status quo,* occurs in a most gradual fashion, and is achieved by means of the selfsame stylistic feature of two different sets of rhetorical questions. Thus, incipient doubts as to the portents of the poet's amorous entanglements are first voiced in the manner of a rhetorical question, pure and simple, with no definite stance taken on the issue, in *Sí è debole il filo* (XXXVII):

> chi mi conduce a l'esca
> onde 'l mio dolor cresca? (54-55)

The questions that follow in *Lasso me* are likewise rhetorical, but there is a major departure from that earlier position in that now an answer is being supplied, whereas previously it had only been implied:

> Che parlo? o dove sono? e chi m'inganna,
> altri ch'io stesso e 'l desïar soverchio? (31-32)

This situation is rationalized on several occasions, and the *Secretum* serves also in this instance as a sounding board. Augustine's ironic pronouncement on the two "cathene," *amor et gloria,* thus reappears in the *Canzoniere* in an interesting about-face. Augustine had said: "earum pulchritudine delectatus, non cathenas sed divitias arbitraris" (II, p. 132), yet his quip has now become an opinion espoused by his erstwhile opponent:

> dissi: Oimè, il giogo, et le catene e i ceppi
> eran piú dolci che l'andare sciolto.
> Misero me, che tardo il mio mal seppi;
> et con quanta faticha oggi mi spetro
> de l'errore, ov'io stesso m'era involto! (LXXXIX, 10-14)

The rationalizing aspect present here will be paralleled in its explicitness only by the sonnet *S'amor non è* (CXXXII), which will be discussed later in another connection. As to the *Secretum,* its prose in this instance, too, provides an analysis of the poet's stance in a much more extensive review of the different aspects involved. It comes in the end to a clear and unequivocal resolution in the exchange in book

III, where both speakers resort to quotations from Terence's *Eunuchus*. The remarks preceding this contest had indicatively revolved around the issue of Petrarch's being attracted to Laura "non minus nominis quam ipsius corporis splendore" (III, p. 158), and all the evils inherent in love were then enumerated by Augustine. Anticipating Petrarch's expected reply that these vices would be moderated by dint of reason, Augustine's Terence quotation then centers around that issue of "cum ratione insaniare," precisely the mode represented by that willing acceptance of self-deception, of conscious illusion. It is small wonder, then, that Petrarch's own reply contains the statement: "vivus densque pereo" (p. 160).

This *amantum infame privilegium,* the mode of conscious adoption of illusion itself, in the *Canzoniere* then comes most clearly to the fore in three compositions, all of them canzoni, which are placed in close sequence at the center of the first part. In the first of them, *Se 'l pensier che mi strugge* (CXXV), which reads as a sort of prelude to CXXIX, there seems to emerge the concept of an illusion that is self-sufficient precisely because it knows that it is self-deceptive. We hear, therefore, no further questions, but, rather, a wise caution against more certainty which, in such a situation as the present one, may be of evil:

> Ovunque gli occhi volgo
> trovo un dolce sereno
> pensando: qui percosse il vago lume.
> . . . .
> Cosí nulla se 'n perde,
> et piú certezza averne fora il peggio. (66-68; 75-76)

The immediately following *Chiare, fresche et dolci acque* (CXXVI) in more ways than one represents a pendant to *Se 'l pensier che mi strugge*. Metrically, they are both intended to be "rustic" compositions,[16] but also in that deeper sense which—conversely to Augustine's *caveat* against solitude—sees in the simple life and in seclusion the most propitious environment that may be conducive to the imagination.[17] It is a

16. For a full discussion of the canzone's meter see Mario Fubini, *Metrica e poesia*. I. *Dal Duecento al Petrarca* (Milano, 1962), pp. 307 ff.

17. Rather indicative in this respect is that reference, in the *Secretum* (II, p. 120), to Avignon as "mestissimam turbulentissimamque urbem terrarum omnium." After all the shortcomings of city life have been cited in the following, Petrarch ends his part sarcastically with a quote from Horace: "I nunc et versus tecum compone canoros." From the same epistle of Horace (II, 6), even Augustine then quotes assentingly: "Silva placet Musis, urbs est inimica poetis." The concept appears in several of the *Metricae,* as it is often discussed in the letters. There are also many references to it in the *Canzoniere,* where *Solo et pensoso* (XXXV) is devoted entirely to a discussion of this aspect.

setting that *par excellence* allows for the monologizing so prevalent in these compositions. Thus, *Chiare, fresche et dolci acque,* after an initial invocation, reverts to a monological situation in which illusion freely reigns over the whole span of human experience from the past to the future: "Tempo verrà anchor forse / ch'a l'usato soggiorno / torni la fera bella e mansüeta" (27-29). An almost perfect symbiosis is reached between nature, the beloved, and the poet in the famous fourth stanza.[18] The all-pervading power of that illusion, however, is then analyzed in the last stanza where the distance is clearly perceived that separates the beloved of the illusion from the one of reality:

Cosí carco d'oblio
il divin portamento
e 'l volto e le parole e 'l dolce riso
m'aveano, et sí diviso
da l'imagine vera,
ch'i' dicea. . . . (56-61)

No matter which interpretation we give to this much debated passage, whether we conceive of *imagine vera* as the real Laura, distinct from that illusory and divine one (H. Friedrich), or as "vera opinione" (G. Leopardi[19]), or "realtà" (D. Ponchiroli), or merely as "nature": in all cases it represents a dimension different from that earlier illusion which is consciously perceived as such. That this gap is seen, and that the illusion realized as such is yet willingly sought is apparent from the last two verses of the stanza: "Da indi in qua mi piace / questa erba sí, ch'altrove non ho pace" (64-65).

Di pensier in pensier, di monte in monte (CXXIX) already in its opening verse aligns the concept of illusion and imagination with nature. It is significant that within the syntactic as well as tonal parallelism of that line the realm of illusion is yet conceded the upper hand, appearing, as it does, in first place in an *endecasillabo a maiore.* It is thus not only being accorded mere sequential precedence, but also that of stress in a *settenario tronco.* The atmosphere of solitude and reflection soon becomes one of torment and vexation when in the second stanza the question is raised as to whether a definite mending of the poet's ways

18. On the importance of this feature in the history of the motif see Hugo Friedrich, *Epochen,* p. 258: ". . . das Einswerden von Natur und Frau und Liebendem. Eine solche dreifache Durchdringung gab es nirgendwo in der Lyrik vor Petrarca."

19. Leopardi in his commentary speaks of being "diviso dalla imagine vera, cioè alienato dalla vera opinione, dal concetto vero." *Rime di F. Petrarca con l'interpretazione di Giacomo Leopardi* (Firenze, 1864), p. 121.

("questo mio viver dolce amaro," 21) may not eventually turn out to be ill-advised: "Forse anchor ti serva Amore / ad un tempo migliore; / forse, a te stesso vile, altrui se' caro" (22-24).

After this strongest, yet illusive argument against any change of the *status quo* has swept away all reasoning, the image of the beloved is promptly projected into nature ("et pur nel primo sasso / disegno co la mente il suo bel viso," 28-29). The poet is indeed aware of the deceptive aspect of this illusion, yet it is being recognized as a means to overcome all distance, of space and time, as well as of averse feeling; it is thus not rejected but actively pursued:

> sento Amor sí da presso,
> che del suo proprio error l'alma s'appaga:
> in tante parti et sí bella la veggio,
> che se l'error durasse, altro non cheggio. (36-39)

Stanza III then brings an almost rhapsodic enumeration of the diverse aspects this illusion takes, it re-emphasizes the familiar contention that the beauty of the beloved grows in proportion with the solitude of the environment, and in the end it testifies to that ensuing disillusion when reality takes over:

> I' l'ò piú volte (or chi fia che mi 'l creda?)
> ne l'acqua chiara et sopra l'erba verde
> veduto viva, et nel tronchon d'un faggio
> e 'n bianca nube, sí fatta che Leda
> avria ben detto che sua figlia perde,
> come stella che 'l sol copre col raggio;
> et quanto in piú selvaggio
> loco mi trovo e 'n piú deserto lido,
> tanto piú bella il mio pensier l'adombra.
> Poi quando il vero sgombra
> quel dolce error, pur lí medesmo assido
> me freddo, pietra morta in pietra viva,
> in guisa d'uom che pensi et pianga et scriva.

And yet, the last stanza nevertheless reaffirms that mode of conscious illusion that is conjured up again with the same promissory adverbial phrase of lingering hope with which it had been introduced in the second one:

> Poscia fra me pian piano:
> che sai tu, lasso? forse in quella parte

or di tua lontananza si sospira.
Et in questo penser l'alma respira. (62-65)

Thus, the canzone begins, and ends, with an affirmation of the principle of illusion against all realities. In between, there is articulated the complete course and evolution of this mode: the active search of illusion (disegno co la mente), the implicit recognition of that illusion as being deceptive (se l'error durasse), its conscious embracing (altro non cheggio), its variations (nel primo sasso; ne l'acqua chiara; sopra l'erba verde; nel tronchon d'un faggio), the disillusion (quando il vero sgombra quel dolce error).[20] Just as the second stanza had prepared the way for the mode of illusion with that promissory *forse,* thus the last stanza, by the same token and with the same adverb, denoting a state between full affirmation and explicit negation, reaffirms the dimension and mode of conscious illusion.

Di pensier in pensier is thus the most prominent, yet by far not the only example of this mode expressed as a viable solution of the poet's dilemma in the *Canzoniere.*[21] The concern with this mode is evident

20. The connection with *Met.* I, 6, is obvious. On the transformation of certain themes see Adelia Noferi, *L'esperienza poetica del Petrarca* (Firenze, 1962), pp. 221 ff. Especially p. 222: "In essa [*Met.* I, 6] troviamo appunto tutti i temi di quelle rime, ma disposti su quel fondo autobiografico e psicologico, che la poesia in volgare aveva interamente consumato . . . ."

21. As this aspect was traceable in the *Secretum,* so it is in the letters; and the *Familiari* in the single instances may prove in the end to be more reliable in witnessing the evolution of this mode of conscious self-deception, illusion. It is indicative that, even when reference to illusion is made in an entirely different context, the passage nevertheless establishes a connection, a parallel with amorous experience. Thus, in *Fam.* VII, 12, 5, to Giovanni dell'Incisa, where Petrarch deplores the death of Franceschino degli Albizzi, a young Florentine relative of his who at some time had been a house guest in the Vaucluse, the power of deceptive illusion is discussed with respect to the young man passed away recently. Yet, the passage then turns for a parallel to amorous experience as if it were the matrix for such situations: "Sed ego, iure quodam meo quod amantium omnium est comune, fictis congressibus atque colloquiis invise moras solabar absentie meque ipsum, ut fit, quadam cum voluptate fallebam." Then it proceeds to confirm the poet's own experience with that quote from Vergil's eighth eclogue, that appears also in the *Secretum* (III, p. 142): "An qui amant ipsi sibi somnia fingunt?"

The same procedure is followed in a letter to Francesco Nelli (*Fam.* XIII, 4, 8). The tenor of the letter is on the whole businesslike, but upon recalling Nelli's affectionate remembrance, Petrarch will borrow his imagery again from the realm of amorous experience: ". . . meque post Alpes ac maria plus quam linceis oculis, plusquam aprinis auribus insigni quodam et vulgato amantum privilegio **absentem absens audisque videsque**—imo vero ubilibet presens es—etsi te tacente nota sunt, michi iuvat tamen audire. . . ." This passage is interesting in more than one respect, for it resembles too closely the one in the *amor* discussion of the *Secretum* where Augustine passes in review possible remedies for his lovelorn interlocutor, chiding above all that selfsame *amantum infame privilegium:* "Ubicunque fueris, quocunque te verteris, relicte vultum et verba contemplaberis

throughout the whole work, yet particularly so in its first part. It may be expressed as an incidental recognition, as in the canzone *Poi che per mio destino* (LXXIII, 78): "E vivo del desir fuor di speranza," or in an almost prosy and matter-of-fact statement as in the canzone *I' vo pensando* (CCLXIV, 91-94), which equally leaves no doubt that its poet is aware of the delusive quality of his illusion and its aspect of make-believe: "Quel ch'i' fo veggio, et non m'inganna il vero / mal conosciuto, anzi mi sforza Amore, / che la strada d'onore / mai nol lassa seguir, chi troppo il crede." In other instances, an entire composition may be based on this mode of conscious illusion, as is the case with the sonnet *Beato in sogno* (CCXII), which derives its particular importance from the fact that it is also an "anniversary" composition. That is, the mode of conscious illusion being the theme of the poem, it is almost projected, as it were, into that span of "venti anni, grave et lungo affanno" (12). Moreover, the sonnet is fashioned almost entirely after proverbial phrases and has thus that inexorable and apodictic aura of the maxim about it as if to represent the poet's experience in a finite sense, and to reinforce the aspect broached in the opening lines: "Beato in sogno et di languir contento, / d'abbracciar l'ombre et seguir l'aura estiva."[22]

A last instance of the mode of conscious self-deception and illusion that should be pointed out here is the sonnet *S'amor non è* (CXXXII). In the two quatrains, a veritable battery of rationalizing rhetorical questions tries to pinpoint the cause of the poet's situation. Beginning in the first quatrain with a disquisition on the nature of love and its effects on the poet, in the second one the discussion moves on to probe the poet's own part in it:

S'a mia voglia ardo, onde 'l pianto o lamento?
S'a mal mio grado, il lamentar che vale?
O viva morte, o dilectoso male,
come puoi tanto in me, s'io nol consento?

The poet's own answer which is provided in the first tercet clearly

et, quod est amantum infame privilegium, illam absentem absens audies et videbis" (III, p. 166). There should be little doubt that this constitutes further evidence to uphold Hans Baron's thesis as to the later insertion of the *amor* discussion paragraph as it now stands in the *Secretum*. It would also supply us with a reliable *terminus ad quem* that would credibly attest to a revision of the *Secretum* as late as 1352, the date of Petrarch's letter to Nelli.

22. Although none of the commentaries refer to it, it does not at all seem implausible—*maxime iudicant aures*—that there may be an allusion to the final verse of Statius' speech at the end of *Purg.* XXI (133-136), as Petrarch here indeed "dismenta" (as had Statius) "nostra vanitate / trattando l'ombre come cosa salda."

points to his being a willing part in these happenings ("Et s'io 'l consento, a gran torto mi doglio," 9), and then proceeds to suggest that most ubiquitous image of *naufragio, naufragium,* so prevalent a symbol in all of Petrarch's work ("Fra sí contrari vènti in frale barca / mi trovo in alto mar senza governo," 10-11).

Petrarch himself has established here a connection with a symbol that by its own implications is intrinsically linked with the mode of conscious self-deception and illusion. In a letter to Lelio he once said: "Multum est, frater, vana expectatione liberari" (*Fam.* III, 20, 7). And yet, to discover not simply illusion, but its uses, to proceed from living with an illusion to objectively acknowledging and sanctioning it, is but a minor step. This minor step, however, implies a knowledge and an acceptance of defeat. And it is here that we see a close connection of this mode of illusion, consciously perceived as being deceptive yet retained as a viable alternative, with other aspects within that paronomastic web of the *Canzoniere.* For one, Phoibos Apollon, one of the implied pendants in that binomialism of *amor et gloria,* Laura and *lauro,* seems to enjoy his preeminent place in the *Canzoniere* not only because he is the God of the Muses, but also because one of his sacred trees was the laurel. Yet the laurel is not only the symbol of fame acquired through poetry, it is, also, the tree into which the nymph Daphne turned to spurn once and for all her suitor, and as such it is also a symbol of defeat. Thus, Phoibos Apollon is also an *exclusus amator,*[23] a rejected lover, as was indeed Petrarch himself.

There are yet further parallels. As Daphne's beauty grows with every step by which she withdraws and flees ("auctaque forma fuga est," *Met.* I, 530), so does distance enhance Laura's beauty ("et quanto in piú selvaggio / loco mi trovo e 'n piú deserto lido, / tanto piú bella il mio pensier l'adombra." CXXIX, 46-48), since every action by which Laura denies herself makes her more attractive (cf. the sonnet to Orso dell'Anguillara, XXXVIII). Furthermore, Phoibos Apollon would not simply—in the Ovidian version—accept his defeat and lay down his garland at the doorstep, as it were, of his spurning beloved. He would instead crown himself with the symbol of his defeat ("semper habebunt / te coma, te citharae, te nostrae, laure, pharetrae." *Met.* I, 558-9).[24] There would be no imprecations, no *paraclausithyron,* there would

23. On this concept see Frank O. Copley, *Exclusus Amator. A Study in Latin Love Poetry.* Philological Monographs Published by the American Philological Association, XVII (Baltimore, 1956).

24. This aspect of Apollo's crowning himself comes out even more clearly in the collection of the *Fabulae* that goes under the name of Hyginus, but actually dates from the second century A.D. It thus furnishes interesting criteria as to the

be, instead of the plea, a paean. There would be song and praise of the beloved. The selfsame psychological stance may be observed in Petrarch. His pleading with Laura throughout the first part of the *Canzoniere* is paradigmatically echoed in the sixth stanza of the sestina *A qualunque animale* (XXII), which reasserts the link with the Daphne myth:

> Con lei foss'io da che si parte il sole,
> et non ci vedess'altri che le stelle,
> sol una nocte, et mai non fosse l'alba;
> et non se trasformasse in verde selva
> per uscirmi di braccia, come il giorno
> ch'Apollo la seguia qua giú per terra.

There is, then, equally, the paean of Laura ("l'arboscel che 'n rime orno et celebro," CXLVIII, 8), best represented by the sonnet *Benedetto sia 'l giorno* (LXI) with its anaphora of praise and that most explicit last tercet:

> et benedette sian tutte le carte
> ov'io fama l'acquisto, e 'l pensier mio,
> ch'è sol di lei, sí ch'altra non v'à parte.

Among the multiple and divergent connotations originating within the realm of the Laura-myth, this is not one to be dismissed out of hand, although it has hardly received any attention.[25] There should be little doubt as to its representing a category of its own within the kind of polysemantic system any shrewd application of paronomasia will establish. Indicative with respect to the implied connection is the evidence furnished by the sonnet *Apollo, s'anchor vive il bel desio* (XXXIV), which conceives of the God's experience as being identical with that of the poet ("l'onorata et sacra fronde, / ove tu prima, et poi fu' invescato

---

development of taste and interpretation above all of mythological subjects. The respective passage in the *Fabulae* concerning our discussion reads: "Apollo Daphnen Penei fluminis filiam uirginem cum persequeretur, illa a Terra praesidium petiit, quae eam recepit in se et in arborem laurum commutauit. Apollo inde ramum fregit et in caput imposuit." *Hygini fabulae,* ed. H. J. Rose (London, 1934), p. 142.

25. Among the more recent studies on the subject should be mentioned Ugo Dotti, "Petrarca: il mito dafneo," *Convivium,* XXXVII (1969), pp. 9-23. The subject of myth is also discussed by Eberhard Leube, "Petrarca und die alten Götter. Zum Bild der antiken Mythologie in der *Africa* und im übrigen lateinischen Werk des Dichters," *Romanistisches Jahrbuch,* XI (1960), 89-107. Both of them, however, make no reference to the particular aspect of the myth we are pursuing here.

io," 7-8), and in an ambiguous fashion at that, since *invescare* carries with it the connotation of being caught as by bird lime.[26] On the other hand, both Laura and Daphne are identified in terms of the laurel which is, as has been pointed out earlier, not exclusively a symbol of fame for the purposes of the *Canzoniere* ("sí vedrem poi per meraviglia inseme / seder la donna nostra sopra l'erba, / et far de le sue braccia a se stessa ombra," 12-14). If there is some foundation to the assumption that the sonnet in question was to be the introductory poem in the first form of the *Canzoniere,* it was no doubt to stress this theme in a more salient manner than the subsequent arrangements let us surmise. The shift that obviously occurred from an emphasis on classical mythological subjects and their derivatives to a more religiously oriented whole is referred to by Petrarch himself in one of his letters to Francesco Nelli.[27] Nevertheless, the role of Phoibos Apollon in a system of paronomastic interdependencies with their multifarious meanings did not only lend itself as a most fruitful and polyvalent referent throughout the structured whole of the *Canzoniere,* and as a symbol and guarantor of that fame its poet aspired to, but also as a symbol of this poet's defeat in that most tenuous of human transactions which is love.

From such a vantage point we might perhaps also have a more enlightening look at the symbolic image already mentioned as recurring so often in Petrarch's writings, that of shipwreck. *Naufragium, naufragio,* indeed seems to be a parallel image to that of the *exclusus amator* in that it represents a situation that implies rationalization of the poet's

26. This image is used in the same derogatory sense and with similar ironic implications in relation to Dante by Beatrice in the scene where she presents him with the principle of repentance, *Purg. XXXI* (58-61): "Non ti dovea gravar le penne in giuso, / ad aspettar più colpi, o pargoletta / o altra vanità con sì breve uso. / Novo augelletto due o tre aspetta."

27. There Petrarch, with respect to this change in his orientation, says: "Ego non permittentibus solum sed plaudentibus Musis et secundo fieri rear Apolline, ut qui iuvenilibus iuventam studiis dedi, maturiorem etatem melioribus curis dem. . . . Denique sic statutum fixumque animo est, si ex alto dabitur, inter hec studia et has curas spiritum exhalare. Ubi enim melius possim aut quid agendo tutius hinc abeam, quam amando et memorando et laudando semper Eum, qui nisi me semper amasset, nichil penitus vel, quod minus est nichilo, miser essem, et si eius amor erga me finem habuisset, mea finem miseria non haberet? Amavi ego Ciceronem, fateor, et Virgilium amavi, usqueadeo quidem stilo delectatus et ingenio ut nichil supra . . ." (*Fam.* XXII, 10).

One cannot help but notice the parallel development in St. Augustine's *Confessiones* (I, 13), where he admits that he once cherished *poetica illa figmenta:* ". . . mihi erat . . . dulcissimum spectaculum vanitatis equus ligneus plenus armatis et Troiae incendium atque 'ipsius umbra Creusae'." But then comes the denouncing of those "venditores grammaticae vel emptores," and all they stand for, and later there will be that ironic reference to Cicero: "Perveneram in librum cuiusdam Ciceronis" (III, 4).

position. We are speaking here of course of instances where it is used in the context of the poet's amorous experience. As the *exclusus amatòr* is, in a sense, a *naufragato,* so the *naufragato* is, on the other hand, a rationalizer parallel to that cherisher of his own deceptive illusion.[28] As the unconditional acceptance of that illusion, recognized as deceptive, presupposes a process of rationalization that is aware of the premises as well as of their outcome, thus, from the vantage point of a precarious rescue, the *naufragato* ponderingly looks upon the perils and obstacles that were the cause of his foundering.

It is in this fashion that Petrarch had conceived of Vaucluse—in the *Metrica* to Giacomo Colonna (I, 6)—as his secure port from where to gaze out at the sea, cause of, and witness to, his failure; a place, also, where he could pander to his *atra voluptas* and live forever unperturbed in his illusion, because it was the seclusion and remoteness of the "chiusa valle" which alone allowed such fancy. The symbolic image of the broken oar, which the poet wishes to lay down at the votive altar, appears in this passage, followed by the description of Vaucluse, asylum and refuge, were he can recall and ponder the shipwrecks of his past:

> . . . . Comitantibus ergo
> his animum curis, dum singula mente revolvo,
> hoc procul aspexi secreto in litore saxum:
> naufragiis tutumque meis aptumque putavi:
> huc modo vela dedi; nunc montibus abditus istis,
> flens mecum enumero transacti temporis annos. (120-125)

Thus, the image of the storm on the high sea is symbolically linked to the poet's love and is also seen, therefore, in relation to his salvation. It depends on the nature of the sinner that little progress could ever be expected on the road toward that salvation. An early reference to the situation presents it already in the same terms as it will appear later in the canzone to the Virgin, last testimony to a situation that essentially had remained unchanged. Thus, already in 1331, in a short letter to Cardinal Giovanni Colonna, Petrarch confesses: "Me

28. It is this aspect that no doubt is one of the roots of that over-extensive use of oxymora, such as *dolce-amaro,* indicating two states that should be mutually exclusive, yet either of which can only be defined through the other and receive its particular meaning through it. Each complements the other in such a way that the particular frame of mind would be unthinkable, in the last analysis, if it did not contain an element of both. They would thus involve not a contradiction, but rather a *coincidentia oppositorum.*

scilicet, peccatorum meorum nodis[29] implicitum, nondum in portum potuisse confugere, sed in eadem tempestate, qua me discedens reliquisti iactatum, fluctibus herere" (*Fam.* II, 5, 6). The metaphor of the ship of life and the invariable and potential danger of shipwreck are therefore ever present in Petrarch's work. He was so obsessed by the theme (and its poetic potentialities) that he devoted one of the *Canzoniere*'s nine sestine entirely to the subject. Being one of the most complicated verse forms, the sestina's six recurrent rhyme words allow, and demand, utmost concentration and restriction, and their choice equally reveals the particular concern of the poet. In the case of *Chi è fermato di menar sua vita* (LXXX), it revolves in fact around a cluster of key words that indicate Petrarch's concern for salvation: *vita-scogli-legno-fine-porto-vela.* The mutual relations between them are obvious, and the close alignment of *vita-fine,* and *legno-porto,* seen in relation to the imponderables of *scogli* and *vela,* already gives an indication of the direction in which the sestina was planned to move. In comparison with the concern for the poet's salvation, the theme of his amorous involvement is not given extended treatment here, yet when it appears it is in that powerful symbolic correlation of wind (Laura) and fate:[30]

> L'aura soave a cui governo et vela
> commisi entrando a l'amorosa vita
> et sperando venire a miglior porto,
> poi mi condusse in piú di mille scogli. (6-10)

A passage in the *Secretum* shows that same concern for the poet's salvation, yet Augustine's reference to shipwreck in the discussion of *accidia* has almost the function of an *exemplum* that provides gratuitous experience:

Itaque velut insistens sicco litore tutus, aliorum naufragium spectabis et miserabiles fluitantium voces tacitus excipies; quantum ve tibi turbidum

29. This metaphoric use of *nodus* reappears also rather frequently in the poetry of the *Canzoniere.* Cf. CCLXIV, 82-83: "la mia barchetta . . . / è ritenuta anchor da ta' duo nodi?" LIX, 17: "non vo' che da tal nodo Amor mi scioglia." CCLXXI, 1-2: "L'ardente nodo ov'io fui d'hora in hora, / contando, anni ventuno interi preso."

30. In his discussion of the metaphor of the ship of life, and of state, in Greek thought, Viktor Pöschl concludes: "Damit eng verknüpft ist das metaphorische Band, das in der Vorstellung der Antike zwischen Wind und Schicksal besteht und in der Äneis mehrfach begegnet." *Die Dichtkunst Virgils* (Wiesbaden, 1950), p. 82. In the corresponding note, he mentions Petrarch's *Passa la nave mia colma d'oblio* (CLXXXIX), as "eine der mächtigsten Erneuerungen des antiken Symbols." Adelia Noferi, on the other hand, in connection with the *Secretum* passage points to the frequent occurrence of the image in religious literature, citing in particular S. Pier Damiani's *De Divinia Omnipotentia* (*L'esperienza,* p. 276).

spectaculum compassionis attulerit, tantum gaudii afferet proprie sortis, alienis periculis collata, securitas. (*Secretum,* II, p. 126)

Here is again implied that aspect of *securitas* which also represented an important element in the *Metrica* to Giacomo Colonna, yet it is a gratuitous *securitas* before the weathering of one's own storm which knows of failure only vicariously. When Petrarch later in his life, in a letter to Socrates in 1350, complained about the—real or imagined—loss of many of his friends, he would again return to the same image of shipwreck. But then, the experience of *naufragium* no longer was conceived as a potential one, and the letter begins by portraying him in the likes of one who, having escaped shipwreck, sits dry-eyed and without illusions on the shore, counting his losses:

Ut compressis aliquando gemitibus sedatisque suspiriis atque animi turbinibus, infracta voce siccisque oculis te alloquar, sic me audies quasi hominem naufragio elapsum fessum ve querimoniis, sedentem in litore, mestum quidem sed iam fletu abstinentem et parvas magne fortune reliquias recensentem. (*Fam.* IX, 2; 1)

The focus of the image varies slightly from what it was in the earlier *metrica* to Giacomo Colonna to more religious concerns in other, and mostly later, instances, conforming to the opinion expressed in the letter to Francesco Nelli. Yet it remains linked to the poet's amorous experience, and its major characteristic remains intact: that of a state of reflection on an experience which may be circumscribed by terms such as failure and defeat.[31] Thus the image of the *naufragato* as well as the concept of the poet abiding by deceptive illusion as a consequence of his reasoning, seem but two aspects of one and the same frame of mind. Central to both of them is the state of pondering, weighing, reflecting, mirroring. As Augustine had said: "Inventa sunt specula, ut homo ipse se nosceret" (*Secretum,* III, p. 184). It is in the sense of an ever-present warning, then, that the potentiality of *naufragium* is conceived, not so unlike that forever re-enacted nightly temptation by the snake in Dante's *Valletta dei principi negligenti.* But for Petrarch this is not quite the innocuous ritual yet; it still denotes an actual situation of which he is

31. In her discussion of the particular portents of *naufragium,* Adelia Noferi stresses the sense of relief imparted by it: "il piacere di un naufragio sofferto e superato" (p. 276), citing in support a passage from *De vita solitaria,* and sonnet XXVI, 1-4. In particular, she points to the chances of potential transformation the concept affords the poet: "Il 'presente' del *Secretum* e della *Vita Solitaria* non è in realtà che dolore, tempesta, naufragio . . . , ma da questo naufragio emergeranno le cose salvate dalla memoria, con quel di più di dolcezza che è dato dal saperle colme di un valore inestimabile per il fatto stesso di averle perdute; ed alla fine saprà che il solo modo per rendere dolce, prezioso quel 'naufragio' stesso, è di conservarlo, dorarlo, trasfigurarlo nella memoria" (p. 276).

the protagonist. Still in the last composition of the *Canzoniere,* addressing the Virgin as "di questo tempestoso mare stella" (67), Petrarch will conceive of himself as "in terribile procella," and "sol, senza governo." The boat of his life was still held back on the high seas by those selfsame two "nodi", as he had depicted it in *I' vo pensando:*

> Che giova dunque perché tutta spalme
> la mia barchetta, poi che 'nfra gli scogli
> è ritenuta anchor da ta' duo nodi? (81-83)

Petrarch had not unwittingly arrived at this state of affairs. It was almost staged, arranged, set, for him to probe the depths of his own psyche. And after all, his situation was not much unlike that created by the proposal which his precursor in the arts of renunciation, Phoibos Apollon, had made to Daphne: she was to flee with less speed, but he then, too, would reduce his own: "Moderatius, oro, / curre fugamque inhibe, moderatius insequar ipse" (*Met.* I, 510-511). Thus, the distance between suitor and pursued would be maintained unaltered, remaining the same as before in a situation of flight eternal: Daphne, in the last analysis, was never to be reached, as Laura was to remain a "princesse lointaine." Conscious illusion, then, was in effect to be an assurance of a distance that was willingly sought, though it was always measured against the woman in the flesh. It was entertained not because it would bring the poet closer to Laura, but because it insured that the distance between them would never be reduced—like that between the god and the nymph.

When, in October 1359, Petrarch wrote to Boccaccio that long letter from the countryside in Pagazzano, discussing the problems of *imitatio,* he mentioned that he had included unawares into his *Bucolicum carmen* a verse from the seventh book of Ovid's *Metamorphoses* which he wanted Boccaccio to replace in his copy by one of his own he sent along. As Petrarch checked his source, he certainly must have run through the preceding paragraphs and chanced upon those words of Medea's to Jason, after her decision to let him have the magic herbs: "Quid faciam, video: non ignorantia veri / decipiet, sed amor" (*Met.* VII, 92-93), and he must have found his own experience confirmed. But as surely as Petrarch was aware that he was abiding by an illusion, he also knew that this illusion had saved him not once, but twice, thus fulfilling a double purpose: reaching for the unreachable, yet never forcing him to prove to himself that what he had reached was but a most beautiful Fata Morgana. Because, in the final analysis, he did not want what he seemed to want, as his *alter ego* so aptly put it in that description of the eternal dilemma of lovers in the Secretum: "Volo, nolo, nolo, volo."

Having thus discovered the uses—and through them doubtless also the dangers—of illusion, Petrarch is perhaps not so much "primo infermo di un'infermità che corre attraverso tutto il mondo e la poesia moderna" (Croce), as a most sensitive man who had realized the potentials of a mode of living, an approach to aspects of reality, which later poets would not only sanction but consider indispensable to their respective philosophies. Realizations of this can be detected in beginnings in Lorenzo de' Medici's *Comento,* more profusely in Tasso's poetry, and then above all in the writings of that other cherisher of illusion, Giacomo Leopardi, who would maintain that illusions form part of the very system of this world, and that "tutto il reale essendo un nulla, non v'è altro di reale né altro di sostanza al mondo che le illusioni."[32]

32. Giacomo Leopardi, *Zibaldone di pensieri,* in *Tutte le opere di G. Leopardi,* a cura di Francesco Flora (Milano, 1961), vol. I, p. 126.

Leopardi's opinions on the merits of illusion are found above all in his *Zibaldone,* where he follows the debate from Theophrastus to Cicero's *De officiis* (*Zibaldone,* 316-318). Concluding his observations, he maintains: "Così si vede che appunto chi conosce e sente più profondamente e dolorosamente la vanità delle illusioni, le onora e desidera e predica più di tutti gli altri, come Rousseau, la Staël ecc." (*Zib.,* 318). Of interest here are of course especially those remarks which reflect upon illusion that has been perceived as deceptive, such as the following: "Le illusioni per quanto sieno illanguidite e smascherate dalla ragione, tuttavia restano ancora nel mondo, e compongono la massima parte della nostra vita. E non basta conoscer tutto per perderle, ancorché sapute vane" (*Zib.,* 213). And further: "Il più solido piacere di questa vita è il piacer vano delle illusioni" (*Zib.,* 51).

Judging from the remark he made on a verse of Tasso's ("E da l'inganno suo vita riceve," *Gerusalemme liberata,* I, 3): ". . . anzi può applicarsi ad ogni genere di viventi" (*Zib.,* 3761), he must have read other writers with an eye for the position they took with respect to illusion, yet his commentary on Petrarch's *Canzoniere* is singularly devoid of remarks in this respect. There are remarks in the *Zibaldone* on the relation of solitude to illusion (*Zib.,* 490), for example, but we would look in vain for a similar discussion in his commentary on *Solo e pensoso,* or *Di pensier in pensier.*

VIII

THE MYTH OF APOLLO AND DAPHNE IN PETRARCH'S *CANZONIERE*:

The Dynamics and Literary Function of Transformation

by Marga Cottino-Jones
University of California at Los Angeles

The rich complexity of the poetic texture in Petrarch's *Canzoniere* seems to derive from the significant interplay of traditional themes and characterizations with unusual forms and techniques of expression. This becomes evident in Petrarch's use of a suggestive and dynamic technique of literary rendition, which takes the form of a transformational process of Ovidian derivation. Through this process, any emotional as well as rational level of human experience is—for representational purposes—transferred onto another level of experience and thus externalized in terms of the natural environment. To visualize this concept, one may recall, for example, the sestina "Giovene donna sotto un verde lauro," where the beloved woman is emotionally rendered in terms of the natural environment as "duro lauro/ch'à i rami di diamante, et d'or le chiome" (XXX, 23-4); or the canzone "Ne la stagion che 'l ciel rapido inchina," where she becomes "una fera che mi strugge . . . che s'appiatta et fugge" (L, 40-2); or still again the sestina "L'aere gravato et l'importuna nebbia," where the poetic persona becomes one among the many elements of a winter landscape: "Et io nel cor via più freddo che ghiaccio/ò di gravi pensier' tal una nebbia,/qual si leva talor di queste valli,/serrate incontra agli amorosi venti . . ." (LXVI, 7-10).

The dynamics of this literary process of transformation and its poetic function in the total overview of the world of the *Canzoniere* is a problem still to be investigated fully in its many aspects.[1] In partic-

1. Some of the main works that touch on this problem are: D. Alonso, "La poesia del Petrarca e il petrarchismo: Mondo artistico della pluralità," *Lettere Italiane,* XI (1959), 277-319; T. Bergin, *Petrarch* (New York: Twayne, 1970); U. Bosco, *Francesco Petrarca* (Bari: Laterza, 1961); P. Camporesi, "Il tema dell' 'adynaton' nel *Canzoniere* del Petrarca," *Studi Urbinati,* XXVI (1952), 199-202; F. Chiappelli, *Studi sul linguaggio del Petrarca: La Canzone delle visioni*

ular, one aspect of this transformational technique, the one connected with the myth of Apollo and Daphne and the motif of the *lauro,* seems worthy of being singled out.[2] Clear references to the myth of Apollo and Daphne are to be found only in the part *In Vita* of the *Canzoniere,* with a higher frequency prior to LI than subsequently (V, VI, XXII, XXX, XXXIV, XLI, XLIII, LI, CXXXVIII, and CXCVII). The motif of the *lauro,* instead, appears in both parts *In Vita* and *In Morte,* although its frequency is higher in the former, where, in its many forms of *lauro, alloro, arbore, arboscello,* it appears connected, other than with poetic glory and the woman, with the myth of Apollo and Daphne in thirty-one compositions: V, VI, VII, XXIII, XXIV, XXVIII, XXIX, XXX, XXXI, XXXIV, XLI, XLIII, LI, LX, LXIV, LXVIII, CVII, CXIX, CXLII, CXLVIII, CLXI, CLXXXI, CLXXXVIII, CXC, CXCV, CXCVI, CXCVII, CCXXV, CCXXVIII, CCXXX, CCXLVI, CCLXIII. In the part *In Morte,* on the other hand, the *lauro* stands always for the woman and especially for her quality of perfect chastity in eleven compositions:[3] CCLXVI, CCLXIX, CCLXX, CCCXIII, CCCXVIII, CCCXXIII, CCCXXV, CCCXXVII, CCCXXXVII, CCCLIX, CCCLXIII. This pattern seems already to point out a clear development in the specific use made by Petrarch of both the myth and the motif; in fact, from an initial rendering of the mythological tradition in unqualified imitative terms, openly comparing the poetic persona's

(Firenze: Olschki, 1972); G. Contini, "La lingua del Petrarca," in *Il Trecento* (Firenze: Sansoni, 1953), pp. 93-120; G. Di Pino, "Poesia e tecnica formale nel *Canzoniere* petrarchesco," in *Stile e Umanità* (Messina-Firenze: G. D'Anna, 1957), pp. 33-63; F. Figurelli, "Le cinque canzoni centrali della prima parte del *Canzoniere* del Petrarca," *Annali dell'Istituto Superiore di sc. e lett. Santa Chiara di Napoli* (1957), 215-251; G. Herczeg, "Struttura delle antitesi nel *Canzoniere* petrarchesco," in "Petrarca e il Petrarchismo," *Studi Petrarcheschi,* VII (1961), 195-208; F. Neri, "Petrarca e le rime dantesche della Pietra," *La Cultura,* VIII (1929), 389-404; A. Noferi, *L'esperienza poetica del Petrarca* (Firenze: Le Monnier, 1962); A. Romanò, "I sonetti dell'aura," *L'Approdo,* II (1953), 71-78; N. Sapegno, *La poesia del Petrarca* (Roma: Bulzoni, 1970); A. Schiaffini, "Il lavorio della forma in Francesco Petrarca," in *Momenti di storia della lingua italiana* (Roma: Edizioni di storia e letteratura, 1953²), pp. 57-60.

2. This topic is present in the critical discussions of C. Calcaterra, *Nella selva del Petrarca* (Bologna: Cappelli, 1942) and in U. Dotti, "Petrarca: Il mito dafneo," *Convivium,* XXXVII (1969), 9-23.

3. The same seems to hold true also for verbs, such as *trasformare* and *cangiare,* that are more frequently used in the part *In Vita* than in that *In Morte,* as it is visible in the total of 12 (8 *trasformare* in 7 compositions and 4 *cangiare* in 4 compositions) in *In Vita,* and only 3 *cangiare* in three different compositions (CCCXLIX, CCCL, CCCLXI) in *In Morte.* See K. McKenzie, *Concordanze delle Rime di Francesco Petrarca* (Torino: Bottega d'Erasmo, 1969), Photolit. reprodution of 1912 edition.

love experience with Apollo's, the poet moves to a more complex handling of both myth and motif through a total involvement of human, natural, and supernatural elements. In this second phase, direct references to the myth of Apollo and Daphne tend to disappear and a still further process of development takes place: from a more general handling of the *lauro* as symbol of the transformed woman and thus of the transfiguration of reality into poetry or art, the poet arrives at a definite moralizing interpretation of the process of transformation from living flesh into unfeeling object, whereby the *lauro* represents virginity and total virtue in the woman (see especially CCCLIX).

This moralizing interpretation, however, is not new and goes back to anagogic explications of classical writers offered by medieval exegetes. In the case of Ovid's *Metamorphoses*, we know for sure that many commentators competed in the boldest moralizations of such a text, as is still visible, for instance, in John of Garland's *Integumenta Ovidii,* John of Virgil's *Allegoriae librorum Ovidii Metamorphoseos,* and the famous *Ovide moralisé.*[4] In John of Virgil's work, we read the following moralizing interpretation of Daphne's transformation:

9. Nona transmutatio est de Dane conversa in laurum. Allegoria est hec. Per Phebum intelligo pudicam personam et castam, per Dapnem ipsam pudicitiam quam insequitur casta persona. Per Danem converti in arborem intelligo quod pudicitia radicatur in corde illius qui insequitur eam. Per laurum signatur virginitas eo quod semper est virens et redolens. U. d. e.:

Ille pudicitiam sequitur pro posse fugacem. (sic)
    Qua tandem pressa rara corona datur. (sic)
Laurus odora virens designat verginitatem (sic)
    Nam viret et redolet virginitatis odor (sic)
Lubrica virginitas fertur de flumine nata (sic)
    Nam dilapsa semel non revocanda fuit (sic)
At si continuis servet quis passibus illam (sic)
    Tunc radicata est et viridente coma. (Lib. I, 9, 39-46)

Here we have a clearly allegorical interpretation of Apollo as a chaste being pursuing Daphne, who allegorically represents the virtue of chastity; her transformation into a laurel becomes the visual representation of the rooting of chastity in the heart of the person who pursues it, while the laurel itself is seen as the symbol of virginity, always green and fragrant.[5]

4. Johannes de Virgilio, *Allegorie librorum Ovidii Metamorphoseos,* ed. F. Ghisalberti, *Giornale Dantesco,* XXXIV (1929-31), 1-110; *Ovide moralisé, Poème du commencement du quatorzième siècle*... ed. C. De Boer (Amsterdam: Johannes Müller, 1915).

5. This same motif of the laurel rooted in the heart is to be found also in the *Canzoniere,* and specifically in poems CCXXVIII, CCLV, and CCCXVIII, where the laurel symbolizes the woman whose presence is deeply rooted in the poet's heart.

A very similar interest in moralizing upon the same fable is visible also in De Boer's "Summary to the First Book" of the *Ovide moralisé:*

> . . . Vient d'abord une "histoire," c'est–à–dire une explication réelle: Dane, fille du Penée, poursuivie par Apollon, est changée en laurier; cela veut dire que le soleil et l'humidité du fleuve Penée y font naître des lauriers. Mais peut-être une autre "histoire" est-elle préférable: il n'y a qu'à retrancher du récit ce qu'il a de merveilleux. Une jeune fille chaste, en fuyant un homme qui voulait lui faire violence, tomba d'épuisement et mourut au pied d'un laurier. Quant à la "sentence prouffitable" qu'on peut tirer du récit, la voici: Dane, fille d'un fleuve, c'est-à-dire douée d'un tempérament froid, représente la virginité; elle finit par être changée en arbre, parce que la parfaite pureté ne connaît plus aucun mouvement charnel, et cet arbre est un laurier, qui, comme la virginité elle-même, verdoie toujours et ne porte pas de fruit. Le rôle donné à Phébus est ici peu clair: l'auteur a suivi "l'integument," qui l'appelle "dieu de sapience;" mais la façon dont le commentateur latin se représente le rapport de ce dieu avec la virginité figuree par Daphné (sic) est obscure pour nous et l'a été pour son imitateur. Celui-ci ajoute d'ailleurs, de son cru, une "autre sentence": Dane représente la vierge Marie, aimée par celui qui est le vrai soleil; Apollon se couronne du laurier qui est Dane; c'est Dieu qui s'enveloppe du corps de celle dont il fait sa mère. (p. 56)

In this passage, the motif of transformation of living and mobile human flesh into a firmly rooted and unproductive element of nature and into an eternally immutable laurel is envisioned as the essential means to achieve eternal purity, which will remain such only through the elimination of all carnal instincts. Clearly religious implications are offered in the relationship of the character of Apollo to Christ, that of Daphne to the Virgin, and the image of the laurel to the crown of glory in Paradise.

In the fourteenth-century poem, these points, and particularly the close relationship between the laurel and virginity, are conveyed as follows:

> Dané, qui si isnelement
> Fuioit charnel atouchement
> Et puis fu en arbre muee,
> C'est: que cuer et cors et pensee
> Doit garder enterinement,
> Sans nul charnel esmouvement,
> Sans pensé de corruption
> Et sans nulle interruption,
> Qui veult estre vierge parfaite,
> Et lors sera elle arbre faite,
> Que nulz vens ne puet eslocier,
> Car si con li vens, pour hocier,
> Ne puet le fort arbre mouvoir,

Ne doit flescir ne esmouvoir
Vierge cuer en nulle maniere
Dons ne promesse ne proiere,
Qui tout sont vent de vanité,
A perdre sa virginité.
Dané fu muee en lorier
Plus qu'en chesne ne en cerisier
N'en nul autre arbre que l'en voie,
Quar si com li loriers verdoie
Et nul temps ne pert sa verdure,
Ne pour chalour ne por froidure,
Ains verdoie en toute saison
Sans fruit faire, ausi par raison
Doit virginitez verdoier
Et vivre sans fructefier,
Qu'onques n'avint ne n'avendra,
Qui viergement se contendra,
Qu'il puisse fere engendreüre,
Fors cele qui contre nature
Enfanta son pere et son mestre,
Dieu, qui de la Vierge volt nestre,
Qui sagement en charité
Gardera sa virginité,
Et parseverer i porra
Jusqu'a la fin. Dieus li donra,
En signe et en non de victoire,
En sa grant delitable gloire,
Coronne que les vierges ont
Qui ou ciel coronnees sont. (I, 3173-3214)

The pagan myth of Apollo and Daphne is seen here as a pre-enactment of the future myth of the Virgin, whose virtue made her worthy to give birth to Christ for the glorification of all mankind. The *Ovide moralisé* thus conveys a revealing example of the method by which, as late as the beginning of the fourteenth century, classical works were analyzed and interpreted in allegorical terms so as to make them acceptable to the Christian mentality in search of spiritual enlightenment.

The application of this moralizing approach to classical myths in Petrarch's *Canzoniere* testifies to the poet's "moralizing" intentions, particularly as expressed in the motif of the *lauro,* which he often connects with the myth of Apollo and Daphne. At the same time, the use of both devices seems to go beyond the merely didactic intentions of medieval exegeses, and these devices become, in fact, functional in contributing to the poetic essence of the world of the *Canzoniere*. Daphne, for instance, is the ever-escaping heroine, the feminine element eternally fleeing her suitor's amorous efforts to conquer her and thus destroy the uniqueness of her essential virtue and beauty. While Laura emerges as Daphne, the poetic persona, through this correspondence of characters and emotions, succeeds in objectifying his affections by rendering visually, in terms of the natural environment, his own desires and failures as well as the fluctuating occurrences of love and life. Furthermore, in the poetic texture of the work, the motif of the transformation of a fleeing creature into a fixed, rigid, solid substance, such as the tree from whose everlasting leaves poetic crowns are made, also creates another important image of mutation: from life into something immovable, eternal, ever-present—in other words, into art. The perfection of love cannot be reached through the fleeting movements of life, but rather in the immutability of poetry, symbolized by the evergreen leaves of the laurel. The myth of Apollo and Daphne and the motif of the *lauro* are handled in such a way in the *Canzoniere* as to convey these two important aspects of the process of transformation: the shift from motion to fixity, and the crystallization of life into poetry, which are so essential to Petrarch's poetic world.

It is the purpose of this study to investigate the literary function of the transformational technique involved in the Daphne myth and in the image of the *lauro* within the poetic texture of the *Canzoniere*. The main object of this research will be to identify the principal compositions where either myth or image—or both—appear and to emphasize their importance as dynamic forces functionally relevant to the rich complexity of Petrarch's poetry.

In sonnet V, "Quando io movo i sospiri a chiamar voi,"[6] we find the first mention of the *lauro* in connection with the myth of Apollo and Daphne, in a rather new interpretation of the *topos* of modesty, whereby the poetic persona's artistic endeavors are seen as the product of a "lingua mortal presuntuosa:"

> se non che forse Apollo si disdegna
> ch'a parlar de' suoi sempre verdi rami
> lingua mortal presumptuosa vegna. (V, 12-14)

In these verses a disdainful Apollo, possessor of the "sempre verdi rami" sung by the poet, gives the first clue for the interpretation of Daphne as LAU RE TA and viceversa. At the same time, Apollo's disdain for the poetic persona implies the presence of a rivalry between them both in love and in the poetic endeavor. Emulation of the god of poetry is an

6. All quotations are from G. Contini's edition of the *Canzoniere* (Torino: Einaudi, 1964).

ambitious task which will become more and more intriguing to the poet in his constant effort to reach out and possess those "sempre verdi rami," which slowly become the symbol of both love and poetic perfection. The relationship between the *lauro* and poetry, clearly implied for the first time in these verses, will be more and more frequently used in the *Canzoniere* as a poetic theme.

An identity between Laura and Daphne is also suggested in sonnet VI, "Sí traviato è 'l folle mi' desio" through the motif of flight, which, by being so intrinsically related to the theme of transformation, is essential to the myth of Apollo and Daphne. The woman is seen by her lover as being

> 'n fuga . . . volta,
> et de' lacci d'Amor leggiera et sciolta
> vola dinanzi al lento correr mio. (VI, 2-4)

The antithesis between the woman's swift flight and the lover's slow pursuit rests heavily on the power of *Amor:* the woman is free from the "lacci d'Amor" while her lover is "in signoria di lui." This contrast therefore conveys the theme of the inaccessibility of the woman and the lover's frustration. The motif of the flight and unsuccessful pursuit develops through the two quatrains and the first tercet of the sonnet, and it is only in the second and final tercet that, with no transitional explanation, the object of the pursuit appears suddenly transformed into the natural element of the

> lauro onde si coglie
> acerbo frutto, che le piaghe altrui
> gustando, afflige piú che non conforta. (VI, 12-4)

The outcome of the transformation—the *lauro* and the *acerbo frutto*—and the effects that the lover derives from the tasting of the *frutto* which "afflige piú che non conforta," seem to be of greater interest to him in this sonnet than the actual instant and phenomenon of the transformation itself. This must be related to the internal logic of this specific composition, in which the poetic attention is aroused by a mental and spiritual condition clearly specified as complex in the very first line, where both the adjectives *traviato* and *folle* convey the connotation of an unhealthy deviation of both soul and mind. This condition is then further investigated through an act of memory which projects the scene of the woman's flight and the lover's unsuccessful pursuit. This poetic situation recreated by memory provides, in effect, the core of the composition and is dramatized by the antithetical references to the woman "de' lacci d'Amor *leggiera* e *sciolta,*" who "*vola* dinanzi al *lento* correr" of the lover. The latter is held back by the *freno* of *Amor* under whose power he is doomed to remain until death. This poem thus evolves from the poetic persona's recollection of his own unsuccessful pursuit of the beloved woman. Both myth and image operate in these two sonnets on an imitative level based on a displacement through an act of memory, by which the poet sees himself as Apollo and the beloved woman as Daphne.

While in sonnets V and VI the "verdi rami" and the laurel are contemplated as non-dynamic symbols of impotence in the post-transformational period of immobility and passivity, sestina XXII, "A qualunque animale alberga in terra" presents in action the motif of transformation, forcefully prepared for by the dynamic contrast arising in the first five stanzas between the poet's individual situation and the world around him. While night brings peace to "qualunque animale alberga in terra" (1), be it man ("qual torna a casa") or beast ("qual s'anida in selva") (5), the poet, who never has "triegua di sospir' col sole" (10), cannot help but wander aimlessly "lagrimando, et disiando il giorno" (12). Furthermore, the transformation of human into natural elements is already foreshadowed through the vision of the poet as "facto di sensibil terra" (16), or as "un huom nudrito in selva" (17), or as "mortal corpo di terra" (23), or, finally, as transformed into "trita terra" (27) after death. On the other hand, as soon as the beloved though cruel woman is introduced, the transformation motif works openly: in fact, she is audaciously presented in non-human terms:

> Non credo che pascesse mai per selva
> sí aspra fera, o di nocte o di giorno,
> come costei ch'i' piango a l'ombra e al sole. (XXII, 19-21)

Here, the human quality is limited to the poet's crying, while the animal-like quality is emphasized—*pascesse, selva, aspra fera.* This clearly atypical human situation, developed against a totally natural background, prepares for the climactic sixth stanza, where all previous motifs are reiterated in order to highlight the process of transformation taking place:

> Con lei foss'io da che si parte il sole,
> et non ci vedess'altri che le stelle,
> sol una nocte, et mai non fosse l'alba;
> et non se transformasse in verde selva
> per uscirmi di braccia, come il giorno
> ch'Apollo la seguia qua giú per terra. (XXII, 31-6)

The aura of utter unreality is emphasized by the series of adynata with its repetitive use of the past subjunctive verbs *foss', vedess', mai non fosse, non se transformasse,* which imply only hypothetical possibilities. Also, the time category, moving from evening ("da che si parte il sole") through night ("sol una nocte") to the impossible dream of a dawn which never comes ("et mai non fosse l'alba"), underlines the exceptionality of the situation, and prepares for the sudden transformation of the woman "in verde selva" and the climactic leap in time and experience brought about by the dramatic insertion of the Apolline myth into the poet's personal love situation:

come il giorno
ch'Apollo la seguia qua giú per terra. (XXII, 35-6)

Here the woman, transformed symbolically into Daphne, acquires a mythical reality outside any boundary of time, just as alive and eternally unreachable in the "then" time of Apollo's pursuit "qua giú per terra," as she is in the "now" time of the poet's attempt to hold her in his arms for fear "se transformasse in verde selva." Moreover, in his involvement with such a mythical creature in her everlasting natural essence, the poetic persona, too, participates in another reality, and becomes himself a projection of Apollo in his double function of disappointed lover and impassioned poet. In this way, the transformational motif presented in this last stanza, besides representing the climactic poetic moment for which all the other stanzas of the sestina have been preparing, succeeds in creating a mythical atmosphere of mysterious interrelationships where human qualities are infused into natural elements, human subdivisions of time are overcome in an eternal present, and human beings are absorbed into superhuman conditions. This whole poem, then, actually constitutes one of the most successful examples of the complex and fascinating climate of the *Canzoniere,* consisting of a synchronization of the various levels of experience therein infused—the human-emotional, the natural, and the super-human-mythical. The purely imitative use of the myth of Apollo and Daphne is thus surpassed in favor of a more complex rendition of the poet's love experience now involving a many-faceted form of reality.

The same seems true of canzone XXIII, "Nel dolce tempo de la prima etade," probably written in 1333 or even earlier, but re-elaborated many times afterward, thereby proving once more that Petrarch, from the time of his youth, was interested in the metamorphosis motif inspired by Ovid. The initial move towards a total vision of eternal mutation is given here by a new rendition of the transformational process in relation to the *lauro*; that is, by the poetic persona's own transformation into "un lauro verde/che per fredda stagion foglia non perde" (39-40). The transformation of the lover into the beloved person is characteristic of the process of love, restated also in sonnet LI, "Poco era ad appressarsi agli occhi miei,"[7] and, more specifically, in the *Trionfo d'Amore*, where the "amante ne l'amata si trasforma" (III, 162). To fall deeply in love, thus, is almost to transform oneself into the beloved person: the poetic persona of the canzone is overcome by his great passion and this first moment of overpowering love is symbolically rendered by his transformation into the green laurel which in turn symbolizes Laura, the beloved woman, in all her virginal beauty and poetic glory:

Amor . . .
prese in sua scorta una possente donna,
. . . .
e i duo mi trasformaro in quel ch'i' sono,
facendomi d'uom vivo un lauro verde
che per fredda stagion foglia non perde. (XXIII, 22-40)

As such, this transformation represents the initial moment of all the cyclical changes in natural or animal form which, in response to the force of love, the human element, the "uom vivo" undergoes, in Ovidian terms: first, into "cigno," the swan symbolic of poetic song; then, into "sbigottito sasso," emphasizing the fixity of an object paralyzed by love; then again, into "una fontana a pie' d'un faggio," conveying the compassionate, elegiac mood of tears; later on, the lover is split in two—his body hardened into a natural element such as "dura selce," and his soul etherealized into air like a "scossa voce"; and, finally, he is swiftly camouflaged as a "cervo solitario et vago," to be eventually immobilized forever under "la dolce ombra" of "il primo alloro," which closes the series of transformations in a perfected circle. Each transformational moment seems to be connected with either the presence of the beloved

7. Another mention of the same process is to be found in this sonnet, which provides some points of comparison with canzone XXIII, specifically in relation to two moments of the transformation, that is, the change of the poetic persona into the woman and then into a stone; and in both cases, bringing the transformation one step further. In fact, while in the canzone the first change is presented in the process of taking place, here in the sonnet it is given as already completed: "non posso trasformarmi in lei / piú ch'i' mi sia" (5-6). As to the second change, the transformation is precisely defined in terms of specific stones:

di qual petra più rigida si 'ntaglia
. . . . sarei,
o di diamante, o d'un bel marmo biancho. (LI, 7-9)

woman as an essential object of the landscape, or her absence. The presence of the woman seems to create, at least in three of the four cases where it occurs, constant fixity and rigidity of reaction in the lover: she has a Medusa-like influence on him. In fact, the first, third, and fifth metamorphoses into *lauro, sasso,* and *dura selce,* prove it. The absence of the woman, instead, provokes the lover into unceasing movement in search of her, as proved by the metamorphosis into *cigno* and *fontana.* The introduction of the swan for the second metamorphosis, with its mythological connotations of sorrow, implies that the further effects of the woman's absence are tears, lamentations, unhappiness, and vain search:

> Né meno anchor m'agghiaccia
> l'esser coverto poi di bianche piume
> allor che folminato et morto giacque
> il mio sperar che tropp'alto montava:
> ché . . . .
> . . . . solo lagrimando
> là 've tolto mi fu, dì e nocte andava,
> ricercando dallato, et dentro a l'acque;
> . . . .
> ond'io presi col suon color d'un cigno. (XXIII, 50-60)

Everything here suggests a new sentimental scenery: before, in the vision of the *lauro verde,* there was immobility and silence; now, since the cause of fixity has disappeared, immobility is replaced by wandering movement in search of the lost love, and silence by resounding lamentations and loud mourning. A change in color is also observed in the transformation of the *lauro verde* into the *bianche piume* and the *color d'un cigno;* the color white indicates a condition of tragic sorrow bordering on death, implied further on in the expressions "anchor m'agghiaccia," "folminato et morto giacque/il mio sperar," and "solo lagrimando," with their connotations of frozen solitude and despair. In these connotations of frozen rigidity, the previous element of fixity externally conveyed by the *lauro* is internalized into a spiritual and emotional rigidity which foreshadows the next metamorphosis and the return to an external form of rigidity and fixity conveyed by the *sasso.*

The same elegiac tone of tearful lamentation predominates, then, in the following scene, portraying the further wanderings of the lover-swan, singing "in sí dolci o in sí soavi tempre . . . gli amorosi guai." (64-5) The mood, however, dramatically changes with the sudden reappearance of the woman, whose complex, sentimental essence is rendered in the oxymoron "la dolce et acerba mia nemica." (69) At the same time, the drastic effect of her presence on the lover-swan is dramatically portrayed through her taking away the lover's heart, by which action his falling prey once again to passionate love is powerfully stressed. Furthermore, with the implication of stealing conveyed in the line "Questa che col mirar gli animi fura," the second act of the transformational scene is introduced; that is, the re-enactment of the Batto story (Ovid, *Met.*, II, 685-707):

> Poi la rividi in altro habito sola,
> tal ch'i' non la conobbi . . .
> ed ella ne l'usata sua figura
> tosto tornando, fecemi, oimè lasso,
> d'un quasi vivo et sbigottito sasso. (XXIII, 75-80)

A more complex form of transformation is here taking place: first, in the woman, who appears "in altro habito" and then, "ne l'usata sua figura/ tosto tornando," strongly suggests a comparison between the figure of Mercury in the Batto story and herself; secondly, in the lover, who is transformed into "vivo et sbigottito sasso." This connotation of human feeling ascribed to the stone by the two qualifying adjectives *vivo* and *sbigottito,* maintains the implication of change from animate to inanimate objects, which is further strengthened by the effect and power that the woman still has on the lover-*sasso* whom she "tremar . . . fea dentro a quella petra." (82) This prepares the ground for the following transformational scene of the *petra* back into a human being, unable, however, to use his voice since his "vive voci . . . erano interditte," (98) and compelled to manifest his feelings only by writing: "ond'io gridai con carta et con incostro." (99) The motif of wandering and lament is evoked by another moment of solitude so as to prepare the scene for a new transformation:

> Ed io non ritrovando intorno intorno
> ombra di lei, né pur de' suoi piedi orma
> . . . .
> . . . . . . sentí' me tutto venir meno,
> et farmi una fontana a pie' d'un faggio. (XXIII, 108-117)

This change into an inanimate element, endowed however of a connotation of motion due to the running quality of water, seems to preserve in the transformed object the fundamentally human qualities of sensibility and movement, while the objectified condition everywhere suggests a tendency towards immobility and rigidity. Eventually the alternation between a fixed condition and a wandering one is coordinated in the combined transformation of the lover's "nervi e l'ossa . . . in dura selce" (137-8)—conveying fixity—and of his soul into "scossa/voce . . . de l'antiche some" (138-9), suggesting the wandering of a "spirto doglioso . . . per spelunche deserte et pellegrine" (141-2).

The whole transformational move is thus stimulated through constant change: from a vegetative element (the *lauro*), to an animal (the *cigno*), to an objectified form (the *sasso*), to a fluid natural object (a *fontana*), to the coordinated vision of (1) fixity in *dura selce*—combining the objectified quality of the *sasso* with the vegetative one of the *lauro*—and of (2) motion in *scossa voce*—which transposes into air the quality of fluidity contained in the *fontana* image—and, finally, to the *cervo solitario et vago,* which relates, in its animal substance, to the *cigno* of the second transformation, thus preparing in this mirrored pattern for the return of the lover-*lauro* to the *lauro* whose "dolce ombra/ogni men bel piacer del cor mi sgombra." (168-9) The vision therefore closes on the same image which had opened the poem, thus creating a circular cycle of transformation.

Many powerful images and figurative as well as rhythmical constructions are used in the texture of this canzone in order to convey more subtle suggestions of transformation, such as "allor che folminato et morto giacque/il mio sperar che tropp'alto montava" (52-3); or "ond'io presi col suon color d'un cigno" (60); or "tremar mi fea dentro a quella petra" (82); or "ma fui ben fiamma ch'un bel guardo accense" (164). Furthermore, one can notice a conscious use of specific verbal devices which repeatedly stress the process of transformation in action. The verb *trasformare* itself is used twice in the canzone: (1) at the very beginning of the process (when the poetic persona is the object of the transformation), so that it triggers the whole series of mutations to follow: "e i duo mi *trasformaro* in quel ch'i' sono" (38); and (2) at the end, in order to stress the last scene of the mutation (where the poetic persona has become the agent of his own transformation, thus relating himself totally to the natural world around him): "et in un cervo solitario et vago/di selva in selva ratto *mi trasformo*" (158-9). Verbs synonymous with *trasformare* are found in specific dramatic moments of the canzone in order to underline changes in the poetic mood, as well as within the poetic persona. Such is the case with the statement made at the initial moment of poetic recollection

> I' dico che dal dì che 'l primo assalto
> mi diede Amor, molt'anni eran passati,
> sí ch'io *cangiava* il giovenil aspetto; (XXIII, 21-3)

where the category of time is conveyed through the verbal form *cangiava* in a poetic language congenial to the general transformational mood of the canzone.[8]

Furthermore, we find similar uses in the first transformation of the poetic persona—into a *lauro verde*—which is dealt with more amply than the others through the abundant use of verbal devices stressing each individual facet of the transformational process taking place. The verb *fare* with the meaning of *trasformare* is used twice: (1) "facendomi d'uom vivo un lauro verde" (39), and (2) "i capei vidi far di quella fronde" (43). Other synonyms of *trasformare* are used in "i piedi . . . *diventar* due radici" (45-7) and " 'n duo rami *mutarsi* ambe le braccia" (49); finally, the fixed condition of the transformed self is rendered with the image "la *trasfigurata* mia persona" (42). There are, therefore, six verbal expressions used in order to specify this single transformation of the poetic persona into a *lauro verde,* while for the following six transformations—into *cigno, sbigottito sasso, fontana, dura selce, scossa/ voce,* and *cervo solitario et vago*—only eight verbal devices in all are employed: two for the transformation into *sbigottito sasso*—offering *fare di* with the meaning of *trasformare in:* "fecemi . . . d'un quasi vivo et sbigottito sasso" (79-80) and the bold expression *spetra:* "Se costei mi spetra" (84)—one for the transformation into a fountain—"e *farmi* una fontana a pie' d'un faggio" (117)—one for the mutation into a tree—"i nervi et l'ossa/mi volse in dura selce" (137-8)—one past participial form for the metamorphosis into a voice—"e cosí *scossa/* voce rimasi *de* l'antiche some" (138-9)—one for the restoration to human form—"ritornai ne le terrene membra" (145)—and two for the transformation into a deer:

> i' sentí' *trarmi de* la propria imago
> et in un cervo solitario et vago
> di selva in selva ratto *mi trasformo.* (XXIII, 157-8)

It is evident from the preceding discussion that the technique of transformation is essential to the poetic world of this canzone. At the same time, among the many transformational scenes, the prominence accorded to the metamorphosis of the poetic persona into a *lauro* is particularly significant in that it opens and closes the transformational cycle and the canzone itself and is richly endowed with stylistic devices functional to the poetic context of the work. The technique of transformation, and especially the motif of transformation into a *lauro verde,*

8. On the special use of time in the *Canzoniere,* see G. Caione, *Il sentimento del tempo nel Canzoniere del Petrarca* (Lecce: I.T.E.S., 1969).

are the key elements which move the poetic action into a spiralling world of changes. The image of the *lauro,* while hinting at the thematic combination of *lauro*=woman=poetic fame, works specifically to convey the conflict of the transient and ever-fleeting quality of human feelings (and particularly of human passion) with the aspiration to perfection and immutability.

The motif of the *lauro* is also an important constituent of the emblem poem "Giovene donna sotto un verde lauro" (XXX).[9] Through the abundant use of adjectives relating to the lauro—"verde lauro" (1), "dolce lauro" (16), "duro lauro" (23), "vivo lauro" (27), "ben colto lauro" (36)—the internal motivation for creating a parallelism between woman and *lauro* appears, first in affective terms, with the identity between woman=*dolce lauro* and *vivo lauro*=love; and then in visual terms, with a parallelism between woman=*duro lauro* and *ben colto lauro*=poetry.

Here the theme of transformation is embedded in the motif of the *lauro,* which is presented in a post-transformational condition as animated by the emotional energy of the lover, through whom woman, natural landscape, and cyclical time become one. This is clearly implied in the third sestet:

> o colle brune o colle bianche chiome,
> seguirò l'ombra di quel dolce lauro
> per lo piú ardente sole et per la neve,
> fin che l'ultimo dí chiuda quest'occhi. (XXX, 15-9)

Here the use of adjectives is the stylistic means for visually portraying the transformational process: the passage from *brune* to *bianche chiome* stresses the mutation of the lover's personal time from youth to old age, and eventually to death, as suggested in the line "fin che l'ultimo dí chiuda quest' occhi." This line concludes the sestet with a very powerful image: the *occhi,* which in the first three stanzas pertain directly to the lover, relate to the woman in the fourth and fifth stanzas, and eventually, in the sixth stanza, to the future readers of the poem. The first action that involves the lover's eyes is the vision of the woman and the everlasting fascination she radiates: "mi piacquen sí ch'i' l'ò *dinanzi agli occhi*/ed avrò sempre" (5-6), so that the *occhi* here imply the woman's unremitting hold on her lover's life. The second time the image of the eyes appears, it is in the context of the extraordinary effect of such a vision, which is conveyed through the powerful sequence of adynata stressing impossible

9. For a discussion of this poem, see also R. M. Durling, "Petrarch's 'Giovene donna sotto un verde lauro,'" *MLN,* 86 (1971), 1-20.

changes in the woman-*lauro,* in the lover, and in nature:

> Allor saranno i miei pensieri a riva
> che foglia verde non si trovi in lauro;
> quando avrò queto il core, asciutti gli occhi,
> vedrem ghiacciare il foco, arder la neve. (XXX, 7-10)

Finally in the last line of the third sestet, a vision of death is implied through the image of the *occhi* ("fin che l'ultimo dí chiuda quest'occhi"). The image of the *occhi,* thus, in its connection with the lover, has conveyed the full life cycle of the love experience, from the birth of love, through a lifetime of unrequited, sorrowful love, until the very moment of death.

In the following two stanzas, the rhyme word *occhi* no longer relates to the lover, but is connected in three instances with the woman's physical beauty. In line 19—"Non fur già mai veduti sí begli occhi"—the beauty of the woman is precisely identified with the *begli occhi,* a traditional cause of the birth of love in the poet, and at the same time a connecting element between woman and lover in the general connotation of the love vision implied by the same image in both contexts. Lines 26-27—"con vera pietà mi mostri gli occhi/l'idolo mio, scolpito in vivo lauro"—bring out the same hypothetical mood already conveyed in lines 7-10, in the context of the many adynata used therein, and propose therefore a restatement of the lover's helpless condition. The last appearance of the image related to the woman in the congedo—"vincon le bionde chiome presso agli occhi"—stresses again the dominating motif of the woman's beauty, which is the prime cause of her lover's suffering and eventual death, previously mentioned in line 18. Even in the cases when the image of the *occhi* relates to the woman, its main function in the poetic context is to reformulate the three essential steps of the lover's life story as previously conveyed by the same image in connection with his love experience. The man's love and the woman's beauty are thus correlated through the same motif of the *occhi,* which appears constantly in dynamic connection with the changing world of nature that forms the backdrop of this love story. The lover will in fact always have his woman "dinanzi agli occhi . . . ov'io sia, in poggio o 'n riva" (5-6), while his hypothetical desire to put an end to his sorrow and have "queto il core, asciutti gli occhi" (9) corresponds to the impossibility of phenomena such as "ghiacciare il foco, arder la neve" (10). Eventually the lover will follow "quel dolce lauro/per lo più ardente sole et per la neve,/fin che l'ultimo dí chiuda quest' occhi" (16-18). This last correlation seems to create the appropriate context for the insertion of the lover's personal experience of love and death into the eternal natural process of seasonal time, expressing a sentimental-mythical correspondence between "ardente sole," or summer, and his love and "neve," or winter, and his death. This correspondence is further stressed in the last stanza, where the lover precisely describes for the last time his own emotional condition in terms borrowed from the natural world:

> Dentro pur foco, et for candida neve,
> sol con questi pensier', con altre chiome,
> sempre piangendo andrò per ogni riva,
> per far forse pietà venir negli occhi
> di tal che nascerà dopo mill'anni. (XXX, 31-5)

Here the same image of the *occhi,* presented in the context of the lover's personal experience of love and sorrow, with a dynamic leap towards the future, introduces into the world of the poem a new human dimension in the future, unidentified audience of human participants in the love story herein narrated. In this way the personal experience involving the lover and his woman becomes projected also onto a universal, human time-category, which provides it with a wider human perspective. The correlation, thus, of the image of the *occhi* with all these different motifs here points—even more clearly and precisely than in the previous poems—to the close relationship between a personal and a universal view of love as well as to that between the cyclical mutations of natural phenomena and the lover's personal mutations in life.

To return to the central third sestet of the poem and to its transformational theme, the adjective *dolce* is here the clue for the emotional animation of the image of the *lauro.* This stresses the already accomplished metamorphosis of the woman into the *lauro,* which will be hinted at again in a similar way later on in the vision of the *vivo lauro* (27), and will be recreated in the gem imagery of the following sestet in terms of colorful preciosity "a pie' del duro lauro/ch'à i rami di diamante, et d'or le chiome" (23-4). This last example of visual imagery in terms of precious gems gives this poem its emblematic quality, further stressed by the colorful representation given in the congedo:

> L'*auro* e i *topacii* al *sol* sopra la *neve*
> vincon le *bionde* chiome presso agli occhi
> che menan gli anni miei sí tosto a riva. (XXX, 37-9)

The woman is here reinstated from her previous condition of *vivo lauro* in her womanly attributes of *bionde chiome* and powerful *occhi,* whose beauty is superlatively activated in terms of precious visual imagery with the "auro e i topacii." At the same time, the continuous transformational process of the poetic persona's love experience is visually rendered through the naturalistic suggestions of a seasonal cycle implied especially in the expression "al sol sopra la neve." Also suggested in this last line is a close antithetical relationship which tightly connects the woman's personal time of eternal coldness opening the poem ("non percossa dal sol molti et molt'anni") and the lover's own personal time experience of eternal slavery of love which closes the poem with a further implication of death ("che menan gli anni miei sí tosto a riva"). The category of time thus endows the lover's own personal experience with a cyclical relevance built upon the woman's mythical time experience, as well as upon the seasonal cycle of nature. Furthermore, the myth of Daphne is here still working through the image of the *lauro:* a Daphne visualized not in movement, in fleeing race, but rather in her post-transformational condition as an untouchable creature of pure and precious beauty that the poetic persona can approach only by projecting his love and torment towards a future of eternal poetic achievement.

The same interconnection between human and natural world is present in sonnet XXXIV, "Apollo, s'anchor vive il bel desio," where also the element of mythical time is introduced to underline the connection between the poet and Apollo, both visualized in their everlasting *desio* for "l'amate chiome bionde" (3) and "l'onorata et sacra fronde/ ove tu prima, et poi fu' invescato io" (7-8). The identity between Apollo and the poet is here maintained both on the level of the "amorosa speme" and on the one of poetic inspiration which is here conveyed in terms of natural description figuratively implying the desert of the mind through expressions such as *pigro cielo, tempo aspro et rio,* and *vita acerba.* The poem closes on a conceivably positive vision of the woman, suggesting a return of beauty and love, as well as a potential recuperation of poetic inspiration:

> sí vedrem poi per meraviglia inseme
> seder la donna nostra sopra l'erba,
> et far de le sue braccia a se stessa ombra. (XXXIV, 12-4)

This poem develops further the dramatic connection between Apollo and the poetic persona, discovered in the sestina "A qualunque animal alberga in terra" (XXII) and later on amplified in sonnets XLI and XLIII, and especially in CLXXXVIII dedicated to "Almo Sol."[10] It also revealingly discloses the pattern of intercommunication between the

10. See C. Segre's reading of this poem in M. Corti and C. Segre, *Metodi attuali della critica in Italia* (Torino: ERI, 1970), pp. 328-330.

human and the natural worlds so clearly conveyed in sestina XXX, "Giovene donna sotto un verde lauro." In fact, the vision of the woman in the first line of that sestina reappears in the last two lines of this sonnet, where "la donna nostra" is viewed in more active terms as if to emphasize her own willful intention to become what she actually is: to wit, she is portrayed in the self-activating process of transforming herself into that same tree that she already symbolically represents: "e far de le sue braccia a se stessa ombra."

Another rendering of the presence of the *lauro* is to be found in sonnet LX, "L'arbor gentil che forte amai molt'anni," where the interconnection between the tree and poetic inspiration is again strongly stressed, and the transformation of the *lauro* from *dolce* to *spietato* causes creative impotence in the poet.

In all these last compositions (XXXIV, XLI, and LX), the poetic interest focuses on a post-transformational time and object, and especially the close dependence of poetic inspiration upon the already transformed *lauro*. The same holds true for another poem, "Se voi poteste per turbati segni" (LXIV), where, however, the *primo lauro* is seen as deeply rooted in the poet's heart—so as to imply an internalization of the woman's entity into the most intimate essence of her lover's personality. One cannot speak of transformation here; at the same time, also in this case both the woman and her lover's most human element—his heart—are rendered in terms of the natural world: "gentil pianta in arido terreno" (9). The presence of the woman as *altera fronde,* strictly connected with artistic inspiration "di cui conven che 'n tante carte scriva," (4) is visible again in sonnet LXVII, "Del Mar Tirreno a la sinistra riva," where the natural world becomes again the backdrop for the sorrow and solitude of the poetic persona in love.

Up to this point, while tracing the theme of transformation in the *Canzoniere,* we have noticed two specific moments in its development: one that is present in V, VI, XXII, XXIII, and XXX, where the process of transformation is carefully analyzed and a total interaction of human, natural, and often supernatural worlds is dynamically conveyed; and the other, present in XXXIV, XLI, XLIII, LX, and LXIV, where the poetic interest is focused on the post-transformational period and on the influence which the transformed *lauro* has on the creative inspiration of the lover.

The next moment, developing later, after a good number of poems where the lauro motif does not appear, will offer a still different perspective. After a mention of the *lauro* as symbol of the beloved woman eternally present in the lover's mind in "Solo d'un lauro tal selva verdeggia" (CVII, 12), and a brief vision of the *verde lauro* as the image of poetic fame presented to the poet by the personification of glory—"di verde lauro una ghirlanda colse,/la qual co le sue mani/ intorno intorno a le mie tempie avolse" (CXIX, 103-5)—a new outlook on the *lauro* and its *frondi* is conveyed by sestina CXLII, "A la dolce ombra de le belle frondi." In the first four stanzas, the *leggiadri rami* and *verdi frondi* stand for the poetic persona's love experience projected on a nocturnal background made of *poggi, erbe, rami, selve, sassi, campagne,* and *fiumi.* The *lauro* represents the youthful time of love, "quel primo tempo" (9) when no other interests existed for the lover but finding refuge under the "ombra . . . de la pianta piú gradita in cielo" (11-2) and, if obliged to depart, returning "devoto ai primi rami" (22). In line 26, "quanto è creato,/vince et cangia il tempo," the category of time is introduced to justify also the change the lover is undergoing, and by which he plans to "fuggir gl'invescati rami" (29) and choose "altro sentier di gire al cielo" (35). The poetic persona thus is here implying a need for a change of love as well as of life experience, while using the same kind of imagery constantly employed in the depiction of his former situation:

> Altr'amor, altre frondi et altro lume,
> altro salir al ciel per altri poggi
> cerco, ché n'è ben tempo, et altri rami. (CXLII, 37-40)

The lauro thus becomes an object of the past, inasmuch as in its quality of immutability it has become obsolete and unfitted to coexist with the constant changes taking place in the world around it. In fact, time, in its everchanging movements, influences all natural elements and their emotional human coordinates, as suggested in "l'aura amorosa che *rinova* il tempo," (5) or in "né già mai ritrovai tronco né frondi . . . che non *mutasser* qualitate a tempo," (16-8) or again in "Selve, sassi, campagne, fiumi et poggi,/quanto è creato, *vince et cangia* il tempo," (25-6) etc. Only the lauro is immutable in its post-transformational condition of everlasting *verdi frondi* and *primi rami.* These adjectival qualifications, *verdi* and *primi,* point out the dynamic conflict between the *lauro's* condition of eternally youthful unchangeability (derived from its supernatural transformation) and the lover's emotionally youthful involvement, bound to change with the natural course of human life. The uniqueness of the *lauro* is thus once more stressed in this composition where it alone remains unchanged by the powerful influence of time. It is as if once the post-transformational time has set in, no mutation is expected any longer for the *lauro,* and even its poetic function seems to change.

The appearance of the expression "invescati rami" (which will return also in CXCV, "Di dí in dí vo cangiando il viso e 'l pelo" in the same context of changing time and interests, as well as in CCXI, "Voglia mi sprona, Amor mi guida e scorge," where the lover's heart "s'invesca" in the *lauro's* branches) conveys a moralistic implication suggestive of a spiritually sterile love to be found also in the poet's desire to follow "altro sentier di gire al cielo/et di far frutto, non pur fior' et frondi." From now on, then the image of the *lauro,* static and sterile, appears mostly in conjunction with a memory of youthful love (i.e., CXLVIII, "Non Tesin, Po, Varo, Arno, Adige et Tebro," or CLXXXI, "Amor fra l'erbe una leggiadra rete," or CLXXXVIII, "Almo Sol, quella fronde ch'io sola amo," or CXCV, "Di dí in dí vo cangiando il viso e 'l pelo," or CXCVII, "L'aura celeste che 'n quel verde lauro," or still CCXLVI, "L'aura che 'l verde lauro e l'aureo crine"), or with an inspirational view of the *lauro* as symbol of poetic glory (as in CLXI, "O passi sparsi, o pensier vaghi et pronti" and CXC, "Una candida cerva sopra l'erba"). Eventually, in two other compositions, the two connotations of youthful love and poetic fame are clearly conveyed together. In CCXXVIII, "Amor co la man dextra il lato manco," the *lauro* is directly visualized inside the lover's heart: "Amor . . . piantòvi entro in mezzo 'l core/un lauro verde," as already suggested in LXIV, introducing thereby a convention typical of thirteenth-century poets, for whom the woman's presence is constantly recreated inside the lover's heart. What is new here is the technique employed, consisting exclusively of natural imagery which also plays an important rôle in the spiritual qualifications of the woman herself:

> Fama, Honor et Vertute et Leggiadria,
> casta bellezza in habito celeste
> son le radici de la nobil pianta. (CCXXVIII, 9-11)

The same combined connotation is particularly vivid in sonnet CCLXIII, "Arbor victorïosa trïumphale," where the *lauro* is clearly represented as "honor d'imperadori e di poeti" and at the same time intimately linked to the lover's own personal history of love and sorrow: "quanti m'ai fatto dí dogliosi et lieti/in questa breve mia vita mortale!" (3-4). Here again the vision of immutability is stressed, especially in the representation of the woman's virtue, which reminds us of the moralizing interpretation of the Daphne myth of earlier times:

> L'alta beltà ch'al mondo non à pare
> noia t'è, se non quanto il bel thesoro
> di castità par ch'ella adorni e fregi. (CCLXIII, 12-4)

It is revealing that on this final note of intimate correlation between fame and chastity, combined in the image of the *lauro,* the part *In Vita* of the *Canzoniere* ends.

In investigating thus the literary function of the myth of Apollo and Daphne and the image of the *lauro* up to this specific point in the *Canzoniere,* it has become evident that both devices work dynamically in the poetic context every time that the sentimental experience of the poetic self is projected towards a more universal form of life, which includes the cyclical alternation of natural forces. The myth and the image actively animate the poetic context in a poignant interaction of human, natural, and even supernatural energies. This poetic mood, however, is short-lived. The poet tends increasingly to close in on a more intimate view of his sentimental experience, and while the openly active myth of Daphne nearly disappears, the image of the *lauro* is reduced more and more to an almost completely spiritualized connotation. This trend continues to its extreme consequences in the part *In Morte.*

In this section of the *Canzoniere,* the *lauro* is introduced less frequently, and only in order to symbolize the beloved woman, as in CCLXIX, "Rotta è l'alta colonna e 'l verde lauro," where the lamentations for the loss of the poetic persona's *doppio thesauro* are the mourning sounds of a deprived soul, who finds potential relief only in the memory of a past that will never return. This is clearly intimated in canzone CCLXX, "Amor, se vuo' ch'i' torni al giogo antico," where the woman with all her in-life qualities returns momentarily in the dream vision of her lover, and through memory is reborn to poetic life in a mythical springtime return of love and nature:

> . . . la sua vista dolcemente acerba,
> la qual dí et notte piú che lauro o mirto
> tenea in me verde l'amorosa voglia,
> quando si veste e spoglia
> di fronde il bosco, et la campagna d'erba. (CCLXX, 64-8)

The presence of death, however, brings back the reality of solitude and sorrow at the end of the poem, where the poetic self's personal situation is precisely recreated in clear-cut descriptive terms:

> Morte m'à sciolto, Amor, d'ogni tua legge:
> quella che fu mia donna al ciel è gita,
> lasciando trista et libera mia vita. (CCLXX, 106-8)

The same conflict between a nostalgically remembered, dream-like past and a present of loneliness and silence, recurs in CCCXVIII, "Al cader d'una pianta che si svelse," and especially in CCCXXVII, "L'aura et l'odore e 'l refrigerio et l'ombra." Here all positive implications are connected with the presence of the *lauro,* and "sua vista fiorita" in the past is antithetically compared with the present status of things where the lover is deprived of its presence and confines himself to a poetic hymn for its *memoria eterna* (14). A similar experience is voiced in CCCXXXVII, "Quel, che d'odore et di color vincea" with a more intense tone of intimate affection in the verses

> dolce mio lauro, ove habitar solea
> ogni bellezza, ogni vertute ardente, (CCCXXXVII, 5-6)

which convey a note of more personalized melancholy.

The more traditionally Christian image of the *lauro* as symbol of chastity reappears in three other compositions of the *In Morte* section. The sonnet CCCXIII, "Passato è 'l tempo omai, lasso, che tanto," in the general vision of death and disappearance of the most beloved features of the woman—such as " 'l viso sí leggiadro et santo" (5) and "i dolci occhi" (6)—presents the image of the woman's triumph "in cielo/ornata de l'alloro" (10-1)— a neat preamble for the *Trionfo della Pudicizia.* The mention of the "rami santi/ . . . d'un lauro giovenetto et schietto" (25-6) in canzone CCCXXIII, "Standomi un giorno solo a la fenestra," brings about the same metaphorical connotation of chastity and holiness, found also in canzone CCCLIX, "Quando il soave mio fido conforto," where it is interpreted in its symbolic meaning by the woman herself as she appears in the dream-vision of the lover. The woman is here seen holding two branches—"Un ramoscel di palma/et un di lauro" (6-7)— whose meaning she explains:

> vinsi il mondo et me stessa; il lauro segna
> trïumpho, ond'io son degna,
> mercé di quel Signor che mi die' forza. (CCCLIX, 50-2)

The presence of the *lauro* is thus intimately connected with the virtue of chastity embedded in the character of the woman, who becomes herself the direct judge and interpreter of her own personal moralizing experience. With this final restatement made by the woman-*lauro* of her own spiritual essence, the presence of the image of the *lauro* recurs no further in the *Canzoniere.*[11] It has worked in the poetic texture of the poems towards two rather different functions in respect to two fundamentally diversified moods: one which inspires effectively the first one-

11. *Lauri* appears once more in a generalized vision of death and decay in sonnet CCCLXIII: "spenti son i miei lauri, or querce et olmi" (4).

seventh of the compositions (roughly the first fifty), and the other, the remainder. In accordance with the mood of the first poems where both myth and image appear, the everchanging, fleeting characteristics of love and life are almost exclusively signified through those two poetic devices, both of which denote the transformation of a human being into the *lauro,* from an ever-moving creature in flight into a rigid and immutable element of nature. In this first moment, the accent is essentially on the motif of change, as if the poet's main interest were captivated by the fascinating, instantaneous process of a universal condition of eternal change. In all the following compositions, instead, in accordance with a more internalized mood of spiritual analysis, the focus is on the post-transformational time, on the eternally unchangeable image of the transformed *lauro* and its essential symbols of artistic fame (connected with the poetic persona) and of immutable chastity (connected with the woman). The *lauro* becomes then the only image capable of connecting the two main characters of the love story narrated in the *Canzoniere:* it projects their relationship onto a spiritual level thus providing a poetic solution to the irreconcilable conflict between love and chastity, between desire for fame and Christian virtue. The fixity of the *lauro* becomes in this way essential in the human world of natural change which provides the backdrop for the poetic action, since it is only through the immutability of virtue that mortal love can be transformed into spiritual love, and the *lauro* can triumph over the uncontrollable forces of the constantly changing world of nature and man.

If we consider now the *Canzoniere* as a whole and what its poetic essence might be, a basic pattern of antithetical relationships seems to emerge. There are in fact two protagonists, the poetic persona and his beloved woman, each of them representing a specific aspect of love, conflictingly related to one another: the former's based on a natural desire, the latter's articulated around a spiritual and virtuous aspiration to heavenly love. These antithetical forms of love point, in turn, to two different directions in life, that is, life on earth versus life in heaven. Love, moreover, in its natural form, shows a tendency to conflicting experiences, such as happiness versus sorrow, hope versus despair, illusion versus reality, peace versus war, serenity versus anguish, desire versus sense of guilt, etc. In addition, the poetic self's personal experience develops around central conflicts in so far as his need for poetic communication is sometimes poignantly projected outward into the world of nature, while at other times it is more soberly directed to the intimacy of the self. As important components of the poetic context, the main themes of time and memory also move on a constantly conflicting path, now recuperating the past with a bold repossession of human experiences—otherwise lost for ever, and now extending towards an undefined future, as dreams and hopes unfulfillable in the reality of the present. Cyclical recurrences, then, project all these conflicting trends onto a natural world context and, in so doing, discover revealing correspondences within the human world of the poetic self.

Dynamic conflict thus being the core of the poetic essence of the *Canzoniere,* and change, or at least attempts at change, being the dramatic outcome of conflict, our inquiry into the literary function of transformation becomes relevant also in the discussion of the problem of poetic essence. Through the analysis of the process of transformation offered in these pages, the basic conflict between the two protagonists has been visualized, as well as the antithetical correspondences between the aspects of love and life that each represents. The transformational process into natural, animate and inanimate elements which the poetic self and the woman undergo in some of the compositions discussed here, serves to dramatize the conflicting experiences created by the activating power of love. Furthermore, the occurrences of the image of the *lauro,* symbolizing sometimes a nostalgic desire for a delightful, amorous past, and sometimes a moralizing view of a spiritually enlightened future, convey in a clearly visual form the intriguing play of time and memory as projected through the interiorized complexity of the poetic self. To close, the rendition of human conflicting experiences in terms of the natural world that is realized through the dynamic technique of transformation—as experienced in the myth of Apollo and Daphne and in the image of the *lauro*—is also particularly relevant inasmuch as it conveys in visual form the basic antithetical pattern that is constitutive of the poetic essence of the *Canzoniere.*

IX

PETRARCH AND THE ART OF THE SONNET*

by Christopher Kleinhenz
University of Wisconsin (Madison)

For centuries the sonnet has remained the most popular and the most difficult poetic form in Western literature. The reasons for its predominance are many, and they vary according to the literary tastes of any given age. Nevertheless, poets and critics alike are generally agreed on one point: in the long history of the sonnet Petrarch is the first master of the form. The 317 sonnets that provide the form and essence of the poetic *corpus* of the *Canzoniere* are without doubt one of the finest literary legacies ever bequeathed to mankind. In their attempts to define the excellence of the Petrarchan sonnet, critics praise it for its precision and compactness, for its graceful symmetry and vibrant musicality, and for its noble sentiments and intimate tones. Indeed, in the sonnet Petrarch was able to capture the lyrical quality of his desires and aspirations, to express his internal conflict between love and reason and his simultaneous quest for earthly glory and spiritual salvation, and to compress the rhetorical intensity of moral and political invective.

However, recognition of Petrarch's success with the sonnet has tended to obscure more than one hundred years of pre-Petrarchan poetic activity and creativity in Italy. From 1220, the approximate date of the invention of the sonnet by Giacomo da Lentino, a notary attached to the Imperial court of Frederick II in Sicily, to the third decade of the fourteenth century, when Petrarch first began composing his lyrics, many metrical experiments had taken place and several poetic schools had flourished, each leaving its mark on the literary tradition. In fact, during the period of its origins, the sonnet does possess certain formal and thematic characteristics that anticipate its subsequent development in Italy. Even among the earliest examples, there are traits similar to those that characterize Petrarch's poetry: diversity of subject matter, formal and thematic divisions within the structure, and general artistic sophistication. The excellence of the "Petrarchan" sonnet may be viewed, in part, as the fulfillment of those elements that were present in this form ever since its invention.

* This paper was presented in a slightly different form at the Ninth Conference on Medieval Studies, Western Michigan University, Kalamazoo (May, 1974).

Leaving aside the debatable question of origin,[1] let us consider the few certain facts about the sonnet. The earliest form had fourteen hendecasyllabic lines and was divided by rhyme into two quatrains (or four couplets) and two tercets (or three couplets), either with an alternate scheme throughout (ABABABAB CDCDCD) or with a variation in the tercets (CDE CDE). It is remarkable that today, 750 years after its appearance, the sonnet still has the same basic form. Even more remarkable is that a fixed form emerged at all, for in the Romance literatures there were, with the exception of the *sestina,* no established strophic patterns for the composition of *canzoni, ballate, contrasti,* and so on. At this time, a poet's greatness was measured by his virtuosity, by his originality in the invention of a suitable vehicle for the expression of his thoughts. In terms of artistic creativity, then, the *discordo* must have been one of the most exceptional with its constantly changing meters, rhymes, and strophic patterns. How could the sonnet compete with such formidable opponents? How could a poet restrict his expression to a mere fourteen lines, use the metrical scheme that countless others had employed, and still be "original"? Perhaps, given the fixed form, "success" with the sonnet should more properly be measured in terms of the poet's ability to overcome this "structural disadvantage." Or, the argument could run, because of extensive experimentation in the Duecento and early Trecento, the sonnet form did not remain stable at all. Indeed, in this early period, the sonnet, through its adaptability of form and versatility of content, reveals its potentiality as a mode of poetic expression. On the one hand, we have numerous metrical and structural variations (the disposition of rhymes in quatrains and tercets, *sonetti caudati, doppi, doppi caudati, rinterzati* and *raddoppiati*).[2] On the other hand, we see the sonnet used as the means of communication and for debates (cf. the Provençal *tenso*) and as the basic strophic unit for longer narratives (*Il fiore*) and shorter *corone* (Folgóre da San Gimignano, Cenne da la Chitarra, the so-called *casistica amorosa.*) Moreover, although love was the most popular theme, the sonnet was frequently used for the treatment of moral topics (cf. the Provençal *sirventés*) and philosophical or theological arguments. The traditional rhetorical figures and technical devices were successfully employed in the superficial adornment of the sonnet, embellishments that contributed to the inseparable unity of form and content: *traductio, derivatio, replicatio, amplificatio,*

1. For a good overview of the several theories, see Ernest Hatch Wilkins, "The Invention of the Sonnet," in *The Invention of the Sonnet and Other Studies in Italian Literature* (Roma: Edizioni di Storia e Letteratura, 1959), 11-39.

2. For examples of these modifications in form, see Raffaele Spongano, *Nozioni ed esempi di metrica italiana* (Bologna: Pàtron, 1966).

anaphora, antithesis, internal rhymes, and so on.

Although courtly in origin, the sonnet is the only lyric successfully employed by writers from every social class. Moreover, its many transformations reflect the intense creative activity flourishing in the Italian cities, and, because of its adaptability and versatility, the sonnet emerges as the most important poetic form of the period, the one which mirrors and synthesizes the various contemporary literary tendencies and cultural movements. It would seem, then, that the sonnet fulfilled at least one major goal of these early poets: the creation of a distinctly Italian verse form that would be a viable mode of poetic expression. Moreover, I would suggest that the invention of the sonnet was motivated to a large extent by Giacomo da Lentino's conscious desire to create a uniquely Italian form to rival the excellence and supremacy of the *canzone* and its predecessor, the Provençal *canso*.

While these traditional forms were praised for the difficulty and novelty of their structure, the sonnet, because of its relatively fixed form, contradicted this concept of beauty or originality and proposed, through example, new standards or criteria for excellence. This resulted in the gradual shift of emphasis from form to content and in the seeming paradox of poetic fluidity in metrical fixity. This does not mean, of course, that there was no longer any interest in the form *per se,* for, as I mentioned earlier, the thirteenth century was perhaps the greatest experimental period in Italian literature. Rather, the content was raised to the artistic level of the form, so that the one could complement the other.

To define the art of the sonnet is tantamount to writing the literary history of this period, for such a study would entail the examination of every sonnet by every poet and the consideration of all other pertinent information. Included would be such diverse subjective factors as the poet's general preparation and cultural heritage, his poetic sensibility, and his idea of poetry, as well as the more objective technical elements: metrics, rhymes, themes, images and language. While I can offer no comprehensive definition of the art of the sonnet, I would like to present here some preliminary findings of my investigation.

The sonnets under examination treat the same theme: the poet's remembrance of the first meeting with his lady. I have purposely restricted the subject so as to be able to comment significantly on the diversity of treatment and to demonstrate the essential similarities and, to a lesser extent, the differences in their technique. Moreover, I believe the analysis will show that the art of the sonnet varies according to the poet's general conception of the nature and/or purpose of poetry, a problem that depends ultimately on the complex relationship between the poet, his subject matter, and his intended audience.

Generally speaking, medieval poets conceived poetry as a rhetorical exercise directed toward a specific and immediate audience for the attainment of some pre-established end. Poetry was purposive and incorporated the arts of rhetoric and grammar to accomplish its end. For example, the love lyric was intended to convince the lady of the sincerity of the poet's affection and to persuade her to grant him her love. By describing the benefits to be derived from martial combat, the poet hoped to persuade the reader to undertake a similarly noble activity. In both cases, the poem, although the vital means of expression and communication, is merely the rhetorical adjunct, the linguistic instrument that assists in the pursuit and attainment of a specific end. For most sonnets of the Duecento, the recipient of the poem and its intended audience are the same; thus, the poem remains on the immediate, personal level.

With these three guiding principles in mind (technique, intention, audience), we shall begin our examination by considering the following example by Giacomo da Lentino, the inventor of the sonnet:[3]

Lo giglio quand'è colto tost'è passo,
da poi la sua natura lui no è giunta:
ed io, dacunque son partuto un passo
4 da voi, mia donna, dolemi ogni giunta,
perchè d'amare ogni amadore passo,
in tanta alteza lo mio core giunta:
così mi fere Amor, lavunque passo,
8 com'aghila quand'a la cacc[i]a è giunta.
Oi lasso me, che nato fui in tal punto,
c'unque no amasse se non voi, Chiù-gente!
11 Questo sacc[i]o, madonna, da mia parte:
in prima che vi vidi ne fui punto,
servi[i]vi ed inora[i]vi a tutta gente,
14 da voi, bella, lo mio core non parte.

We are immediately struck by the technical virtuosity, manifested in the play of *traductio,* the equivocal rhymes which inform both the structure and the meaning of the sonnet with uniformity (the same word) in diversity (the different meanings of the words): the poet's single devotion to his lady is expressed through diverse external allusions (the plucked lily, the eagle swooping down on its prey). Metrically, the sonnet divides into two parts, 8—6 (ABABABAB CDECDE). According to meaning, the quatrains may be divided into what could be called "personal" and "impersonal" groupings: the similes drawn from na-

3. Bruno Panvini, ed., *Le Rime della scuola siciliana* (Firenze: Olschki, 1962), 43.

ture open and close the quatrains and comment upon the condition of the poet, which is expressed in the central four verses. As the lily parted from its stem withers and dies, so the poet separated from his lady, his source of life and inspiration, is wracked with pain. As the eagle seizes its victim, so Love inflicts wounds upon the poet. With regard to the quatrains, the "containment" of the necessary personal commentary within the allusive external images reflects the vital, organic nature of the poet's love for his lady, the love which necessarily stems from the external form of his lady.

The content is mirrored in the form. The complementary notions of violence, that of tearing apart (the lily) and bringing together (the eagle) bind the quatrains together as a unit and perhaps also comment on the poet's anguish, whether near or far from his lady. The physical suffering causes the poet to lament his state in vv. 9-10, where we note the use of the Provençal *senhal* (*Chiù-gente*) and, more important, the phrase *nato fui,* which would seem to declare the ever-present, never-changing nature of his love: he was *born* to suffer with love for her. Moreover, although the images in the quatrains allude to the death of the lily and the eagle's victim as facts of nature, here the poet's affirmation that he was born *in tal punto* would serve to emphasize that his condition, one of death in life, is an exception to this universal law. It could also be said that the poet owes his very life to the lady, if *in tal punto* were interpreted to mean *at that precise moment* when he fell in love with her. The equivocal *punto* in v. 12 would make the two verses parallel: thus, *nato fui* and *in prima che vi vidi* would refer to the same moment. The last four verses of the tercets reveal the steadfast love of the poet, who ever since his first meeting with the lady has served and honored her; in fact, his life is one of complete dedication, a faithfulness reinforced by the final declaration that his heart will not stray from her.

The sonnet, then, has run its course, coming around full circle to the introductory image of the separation of lily from stem, lover from lady, a hypothetical separation which the reader now understands to be an impossibility. The violence of the quatrains culminates in the lament, which opens the tercets and then dissolves in the tranquillity of the poet's life of service to his lady. While not becoming individualized, the tone is highly personal throughout; the poet remains anonymous behind his beautiful and ornate mosaic of words and sentiments. Art here is the poet's means of self-expression and personal communication with his immediate audience, the lady. The poem serves in its traditional rhetorical function: the main figure in this egocentric profession of love-service to his lady, Giacomo, as the troubadour, hoped to convince her of the sincerity and desperate nature of his love, in order to reap his reward.

The second example comes from the poetry of Guido Guinizzelli, to whom Dante affectionately referred in the *Divine Comedy* as his literary father (*Purgatorio* XXVI, 97-99) and who is generally considered the originator of the "Sweet New Style." The sonnet *Vedut'ho la lucente stella diana,* while lacking the artificial embellishments of the first, nevertheless possesses an extraordinary power and achieves a remarkable effect through its rhymes.[4]

Vedut'ho la lucente stella diana,
ch'apare anzi che 'l giorno rend' albore,
c'ha preso forma di figura umana;
4 sovr'ogn'altra me par che dea splendore:
viso de neve colorato in grana,
occhi lucenti, gai e pien' d'amore;
non credo che nel mondo sia cristiana
8 sì piena di biltate e di valore.
Ed io dal suo valor son assalito
con sì fera battaglia di sospiri
11 ch'avanti a lei de dir non seri' ardito.
Così conoscess'ella i miei disiri!
chè, senza dir, de lei seria servito
14 per la pietà ch'avrebbe de' martiri.

On a first reading, the sonnet would appear to divide thematically as it does metrically: the quatrains devoted to praise of the lady's beauty, the tercets to her effect on the poet. The first verse contains the three major themes of the sonnet (and perhaps of Guinizzelli's entire poetic *corpus*): the contemplation of the lady (*Vedut'ho*); her luminescence (*lucente*); and her extra-terrestrial nature (*stella diana*). The progression in the rhyme words in the quatrains is striking: *diana* → *umana* (the transformation from the divine to the human); *albore* → *splendore* (from the soft light of dawn to the brilliance of a goddess in her majesty); *grana* → *cristiana* (from red as an earthly color to its Christian symbolic value as *caritas*); *amore* → *valore* (the potentiality of love transferred to its effective power over other beings). It is this final movement from *amore* to *valore* that leads directly, both thematically and structurally, into the tercets, introduced by the dramatic *ed io,* which captures fully the notion of turning in both form and content. Also worthy of note is the type of *coblas capfinidas* repetition of *valore* to aid the transition between quatrains and tercets.

4. Gianfranco Contini, ed., *Poeti del Duecento* (Milano-Napoli: Ricciardi, 1960), II, 469.

The poet is so overwhelmed by the fullness of his lady's beauty and power that he can only emit sighs, while remaining rapt in her presence. This contemplative pose of the poet recalls the first verse of the sonnet that set into motion the entire chain of events: gazing on the star that becomes the lady who completely holds his attention. As the quatrains, the tercets reveal a progression in the rhymes: *assalito* → (*non*) *ardito* → *servito* (from the initial assault to the humble acquiescence to the hoped-for reward); *sospiri* → *disiri* → *martiri* (from the outward manifestation of his torment to the inner desires that he harbors to the combination of the two as complete martyrdom). The second tercet opens with the silent outburst of the poet, who earnestly wants his lady to know his inner desires, but who will remain silent in her presence. The poet's imploration is charged with emotion and interrupts the evenness of the verses, the calmness of the narration, as the emphatic *ed io* had done in v. 9. While the quatrains are characterized by a smoothness of diction, a harmony in themes and concepts, each tercet begins in a forceful manner, with a violence that is then muted in the subsequent two verses. Although the intent is the same here as in the first sonnet, the manner of argumentation has changed radically: the emphasis has been shifted from the poet's anguish to his almost selfless praise of the lady's beauty and virtue. The poet, whose emotions are sublimated into idealistic adoration, shares the spotlight with his lady. Art is still understood as the means of personal communication between the poet and his lady, although its more direct function as a vehicle of self-expression has diminished.

We should preface our remarks on Dante's *Di donne io vidi una gentile schiera* by remembering that the author himself in the *De vulgari eloquentia* classified the sonnet as being an inferior lyrical mode.[5]

Di donne io vidi una gentile schiera
questo Ognissanti prossimo passato,
e una ne venia quasi imprimiera,
4 veggendosi l'Amor dal destro lato.
De gli occhi suoi gittava una lumera,
la qual parëa un spirito infiammato;
e i' ebbi tanto ardir ch'in la sua cera
8 guarda', e vidi un angiol figurato.
A chi era degno donava salute
co gli atti suoi quella benigna e piana,
11 e 'mpiva 'l core a ciascun di vertute.

5. *De vulgari eloquentia,* II, iv. The edition of the sonnet follows Contini, ed., Dante Alighieri, *Rime* (Torino: Einaudi, 1965), 72-73.

> Credo che de lo ciel fosse soprana,
> e venne in terra per nostra salute:
> là 'nd'è beata chi l'è prossimana.

The only technical feature that strikes the reader is the equivocal rhyme (or is it, in fact, identical?), *salute,* in vv. 9 and 13. The first quatrain presents the scene, a group of ladies on All Saints' Day, and then focuses on the lady who comes first, accompanied by Love. The second quatrain is an interesting study in the transformation of the light from the lady's eyes: from a ray of light (*una lumera*) to a burning spirit (*un spirito infiammato*) to an angel (*un angiol figurato*). In fact, in the process the lady herself has assumed a dual nature: woman and angel. Although the quatrains end with the poet in rapt contemplation of the lady, the tercets begin with his turning his gaze to those with whom she comes in contact, noting the effect she has on them. The second tercet centers once again on the lady from the personal perspective of the poet, who then comments on her universal mission (to give beatitude to man) and her immediate beatific effect on the ladies in her company. With this conclusion, we are transported to the beginning of the sonnet and realize that in the space of a mere fourteen lines we have traveled from earth to heaven and back again.

Of utmost importance in this sonnet is the use Dante makes of real events: the specific date (All Saints' Day) and place (undoubtedly Florence, but more importantly any earthly city, *civitas mundi*) provide Dante with the historical basis for his allegory of the lady who has come to lift man up to his eternal beatitude. The allegory of the *Divine Comedy* is founded on this principle, which here infuses the sonnet with a wealth of meanings not possible in the earlier lyric tradition. The sonnet does not dwell on the physical suffering of the poet (as did da Lentino's), nor on the mystical awe combined with mental distress that characterized Guinizzelli's, but rather on the selfless exaltation of the lady in her dual role: as the object of the poet's praiseful adoration and as the bestower of grace on mankind. Thus, the personal vision of the poet in the quatrains and his recognition of her universal implications in the tercets are joined together in perfect harmony, just as the lady reveals herself to be a fusion of human and divine elements. The poet remains a spectator, the lady having become the main character, free to accomplish her human and divine roles, as defined by the poet: that is to say, to minister to him and to the needs of all mankind. Poetic art is no longer solely the means of personal communication with the lady, but rather speaks to all humanity. The expansion of the personal context to include the universal in this sonnet is consonant with the guiding artistic principle of the *Divine Comedy,* in which poetry is the means to the didactic end of revealing to mankind the operation of Divine Justice.

Through these varied treatments of the same theme, we have observed some of the basic technical features of the sonnet tradition in pre-Petrarchan literature: the incorporation of metrical and rhetorical devices; the tension or harmony existing between quatrains and tercets; the quest for identity between form and content; the changing perspective within the composition itself; and the elevation of the subject matter with a subsequent increase in metaphorical allusiveness.

Petrarch was indeed greatly indebted to the preceding tradition for all of these elements, as the following examples will show. The theme under discussion, that of the poet's remembrance of the first meeting with his lady, becomes central to an entire group of sonnets in the *Canzoniere,* which have been called the "anniversary" poems. The sonnet *Era il giorno ch'al sol si scoloraro* recalls that Good Friday (April 6, 1327) when, in the church of Santa Chiara, Petrarch first saw Laura.[6]

Era il giorno ch'al sol si scoloraro
per la pietà del suo factore i rai,
quando i' fui preso, et non me ne guardai,
ché i be' vostr'occhi, donna, mi legaro.
Tempo non mi parea da far riparo
contra colpi d'Amor: però m'andai
secur, senza sospetto; onde i miei guai
nel commune dolor s'incominciaro.
Trovommi Amor del tutto disarmato
et aperta la via per gli occhi al core,
che di lagrime son fatti uscio et varco:
però al mio parer non li fu honore
ferir me de saetta in quello stato,
a voi armata non mostrar pur l'arco.

The most remarkable quality of this sonnet, and indeed of all Petrarch's poetry, is the measured cadence and rich musicality of the verse and the refined diction, three elements that are found infrequently in the previous lyric tradition. Among other features, we note the effect of the postponement of *rai,* the subject of *si scoloraro,* as well as the emphatic initial position of *Trovommi,* or the delicate separation, by means of the vocative *donna,* of the beautiful objects (*i be' vostr' occhi*) from their adverse effect (*mi legaro*). The alliteration of *secur, senza sospetto* provides audible anticipation of his *guai*; the movement in vv. 10-11 reveals Love's quickness and the simultaneity of seeing and feeling.

6. Francesco Petrarca, *Canzoniere,* ed. Contini (Torino: Einaudi, 1968), no. III.

Finally, the hesitancy of Love to attack Laura is described as the negation of the minimal non-hostile action: *a voi armata non mostrar pur l'arco*.

The setting is epic in quality: the crucifixion of Christ, the eclipse of the sun, and the general grief of the faithful; and because of this, its suggestive power is heightened. We see the revelation of Petrarch's sun (Laura) in all her glory, his being transfixed by Love's arrows, and the beginning of his "passion" on a cross fashioned, as it were, from the laurel tree. The quatrains begin and end with the general scene on Good Friday and contain in the inner verses the personal situation, just as universal history provides the frame for a myriad of individual actions. Petrarch's personal drama is connected to Christ's passion by subtle strands: the rays of the sun, dimmed through God's pietà, are transformed into the resplendent, pitiless eyes of Laura that entrap the poet. Whereas Christ atoned for man's sin on the cross, it is ironic here that on the day symbolizing man's redemption and liberation from original sin, Petrarch becomes ensnared by Love. To the universal expression of grief that transcends the earth is joined his own sorrow that is directed earthward, toward himself. The tercets remain on the personal level, first on the manner in which his injury was inflicted and second on the unfairness of Love's action. There is a certain tension in the tercets that results from the opposition between *disarmato* (9) and *armata* (14), a sort of *conflictus* that represents accurately the tormented, unrequited nature of his love and that will prove to be the inspiration for most of his lyrics.

The sonnet *Benedetto sia* reveals the happier side of Petrarch's love:[7]

Benedetto sia 'l giorno, e 'l mese, et l'anno,
et la stagione, e 'l tempo, et l'ora, e 'l punto,
e 'l bel paese, e 'l loco ov'io fui giunto
4 da' duo begli occhi che legato m'ànno;
et benedetto il primo dolce affanno
ch'i' ebbi ad esser con Amor congiunto,
et l'arco, et le saette ond'i' fui punto,
8 et le piaghe che 'nfin al cor mi vanno.
Benedette le voci tante ch'io
chiamando il nome de mia donna ò sparte,
11 e i sospiri, et le lagrime, e 'l desio;
et benedette sian tutte le carte
ov'io fama l'acquisto, e 'l pensier mio,
14 ch'è sol di lei, sì ch'altra non v'à parte.

7. Ibid., no. LXI.

A superficial unity is given to the composition by the anaphora of *benedetto/e*; however, a closer examination shows that there is a dramatic, yet subtle shift in attention in passing from the quatrains to the tercets. The first two verses remarkably display one of the principal characteristics of the sonnet form: the opposing principles of expansion and compression. The temporal limits are first opened so as to deny the existence of any limit whatsoever: *Benedetto sia 'l giorno, e 'l mese, et l'anno.* And then they are closed, reduced to that precise point in time when he fell in love: *et la stagione, e 'l tempo, et l'ora, e 'l punto.* From this, the sonnet could be said to expand the personal into the universal or to compress the universal in the personal. The third verse continues the compression in spatial terms to the exact place where he was bound by Laura's eyes. By concentrating on the grief and the instruments that occasioned it, the second quatrain builds, expands on the time and place of the first: Petrarch in the church on Good Friday. The equivocal rhyme *punto* in vv. 2 and 7 serves to connect the quatrains and, at the same time, to stress their slightly different focus. Similarly, the derivative rhymes *giunto* (3) and *congiunto* (6) reveal through their meaning the progression from the isolated, passive receiver to the active participant, now joined with Love. The first tercet builds on the oxymoron *dolce affanno* (5) by depicting the outward manifestation of his grievous joy. The second tercet passes even further to the final form of these externalizations of emotions, namely his many poems through which he acquires fame for his lady (and for himself, too). The entire sonnet could be called a study in the creative process, from the first inspiration (internalization) to its final concrete expression (externalization) in a work of literature, which is, in this case, a sonnet. The unity through progression is enhanced by the last two verses (*e 'l pensier mio, / ch'è sol di lei, sí ch'altra non v'à parte*), which declare the source of the poet's inspiration to be unique and changeless.

As I believe the preceding analyses have shown, Petrarch was more the perfector of traditional forms than the technical innovator. In the *Canzoniere* he synthesizes the "best" elements from the preceding literary tradition (both Classical and Romance) and reshapes them according to his own artistic principles. His language lacks dialectal elements (Sicilianisms, Guittonianisms), but contains the usual Provençalisms and many Latinisms. Besides attempting to imitate Latinate syntax in the vernacular period, Petrarch renews the Italian poetic vocabulary through use of highly suggestive words and phrases. In fact, the relatively restricted vocabulary of the *Canzoniere* is further evidence of his absolute control over his artistic creation.[8] With regard to the structure of poetry, he achieved, through technical expertise, a more balanced, symmetrical form, both in its entirety and in each individual line.

However that may be, Petrarch's more important contribution to the world of letters may be seen in his role as theoretical innovator. For most, if not all, of his sonnets have been subjected to at least two "creative moments": the original composition and the subsequent inclusion in the *Canzoniere* with all attendant revisions. In the passage from the first to the second moment, from the topical inspiration to the conscious reelaboration, we may also observe a change in Petrarch's attitude toward his art and audience.

He did not write solely for immediate communication with individuals or for consumption by the contemporary world readership; rather, he destined his works to posterity, for the unborn generations whom he addressed in the epistle *Posteritati,* for us modern readers who never fail to marvel at the intimacy, the directness, the vitality of the first sonnet of the *Canzoniere,* beginning *Voi ch'ascoltate.* The preoccupation with posterity did not, however, diminish the importance of that final audience: the poet himself who, in his curious dual role of author and auto-critic, would read, contemplate, and revise in the privacy of his study. To be sure, Petrarch's approach to composition, his constant revision and reworking, would tend to detach the man from his work, and his work from the audience. Moreover, it is possible, indeed it is necessary, to distinguish between Petrarch the poet and Petrarch the protagonist, between the self-conscious artist and the principal character of his self-sufficient creation.

For Petrarch, art, and more specifically poetry, was the only sublunary thing that would continue to exist. Poetry allowed him to project his own individual image forward in time, so that future generations could read of him and see him, as it were, through a number of self-portraits. In his Latin works there are many such pictures: Petrarch the Latin Humanist and ardent student of Holy Scripture emerges in the *Posteritati,* as does Petrarch the philosopher and man of letters in Book I of the *Vita solitaria.* An intimate portrait of Petrarch the social animal, the diplomat, and man of many interests, may be obtained from the numerous letters to friends and acquaintances; the morally-troubled Petrarch conducts a rigorous self-examination in the *Secretum.* All of these diverse components of Petrarch's personality reappear, united, in the *Canzoniere.*

8. For the language, see G. Contini, "Preliminari sulla lingua del Petrarca," which serves as the introduction to the above edition of the *Canzoniere* (pp. vii-xxxviii).

Unlike earlier compilations of lyric poety, the *Canzoniere,* more properly called the *Rerum vulgarium fragmenta,* is preserved in a partially autograph manuscript (Vatican Latin 3195). We may trace the evolution of his thoughts on poetry in the several successive versions of these carefully ordered and continually revised poems.[9]

Petrarch's editorial work would lead us to believe that there is indeed some order to the work, some unifying principle that operates within it, even though the large number of poems would tend to discourage such an analysis and the title *Rerum vulgarium fragmenta* would seem to negate any notion of internal unity.[10] In order to understand Petrarch's intention in the *Canzoniere,* I would suggest that it has a *cornice,* which is similar in function, but dissimilar in appearance, to that of the *Decameron.* The *cornice* or 'frame' of the *Decameron* allows Boccaccio to realize his artistic intention: to grant the writer the same freedom of expression that the painter enjoys. It is this attitude that is at the base of the several defenses of his art in the *Decameron.* Literature can exist and can be justified on its own terms and merits without being purposive, without appealing to an external end, to moral instruction, or to an ethical structure. In the *Rerum vulgarium fragmenta* the introductory sonnet (*Voi ch'ascoltate*) and the concluding *canzone* (*Vergine bella*) serve as the *cornice* which contains the *fragmenta,* the scattered lyrics that reveal through their diversity the many-sided nature of their author.[11] Thus, each lyric, although in itself representing one minute aspect of Petrarch's personality, contributes to the detailed portrait of the author that emerges from the whole. There is no "higher truth" toward which the compilation aspires; there is no moral or intellectual progression in the itinerary of the 366 poems, as there is, for

9. See the fundamental study by E. H. Wilkins, *The Making of the "Canzoniere" and Other Petrarchan Studies* (Roma: Edizioni di Storia e Letteratura, 1951).

10. However, among others, see the recent studies by Adolfo Jenni, "Un sistema del Petrarca nell'ordinamento del *Canzoniere,*" in *Studi in onore di Alberto Chiari* (Brescia: Paideia, 1973), II, 721-732, and Thomas P. Roche, Jr., "The Calendrical Structure of Petrarch's *Canzoniere,*" *Studies in Philology,* LXXI (1974), pp. 152-172.

11. It could be argued that there is a further division within the *Canzoniere:* between those poems *in vita* and those *in morte di Madonna Laura.* However, such a division, if indeed one were intended by Petrarch, would add further support to my contention, for the first section (I-CCLXIII) would then conclude with a sonnet (*Arbor victoriosa triumphale*) and the second (CCLXIV-CCCLXVI) would open with a *canzone* (*I' vo pensando*). Thus, in accordance with my remarks below, the "earthly" section (*in vita*) would be contained in a *cornice* delimited by the "eternal" form of the sonnet, and the "extra-temporal" one (*in morte*) in a *cornice* determined by the variable form of the *canzone.*

example, in the *Vita nuova.* The structure simply contains the lyrics which, freed from their initial topical purpose, become vital elements in this poet-centered poetical universe.

It is significant that the collection begins with a sonnet and concludes with a *canzone,* for the sonnet presents all that is earthly and ephemeral (*che quanto piace al mondo è breve sogno,* 14) and the *canzone* all that is divine and changeless. In this way, it could be said that the lyrics of the *Canzoniere* are contained in a sort of suspended state between time and eternity. Although their subject matter belongs to this world, the poems themselves are immune to the transitory nature of earthly things and aspire toward that permanence that is divine. In effect, the fragmentary quality of life, of Petrarch's life in particular, is captured and preserved in the *Canzoniere* as a sort of eternal monument of man. Petrarch tended to see the past as immutable, far removed from the ravages of time, and I would suggest that he viewed the future in precisely the same way. By directing his works toward posterity, he would enable them to partake of this changelessness. It is especially significant that the mutability of earthly things is expressed in the fixed form of the sonnet, and the stable quality of the divine is represented in the variable form of the *canzone.* This paradoxical interchange of poetic modes is striking, for in it we may understand Petrarch's real intention: to "eternalize" the earthly by means of a fixed form and to "humanize" the eternal by means of a variable form. The sonnet would then become that perfect vehicle by which the work of art conquers time and endures for posterity. In general terms, poetry, for Petrarch, was the only sure way of attaining immortality and of retaining one's individual identity and character, and among the several poetic modes available, the sonnet more than any other had the intimations of an eternal form: rigid in structure, stable in rhythm, sublime in musicality, and adaptable in content.

While synthesizing and perfecting the rhetorical devices of the preceding lyric tradition, Petrarch has also accepted, to a certain extent, the subservient function of poetry as a means to a pre-established end. In the initial creative moment, his poetry was the means of personal communication with Laura, personal friends, God, Christ, the Virgin Mary, and the contemporary readership. In a subsequent creative moment, the sonnets, by themselves and as part of the *Canzoniere,* are intended for posterity, for that audience far removed in time from the present. Poetry for Petrarch, as for Horace and countless others, was eternal, an enduring monument, by which the name of the poet and his subject matter would live on, and because the poet and subject matter of Petrarch's poetry are one and the same, it would seem that he conceived of poetry as the means to an end: worldly glory, the perpetuation of his unique personality through time. However, more than the eternalization of self through poetry understood in the traditional manner, I would suggest that Petrarch's approach to poetic composition, his constant revision and reordering, and his concern with posterity have caused the emergence of a certain aesthetic distance, which separates the poet as creator from his creation, the poem, indeed from the entire universe of poems that will continue to exist in the objective form of the *Canzoniere*, which, complete in itself, is animated by its own system of images, metaphors, and symbols. Finally, in terms of the art of the sonnet, I believe, on the one hand, that Petrarch recognized in that fixed, stable form the means of attaining stability in this world of flux, of preserving his fame for posterity, and of immortalizing the vernacular language, thereby raising it to the level of Greek and Latin; and, on the other hand, I believe that he viewed the sonnet, that perfect artistic creation, as an end in itself, a life force which, reflecting yet remaining separate from its maker, would continue to exist through time. Thus, in fulfilling the potentialities of the sonnet form, Petrarch elevated it to its privileged place in poetry and gave it a life of its own.

X

THE POET-PERSONA IN THE *CANZONIERE*

by Sara Sturm
University of Massachusetts (Amherst)

Poems about poetry are found throughout Petrarch's *Canzoniere*. The importance of poetry as theme, widely recognized in the concept of poetic fame relating Laura and the *lauro,* is established in a variety of contexts and continues with undiminished emphasis from the first poem of the collection to the last. In the *Canzoniere* Petrarch is concerned, as Bosco notes, with the creation of a "poetic myth" rather than with an autobiographical account of his love for Laura,[1] and the emphasis on poetic activity is an essential part of that myth-making. In important recent studies of the *Canzoniere,* Amaturo has pointed to the delineation throughout the collection of "rapporti reciproci fra vita e letteratura, fra psicologia e arte," and Bernardo cites Petrarch's "awareness of depicting a human experience that is infinite in its dimensions and the corresponding infinite struggle to convey the experience through the finite means of poetic language."[2] This relationship and this struggle are dramatized in the *Canzoniere* through the presentation of the poet's continuing effort to give poetic form to his experience. While the experience presented must in many instances be assumed to coincide with that of the author, the poet who records his effort, in whose voice the poetic "story" of the collection is told, is a persona to be distinguished from Petrarch the author of the *Canzoniere* just as the pilgrim Dante is to be distinguished from the author of the *Commedia.* If we acknowledge with Bosco that the patterning of the *Canzoniere* is "inteso a dare l'illusione di una 'storia,' anzi di un diario,"[3] it is in the fictional autobiography of the poet-persona that we may find a major element in the creation of that illusion. Taken out of their context in the body of love-

1. U. Bosco, *Francesco Petrarca* (Bari, 1968), p. 22: "Nella vita dell'uomo, dunque, l'amore per Laura non fu che un episodio; ma un episodio che il poeta lirico vuole rappresentarci come centrale e determinante; un episodio trasformato in 'mito' poetico."

2. R. Amaturo, *Petrarca* (Bari, 1971), p. 356; A. Bernardo, "Petrarch and the art of literature," in J. Molinaro, ed., *Petrarch to Pirandello* (Toronto, 1973), p. 42.

3. Bosco, p. 28.

lyrics and considered in sequence as they are placed throughout the collection, the references to the poet's struggle trace a story of poetic development and of continuing reassessment of the poet's role.[4]

The first poem of the *Canzoniere* establishes the fundamental importance of the poet's activity as theme. The opening utterance contains the principle of the relation between poet and audience:

> Voi ch'ascoltate in rime sparse il suono
> Di quei sospiri ond'io nudriva 'l core
> In sul mio primo giovenile errore,
> Quand'era in parte altr'uom da quel ch'i' sono . . . .[5]

In the intimate context of direct communication, Petrarch addresses himself to his readers as "voi che ascoltate"; but that which they are to hear is not the direct utterance of the *sospiri,* Petrarch's sighs, but rather their sound, the *suono.* The *suono* is in turn that of verses: the sound of the sighing is to be communicated through the *rime sparse* which make up the poet's collection of verses. In one sense it is immediately inappropriate to describe the poet's love-*rime* as *sparse,* since they are brought together in the collection to which he is directing the reader in the opening sonnet.[6] The adjective *sparse* suggests, then, a different sense: the individual poems are collected into a volume, but the love-poetry itself has failed to assume a coherent form. In the second stanza, when the poet writes

> Del vario stile in ch'io piango e ragiono
> Fra le vane speranze e 'l van dolore,
> Ove sia chi per prova intenda amore,
> Spero trovar pietà, non che perdono,

there is a deliberate ambiguity in the syntax of this expression of his hope, which is the expression at the same time of his stated purpose in the presentation of the *Canzoniere* poems. The *vario stile,* it is assumed, will convey his suffering in such a way that through his poems the anticipated effect ("pietà, non che perdono") will be produced in the reader; but the verses also suggest that the reader's *pietà* may be evoked because of the result of the poetic experience, rather than or in addition

4. The present article is a preliminary study to a more detailed evaluation of the function of the poet-persona's "story" in the *Canzoniere.* A number of important aspects of the treatment of poetry in the collection are necessarily omitted here.

5. Quotations are from *Le Rime di Francesco Petrarca,* ed. N. Zingarelli (Bologna, 1964).

6. Amaturo notes the relation of this reference to the critical problems raised by the title of *Rerum vulgarium fragmenta* (p. 241).

to the love-experience itself.[7] In this context, the reference to the poet's *vergogna* in each of the two tercets also includes his poetry as antecedent.[8]

The apparent apology of this opening sonnet has been related to well-known medieval patterns. Montanari notes in it "la figura tipica dell'introduzione medievale," including the author's apology for the limitations of his talent, his inability to do justice to the important theme which he is about to attempt; Dante in invoking the aid of Apollo to tell of his experience of Paradise, for example, refers modestly to his account as "poca favilla" which may nonetheless feed a greater flame. While Petrarch includes numerous apologies of this type in the *Canzoniere,* however, in the first sonnet his apparent apology is not for the inadequacy of his talent, but rather for offering a work made up of *rime sparse,* the final result of a poetic effort which the poet himself questions even while offering it to his reader.[9] Scaglione relates the apology to the experience to be presented in the collection, seeing in it a reflection of a pattern of recantation in which "at the beginning and at the end of the collection of his love lyrics, the poet became accustomed to condemn the very experience he was exalting in the body of his work."[10] While recantation is clearly suggested in the opening poem, Petrarch's reference to *rime sparse* introduces an additional dimension in its suggestion that the experience to be presented is that of the poet as well as that of the lover. The author of the first sonnet looks back over an experience of both love and poetry which he describes as having begun "quand'era in parte altr'uom da quel ch'i' sono," and the entire sonnet suggests an essential ambiguity in the assessment of the poetic effort referred to in the poem. It is this which prepares the unfolding of the poet-persona's story, one of continued striving to present his love in verse.

Both the beginning of love and the poet's first attempts to write of it are detailed in the early poems of the *Canzoniere.* Bernardo, tracing the periodic emergence of the artist's self-awareness in the first fifty lyrics of the collection, calls attention to the poet's return to the "formal qual-

7. We find in these verses "da un lato una sorta di intuitiva, quasi ancora inconsapevole dichiarazione di poetica, l'accenno alle 'rime sparse' e al 'vario stile' implicando l'aspirazione ancora vaga a un unitario *ductus* compositivo; d'altro canto . . . la consapevolezza esplicita che poesia è per lui non sospiro, ma espressione intellettualmente e artisticamente mediata di intimi affanni" (Amaturo, p. 250).

8. As Bernardo explains, "poetry written in this fashion makes of the poet a kind of object of derision in the opinion of the greater part of the people" (p. 36).

9. See F. Montanari, *Studi sul Canzoniere del Petrarca* (Rome, 1958), p. 20.

10. A. Scaglione, *Nature and Love in the Late Middle Ages* (Berkeley and Los Angeles, 1963), p. 19.

ities of poetry" in no. 5, with his attempt "to organize his sighs" in order to pronounce Laura's name, and to mentions of poetry in other early poems.[11] While all of these have implications for the poet's activity, none before no. 20 describe the actual attempt by the poet to write verses about Laura. In fact, they suggest the contrary. In no. 7, encouraging a friend to greater effort, the poet refers generally to the lack of attention and respect accorded poetry in their time ("che per cosa mirabile s'addita/ Chi vol far d'Elicona nascer fiume"). In no. 12 he imagines himself revealing his love to Laura when they have both grown old, the contrast to his present inability to express his love heightened by the use of the single present tense in the poem to confide that her beauty in the present "a lamentar mi fa pauroso e lento." In no. 18, the emphasis is on his silence, his desire to avoid an audience:

> Tacito vo, ché le parole morte
> Farian pianger la gente; et i' desio
> Che le lagrime mie si spargan sole.

Poem no. 20 is the first after the introductory sonnet to deal directly with the poet's efforts, and in it he records his shame that he has not yet celebrated Laura's beauty in rhyme: "Vergognando talor ch'ancor si taccia, / Donna, per me vostra bellezza in rima." This poem and its position, with its explicit introduction to the poet's effort to express his love and admiration in verse, clearly establish the poet-persona. After eighteen poems devoted to his *innamoramento* and initial reactions to his love, the poet of no. 20 is still protesting that a theme such as Laura's beauty is not "ovra da polir co la mia lima," and confessing that in the attempt his "ingegno" "tutto s'agghiaccia," declaring solemnly that so far his poetic effort has met with no success:

> Più volte incominciai di scriver versi:
> Ma la penna e la mano e l'intelletto
> Rimaser vinti nel primier assalto.

It is significant in terms of the relation between love and poetry that his words here recall the first poem introducing his new love, in which he describes his inability to defend himself against Love's first attack (poem no. 2):

> Però turbata nel primiero assalto,
> Non ebbe tanto né vigor, né spazio
> Che potesse al bisogno prender l'arme.

11. Bernardo, p. 37.

The introductory section of the famed metamorphosis canzone (no. 23) clearly relates to both the first sonnet and no. 20 in its indication that the poet's *sospiri* have now become known to many, as he has written so much about his suffering, that "mille penne/ ne son già stanche;" it also introduces, as Bernardo points out, the "therapeutic value" of poetry.[12] The various metamorphoses undergone by the lover are related by their implication for his ability to express his love,[13] and the *commiato* of the canzone emphasizes the relation of lover to poet: while he had not been successful as lover, as detailed in the series of metamorphoses, the poet nonetheless claims that

> . . . fui ben fiamma ch'un bel guardo accense;
> E fui l'uccel che più per l'aere poggia
> Alzando lei che ne' miei detti onoro.

It is evident in the contrast of the two conditions that the poet's ability to exalt his lady in verse is a substitute satisfaction for that of the lover. In the poem immediately following, however, he states that the "onorata fronde," the laurel, had refused him its crown. Because of the "ingiuria" which he suffers, he is not a friend of the Muses, and his own friend must turn for poetry to a "fonte più tranquillo." His exclusive poetic focus on Laura, while supporting his boast at the end of the metamorphosis canzone, is nonetheless recognized by the poet as a limitation which excludes other avenues of poetic development.

In sestina no. 30 the poet expresses his inspiration in terms of the laurel and declares that his weeping may "far forse pietà venir negli occhi/ di tal che nascerà dopo mill'anni." No. 34 again focuses on the laurel, and while it contains no direct reference to the poet's role, it is of particular interest because it was included as the opening sonnet in the first form of the *Canzoniere*.[14] It contains an invocation to Apollo to restore to health "l'onorata e sacra fronde," the laurel, presumably here Laura; but as Amaturo notes, the particular interest of the sonnet "è nell'ambiguità (insita nel mito dafneo) fra il nome della donna amata e l'alloro che dona la poesia: sicché tutta l'invocazione ad Apollo suona anche come preghiera ad aiutare e proteggere una sua nuova stagione poetica."[15]

12. Loc. cit.

13. Ibid., pp. 35, 37-38; and Amaturo, who notes that the poet seems in this poem to delineate both "la storia stessa dei suoi stati d'animo e le successive fasi dei suoi modi espressivi" (p. 260).

14. For a discussion of this first form, see E. H. Wilkins, "The Evolution of the *Canzoniere* of Petrarch," *PMLA*, 63 (1948), pp. 416-419.

15. Amaturo, p. 262.

Even the success of his efforts within the tradition of love lyrics to which the poet has devoted himself is called into question in the pessimistic tones of the next major assessment of his poetic achievement, no. 60, which Amaturo considers the conclusion of an opening cycle of poems in the *Canzoniere*.[16] The laurel, which in his earlier love poetry "fiorir faceva il mio debile ingegno," now has a different effect: "fece di dolce sé spietato legno." His present complaint takes up again the suggestion of an exclusive poetic focus in no. 20: "I' rivolsi i pensier tutti ad un segno," he states, and now, rather than exulting in his achievement, he relates poetry to experience in a more sombre vein, revealing that these thoughts now "parlan sempre de' lor tristi danni." As a result, he thinks of those who had drawn hope from his "rime nove" about love and who must now lose that hope because of his sad example. Sonnet 61, however, forms a sharp contrast to the preceding poem, as if intensifying its statement through that opposition.[17] Each stanza begins with "benedetto" or "benedette," and praises various aspects of the poet's love from its beginning, concluding with a final tercet relating the experience to its poetic record:

> E benedette sian tutte le carte
> Ov'io fama l'acquisto, e 'l pensier mio,
> Ch'è sol di lei, sì ch'altra non v'à parte.

After evoking the tradition of Italian love poetry through the mention of his "rime nove" in no. 60, he tells his own amorous story in terms of that tradition in no. 70. Beginning dramatically—"Lasso me, ch'i' non so in qual parte pieghi/ La speme ch'è tradita omai più volte," he continues with a reference relating his frustration and despair to the terms of the opening sonnet of the *Canzoniere:* "Che se non è chi con pietà m'ascolte,/ Perché sparger al ciel sì spessi preghi?" He then refers to various moments of the love-experience recorded by his predecessors in the Italian love-lyric, moments which refer clearly to the relation between poetry and experience, the deliberate relationship signalled by the use of a verse from an earlier poet as the final verse of each of the first four stanzas. The fifth and final stanza then concludes with the opening line of his own metamorphosis canzone (23), that verse which had introduced his experience as lover and as poet "nel dolce tempo della prima etade," and in this stanza he goes beyond his

16. Ibid., p. 250: "il ciclo iniziale sembra proporsi di riesumare e restaurare . . . le diverse maniere e tendenze della lirica giovanile petrarchesca."

17. See Amaturo, p. 275, who considers sonnets 61 and 62 together to be a sort of "rinnovato proemio" for the development of the myth of Laura.

predecessors to write of his personal difficulty in following their example: "Ma me," he says, "che così a dentro non discerno,/ Abbaglia il bel che mi si mostra intorno;" his own eye is not firm in regarding the "vero splendor," and its weakness is due solely to "la sua propria colpa."

This canzone stands as introduction to the three famous canzoni "sugli occhi di Laura."[18] In the first of these, again hesitant to write of his lady because "l'ingegno paventa a l'alta impresa," the poet attempts to overcome this obstacle through a deliberate focus on a determined theme. Addressing himself to Laura's eyes, "Occhi leggiadri dove Amor fa nido," he solemnly declares that "A voi rivolgo il mio debile stile,/ Pigro da sé, ma 'l gran piacer lo sprona," and this dedication is effective: with the specific inspiration of Laura's eyes, he begins "a dire or cose,/ Ch'ò portate nel cor gran tempo ascose." The body of the canzone is then devoted to this theme of praise, and the initial emphasis on poetry returns in the final stanza with his hope for the success of his poetic endeavor, since from his "amoroso pensero"

> . . . parole e opre
> Escon di me sì fatte allor, ch'i' spero
> Farmi immortal, perché la carne moia.

The second of the three canzoni carries out his stated intent of praising Laura's eyes, yet when he returns to the theme of poetry in the third poem to declare that "per mio destino/ A dir mi sforza quell'accesa voglia," the success of his effort is again called into question in a different sense. While he has overcome his previous inability to express his love in verse, his hope that the writing of poetry might relieve his passion has been disappointed, "Ché 'l dir m'infiamma e pugne;" the very sound of his own words torments him, "Anzi mi struggo al suon de le parole." The poetry, the expression of the passion, is thus duplicating the effect of the experience, the passion itself. The poet's success is the lover's heightened suffering; his hope that he might find "qualche breve riposo, e qualche triegua" in speaking of his love—the hope that had led him to "ragionar quel ch'i' sentia"—now abandons him, although he is compelled to continue his own "amorose note."

The pair of sonnets which follow develop the theme of the poet's weariness which concluded the canzoni sequence. No. 74 begins "Io son già stanco di pensar sì come/ I miei pensier in voi stanchi non sono," and in it the poet, considering his continued effort to express his love

18. N. Zingarelli considers that this use of predecessors "esprime la coscienza di un'arte nuova, e il proposito di richiamare l'attenzione del lettore paragonandola a quella dei predecessori" (p. 533).

in verse, is surprised that his tongue does not fail, "e 'l suono,/ Dì e notte chiamando il vostro nome," asserting finally that "Se 'n ciò fallassi,/ Colpa d'Amor, non già defetto d'arte." Sonnet no. 75, however, answers with a return to the theme of Laura's eyes, citing them as sufficient reason why "io di lor parlando non mi stanco."

The three canzoni about Laura's eyes and the two sonnets which follow summarize the various attitudes toward love-poetry expressed in the beginning section of the *Canzoniere*. When Love compels the poet to write, he considers his ability unequal to the task; then with the direct inspiration of his chosen theme, he begins to say those things which have long been hidden in his heart, and hopes even that his verses may be immortal. But after applying himself to this theme of the praise of Laura's eyes, he finds himself again unsure of his success, complaining that writing of his love increases his pain. He declares his weariness with the effort, but the strength of his inspiration obliges him to continue. The pattern, based on the compelling need to give expression to his love in verse, is one of alternating elation-pessimism about the adequacy of poetry for such a task, and of alternating elation-despair about the effect of the poetic effort on the lover.

Poem 105 opens with the poet's declaration that he will abandon his accustomed form of poetry: "Mai non vo' più cantar com'io soleva, Ch'altri non m'intendeva; ond'ebbi scorno," and in the canzone which follows he forsakes the conventions of the Italian love lyric to express himself in a variety of dissonant modes. In 125 he distinguishes his current poetic style from that of his early poetry: speaking now in "rime aspre e di dolcezza ignude," he laments that he has lost even the comfort that he had once found in writing the "dolci rime leggiadre/ Che nel primiero assalto/ D'Amor usai, quand'io non ebbi altr'arme." These verses recall the "primero assalto" both of Love and of his own first efforts at writing poetry about Laura's beauty (20), his "ingegno" having faltered at the task of attempting love-poetry which he felt could not do justice to his subject; it is his heart which is now "di smalto," and he is nonetheless led to write, like a youth "che dir non sa, ma 'l più tacer gli è noia." Two poems later, the first stanza of no. 127 again takes up the change from his earlier *rime,* but the nature of that change is itself not clear to the poet because even Love's dictation has become difficult to understand:

> Quai fien ultime, lasso, e qua' fien prime,
> Colui che del mio mal meco ragiona
> Mi lascia in dubbio, sì confuso ditta.

He continues to write of his love, however, because his poems again provide temporary relief from his suffering: "i sospiri/ Parlando àn triegua, e al dolor soccorro."

A more positive phase is initiated with the announcement of a new beginning in 131. "Io canterei d'amor sì novamente," the poet resolves, that his song will draw sighs from Laura "per forza."[19] This confident assertion is followed by a poem (146) which seems a deliberate illustration of that new departure, with the expression of the poet's fervent wish that his verses could fill the world with Laura's name. The optimistic note continues in 148 with the revival of the laurel, "l'arboscel che 'n rime orno e celebro," again a "soccorso" for the poet "tra gli assalti/ D'Amore." In 151 Love too again favors the poet's efforts: in indicating in Laura's eyes "quant'io parlo d'Amore, e quant'io scrivo," he shows the poet "quel ch'a molti cela."

Following the renewed confidence about the writing of love lyrics apparent in these poems, 166 abruptly calls into question all of the poet's implied achievement by considering it within a wider poetic context. The poet sighs that had he been true to his early promise, "Fiorenza avria forse oggi il suo poeta," but for him "l'oliva è secca, e è rivolta altrove/ L'acqua che di Parnaso si deriva." This poem, one of the most explicit and forceful statements about the poet's efforts in the *Canzoniere,* relates in particular to two previous poems about poetry. The reference to the "oliva secca" recalls the declaration of his distance from Minerva in 24, his earlier protest of poetic inadequacy. In 60, he had lamented that the laurel no longer protected him from Giove's lightning, and here the reference to Giove's influence on the poet's state recurs radically transformed. The poet is no longer concerned with the determination of the cause of his failure, whether it be "sventura" or "colpa," but rather with its possible remedy, and he declares that he has no hope "se l'eterno Giove/ De la sua grazia sopra me non piove." In this final verse the poetic context has expanded to include a spiritual dimension, in which the recognition of unfulfilled poetic promise concludes with a more general admission of incapacity and failure.

In the remaining poems about the expression of his love for Laura "in vita," the poet attempts the elevation of his subject from the limited tradition of Italian love lyrics to the highest standard of poetry. This

19. Amaturo too notes a new beginning at this point with 130 and 131, which, "tra loro quasi complementari, insieme costituiscono quasi un prologo alla nuova serie" (p. 300). He characterizes the poems thus introduced as a series moving "dalla 'loda' alla 'meraviglia.'"

attempt takes two major forms: an evaluation of the theme of praise of Laura in terms of classical poetry, and the assertion of her "stato divino" beyond human praise. Sonnets 186 and 187, both taking as their subject poetry in praise of Laura, assert specifically that the great classical poets would have chosen to devote their poetry to Laura had they known her.[20] In 203 the poet cites the immortality which his verses may give his love, and in 247 he answers those who might find his praise of Laura excessive with the assertion that it is instead necessarily inadequate, because "lingua mortale al suo stato divino/ Giunger non pote."[21] Other poems which follow repeat his sense of inadequacy in attempting to write of Laura, now expressed in terms of a poetic object beyond mortal description. This reservation is most clearly articulated in 248, "Chi vuol veder quantunque pò natura," in which the poet calls upon those who observe Laura's perfection to witness also that "mie rime son mute,/ L'ingegno offeso dal soverchio lume."

With the expression of the poet's struggle to write of his love a recurring theme in the poems about Laura "in vita," we may expect to find it central also to the fundamental division between poems "in vita" and "in morte." The death of Laura in the *Canzoniere* is presented as a crisis, not only for her lover, but for her poet. From the opening sonnet he has expressed recurring doubts about his activity as love-poet; after the death of Laura, then, what is to become of his poetry? Love urges him in 268 not to abandon his poems about Laura, particularly in order that her fame may be preserved:

> E sua fama, che spira
> In molte parti ancor per la tua lingua,
> Prega che non extingua,
> Anzi la voce al suo nome rischiari,

and the poet also sees in his writing a means to relieve the new suffering occasioned by her death. After these initial reactions, however, there

20. In the opinion of K. Foster, Petrarch's reference in this poem is more general: "though he called his vernacular verses *nugae* and *fragmenta,* he never suggests that the considerable time he spent on them was lost from nobler *literary* undertakings" ("Beatrice or Medusa," in *Italian Studies presented to E. R. Vincent,* ed. Brand, Foster, Limentani; Cambridge, 1962, p. 51). Foster considers the poems declaring that Homer and Virgil would have sung of Laura rather than of their semi-devine heroes to be evidence of this attitude.

21. This twofold effort is strictly in accord with Petrarch's own attitudes toward poetry in the vernacular; as Bernardo points out, "only poetry written in the style of a Virgil or a Homer and containing some of the truths of Christianity was worthy of the name" (p. 40).

begins with 292 a series of six poems which in combination announce a deliberate redirection of his poetic effort.

Part of the complex response to the death of Laura, these six poems detail the evolution of the poet's resolve. The opening verse of the first poem of the series, "Gli occhi di ch'io parlai sì caldamente," relates directly to his former poetry while recalling his dependence on the inspiration of Laura's eyes in the earlier sequence in which he had begun to give expression to his "amoroso pensero." Now, following an extended lament, he concludes in the final tercet:

> Or sia qui fine al mio amoroso canto:
> Secca è la vena de l'usato ingegno,
> E la cetera mia rivolta in pianto.

This seems indeed to be the ending to the poet's story: the "amoroso canto" is over, its inspiration having become "poca polvere." The experience and the poetry of love are to come to an end together. But for the reader attuned to the poet-persona's story, the last verse leaves open a new avenue of expression, a continuation of poetry if not of the "amoroso canto." While the poet's music is "rivolta in pianto," his weeping itself, like his earlier sighing and his earlier song, may find expression in verse.[22]

The poet's sense of the break with his past, with regard to his poetry as well as to Laura, is emphasized in the sonnet immediately following. He regrets that he had not written more of his love lyrics, "le voci de' sospir miei in rima," since many had found them "sì care." At the time of writing them, his intent had been

> Pur di sfogare il doloroso core
> In qualche modo, non d'acquistar fama.
> Pianger cercai, non già del pianto onore.

Now, however, when he would like to please through his poetry, he is unable to do so because with Laura's death he has lost his inspiration ("sì dolce lima,/ Rime aspre e fosche far soavi e chiare"). The memory of Laura still commands his allegiance, and he concludes that "tacito, stanco dopo sé mi chiama." Without her he cannot continue to write poetry as before. Yet again, in the final verse of the sonnet, the possible resolution is implied: that of modifying his love-poems to follow and praise her still, but in a different mode reflecting her altered state.

22. Amaturo notes that in addition to the "commiato alla poesia" in 292, "nel complesso intreccio tematico . . . affiorava tuttavia il presagio e il conforto di una non impossibile ripresa del canto . . . su diverse corde espressive" (p. 341).

It is significant that much of the next sonnet, placed here at a point of psychological and poetic transference, is a beautifully articulated *reprise* of the first sonnet of the *Canzoniere*. The *pietà* justified now by the poet's condition—his "alma d'ogni suo ben spogliata e priva,/ Amor de la sua luce ignudo e casso"—cannot be evoked because there is no one who can tell of his sorrow: "non è chi lor duol racconti o scriva." His weeping is confined within, and cannot reach the ears of others:

> Che piangon dentro, ov'ogni orecchia è sorda,
> Se non la mia, cui tanta doglia ingombra,
> Ch'altro che sospirar nulla m'avanza.

Only poetry would open this inner world to others, and poetry is not now possible. The poem concludes with a note of resignation marking the end of the poet's hopes for his earthly love, clearly reminiscent of the final verse of the first sonnet: "Veramente fallace è la speranza."[23]

The next two poems together, however, lead to a reassessment of the poet's past devotion to Laura. Sonnet 295 moves from the suggestion of a single hope which now remains of Laura, that she observes "nostro stato dal ciel," to a tercet which rings of the *donna angelicata* immortalized in the Italian lyric:

> O miracol gentil, o felice alma,
> O beltà senza exempio altera e rara,
> Che tosto è ritornata, ond'ella uscio!

While poetry is not the subject of this poem, it is implicit in the closing assertion that Laura had become "sì famosa e chiara" not only through her own great virtue, but through " 'l furor mio," the expression in poetry of the poet's ardor. The following poem then begins with an implicit reinterpretation of the poet's experience: "I' mi soglio accusare, e or mi scuso,/ Anzi me pregio, e tengo assai più caro," and after an exaltation of Laura concludes with his expression of pride that even in suffering he had been constant in his devotion to her:

> Togliendo anzi per lei sempre trar guai,
> Che cantar per qualunque, e di tal piaga
> Morir contenta, e vivere in tal nodo.

Never again in the *Canzoniere* will the poet question the worthiness of

23. Amaturo's comments about the early poems "in morte" indicate the possibility for future poetic development: "la situazione sentimentale immediatamente si trasforma nel *topos* letterario della solitudine, dell'abbandono e della morte; da questa consapevolezza prende le mosse il proposito di nuove variazioni, la possibilità di invenzioni in direzioni diverse" (p. 322).

his chosen subject until the debate with Love near the end of the collection, a debate in which his entire poetic involvement with Laura from its first moments to its last is called into question.

Following this reassessment, this exaltation of Laura which serves to justify in retrospect both his love and his love-poetry, the poet rededicates his *canto* to Laura in 297. Even if her beauty and all the traits he had loved "sono spariti," even if "al seguir son tardo," he recognizes a redeeming possibility for his continuing poetic focus: "Forse averrà che 'l bel nome gentile/ Consecrerò con questa stanca penna."[24] He takes up his pen again, accepting the task to which Love had urged him in 268. The stress on his "stanca penna" deliberately underlines this development: at the end of 293 he had declared that he could write no more because Laura "tacito stanco dopo sè mi chiama;" now, despite the weariness of his pen, he is no longer to remain silent. The apparent renunciation of poetry at the beginning of 292 gives way to a new resolve at the end of 297, marking the endpoint of an evolution which is underscored by the time-references of the six poems: all contrast the present to the past, but only the last verse of the last poem of the series indicates a future.

This new poetic endeavor gives rise, however, to redoubled feelings of inadequacy, reflected in a series of three poems, 307-308-309. After reflecting about his earlier poetry in 304 that "l'ingegno e le rime erano scarse/ In quella etate ai pensier novi e 'nfermi," in 307 the poet comes to a new understanding of why he had found himself "lento e fraile" in his early attempts to praise Laura:

> Mai non poria volar penna d'ingegno,
> Non che stil grave o lingua ove natura
> Volò, tessendo il mio dolce ritegno.

In 308, again considering the limitations of that poetry, he uses past experience to draw a further distinction: he had been unable to depict even her beauty adequately in his verses, but in the attempt to write of "la divina parte," "ivi manca l'ardir, l'ingegno e l'arte." The capacity of the poet is here circumscribed not merely by the limitations of art; his "ingegno" and even his "ardir" also fail in the attempt to render the spiritual dimension sensed in his subject "in vita" and "in morte." In the following poem he admits his failure in repeated attempts to present the

24. "Il lungo aggirarsi intorno alla poesia lo ha finalmente condotto a trovare la materia degna di essa, poichè la persona di Laura era sparita e sembrava inaridito il suo ingegno . . . . Riconoscendo la santità di Laura, questa si propone ora di cantare con animo religioso" (Zingarelli, p. 1310).

"alto e novo miraclo" of Laura in verse: "poi mille volt'indarno a l'opra volse/Ingegno, tempo, penne, carte, enchiostri." Even the laurel is "al ciel traslato" in 318. This extended apology culminates in the humble dedication of the final tercet of 327:

E se mie rime alcuna cosa ponno,
Consecrata fra i nobili intellecti,
Fia del tuo nome qui memoria eterna.

The recurring themes of the poems about poetry "in vita" are thus repeated "in morte," with varying emphasis on poetry as a means of relief for suffering, on the dictation of Love, on the laurel in relation to the poet, on the poet's feared inadequacy. Sestina no. 332, which includes *rime* and *stile* among the rhyme-words of each stanza, is a major recapitulation of the relation between poetry and love. The poet once again evokes the tradition of *dolce stil* poetry, and in particular his own "dolce stile,/ Che solea resonare in versi, e 'n rime,/ Volti subitamente in doglia." Because of Laura's death, his sighs no longer find expression. "Ove è condutto il mio amoroso stile?" he demands:

A parlar d'ira, a ragionar di morte.
U' sono i versi, u' son giunte le rime
Che gentil cor udia pensoso e lieto?

While his desire for Laura "in vita" had caused him to weep in such a way that it "condia di dolcezza ogni agro stile," his present weeping, deprived of its hope, is "amaro più che morte." In the definitive conversion of his song into weeping he redefines the *vario stile* of the first sonnet of the collection: "Non à 'l regno d'Amor sì vario stile,/ Ch'è tanto or tristo, quanto mai fu lieto," and in the final stanza he turns again to the audience of the *dolce stil* faithful to whom his earlier love lyrics had been addressed:

O voi che sospirate a miglior notti,
Ch'ascoltate d'Amore, o dite in rime,
Pregate non mi sia più sorda morte.

The relation to the first sonnet of the *Canzoniere,* with its address to "voi che ascoltate in rime sparse il suono/ Di quei sospiri," is obvious in these verses, as is the poet's recognition that he is no longer one of their number. His "vario stile" has given way to weeping expressed only " 'n aspro stile e 'n angosciose rime," and those to whom he now addresses himself, asked to consider the tragic result of his efforts as love-poet, are asked also to second his prayer for an end to his torment. His verses no longer express his "sospiri," but rather take the form of a repeated plea for death.

Other poems continue the recall of his earlier poetic preoccupations, which now assume a definitive tone. In 344 he repeats the contrast of his now perpetual lament to the variations which had characterized his earlier love poetry:

Piansi e cantai: non so più mutar verso;
Ma dì e notte il duol ne l'alma accolto
Per la lingua e per li occhi sfogo, e verso.

Finally, in 354, when he once again asks Love's aid for his "affannato ingegno" and his "stile stanco, e frale" in order to write poetry in honor of Laura in heaven, Love replies that he is unable to respond to the poet's need because "tutto fu in lei, di che noi morte à privi," and concludes sadly: "e basti or questo./ Piangendo il dico, e tu piangendo scrivi." We understand that like the poet's song, Love's dictation, so important in the entire treatment of love poetry, is now "rivolta in pianto;" in so far as it can continue at all, it is dictation in a different key, for a different kind of poetry.

In 359, as if in response to these repeated references to his past poetry, Laura gently reproaches the poet in a dream for his continued lament:

Quanto era meglio alzar da terra l'ali,
E le cose mortali
E queste dolci tue fallaci ciance
Librar con giusta lance. . . .

And it is as if in response to this urging to weigh his efforts with a "giusta lance" that the poem immediately following (360) presents a debate between Love and the poet in which Reason is called upon to decide between their opposing claims. In this canzone, located very near the end of the collection, the lines of crisis are drawn with remarkable clarity as Petrarch pleads his case against Love. The poet levels the charge that because of Love's influence he had not duly loved God nor considered himself, and laments the waste of his talent: "Misero! a che quel chiaro ingegno altero,/ E l'altre doti a me date dal cielo?" From the loss of his freedom due to Love's cruel assault,

Quinci nascon le lagrime e i martiri,
Le parole e i sospiri,
Di ch'io mi vo stancando, e forse altrui.

Throughout the canzone it is not only the lover but also the poet who states his grievance, and it is in terms of poetry as well that Love justifies Petrarch's continued bondage. In response to the poet's allegation that he has been turned by Love from better use of his talents, Love begins with the reminder that in Petrarch's former involvement with words, in his early training as a lawyer, "fu dato a l'arte/ Da vender parolette, anzi menzogne," and continues with the claim that the poet had

> Salito in qualche fama
> Solo per me, che 'l suo intellecto alzai
> Ov'alzato per sè non fora mai.

Love then counters the poet's charges with the accusation of ingratitude, exclaiming that he had given the poet, not only his incomparable lady, but thereby also his song:

> E sì dolce ydioma
> Le diedi, e un cantar tanto soave,
> Che penser basso o grave
> Non potè mai durar dinanzi a lei.
> Questi fur con costui l'inganni mei.

In the following stanza Love underlines the significance of this contribution in terms both harsh and explicit:

> Sì l'avea sotto l'ali mie condutto,
> Ch'a donne e cavalier piacea il suo dire;
> E sì alto salire
> Il feci, che tra' caldi ingegni ferve
> Il suo nome, e de' suoi detti conserve
> Si fanno con diletto in alcun loco;
> Ch'or saria forse un roco
> Mormorador di corti, un uom del vulgo. . . .

But after hearing both parties in this debate, Reason replies only that "più tempo bisogna a tanta lite;" the final chapter alone will indicate which complaint is justified.

The charges and countercharges of this debate, which Cochin termed "una specie d'esame della coscienza poetica,"[25] invite the reader to recall the various phases of the poet's continued struggle and the general

25. Cochin notes that the poem is "molto convenientemente collocata nel posto che occupa, perchè ripiglia e contiene pienamente quei sentimenti tutti dei quali si compone la materia del canzoniere" (cited in *Rime,* ed. Carducci and Ferrari, Firenze, repr. 1965, p. 498).

lines of poetic evolution traced throughout the *Canzoniere.* The first phase, identified as his "primiero assalto," details his hesitant beginning under the compulsion of Love, and his apprenticeship of alternating optimism and despair. He then proclaims a change in his poetry, stresses the inadequacy of his early style for his new situation, and characterizes his new poetry as "aspro." After a second, more positive "new beginning" the pessimistic note soon returns, culminating in the lament about the poetic heights he might have reached had he fulfilled his early promise. He then attempts to elevate his love poetry in praise of Laura to the level of the highest poetic standard, and in terms of this attempt he experiences a renewed sense of poetic inadequacy. After the death of Laura, he resolves to continue his poetry in order to continue her praise, and there are a number of poems in the final section of the *Canzoniere* which form an outline of the type of response suggested by Dante after the death of Beatrice in the *Vita Nuova.* Yet Petrarch, unlike Dante, never fully rededicates his poetry to the glorification of his lady in heaven, and the crisis for the poet occasioned by the death of his earthly lady is never fully resolved. The process of abstraction, the near-success in the creation of a coherent poetic myth, is repeatedly interrupted, and he acknowledges his failure to celebrate Laura's "divina parte." Laura's urging that he reassess his "fallaci ciance" leads to the debate with Love which turns in part on the consequences of the choice of Laura as exclusive theme, and which seems to end the poet's story on an inconclusive note.

The final statement about poetry, however, is not found in the inconclusive debate with Love, but rather in the *Canzone alla Vergine.* Petrarch turns from Laura to address himself in this last poem, not to God directly, but to the Virgin, and the significance of this choice is heightened by the two preceding poems in which he addresses himself to God. Poems 364 and 365, in fact, as Amaturo notes, seem themselves to have a function as epilogue, "una diversa forma di conclusione in tono minore."[26] Yet there is clear evidence that Petrarch intended 366 as his concluding poem, and he makes of it "un *explicit* che presuppone . . . un ripensamento in chiave moralistica del cammino della propria vita e di essa vuole essere la sospirata palingenesi."[27] Throughout the poem there are direct and indirect contrasts between the earthly and the heavenly ladies.[28] In particular, the Virgin can offer aid where Laura had failed.

26. Amaturo, p. 341.

27. Ibid., p. 347.

28. E. Williamson, who sees the sin repented in the poem as concupiscence, discusses the importance of the choice of Mary in terms of this particular emphasis, relating it to the theme of Mary as the second Eve; see "A Consideration of 'Vergine Bella,'" *Italica,* 29 (1952), 215-228.

Of all the lover's grief, his earthly lady knew nothing at all, and had she known she could not have acknowledged his suffering: "ch'ogni altra sua voglia/ Era a me morte," he cries, "e a lei fama rea." But the Virgin sees "il tutto," the whole man, and that which Laura could not offer him, the Virgin can provide: "quel che non potea/ Far altri," he tells her, "è nulla a la tua gran vertute." Williamson considers this specific transfer of the poet's love and hope as Petrarch's "special solution" to the moral dilemma inherent in the tradition of courtly love poetry, that of the courtly lover who seeks a relief from his suffering which "in the very nature of things" is impossible.[29]

Yet it is not only the moral dilemma of the courtly lover which is confronted and resolved in the *Canzone alla Vergine,* but the dilemma of the courtly poet as well. Petrarch renounces the praise of Laura as his poetic focus to assume a new one, the praise of the Heavenly Lady, the Virgin herself. Almost an entire stanza is devoted to the rededication of his poetry, its relation to his earlier poetry again emphasized through contrast:

Ché se poca mortal terra caduca
Amar con sì mirabil fede soglio,
Che devrò far di te, cosa gentile?
Se dal mio stato assai misero e vile
Per le tue man resurgo,
Vergine, i' sacro e purgo
Al tuo nome e penseri, e 'ngegno, e stile,
La lingua, e 'l cor, le lagrime, e i sospiri.

The terms of the transference are specific: the love which he felt for Laura is to be replaced by love for the Virgin, and the poetry through which he had attempted to give significant form to that earthly love will also be dedicated to its new heavenly object. The relation between poetry and experience is once again stated in the final two verses of this rededication of his poetry: "Scorgimi al miglior guado," he begs of the Virgin, "E prendi in grado i cangiati desiri."

In his study of the structure of the final canzone, Williamson observes acutely that "the nature of the poet's sin, the nature of the Virgin, and the nature of the correction are all bound together in a single argument of love, and the argument is made within the frame of an enclosing figure which unites love with its expression in poetry."[30] This enclosing figure, however, points in turn beyond its immediate expression

29. Ibid., p. 223.
30. Ibid., p. 225.

in the *Canzone alla Vergine* to the poet's story articulated throughout the *Canzoniere*. The relation and contrast to the opening poem in particular is clearly marked by verbal recall as well as by thematic continuity. The first sonnet is addressed to "voi che ascoltate," and the reaction desired and expected by the poet from that listener who "per prova intenda amore," will be "pietà, non che perdono." In the final poem, when he addresses himself to the Virgin with the plea that "del comune principio amor t'induca," his prayer is not only for *pietà* but for pardon in the most serious Christian sense. When the poet asks that the Virgin fill his heart with "sante lagrime e pie," so that "almen l'ultimo pianto sia devoto,/ Senza terrestro limo,/ Come fu 'l primo non d'insania voto," we are again confronted with the context of his first weeping, the opening poem of the *Canzoniere:* that opening poem was both the result and the expression of his love, while the ultimate weeping will be his renunciation. In the declaration of his resolve to devote all of his poetic effort to the praise of the Virgin, his "pensieri, e 'ngegno, e stile,/ La lingua, e 'l cor, le lagrime, e i sospiri" brings together once again the major recurring elements in terms of which his activity as love-poet has been expressed, and recalls not only the many poems about these elements individually and together, but also the opening verses of the *Canzoniere*. Even the final words of the *Canzone alla Vergine,* with their totally spiritual sense, relate to the first verses of the opening sonnet: the "sospiri" expressing the poet's troubled love for Laura in verse are indirectly recalled in the reference to his last breath, in the prayer that Christ may receive his "spirto ultimo in pace."

The *Canzone alla Vergine* as a whole is clearly an expression of spiritual crisis, verified in the solemn tones of the poem and in the plea for the Virgin's aid for the penitent's salvation. Like the first poem of the *Canzoniere,* the final canzone invites consideration apart from the body of the collection; a combination of prayer and elegy, it has been generally interpreted in terms of its conformity to traditional patterns of medieval marianic poetry. Yet its relation to the opening sonnet of the *Canzoniere* and its emphasis on the ultimate renewal of poetry lend special significance to its first stanza, an explicit opening generally overshadowed in critical interpretation by the rest of the canzone. The poet records that he begins the poem because he is moved by Love to write poetry of the beautiful lady of Heaven. Addressing himself to the "Vergine bella," he states the reason for the composition of his poem: "Amor mi spinge a dir di te parole." As in the case of his poetry about Laura, it is Love which compels him to write. Iliescu is certainly correct in observing that this love "significa, ovviamente, tutt'altra cosa dalla passione che per tanti anni lo aveva tenuto in catene,"[31] yet there is ample precedent in troubadour poetry for praising the Virgin in the vocabulary of secular love. And as in the case of the poet's earliest love lyrics for Laura, without his lady's inspiration he is unable even to begin his composition: "Ma non so 'ncominciar senza tu' aita." Within this context the phrase which follows, "Invoco lei che ben sempre rispose," assumes the form and position of an invocation to the Muses, and strikes a sharp contrast to his previous expression of failure in his experience as love-poet with Laura as his inspiration.[32] This opening stanza establishes the basis for the disputed unity of the *Canzone alle Vergine:* the rededication of poetry promised in return for the Virgin's aid at the end of the canzone, that promise which so clearly recalls the opening poem of the *Canzoniere,* is a rephrasing in terms of spiritual need of what has been stated in the opening stanza in terms of poetry alone. The Virgin is invoked not only to aid the sinner, but to aid the poet; the object of the poet's love and his Muse are to be one.

It is the *Canzone alla Vergine,* then, which offers the final chapter of the poet-persona's story in the *Canzoniere,* and in it the struggle to interpret and transform the experience of earthly love into a focus worthy of the poet's highest efforts ends in renunciation.[33] It is in this final assessment of the poet's efforts that the final canzone most clearly relates to the opening sonnet of the *Canzoniere.* The mention of *rime sparse* in the opening poem implies the possibility of a different, more coherent form which the expression of the poet's *sospiri* might have assumed, and the references to poetry throughout the *Canzoniere* trace the poet's attempt to articulate that form, to find a poetic expression commensurate with that experience, and to find a relation between poetry and experience which would satisfy both the poet and the lover. In the *Canzone alla Vergine,* while that effort reaches its limit point with the admission of

31. N. Iliescu, *Il canzoniere petrarchesco e Sant'Agostino* (Rome, 1962), p. 93.

32. Williamson notes that in appearance this is the "traditional invocation of help with the composition of the poem, in which Christian poets had substituted the Virgin or the Trinity for the Muses," but sees it in essence to be rather "an invocation of spiritual help that the poet may enter the way of heavenly love" (p. 223). The invocation assumes an additional dimension with regard to poetry, however, when considered within the context of the poet-persona's story throughout the *Canzoniere.*

33. Montanari points to the necessity of keeping in mind that this "non è conclusione vissuta realmente dal Petrarca, bensì conclusione del solo *Canzoniere,*" as the different conclusion of the *Trionfo dell'Eternità* indicates (p. 37). There, "l'amore per Laura era confermato in eterno come nobile elevazione verso Dio."

failure, love poetry itself is ultimately redeemed through rededication. It is the experience of the poet-persona which explains both the ambiguity of the opening poem and the ultimate renunciation and transformation of love-poetry, and it is with reference to the poet-persona's experience that Petrarch adapts the traditional patterns reflected in the first and last poems of the *Canzoniere* to construct a frame for his collection of *rime sparse*.

XI

THE POETICS OF FRANCIS PETRARCH*

by Concetta Carestia Greenfield
Carnegie-Mellon University

Poetry for Petrarch was the catalyst for a humanist awakening, the symbol of a renewed consciousness. Salutati and Boccaccio looked back to Petrarch and Dante as the ones who opened the way for the return of the Muses to Italy. Indeed, if the word Humanism referred to a reawakening centering around the consciousness-expanding power of poetry, Petrarch would certainly be its primary innovator.[1] Completely original in his poetry, he developed in his poetics some of the themes introduced by his Paduan predecessor Albertino Mussato. Petrarch's discussion of poetics was tightly bound up with the major issues of the thirteenth-century intellectual tradition, namely: 1) the conflict in poetics between a humanist-patristic tradition of Platonic inspiration and the new Aristotelianism based on all the translations of Aristotle's *Organon*; and 2) the debate over the legitimacy of classical pagan literature for the Christians. The significance to poetics of the latter debate was to raise questions about the nature of poetical and biblical metaphor, and about the place of poetry within the system of the sciences. These issues colored Petrarch's entire life in addition to his intellectual output. For this reason scholars have devoted considerable attention to his biography, the stages of which reflect the progress of these conflicts of the time.[2]

Petrarch spread the Platonic spirit of Cicero and St. Augustine in Florence. On one occasion he even made a gift of St. Augustine's *Confessiones* to the Augustinian monk Luigi Marsili. Under Petrarch's influence, the medieval Platonic heritage remained the center of the Cenacolo of Santo Spirito in which Marsili and, later, Coluccio Salutati participated.[3] When in Padua, he strenuously fought the dehumanizing

* The following is part of a doctoral dissertation submitted at the University of North Carolina.

1. B. L. Ullman, *Studies in the Italian Renaissance* (Rome, 1955), pp. 11-40, supports the idea that early humanist reawakening means reawakening of poetry.

2. E. H. Tatham, *Francesco Petrarca: The First Man of Letters,* 2 vols. (London, 1925-26); E. H. Wilkins, *Life of Petrarch* (Chicago, 1961).

3. E. Garin, *La letteratura degli umanisti,* in *Storia della letteratura italiana* (1966), III, 7, sees as symbolic of this heritage the gift of the *Confessiones* made by Petrarch to the humanist Augustinian monk Luigi Marsili, who revamped

Aristotelian trend prevailing at the University of Padua in the Faculties of Law and Medicine. A result and expression of this opposition is his *Invectivae contra medicum*.[4] Finally, in France, as Pierre de Nolhac suggests,[5] he came into contact with many classical manuscripts at the Library of the Sorbonne and experienced the heritage of the School of Chartres. French Humanism played an important role in the development of Italian Humanism through the influence of such representatives of the School of Chartres as John of Salisbury, Bernard Silvestris, and Fulbert of Chartres on Petrarch, Boccaccio, and Salutati. The major feature Petrarch inherited from the School of Chartres and transmitted to Italian Humanism was an insistence on the reconciliation of classical poetry with Christianity. This doctrine was based on the Augustinian philosophical argument in the *De doctrina christiana* concerning the Egyptian gold appropriated by the Jews, and on the practical argument of Cassiodorus' *De ordine,* which suggests that grammar, comprising poetry and history in the Middle Ages, was the first of the liberal arts and was necessary for an understanding of Scripture.

While accepting the idea that the liberal arts are necessary to an adequate understanding of Scripture, Petrarch disengages poetry from its ancillary role to grammar, and defines it as an autonomous science, including the traditional disciplines of the patristic and classical heritage and devoid of the anti-classical and technical spirit of the Aristotelian theology and philosophy. Petrarch's main statements on poetical theory are contained in the *Invectivae contra medicum*[6] and in letters among his *Familiares* and *Seniles*. Book III of the *Invectivae* specifically concerns poetics. Its tone is that of a defense, this time not against a Dominican, but against a *medicus*. The *medicus* represents the scholastic approach characteristic of fourteenth-century law, medicine, and theology.

Concurring with Augustine,[7] Petrarch attributes the popularity of

---

the Augustinian spirit in the Florentine circle. Petrarch sides with the Franciscans, i.e., the Augustinian Platonic tradition, against the Dominicans who, in the middle of the thirteenth century, following Albertus Magnus and St. Thomas, abandoned that tradition. Platonic idealism corresponded to the spiritualism of the Franciscan order, while Aristotelian intellectualism corresponded to the rationalism of the Dominicans. Hence a continuous polemic between the two schools of thought.

4. For a discussion of this cultural climate, see G. Toffanin, *Storia dell'Umanesimo* (Bologna, 1933), p. 13, and *Il secolo di Roma* (Bologna, 1942); U. Bosco, "Il Petrarca e l'umanesimo filologico," *Giorn. Stor. della lett. It.*, 120 (1943), 65.

5. Pierre de Nolhac, *Pétrarque et l'Humanisme* (Paris, 1907), I, 39.

6. *Invectivae* in *Francisci Petrarchae Opera Omnia* (Basel, 1581). For the text with an Italian translation see P. G. Ricci's edition in Francesco Petrarca, *Prose,* ed. G. Martellotti et al. (Milan, 1955).

7. *De doctrina christiana* 4.1; 2.50.

dialectic to the decadence of the *humanae litterae*. After the invasion of dialectic, the humanism of the church fathers gave way to speculative commentaries; philosophy and theology became matters of captious argumentation or subtle intellectual games. Thus, the Arab translations of the books of the *Organon* made possible the flow of late medieval dialectic into the body of logic then prevailing at the universities. The mania for syllogism, a cumbersome way of reasoning, became the subject of the debate.[8] According to Petrarch, this disease spread and entrenched itself particularly in England's school of Occam and in Italy's Averroistic University of Padua, most noticeably in its Faculty of Medicine. Petrarch complains in a letter of the accusations against poetry directed to him by a Sicilian dialectician.[9] He notes that this pestilence seems to be peculiar to islands, for in addition to the legions of British dialecticians and logicians, a new horde seems to be arising in Sicily. This is the third pack of monsters to have invaded the poor island of Sicily, their predecessors being the Cyclops and the tyrants. Petrarch goes on to say that these dialecticians are anti-Christian, since their naturalistic beliefs stem from the Arab commentators on Aristotle, rather than from Aristotle himself. To Averroism as a pseudo-science, to dialectic as a pseudo-philosophy, he opposes humanist wisdom, the subordination of the intellectual sphere to the moral one.

Petrarch's emphasis on moral philosophy led him not to a metaphysical but to a practical kind of wisdom, much like the philosophy of *bene vivendi* developed by Cicero in his *Tusculan disputations*. The Thomist negation of the cognitive value of poetry is itself to be discounted in view of poetry's esthetic and moral impact, according to Petrarch. In this issue Petrarch sided with the Franciscans, heirs of the Platonic-Augustinian tradition by virtue of its coincidence with their basic spiritualism.

The Aristotelian doctor who makes his charges against poetry is addressed by Petrarch as "Ypocras et Aristoteles secundus,"[10] by which Petrarch means someone who is versed in naturalistic science and syllogism. The first charge of the *medicus* is based on the premise that

8. *Secretum* 1.1 in *Prose,* p. 52. "Ista quidem dyalecticorum garrulitas nullum finem habitura, et diffinitionum huiuscemodi compendiis scatet et immortalium litigiorum materia gloriatur; plerumque autem, quid ipsum vere sit quod loquuntur, ignorant."

9. *Familiares* 1.7. See the critical ed. by Rossi-Bosco, 4 vols. (Firenze, 1933-42). Cf., among others, P. O. Kristeller, *Renaissance Thought II* (New York, 1965), pp. 111-118.

10. *Invectivae* in *Prose,* p. 648.

what is not necessary is not worthy and noble. Petrarch, however, undoes the logic of the syllogism. If necessity argues true nobility, the farmer and the carpenter are truly noble and the ass and the cock are nobler than the lion and the eagle. So necessity does not always imply nobility. In fact, the contrary is sometimes true, since it is obvious that the eagle is no less noble than the cock, although it is less necessary than the cock. The fact that the art of medicine is more necessary makes it only an *ars mechanica.* How does the doctor dare to proclaim himself a follower of Aristotle if he ignores the basic distinction made in the *Metaphysics* (983a 10-11) between the productive and theoretical arts? With this distinction Aristotle locates the *artes mechanicae* among the productive arts. On the other hand, Aristotle holds the theoretical arts in higher esteem because they pursue knowledge for its own sake rather than for utilitarian goals. Since goals are proper to the *artes necessariae* or *artes mechanicae,* they are less noble and the syllogism of the doctor turns out to be incorrect even in Aristotelian terms.

Continuing in this vein, Petrarch argues that the doctor should understand the limits of his trade, insofar as its nobility is concerned, from the fact that there are many doctors but only a few poets. As Horace said, "neither men nor the gods, nor the booksellers allowed the poets to be mediocre" (*Ars Poetica* 372-3), and it is for this reason that they are few and good. Poetry's gratuity is the mark of its superiority; its lack of necessity makes it a theoretical art, hence more worthy than medicine.

The doctor had subsequently argued that since medicine cures the body and helps people to live better, it is on the same level as ethics and poetry. But Petrarch counters by observing that medicine is directed to the cure of the body and is, therefore, at the service of the body. In the same way the liberal arts, as they aim at the benefit of the soul, are at the service of the soul. Now since the soul clearly leads the body and stands above it, it follows that the liberal arts lead and are above the arts which aim to cure the body. Nor should the doctor think, continues Petrarch, that poetry is not a liberal art simply because it is not mentioned in the traditional division of the arts. It is true that poetry is not mentioned by Hugh of St. Victor in his *Libri septem eruditionis,* where he says that the liberal arts include grammar, rhetoric, dialectic, arithmetic, music, geometry, and astronomy, distinguishing them from the *artes mechanicae* including *lanificium, armatura, navigatio, agricultura, venatio, medicina,* and *treatricum.* But poetry goes without mention here because, along with history, it is included in grammar, the leading art. Nobody would deny the existence of philosophy simply because it is not mentioned among the seven liberal arts, and since grammar subsumes poetry, Petrarch concludes that the place of poetry among the liberal arts is so obvious as to have been taken for granted.

In the next point of controversy, the doctor argues that a science is *firma et impermutabilis,* while poetry is a matter of variable meters and words and is, therefore, not a science. Petrarch counters that the doctor should inquire what this variation means before excluding poetry from the sciences, for what changes is words, while the things remain "upon which the sciences are founded."[11] Science, too, uses words which change according to historical periods, yet it is not judged wholely on the words it uses. Poetry is a science "firm and immutable," as is obvious from the fact that its exercise lends eternity to the poet. It gives the poet a glory which Petrarch's *Secretum* identifies with the particular achievement of the poet in society: through his poetry the poet survives beyond his bodily death. Since poetry transcends the finite barriers of the human life span, it has no time limits and assures the survival of worthwhile human endeavour. Poetry sets itself against the transitoriness of other human values, as a means to eternity. Being eternal, then, its laws remain the same from antiquity to modern times. Hence poetry is a science.

Another accusation made by the doctor is that poets are the enemies of religion: "What do you think of Ambrose, Augustine, Jerome, Cyprian, the martyr Victorinus, Lactantius and all the other Christian writers," asks Petrarch, "since you accuse the poets of being enemies of religion?"[12] He adds that poets have always been concerned with divine matters, and many of them have defended the existence of a unique God. On the other hand, doctors have not become any healthier for reading the treatise of Galen and the Greek treatises based on a naturalistic approach. Furthermore, the doctor seems to ignore the opinion of the philosopher Aristotle, of whom he proclaims himself a follower. In *Metaphysics* 983b 29 Aristotle calls the poets "theologians," since these ancient poets were striving for an understanding of God even more than the philosophers were. Privately, poets believed there was only one God, although the people in those times were uncultured and incapable of understanding concepts of monotheism. Homer thus presented them with images that they could grasp, images of many gods who, in a fashion similar to men, committed crimes and fought with one another.

11. *Invectivae* in *Prose,* p. 648: "In quibus scientiae fundatae sunt."

12. *Invectivae* in *Prose,* p. 648. "Quid de Ambrosio, Augustino et Ieronimo, quid de Cypriano, Victorinoque martire, quid de Lactantio ceterisque Catholicis scriptoribus sentias?"

In this way, Homer indicated that since a multiplicity of gods led them to disputes much as it does with man, there must be some sort of supreme being to inspire harmony.

Poetry is theology for Petrarch as well. In the *Familiares* (10.4), he writes: "Poetics is not very different from theology. Are you amazed? Actually I could easily say that theology is that form of poetics concerning itself with the godhead. Christ is described now as a lion, now as a worm, and is this not a form of poetry? It would be a long matter to enumerate all the other similar images which can be found in Scripture."[13] Considering their relationship further, Petrarch says that poetry and theology are identified not only because the ancient poets were theologians, but also because poets and theologians shared a figurative language whose main element is the metaphor. This language was invented by the ancient poet-theologians: in their desire to understand the first causes, struck by the worth and nobility of these generative principles, they built temples and established ministers and a cult to celebrate them. In order to pray and implore the divinity, they had to create a language more noble than the colloquial one, suitable to address the divinity, so they invented poetry. This is a particular form of speaking and writing involving *numerus,* which confers *suavitas.*[14] This form was called poetry, and the people who used is were called poets. Since it was born out of the need to communicate and address the divinity properly, it is a divine form of speech shared by Scripture; however, while poetry and theology have a common means of expression, their subject-matter remains different. For theology always speaks of true facts and presents true gods, while poetry has often portrayed fictional events and false gods. Except for this difference in subject matter, then, poetry and theology basically involve the same literary forms. So there is a tradition which emphasizes the literary quality of Scripture and notices the poetical language used in such works as Jerome's *Breviary,* St. Augustine's *Enarrationes in Psalmos,* and Cassiodorus' Exposition in his *Psalterium.* St. Augustine himself saw David as a poet, and interpreted the Psalms allegorically. Petrarch provides an allegorical interpretation of his *Bucolics* in much the same vein as

13. The Latin text with an Italian translation appears in E. Garin, *Il pensiero pedagogico dell'Umanesimo* (Firenze, 1958), p. 32. "Miraris? parum abest quin dicam theologiam poeticam esse de Deo: Cristum modo leonem modo agnum modo vermem dici, quid nisi poeticum est? mille talia in Scripturis Sacris invenies que persequi longum est."

14. Garin, *Il pens. ped.,* p. 32. "Id quadam non vulgari forma, sed artificiosa et exquisita et nova fieri oportet." See also Isidore's *Etymologiae* 8.7, 1.3; Suetonius, *De poetis* 2; and Boccaccio's *Gen. Deor.* 14.7.

St. Augustine had done with the Psalms (*Fam.* 10.4; 10.3).

The *suavitas* of the poetical language, its allegorical veil, the doctor counters, is a form of obscurity which, just as it creates wonders, deceives the reader. Petrarch, however, defends the obscurity of poetical allegory, likening it to that of Scriptural allegory.[15] Following the Augustinian argument, he says that the divine word must be obscure, for it is the expression of an inconceivable power, access to which must be rendered difficult to make its understanding pleasing and wondrous. Similarly, poetry uses allegory to signify things not easily understood in a way which stimulates the intelligence of the reader to understand them. Thus, with the allegorical *sermo ornatus* the poet creates wonders, as Horace also noted; the creation of wonder is a main characteristic of poetry. So *veritas* is hidden under the ornamentation of allegory. And beauty resides both in this cortex and in the *veritas* hidden by the cortex, because content and form complement one another. The cortex creates in the reader a sense correlative to the *veritas,* as St. Augustine found in Scripture; Petrarch extends this power to poetry.

It bears noting here that although Petrarch is moved to emphasize that both form and content must be given proper care, it is the *stylus* or *sermo ornatus,* as he calls it, which must be particularly cultivated by the poet. Petrarch's notion of style is a very complex one, as it involves not only poetics but the "expression" of all the *humanae litterae.* It is strictly related to the concept of imitation. In the *Familiares* 1.8 he says: "Like the bees, who do not regurgitate the flowers as they find them but combine them to make wax and honey, . . . so words and style should be our own although composed out of many. . . . Some are like silk worms, which spin everything out of themselves. Let us, however, peruse the books of the wise."[16] The invitation here is to read carefully the form of expression of the classical writers and to retain their spirit, *from which all*

15. *Invectivae* in *Prose,* pp. 669-70. "Quid sermo ipse divinus, quem etsi valde oderis, tamen aperte calumniari propter metum incendii non audebis? Quam in multis obscurus atque perplexus est. Cum prolatus sit ab eo Spiritu Sancto. . . ."

16. Garin, *Il pens. ped.,* p. 31. "Apes in inventionibus imitandas, que flores, non quales acceperint, referunt, sed ceras ac mella mirifica quadam permixtione conficiunt . . . . Illud affirmo: elegantioris esse solertie, ut, apium imitatores, nostris verbis quamvis aliorum hominum sententias proferamus. . . . Rursus nec huius stilum aut illius, sed unum nostrum conflatum ex pluribus habeamus; felicius quidem, non apium more passim sparsa colligere, sed quorundam haud multo maiorum verminum exemplo, quorum ex visceribus sericum prodit, ex se ipso sapere potius et loqui, dummodo et sensus gravis ac verus et sermo esset ornatus . . . . Perscrutemur doctorum hominum libros."

things follow, not simply to copy them: "Like a father and a son whose features and dimensions are different yet have in common what the painters call 'air.' Do not copy words and expressions, but inspire the general 'air.' "[17] "Mix the old with the new."[18] Imitation is then intended as an invitation to be alert to the general "air," i.e., to the spirit or style of the ancient writers.

While the Thomist movement and even some famous Christian writers de-emphasize form and style, often seeing them as a useless adjunct, Petrarch conceives of style as an integral part of content, by virtue of its formative power over content. Later Petrarch clearly felt a conflict between his attachment to form and the disregard of it by famous Christian writers, whom he otherwise admired:

> I loved Cicero, I admit, and I loved Virgil; . . . similarly I loved, of the Greeks, Plato and Homer. . . . But now I must think of more serious matters. My care is more for salvation than for noble language. I used to read what gave me pleasure, now I read what may be profitable. . . . Now my orators shall be Ambrose, Augustine, Jerome, Gregory; my philosopher shall be Paul, my poet David. . . . But although I put the Christian writers first, I do not reject the others. I seem to love both groups at once, provided that I consciously distinguish between those I prefer for style and those I prefer for content.[19]

The doctor's final objection concerns a passage in Boethius' *De consolatione Philosophiae* (1.1.8). Boethius narrates that at his death-bed the poetical Muses came to comfort him, but Philosophy sent the "scenicas meretriculas" away and wished for the presence of her muses ("meae Musae"). Following Priscian's grammatical reasoning, the doctor tries to establish that the "meae" refers to philosophical Muses rather than to poetical Muses in general. Petrarch laughs at the internal contradiction inherent in the doctor's argument, for it seeks to undermine the existence of poetry by borrowing explanations from the field of grammar. In his turn, Petrarch argues that the Muses have always been muses of poetry. By calling them "meae," the personification of Philosophy means that the Muses, in general, are close to her, for philosophers have frequently dealt with poetics, as Aristotle's *Poetics* proves. Actually, Lady Philosophy in Boethius differentiates between the theatrical and other kinds of poetry, which Petrarch uses as evidence that theatrical poetry has too often deviated from the path of truth. But this is not a fault peculiar to poetry. All good things have an impure side, just as

17. *Familiares* 22.19; English translation in Morris Bishop, *Letters from Petrarch* (Bloomington and London, 1966), p. 198.
18. *Seniles* 2.3 in Garin, *Il pens. ped.*, p. 38: "Veteribus nova permisce."
19. *Fam.* 22.10 in Bishop, p. 191.

oil has dregs and philosophy has Epicurus. In fact, philosophy, like poetry, has been accused of impurity. In Book VIII of the *Confessiones* (2.3), St. Augustine writes that the books of the philosophers are filled with deceptions and lies; yet by this he does not mean to condemn philosophy, for in the same book he extensively praises Platonic philosophy. He condemns only that branch of philosophy which by the use of limited rational syllogisms claims to arrive at unconditional truths. The impure part of poetry comes from the dramatic poets condemned by Plato in the *Republic* (398a and 606-607) because the theater had become unworthy of the majesty of the gods. But epic poets like Homer and Virgil have never written drama. Thus, the condemnation should not be extended to them.

To sum up Petrarch's poetics, we find it an elaboration of the rhetorical and Platonic tradition against the new Aristotelianism. He mentions Thomas Aquinas only once, but opposition to a technical, dehumanized theology, philosophy, and poetry runs through his entire work. For Petrarch, poetry is a theoretical art because it makes use of grammar and all the other liberal arts. What raises poetry above grammar and the other liberal arts is the poetical language it shares with the Bible. This language has divine origins because it was invented to speak about the gods. Furthermore, it serves as a vehicle for divine revelation, not only on account of its content and origins, but because with its allegorical form of expression it has the air of divine truth, from which every truth proceeds. With its language, then, poetry holds to the spirit of things, and the *stylus ornatus* is the specific characteristic of poetry which gives it a formative power unsurpassed by any other art. In addition, poetry immortalizes the poet through posterity, a theme dear to Petrarch's sonnets in the *Canzoniere*. For insofar as the poet avails himself of the classical poets, imbuing their style with the spirit of his own times, his poetry will come to have enduring force.

Petrarch's poetics is particularly influenced by Platonism.[20] In Book VIII of St. Augustine's *De civitate Dei,* he read about the superiority of Platonism to all other philosophies. And in the work of St. Augustine, Petrarch found much correspondence with Christian Fathers.[21] He knew Plato, too, through Macrobius' *Somnium Scipionis*. He knew Chalcidius' version of the *Timaeus* and Apuleius' *De Platone et eius dogmate*.[22] In addition to this indirect tradition, the School of Chartres

20. P. P. Gerosa, *Umanesimo cristiano del Petrarca* (Torino, 1966), p. 246.

21. *De Remediis* 11.119; *Fam.* 22.5.

22. Giovanni Gentile, "Le traduzioni medievali di Platone e Francesco Petrarca," *Studi sul Rinascimento* (Firenze, 1936); Roberto Weiss, *Il primo secolo dell'Umanesimo* (Roma, 1949).

handed down to him the ideal of a reconciliation of paganism and Christianity, of classical humanist wisdom and the newly rediscovered Aristotle.[23] The direct influence of John of Salisbury of the School of Chartres on Petrarch has been recently pointed out by Paolo Gerosa.[24] Like John of Salisbury in the *Metalogicon,* Petrarch considers logic a science of persuasion involving basically moral criteria and directed toward practical aims. All this is not to say that Petrarch did not recognize Aristotle's scientific acuity. Petrarch, however, calls Aristotle a student of Plato: "Aristotle, a disciple of Plato, was a man of great intelligence and eloquence; though not comparable to Plato, nevertheless he easily surpasses quite a few."[25] Petrarch's Platonism is of extreme importance, for he is the transmitter of the Platonic heritage in poetics to the Florentine humanists. This tradition was not transmitted without influence from medieval thinkers; Gerosa's investigation of Petrarch's sources indicates that the medieval heritage was his firm cultural background, while he emphasized the classical sources as a "discovery."[26] Thus, his poetics reflect that humanist tradition which, issuing from the classical and Platonic tradition, became crystallized in the system of St. Augustine. This tradition was transmitted to the Renaissance by such early humanists as Mussato, Petrarch, Boccaccio, and Salutati.

23. Pierre de Nolhac, ch. ix.

24. Gerosa, p. 248.

25. *Rerum memorandarum* 1.26. "Aristoteles, Platonis discipulus, vir excellentis ingenii et eloquii, Platoni quidem impar, sed multa facile superans."

26. Gerosa, p. 258, lists all the medieval thinkers who, like the rings of a long chain, connect St. Augustine to Petrarch.

XII

PETRARQUE ET LE LANGAGE

by Arnaud Tripet
University of Chicago

"Aux uns la prison et la mort, aux autres la transhumance du Verbe."
René Char

1. *Homo loquens*

Le beau discours renvoie à l'excellence du discourant. "Tel est l'homme, tel est son discours", dit Sénèque.

L'on a souvent parlé de l'évolution qualitativement négative de l'art oratoire dans les temps anciens. Soit en Grèce, soit à Rome, la rhétorique, pratiquée originellement selon les exigences objectives de sa perfection, dégénéra, dit-on, par les soins de ses adeptes, trop soucieux d'exploits retentissants et plus attentifs à leurs intérêts privés qu'à la vérité et au bien collectif. Les Anciens eux-mêmes nous ont livré ce schéma; l'affrontement de Socrate et des sophistes, le découragement tacitien devant la décadence de l'art oratoire et des condition disparues de son existence, constituèrent, de l'humanisme jusqu'hier, des scènes typiques et des points de référence obligatoires de la lutte historique entre un usage vertueux du langage au sein de la société, et la finalité coupablement égocentrique de sa pratique.[1] Il faut faire la part de la réduction catégorique d'autrui que l'esprit polémique opère volontiers: de même qu'on est toujours le barbare de quelqu'un on est souvent le sophiste de ses ennemis. Et ceci de tout temps. Il est bien difficile, en effet, de ne pas imaginer un parallélisme étroit et nécessaire entre la naissance d'une conscience artistique de la parole et, d'autre part, l'émergence de la vanité et d'une intention intéressée. Au coeur même de l'école, dès son origine, mais aussi dans chaque expérience individuelle et en tout point de l'histoire, surgit pour l'éloquence la tentation de l'effet en retour et les périlleuses conséquences d'une paternité complaisante.

Au versant de la décadence possible répond cependant le versant de l'ascèse, non moins lié, sans doute, à la vanité, mais dérivant alors du sentiment plus austère d'une noblesse de caste. Une sorte de législation s'instaure très tôt dans l'image du parfait orateur, où la perfection du

1. Voir notamment U. Foscolo, *Dell'origine e dell'ufficio della letteratura, Edizione nazionale* (Firenze, 1933), pp. 25-30.

discours postule explicitement celle du discourant. "Qui parle bien est beau et bon", dit Platon. Conséquence ou condition? La question est d'importance, mais quelle qu'en soit la réponse, que celle-ci révèle une généralisation discutable du talent ou fonde la thèse exigeante d'un discours-reflet, qu'elle soit d'un versant ou de l'autre, il est sûr que la formule platonicienne trahit la volonté de lier clairement, chez l'artiste de la parole, la bonté productrice et la beauté produite, la vertu et l'art, l'éthique et l'esthétique. Cette communication proclamée par le philosophe athénien et répétée à satiété par les théoriciens de l'éloquence latine, passera dans le moule chrétien, par les soins entre autre d'un saint Augustin, rhéteur et platonisant. A la charnière d'une religion des formes et d'une religion de l'âme, il accueille, de l'antiquité, l'instabilité éthico-esthétique que traduit le vocabulaire ambivalent des rhéteurs classiques—l'on sait combien le *recte dicere* de Quintilien appelle l'idée de rectitude—et la transmet au monde chrétien, qui multipliera, particulièrement dans l'aire gothique et courtoise, les effets d'une esthétisation de l'âme humaine. A l'idée précédemment dominante d'une beauté qui inclut le bien, succèdera le règne d'un bien qui est beau.

"Anime belle", dira Pétrarque des héros d'autrefois. Pour en arriver à une telle ferveur, il a fallu que les forces de la synthèse éthico-esthétique de l'éloquence antique, patronées de loin par le platonisme, rencontrent un terrain où la croyance du destin éternal de l'âme humaine dépendît de son passage ici-bas, de son apparition, de ses preuves, de la manière décisive dont elle s'est fait *voir* et si possible admirer. Il fallait, en d'autre termes, que le monde d'héroïsme et de sagesse véhiculé par l'éloquence des Anciens opérât sa jonction avec le grand courant de la sainteté chrétienne.

La couleur particulière de l'humanisme pétrarquien, si fécond, dans ses conséquences pour l'humanisme occidental tout entier, tient à cette confluence; mais aussi aux problèmes d'homogénéité que cette rencontre pose, et à la synthèse effective, et obstinément conquise, qu'elle nécessite. L'on sait combien Pétrarque lutte pour établir la légitimité de la leçon des Anciens pré-chrétiens. Il n'est pas le premier à répondre au défi des dogmatiques et des puristes en matière de croyance. Dès l'aube du christianisme cultivé, à Alexandrie en particulier, l'on n'avait pu échapper au problème d'un langage saturé d'images incompatibles avec les vérités révélées, mais seul capable, soit dans la poésie, soit même dans la constitution d'une exégèse proprement chrétienne, de fournir des instruments subtiles et robustes.

Les besoins et les moyens se répondent. Cela est vrai de la culture chrétienne à l'époque impériale, et, au delà, dans le monde byzantin; cela est vrai de toutes les Renaissances, qu'elles soient carolingienne ou contemporaine des premières cathédrales, mais aussi des trois décennies (1340-1374) que Pétrarque marqua de sa présence active, inquiète et exigeante. Si toute Renaissance débute par une reprise en charge des pouvoirs du *logos,* il convient d'assigner à l'humanisme pétrarquien, à ces retrouvailles extraordinairement passionnées d'un langage oublié (non point tellement du latin en tant que tel, que d'un certain "langage" du langage), la place inaugurale dans ce qui, par lui, devint la Renaissance. Cette Renaissance qu'il ne prévoyait que très obscurément, et pour certains pas du tout, développa, il faut bien le dire, en mille sens différents les germes du Trecento.[2] Cependant, une chose semble constante dans les conclusions auxquelles peuvent conduire les discussions infinies sur la périodisation et l'essence de cette catégorie historique, et c'est ce qu'on pourrait appeler l'enjeu humain de l'aventure formelle, de l'éloquence verbale aux arts de l'espace ("cosa mentale" selon Leonardo). Si paganisante ou hédoniste qu'ait pu être parfois la recherche du beau au Quattrocento et au Cinquecento, il appert néanmoins qu'une sorte de passion anime toujours à cette époque l'activité qui se déroule dans le monde d'une perfection sensible. Quant à l'insouciance apparente de certains produits du monde médicéen, ne peut-on y voir la traduction d'une angoisse? Ne peut-on deviner dans ce formalisme raffiné et même ludique, l'aveu indirect d'un vide à combler? Que l'on opte, à l'égard de la Renaissance, dans les oeuvres déployées dans l'espace ou celles dites "sermocinales", pour la thèse d'une esthétique passionnée, ou d'un art désenchanté (bien qu'enchanteur), le choix décisif de la forme s'inscrit de toutes façons dans une perspective où le visible est aux antipodes de l'indifférence, car il est le produit d'une opération décisive, toute valeur vécue, qu'elle relève du bien ou du beau étant conçue alors comme quelque chose d'essentiellement perceptible.

A l'origine il y avait bien Pétrarque, avec cette soif de bien faire dans le court laps de la vie, cette crainte panique d'être surpris par la mort, en état de péché, sa croyance proche d'un certain esprit d'enfance, en un Dieu un peu comptable et facilement réductible dans son infinie sagesse à l'économie d'une sagesse finie et humaine, un Dieu où l'on ne se perd assurément pas, au bout des avenues d'une nuit mystique, mais qui grâce aux médiations des âmes élues, de la Vierge et du Christ communique avec le monde d'ici-bas et autorise par ce rapport et ce regard le sentiment d'une issue possible de l'intention dans le faire et

2. E. Gilson, "Sur deux textes de Pétrarque", *Studi petrarcheschi,* VII (1961), discuté dans mon *Pétrarque ou la connaissance de soi* (Genève, 1967), p. 123, n. 9.

des valeurs dans le visible. Un christianisme de confessional, à première vue, et où l'objet visé par la connaissance est—contrairement à la démarche dantesque—l'homme bien plus que Dieu. Aussi bien le bréviaire idéal de Pétrarque contient-il d'abord des exemples et peu ou pas de méditations sur la transcendance; chrétiennement, il est l'homme des *Fioretti,* plutôt que du *Breviloquium* bonaventurien; et s'il puise très largement dans l'oeuvre augustinienne, c'est aux *Confessions* qu'il revient toujours.

Ce qui prime pour lui, c'est le bien vécu, la vie comme mise au jour de la vertu. Et la raison première qui l'attache aux Anciens procède de leur caractère exemplaire à cet égard. Pour Pétrarque, il n'y a qu'une manière d'être homme, c'est la vertu, et comme son christianisme sera, en ce sens, anthropocentrique, son humanisme culturel (archéologique) s'accordera naturellement avec sa conception vertuiste de la religion. Quand on lui demande, ou quand il se demande, s'il n'aime pas trop la littérature, il n'a nulle peine à justifier son goût en le rapportant au goût d'une vertu, d'une grandeur et d'une gravité que la tradition littéraire lui transmet. Dans la relation des *res gestae* magnifiées et exaltantes, l'ambition bien comprise d'une vie vraiment humaine puise une sorte d'équivalent moral de l'oxygène. L'on a l'impression que l'exemplarité proclamée par l'historiographie antique se met à jouer, chez lui, sur le plan individuel; bien plus, que Pétrarque se reconnaît en Scipion, héros et lettré, parce que les lettres pour lui englobent l'héroïsme comme ressurgence possible, et, pour ainsi dire véritable, des faits dans le souvenir effectif de l'écrit. Ainsi, sans renoncer au *nous* collectif auquel aboutit la visée des *exempla* dans la pensée antique, Pétrarque confère à ceux-ci un rebondissement nouveau en direction d'un moi pour lequel ils vivent d'une nouvelle vie, car c'est lui qui les ressaisit dans la mise en forme de l'enthousiasme et d'une beauté inédite. La fusion du beau (dont il est capable) et du bon que son espoir caresse, il ne cesse de la tenter tout au long de sa carrière, comme l'alchimiste s'évertue après la pierre philosophale; et comme pour celui-ci, la noblesse du propos entraîne chez l'humaniste une sorte de pureté, dont il se sent le dépositaire, la pureté finale, et bien hypothétique ici-bas, éclairant et purifiant par avance, celui qui s'achemine vers elle. Voilà qui explique le caractère à la fois épidictique (Laure, les Anciens) et satirique (combien de "méchants"!) de l'oeuvre de Pétrarque; l'alternance en elle de l'admiration et du mépris; car à la première se rattache, à l'égard de la pureté, une volonté d'orientation, tandis que le second révèle, surtout, une sorte de conscience de l'acquis. Quelle soit la preuve d'un arrachement accompli ou en train de s'accomplir, la littérature revendique le privilège transformant de l'acte, de la valeur en acte, pour dire mieux. Quelle chance pour elle que la pensée du temps soit encore dans le prolongement d'une mentalité et d'une méthode normatives, que la grammaire et la logique scolastique, avec leur absence de risque, d'enjeu et d'ouverture, surtout dans les formes dégénérées d'une application devenue souvent mécanique, soient encore dans leur prestige! La littérature peut alors plus aisément se définir, saisir radicalement sa différence, opposer aux arts du fonctionnement un art de l'expérience valorisante et d'une vertu qui trouve dans l'irradiation du langage cet élément dynamique, visible et communicatif qui lui permet de s'y reconnaître.[3] Cette revendication a été étudiée sur le plan des luttes historiques, comme la volonté d'obtenir pour la rhétorique la place d'honneur que les humanistes estimaient lui revenir de droit dans un *trivium* déséquilibré selon eux par les maîtres de l'Université.[4] Pétrarque appartient à cette lutte au niveau des principes et il est moins sensible que d'autres à l'enjeu économique et social de cet affrontement entre les tenants de la culture officielle et la *novitas* qu'il incarne. Quand en 1340, la Sorbonne et Rome lui offrent en même temps la couronne de poète, il choisit le patronage de Robert d'Anjou et le Capitole, c'est-à-dire l'humanisme de la cour de Naples et l'Antiquité, non la grande école parisienne et son siège théologique. Abstraction faite de l'intérêt immédiat que Pétrarque pouvait indéniablement y trouver, un tel choix apparaît essentiellement comme un fait symbolique, confirmé par mille passages des lettres et par maintes diatribes en forme contre la culture de son temps, en particulier l'aristotélisme scolastique et son formalisme envahissant, l'averroïsme et son naturalisme mal-pensant. Mais, à nouveau, ce n'est pas au niveau du professionalisme, mais d'une profession de foi, que doivent se situer ces textes où Pétrarque attaque et se justifie; ce qui est en cause, ce n'est pas un prestige institutionalisé mais l'efficacité et le sérieux de cette alchimie nouvelle ou renouvelée qui associe dans un même mouvement valeur et vie, beauté et vertu.

2. *Le bien*

Dira-t-on qu'il suffit à Pétrarque de proclamer la vertu pour qu'il se sente persuadé de la posséder et de la pratiquer? Revivre en esprit, est-ce pour lui vivre effectivement, et peut-il s'identifier, sans éprouver le sentiment d'une usurpation, à un mérite qu'il se contente de recon-

3. Consulter E. Garin, *L'Umanesimo italiano* (Bari, 1952); C. Vasoli, *La Dialettica e la retorica dell'umanesimo* (Milano, 1967).

4. P. O. Kristeller, *Renaissance Thought: The Classic, Scholastic and Humanistic Strain* (New York, 1961).

naître et d'exalter? Toutes ces questions, il faut les poser, non à la conscience d'un Pétrarque hypothétiquement vivant, mais au mouvement intime de son oeuvre. En d'autres termes, est-on en présence d'un monument, constitué par de faciles substitutions, où l'action vertueuse des autres, inscrite dans le prolongement d'un jugement, d'une intention et d'un amour parfaitement pétrarquiens, apparaîtrait à son tour comme une émanation pétrarquienne? Si, dans le rapport entre l'éthique et l'esthétique réside, comme nous le croyons, le germe et l'enjeu de cette oeuvre, il sera difficile de lui reconnaître une grandeur authentique et d'admettre, en même temps, les données d'une magie aussi médiocre. Certes, la tentation existe chez Pétrarque, quand il se place de côté de l' "acquis", et se drape à l'antique, de se croire corps et bien dans le monde qui naît de son désir et de sa plume. Une certaine suffisance, parfois polémique, un goût prononcé pour un discours puisant aux sources de la sagesse et, parallèlement, une attitude de familiarité envers les possesseurs prestigieux de cette sagesse, tout cela peut créer, chez le lecteur, qui dans son ignorance fonctionne alors comme un utile "repoussoir", le sentiment fortement sollicité que celui qui parle et qui sait, est ce qu'il sait, et qu'il engendre ce qu'il dit. Mais la tentation est conjuré dans le discours même.

Dans le discours pétrarquien, nous avons vu que l' "acquis" n'est qu'une des tendances à l'oeuvre, et qu'il en est une autre qui est la tendance à acquérir, la conquête. Si facilement qu'il se mette parfois au diapason de l'univers des Anciens, par exemple, Pétrarque, le plus souvent, s'emploie visiblement à s'en approcher, à les pendre à témoins des efforts qui le conduisent vers eux, à les placer sur sa route pour mieux enregistrer un cheminement, un dépassement, et *se* conduire, avec leur aide, au-delà de lui-même. C'est là un des sens principaux du dialogue chez Pétrarque. Et à cet égard, l'on peut dire que presque tout est dialogue dans son oeuvre, car, même quand l'autre n'apparaît pas explicitement comme *persona,* on trouve le plus souvent très clairement posé ce par quoi (et non seulement ce sur quoi) Pétrarque s'efforce de bien penser, le mètre, ou, qu'on pardonne le mot, le maître de sa pensée en acte. Pétrarque écrit constamment sous le regard de juges qu'il insère à titre de citation, de référence, de correspondant fictif dans l'économie de son discours, de manière à s'obliger. Il constitue son *surmoi* en Olympe actif, dans le drame dont il est le protagoniste agissant et "agi". Et tandis que par rapport au lecteur, il parle souvent en maître, il se comporte, parfois dans le même texte, comme le disciple d'une valeur précédemment incarnée, quand il veut (mais, au fond, ne le veut-il pas toujours?) voir s'accomplir sous ses yeux une transformation qui associe au mieux-dire, un mieux-être. La retouche est la forme maîtresse de cette opération. Elle marque d'une part une supériorité qui se construit; elle fonctionne, ainsi, dans une perspective "magistrale". Mais elle marque, d'autre part, l'effort d'une âme en quête d'une vérité qu'il faut conquérir pouce par pouce; et cette vérité toujours provisoire avoue à chaque étape son approximation, et une imperfection qui ne s'estompe que progressivement.

La retouche est, en somme, la forme dynamique d'un dialogue de Pétrarque avec lui-même, entre un état illusoire et un état véridique, et cela, sous l'égide d'une Vérité (*Secretum*) ou de porteurs de vérité (Laure, les Anciens, la Raison du *de Remediis,* saint Augustin dans le *Secretum*) qui sont le repère nécessaire d'une distance à parcourir. Sur cette route, dont Pétrarque figura si éloquemment les difficultés dans sa lettre relatant son ascension du Mont-Ventoux, chaque étape est une conquête. Sur cette route où se meuvent à la fois l'homme en marche et le discours humain, s'accomplit un pélerinage coûteux, et dont l'orientation, constamment rectifiée, est assumée par une mémoire et un amour vigilants.[5]

3. *Vérité et beauté*

Pour l'humaniste et le chrétien, la seule connaissance qui compte est celle qui se rapporte directement à la vie et à la survie de l'homme. Pétrarque s'engage sans hésiter dans ce chemin hors duquel il ne voit pas seulement l'éventualité d'un vagabondage, mais la menace de l'erreur. C'est ainsi qu'il proclame l'inutilité entre autre des sciences naturelles et accuse ceux qui s'y adonnent de complaisance pour l'illusoire. Son "invective" contre les quatre averroïstes padouans est bien connue, et elle nous permet de surprendre Pétrarque dans sa tentative la plus approfondie d'autojustification face aux doutes dont pouvait être l'objet le sérieux de ses études. A l'objection averroïste que bien parler n'est pas nécessairement dire vrai, l'humaniste rétorque que la vérité, la vérité vraie, celle qui nous concerne vraiment, ne peut s'énoncer que dans un langage qui nous touche, le langage de Cicéron, par exemple, de préférence à celui dans lequel nous sont parvenues les leçons d'Aristote. Il s'applique évidemment à délimiter les articles positifs de son orthodoxie, s'en remettant prudemment à un minimum officiellement inattaquable et qu'il appelle la vérité du Christ. Mais le point névralgique et l'originalité de ces lettres polémiques tient davantage à cette foi qui les imprègne et qui affirme la parenté profonde des lois qui gouvernent la vérité

5. F. Tateo, *Dialogo interiore e polemica ideologica nel* Secretum *del Petrarca* (Firenze, 1965).

et de celles qui assurent au langage son efficacité plénière. L'idée que la force du langage puisse servir au mensonge et que le diable est un maître discoureur ne l'effleure pas. Il n'y veut pas penser (si ce n'est en y associant l'idée des "dialectici" modernes), comme si une certaine virginité du *logos* pouvait être tenue pour bien autre chose qu'un songe de l'âge d'or ou un souvenir édénique.

S'il accorde que Cicéron n'est pas chrétien c'est de la plus mauvaise grâce du monde et uniquement parce qu'on l'oblige à endosser cette vieille querelle "patristique" qui l'assomme, et où il s'embrouillerait complètement, n'était l'apparente rigueur d'une machine rhétorique toujours prête à fonctionner. Il n'y eut pas de réponse à cette mise au point de Pétrarque, du moins à notre connaissance. Avouons que les philosophes padouans auraient eu là beau jeu. Ce qu'ils auraient sans doute dénoncé n'est que trop évident: à savoir qu'une vérite qui se poursuit en liaison si étroite et si avouée avec une recherche de l'épanouissement intérieur, de l'équilibre et du salut court de graves risques, et que son objectivité pourrait ne mériter que fort peu de crédit. Mais à une attaque de ce genre Pétrarque était en mesure d'opposer une sereine indifférence. Car, au-delà de l'agacement que cause à sa vanité un certain refus de la jeunesse contemporaine, au-delà même de la stupeur indignée (mais partiellement retenue) qu'il éprouve à voir l'hostilité des tenants d'une culture qui lui semble dépassée, à l'égard des valeurs qu'il reconnaît et qu'il vit, ce qui pour lui ne fait aucun doute, c'est la sainteté du langage alors précisément qu'il est polarisé par un monde de valeurs, qui, ainsi que nous l'avons vu, opère chez le disant une purification "intentionnelle", condition préalable et fin téléologique d'une parole déployée. Il y a là, tout compte fait, une sorte de conviction intime qui dérive de la révélation chrétienne (nécessité de s'intéresser à un salut qui est aussi la voie de la vérité), des exemples anciens, révélation d'une autre sorte, mais non moins irréfutable, et enfin, d'une expérience littéraire qui trouve dans le prestige de semblables instances le sentiment d'une véritable bénédiction et la confirmation la plus autorisée. Que l'on éprouve en présence d'un tel éventail de raisons sous-jacentes l'impression tout à la fois d'une certaine naïveté et d'un agencement commode, il est difficile de le nier. Les prémisses d'une telle expérience ont quelque chose de peut-être trop massif pour ne pas être un peu fragile. Nous retrouvons, au niveau de la vérité, une tension que nous venons de surprendre entre l'éthique et l'esthétique et qui engageait Pétrarque à joindre littérairement les mérites à la grâce et les oeuvres à la foi.

Dans la mesure où il consacre l'alliance de principe entre le moi et la vérité, le discours pétrarquien semble bien contenir, malgré le "bon ange" du salut (intérêt égocentrique et vérité), le germe d'une illusion contre laquelle il convient de se prémunir. Or, nous surprenons précisément dans l'écriture du philosophe moral et du poète un effort qui va constamment en ce sens.

Examinons d' abord le mécanisme de la tentation; le remède en apparaîtra plus spécifiquement. On pourrait réduire cette tentation à une sorte d'avatar de ce que Schiller devait appeler "poésie sentimentale". En effet, Pétrarque, tout au long de son oeuvre, vise Pétrarque; son mouvement le plus naturel est celui de la réflexion ou de la réflexivité. Mais, il vise aussi la vérité; et il est bien obligé de lui accorder un statut distinct, et, en un premier temps au moins, un statut extérieur. On lui voit, en effet, souligner ce caractère en faisant apparaître la vérité comme une révélation d'en-haut, la matière d'un credo, une allégorie. Cependant la contrepartie "sentimentale" ne tarde pas à s'imposer. L'extériorité va s'intérioriser; et ce sera pour le meilleur et pour le pire.

Pour le meilleur, car cette assimilation fait partie de ce que nous avons appelé la "conquête", le perfectionnement de soi dans l'exercice ardu d'une vérité approchée. C'est là ce qui donne à l'oeuvre de Pétrarque l'allure d'une vérité vécue, car même dans les moments où l'humaniste déverse, presque sans les filtrer, les flots d'un savoir accumulé, on devine l'enthousiasme, la volonté démonstrative, l'expérience, laquelle semble suggérer, au-delà de la compilation, que ce qui est dit n'est pas simplement une chose sue, mais une chose apprise. Pétrarque va le plus loin possible dans ce processus d'intériorisation: la Providence même s'y est intéressée; elle lui a montré la voie royale de l'excellence en lui faisant aimer, sans qu'il les comprît encore, Cicéron et Virgile, et en l'attachant, dès l'aube de sa vie, à cette vérité du Christ, dont il a eu le tort de s'éloigner momentanément, à l'âge des passions.

Mais pour le pire aussi, car cette assimilation le conduit à se prendre pour la vérité, et à se mettre, pour cette raison même sur le devant de la scène. La vérité ontologique se voit relayée par la vérité pétrarquienne, une vérité proférée par Pétrarque et qui s'identifie en dernier ressort avec la vérité *sur* Pétrarque, et la connaissance qu'il peut et que nous devons en avoir. Tel est le piège de l'éloquence valorisante et de l'humanisme sotérologique. La discrimination orthodoxe de la vérité n'ayant pas conjuré les démons de l'égocentrisme, Pétrarque va procéder à une discrimination de soi-même, et dégager sa responsabilité de cette image vraie, qui se substitue trop volontiers, il le sent bien, à l'image du vrai. Pétrarque va partir à la recherche d'une obliquité qui révèle le moi non comme un objet *donné,* mais comme une physionomie dérivée.

Là encore, la littérature vient à son aide, car elle lui permet, par le style qui traduit l'homme, d'être constamment présent, mais sans se proposer explicitement dans une sorte d'autoportrait. Il se montre en action, au travail, en posture courageuse, lucide; et c'est le lecteur qui tirera de l'exemple d'un comportement la conclusion généralisante d'un trait ou d'une opinion. Il n'est que de lire ce qui s'approche le plus de l'autoportrait en forme, la lettre à la *Postérité* et le *Secretum.* Dans le premier cas, l'on s'aperçoit que ce qui importe à Pétrarque, c'est d'imposer au lecteur l'image de quelqu'un qui sait parler de soi, bien plus que de construire un ensemble de traits ou d'événements directement "épidictiques". Ceux-ci sont volontairement ramenés à une sorte de norme typique pour mieux traduire l'aptitude latente à l'équilibre et à la mesure. Les traits de l'autoportrait visé se dégagent de l'écriture même et de l'esprit qui y recourt.

Pour le *Secretum,* la vertu actuelle de celui qui parle de soi est encore plus apparente puisqu'elle est le fondement éthique de la confession. Le courage est ici le viatique d'une entreprise conquérante, où le moi doit accepter de se renoncer pour se réformer. Mais se renonce-t-il? Et le caractère fondamentalement égocentrique du salut et de la vérité n'entraîne-t-il pas, fût–ce obliquement, pour sauver les apparences, le retour presque nécessaire d'une mise en forme de soi, qui ressemble quelque peu à un privilège? Celui, notamment, d'ajouter à la satisfaction de déployer tant de courage, celle, accordée indirectement par la bouche de saint Augustin, d'une reconnaissance de bonne conduite sur un certain nombre de points. L'on a l'impression aussi que le saint exagère juste assez sa sévérité pour que, quelquefois, François puisse, sinon le réfuter (la solution reste en général ouverte), mais faire entendre que la vérité n'est pas si noire. L'on voit que, de deux manières, l'auteur recourt dans cette confession à une obliquité finalement avantageuse.

Mais, dira-t-on, le *Secretum* est oeuvre intime; il n'est pas vraiment destiné à être lu et l'objectivité qui devrait naître dans l'esprit d'un lecteur reste donc à l'état de puissance. A cela, une réponse fort simple. Saint Augustin, au moyen de son approbation, et François de sa résistance légitime, fonctionnent à l'intérieur de l'oeuvre comme des lecteurs qui dégageraient la vérité à partir de l'extérieur et de manière dérivée. Plus généralement, ils sont des lecteurs, des points de vue, en même temps que des peintres de la réalité intérieure, et cela d'autant mieux qu'ils sont deux et que ce que chacun dit est à la fois une manière d'être pétrarquienne traduite dans l'écriture, et la lecture de ce qui vient d'être dit par l'autre et qui était également une manière d'être pétrarquienne. L'on se trouve ainsi, en présence, non seulement de deux niveaux de conscience, la conscience immédiate de François et la conscience déontologique d'Augustin, mais aussi des deux faces de l'image pétrarquienne: l'image suggérée par l'allure du dire et l'image constituée dans la synthèse de la lisibilité.

Grâce à un processus de théâtralisation extrême, ce dialogue avec soi-même, qui en tant que tel, reproduit une expérience commune chez Pétrarque, parvient donc à supprimer la nécessité du lecteur, chacune des deux *personae* lisant l'autre. Exemple d'oeuvre fermée, puisque l'image sollicitée est recueillie à l'intérieur, mais où l'expression favorable et oblique (oblique pour ne pas être trop favorable) n'échappe pas, surtout si l'on se rappelle que le langage augustinien qui s'y trouve procède d'une dictée pétrarquienne et que l'ignorance dans laquelle on tiendra peut-être le public de cette oeuvre intime, n'empêchera pas un lecteur au moins de reconnaître dans la force explicite de cet autre qu'est saint Augustin (mais autre par le nom seulement) quelque chose qui lui appartient, puisqu'il a su le mettre en oeuvre; et ce lecteur est Pétrarque lui-même. On lit dans le *Prohemium:*

> Hoc igitur tam familiare colloquium ne forte dilaberetur, dum scriptis mandare instituo, mensuram libelli huius implevi. Non quem annumerari aliis operibus meis velim aut unde gloriam petam (maiora quedam mens agitat) sed ut dulcedinem, quam semel ex collocutione percepi, quotiens libuerit ex lectione percipiam.

Si narcissique qu'elle soit, la satisfaction renouvelée du lecteur de soi-même, reproduit bien le modèle connu d'une suggestion émise par un texte et d'une représentation déduite dans une lecture.

En fait ces quelques lignes et tout le dialogue intérieur qu'il annonce nous placent devant les aspects les plus significatifs de la pratique et de l'idéologie pétrarquienne en matière de langage. D'abord la dialectique de l'acquis et de l'acquisition; l'acquis étant la conséquence d'une familiarité, ennoblissante pour l'auteur, avec la grandeur et la sainteté du monde dans lequel son écriture humaniste et chrétienne l'introduit; l'acquisition étant le recours qui permet de maîtriser l'apparence, inévitable en l'occurrence, d'une assimilation *a priori* de l'éthique par ce qui, en fait, ne relève que de la sphère esthétique. Ce recours dont la marque stylistiquement la plus visible est la correction et la retouche (le tâtonnement zigzagant du *Secretum*) emprunte au langage même et à sa dimension ouverte (Saussure dirait linéaire), la possibilité d'obvier à ce qui dans le langage et dans sa fixation "monumentale" peut exprimer l'*a priori* abusif d'un embellissement de l'âme, cet "acquis" que la présence toute naturelle d'un saint trahit ici, comme le fait ailleurs celle des Anciens, auxquels l'humaniste se prend à écrire.

La deuxième tension se rapporte à l'annexion du vrai, plutôt qu'à celle du bien. Dans un réseau de notions où circule le moi, Pétrarque s'offre d'abord l'assurance d'une identité possible entre ce moi et la vérité. Si la vérité est un certain langage, ce langage est créé et reçu par le moi, d'où possibilité d'une jonction moi-vérité, confirmée par le lien théologique d'un salut égocentrique et véridique, non moins que linguistique. Mais là encore, grâce aux ressources du langage, Pétrarque corrige les effets inadmissibles d'un langage trop généreux. Il s'emploie à incarner la vérité hors de lui et, surtout, il s'attache à dégager par l'implicite et par l'obliquité d'un style, sa responsabilité directe dans une entreprise qui est constamment sollicitée par la réalité du moi. Si le problème de mon identité finit ainsi par absorber presque complètement le souci de vérité, il ne sera pas dit que ma vérité puisse assumer l'apparence d'une sorte de dogme. Elle sera tout au plus la généralisation d'un exemple vivant dans l'esprit du lecteur, image vraie, dont les autres feront (ou ne feront pas) la vérité.

Enfin, troisième (et nouvelle) tension, admirablement signifiée dans le titre du dialogue (*De secreto conflictu curarum mearum*) et dans la thématique de sa troisième partie (Laure, la gloire), la littérature qui est forme bénéficie évidemment des avantages de la beauté: elle possède le pouvoir de plaire et d'habiter la mémoire des hommes; elle transmet la grandeur morale de l'héroïsme qu'elle chante et *se* transmet elle-même comme chant durable et prestigieux. Elle est siège et création d'une valeur éternelle. Mais est-elle éternelle? Dans les *Trionfi,* le *de Remediis* et le *Secretum* Pétrarque s'interroge, sans parvenir à se résoudre, sur la valeur de la gloire. L'intérêt pour nous est qu'ici le topos antique, que la vanité pétrarquienne ne pouvait pas ne pas accueillir avec faveur, rencontre une résistance. La forme qui peut tant, Pétrarque ne se cache pas qu'elle ne peut pas tout; que le temps et une deuxième mort, celle de la gloire, finissent par la vaincre. Dans un même mouvement, la bouche d'Augustin condamnera l'amour de Laure et celui de la gloire. Voisinage éclairant, et qui nous montre que pour Pétrarque, la même inanité menace, d'une part la beauté perçue et chantée de la dame, d'autre part la beauté produite et multipliée de l'écriture: dans les deux cas le confesseur stigmatise l'illusion d'une valorisation excessive de la forme. François aimerait-il Laure si elle était laide? N'avoue-t-il pas dans son amour de la gloire un goût immodéré pour l'opinion? Il y a dans la forme une aimantation aliénante. Elle se nomme tantôt fascination érotique, et Pétrarque s'applique, dans un effort remarquable, à lui ôter toute connotation spirituelle; elle se nomme aussi la gloire et relève de l'extériorité du paraître: de ce qui, en moi, est visible et doit être vu (*videndum*).

Accueillie dans la beauté de son épiphanie, la créature (Laure) est cause d'aveuglement; il faut comprendre que sa vraie beauté est *secrète,* qu'elle réside en Dieu, pouvoir éternel et invisible, et ne s'accorde qu'au regard intérieur (symboliquement: en songe et outre-tombe). N'en va-t-il pas de même pour cette autre manifestation de la beauté qu'est la création artistique? Si je lie mon destin à la forme que je produis, je m'éloigne de moi-même, de mon centre intime—qui est aussi mon rapport avec Dieu. Car je commets à un mouvement qui va vers autrui, ce qui ne devrait aller qu'à soi-même: le bien, le vrai et même le beau. Une volonté de régression sur des positions authentiques qui postulent, dans une adhésion au silence, le secret et la transcendance, apparaît comme l'aboutissement naturel de cette prise de conscience. Augustin décrète qu'il y a mieux à faire qu'à écrire. François n'aura pas le coeur de l'accepter sans autre et l'on sent dans sa détermination finale, non moins que dans les propos très "littéraires" du *prohemium* que nous avons cités, qu'il n'est pas disposé à abandonner son oeuvre (*maiora quedam*), ni à travailler désormais dans l'anonymat. Mais la dimension du silence a été indiquée;[6] un au-delà ou un en-deçà de la parole, plus précieux que la parole a été posé. Or, soit dans l'alternance rythmée du son et du silence soit dans une volubilité qui s'impose pour combler le silence, soit, au contraire, dans une parole pauvre et essentielle se détachant sur le grand mutisme de Laure et de Dieu, le silence est partout présent dans cette oeuvre. Comme dans les tensions précédentes, nous trouvons derechef la forme d'un recours, qui pallie de l'extérieur (le silence) une tentation née de l'idolâtrie littéraire, mais, comme précédemment, il se combine à l'intérieur et littérairement avec la tendance qu'il essaie de dominer, pour former la résultante du discours. C'est dans une tension que naît donc l'harmonie pétrarquienne, dans l'adhésion et la crainte, dans l'enthousiasme et le scrupule. S'il est le premier à croire, comme il le fait, à la sainteté du langage, s'il hérite pour la transmettre à l' "âge de la forme" la foi en un *logos* qui conduit à une actualisation, en l'homme, de toutes les valeurs que l'antiquité et le christianisme ont proposées, Pétrarque, et c'est là sa richesse, est aussi le lieu où le langage se trouve en état de crise. Son oeuvre en est le produit, qui se propage dans un paradoxe répété: celui d'une correction qui s'avère actuelle, plutôt que préalable, d'un objet qui coïncide avec la vue d'un artisan au travail, et d'un discours que le silence traverse avant d'en triompher.

6. J. E. Seigel, "Eloquence and Silence in Petrarch," *Journal of the History of Ideas* (1965), 147-174.

XIII

PETRARCH AND THE FREEDOM TO BE ALONE

by Douglas Radcliff-Umstead
University of Pittsburgh

Throughout his life Petrarch felt an intense need to escape from the turmoil of active participation in the world's affairs. What the poet longed to enjoy was a sense of being at complete peace with himself. By wandering in the forests near Vaucluse, seeking the source of the River Sorgue in a mysterious grotto, or scaling the slopes of Mt. Ventoux Francis Petrarch was attempting to discover in the solitude of those natural retreats a feeling of tranquillity which might soothe the anguish of his heart. What the savage landscape usually offered the poet was an analogue to the constant unrest of the poet's emotions. Perhaps the word that best expresses Petrarch's frenetic and vain quest for a peaceful asylum is *"errore,"* which signifies not only the many wearisome journeys that the writer undertook but also the state of sweet "illusion" where the poet's dreams would be realized. It is this "errando" rhythm which characterizes poems like "Solo e pensoso," "Per mezz' i boschi inospiti e selvaggi," and especially "Di pensier in pensier" where Petrarch recorded how he sought to calm his "alma sbigottita" by finding in nature the illusory image of his desire. The opening line of one of the writer's sonnets unhesitatingly declares his eagerness to flee the company of insensitive and inquisitive persons for the seclusion of river banks and forests: (no. CCLIX) "Cercato ò sempre solitaria vita." But the error could not last, and in the third book of his *Secretum* the poet had to admit that his frequent sojourns in the country had brought him no permanent feeling of inner peace. With all the self-contradictions of a soul in error, Petrarch even confessed in a sonnet like no. CCXXXIV his inability to endure being alone with his haunting thoughts in the privacy of his room:

> e 'l vulgo, a me nemico ed odioso,
> (chi 'l pensò mai?) per mio refugio chero:
> tal paura ò di ritrovarmi solo.

Petrarch's passionate spirit yearned for the calm of solitary withdrawal but recoiled before the frightening confrontation with its inner desolation.

Three years after Petrarch made the agonizing confessions of his spiritual inadequacy in the *Secretum,* he begun to write the treatise *De vita solitaria* in 1346. It would be tempting for a critical reader to regard the treatise as a text where the poet was looking for a solution to his personal problems. The ideal state of solitude which the treatise proposes could be viewed as the author's capitulation to amorous passion and the wearisome *"accidia"* which exhausted him emotionally.[1] It will be the intention of this essay, however, to demonstrate that in writing the *De vita solitaria* Petrarch was advocating an ideal of creative leisure which would permit an individual—any individual—to cultivate to the full his intellectual capabilities. Although the author readily admitted that he was describing the benefits of solitary life which brought him pleasure, his treatise is far from being a literary exercise in self-indulgence. For by leisure, as we shall see, Francis Petrarch did not signify self-consuming idleness but the freedom to withdraw and pursue a program of studies and writing which would bring glory both to an individual and to all of humanity. The ideals of leisure and freedom which inspire the Petrarchan treatise remove it from a Narcissistic preoccupation with flight from emotional problems and reveal it as anticipating the aim of creative self-realization in Cardinal Newman's text *The Idea of a University* and Josef Pieper's essay *Leisure, the Basis of Culture.* Since the fourteenth-century poet well understood that the leisure brought about by solitude could degenerate into a destructive idleness, he recommended a nearly ascetic discipline of calmness, equitableness and moderation which would sustain an individual in the life of withdrawal. Solitude would thus provide the opportunity for the cultivation and refinement of an individual's intellectual potential. Rather than displaying the tormenting *"errore"* of the poems of solitude or the agonizing spirit of confession of the *Secretum,* the treatise *De vita solitaria* advances an educational program to lead men to the tranquillity of wisdom.

Petrarch's scholastic method of citing the examples of pagan figures, early Christian hermits and medieval theologians to support his argument lends itself perfectly to the basic educational problem raised by Cardinal Newman: the creation of a valid culture by conjoining religious asceticism to intellectual discipline.[2] Humanist that he was,

1. In a lecture delivered before the University of Pittburgh's program in Medieval and Renaissance Studies, Professor Donald Nesti of Duquesne University asserts that the *De vita solitaria* should be judged an exercise in Narcissistic self-concern. Nesti holds that Petrarch's compulsive flight to solitude might be summarized by the words *amore, dolore, accidia, stanchezza, pace.*

2. See *The Idea of a University* (Garden City, N.Y.: Doubleday, 1959), p. 26.

Petrarch explored the totality of man's experience from pagan antiquity to his own times to demonstrate how history's self-surpassing individuals have derived their inner strength through love of the solitary life. In the opening chapter of the seventh tractate in Book II, the author makes a general observation that philosophers require solitude in order to be able to penetrate the inner mystery of things. Leisure permits the philosopher to enjoy a spiritual silence which leads to contemplation of eternal Essences. Petrarch's view of the role of a philosopher is in the Platonic tradition wherein the rational man must ascend the mountain of solitude to gaze into that supreme Good which comprehends all the other timeless Ideas. The Italian poet, who did not have a direct acquaintance with the Platonic dialogues, failed to appreciate Plato's insistence on man's service to the state. In the ideal society of Plato the individual does not have the freedom to withdraw; only a few specially gifted philosophers may arrive late in their lives at the vision of the Eternal. Petrarch, like Pieper in the twentieth century, felt that the interests of society were best served when certain individuals were allowed to seclude themselves for devotion to study and creativity.

Aristotle, much more than Plato, affirms the necessity for leisure to enable men to behold truth. Once the individual has been freed from utilitarian concerns, he can enjoy contemplation as an inner state of the soul where his intellect may grow aware of truth. Aristotle's specific term for leisure is *scholé,* which cannot be experienced in military, political or everyday affairs. The "scholar" alone can reach knowledge of the highest good. In the *Nicomachean Ethics* Aristotle observed that only the philosopher possesses the independence of spirit to concentrate his faculties on the supreme felicity of the contemplative life: ". . . Again, what we have called self-sufficiency must belong principally to the contemplative activity. For whereas the philosopher, as well as the just man or one possessing any other virtue, requires the necessities of life, once they are sufficiently endowed therewith, the just, temperate or brave man still needs people toward whom and with whom he may act justly, temperately or bravely, but the philosopher can contemplate truth even when all alone. . . . The self-sufficiency, leisureliness, unweariness (so far as this is possible for human beings) and all the other attributes ascribed to the supremely happy man are evidently those connected with the contemplative activity of man, it follows that this will be man's complete happiness. . . ."[3] A man of a

3. *Aristotle's Ethics,* trans. John Warrington (London: Dent, 1963), pp. 228-229.

truly scholarly disposition must be beyond labor, and Petrarch—whether in rustic retirement or in attendance of a court like that of the Visconti—never considered himself a functionary who had to labor in the service of another. The Italian poet of the fourteenth century demanded for himself the same freedom for contemplation which Aristotle had deemed necessary for man to attain a nearly divine life of reason.

In contrast to Aristotle's devaluation of the military or political life as the way to supreme self-realizing, Cicero insisted that service to society afforded persons of ability the opportunity to use knowledge for practical benefits. Active involvement in the affairs of the world, according to the Roman statesman, would enable men of study and learning to influence the destiny of the state and protect the best interests of the commonweal. Despite his admiration for the eloquent style of the ancient orator, Petrarch feared that a life of constant public occupation would prevent him from pursuing knowledge. In the second chapter of Book I, Third Tractate, Petrarch cites a passage from Cicero's *De officiis* which recommends that men should imitate the example of Hercules by toiling for others rather than live in seclusion. Although the Italian author would prefer to agree with Cicero's observation, he declared that nowhere in contemporary society could he find individuals whose public service actually resulted in improving the world. Petrarch felt that an individual who concerned himself with the affairs of others ceased to be the master of his own life and therefore could never enjoy the serenity of mind which solitude might grant. In examining the events of Cicero's life, the Italian writer remarked in Book II, Eighth Tractate, Ch. Two, that it was the need for an audience which caused the Roman orator to prefer an active public career in a metropolitan center over the pleasures of rural retreats. Along with this keen intuition into Cicero's longing for the approval and attention of an admiring populace, Petrarch further noted that after political reverses forced the Roman orator into exile at remote villas, Cicero used his involuntary isolation to compose those works which placed him among the foremost Latin philosophers. The ancient Roman writer possessed the discipline not to allow himself to become dissipated by seclusion but to devote himself to the contemplative life. Petrarch closed his argument for solitude over active public service by observing how in time Cicero himself came to recognize the advantages of retirement and declared his love for a *"literata solitudo"* before all other pleasures.

Of all the ancient writers who praised solitude Petrarch considered Horace to be the most congenial to his ideal of leisure. Horatian Epicureanism consisted in seeking freedom from laboring for others in order to create a private zone of life for meditation on virtue and wisdom. A greatly restrained hedonism without self-abusive excesses could result in a state of mental repose conducive to literary creation. Petrarch saw in Horace a kindred soul who had rejected lofty public posts in the imperial administration for an unexciting life at his villa. In the second book of *De vita solitaria* Petrarch states that no poet ever found solitude as friendly and rewarding as did Horace. Both the ancient poet and the modern Italian writer agreed in viewing cities as places of continual vexations and empty distractions. Neither author believed that his withdrawal should be attributed to selfish motives. Each asserted a primary obligation to the full development of self, which in their cases was manifested by devotion to literature. Both Horace and Petrarch after him sought to flee the commotion of cities for the inspiring quiet of the country.

Petrarch did not hesitate to include the example of a pagan Epicurean poet like Horace alongside the self-denying experiences of Christian desert fathers. The ancient Latin poet as well as the religious hermits had chosen solitude as a guide, and Petrarch thought that the ascetic and the hedonist both contributed insights for the proper employment of the solitary life. Francis Petrarch wished to be thought of as a Christian, if only as an errant one. Although he would never emulate the frightening austerity of the desert fathers, the Italian author recognized in their severe withdrawal an absolute standard of rigid discipline for a Christian's struggle to gain salvation. The desert fathers regarded solitude as a challenge whereby one tames his passions and earns the right to meditation on the divine. As the *athletae Dei,* the desert hermits saw their ascesis as a spiritual exercise for the correct ordering of their lives.[4] Withdrawal allowed them to cultivate virtues like humility, magnanimity and gentleness; and even if Petrarch himself did not possess any of those virtues to a great degree, his argument for the beneficent effects of solitude still remains valid with the example of the desert fathers, who never succumbed to idle self-indulgence. In Ch. Six of Book II's third tractate the Italian author specifically refers to St. Jerome's decision to forsake the comforts of life in Rome to withdraw to a savage desert, so as to come to terms with God and avoid the damnation of Hell. Jerome did not feel that ascesis was incompatible with literary culture, and during his stay in the desert he mastered Hebrew. Petrarch observes that although solitude strengthened Jerome

4. See Helen Waddell, *The Desert Fathers* (Ann Arbor: University of Michigan Press, 1971), pp. 10-16.

in his resolve to resist passion, the saint never returned to the temptations of Rome but chose refuge in Bethlehem. From this remark it appears evident that the Italian author never intended to practice the seclusion of a hermit. For Petrarch the solitary man is one who returns periodically to the city, refreshed by his retreat and prepared to renew the struggles of daily life.

Rather than follow the total retreat of an ascetic, Petrarch longed to imitate the example of St. Augustine in reconciling the active and contemplative lives. In his vision of history Augustine recognized that the celestial city must forever remain man's goal as his one true home. But as the saint declared in *De doctrina christiana,* man in his earthly pilgrimage may make use of this world provided he does not let his heart rest in it as an end unto itself. Augustine, while scrupulously refuting the Manichaean rejection of the world as basically evil, repeatedly warned others of the danger of finding peace in the earth alone. In those moments when Petrarch came closest to experiencing a superficial mundane contentment, it was always the admonitions of Augustine which awakened the poet to his spiritually perilous situation. The episode during the ascent of Mt. Ventoux, where the Italian writer casually opened Augustine's *Confessions* and read the saint's appeal for men to look inwardly rather than gaze in satisfaction at the earth's wonders, reveals how Petrarch relied on the Bishop of Hippo as a guide for his moral conduct. While always admitting that the life of contemplation is the ideal to which men should aspire, Augustine commented that man must carry out the necessary toils of this world: ". . . otium sanctum quaerit charitas veritatis: negotium iustum suscipit necessitas charitatis (*De Civ. Dei,* xix, 19)." This distinction between a sacred *"otium"* and a righteous *"negotium"* pointed the way by which man could reach the eternal without denying the life of earth. Even though Petrarch never arrived at Augustine's genuine moment of conversion where the saint succeeded in renouncing worldly desire, the Italian poet learned from the Christian father that the city of God is ultimately to be discovered within oneself. In Ch. Five of the second book's third tractate in *De Vita Solitaria* Petrarch notes that Augustine's confrontation with truth occurred after the troubled philosopher took refuge in the country at Cassiciacum; in that rural retreat the saint at last triumphed by turning totally to God to derive the absolute power of will necessary for transcending himself. Petrarch also quotes a passage from Augustine's commentary on the Gospel according to St. John that illustrates how the philosopher regarded solitude as a state of mind free from external disturbance which permitted one to behold the redeeming light of

God: "Difficile est in turba videre Cristum: solitudo quedam necessaria est menti nostre, quadam solitudine intentionis videtur Deus. Turba strepitum habet; visio ista secretum desiderat."[5] Augustine's experience showed the Italian poet that man's vision of God depends on an isolation of attention. Although Petrarch's own *Secretum* reveals that the poet did not possess the saint's constancy of will, the Italian writer considered solitude as ideal for founding the heavenly city within one's soul.

Petrarch's conception of leisure and solitude is part of an attitude which has been called "mystical humanism."[6] Perhaps a more appropriate term would be "spiritual humanism" wherein the scholar employs his leisure not in the corporally mortifying discipline of the ascetic but in intensive study free from the turmoil and distractions of the city. The audience to whom Petrarch addresses the *De vita solitaria* is the studious who will understand that the intellect must be allowed to be "always at play" like divine wisdom itself in order for knowledge to come to man as a flashing illumination from heaven. The Italian poet hopes to gain the approval of the highly-educated for his efforts to justify the necessity of freedom for study: "De his ergo alii ut libet, quanquam facile consensuros vero eruditorum animos atque ora confidam" (p. 296). Petrarch finds encouragement in the knowledge that his views will be appreciated by Philippe de Cabassoles, to whom the treatise is dedicated. If one kindred soul, like the bishop of Cavaillon, agrees with the poet's recommendations for scholarly retreat, Petrarch feels that his appeal for the cultivation of the mind will not be wasted. While never denying that the true foundation for a life of peace is in God, the poet seeks to point out a way to create harmony of spirit through the leisure of study.

Before the Italian author proceeds in his treatise to present a satirical set of contrasting portraits between the troubled *homo urbanus* and the serene *homo solitarius,* he declares that in solitude he desires to discover a self-surpassing tranquillity: "Neque enim solitudinis solum nomen, sed que in solitudine bona sunt laudo. Nec me tam vacui recessus et silentium delectant, quam que in his habitant *otium et libertas*" (p. 300, italics our own). By freedom Petrarch intends the ability to flee the sins of men, to escape the hateful preoccupations of populous urban centers. The Petrarchan *"otium"* recalls Aristotle's *"scholé"* of

5. *De vita solitaria,* in Francesco Petrarca, *Prose,* ed. G. Martellotti (Milan: Ricciardi, 1955), p. 440. All subsequent page references will be from this edition.

6. See Luigi Russo, *Ritratti e disegni storici,* 3rd series, I (Florence: Sansoni, 1960), 267.

the contemplative nature and anticipates Pieper's "leisure" as the foundation of civilized life. Solitude is where the soul dwells in contemplative silence. Petrarch frequently employs the word *"strepitum"* to designate the noisy agitation in the daily life of the *homo urbanus* or *occupatus,* who never succeeds in enjoying moments of quiet even during the late hours of the night, since he must always be scheming to defeat his enemies and advance new projects of deception. The true condition of the *homo urbanus* is one of slavery, total dependence on others who may offer opposition to or participate in his intrigues. This man of affairs is never alone, not just at those times when his richly laden banquet table is surrounded by a crowd of ambitious flatterers, but also when no one else is physically present; for the *homo urbanus* is constantly thinking of others and how he might exploit them for his own ends or frustrate their designs upon him. The preoccupied man of the city is not even master of himself as the passions of avarice, lust and wrath dominate his every waking hour and never concede him an instant of peace. Throughout this description of the *homo urbanus* Petrarch maintains an ironical detachment which is perhaps the chief stylistic characteristic of the *De vita solitaria,* so that the book should appear as a general treatise on a particular way of life and not as an anguished book of confessions. The picture of urban life presented in *De vita solitaria* never reveals the nauseating sense of spatial constriction and physical oppression as evidenced in this passage from the *Secretum:*

> Quis vite mee tedia et quotidianum fastidium sufficienter exprimat, mestissimam turbulentissimamque urbem terrarum omnium, angustissimam atque ultimam sentinam et totius orbis sordibus exundantem? Quis verbis equet que passim nauseam concitant: graveolentes semitas, permixtas rabidis canibus obscenas sues, et rotarum muros quatientium stridorem aut transversas obliquis itineribus quadrigas; tam diversas hominum species, tot horrenda mendicantium spectacula, tot divitum furores: illos mestitia defixos, hos gaudio lasciviaque fluitantes; tam denique discordantes animos, artesque tam varias, tantum confusis vocibus clamorem, et populi inter se arietantis incursum? (Martellotti edit., p. 120)

Whereas the intensity of the portait of an aesthetically disgusting and tumultuous city finds correspondence in the confusion of Petrarch's soul as the poet confesses in the *Secretum,* the sketch of the *homo urbanus* in the later treatise merely exhibits the author's desire to represent the splendid emptiness in the life of any individual who blindly accepts the values of the urban world and struggles to secure a position of wealth and authority.

A life beyond struggle and desire assures for the *homo solitarius* an undisturbed calm which sustains him throughout his daily tasks. The retired man never enters into intrigues, and consequently he has no need for allies and no fear of opponents. With his conscience at rest, the *homo solitarius* remains his own man, never depending on others to satisfy his wishes. The morning strolls of the solitary man out into the woods bring to mind those excursions in birding groves which the exiled Machiavelli was later to describe in a letter of December 10, 1513, to Francesco Vettori. Both the retired man and the deposed Florentine official come to experience in the woods a meditative tranquillity. There is of course a significant difference in the personal situations of Petrarch's ideal *homo solitarius* and Machiavelli. The Florentine secretary did not choose retirement at San Casciano; it was thrust upon him, and like Cicero before him Machiavelli took advantage of his enforced leisure to compose his masterworks. A rule of moderation without severe self-denial guides the solitary man and makes him content with his simple fare and unpretentious abode. Although the retired man occupies himself principally with his readings and literary projects, he does not live in forgetfulness of God. He begins every day with prayer, and the redemptive promise of the Holy Spirit is never far from his constant reflections on human destiny. Petrarch's inclusion of prayers in the daily regime of the *homo solitarius* should not be dismissed as a concession to conventional religious practice.[7] The Italian author warns his readers that in the leisurely life one does not look to others as guides, censors or sources of comfort. The Christian man of solitude has the consolation that his Savior is always present in person. In Ch. Eight of the fourth tractate in Book I, Petrarch expressly disagrees with the recommendations of Cicero and Seneca that the solitary individual should select an imaginary witness to his acts. The Christian does not need to imagine that another—even an illustriously virtuous figure from antiquity—is looking over his shoulder in approval or disapproval. Petrarch's man of retirement is one who has arrived at independence of judgment by carefully examining his own needs without relying on the inconstant esteem of other persons. Christ, in the evaluation of the Italian poet, is that sole Other who will witness the individual's actions and speak to him as the voice of conscience. The *homo solitarius,* unlike the man occupied with worldly affairs, can remain forever receptive to the spirit of Christ which will descend upon him in the tranquil recesses of his retreat.

7. See the introduction by Jacob Zeitlin to his translation of *The Life of Solitude by Francis Petrarch* (Urbana: University of Illinois Press, 1924), p. 57, where he denies the deep strain of Christian mysticism in the treatise and finds only the "self-centered virtue of the Epicureans."

Petrarch recognizes that the existential status of the solitary man is that of a modest rank in the hierarchy of virtues. He follows Plotinus in assigning the affection for leisurely studies to the purgatorial virtues (Bk. I, Tr. 4, Ch. 2). The solitary scholar is one who has attempted to use his leisure to eradicate those fierce passions which blind men from the illumination of divine grace. Beneath the purgatorial virtues stand the political virtues, which are attained only by those persons whose worldly commitment aims not only at self-perfection but also the improvement of the state. The man of political virtues may succeed in moderating his passions; he never transcends them. Virtues of perfect men occupy a third level, and Petrarch doubts if such perfection has ever existed. On the highest level are the exemplary virtues beyond time and space in the mind of God, from which the lower degrees originate. Even though the Italian author attributes a secondary rank to the virtues of the solitary life, he regards them as the supreme level of attainment for all but the most perfect souls. The Petrarchan man of leisurely retirement is capable of performing what Pieper has called "celebration," where mental calm, relaxation, and effortlessness emerge together as the virtuous soul opens to divine worship.[8] Withdrawal from human society and the voluntary renunciation of worldly treasures may be rewarded in an eternal state of beautitude for the solitary man whose contemplative leisure has made him attentive to the voice of Christ.

Solitude for the desert fathers was a means to restricting the self so that only its divine aspect would remain in ascendance. For Petrarch solitude appears as a means for expanding the self which would become *"capax Dei"* as it comes to comprehend eternity. To those critics of solitude who accused retreat of being a form of death the Italian author answered with the words of Seneca: "Otium sine literis mors est, et hominis vivi sepultura." It is not so much self-satisfaction as intellectual self-cultivation to which Petrarch thought solitude must be directed. The study of literature provides the educational program by which reason can exercise itself. Petrarch, like Cardinal Newman several centuries after him, stressed that the cultivation of the intellect was an end in itself and should never be directed toward a venal goal as a reward for the mere accumulation of knowledge:

Ad quas hodie discendas magno rei familiaris impendio, sed multo maxima lucri spe, pueri a parentibus non quasi ad liberale gymnasium, sed velut ad

8. See *Leisure, the Basis of Culture,* trans. Alexander Dru (New York: Pantheon Books, Inc., 1952), p. 71. Pieper, p. 75, expresses a serious reservation about the limitations of humanism where leisure, once it is separated from divine worship, becomes idleness.

servile mercimonium destinantur, ut mirari nemo habeat eos venaliter et avare literis uti, quas ut venderent quesierunt, et quibus improba spe non sibi centesimum fenus, sed millesimum statuerunt. (p. 330)

The Italian author believed that the study of literature in time of leisure should form a school of generosity where the sole enrichment would be that of the spirit. This program of personal refinement would totally exclude the instrumental use of education for professional training. For Petrarch the true philosophers are those who genuinely love wisdom and not the salaried "cathedrarios" (p. 524) who merchandize their knowledge. This gratuitous view of scholarship would later be echoed by Newman as his *beau ideal* for a university education which would not emphasize the acquisition of facts but the gaining of a clear, calm and accurate vision of reality.[9] The cultivation of the intellect requires solitary leisure for the scholar to arrive at that lustrous vision.

Petrarch's ideal of scholarly retreat should not be regarded as an apology for misanthropic seclusion. The *homo solitarius* is not a recluse who locks his door to persons of merit. While never depending on the opinions of others, the scholar wishes to share the delights of his rustic sojourn with companions sensitive to the joys of retreat. Petrarch even asserts that he would rather abandon solitude than renounce friendship. In a friend the poet admits that he is looking for a reflection of himself ("in quo se se videant," p. 376), and it is here that a critical reader might accuse Petrarch of Narcissistic self-gratification in selecting friends of a kindred disposition. Actually the attitude of the Italian writer very much resembles that of the nineteenth-century American transcendental philosopher Ralph Waldo Emerson, according to whom a friend should be chosen because he reflects the best qualities of an individual. The Petrarchan solitude is not a closed experience. While disturbing crowds are excluded from the solitary recesses of the scholar, the comfort of friendly and intelligent conversation is made welcome.

In the final two chapters of the fourth tractate in Book I the author examines the benefits of the freedom which the retired man enjoys. Petrarch reiterates the precious ability of the solitary scholar to stand without need of compelling others to recognize him. There is no contradiction between the repeated affirmations of moral independence and acknowledgment of an openness to friendship, for among friends the attitude of constraint which prevails in the daily relationships of the *homo urbanus* is altogether absent. The scholar has the advantage over involved persons of being able to detach himself and serenely contemplate the rush of events throughout the world. This intellectual distance is

9. Cf. *The Idea of a University*, p. 160.

not a form of alienation, another aspect of the *"accidia"* which frequently deprived Petrarch of the will toward creativity, but that state of inner tranquillity where the solitary scholar dwells as if looking down upon the earth from a lofty tower. Not only does the *homo solitarius* experience a spatial detachment but also a temporal mobility which permits him to travel across the ages to converse with the great individuals of the past. Literature offers the opportunity for one to reflect on the thoughts of those persons who have been the guardians of civilization. The nearly ecstatic tone of Petrarch's language in describing the solitary reader's flight across the ages brings to mind the rapturous passage in the Vettori letter where Machiavelli relates how with the coming of evening he discards his garments dusty from the day's tasks and dons his lordly robes to enter into the courts of the ancients who speak to him from their writings. This experience of literature is not merely a passive one, for the scholar uses his free time for his own writings: "Vacuitatem vero seu vacationem dici mavis literarum atque artium fontem esse" (p. 360). Re-echoing the words of Horace, the author declares that the solitary man of letters creates monuments which will endure longer than those of bronze or marble. This disciplined scholar does not yield to the enervating melancholy of *"accidia"* but devotes his hours of leisure to literary pursuits that may promise terrestrial immortality.

Throughout the sixth and final tractate of Book I, Petrarch studies the situation of man dwelling within the confusion of the city, pointing out the tedium which reigns in an urban setting. The writer does acknowledge the possibility of there being an *"homo solitarius in urbe"* (the terminology is our own and not Petrarch's), when an individual is vitally aware and resists the agitation about him. The everyday scene in a typical city, however, is one of individuals hurrying along at a frenetic pace, never able to pause for a few seconds as they dash from one meaningless encounter to another. Petrarch cites Seneca's description of the aimless man who cannot determine a firm destination for his life: "ignoranti quem portum petat, nullus suus ventus est" (p. 386). It is the author's express intention to urge his readers to establish a zone of calm within their restless hearts and then to withdraw to a tranquil recess. This need for inner stability doubtless reflects the author's own *"errore"* from one troubled state to another, but the chapters in the *De vita solitaria* do not convey an impression of the author's agitated soul. In the treatise Petrarch concentrates his attention on demonstrating the errors of the *"homines urbani"* who enslave themselves to every passing fashion and neglect to become concerned with what is solely important: their eternal destiny. The author will close the first book with the observation that it is less difficult to rule cities and kingdoms or command armies than it is to govern the heart which remains forever rebellious to the sway of reason. By seeking out a life of solitary repose, the individual whose heart resembles a demoralized and endangered city may find eternal liberation.

Petrarch's *homo solitarius* is one who has become master of human time, which he does not allow to pass by in wasteful idleness but organizes in a meaningful pattern of creative endeavors. The projects of the present moment carry on the work of the glorious men of the past and will be remembered by future generations. In his treatise *De vita solitaria* Petrarch portrayed that man of imagination and sentiment whom Cardinal Newman was later to call the gentleman scholar. The cultivated intellect of the solitary scholar reflects a clarity of vision of one who has overcome the dark restlessness of the soul by discovering in leisure the illuminating peace of spiritual freedom. With the *De vita solitaria* Petrarch represented the individual's quest to withdraw from the destructive tensions of the earthly city, so as to cultivate in leisurely solitude the divine principle within himself.

XIV

NOTES ON THE RHETORIC IN PETRARCH'S *Invective contra medicum**

by Conrad H. Rawski
Case Western Reserve University

For Morris Bishop
Quid prodest temet studiis librorum
Tam brevis vitae morulas dicasse
Corpus ac fractum macerasse tantum,
Si nihil audes?
—Notker

THE *Invective contra medicum.* The *Invective contra medicum,* completed in 1353, is the earliest of Petrarch's four formal contributions to a literary genre which, in Highet's words, was born in the stone caves, whose parent on one side was anthropoid, and on the other lupine: Invective, the grim gruff old ancestor of satire with the one purpose, to destroy the enemy.[1] All of Petrarch's invectives are diatribes against specific individuals who have aroused his *saeva indignatio.* He uses historical materials and the contemporary subject literatures; *exempla,* fables, dramatic incidents, fictional experiences, anecdotes, proverbs, and homilies;[2] sarcasm, irony, mockery, raillery, exaggeration, and understatement;[3] and a rich vocabulary of succulent mordancy.[4] He uses

* A short preliminary version of this paper was read at the Ninth Conference on Medieval Studies, Western Michigan University, 1974.

1. G. Highet, *The Anatomy of Satire* (Princeton: Princeton University Press, 1962), 151, 156. The later invectives are *Contra quendam magni status hominem* (1355); *De sui ipsius et multorum ignorantia* (1367); and *Contra eum qui maledixit Italie* (1373).

2. *Francesco Petrarca: Invective contra medicum; Testo latino e volgarizzamento di Ser Domenico Silvestri,* ed. P. G. Ricci (Rome: Edizioni di Storia e Letteratura, 1950), henceforth cited as *CM,* III, 573-577. Cf. M. Schiavone's Latin-Italian ed., F. Petrarca, *Invettive contro un medico* (Milan: Marzorati, 1972), 115.

3. Cf. R. C. Elliott, "Satire" in *Encyclopedia of Poetry and Poetics,* ed. A. Preminger (Princeton: Princeton University Press, 1965).

4. In the four invectives this vocabulary is deployed on various levels of intensity. As such it is limited to the relatively few available expletives of personal abuse [e.g., *ridicule animal* (*CM* II, 22), *asellus* (*CM* I, 299; *Contra eum,* in

satire and satiric stance, but is not guided by the norms of the satirist:[5] *Relege nunc epistolam illam meam que te furere fecit et faciet mori*—reread now that letter of mine which made you rage and which shall make you die.[6] He writes to kill.[7]

The events which led to Petrarch's "four books of invectives against the physician"[8] may be briefly summarized as follows (Detail 1).[9]

In December 1351, Pope Clement VI fell ill. On March 12, 1352, Petrarch addressed to the Pope *Fam.* V, 19, the letter *unde tota lis oritur*

Francisci Petrarchae ... Opera (Basel, 1581), henceforth cited as *1581:* 1079), *belua* (*CM* I, 397), *canis* (*CM* II, 471, etc.), *corvus* (= Alain de Lille, *Distinctiones, PL* 210, c. 754—*Contra eum, 1581:* 1073), *upupa* (*CM* II, 543-554), *mendacii amicus* (*CM* I, 390, 401; *Contra eum, 1581:* 1085), *os impurum* (*CM* I, 201; *Contra eum, 1581:* 1074), *iurgator improbus* (*CM* III, 591), *stultus* (*CM* II, 6, 437 etc.; *De sui ipsius, 1581:* 1056; *Contra eum,* ibid., 1068), *ydiota* (*CM* IV, 387), etc.]—yet Petrarch uses these often in elaborate aggregates of insult [e.g., *CM* II, 71-73; III, 510-517; IV, 332-333, 415-445; *Contra quendam,* in Fr. Petrarca, *Prose,* ed. G. Martellotti (Milan-Naples: Ricciardi, 1955), henceforth cited as *Prose,* 708—with allusion to Dante, *Parad.* XXI, 130-134].

5. G. Highet, op. cit., 155-156; R. C. Elliott, op. cit., 738-738; N. Frye, *Anatomy of Criticism* (Princeton: Princeton University Press, 1957), 223-239.

6. *CM* II, 89-99. This remark may suggest that the puzzling statement *CM* I, 446-447: [*tu*] *qui . . . medicine nomine mortem michi literarum tuarum in fine denuncies* could refer to a figure in a lost letter to Petrarch, rather than a threat of physical death. Cf. E. H. Wilkins, *Studies in the Life of Petrarch* (Cambridge, Mass.: Mediaeval Academy of America, 1955), 109.

7. Petrarch discusses this kind of invective in *De sui ipsius* (*1581:* 1059):

> Incidunt vero . . . et acriores dissensionum causae, non invidia studiorum sed profundis flammantes odiis. Nam Sallustii in Tullium, atque Aeschinis in Demosthenem, horumque in illos invectivae, non ingenia, neque stylos arguunt, sed mores amarumque aliquid et hostile, imo pacatum nihil in se continent, nullae ibi facetiae, nullus iocus, sed certamen longe aliud, quam quod de literis, aut pro gloria sumi solet.
>
> Sometimes it is not envy for the great learning of the rival, but deeply rooted hatred that has made much sharper strife flare up . . . . In the Invectives of Sallust against Cicero and those of Aeschines against Demosthenes and vice versa, the insults are launched against the character of the attacked, not against his genius or style. They are full of bitterness and hostility and show not the slightest hint of a peaceful mood. There is no room for facetiousness or joke. It is a struggle of quite another kind than is usually fought in literary matters or for fame.

Does this statement suggest the kind of editorial revisions Petrarch may have made in the missive texts when he prepared the manuscript of *CM*?

8. *Misc.* 1: *Quattuor Invectivarum libros dicam....* E. H. Wilkins and G. Billanovich, "The Miscellaneous Letters of Petrarch," *Speculum,* 37 (1962), 227.

9. C. H. Rawski, *Petrarch and the Physician: A Preliminary Essay,* forthcoming; cf. *Abstracts of the Papers Presented at the Seventh Conference on Medieval Studies* (Kalamazoo: Western Michigan University, 1972), 38.

—which started this whole feud.[10] He urged the Pontiff to select a physician "known not for his eloquence, but for his knowledge and integrity"[11] and to shun the crowds of prattling doctors who confuse Hippocratic action with Ciceronian oratory. One of the papal physicians (probably representing a group of physicians) immediately replied with a critical letter *in oratione soluta* (MD 1—not extant).[12] Infuriated by this attack from someone he had not addressed, Petrarch wrote a rejoinder[13] in form of a very long letter to *procaci et insano medico*—an arrogant and insane physician.[14] Pope Clement VI died, December 6, 1352. Nevertheless, the physician did reply at length in January or February 1353 (MD 2—not extant). While still at Vaucluse, Petrarch retaliated with a counterblast in three parts, and challenged the doctor to renew the battle within a year's time.[15] He never replied.

Shortly after moving to Milan in the summer of 1353, Petrarch combined his rejoinder of 1352 and the counterblast, and established from these missive texts, no longer extant, the text of the *Invective contra medicum i-iv*.[16] Book i addresses the doctor's reply (MD 1) probably item by item, and perhaps in the same order as in MD 1.[17] Book ii serves

10. *CM* II, 401. Cf. *Sen.* XVI, 3: *epistolam illam* [i.e., *Fam.* V, 19], *quae fons odiorum fuit omnium.*

11. *Fam.* V, 19, 5.

12. *CM* IV, 477: *ut a sene iam senior soluta oratione lacesserer* . . . . Note also *CM* IV, 250-251: *Non ego te carmine aut ullo poetico mucrone confixeram, sed pedestri solutoque sermone leseram.* . . . In contrast to *oratio perpetua* and the structured use of the periodic sentence, *oratio soluta* denotes a simple linear order of words and prose statements, *qualis in sermone et epistolis* (Cicero, *De oratore* III, 48, 184; Quintilian, *Institutiones* IX, 4, 10; Aquila [Halm, *Rhet. lat. min.*, 1863], 18; Isidore, *Etymologiae,* I, 38, 2. Examples, e.g., *Ad Herennium* IV, 54, 68). On the whole issue, A. Scaglione, *The Classical Theory of Composition from its Origins to the Present.* University of North Carolina Studies in Comparative Literature, 53 (Chapel Hill: University of North Carolina Press, 1972), 24-28.

13. The term is by E. H. Wilkins.

14. *Fam.* XV, 6, 2.

15. *CM* IV, 453-454.

16. Cf. above, note 2.

17. In the counterblast Petrarch refers explicitly to leaving the order of arguments in MD 2:

> Sed ego iam hinc ordinem tuum amplius non sequar, quippe qui nullo modo michi videor ordinatius dicturus, quam si longissime discesserim ab ordine libri illius quem michi serio, ut asseris, remisisti, ut aperte conicerem qualis tibi repentinus ac tumultuarius stilus esset si lucubratus ac serius talis est. *CM* II, 289-293.

> From here, I shall not follow your order any longer, because I simply fail to see how I can state anything in better order, save by departing at great length from the order of that book, which you sent me, as you claim,

as an elenchus dealing with the issues raised in the doctor's counter-rejoinder—to use Wilkins's term (MD 2). Book iii is in two parts: a defense of poetry, and an argument refuting as dysfunctional a relationship between medicine and rhetoric. Book iv extols the life of solitude.

Apologiae conclusio. In its present form, Petrarch's work ends with an apology to the reader, in which Petrarch regrets that *mordacissimus conviciator,* the ferocious slanderer, forced him *humilem solivagumque ruricolam,* a humble countrydweller walking in solitude, "to boast, and say vain and prideful things about himself; and to defame another person."[18] But, he adds, I know that the great orators, both Greek and Latin, and, which is more surprising, the holy Fathers of the Church have often engaged in verbal combat *(certamen verborum).* He cites as examples the pseudo-Ciceronian *Controversia Sallustii adversus Ciceronem;* Aeschines vs. Demosthenes; St. Jerome, *In Rufinum*; and the invectives of St. Augustine.[19] The concluding passage assesses the doctor's action and justifies Petrarch's response:

Ita, si fortassis hoc calle famam petit, nequicquam insanierit. Sin turbasse otium, et silentium meum interrupisse contentus est, quod decreverat implevit; aliquot michi dies eripuit quos nemo restituet, et a meis tramitibus abductum, ad durum et insolitum iter traxit. Quidni igitur turber, temporisque iacturam querar nec michi nec alteri fructuosam, nisi quantum studioso homini, modo animi crimen absit, et data sit occasio non quesita, in omni genere orationis exercendus est stilus? En in demonstrativo genere exerceor; mallem in laudibus exerceri. Ceterum ut aliquando sit finis, is qui hanc michi necessitatem imposuit, in alienis finibus non inveniens quod querebat, revertatur ad proprias febres; tu lacessito faveas, lacessentem oderis, et valeas precor. (*CM* iv, 580-592)

in all sincerity, in order to interpret clearly that hasty and confused style of yours, if it is really meant to convey something that is carefully thought out and serious.

---

18. *CM* IV, 465; cf. also *Misc.* 1, and E. H. Wilkins, *Petrarch's Eight Years in Milan* (Cambridge, Mass.: Mediaeval Academy of America, 1958), 142-146.

19. *CM* IV, 491-501. The first two are also cited *CM* I, 429-430, and reappear in a longer list of invectives in *De sui ipsius* (note 7, above). *Odium . . . nec mereor nec metuo*—Hatred . . . I certainly do not deserve nor do I fear it: *Fam.* I, 1, 17, transl. M. Bishop, *Letters from Petrarch* (Bloomington: Indiana University Press, 1966), 18: Petrarch enjoyed a good fight. He seems to have counted the Sallust invective among his favorite books (1343 or earlier; cf. B. Ullman, *Studies in the Italian Renaissance,* Rome, Edizioni di Storia e Letteratura, 1955, chap. VI), and recalls repeatedly how he fearlessly defied Brizio Visconti with *Met.* II, 11 and 18 (*CM* IV, 472-475; *Contra quendam,* in Petrarca, *Prose,* 698; 704-706; 708: *fulgentem galeam sprevi . . .*). Cf. C. H. Rawski, *Petrarch: Four Dialogues for Scholars* (Cleveland: Press of Western Reserve University, 1967), 182 n. 18.

If, perhaps, he [i.e., the doctor] thought this was a way to fame, he ranted in vain. But if he wanted to disturb my peace and break my silence, he did accomplish his purpose. He has robbed me of several days which no one can give back to me, has forced me off my usual paths and dragged me down a hard, strange road. So, why shouldn't I be angry and fret about the waste of time spent neither fruitful to me nor to anyone else, if not for the fact that a man of letters, with no malice in his heart, and in a situation not of his making, must practice with his pen all genera of oratory available to him? Look! I am practicing *genus demonstrativum*; I prefer practicing *laudes*. Thus, if ever there is to be an end to this, let him who has forced upon me this necessity, who has not found 'in regions strange to him' that which he sought, go back to his old fevers. You, I beg to favor him who was hurt, to hate the one who hurt, and to stay well.

As such, this *conclusio* does not seem to display the "honied charm of resounding words" found by Boccaccio in Petrarch's prose.[20] If we examine the passage for *elocutionis virtutes et vitia*[21] we find a traditional, somewhat old fashioned text situation with (1) little attention to word sequence, as indicated by repetition of equally long words, reduplication of vowels, clustering of consonants, the *m inlisa vocalibus,* and a flagrant instance of assonant phonetic complication (syllabic jointure); (2) simple *tropi* (*metonymia* and *periphrastic synecdoche*); (3) a few word figures, the most ambitious among them the final pleonastic *isocolon,* using anaphoric *polyptoton* and epiphoric *variatio* within a zeugmatic parenthesis; and (4) the old medieval *cursus* and *cursus*-related *clausulae* (Detail 2). The sentence structure is certainly not casual. There is a hint at *protasis*—suspense, and *apodosis*—resolution in the "if A then B" pattern:

α *Ita si* (1-2) β *sin* (3-9),

leading to the intensifying thought figure of pathetic query (*interrogatio*): γ *Quidni igitur turber . . .* ? (10-17), which creates the emphatic climax δ (18-19). Then the fall off (20-23) and the quietly elaborate ending (24-26) as a bid for elegance.

20. . . . orator suavis et iucundus ex quo opera eius tam prosaica, quam metrica, quae plura extant, tanto splendore refulgent, tanta suavitate redolent, tanto florido ornatu spectabilia sunt, et lepore sonantium verborum mellifluo et sententiarum succo mirabili sapida, ut caelestis ingenii artificio potius, quam humani fabre facta credantur. (*1581: Epistola dedicatoria,* † 2vo.)

21. For an inclusive modern discussion of the rhetorical theory of style and the relationships to *elocutio* touched upon in this paper, see A. Scaglione, op. cit., espec. 14-96.

The tone is calm, as befits the figure of the humble countrydweller invoked by Petrarch.[22] Among the references to earlier portions of the text[23] is a reprise-like return to the motif of the doctor being *in alienis finibus*—in regions strange to him, as charged at the beginning of *CM* I.[24]

And there is the reference to the stylistic genre in which the preceding four books of invective are written: *en, in demonstrativo genere exerceor,* followed by *mallem in l a u d i b u s exerceri.* This makes the first phrase *synecdoche,*[25] since the task of *genus demonstrativum* includes both praise and censure. Petrarch may have had in mind the old school sentence *nam vituperatio, quae contraria est laudis* (which exhibits the unusual sequence censure-praise required here);[26] or, as we note his use of the plural *laudes* (rather than the singular which appears in most of the old definitions we may assume Petrarch knew),[27] a Ciceronian passage, such as *Brutus* xii, 47:

cum [Gorgias] singularum rerum laudes vituperationesque conscripsisset, quod iudicaret hoc oratoris esse maxime proprium, rem augere posse laudando vituperandoque rursus affligere.

[Gorgias] writing particularly in praise or in censure of given things, since he held that it was the peculiar function of oratory to magnify a thing by praise, or again by disparagement to belittle it.[28]

22. *CM* IV, 416-436, 575; I, 71-73; *et passim.*

23. Cf. above, notes 19, 22. "His . . . fevers": *CM* IV, 591; I, 309.

24. *CM* I, 19-20: *te, scilicet, egressum tuis alienis finibus oberrare; CM* IV, 590-591: *in alienis finibus non inveniens quod querebat.* The argument is that of *artis officium* (e.g., Quintilian, *Inst.* II, 21) and parallels in essence Brunetto Latini's comment:

4. Raison coment: li office de fisicien est a faire cures et medecines por saner, et sa fins est saner par ses medecines et briefment. L'office de rectorique est a parler penseement selonc les ensegnemens de l'art, et la fins est cele chose pour quoi il parole.
5. La matiere de retorique est ce de quoi li parliers dist, ausi comme les maladies sont matieres dou fisicien.

Li Livres dou Tresor III, 2, 4-5, ed. F. J. Carmody (Berkeley: University of California Press, 1948), 319.

25. Isidore, *Etym.* I, 37, 13; see Detail 2, below. Note also *Fam.* I, 11, 1: *Experiri vis, ut arbitror, in demonstrativo cause genere quid possim. In laudibus potius quam in contrario me probasses!*

26. Cf. also *CM* IV, 11: *Quos vituperare vis laudas.* The same sequence occurs Augustine, *De doctrina* IV, 19, 38: *cum aliquid vituperatur sive laudatur.*

27. E.g., *Ad Herennium* III, 6, 10; Cicero, *De inv.* I, 5, 7; Quintilian, *Inst.* III, 7; Cassiodorus, *Inst.* II, 3; Isidore, *Etym.* II, 4, 5; Brunetto Latini, III, 2, 9, etc.

28. Cicero, *Brutus,* transl. H. M. Hubbell, Loeb Classical Library [=LCL] (Cambridge, Mass.: Harvard University Press, 1939), 49. An allusion, "mysteriously meant," inviting the text identification Gorgias=Petrarch at the very beginning of *CM* is certainly within the realm of the arcane Petrarchan *iocus* for intimates.

The characteristics of this *conclusio* may be determined by the apologetic purpose of the entire postscript to the reader. We have yet to investigate similar passages in other Petrarchan texts. But it is noteworthy that the culminating statement, elaborately introduced and positioned, and somewhat unusually phrased, stresses a specific *genus dicendi* and the fact that Petrarch just has practiced it, that the four books of *CM* are thus *exercitamenta in genere demonstrativo* and to be read as such. Petrarch referred frequently to rhetorico-stylistic matters, which had also prominently figured in his recent experiences at the papal Curia in Avignon.[29] But, if I am not mistaken, this specific technical pronouncement *ex post facto,* is unusual. Petrarch shared Cicero's view: *oratori minimum de arte loqui, . . . multo maximum ex arte dicere* —for an orator it is a very slight thing to talk about art . . . by far the most important thing is to speak in accordance with the principles of his art,[30] and considered himself a practitioner, unlike Quintilian, who, as a teacher of orators, served as a sharpening *cos*—whetstone rather than as *gladius*—the flashing blade.[31] Petrarch's purpose may have been to represent the edition in bookform of his diatribes as a stylistic exercise in a genre with a long and distinguished tradition, well established in the communication theory of his time, and thus more acceptable to the kind of reader he had now in mind.[32] The same un-

29. E. H. Wilkins, *Life of Petrarch* (Chicago: University of Chicago Press, 1961), 109-110. Closely related to these issues, *Fam.* I, 1 and 3; and the letters addressed to Tommaso Caloria, I, 2; 7-12; on these, G. Billanovich, *Petrarca letterato* (Rome: Edizioni di Storia e Letteratura, 1947), 48-55.

30. Cicero, *De inv.* I, 6, 8 = *Fam.* XXIV, 7, 5.

31. *Fam.* XXIV, 7, 6; cf. Horace, *Ars poet.*, 304-305:

> . . . . . . ergo fungar vice cotis, acutum
> reddere quae ferrum valet, exsors ipsa secandi;
> munus et officium, nil scribens ipse, docebo . . .

(not noted in the editorial apparatus, *Edizione nazionale* of Francesco Petrarca, *Le Familiari,* vol. IV (Florence: G. C. Sansoni, 1942), 242, *11.* 48-49). Cf. Thomas Wilson's *Rule of Reason* (1551): ". . . to be but as a spurre or a whet stone, to sharpe the pennes of someother, that they may polishe, and perfect, that I have rudely and grossly entered," as quoted in W. S. Howell, *Logic and Rhetoric in England, 1500-1700* (Princeton: Princeton University Press, 1956), 13.

32. *Fam.* I, 1, 29:

> ut geminus sit labor: cogitare quisnam ille sit cui scribere propositum est, qualiter ve tunc affectus, cum ea que scribere instituis lecturus est.
>
> So the writer has a double task: to envisage the person he is writing to, and then the state of mind in which the recipient will read what he proposes to write. (Transl. M. Bishop, op. cit., 20.)

In return, Petrarch expected the reader

> "whoever he may be, to be thinking of me only, and not of the marriage of his daughter or of nocturnal company or of the plots of his enemies or

erring sense that guided him when editing the great collection of the *epistolae familiares*[33] may have suggested to him that without some common base of agreement or interest "personal pique goes out of date very quickly"[34]—hence the assurance that all that had been said is, after all, epideictic discourse:[35] *lector, intende, letaberis*[36]—Petrarch did not have to say it! The statement could also represent a last ironic *aculeus*—dart[37] against the doctor, whose missives, probably, were carefully arranged in accordance with the dialectic protocol of academic disputation (which may have made him accuse Petrarch of lacking in logic and call Petrarch's works homilies[38]). By shifting the reader's attention in retrospect from heated argument of proof, a *dubium* which has to be decided in its own right, to the *certum* of narrative vituperative oratory, Petrarch defeats "the clenched fist" of logical syllogism with the "open palm" of rhetorical *enthymema*[39] and the credibility of interesting, in-

> of an appearance in court or of his household or his fields or his treasure: I want him to be with me, at least while he reads. If business matters are pressing, let him postpone his reading: when he starts to read let him lay aside the cares of his business and his property, and devote his attention to what is under his eyes. If he does not like that, let him cast my writings aside: he would gain nothing from them. I do not want him to be negotiating and reading at the same time; and I do not want him to read without care what I have written not without care."

Fam. XIII, 5 (to Francesco Nelli, August 9, 1352; transl. E. H. Wilkins, *Petrarch at Vaucluse* (Chicago: University of Chicago Press), 1958, 130.

33. Cf. *Fam.* I, 1; P. Piur in *Vom Mittelalter zur Reformation,* ed. K. Burdach, vol. I, 2 (Berlin: Weidmannsche Buchhandlung, 1928), chap. 7; *Edizione nazionale* of Francesco Petrarca, *Le Familiari* vol. I, ed. V. Rossi, "Introduzione" (Florence: Sansoni, 1933).

34. N. Frye, op. cit., 224.

35. This raises the question of later interpolation for some of the digressive *exempla* and more elaborate patterns and devices—and, of course, the question of excision of text, which cannot be answered. Cf. also, above, note 7.

36. Apuleius, *Metam.* I, 1 = *Fam.* I, 1, 12.

37. Augustine, *De doctrina* III, 19, 29: *Videant ergo quam sibi arduum sit atque difficile nec laudis esca illici, nec contumeliarum aculeis penetrari....*

38. *CM* II, 428; III, 573-577. It seems probable that the relationship between the texts composed by the physician and by Petrarch was akin to the Boethian juxtaposition of dialectic and rhetoric (*De differentiis topicis* IV; *PL* 64, cc. 1205-1206), which McKeon describes as follows:

> dialectic uses interrogation and response, and its arguments are set forth in syllogisms; rhetoric uses continuous speech involving enthymemes; the end of dialectic is to force what one wishes from an adversary, that of rhetoric to persuade a judge. R. McKeon, "Rhetoric in the Middle Ages" in *Critics and Criticism,* ed. R. S. Crane (Chicago: University of Chicago Press, 1952, 1968), 271; cf. also, ibid., 273.

But note E. Raimondi in *Studi Petrarcheschi,* 4 (1951), 257-58.

39. Cicero, *De fin.* II, 6, 17; *Orator,* 113; *Acad. quaest.* 2; Quintilian, *Inst.* II, 20, 7; Sextus Empiricus, *Adv. mathematicos* 2, 7; Isidore, *Etym.* II, 23, 1-3. Cf.

formative *exempla,* presented in a stylish way—the poet's revenge.[40] *Materia et partes artis. Genus demonstrativum* is one of the three Aristotelian rhetorical *genera* whose 'office' it is *ad persuadendum accommodate dicere*—to speak in a manner adapted to persuade.[41] *Genus iudiciale* and *genus deliberativum,* Brunetto Latini's *jugement* and *conseil,*[42] address the listener or reader, be he judge or jury, primarily as decision maker between *iustum / iniustum* and *utile / inutile.* As epideictic oratory of praise (*honestum*) or censure (*turpe*), *genus demonstrativum* (Latini's *demoustrement*)[43] requires no action of this kind.[44] It is to be witnessed, to be experienced by intellectual and emotional participation as a member of the audience, as it were, and to be judged (*aestimatio*) in terms of information (*docere*),[45] interest (*delectare*),[46] and emotional appeal (*movere*).[47] In order to convince (*per-*

---

also Boethius, *De diff. top.* IV; *PL,* 64, cc. 105-06, 1177. Note the reference to *armatum enthimemate bisacuto, Fam.* I, 7, 6 (in reference to Juvenal, VI, 446-450, one might assume:

> Non habeat matrona, tibi quae iuncta recumbit,
> Dicendi genus, aut curtum sermone rotato
> Torqueat enthymema, nec historias sciat omnes,
> Sed quaedam ex libris et non intelligat).

On this analogy, W. S. Howell, "Nathaniel Carpenter's Place in the Controversy between Dialectic and Rhetoric," *Speech Monographs,* 1 (1934), 20-41.

40. On the shifting conceptions of rhetoric in the Middle Ages, R. McKeon, op. cit., 260-296.

41. Cicero, *De or.* I, 31, 138.

42. *Li Livres dou Tresor* III, 2, 8 (Carmody, op. cit., 320).

43. Ibid.

44. Augustine conveys something of this attitude in his remarks about listening to the sermons of St. Ambrose, *Confess.* V, 13, 23:

> Studiose audiebam disputantem in populo, non intentione qua debui, sed quasi explorans eius facundiam . . . et *verbis* eius suspendebar intentus, *rerum* autem incuriosus et contemptor adstabam et delectabar sermonis suavitate.
>
> And I listened diligently to him preaching to the people, not with the intent I ought, but, as it were, trying his eloquence . . . and I hung on his *words* attentively; but of the *matter* I was a careless and scornful looker-on and I was delighted with the sweetness of his discourse. (Transl. E. B. Pusey; italics mine.)

Cf. also Petrarch, on his youthful reading of Cicero, *Sen.* XV, 1: *Et illa quidem aetate nihil intelligere poteram, sola me verborum dulcedo quaedam et sonoritas detinebat, ut quicquid aliud vel legerem vel audirem, raucum mihi longeque dissonum videretur* (*1581:* 946).

45. *docere* (the *prodesse / monere* in Horace, *Ars poet.* 33, 334) is the intellectual aspect of *persuasio* in form of *narratio* (using *oratio perpetua*) or the dialectical argumentatio (using *oratio concisa*). Cf. Quintilian, *Inst.* IV, 2, 79; and, above, note 38.

46. Quintilian, *Inst.* VI, 2, 8.

47. Quintilian, *Inst.* XII, 10, 59.

suadere)[48] discourse *in genere demonstrativo* must achieve appropriateness in these terms.[49] This *aptum* involves an *inward* component concerning the content (*res*) and form (*verba*) of the text (*opus*); and an *outward* one concerning the effect on the listener/reader.[50] The basic situation of *CM* as a rhetorical work can be diagrammed as follows:

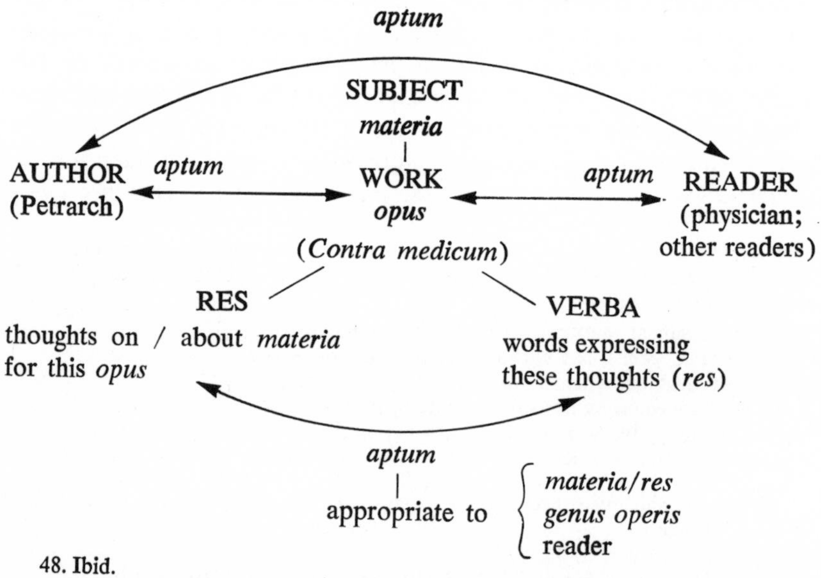

48. Ibid.

49. Cf. Augustine, *De doctrina* IV, 26, 57, discussing *genus demonstrativum* for the Christian orator:

> Illa quoque eloquentia generis temperati apud eloquentem ecclesiasticum, nec inornata relinquitur, nec indecenter ornatur: nec solum hoc appetit ut delectet, quod solum apud alios profitetur; verum etiam in iis quae laudat, sive vituperat, istis appetendis vel firmius tenendis, vult utique obedienter audiri. Si autem non auditur intelligenter, nec libenter potest. Proinde illa tria, ut intelligant qui audiunt, ut delectentur, ut obediant, etiam in hoc genere agendum est, ubi tenet delectatio principatum.
>
> For the Christian orator, eloquence of the moderate style must be neither altogether without ornament, nor unsuitably adorned, nor is it to make the giving of pleasure its sole aim, which is all it professes to accomplish in the hands of others; but in its praises and censures it should aim at inducing the listener to strive after or hold more firmly by what it praises, and to avoid or renounce what it condemns. If it cannot be heard with understanding, it cannot be heard with pleasure. Hence, those three qualities of being clear, enjoyable, and persuasive are to be sought also in this style—delight, of course, being its primary object.

Petrarch knew Augustine's Book: *Sen.* XV, 6 (*1581:* 734).

50. Cicero, *Orator* 22, 74: *decere* [declarat] *quasi aptum esse consentaneumque tempori et personae; quod cum in factis saepissime tum in dictis valet, in*

Augustine summarized this from the practitioner's viewpoint in *De doctrina christiana* IV, 4, 6:

Ubi autem benevolos, intentos, dociles aut invenerit, aut ipse fecerit, caetera peragenda sunt, sicut postulat causa. Si docendi sunt qui audiunt, narratione faciendum est, si tamen indigeat, ut res de qua agitur innotescat. Ut autem quae dubia sunt certa fiant, documentis adhibitis ratiocinandum est. Si vero qui audiunt movendi sunt potius quam docendi, ut in eo quod iam sciunt, agendo non torpeant, et rebus assensum, quas veras esse fatentur, accommodent, maioribus dicendi viribus opus est. Ibi obsecrationes et increpationes, concitationes et coercitiones, et quaecumque alia valent ad commovendos animos, sunt necessaria.

But once that his [the Christian orator's] hearers are friendly, attentive, and ready to learn, whether he has found them so, or has himself made them so, the remaining objects are to be carried out in whatever way the case requires. If the hearers need teaching, the matter treated of must be made fully known by means of narrative. On the other hand, to clear up points that are doubtful requires reasoning and the exhibition of proofs. If, however, the hearers require to be roused rather than instructed, in order that they may be diligent to do what they already know, and to bring their feelings into harmony with the truths they admit, greater vigour of speech is needed. Here entreaties and reproaches, exhortations and upbraidings, and all the other means of rousing the emotions, are necessary. (Transl. by J. F. Shaw)

The rhetorical task involved (1) *inventio*—seeking out competently, with talent (*natura*) and ingenuity (*ingenium*), the subject matters for the *exordium, narratio, argumentatio,* and *peroratio*;[51] (2) *dispositio*—the careful ordering of these matters; and (3) *elocutio*—the expression through language (*vestire atque ornare*)[52] of the matters discovered by *inventio* and ordered by *dispositio,* which comprises the virtues (*virtutes*) and vices (*vitia*) of latinity and three styles (*genera dicendi*): the *subtile*—humble expository prose; the *medium*—prose to delight and entertain; and the *grande*—prose to shock and to move.[53] These require-

vultu denique et gestu et incessu—'propriety' is what is fitting and agreeable to an occasion or person; it is important often in actions as well as in words, in the expression of the face, in gesture and in gait.... Transl. H. M. Hubbell, *Cicero: Brutus. Orator,* LCL (Cambridge, Mass.: Harvard University Press, 1939), 361. Cf. *Ad Herenn.* III, 11, 20-15, 27; and the detailed treatment of *pronuntiatio* in Quintilian, *Inst.* XI, 3.

51. Based on Aristotle, *Rhet.* 3, 13: Quintilian, *Inst.* III, 9, 1; *Ad Herenn.* I, 3, 4; Cicero, *De inv.* I, 14, 19; Isidore, *Etym.* II, 7, 1; Brunetto Latini, III, 14, 1; etc.

52. Cicero, *De orat.* I, 31, 142.

53. Cf. the specific references to the three styles: *grandiloquus/gravis; moderatus/mediocris; humilis/extenuatus* [*Ad Herenn.* IV, 8, 11] in *Fam.* XIII, 5, 16 (to Nelli, 1352); *Fam.* I, 1, 16; XXII, 10; XXII, 2, 17. Note also, *CM* IV, 410-445.

ments are interconnected, *inventio* dealing with *res, elocutio* with *verba,*[54] and *dispositio* with both *res* and *verba.* Together with memory (natural and artificial) and voice, countenance and gesture[55] required for actual oratorical delivery, they describe the main parts of rhetoric.[56]

These subjects are not purely denotative. There are rules to be observed. Conveyed by *doctrina* and acquired through *disciplina,* they form the *scientia,* which coupled with talent (*natura*) and industry (*exercitatio; imitatio*) produces the rhetorical competence needed for good work, the *virtus operis.*[57]

Even a superficial reading of *CM* within these contexts reveals a multiplicity of relationships, some evident, some suggested, varying in order and function, often entangled, elusive, and perplexing. The problem of interpretation is formidable.[58] Here, I can only attempt to sketch a few first results, which, I think, are not altogether uninteresting (this phrase using, of course, the rhetorical tropus *litotes*).

54. *Elocutio* is thus related to *grammatica.* Yet, *grammatica* is primarily *ars recte dicendi* (correct usage), *elocutio, ars bene dicendi* (effective usage). Petrarch refers to *res* and *verba CM* III, 166-167 (see below, p. 266 [10], *Prose,* 658) = *Fam.* III, 14, 5.

55. Geoffrey of Vinsauf, *Poetria nova* (early thirteenth century), 83-85, echoes Ciceronian advice (above, n. 50):

> . . . . . . Labor finalis: ut intret in aures,
> Et cibet auditum, vox castigata, modeste
> Vultus et gestus gemino condita sapore.

> The final concern is to ensure that a well-modulated voice
> enters the ears and feeds the hearing, a voice seasoned with the
> two spices of facial expression and gesture.

English transl. by M. F. Nims, *Poetria Nova of Geoffrey of Vinsauf* (Toronto: Pontifical Institute of Mediaeval Studies, 1967), 18.

56. Cf. A. Scaglione, op. cit., 18-24.

57. Cf. H. Lausberg, *Handbuch der literarischen Rhetorik* (Munich: M. Hueber, 1960), I, 47-64. The useful bibliography, ibid., vol. II, 605-638, is conveniently implemented by J. J. Murphy, *Medieval Rhetoric* (Toronto: University of Toronto Press, 1971); and the Basic Bibliography in A. Scaglione, op. cit., 405-417.

58. The difficulties inherent in rhetorical text analysis have been carefully explored by McKeon, who points to the ever varying differences concerning the subject matter and purpose of rhetoric.

> The theoretic presuppositions which underlie the shifts and alterations of rhetorical doctrines are readily made to seem verbal and arbitrary preferences, for in the course of discussion all the terms are altered in meaning, and the contents and methods of each of the arts are transformed when grammar, rhetoric, poetic, dialectic, and logic change places or are identified with another, or are distinguished from one another, or are subsumed one under another.

(R. McKeon, op. cit., 261.)

In demonstrativo genere exerceor

1. *Michi tecum pugna est.* The personal quarrel between Petrarch and the physician described in the abrupt, vehement opening of *CM,* is stated in the terms of rhetorical combat. The case (*causa*) concerns a concrete issue, a *quaestio finita,* in which Petrarch's deed, the letter to Clement VI, has been challenged by the physician, who is the accuser (*actor*). Petrarch, the *auctor* of this *factum,* is the accused (*reus*).[59] His opening reply establishes the state (*status*) of the action. It can be interpreted as the 'strong' denial of *coniectura* (*'non feci'*) or the 'weak' restrictive pleas (*'feci, sed . . .'*) of *finitio, qualitas,* or *translatio* (Detail 3)—in the course of the invectives he has recourse to all of them—but, as a denial of guilt, it initiates conflict: *pugna,* Quintilian's term,[60] which promptly appears in the first paragraph. For the initiated, attuned to the patterns of statement, the various states of plea (*status*) now become battle positions in the ensuing contest, in which the combatants and their 'troups' fight with verbal blades and shafts, and score or suffer injuries, which are medicated by the use of rhetorical *remedia.*[61] This is the *certamen verborum,*[62] deadly serious and, yet, *ludus*—action to be beheld.[63] This notion anticipates a good many features of *CM* which, as such, puzzle and alienate.

The interpretation of this opening as a statement of *status causae* is supported by the fact that the reader remains uninformed about the circumstances behind the conflict. The opening is an *insinuatio,* a special kind of *exordium,* which seeks to accomplish the traditional purpose *ut attentos, ut dociles, ut benivolos auditores habere possimus*—to have hearers who are attentive, receptive, and well-disposed,[64] by devices, such as surprise, 'dissimulation,' and 'indirection'[65]—a type of *exordium* appropriate when the adversary already has had his say (i.e. in MD 1) and, with it, the opportunity to place the *causa* under the cloud of *genus turpe*—being a shameful matter.[66] However, Petrarch may have provided

59. Invoking Cicero, *Pro Q. Ligario* I, 2, he tells the doctor: "*Habes* igitur quod est accusatori maxime optandum, *confitentem reum.*" (*CM* IV, 27.)

60. Quintilian, *Inst.* VII, 1, 8. Cf. the reference to *pugnando, CM* IV, 522.

61. Cicero, *De inv.* I, 21, 30: *ut vulneri praesto medicamentum est. . . .*

62. *CM* IV, 493.

63. *CM* II, 391-393, etc. On this, J. Huizinga, *Homo ludens* (Basel: Pantheon, 1938), 142-143; chaps. vi and ix.

64. *Ad C. Herennium* I, 4, 6; transl. H. Caplan, LCL (Cambridge, Mass.: Harvard University Press, 1954), 13. Cf. Augustine, *De doctrina* IV, 4, 6, above, p. 259.

65. Cicero, *De inv.* I, 15, 20: *Insinuatio est oratio quadam dissimulatione et circumitione obscure subiens auditoris animum.*

66. *Ad Herenn.* I, 6, 9.

a first *prooemium* (the direct opening) by placing the letter to Clement VI before the text of *CM*. Be that as it may, a number of early manuscript versions of *CM* include the Clement letter or the explanatory *Misc.* 1 of 1375 (Detail 4). The early editions of Petrarch's works (1496-1581) print both *Fam.* v, 19 and *Misc.* 1., the latter as *Epistolaris praefatio,* before the text of *CM*.

2. *Quod constat laude et vituperatione.*[67] If the general concept of rhetorical status and its bellicose stance accounts perhaps for much of the "unamiable arrogance and touchiness" the late Morris Bishop found in Petrarch's work,[68] the subjects of praise and censure as listed in the rhetorical texts provide interesting comment on some specific passages in *CM*.

The protracted exchange aimed at the doctor's swarthy but ashen complexion may serve as an example. *CM* I, 240 comments on the doctor's sallow, unhealthy looking face as ill becoming a man who promises others the health he does not appear to possess himself. When the doctor replied, ascribing his pallor to a lack of sleep due to frequent vigils spent in philosophical studies, Petrarch counters with a bizarre diatribe[69] based on *Genesis* xxx, 35-40, stating that just as Jacob's varicolored rods affected the color of his sheep, so the color, odor, and taste of the stools the doctor examines daily, affects the color of his face: *Ab obiectis inquam stercoribus et colorem et odorem traxeris et saporem.* This jars the modern reader's image of Petrarch.[70] Yet the rhetorical *savoir faire* permits that *homines laudantur vel vituperantur ex corpore*— as to features of the body, especially *ex pulchritudine*—physical beauty (or the absence thereof) and relevant details; as well as *ex robore vel infirmitate*—vigor or weakness of the body. The licit *argumenta a persona*[71] include reference to the two sexes and their actual or assumed

67. Quintilian, *Inst.* III, 7.

68. M. Bishop, *Petrarch and His World* (Bloomington: Indiana University Press, 1963), 315.

69. *CM* II, 157, 565, 610-639.

70. Es ist ein hoechst unerquicklicher Krieg . . . gewinnt man doch, wenn man die Invectiven zu lesen beginnt, den Eindruck, als wenn der sonst so wuerdige und moraleifrige Petrarca, wie von einem ploetzlichen Wahnsinn befallen, nach Art eines verwilderten Menschen mit Steinen und Scherben um sich wuerfe . . . .

G. Koerting, *Petrarcas Leben und Werke* (Leipzig: Fuess, 1878), 619. In essence, the argument parallels closely physiognomic texts, such as Galen (Kuehn XIX, 253 = Maimonides, *Aph.,* Particula 24), as cited in L. Thorndike, *A History of Magic and Experimental Science* (New York: Columbia University Press, 1923), I, 176-177. Cf. also p. 264, and notes 82, 83, below.

71. Quintilian, *Inst.* V, 10; E. de Bruyne, *Études d'esthétique médiévale* (Bruges: De Tempel, 1946), II, 173-202.

proclivities,[72] age, family background, and nationality, to *educatio* and *disciplina, habitus corporis,* social class, *animi natura,*[73] occupation, etc., even play on the names of persons,[74] and flattering or deprecatory remarks on emotional states. A number of other passages in *CM* seem to fit smoothly into the rhetorical schemes of praise and censure for humans, works, deeds, activities, places, towns, animals, trees, etc.—all of which suggests that Voigt may have been correct in surmising that *CM* was motivated primarily not by hatred of a person or a profession, but by Petrarch's desire to prove himself an adversary of Ciceronian [or Augustinian?] stature[75]—an observation which may have implications far beyond the text of *CM*.

3. Topics and *sententiae*. The text of *CM* displays a rich substratum of themes, allusions, and images, elaborately developed, briefly stated, or just touched upon, which is clearly related to rhetorical tradition, yet thus far scarcely dealt with in the Petrarchan literature. We have just mentioned the sequence on the doctor's complexion: it constitutes just one, gross, instance of the archetypal *vultus* topic, the expressive face, the telltale countenance that indicates one's feelings independent of his will.[76] The topic rings through literature from Homer well past Goethe's times, and was acknowledged as a tool of rhetorical practice since early an-

72. Cf. Quintilian, ibid.: *ut latrocinium facilius in viro, veneficium in femina credas.*

73. Quintilian, ibid.: *etenim avaritia, iracundia, misericordia, crudelitas, severitas aliaque his similia afferunt frequenter fidem aut detrahunt, sicut victus luxuriosus an frugi an sordidus, quaeritur.*

74. Quintilian, *Inst.* IX, 3, 70: *cur ego non dicam, Furia, te furiam?*

75. Dennoch ist es nicht so sehr der Hass gegen einen einzelnen Menschen oder einen Stand, der Petrarca reizte, als vielmehr das Verlangen, sich als redegeruesteten Cicero zu zeigen.

G. Voigt, *Die Wiederbelebung des classischen Altertums,* 2nd ed., vol. II (Berlin: G. Reimer, 1881), 449.

76. Augustine, *De doctrina* II, 1, 2. The medieval literature abounds with matter of fact statements, such as Geoffrey of Vinsauf, *Poetria nova,* 974-977:

Quid dat formido? pallere. Quid ira? rubere.
Quidve superba lues? turgere. Resumimus ergo.
Formido pallet. Rubet ira. Superbia turget.

What does fear produce? Pallor. What does anger cause? A flush.
Or what, the vice of pride? A swelling up. We refashion the statement thus:
Fear grows pale, anger flushes, pride swells.

(M. F. Mims, op. cit., 51.) Cf. also the old encyclopedic handbooks, such as Aelian, *Var. hist.* III; Isidore, *Etym.* XI, 1, 34; Hrabanus Maurus, *De universo* VI, 1 (*PL* 111, cc. 147-148). D. G. Morhof, *Polyhistor literarius* I, 115, 18 (1688; last edition, ed. I. A. Fabricius, Luebeck, P. Broeckmann, 1747) still summarizes the literature on *honestatem vultu, verbis, facto exprime.*

tiquity. Reinforced by scriptural usage,[77] it entered everyday discourse as a figure of speech. Petrarch used it as such,[78] and as a rhetorical topic,[79] bending back upon itself the old device,[80] aware of the fact that it was part of the ordinary speech of men who are content to use the vulgar idiom.[81] As far as *CM* is concerned, the *vultus* topic must also be considered in relation to the medical literature. Petrarch's insult may have been doubly painful to one familiar with the demands of Hippocratic decorum,[82] and the symptomatic significance associated with *vultus* in contemporary medical practice.[83] Is this another instance of *iratus iocari?* The question of Petrarch's familiarity with these matters is yet to be addressed.

The lengthy argument about Petrarch's alleged disrespect for old men elaborates the time honored *puer-senex*—Boy and Old Man topic[84]

77. For *CM* note particularly *Prov.* 21, 29; *Vir impius procaciter obfirmat vultum suum*—(Douay:) The wicked man impudently hardeneth his face.

78. In *Fam.* XV, 6, Petrarch says of the doctor *signa quedam pertinacis atque arrogantis inscitie in vultu hominis legi.* He 'reads' Giovanni Malpaghini's face, *Sen.* V, 5—cf. C. H. Rawski, *Four Dialogues* . . . . , 83; 202, n. 36. Note also *Contra eum* (*1581:* 1068): *nec vultu nec nomine notus* and *De remediis* II, 118 (*1581:* 207): *quid tam horrificum vultum Caesaris habuit* . . . .

79. E.g., *Secretum* III: *Hinc pallor* . . . (*Prose,* 133).

80. R. McKeon, op. cit., 262. Cf. *Fam.* XXII, 2, 17: *ut in vultu et gestu*. . . . Allusion not noted in the editorial apparatus of the *Edizione nazionale* of Francesco Petrarca, *Le Familiari,* IV (1942), 107, see above, notes 50 and 55.

81. Augustine, *De doctrina* III, 29, 40:

> Quamvis pene omnes ii tropi, qui liberali dicuntur arte cognosci, etiam in eorum reperiantur loquelis, qui nullos grammaticos audierunt, et eo quo vulgus utitur sermone contenti sunt.

> Yet, nearly all these tropes which are said to be learned as a subject of liberal education are found even in the ordinary speech of men who have not studied grammar and are content to use the vulgar idiom.

A good example is *cor lapideum,* a hyperbolic exclamation, which was accepted into scriptural usage (Ezech. 9, 19; 36, 26), entered colloquial speech, and was rhetorically used by Petrarch.

82. Hippocrates, *The Physician* I: "The dignity of the physician requires that he should look healthy, and as plump as nature intended him to be." Transl. W. H. S. Jones, *Hippocrates,* LCL, II (Cambridge, Mass.: Harvard University Press, 1929), 311. Note also, Hippocrates, *Decorum* II, ibid., 281.

83. Cf. Hippocrates, *Prognostic* II, W. H. S. Jones, op. cit., 9, 11, 17; and the later texts on diagnosis and physiognomy (defined by Albertus Magnus as the "science which divines a man's character from the physical form of the various parts of his body"), of which *vultus* is a major subject; cf. L. Thorndike, op. cit., vol. II, 328-329, 575, 887, 910.

84. *CM* II, 504; IV, 33; cf. also *Fam.* I, 7, 18: Seni autem. . . . On related Petrarchan passages, E. Raimondi, op. cit., 241-242, and C. H. Rawski, op. cit., 77, 200, n. 6. On the topos, E. R. Curtius, *European Literature and the Latin Middle Ages* (New York: Pantheon, 1953), 98-101, 103-104, 202, 381, 424, 427.

with, I think, some further stress on Seneca and Augustine.[85] We encounter also topics, such as *fiducia*—self-confidence (in digressive discussion), Curtius' inexpressibility topos 'India',[86] which Petrarch used frequently;[87] and personal information turned into formal motif, as 'being coerced': *avidissimus pacis in bellum cogor;*[88] or 'hasty reply'—*scribere raptim et ex tempore* driven by *undosi pectoris motus.*[89]

Here belong also the furnishings of John of Garland's *rota Virgilii*—Virgil's wheel, which links the works of Virgil with the three styles, and assigns corresponding attributes.[90] Petrarch may or may not have known this school diagram of three segments arranged in a circle; he certainly adhered to its stipulations in his choice of trees, locale, social rank etc. (Detail 5)—which may serve to remind us that Petrarch's relationship to the *artes dictaminis* is yet another topic waiting to be studied.[91]

85. E.g., Seneca, *Ep.* 36, 4; Augustine, *De doctrina* IV, 3, 4.

86. E. R. Curtius, op. cit., 160.

87. *CM* I, 98; *Secretum* III (*Prose,* 166); *Contra quendam* (*Prose,* 700-702); *Fam.* IX, 13, 8; X, 1, 21; XII, 2, 37; XIII, 8, 12; XV, 4, 4; XVII, 3, 21; XXII, 12, 5; XXIV, 8, 1; *Sen.* XVI, 7 (*1581:* 958), etc.

88. *De sui ipsius* (*1581:* 1036); cf. *CM* I, 10; IV, 465, 489-490, 591, etc.; *Misc.* 1.

89. *Fam.* IV, 1, 35; *CM* I, referred to in *Fam.* XV, 6; and the composition of *De sui ipsius* (*1581:* 1035). E. H. Wilkins, *Petrarch's Later Years* (Cambridge, Mass.: Mediaeval Academy of America, 1959), 118. It is interesting to note that Petrarch does not hesitate to adjust old school topics to his purpose, e.g., the startling relationship between the graduation ceremony in *De remediis* I, 12 (C. H. Rawski, *Four Dialogues . . .*, 27, 118, n. 145) and the example of *apostrophe* in Geoffrey of Vinsauf, *Poetria nova,* 435-458, replete with reference to Horace, *Ars,* 139:

Omnes accurrite: nam mons
Parturiet, sed erit mus tandem filius eius. (446-447; compare *CM* II, 22-34.)

90. E. Faral, *Les arts poétiques du xii*e *et xiii*e *siècle* (Paris: Bibl. de l'École des Hautes Études, 1924, repr. 1962), 87-88; E. R. Curtius, op. cit., 231-232; E. de Bruyne, op. cit., I, 233, II, chap. 1, 3; and T. Lawler's forthcoming edition of *The Parisiana Poetria of John of Garland* (New Haven: Yale University Press). The 'ascending' sequence of *Eclogues, Georgics, Aeneid* is observed in the arrangement of most older editions of Virgil's *opera omnia.*

91. G. Billanovich, *Petrarca letterato . . .*, 47-48, touches upon this question in regard to the *cursus.* Here beckon also questions pertaining to the rôle of older sources and materials transmitted in the medieval texts: thus, e.g., the entire section on ancient meters in John of Garland's *Parisiana poetria,* VII, 1929-1984, is based on Augustine, *De musica* II, 8, 15, *Quae nomina pedum Graeci instituerint,* with Augustine's 28 items rearranged as follows: 1, 4, 3, 2, 5, 12 ("*Aeneas*"), 8 ("*Erato*"), 6, 7 ("*carina*"), 10, 9, 11, 13, 28, 21, 22 ("*cantilena*"), 23 ("*Saloninus*"), 19, 20, 18, 14, 24, 15, 25, 16 ("*Menedemus*"), 26 ("*Demosthenes*"), 17, 27 ("*Fescenninus*"). On similar Augustinian references in Aribo's *Musica* (late eleventh century) cf. C. H. Rawski in *Natalicia Musicologica Knud Jeppesen,* ed. B. Hjelmborg & S. Sørensen (Copenhagen: W. Hansen, 1962), 26-28.

Petrarch's *sententiae,* that exuberant repertory of *arricchimenti emblematici,*[92] serve two related functions: to intensify the subject at issue or summarize it in capsule form (*res*); and to enhance the text with a delightful saying (*verba*).[93] Out of context, these "precise sentences"[94] lose momentum and fail to convey the vibrant texture of the passage into which they have been deftly placed. With these limitations, the following examples attempt to illustrate the rich gamut from simple factual succinctness to effulgent turn and sinewy thrust of phrase that often approaches pure *ornatus.*

2 3 2 1
(1) lingua animi sera est (ii, 9)

2 2 2
(2) nullus opus est verbis (iii, 512)

α β × β′ α
(3) si bene dixisses, audisses bene (i, 442)

4(?) 4 4 4
(4) *calcanda* est enim ignorantia superborum, humilium *sublevanda* (ii, 330)

3 3 3 3
(5) *superbo* libertas omnis *superbia* videtur (ii, 123)

3 3 3 3
(6) tam decet ornatus *medicum,* quam *asellum* falere (iii, 763-764)

(7) ridete omnes, plaudite, fabula acta est (iv, 381; cf. *SN* 18)

2 2
(8) male *concluditis,* falsum *dicitis,* pueriliter loquimini (iv, 98-99)

α α β × β′
(9) laudatur philosophia, sed non omnis: laudatur *verax, fallax*
α′
carpitur (iii, 242-243)

(10) omnium una ratio est: mutantur verba, manerent res (iii, 166-167)

(11) mensura vestra fatui cunta metimini: nec gigantem nanus edificans nec formica cogitat elephantem (ii, 316-318)[95]

92. E. Raimondi, op. cit., 259.

93. On *sententia,* which is not closely identified in this paper, cf. G. Paré *et al., La Renaissance du xii*ᵉ *siècle: Les écoles et l'enseignement* (Paris: J. Vrin, 1933), 267-274.

94. Cf. *De remediis* I, prefatory letter (*1581:* ††† 4).

95. On other zoological similes cf. E. Raimondi, op. cit., 243, *et passim.*

(12) talem me genuit *natura,* accessit consuetudo nature *emula,* accessit studium et iugis *cura* (iv, 16-17)

This brief glance at the *sententiae* leads directly to the central rhetorical *aptum,* the words, expressions, figures, and turns of phrase intended to delight the attentive listener/reader.

4. *Ornatus.* The text of *CM* bristles with the devices of *ornatus elocutionis.* Some are used simply, matter of fact—colloquially, it seems. Here belong

hyperbolic exclamations (metaphoric *antonomasia*)—*o callidum ingenium* (ii, 535), *o stolidum caput* (iv, 334);

rhetorical query—this with loose jointure, *Quid enim—lector oro te—quid est . . .* (iv, 503-504);

periphrasis—this concerning the death of the Pontiff, hence *necessitate, si ergo tunc nature debitum persolvisset* (i, 100-101), *cetera sileo* (not mentionable in polite discourse—ii, 559);

ironia—*sed, nisi fallor, utilem* sibi, tibi *forte non ita* (chiastic—i, 132), *quasi de consolatu aut pretura . . .* (i, 358), *vicisti cavillator acutissime, plus confiteor quam accusas* (iv, 445-446), with *regressio:* ars nobilissima tu*que preclarus medicus.* Illa, *ut est mechanicarum penultima, sic omnium prima artium.* Tu, *ut non tantum ultimus, sed hostis es, sic medicorum omnium sis princeps* (iii, 651-653);

antitheton—*quos* vituperare *vis* laudas (iv, 11), *fecisti* optime, *quamvis* pessima *voluntate* (iv, 15);

simple *paronomasia*—*nec verbis, sed verberibus coercendus* (iii, 600),[96] *philosophicos locos, tabificos iocos* (ii, 28), *mendice medice* (iv, 149); and various forms of

2 2

isocolon—*me fatente et favente* (iv, 31), *male* concluditis, *falsum* dicitis, *pueriliter loquimini* (iv, 98-99), *crede michi, si placet, plures* te *quotidie* impellunt, *plures melioresque* me diligunt (iv, 79-80), *rhetores esse vultis,* ridente *Tullio,* indignante *Demosthene,* flente

×

Ypocrate, populo pereunte (iv, 662-663), *Disce iam iurgator, vel mordere profundius, vel silere* (iv, 396-397).

And there is a group of carefully contrived passages, often combining elaborate insult and complex rhetorical devices to be savored. Read today, many do not escape the *vitium* of heavyhanded preciousness. But some have kept over the centuries the playful, sportive élan that

96. Cf. *Fam.* XVI, 12, 1; VII, 17, 7.

fired their mordancy. For instance, the glittering *enumeratio* with increase and *isocolon* (iii, 681-685):

> *Accusare,* excusare, consolari, irritare, *placare animos,* movere lacrim*as atque comprimere,* ascendere ir*as et extinguere,* colorare factum, avertere infamiam, transferre culpam, suscitare suspitiones: oratorum propria sunt hec; medicorum esse non noveram.[97]

Or the roaring ironic *anaphoras* (ii, 31-32; iv, 377-380):

> *Accurrite* philosophi, *accurrite* poete, *accurrite* studiosi; quicunque usquam scribendis libris operam datis, *accurrite.*[98]
>
> *Dic* age, *dic*[99] secure, nil timueris: tuam auream eloquentiam expectamus. *Dic,* rhetorice imperator, *dic,* Galiene Demosthenes, *dic,* bone Cicero et Avicenna.

5. Stylistics. In general, these features of *elocutio* reflect the established rhetorical armamentarium of Petrarch's time. This is not surprising. Like Chaucer, Petrarch learned "out of olde bokes."[100] What, I think, is surprising is the absence of conspicuous instances of usage modelled in imitation of Cicero or the many other authors of Latin an-

97. *De vita solitaria* II, 10, 7 (*Prose,* 582-584):

> Surge, veni, propera: linquamus urbem mercatoribus, advocatis, prosenetis, feneratoribus, publicanis, tabellionibus, medicis, unguentariis, lanionibus, cocis, pistoribus atque fartoribus, alchimistis, fullonibus, fabris, textoribus, architectis, statuariis, pictoribus, mimis, saltatoribus, cytharedis, circulatoribus, lenonibus, furibus, hospitibus, circumscriptoribus, maleficis, adulteris, parasitis ac scurris edacibus, odorem fori vigili nare captantibus, quibus ea felicitas una est, illi inhiant: nullus autem nidor in montibus, et solitis ac placitis caruisse supplicium. Sine illos: non sunt nostri generis.

Compare the list in George Gascoigne, *The Droomme of Doomes day* I, of 1576: *The Complete Works,* ed. J. W. Cunliffe (Cambridge: University Press, 1910), II, 259. Gascoigne translated some of the dialogues in *De remediis* I (cf. C. H. Rawski, "Petrarch's Dialogue on Music," *Speculum,* 46 (1971), 309, n. 9; 310, n. 14; 312-313, n. 26; 314, n. 37). Note also, *De remediis* II, pref. (*1581:* 106):

> Nam ut sileam reliquos motus, velle, nolle [*Secretum* III, *Prose* 154 = Terence, *Phormio,* 949; cf. *Romans,* 7, 19], amare, odisse, blandiri, minari, irridere, fallere, fingere, iocari, flere, misereri, parcere, irasci, placari, labi, deiici, attolli, titubare, subsistere, progredi, retroverti, inchoari, desinere, dubitare, errare, falli, nescire, discere, oblivisci, meminisse, invidere, contemnere, mirari, fastidire, despicere, simulque suspicere, et quae sunt eiusmodi, quibus utique nihil incertius fingi potest, quibusve sine ulla requie ab ingressu usque ad exitum fluctuat vita mortalis.

98. Cf. Geoffrey of Vinsauf, *Poetria nova,* 446, *Omnes accurrite,* above, note 89.

99. Parody of Virgil, *Georg.* IV, 4, 358: *duc, age, duc ad nos . . .* ?

100. *Parliament of Fowls,* 24; cf. Huppé-Robertson, *Fruyt and Chaf* (Princeton: Princeton University Press, 1963), 104-105. Note also E. Norden's reminder to consider Petrarch's contemporary background: *Die antike Kunstprosa* (Leipzig: B. G. Teubner, 1898, repr., Dresden, 1958), II, 732-736 and M. Baxandall, *Giotto and the Orators* (Oxford: Clarendon Press, 1971), 4-5.

tiquity so well known and cherished by Petrarch.[101] The rhetoric of *CM* is clearly aware of the Old and New Rhetoric and, more so, perhaps, Augustine's advice to the Christian orator and disputant.[102] But its stylistic texture is primarily akin to the devices of medieval vituperative prose and the usage established in the old encyclopedic texts, the *artes dictaminis,* and the handbooks of preaching.

The same is true of the overall arrangement, the *forma sive modus tractandi.*[103] Petrarch's handling of *interrogatio* and *subiectio*—rhetorical query and fictive dialogue, for instance,[104] seems to recall St. Bernard[105] and the Victorines rather than Ciceronian models. The tone of *CM,* relentlessly shrill though it may sound to us, reflects essentially the Augustinian formula of varied diction based upon a mix of styles which, in ascending order, primarily serve to inform, to delight, and to move.[106] Much of the text proceeds on the middle level, becomes *humilis* in digression, description, and narration of *exempla,* and rises to grandiose climaxes which seem to reflect very little of the *magnum eloquium* of the ancients. The text of *CM* thus bears out Petrarch's own spirited remark to Nelli, that hardly anybody in his day could write in Cicero's *stilus gravis*, few, *moderatus,* many more, *humilis,* below which lies the age old *verborum potius plebeia quedam et agrestis et servilis effusio*—mass of common words, rude and motley, of the vulgar multitude.[107] The language in *CM* lacks the careful elegance so admired by the Latin prose writers of the *quattrocento.*[108] But it conveys often a compelling gesture of robust immediacy, which sets it apart from, both, the man-

101. A superficial examination of related texts indicates that, *if* there are new models used in *CM,* they come from Seneca.

102. In medieval times Cicero, *De inventione* and the *Ad C. Herennium,* which was ascribed to Cicero, were known as the *Rhetorica prima* or *vetus,* and the Rhetorica *secunda* or *nova.* Cf. W. S. Howell, *Logic and Rhetoric . . . ,* ch. 3, ii; G. Kennedy, *The Art of Rhetoric in the Roman World* (Princeton: Princeton University Press, 1972), 106-148, *et passim*; *Ad C. Herennium,* ed. H. Caplan, LCL (Cambridge, Mass.: Harvard University Press, 1954), Introduction, vii-viii; on Augustine, H.-I. Marrou, *Saint Augustin et la fin de la culture antique* (Paris: De Boccard, 1938), I, ch. iii and iii, ch. vi. Cf. also E. Auerbach, *Literary Language and Its Public in Late Latin Antiquity and in the Middle Ages* (New York: Pantheon, 1965), ch. i.

103. Letter to Can Grande della Scala, 9, *Le opere di Dante; Testo critico della Società Dantesca Italiana* (Florence: R. Bemporad, 1921), 439.

104. E.g., *CM* II, 446-459; IV, 110-111, 297-316; etc.

105. *Sermo de duodecim stellis, Breviarium romanum, 15 sept. in ii Nocturno,* lectio vi.

106. Augustine, *De doctrina* IV, 17, 34, based on Cicero. Cf. above, pp. 257-9.

107. *Fam.* XIII, 5, 16; cf. above, p. 259.

108. M. Baxandall, op. cit., I, 1, *passim.*

nered academic style of Petrarch's age and "die mumienhafte Diktion der Spaeteren."[109]

As far as Petrarch's reader was concerned the distinctive contribution of *CM* was not its style and form; probably, not even its immediate *raison d'être,* the brawl with the Pope's physician. *CM* contained interesting, new *exempla* and arguments. It addressed subjects the contemporary significance of which, though yet to be explored, is highly probable. These timely, new materials, within a curious, if not somewhat sensational framework, and written by one of the foremost literary figures of the day, may well have been the main attraction for Petrarch's contemporaries. Blurred by time, they lost their appeal for a new generation: The *CM* grew old—its anger spent, its stories dated, a thoroughly 'medieval' piece of indifferent oratory.[110]

CONCLUDING NOTE. It should be carefully stressed that these remarks report a mere handful of preliminary results obtained by way of speculative application of a synoptic instrument based on the major rhetorical Latin texts from Cicero's age to the arrival of the New Logic during "the latter part of the twelfth and the greater part of the thirteenth century."[111] In order to qualify as reliable new evidence, these results have to be broadly established—at least, for all four of the great invectives—and to be tested against the texts Petrarch knew and used, or could be reliably assumed to have known and used—which is not an easy task.

Only then will we be able to grasp some of the main features of rhetoric and style in Petrarch's Latin texts.

109. E. Norden, op. cit., II, 769. On the whole issue, A. Scaglione, op. cit., chs. ii, iii, and the important historical remarks, 359-363.

110. Cf. Bruni's matter of fact remark in 1401: [Petrarca] *scripsit etiam* Invectivas, *ut non solum poeta, sed etiam orator haberetur . . . . . . neque quicquam in orationibus quod non artem rhetoricam magnopere desideraret. Ad Petrum Paulum Histrum,* I: *Prosatori latini del Quattrocento,* ed. E. Garin (Milan–Naples: Ricciardi, 1952), 72.

111. R. McKeon, op. cit., 273. The "old" logic consisted of Boethius' Latin translations of the logical works of Aristotle known before the middle of the twelfth century, i.e., the *Categoriae* (*Liber praedicamentorum*), *De interpretatione,* and the *Isagoge* of Porphyry; the "new" logic, of the remaining books of the *Organon,* the *Analytica priora, Analytica posteriora, Topica,* and *De sophisticis elenchis,* rediscovered and newly translated in the mid-twelfth century.

Detail 1. Petrarch's *Invective contra medicum*: Documentation*

Pope Clement VI falls ill		December, 1351
Petrarchan references to Clement's illness		
Fam. xii, 4 to Francesco Nelli		January 13, 1352
xii, 5 Francesco Nelli		January 18
xii, 6 Philippe de Cabassoles		February 1
Events leading to Petrarch's letter to Clement		
Sen. xvi, 3 (see below)		
Letter to Clement VI—*Fam.* v, 19		March 12
(Reply by a papal physician—MD 1	no later than	March 18 or 19)
Petrarch's rejoinder		
(Invective i—missive form) [*Epistola*] *in procaci et insano medico*	late in March	
On the writing of the rejoinder		
Fam. xv, 5 to Pierre d'Auvergne		April 3
xv, 6 Pierre d'Auvergne		April 17
Pope Clement VI dies		December 6, 1352
(Counter-rejoinder by the physician—MD 2	early in	1353)
Petrarch's counterblast		
(Invective ii, iii, iv—missive form) while still in Provence		
Revision as *Invective contra medicum, i-iv*		Milan, 1353
Book i	rejoinder (1352)	
Books ii, iii, iv	counterblast (1353)	
The *Invective* in retrospect		
Misc. 1 to Giovanni Boccaccio		July 12, 1357
Sen. xvi, 3 Francesco da Siena		May 1, 1372
Sen. xv, 11 Benvenuto da Imola		February 9, 1373

*Based on E.H. Wilkins, *Studies in the Life of Petrarch; Petrarch's Eight Years in Milan;* and *Petrarch's Later Years* (Cambridge, Mass.: Mediaeval Academy of America, 1955, 1958, 1959).

Detail 2. *Apologiae conclusio* (iv, 580-92)

		clausulae	*tropi*	Word figures
1	Ita, si fortassis hoc calle famam *petit*	V		homoeoteleuton (1–2)
2	necquicquam *insanierit.*	8 s.◡–		
3	Sin turbasse otium	med		
4	et silentium meum interrupisse contentus est,	T		
5	quod decreverat *implevit:*	8 s. ◡ –		homoeoteleuton (5–6)
6	aliquot michi dies *eripuit*	T		hyperbaton
7	quos nemo restituet,	T		
8	et a meis TRAMITIBUS abductum,	(V)	metonymia	
9	*ad durum et* insolitum ITER *traxit.*	V	metonymia	
10	Quidni igitur turber,	P		
11	temporisque iacturam querar	V		
12	*nec* michi *nec* alteri fructuosam	(V)		anaphora
13	nisi quantum studiosi homini,	(T)		
14	modo animi crimen absit.	V		
15	et data sit occasio non quesita,	V		
16	in omni genere orationis	V		
17	exercendus est *stilus*?	P	synecdoche	
18	En in demonstrativo genere exerceor;	T		
19	mallem in laudibus exerceri.	V		
20	Ceterum, ut aliquando sit finis,	P		
21	is qui hanc michi necessitatem imposuit,	T		hyperbaton
22	*in alienis finibus non inveniens quod querebat*	V	periphrasis	
23	revertatur ad *proprias febres*;	P	synecdoche	
24	tu *lacessito* faveas,			pleonasmus, isocolon, polyptoton, epiphoric variatio (24–26)
25	*lacessentem* oderis,			
26	et valeas precor.	P		zeugma (see below, p. 273)

The schema is as follows:

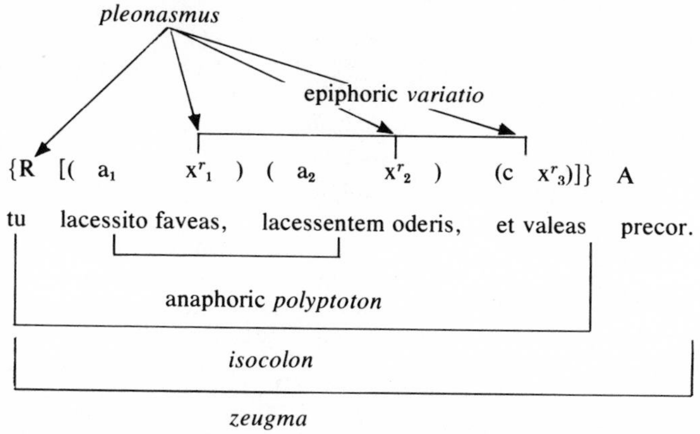

Symbols: + London, Brit. Mus. Harl. 6348, f. 23*ro* (referred to as *H*)
v *m* between two vowels ⌐¬ reduplication of vowels
‿ consonantic jointure =‿= syllabic jointure ( ) modified

Abbreviations: med *cursus medius;* P *cursus planus;* s syllable; T *cursus tardus;* V *cursus velox*

On the *cursus* I have found very helpful A. Marigo, "Il 'cursus' nella prosa latina dalle origini cristiane ai tempi di Dante," *Atti e Memorie d. R. Accad. Scienze Lettere e Arti di Padova*, N. S. 67 (1931), 321-356. For further commentary on the technical terms briefly glossed below, see the respective entries in *Encyclopedia of Poetry and Poetics*, ed. A. Preminger (Princeton: Princeton University Press, 1965).

lines 1-2 5-6-(9)	homoeoteleuton	sequence of sentence portions with assonant ending Isidore, *Etym.* i,36,16: *h. est, quum uno modo verba plurima finiuntur*
6; 21	hyperbaton	separation of two syntactically related words by interpolation of another word or sentence portion *Etym.* i,37,16: *transcensio, cum verbum aut sententia ordine commutatur*
8	*H*:	*obductum* (?)
8; 9	metonymia	replacement of a word by another related one which serves as *signum* *Etym.* i,37,8-10: *transnominatio ab alia significatione ad aliam proximitatem translata*
10	*H*:	*turbarer* changing P to 8 s. – ◡
12	anaphora	parallel beginning of two sentence portions

		Etym. i,36,8: *a. est repetitio eiusdem verbi per principia versuum plurimorum.* As such, *nec . . . nec*, with correlative particle, hardly qualifies as *anaphora*, but note:
	H:	*nec alteri fructuosam*
13	*H*:	*studioso*
17; 23	synecdoche	naming a part to denote the whole, or vice versa. (Petrarch uses *stilus* in both senses. The assumption *stilus* = writing tool seems warranted by the singular. Domenico Silvestri translates *lo stile* [Ricci, p. 201, 743]; cf. also John of Garland [?] *Opus synonymorum* [P. Leyser], 435.) *Etym.* i,37,13: *s. est conceptio cum a parte totum, vel a toto pars intellegitur*
20-21	*H:*	*finis in iis, qui*—avoiding syllabic jointure
21	*H:*	*hanc necessitatem michi imposuit*—avoiding hyperbaton
22	*H:*	*quid querebat*
	periphrasis	expression by paraphrase, often metaphoric *Etym.* i,37,15: *p. est circumloquium, dum res una plurimis verbis significatur . . . Hic autem tropus geminus est. Nam aut veritatem splendide producit, aut foeditatem circuitu evitat*
24	*H:*	*Tu*
	pleonasmus	added word, not required syntactically, for purposes of emphasis and intensification *Etym.* i,34,6: *p. adiectio unius verbi supervacua* (cf. e.g., *CM* iv, 249-256)
24-25	(anaphoric) polyptoton	repetition with varied case at beginning of sentence (portion) *Etym.* i,36,17: *p. est, cum diversis casibus sententia variatur*
24-26	(epiphoric) variatio	repetition of verbs of identical inflection at end of sentence portion *Carmen de fig. vel schem.* Halm, 169: μεταβολή *. . . si verbum varie mutes*
	isocolon	parallel coordination of two or more sentences (sentence portions) *Ad Herennium* iv,20,27: *Conpar* [i.e., isocolon] *appellatur quod habet in se membra orationis . . . quae constent*

	ex pari fere numero syllabarum. Hoc non denumeratione nostra fiet—nam id quidem puerile est—'sed tantum adferet usus' et exercitatio facultatis, ut animi quodam sensu par membrum superiori referre possimus . . .
zeugma	parenthesis of two or more statements related to one verb *Etym.* i,36,3: *z. est clausula, quum plures sensus uno verbo clauduntur, quae fit tribus modis. Nam aut in primo, aut in postremo, aut in medio id verbum ponitur, quod sententias iungit*

Detail 3. *Pugna rhetorica*

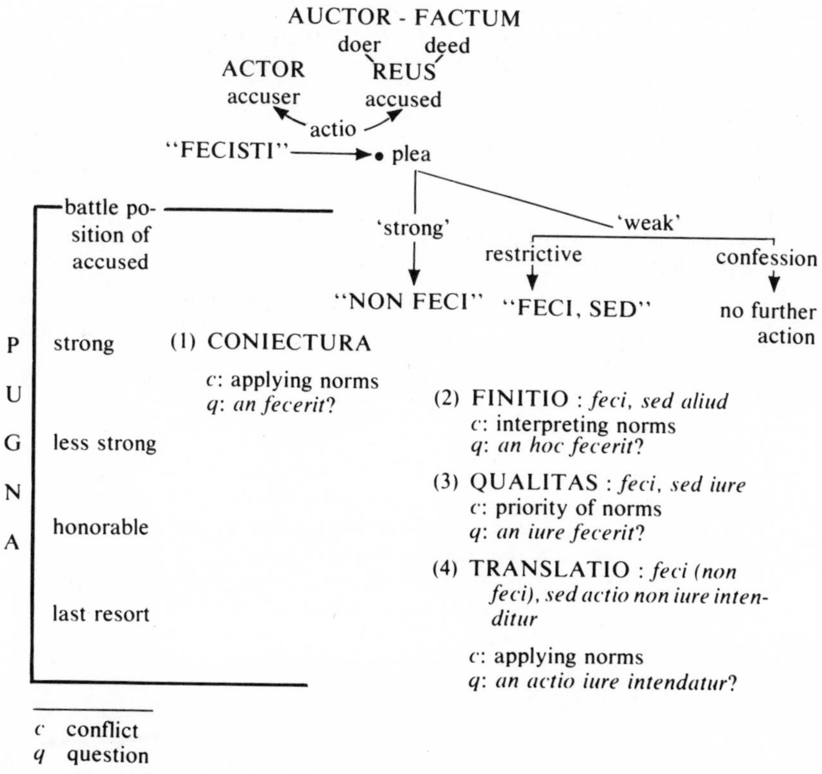

Detail 4. Manuscript Sources (in roughly chronological order)

	Ricci α	Ricci β	Other	*Fam.* v,19	*Misc.* 1
	CM i, 400-402: *Id si michi non crederis*	*CM* i, 51-55: *Quo consilio cur in me*			
s. XIV					
	Rome, Vat. lat. 4518 belonged to Lapo da Castiglionchio			—	f
	Florence, Laur. xxvi sin 8 written by Tedaldo della Casa; dated Oct. 6, 1379			—	p
		London, Brit. Mus. Harl. 6348		p	—
		Paris, B.N., lat. 8751[a]		i	—
			Paris, B.N., lat. 16322*	i	—
			Paris, B.N., lat. 14582*	i	—
s. XV					
	Florence, Bibl. Riccardiana 1176			p	—
	Rome, Vat. lat. 4527 written by Simone Alidosi; dated July 4, 1405			i	—
		Olomouc, Bibl. Capit. 509		i	—
	Rome, Vat. lat. 3355			?	—
		Urbino, 333		—	?

Abbreviations:
f follows text of *Contra medicum*
i included elsewhere in the manuscript codex
p precedes text of *Contra medicum*
* cf. P. de Nolhac, *Pétrarque et l'humanisme* (Paris: H. Champion, 1907), ii, 304-306.

Detail 5. *Rota Virgilii*

	STYLUS		
	HUMILIS	MEDIOCRIS	GRAVIS grandiloquus
status	*pastor otiosus* shepherd	*agricola* farmer	*miles dominans* soldier
figurae	Tityrus, Meliboeus	Triptolemus, Coelius	Hector, Aiax
animal	*ovis* sheep	*bos* cow	*equus* horse
implement	*baculus* crook	*aratrum* plow	*gladius* sword
locale	*pascua* pasture	*ager* land	*urbs, castrum* town, castle
tree	*fagus* beech	*pomus* fruit tree	*laurus, cedrus* laurel, cedar
Virgil	ECLOGUES	GEORGICS	AENEID

Ille ego qui quondam gracili modulatus avena
Carmen, et egressus silvis vicina coegi,
Ut quamvis avido parerent arva colono,
Gratum opus agricolis: at nunc horrentia Martis.

XV

PETRARCH'S *SINE NOMINE 10*: THE HISTORICAL PSEUDONYMS AND ART SYMBOLISM

by John E. Wrigley
University of North Carolina (Charlotte)

I. A modern historian has suggested that the establishment of the papacy at Avignon on the east bank of the Rhone (1305-1378), during the pontificates of seven popes, resulted in large part from a shift in the center of Christendom's gravity from Rome to northern Europe.[1] Many scholars disagree concerning matters of emphasis, causes, effects, and the relative weight of evidence in the interpretation of this era. Ludwig Pastor (1854-1928) devoted his productive years to the writing of a massive documentary history, which in the earlier of sixteen volumes presents a melancholy view of this age. Nevertheless, he concludes that the condemnation of the popes of Avignon has been based in great measure on Petrarch's unjust representations, to which, in later times and without examination, an undue historical importance has been attached.[2] In the judgment of several historians, Pope Clement VI (1342-1352) was the most important among the pontiffs of his time.[3] However, he has also been alleged to have committed acts of gross immorality.[4] Even Monsignor Guillaume Mollat, probably the most significant contemporary revisionist historian of the Avignonese papacy, admits that an embarrassing list of allegations against the virtue of Clement has been collected from the writings of Francis Petrarch.[5]

A British scholar observes that it has long been usual to reprove the Avignonese popes for their rapacity, a degree of moral turpitude, and to allege that their refusal to return to Rome resulted from unwillingness to abandon the delicious wines of Provence. He concludes: "It is

1. Yves Renouard, *The Avignon Papacy 1305-1403,* trans. Denis Bethel (Hamden, Connecticut: Archon Books, 1970), p. 32.

2. Ludwig Pastor, *The History of the Popes from the Close of the Middle Ages,* trans. F. Antrobus (London: Kegan Paul, Trench, Trubner and Co., 1938), vol. I, pp. 66-69.

3. Ibid., p. 88.

4. Ibid., p. 92.

5. Guillaume Mollat, *Les Papes d'Avignon (1305-1378)* (Paris: Letouzey et Ané, 10th ed. 1965), pp. 91-92.

doubtful if the first branch of this charge can be proved; and the second is certainly unjust."[6] Most of the charges which general opinion has levelled against the popes of Avignon go back ultimately to their alleged secularization of the papacy, their concern for temporalities at the expense of spiritualities, and their abandonment of Italy. These themes originate with Petrarch and have traditionally influenced the interpretation and translation not only of his writings, but the evaluation of the entire period during which he wrote. The basic source for these views is his collection of anonymous letters known as the *Sine nomine.*[7]

A critical examination of several letters of this collection has resulted in a tentative solution of a few problems connected with the collection. Previously their number was variously believed to have been nineteen, twenty, or twenty-one. Paul Piur provides the texts of a preface and nineteen letters. Ernest Hatch Wilkins believed that there was a missing letter, which he labelled *Sine nomine x.*[8] The Vatican Library index of the manuscript collection lists, but the collection does not apparently possess, a letter from Lucifer allegedly written by Petrarch and considered to have been part of the *Sine nomine.*[9]

Earlier studies, therefore, have sought to establish the validity of the number of texts edited by Piur. Subsequent investigations concerned themselves with the identification of literary pseudonyms employed by Petrarch in *Sine nom.* 1 and 13, as well as attempted to establish a meaningful historical setting for each of the satires and an explanation of their content.[10]

6. Peter Partner, "Papal Finance and the Papal State," *History Today,* VII (1957), 766-774.

7. Paul Piur, *Petrarcas 'Buch ohne Namen' und die päpstliche Kurie* (Halle/Saale: Max Niemayer, 1925) provides a critical text and traditional analysis of the letters. Norman Zacour, *Petrarch's Book Without a Name* (Toronto: The Pontifical Institute of Mediaeval Studies, 1973) provides the first complete English translation of the texts edited by Piur.

8. E. H. Wilkins, *Studies in the Life and Works of Petrarch* (Cambridge, Massachusetts: The Mediaeval Academy of America, 1955), p. 146. See John E. Wrigley, "A Presumed Lost Petrarchan Letter: *Sine nomine X,*" *Medium Aevum,* XXXVII (1968), 293-306 for an identification of this letter with *Sine nom.* 12.

9. John E. Wrigley, "The Devil and Francis Petrarch," *The Library Chronicle* (University of Pennsylvania), XXXIII (1967), 75-96 provides a text, translation, and commentary of an *Epistola missa Clementi Pape Sexto,* of which the Van Pelt Library possesses the printed text originating about 1540.

10. John E. Wrigley, "A Papal Secret Known to Petrarch," *Speculum,* XXXIX (1964), 613-634 analyzes the preface and *Sine nom.* 1; "A Rehabilitation of Clement VI: *Sine nomine* 13 and the Kingdom of Naples," *Archivum historiae pontificiae,* III (1965), 127-138 attempts to identify Semiramis, Dionysius, Pericles, and Alcibiades.

The current trend toward historical revision of traditional interpretations of fourteenth-century papal Avignon suggests that a new examination of Petrarch's allegedly anti-Avignonese compositions, the *Sine nomine,* might profit from modern knowledge of the milieu in which the poet wrote and rewrote these letters. This present study fixes attention on *Sine nom.* 10, of which Wilkins has written: "Clement himself appears under the names of Nimrod (a reference to his building and his hunting) in Nos. 8 and 10, as Cambyses (a reference to his extravagances) in No. 10, and as Julian (the Apostate) in No. 6. . . ."[11] This identification of the same historical personage by two different symbolic names in the same composition is a technical contradiction which reduces the ironic force of the satire, generalizes the thrust of the humor, and lessens the direct meaning of the literary piece, which Petrarch, a master artist, has carefully constructed. At the close of his translation of *Sine nom.* 13 Wilkins remarks: "Dionysius and Pericles stand for Clement VI. . . . Who is represented by the name Alcibiades we do not know."[12] An earlier examination of *Sine nom.* 13 has identified the name Semiramis with Queen Joanna I of Naples and has offered evidence for the identification of Pericles with Louis of Taranto, of Dionysius with Angelo Acciaiuoli, and of Alcibiades with Niccolò Acciaiuoli.[13]

The satirical sense of *Sine nom.* 10 demands that this letter be related in its theme to *Sine nom.* 13, since the name Semiramis is common to both. Also the name Nimrod must be identified with Clement VI since, unlike the other pseudonyms of the composition which spring from classical literature, this appellation is taken from the Old Testament, which describes Nimrod as ". . . the first to be a mighty hunter before the Lord. . . . The beginning of his kingdom was in Babylon."[14] The sale of Avignon was concluded on 9 June 1348, when for a sum of 80,000 florins Joanna, queen of Sicily and countess of Provence, transferred the city to Clement VI, although it continued to remain under the jurisdiction of the Holy Roman Emperor. Pope Clement and Queen Joanna thus become Petrarch's Nimrod and Semiramis, co-founders of Babylon.[15]

11. Wilkins, *Studies,* pp. 111-112.

12. E. H. Wilkins, *Petrarch at Vaucluse* (Chicago: University of Chicago Press, 1958), p. 96. See Gilbert Highet, *The Anatomy of Satire* (Princeton: Princeton University Press, 1962), p. 3, where he makes the point that satire ". . . pictures real men and women, often in lurid colors, but always with unforgettable clarity."

13. Wrigley, "A Rehabilitation of Clement VI," pp. 132-135.

14. Gen. 10:8-10.

15. Emile G. Léonard, *Les Angevins de Naples* (Paris: Presses Universitaires de France, 1954), pp. 358-360.

Quite early in his pontificate Clement began to negotiate the election of an anti-emperor to oppose the excommunicated incumbent, Lewis of Bavaria. The pope's choice was his former pupil, Charles, count of Luxembourg and son of King John of Bohemia. During April 1346 John and Charles appeared in Avignon and on 22 April Charles swore an oath of fidelity to the pope. Three months later, on 11 July 1346, a select group of pro-papal electors made the election of Charles seemingly valid, and on 26 November that same year, he was crowned with the iron crown by a pro-papal appointee, the archbishop of Cologne. The new emperor shortly returned the papal favor by ceding to the pope, on 1 November 1348, all imperial rights and privileges over Avignon.[16] Some years later Petrarch in a letter to Charles IV remarked that he had seen him on the occasion of his visit to Clement, but at the time he did not know who the emperor was.[17] This latter remark bears some hint of irony, since Charles' action toward Avignon was in direct conflict with the poet's antiquated concept of church-state unity because Petrarch thought of the city of Rome as the only possible center of a valid symphonic imperial and papal government.

Sine nom. 10 becomes more meaningful, both as artistic satire and as historical evidence, if it is interpreted as an attack on Clement VI under the name of Nimrod; on Queen Joanna I of Naples as Semiramis; on Louis of Taranto as Cambyses; on Charles IV as Minos; and on Cola di Rienzo, who will be introduced somewhat later, as the Minotaur.

The identifying characteristics of both Semiramis and Cambyses are the twin crimes of incest and murder. Both are accused of murdering and of marrying relatives.[18] Queen Joanna and Louis of Taranto both endured the double infamy of suspected complicity in the murder of her husband, Andrew of Hungary, and public admission of mutual incest.[19] Petrarch describes Cambyses as he "before whom royalty is carried in a sedan chair, then dashed to the ground, fed with his own

16. Stephanus Baluzius, *Vitae paparum Avenionensium,* ed. G. Mollat, 4 vols. (Paris: Letouzey et Ané, 1914-1922), II, 372-373; 468. See Clément VI, *Lettres se rapportant à la France,* eds. E. Déprez, J. Glénisson, G. Mollat, 3 vols. (Paris: De Boccard, 1901-1961), II, col. 508; Edward Tatham, *Francesco Petrarca,* 2 vols. (New York: Sheldon Press, 1925-1926), I, 267; II, 303-307.

17. Francesco Petrarca, *Le Familiari,* ed. V. Rossi and U. Bosco, 4 vols. (Florence: Sansoni, 1933-1942), *Fam.* XIX, 4.

18. Herodotus, *Histories* III, 27-38; Hyginus, *Fabulae* CCLX, CCXLIII, CCLXXV.

19. Léonard, *Les Angevins,* tables III and IV; *Corpus juris canonici,* ed. A. Friedburg, 2 vols. (Leipzig: 1955), I, cols. 1431-1436, arbor affinitatis, declaratio affinitatis, declaratio arboris affinitatis.

gore, and finally reduced by this insolent prince to a miserable death." Queen Joanna, Andrew of Hungary, and Louis of Taranto are all cousins, sharing a common ancestor, King Charles II of Naples. Unlike Andrew, however, Louis of Taranto consummated his union with Joanna without benefit of duly authorized clergy or before papal dispensation was obtained from the triple invalidating impediments of "affinity," "public decency," and *ad cautelam* "crime."[20] Petrarch's allusion in *Sine nom.* 10 to "the untimely death of Valentinian the Younger" is a plausible link with the poet's opinion that Louis of Taranto was the guilty party responsible for garroting young Andrew, who was dashed headfirst from a balcony to a garden below and choked to death on his own blood.[21] Louis, therefore, seems to fulfill adequately the characteristics necessary to be identified in this letter as Cambyses.

The characters, Minos and Minotaur, in *Sine nom.* 10 must also be related to historical actors prominent in the fourteenth century. Minos is of course a royal person, and the Minotaur (that creature half-man, half-bull) is "Minos' bull," for which Daedalus constructed the labyrinth in which to hide the monster.[22]

Cola di Rienzo, as is well known, seized power in the city of Rome on 20 May 1347. Petrarch was delighted.[23] The poet's joy, however, did not long endure. Papal government was restored in Rome after a revolt against Cola on 15 December 1347.[24] Early in March of 1348 Cola fled to the protection of King Louis of Hungary, who had invaded Naples seeking vengeance for the murder of Andrew. Clement VI demanded the surrender of Cola from King Louis, of whom the pope asked the imprisonment of the fugitive and his delivery to Avignon for trial and punishment.[25] However, the Black Death arrived in Naples before the papal letter and Louis scurried home to Hungary, while Cola

20. Decretal. Gregor. IX. lib. iv. Tit. i. cap. viii; Tit. vii; Tit. xiv; Tit. xix.

21. Baluzius, *Vitae,* I, 243 ff. gives several contemporary accounts of the murder.

22. Herodotus I, 171; III, 122; VII, 169, recites the history of Minos. Plutarch, *Theseus* 17-21. See Pierre de Nolhac, *Pétrarque et l'Humanisme,* 2 vols. (Paris: Champion, 1907), I, 208; II, 72, 127 for Herodotus. See I, 28; II, 128, 274 for Plutarch.

23. Konrad Burdach and Paul Piur, *Briefwechsel des Cola di Rienzo* (*Vom Mittelalter zur Reformation,* ed. Konrad Burdach, Vol. II; Berlin: Weidmannsche Buchhandlung, 1912-1928), part 3, contains all of the tribune's letters, all those addressed to him, and all known letters referring to him.

24. Clément VI, *Lettres se rapportant à la France,* II, 448-449, no. 3786; 453, nos. 3800-3803; 459-460, nos. 3834, 3837, 3838; 462-467, nos. 3851-3852.

25. Ibid., pp. 463-467, no. 3852, 7 May 1348.

took refuge with a group of hermits on Mount Majella in the region of Abruzzi near Sulmona.[26] In July of 1350 the fugitive unexpectedly appeared in Prague to summon Charles IV to Rome for the traditional coronation and a symbolic restoration of the ancient empire.[27] During August Pope Clement learned of Cola's presence in Prague and abruptly ordered the emperor and the archbishop to send their guest to Avignon.[28] Almost a year later Cola, "son of Belial and the father of sinners," was removed from the fortress of Radnitz on the Elbe river and delivered to the papal gendarmes.[29] Roger de Molineuf and Hugh de Charlus under the supervision of the bishop of Spoleto arrived in Avignon with their prisoner on 10 August 1352. The Minotaur, Minos' bull, had been captured and was forthwith enclosed in the papal labyrinth with the aid and cooperation of his former protector, Charles IV, the Holy Roman Emperor. Petrarch was outraged.[30]

Petrarch's knowledge of Herodotus formed his subjective idea of Minos, the Minotaur, and the labyrinth, the last of which is thus described by the classic Greek historian.

> Moreover, they resolved to leave a common memorial, and for this they built a labyrinth. . . . I myself saw it and it is great beyond description. Indeed, if all the walls and other great works built by the Greeks were added together, they would not equal this labyrinth for the labor and cost of the building. . . .
>
> The corridors separating the rooms and the ways going hither and thither through the courts, which are most richly colored, disclose endless marvels to one who goes from a court to rooms and from rooms to colonnades, from those to more corridors, and from rooms to more courts. All these are roofed with stonework like that of the walls.[31]

Herodotus reports that Minos and Sarpedon, sons of Europa, contend

26. Iris Origo, *Tribune of Rome: A Biography of Cola di Rienzo* (London: Hogarth Press, 1938), pp. 168-189.

27. Ibid., pp. 190-210.

28. Clément VI, *Lettres closes, patentes et curiales,* eds. E. Déprez and G. Mollat (Paris: De Boccard, 1901-1961), fasc. 2, p. 318, nos. 2284-85, 17-18 August 1350.

29. Ibid., p. 363, no. 2584; p. 365, nos. 2596-7; p. 366, no. 2601. Felix Papencordt, *Rienzi et Rome à son époque,* trans. Léon Boré (Paris: Lecoffre, 1845), p. 272, fn. 1 cites all pertinent references except the papal letters. He erroneously concluded that Cola arrived in Avignon on 10 August 1351.

30. Prof. William Melczer, Syracuse University, in "Cola di Rienzo and Petrarch's Political Solitude," a paper delivered on 8 April 1974, The Folger Shakespeare Library, World Petrarch Congress, stated: "Petrarch never really grasped any salient aspect of the historic components of his age. . . ."

31. Herodotus II, 148.

for the rule of their father, and ultimately Minos is the victor.[32] The imperial rule of Europe is mirrored in Petrarch's satire which sees Minos, Charles IV, anti-emperor of Clement VI, triumph over the excommunicated imperial incumbent Lewis of Bavaria and his short-lived successor, Gunther of Schwarzenburg, the symbolic Sarpedon.[33] Babylon and the throne of Europe fall into the hands of Minos. The suggestion that Cola di Rienzo is the Minotaur is based upon his relationship with Minos; his entrance into the city of Avignon; and his imprisonment by both emperor and pope in the Babylonian labyrinth, for Petrarch the land of exile, the papal palace, synonymous with Egypt. Shortly after the day on which Cola entered Avignon, Petrarch alleges that he sat himself down and penned an account of Cola's arrival, which in part is as follows:

> Cola di Rienzo, once the awe-inspiring tribune of Rome, now the most miserable of persons, arrived today at court. Rather, he has not arrived, but has been dragged as a prisoner. What makes it so much worse is that he is not entitled to pity, miserable though he be. Instead of a noble death on the Capitoline Hill, he has allowed himself to be taken prisoner by a Bohunk and a Frog. He has brought shame upon his own name, upon the name of Rome, and upon the republic. . . .
>
> . . . To go on with my tale. He who formerly filled with fear wicked men everywhere, and filled honest men with joy and hope, entered the court humbled and despised. He who was in the past accompanied by the entire population of Rome and all the princes of Italy, was led by two guards through a curious crowd which had come to see the face of a man whose name only yesterday enjoyed glorious renown. Worst of all! A Roman king sent him to a Roman pope. . . .[34]

A problem now arises with the identification of the Minotaur as a pseudonym for Cola di Rienzo. If that identification be correct, then the commonly accepted date for the unrevised composition of *Sine nom.* 10 must be wrong. Wilkins places the probable composition of this letter (addressed at Avignon to Nelli) between 1 October 1351 and 1 April 1352. Wilkins also designates this letter among the more noteworthy of the twenty-five extant compositions which the poet wrote in

32. Herodotus I, 173.

33. G. Mollat, *Les Papes,* pp. 350-361. See Gilbert Highet, *The Classical Tradition* (New York and London: Oxford University Press, 1949), p. 88 where he declares: "Petrarch was a synthesis of Greece and Rome with modern Europe . . . . He was more modern, by being more classical."

34. *Fam.* XIII, 6; Wilkins, *Petrarch at Vaucluse,* pp. 132-140 provides a more complete translation of this letter, which he dates 10 August 1352. The author of this essay has translated the selection. The passage parallels Herodotus III, 27.

Avignon about this time.[35] Quite significantly *Fam.* XIII, 6 is also addressed to Nelli 10 August 1352 and has the entrance of Cola di Rienzo into Avignon as its entire theme.[36] Wilkins quite correctly relates *Sine nom.* 10 with Petrarch's *Met.* III, 21 and III, 22, all of which develop the labyrinth motif. Without offering his reasons, however, he states: "*Sine nom.* 10 was written on 13 January 1352 or soon afterwards. . . ."[37] Nevertheless Wilkins also recognizes that *Sine nom.* 13 is "exactly in the mood of *Sine nom.* 5, 6, 8, 10, and 11."[38] Previous independent studies of *Sine nom.* 13 have, however, suggested that Wilkins cannot be wholly correct in his identification of Semiramis with the Countess of Turenne, nor in his firm dating of that composition.[39]

Petrarch's interest in Avignonese, Roman, Neapolitan, and imperial politics would seem to demand some satirical comment on the sudden decline of Cola di Rienzo's power, especially if two letters are included in the *Sine nomine* to commemorate his rapid rise to fame.[40] *Sine nom.* 10 seems to suggest a composition of four related themes. The first two concern the separation of Babylon from Italy; the second two concern the firm establishment of a labyrinth outside Italy. Charles IV and Cola quite appropriately fit the satire of the concluding half of the composition. *Sine nom.* 10 therefore was probably composed, at least in part after 10 August 1352, probably the correct date of *Fam.* XIII, 6 which describes Cola's entry into Avignon sometime shortly before the letter was addressed to Nelli.

In addition to criticizing the firm foundation which Clement created for the papacy in Avignon through his purchase of the city, his encircling walls, his interior decorations, his expansion of the palace, his exemption from imperial control, *Sine nom.* 10 also takes to task the growing bureaucracy. Benedict XII ran the church with a small staff

35. Wilkins, *Studies,* pp. 90 and 111. See Piur, p. 363, whom Wilkins follows for the date of origin. Arnaldo Foresti suggests that *Sine nom.* 10 was addressed to Nelli from Avignon and has assigned 18 January 1352 for the date of composition. Arnaldo Foresti, *Aneddoti della vita di Francesco Petrarca* (Brescia, 1829), pp. 209-212.

36. Wilkins, *Petrarch at Vaucluse,* p. 132.

37. Wilkins, *Studies,* p. 117.

38. Ibid., p. 119.

39. G. Mollat, "Clément VI et la vicomtesse de Turenne," *Mélanges d'archéologie et d'histoire,* LXXIII (1961), 375-389; John E. Wrigley, "A rehabilitation of Clement VI: *Sine nomine* 13 and the Kingdom of Naples," *Archivum historiae pontificiae,* III, cited above.

40. *Sine nom.* 2 and 3 are suggested as such by Wilkins. In my view *Sine nom.* 2 does not refer to Cola, but to Clement VI satirically described as the nuncio of Christ.

housed in a simple palace.[41] During the pontificate of Clement VI the number of curial officials listed by name and title is almost triple the number recorded as employed in his predecessor's pontificate.[42] Under Clement VI the number of persons in administrative and domestic offices reached a level never exceeded during the entire Avignonese period.[43]

It is of this bureaucratic and domestic staff and the cost of their maintenance that Petrarch complains in the final paragraph of *Sine nom.* 10. There Petrarch writes:

The subscription of my letter puzzles you. No wonder! You are astonished at the discovery of a heretofore unknown triplet named Babylon, since you have read previously only of the Babylonian twins, one formerly in Assyria where Semiramis became famous, and the other still flourishing in Egypt where Cambyses rules. You are therefore puzzled at the possibility of still another contemporary Babylon, for you are aware that certain of our friends regard Rome as a kind of Babylon owing to the vast power and the extent of her possessions which she formerly controlled. But Rome obviously is not in question here, since you remember that I have always regarded her as a holy, sacred and queenly city.

Stop struggling to solve the riddle. This corner of the planet has its unique Babylon. Where is there, I ask you, in the entire western world, a more suitable location for a city of confusion? Although the founder is unknown, its proprietor is famous. For good reason, therefore, the shoe fits.

Believe me! Everything appropriate to the name is here; *Nimrod, powerful over the land, a great hunter before the Lord* seeking to reach heaven with his sky-flung towers; Semiramis is here with her bow and arrow; and Cambyses, more insane than his oriental predecessor, before whom royalty is carried in a sedan chair, then dashed to the ground and fed with his own gore, and finally reduced by this insolent prince to a miserable death.

I cannot quote poets for this is not a Pierian essay, nor will I refer you to the historians. Consult instead the catholic commentators, especially Augustine on the Psalm which begins the same way many of my letters to you have ended.[44] There you will discover the meaning of the name *Babylon*. After

41. Benoît XII, *Lettres closes et patentes,* ed. J. M. Vidal (Paris: De Boccard, 1913-1942), Index, cols. 2-4, lists a total of 130 Avignonese curial officials by name and office. It is clear that most of these did not live in the papal palace and many did not reside in Avignon, but served a term at a time in rotation.

42. Clément VI, *Lettres se rapportant à la France,* fasc. VI, Tables, pp. 4-7, lists 374 Avignonese officials by name and office.

43. Bernard Guillemain, *La Cour pontificale d'Avignon: étude d'une société* (Paris: De Boccard, 1962), pp. 444-445; K. Schäfer, *Die Ausgaben der Apostolischen Kammer unter Benedikt XII, Klemens VI, und Innocenz* VI (Paderborn: Schöningh, 1914), pp. 484-7.

44. Psalm 136 [137]: "By the streams of Babylon we sat and wept when we remembered Sion."

reading his definition you must agree that the name applies no less appropriately to the Euphrates. or to the Nile, than to the Rhone. Nor can you be surprised when I remind you that St. Ambrose (in his book mourning the untimely death of Valentinian the Younger) also uses the same synonym in his description of the Rhone.

Having severed one root of your amazement I am going to attack the second. No doubt you are equally puzzled by the prospect of a fifth labyrinth, since you will discover, I believe, that most authors mention only four. In their writings only Egypt, Lemnos, Crete, and Chiusi of Italy are mentioned. They are silent about the most inextricable and worst of all, the labyrinth of the Rhone, either because it did not exist at the time of their writing or because they were ignorant of it. But I have often mentioned it.

Not a single characteristic of a labyrinth is missing; a frightening prison; a crazy house of shadowy darkness; an urn tossing about the fate of humanity; an imperial Minos, a gluttonous Minotaur; and *monuments of the hunter*.[45] The only things missing are aids to salvation; love of God and man; fidelity to promises; friendly counsel; a mute guide pointing out the twisting turns obstructing the exit; an Ariadne; or a Daedalus.

Gold is the only hope of salvation. Gold placates the cruel ruler, gold restrains the savage monster, gold shows the way to the hidden exit, gold crushes the rock and forges the iron bars, gold melts the frozen-faced doorman, gold opens the gates of heaven. What else? Christ is sold for gold![46]

II. The contents of *Sine nomine* 10, 12, and 13 become more meaningful when read against the light of particular events in the history of Avignon, the Holy Roman Empire, and Naples.[47] *Sine nom.* 10 appears therefore to be a satire with four distinct but interrelated themes. The first concerns the artistic decoration of the papal apartment, the heart of Babylon. The second describes the chief actors in the creation of the new Babylon. The third takes up the labyrinthine characteristics of the new architecture. And the fourth is a general description of the tremendous sums of money required both to decorate the physical plant and to support the administrative personnel who control the new papal labyrinthine Babylon, independent of, but related to, the

45. Piur, op. cit., pp. 200-201, provides the critical Latin text. Two words constitute a minor problem: *veneris* or perhaps *venoris*. If the first reading be correct, then the allusion is perhaps an ironic reference to the pregnancy of Joanna. If the second be correct then the allusion is probably an ironic reference to the frescoes of the papal bedroom, The Room of the Stag.

46. Paul Piur, *Petrarcas 'Buch ohne Namen' und die päpstliche Kurie* (Niemeyer: Halle, 1925), pp. 197-201 and 352-364.

47. John E. Wrigley, "A Presumed Lost Petrarchan Letter," *Medium Aevum*, XXXVII (1968), 293-306 offers a commentary and translation of *Sine nom.* 12, Id., "A Rehabilitation of Clement VI: *Sine nomine* 13 and the Kingdom of Naples," *Archivum historiae pontificiae*, III (1965), 127-138 does the same for *Sine nom.* 13.

new empire. Francis Petrarch's interest in art and architecture is well known, but in his writings he gives evidence of esteem for only two contemporary artists, Giotto and Simone Martini. During his early mature years Simone was his favorite painter, although later in his old age Giotto became for Petrarch "the prince of our age."[48]

As early as at the age of thirty-six Petrarch manifested a great interest in the work of Simone Martini, while he came into possession of his precious portrait by Giotto only when he was more than sixty years old. According to his testament Petrarch received the Giotto portrait, probably as a gift, from his friend Michele di Vanni, a member of the important Albizzi family of Florence, with whom the poet became acquainted in Venice about 1365.[49] Petrarch immediately became so attached to Michele that he warmly recommended him to Boccaccio, saying: "At the present time I have [in Venice] a new and very dear friend, Michele di Vanni; if I am dear to you, I wish you to be dear to him also. Amen, I say to you I have not found such great faith in Israel. Farewell."[50] Scholars conclude on the basis of this letter that Petrarch obtained this painting sometime between 1365 and 1370.

Much earlier, when Petrarch was about thirty-four years of age a manuscript of Virgil, formerly owned by his father, which had been stolen several years before, again came into the poet's possession. This manuscript contained the *Bucolics,* the *Georgics,* and the *Aeneid,* each with a commentary by Marius Servius Honoratus. On the verso of the second guard leaf appears a frontispiece allegedly designed by Petrarch himself, but painted (according to a note on the page in the poet's hand) by Simone Martini. Petrarch may have specified that the picture should contain the figures of Virgil, as a poet with pen and book, seated under a laurel tree; of Servius, an interpreter drawing open a curtain; of a man with a pruning hook, representing the *Georgics*; and of a shepherd with sheep, representing the *Bucolics.* Two scrolls appear at the bottom of the scene. On each of the scrolls Petrarch personally penned a rhymed Latin couplet, and below the painting he wrote:

> Virgil of Mantua created the song
> Sienese Simon painted with finger long.[51]

48. Cesare Gnudi, "Giotto," *Encyclopedia of World Art,* 15 vols. (New York: McGraw-Hill, 1958-1968), vol. VI, cols. 339-356; Giovanni Paccagnini, "Simone Martini," *Encyclopedia of World Art,* vol. IX, cols. 502-508 and plate 337.

49. Giuseppe Billanovich, *Petrarca letterato: Lo scrittoio del Petrarca* (Rome: Storia e Letteratura, 1957), p. 275, note 1.

50. Ibid.

51. François Enaud, "Simone Martini à Avignon," *Les Monuments historiques*

After 1340 Petrarch also allegedly commissioned Simone to paint a portrait of his beloved Laura. Of one thing scholars are certain; Petrarch from an early age was passionately interested in all forms of art, and that concern manifested itself in many of his own artistic literary compositions. The poet not only lavishes praise on those whose works he admires, but also heaps scorn on those whose works he rejects.

While Petrarch's patronage of Simone Martini and lavish praise of Giotto have been widely appreciated, far less clearly understood have been the poet's writings which satirically attack the art and architecture inspired by the patronage and direction of Pope Clement VI (1342-1352). During the Avignonese pontificate of this pope a dramatic and important change took place in art, which had a powerful impact on the later development of the Renaissance throughout Europe. The pontificate of Benedict XII (1334-1342) marks the close of one era, the reign of his successor, Clement VI, the beginning of another. Petrarch, perhaps, more clearly than anyone else recognized the reality of this change, but he reacted against the moral implications he read into it.

In another context, art historians are also familiar with the "important change in style and taste around the middle of the fourteenth century" so authoritatively illustrated by Millard Meiss.[52] Meiss emphasizes that most of the Florentine masters of the last half of the fourteenth century were "in a sense anti-Giottesque."[53] The situation in Padua, however, was uniquely different, for there the tradition in favor of Giotto's example was quite strong.[54] It is quite probable that Petrarch, who had been a canon of the Cathedral of Padua since 1349, from which he received a major portion of his income, had something to do with the maintenance of this traditional appreciation of Giotto.[55] About the very same time that Petrarch was drawing up his will in Padua, by which he bequeathed his painting to Francesco da Carrara, a group of Paduan disciples of Giotto, which included Altichiero of Verona, Jacopo Avanzo of Padua, and Giusto de' Menabuoi, adapted Petrarch's chief historical work, *De viris illustribus,* for the decoration

---

de la France, nouvelle série, IX (1963), p. 117 and p. 173 note 10; Giovanni Paccagnini, "Simone Martini," *Encyclopedia of World Art,* op. cit.

52. M. Meiss, *Painting in Florence and Siena after the Black Death* (Princeton: Princeton University Press, 1951), pp. 6-7.

53. Ibid.

54. *Petrarch's Testament,* ed. and trans. Theodor E. Mommsen (Ithaca, New York: Cornell University Press, 1957), pp. 1, 21-25, 78-81.

55. Ernest Hatch Wilkins, *Studies in the Life and Works of Petrarch* (Cambridge: The Mediaeval Academy of America, 1955), pp. 21-23 concerns this canonry.

of the great hall of the Carrara palace, which was commissioned by Francesco da Carrara. These men were certainly known to Petrarch and among them were to be found some of "the masters of art" who were "stunned" by the beauty of his Giotto painting.[56] Of contemporary artists Petrarch states: "I know only two painters of outstanding and beautiful works: Giotto, a citizen of Florence, and . . . Simone of Siena."[57] Without doubt Simone and Giotto are the two most important painters of the first half of the fourteenth century, but their fame must not be permitted to overshadow that of their successors, for artistic creativity did not cease with the death of either Giotto about 1337, or of Simone about 1344.

Simone Martini was called to Avignon during the pontificate of Pope Benedict XII, who died on 25 April 1342. Benedict was a man of ascetic taste with an exalted sense of duty, a dedication to justice, energetic, tenacious, rigidly determined to suppress abuses, personally austere, and fond of restraint in art and in architecture. His successor was Clement VI, unanimously elected, after a conclave of only three days, on 7 May 1342.[58]

Weariness of the cardinals with the rigid, austere, autocratic, ascetic rule of Benedict, especially attracted them to the contrasting qualities of Cardinal Pierre Roger, urbane, gentle, pliant, aristocratic, and of delicately balanced intellectuality.[59] The Sacred College hoped, and as subsequent events proved with almost prophetic foreknowledge, that Clement's pontificate would take an entirely different direction from that of Benedict. The new pontiff took for the principal rule of his pontificate the maxim of that emperor who declared: "No one should leave the presence of a prince dissatisfied." Another of his mottos was: "A pontiff should be concerned with the welfare of his subjects." Upbraided by some for his extreme generosity in contrast with former rulers of the See of Peter, he replied: "My predecessors did not know how to be pope."[60] Nowhere is the contrast between the pontificates of Benedict and of Clement seen more clearly and dramatically than in the construction and artistic decoration of Petrarch's labyrinthine Bab-

56. Theodor E. Mommsen, "Petrarch and the Decoration of the *Sala Virorum Illustrium* in Padua," *Art Bulletin,* XXXIV (1952), 96-102. For an illustration of *De viris illustribus* see *Encyclopedia of World Art,* vol. X, col. 158, plate 76. For Petrarch's influence on subsequent artists see E. H. Wilkins, *The Triumphs of Petrarch* (Chicago: University of Chicago Press, 1962), p. V; also *Encyclopedia of World Art,* vol. XV, p. 442 for several references to the poet's effect.

57. *Fam.* V, 17.

58. Mollat, *Les Papes,* pp. 68-83.

59. Ibid., pp. 84-85.

60. Baluzius, *Vitae,* I, 275, 298; Mollat, *Les Papes,* p. 86.

ylon, the papal palace at Avignon, almost the whole of which presently remaining is work commissioned by one or the other of these two popes.

Less than two years after the election of Pope Clement VI, Avignon's chief papal painter, Simone Martini, died, probably before 9 July 1344.[61] Earlier the architect of Benedict's simple dwelling, Pierre Poisson, lost his position of director of works and was replaced with Jean de Loubières by Pope Clement, who complained that his papal predecessor had left to him a dwelling, *tamquam tabula rasa.* Originally there were few frescoes or interior decorations in the simple palace which Benedict had created from the expanded episcopal palace of old Avignon. Clement, Jean de Loubières, and a new master painter, Matteo Giovannetti da Viterbo created a new palace "which is almost a city and is, therefore, the symbol of the new papacy."[62] During the decennial pontificate of Clement VI, the classical forms of Italy and the naturalism of Avignon were intermingled as never before in art to produce additional inspiration for that phenomenon ultimately labelled the Renaissance.[63]

The importance of the artistic and cultural changes, which occurred between 1342 and 1352, must not be permitted to overshadow the more profound and meaningful ecclesiastical and political developments of which the art and architecture are visible remaining evidence. During this period a new bureaucracy was developed, a new seat for the Roman curia was established, a new residence for the pope was constructed, and a new capital for Christianity was created. Petrarch, whose own considerable talents were the product of a unique blend of French naturalism with Italian classicism, was outraged. Although the poet perceived the changes taking place in art, architecture, politics, ecclesiastical affairs, theology, language, and economic life, he did not wholly understand them. His literary compositions frequently express the complete destruction of his fantasized world, idealized as the past perfect union of an empire without flaw joined to the Church of Christ

61. Enaud, op. cit., pp. 116 and 172. The death register of the church of St. Dominic, Siena, records as of 4 August 1344: "Magister Simon Pictor mortuus est in curia." Town records of Siena dated 5 May 1344 record a payment of taxes by Simon, absent on that date, "in chorte di papa."

62. Enrico Castelnuovo, *Un pittore italiano alla corte di Avignone* (Turin: Einaudi, 1962), pp. 23-29; Franciscus Ehrle, *Historia Bibliothecae Romanorum Pontificum* (Rome: Vatican Press, 1890), pp. 587-700, cap. IV, no. 2, "De historia palatii avenionensis," published the original references in connection with the construction and ornamentation of the palace.

63. Castelnuovo, p. 27 for the peculiar importance of this pontificate in art and architecture.

instituted in apostolic poverty, dedicated to crucifixion for salvation of humanity, and divinized by identification with his favorite theologian's neo-Platonic concept of the City of God.

Two rooms of the renovated palace in Avignon require the focus of our attention in order to understand the nature of this major ecclesiastical transition and of Petrarch's response to the significant events contemporary with this climatic period of his life and creativity. These rooms are: the space chosen by Clement VI for his bedroom; and the bedroom of Benedict XII changed by Clement into his study. The first of these is known as the Room of the Stag; the second, as the Papal Study.

Upon election, Pope Clement VI ordered the brilliant architect Jean de Loubières to begin construction of an enlarged palace in accord with the new pope's style of life, his function, and his need for additional floor space in light of the role he, with a greatly increased staff, intended to play in world affairs.

Without examining the many new rooms, chapels, courts, towers, service stairs, bridges, and walls added by Jean de Loubières, the observation must be made that nothing of this kind ever existed in the old palace of Benedict XII. Almost as soon as one piece of new construction was completed, a swarm of artists invaded the space to paint every square inch of walls, ceiling, rafters, doors, columns, embrasures, and mullions. Decoration of the interior was begun in 1343 with a group of painters under the direction especially of Matteo Giovannetti da Viterbo, Pietro da Viterbo, Robin de Romans, and Enrico d'Arezzo.[64] The presence of this last mentioned artist, a native of Petrarch's birthplace, did nothing to lessen the poet's paranoid rage. As early as 18 May 1343 Pope Clement VI ordered his bed moved into the Room of the Wardrobe, which ultimately became known as the Room of the Stag. Here he slept at night although for several years as many as four artists worked during the day on the frescoes.[65] The pope had become Petrarch's Nimrod.

The Room of the Stag becomes the focal point for Petrarch's satirical letter, *Sine nomine* 10. This letter can be understood in its entirety only through analysis of the administrative, political, and artistic decisions which Clement VI simultaneously made in order to give the church a new direction, which both he and the College of Cardinals

64. Castelnuovo, op. cit., p. 34.

65. Ehrle, *Historia*, pp. 626-629. Decoration of this room began on 7 September 1342 and was still going on on 6 September 1344. The pope's new bed was built in the room before December 1342.

deemed necessary in order to accelerate the institution's adaptation to the emerging modern age.

Incontestably, Matteo Giovannetti da Viterbo is the artist responsible for the plan and execution of the frescoes in the Room of the Stag, although he was assisted by Pietro da Viterbo, Enrico d'Arezzo, and Robin de Romans.[66] The master artist, Matteo Giovannetti, is credited with firmly establishing the great Sienese tradition in Avignon, where he painted for the popes for more than a quarter century, from 1342 until his death in 1368. Here in this international capital he developed to the extreme the arabesques of Simone Martini, although under the influence of the local naturalism he handled them in a more realistic and less luxurious manner. In the exciting and cosmopolitan atmosphere of Avignon, with the encouragement of the innovative pope, Matteo experimented, achieving exceptional results by combining complex spatial arrangements, naturalism, symbolism, and secular drama in the very heart of the papal palace and also across the Rhone in the Chartreuse du Val de Bénédiction at Villeneuve-lez-Avignon.

The frescoes of the Room of the Stag illustrate the climactic changes inaugurated by Pope Clement VI. This papal bedroom is not apparently illustrated with scenes inspired by biblical, theological, or historical themes, but with very fashionable, contemporary, and dramatic scenes of hunting, fishing, and other outdoor activities of field and stream. The west wall depicts three huntsmen chasing a stag, the fresco which gives the room its modern name. On the north wall a complex fishing scene is represented. Grouped around a fish pond, four men strive to catch fish, each demonstrating a different style of the same sport; one uses a casting net, another a scoop net, a third sits contentedly beside the pool with a handline, while the fourth stands tensely prepared to launch an arrow from his bow toward his swimming victim. To the left of this fresco a variety of bird hunting styles are illustrated. In one scene a stalker holds a birdlimed club, while to the right a companion attempts to lure the birds with a reed pipe. The east wall pictures three youths gathering fruit knocked to the ground by a small boy perched in a tree. This same wall depicts a falconer, hawk in hand, magnificently clothed in purple tunic with blue stockings and matching cloak, followed by two hounds, probably retrievers. The falconer stands face to face with a well-dressed companion carrying a red sack slung over his shoulder.

The south wall has a fresco of debatable interpretation. Some suggest that scantily-clad young women are in the process of undressing

66. E. Castelnuovo, op. cit., p. 34; Ehrle, *Historia,* pp. 626-629.

in order to bathe; others conclude that young boys are preparing to swim. In either case the human forms are insufficiently sensuous to reflect unfavorably upon Pope Clement's choice of subjects to inspire sweet dreams.

Finally the cycle is completed by a scene below the window at the far right, where a second child sits in a tree observing a richly costumed youth unleash a ferret to pursue a rabbit, which turns its head toward his pursuer while other rabbits nearby scurry off with frightened leaps into the dense foliage of a thicket.

An adjoining room, the former bedroom of Benedict XII, was also redecorated and became Pope Clement's study. Here, too, the motif seems to be completely naturalistic, profane, and without any obvious religious symbolism whatsoever. Today, although poorly restored, this room appears to us as it did after Clement's artists had completed their work. Sinuous intertwining leafy vines cover all four walls. At intervals an occasional robin can be seen. Wide geometric panels border the frescoes where they meet the timbered ceiling, whose main beams are also decorated with geometric designs. Near the windows, cages for birds or animals are painted as hanging among the vines. The polychrome decoration follows a single pattern of stylized foliage and geometric forms. Every other room of the palace was decorated with scenes directly inspired by a biblical idea or a theme from ecclesiastical history or tradition. In the papal apartments alone, however, the paintings seem uniquely secular, humanistic, natural, and profane.

Petrarch's greatest scorn in *Sine nom.* 10 is reserved for Nimrod, "the great hunter," Pope Clement VI. We have seen that the papal study of the pope was the space used by his predecessor for his bedroom. Apparently Benedict planned to have both his bedroom and his study painted in similar or identical fashion, since traces of a common older design have been found under the paintings which eventually covered the walls of the Room of the Stag. The theory thus develops that the painting of these rooms was under way when Benedict XII died. Clement ordered an entirely new design for his bedroom, a design which would illustrate the more modern ideas and techniques of the new artist, Matteo Giovannetti, whom Clement placed in charge after the death of Simone Martini. Apparently Clement chose to complete, change, or renew a design which Benedict might have already approved for his bedroom.[67]

Unfortunately the heavy hand of restoration, shortly after the discovery of these frescoes in 1906, has obscured some details of perspec-

67. Castelnuovo, op. cit., pp. 32-35.

tive which probably were an important part of the original artistic form. Pope Clement's study is designed as a rustic arbor covered with vines, branches, and leaves. The artistic purpose is to create the illusion of a porch or veranda open to the viewer on the three sides of his perspective from where he sits. The walls are decorated with long intertwining spirals of foliage. Although the illusion is not perfected, the idea is essentially Italian and, for this period, unique insofar as this single theme encompasses all four walls in a kind of primitive attempt at trompe l'oeil. Several birds, squirrels, and two bird cages are included in the fresco.

Originally one large window which overlooked a garden admitted light to the room. The window faced east, but in 1365 that wall was sealed and the existing window on the wall to the north was opened.[68] This room of foliage design, which measures approximately twenty-three by sixteen feet, is joined to the room of the Stag by means of a narrow, short, right-angle corridor and five steps.

Several scholars have placed great emphasis upon the purely profane and naturalistic themes employed in the decoration of these two rooms, and suggest, as Petrarch probably does also, that these artistic achievements dramatically illustrate the secularization of religion which took place during the Avignonese papacy of Pope Clement VI.[69] However, another interpretation seems at least equally probable. The decoration of these two rooms offers evidence for an attempt to adapt the tradition-bound Roman papacy to a modern mode of thought and action required of an institution seeking to play a leading role in European life. Clement VI, unlike Petrarch, sees Avignon not as a refuge from Rome, but as the birthplace of a modern papacy divorced from the limitations of Roman traditions. Reform is a theme of the pontificate and of its art.

The decoration of his bedroom and of his study reveals not a secularization of the Church, but rededication of the institution to newly perceived ideals. The paintings suggest Clement's perception of an evolving role of the Church with regard to the human nature of man and his natural world. If this interpretation is correct, then these two rooms are of the utmost importance for the history of the Renaissance, since they are among the earliest examples, if not the earliest, of religious art patronized by the papacy, the form of which is so completely

68. Sylvain Gagnière, *Le Palais des papes d'Avignon* (Nancy: Caisse nationale des monuments historiques, 1965), pp. 28-30.

69. Castelnuovo, "Pittura profana e naturalismo avignonese," in *Un pittore italiano alla corte di Avignone*, pp. 30-46.

identified with naturalism and a profane theme that their religious allegory has escaped recognition by those scholars who have studied the rooms most closely. Scholars have been so confident as to the naturalism and secularism of these "monumental" paintings that they have questioned the identification of the art of the Room of the Stag with the work of Matteo Giovannetti, since all of his other known works are obviously biblical or ecclesiastical in inspiration.[70]

The role of Petrarch in the proto-Renaissance has in effect obscured the important part played by the Avignonese Papacy in the dramatic changes which took place in art, literature, architecture, and politics during and after the period of Avignon. Erwin Panofsky has emphasized that every distinguishable portion of history must have a certain unity, and the historian who wishes to verify this unity must try to discover intrinsic analogies between such disparate phenomena as the arts, literature, philosophy, social and political currents, religious movements and all other forms of human activity. He quite rightly observes that the mentality which deemed it necessary to illuminate faith through reason, and to clarify reason by an appeal to imagination, also felt bound to make imagination clearer by an appeal to the senses.[71]

Petrarch had a clear understanding of this idea with regard to poetry, where he applies the new developments of his cultural environment to the forms of his personal artistic expression. But his scathing denunciation of similar innovative forms produced by ecclesiastical and political administrators, architects, theologians, painters, and philosophers in response to the same environment have resulted in a distorted picture of the fourteenth century by writers who lean too heavily on a poet whose personal myopic interpretation of the age is often most attractively expressed and conveniently available. Petrarch must not be interpreted as a phenomenon unique in the fourteenth century, but as a representative innovator in an age characterized by innovation in all forms of human activity. Pope Clement, for example, is not only Pe-

70. Florens Deuchler, "Szene mit Fishern" in *Das Hohe Mittelalter,* ed. Otto von Simson, vol. VI of 18 vols. of *Kuntsgeschichte,* ed. Kurt Bittel and others (Berlin, 1972), VI, no. 123, pp. 138-139, says: "Die Autorschaft Giovannettis ist freilich nicht allgemein anerkannt; so wurde auch der Versuch unternommen, die Fresken, überraschend abenso durch ihre Monumentalität wie durch ihre profanen, der Alltagswelt entnommenen Themen, einem französischen Meister zuzuschreiben."

71. Erwin Panofsky, *Gothic Architecture and Scholasticism* (New York, 1957), pp. 1-2 and 37-42; "Renaissance and Renascences," *Kenyon Review,* VI (1944), 201-236; "Classical Mythology in Mediaeval Art," *Metropolitan Museum Studies,* IV (1933), 228-280.

trarch's single most generous benefactor, but the moving spirit behind a variety of innovations whose full effect is only gradually realized subsequently during the century following his pontificate.

The role of Avignon as a center of Renaissance ideas and of reform has been, perhaps, unduly neglected by scholars. Subtle changes in European life were introduced by the residence of the popes on the shores of the Rhone. For example, Simone Martini's painting on the frontispiece of the Ambrosian Virgil may not have been planned by Petrarch, as alleged, and may have far greater significance than mere relationship to the works of the classic poet Virgil. The figure holding a pruning hook is of peculiar importance. Cesare Ripa first published his *Iconologia* at Rome in 1593. Here he describes how to represent pictorially the idea of *reform.* This abstract concept is to be personified by an old woman in simple dress, who in her right hand holds a pruning knife and in her left hand an open book showing the words:

> The loss of dead laws is no disadvantage.[72]

The writings of medieval jurists, glossators, and commentators of Roman and canon law with respect to Renaissance theories of art and literature have too rarely been taken into serious consideration by historians. During the fourteenth century the intelligentsia was represented largely by learned jurisprudents, who (although eventually they might become poets, artists, humanists, highly-placed ecclesiastics or royal officials) started their career by studying Roman law.[73] Most university students trained and demonstrated their wits by commenting upon a classical text, the body of Roman law, which had been handed down from antiquity almost in its entirety. Despite Petrarch's frequently stated dissatisfaction with his own studies in law both at Montpellier and Bologna, he was obliged to inform posterity:

> I studied the whole body of civil law, and would, as many thought, have distinguished myself later, had I continued my studies. But I gave up the subject altogether as soon as I no longer was forced to observe the wishes of my parents. My reason was that *(despite the dignity of law, undoubtedly very great, and its numerous references to Roman antiquity which always delighted me)* I felt the subject habitually degraded by its practitioners.[74]

72. Gerhart B. Ladner, "Vegetation Symbolism and the Concept of the Renaissance" in *De artibus opuscula XL: Essays in Honor of Erwin Panofsky,* ed. Millard Meiss, 2 vols. (New York: New York University Press, 1961), I, 303-322; the quotation is from Lucan, *Pharsal.* III, 119 (translation mine).

73. See Norman Zacour, *Talleyrand: The Cardinal of Périgord (1301-1364)* (Philadelphia: American Philosophical Society, 1960), pp. 10-15.

74. F. Petrarca, *Epistolae de rebus familiaribus et variae,* ed. J. Fracassetti, 3 vols. (Florence: Le Monnier, 1859), I, 5-6.

Aristotle's *Physics* was translated into Latin sometime after the year 1200, and his *Poetics* around 1250. His maxim "Art imitates nature," therefore, became increasingly well known after this period when a new emphasis was given the study of Aristotle's works by the scholastic philosophers.[75] There were, however, other channels by which knowledge of this Aristotelian doctrine could have been transmitted much earlier and in an indirect fashion to western Europe.[76] Justinian's *Digest* and *Institutes* reproduced the essence of Aristotle's maxim with special reference to the prosaic law of adoption and in a general sense to the practice of law itself, a sense far removed from painting, sculpture, or poetry.[77] Nevertheless the reasoning of the law is clear. Jurisprudence as an art imitates nature just as every art is supposed to do, and thus the law of adoption imitates nature by means of an artistic fiction. For example, although a blood relationship may not exist, an older man may legally recognize a younger man as his son, since this is a fictitious model based on a natural human relationship.

This legal and philosophical principle had great influence on the development of late medieval symbolism in art and literature, which is directly related to the Renaissance. The metaphor of a vegetative renascence resulting from a trauma, as the expression of the self-awareness of a new era, must be admitted with a high degree of probability.[78] One of the earliest examples in the Italian language of Roman vegetative ideas applied to the concept of rebirth or renascence is found in Dante's description of the earthly paradise in his *Purgatorio,* Canto XXXII, where the poet speaks of a tree deprived of blossoms and leaves which bursts forth in new flowering when Christ ties the chariot of the Church to its trunk:

> I heard 'Adam' murmured by all: then they encircled a tree despoiled of flowers and of other foliage on every bough. . . . Thus around the sturdy tree they cried; and the animal of two natures: 'Thus is preserved the seed of all righteousness.' And turning to the pole which he had drawn, he dragged it to the foot of the widowed trunk, and that which was of it he left bound to it.
>
> As when the great light falls downward mingled with that which shines behind the celestial Carp, our plants become swollen, and then renew them-

75. Ernst H. Kantorowicz, "The sovereignty of the Artist" in *De artibus opuscula XL,* op. cit., I, 267-279.

76. Ibid., p. 269.

77. *Corpus juris civilis,* eds. T. Mommsen and P. Kreuger, 3 vols. (Berlin: Weidmann, 1954), I, 29 (Dig. I, 1, 1): *jus est ars boni et aequi;* I, 5 (Inst., I, 11, 4): *adoptio enim naturam imitatur.*

78. Gerhart B. Ladner, op. cit., p. 305. See J. Trier, "Zur Vorgeschichte des Renaissance-Begriffs," *Archiv für Kulturgeschichte,* XXXIII (1950), pp. 45-49.

selves, each in its own color, before the sun yokes his coursers under another star, so disclosing a color less than of roses and more than of violets, the plant renewed itself, which at first had its boughs so bare.[79]

This canto of Dante's *Purgatorio* demonstrates the continuity of the concept of vegetative symbolism as applied to the papacy in Avignon and suggests the possibility of the allegorical nature of the subsequent decorative theme of Pope Clement's private apartment as identified with the concept of reform and renaissance. The canto continues:

Therefore I pass on to when I awoke, and I say that a splendor rent for me the veil of sleep, and a call, 'Arise, what are you doing?' As, to see some of the blossoms of the apple tree which makes the Angels greedy for its fruit, and makes perpetual marriage feasts in heaven, Peter, James, and John were led, and being overcome, came to themselves at the word by which great slumbers were broken . . . and all in doubt I asked, 'Where is Beatrice?' And she: 'Behold her under the new foliage, sitting upon its root.'[80]

The concept of Avignon as Babylon is introduced at the end of this same canto when Dante says:

A like monster was never seen before. Secure, as a fortress upon a high mountain, there appeared to me a dishevelled harlot sitting upon it, with bold eyes glancing around. And, as if in order that she should not be taken from him, I saw a giant standing at her side, and now and then they kissed each other. . . . Then full of jealousy, and cruel with anger, he loosed the monster, and dragged it through the wood so far, that he made of that alone a shield from me for the harlot and for the strange beast.[81]

The medieval tradition of symbolic supernatural trees is based on the tree of the knowledge of good and evil (from which the wood of the

79. *Purgatorio,* XXXII, 34-60. Dante's theme here reflects Romans 5: 12-20. The "pole" is the mystic symbol for the wood of the cross of Christ. The "animal of two natures" is the God-man, Jesus Christ. The "carp" is the synonym for the zodiacal constellation Pisces which precedes Aries in spring, when the Ram becomes the sign of the sun. The old frescoes of 1339, covered up by the existing frescoes, seem to reflect the influence of these lines. These translations are adaptations of those of C. E. Norton, L. Binyon, L. G. White, and John Sinclair.

80. Ibid., lines 73-91; Canticle of Canticles, 2: 1-3: "I am a flower of Saron, a lily of the valley. As a lily among thorns, so is my beloved among women. As an apple tree among the trees of the woods, so is my lover among men." Apocalypse 10: 1-9 with the climax "Blessed are they who are called to the marriage supper of the lamb." Matthew 17: 1-13, the Transfiguration of Jesus described in detail following the verse, "Now after six days Jesus took Peter, James and his brother John, and led them up a high mountain by themselves and was transfigured before them." Christ having ascended, Beatrice is found seated at the root of the tree, which is infused with new life by the revitalized Church.

81. Ibid., lines 130-131; Apocalypse, 17 and 18 describe the rise and fall of Babylon. The harlot and the giant represent Pope Clement V and Philip the Fair. The monster is the Church, dragged through the woods from Rome to Avignon in 1305.

Cross of Christ is believed to have been taken) and the tree of life which stood in the midst of the garden of Paradise.[82] Both these trees of the Old Testament are related to the concept of a cosmological tree which rises from the center of the earth and supports heaven.[83] In Christianity the Cross of Christ, which holds the universe together, is such a cosmological tree, identified with the Church as the visible and continuing sign of Christ's power on earth. Thus the parable: "The kingdom of heaven is like a grain of mustard seed, which a man took and sowed in his field. This indeed is the smallest of all seed; but when it grows up it becomes larger than any herb and becomes a tree, so that the birds of the air come and dwell in its branches."[84]

This symbolism of vegetative growth is accepted by scholars as a type of artistic expression which emphasizes the self-awareness of the Renaissance Age.[85] Moreover, metaphors of regrowth and rebirth often combined several different symbols in art especially, for example, when "ornithological symbols of rebirth or rejuvenation, such as the phoenix or the eagle, were joined with symbols of vegetation."[86] If this be true, then the architectural and pictorial innovations of the papal study of Clement VI express his personal conviction that the establishment of the papacy at Avignon is a base for a new reform of the Church which should take a direction other than that chosen by his predecessor, Pope Benedict XII, who gave special attention to the reformation of the Franciscans, Dominicans, Canon Regulars of St. Augustine, and the secular clergy.

The reforms attempted by Benedict were in large measure annihilated by dispensations granted by Clement, who sought to strengthen the Church not by return to the traditional methods of the past, but through identification with the innovative legal, social, economic, and artistic trends emerging in northern Europe. If Boniface VIII had been defeated by confrontation with the power of France, Clement, former intimate counselor of Philip of Valois, would apply the secular principles he had learned in royal service, for the benefit of the Church, which he saw as an institution involved not with an isolated spiritual segment of human life, but with its totality. Man is first a natural being

82. Gerhard B. Ladner, op. cit., pp. 312-313.
83. Genesis, 2: 8-9.
84. Matthew, 13: 31.
85. Gerhart B. Ladner, op. cit., p. 328.
86. Ibid. I am not suggesting that the decorative themes of the papal apartment were inspired by the *Purgatorio*. The point is that classical and scriptural symbolism influence both literary and plastic arts in a similar and continuous manner from antiquity to modern times.

living in a natural world, which is the foundation on which personal spirituality must be built and the whole earthly supernatural order constructed.

The artistic symbolism of the papal study and of the papal bedroom, therefore, reveals not the secularization of the religious ideals of the Church, but rather the re-affirmation of humanistic ideals for all Christianity freed from the limitations imposed by Italian and, especially, Roman papal traditions.

The papal study is decorated with a cosmological tree, reminding Pope Clement that, although in Avignon, he is working in the headquarters of the Church in order to support heaven. The naturalistic theme of the Room of the Stag, the papal bedroom, also lends itself to a probable allegorical interpretation.

The stag symbolizes Christ who is the enemy of the snake or asp, which is often included in medieval bestiaries in the same chapter with the weasel. Psalm 41:2 reads: "As the stag longs for the running waters, so my soul longs for you, O God." Thus the hunters of the stag represent those men who follow Christ in their quest for God. The idea of the purity and nobility of the deer hunter is associated in early Greek poetry with Artemis:

> Now gods and mortals call her
> by her thrilling name: deer-slaying hunter,
> and she is pure of marriage or erotic love.[87]

Oppian, of the late second century after Christ, in his Greek hexameter poetry, the *Cynegetica,* says: "All the race of snakes and deer always wage bitter feud with one another."[88] When the stag knows where the snake is, he tramples it to death, thus symbolizing Christ who destroyed the devil that was unable to endure the tree of knowledge.[89] The horns of the stag also symbolize the Old and New Testaments.[90] The dogs

87. Sappho, *Lyrics in the Original Greek,* trans. W. Barnstone (New York: New York University Press, 1965), p. 103.

88. Oppian, *Cynegetica,* ed. and trans. A. W. Mair, Loeb Class. Libr. (London, 1928), II, 233-234.

89. Florence McCulloch, *Medieval Latin and French Bestiaries* (Chapel Hill, 1962), pp. 88-89 and 172-174. Professors Lazaros Varnos and James Hedges of the University of North Carolina at Charlotte, Department of English, assisted me with these identifications. Professor Aldo Scaglione, Department of Romance Languages, University of North Carolina at Chapel Hill, gave me the benefit of his expert knowledge on key points throughout this study. I am grateful for this generous help.

90. George Ferguson, *Signs and Symbols in Christian Art: With Illustrations from the Paintings of the Renaissance* (New York: 1958), "Stag."

accompanying the hunters are symbols of watchfulness and fidelity after the model of the dog which accompanied Tobias to the house of Raguel and which on the return journey to the home of Tobias "ran before and coming as if he had brought the news, showed his joy by his fawning and wagging his tail."[91]

The fishing scene significantly represents four different types of fishermen, probably the Avignonese successors of Peter the Fisherman: Clement V, John XXII, Benedict XII, and Clement VI, the last of whom commissioned the fresco.[92] The probable interpretation strongly suggests Pope Clement's humanistic concept that not every man can be brought to God with the same method or bait. In Renaissance imagery the fish variously symbolizes Christ, St. Peter, or the restoration of sight to Tobit, father of Tobias. In this fresco the varieties of fish probably represent the human race, the particular object of Clement's concern as to how men can be brought to faith in Christ.

The scene featuring the apple tree represents the Crucifixion of Jesus by which (Christian theology teaches) the fruits of the redemption are distributed to men for their salvation, but not without their cooperation, free will and personal effort. The apple-pickers, therefore, are pictured in various attitudes of labor. They are earning their reward by the sweat of their brow.[93] In Latin the word *malum* may mean either 'apple' or 'evil.' For this reason the apple tree has been identified both with the temptation of Eve and the wood of the Cross, and thus becomes a symbol of salvation.[94] In early Greek literature Sappho speaks of a virgin thus:

> Like a sweet apple reddening on the high
> tip of the topmost branch and forgotten
> by the pickers—no, beyond their reach.[95]

The child hiding in the tree represents the descent of the Second Person of the Trinity to earth from on high, or the incarnation of Jesus Christ as man.[96] Below this child is a weasel chasing rabbits. Here the

91. Tobias 6:1 and 11: 9. See Sirach 13: 14-17: "Is a wolf ever allied with a lamb? So it is with the sinner and the just. Can there be peace between the hyena and the dog?"

92. Luke 5: 1-11. The pertinent remark to Simon by Jesus is: "Do not be afraid; henceforth thou shalt catch men."

93. Canticle of Canticles 2: 2-3; Genesis 3: 17.

94. Genesis 3: 3. The red apple also suggests drops of blood.

95. Sappho, *Lyrics,* op. cit., p. 43.

96. Eleanor S. Greenhill, "The Child in the Tree: A Study of the Cosmological Tree in Christian Tradition," *Traditio,* X (1954), 323-325.

weasel is a symbolic substitute for the serpent of the Garden of Eden.[97] The rabbits, defenseless animals, are a symbol of men who put their hope of salvation in Christ and His Passion, and although the rabbit also represents lust, salvation in Christ depends upon flight from the tempter, represented by the weasel.

In a sense, the bird hunt dramatically repeats this concept. Birds represent, or suggest, the spiritual life or the pursuit of heaven, as opposed to the pursuit of material or earthly goals. The bird hunter with a club topped with birdlime is in sharp contrast to the bird caller using the lure of a reed pipe. The deadly effects of the allurements of the world are paradoxically illustrated in this very natural scene portraying the dilemma of human existence.

The bathers clothed in white symbolize the new life in Christ obtained through baptism. The allegory is completed by the magnificently dressed royal personage holding a domestic falcon. The concept suggests that through baptism the untamed nature of man is brought under control and he becomes a royal person, heir of Jesus Christ, and descendant of the royal line of King David. The domestic falcon is both a symbol of royalty and of conversion from the uncontrolled life of nature to supernatural life of heaven.[98]

The imagery of the falconer and the bird hunt are of one piece. Their symbolism goes back to ancient Babylon and Egypt, where the nature of the tree of life requires that many birds dwell in its branches. Also the tree rich of fruit and inhabited by birds becomes a symbol of the vitalizing power of kingship.[99] The parable of the mustard seed compares the Kingdom of God to a tree in whose branches many birds dwell, but this parable attributed to Christ clearly reflects the following words of Ezekiel:

Thus saith Lord God: I myself will take of the marrow of the high cedar and will set it: I will crop off a tender twig from the top of the branches thereof and I will plant it on a mountain high and eminent. On the high mountain of Israel will I plant it: and it shall shoot forth into branches and shall bear fruit, and it shall become a great cedar. And all birds shall dwell under it and every fowl shall make its nest under the shadow of the branches thereof.

And all of the trees of the country shall know that I the Lord have brought down the high tree: and have dried up the green tree and have caused the dry tree to flourish. I the Lord have spoken and have done it.[100]

97. Florence McCulloch, *Medieval Latin and French Bestiaries,* p. 186.

98. George Ferguson, op. cit., "falcon"; Florence McCulloch, op. cit., pp. 123-124.

99. Gerhart B. Ladner, op. cit., p. 318, fns. 70 and 71.

100. Ezekiel 17: 22-24.

The most persuasive proof for the probably allegorical interpretation of the paintings in Clement's bedroom, the Room of the Stag, comes from the prophecy of Daniel:

I Nabuchodonosor was at rest in my house and flourishing in my palace. I saw a dream that affrighted me: and my thoughts in my bed and the visions of my head troubled me. Then I set forth a decree that all the wise men of Babylon should be brought in before me and that they should show me the interpretation of the dream. Then came in the diviners, the wise men, the Chaldeans, and the soothsayers, and I told the dream before them. But they did not show me the interpretation thereof. Till their colleague Daniel came in before me, whose name is Baltassar, according to the name of my god, who hath in him the spirit of the holy gods: and I told the dream before him.

Baltassar, prince of the diviners, because I know that thou hast in thee the spirit of the holy gods and that no secret is impossible to thee: tell me the visions of my dreams that I have seen and the interpretation of them.

This was the vision of my head in my bed. I saw and behold a tree in the midst of the earth: and the height thereof was exceeding great. The tree was great and strong: and the height thereof reached unto heaven: the sight thereof was even to the ends of all the earth. Its leaves were most beautiful and its fruit exceeding much, and in it was food for all: under it dwelt cattle and beasts, and in the branches thereof the fowls of the air had their abode. And all flesh did eat of it.

I saw in the vision of my head upon my bed: and behold a watcher and a holy one came down from heaven.[101]

In *Sine nom.* 10 Petrarch alludes to Pope Clement VI ironically as Nimrod, a great hunter before the Lord. A careful search of the chronicles, papal letters, and accounts of expenditures seems to confirm the fact that the only hunting Clement ever did as pope was done while dreaming in his bed in the Room of the Stag.[102]

101. Daniel 4: 1-10.

102. This study was made possible in part by a research grant from the Foundation of the University of North Carolina at Charlotte, Inc.

XVI

NON CHIARE ACQUE

by Eugenio Battisti
Pennsylvania State University and
University of Florence

Questo intervento nasce da una profonda frustrazione.[1] Che la natura nel Petrarca sia un fatto puramente letterario è ora ripetuto con la stessa convinzione con cui, nell'Ottocento, si leggevano il poeta e la sua storia in chiave prettamente biografica, e scovare le fonti latine da cui dipendono i suoi mirabili versi sostituisce, con non molta maggior dignità, il pedante lavoro d'archivio alla ricerca di plausibili alberi genealogici di Laura. E con tutto ciò resta aperto il problema fondamentale: perché Petrarca, a differenza di altri scrittori (e in modo certamente piú conseguente per la sua arte che nei modelli classici come Plinio, da

1. Questa ricerca non sarebbe stata possibile senza un generoso aiuto finanziario da parte dell'Institute for the Arts and the Humanistic Studies della Pennsylvania State University, che mi ha permesso, fra l'altro, di rivisitare sistematicamente, per l'occasione, i luoghi petrarcheschi, e di acquistare vari microfilms di manoscritti trecenteschi. Si è trattato di una lotta col tempo, vinta esclusivamente per merito di questo liberale sovvenzionamento.

I limiti della ricerca stessa sono stabiliti dalla mia specializzazione in storia dell'arte, né le conclusioni intendono andare al di là della problematica visiva, anche se le tentazioni sono molte. Poiché manca, finora, una trattazione moderna d'insieme, a mo' di bibliografia ragionata indichiamo qui un gruppo di autori cui si deve l'impostazione moderna del problema dei rapporti fra il Petrarca e le arti. Per l'influsso latamente estetico resta fondamentale il saggio di L. Venturi, "La critica d'arte e Francesco Petrarca", in *Annali della Cattedra Petrarchesca,* II (1931), 442-3, cui si ricollegano Eugenio Battisti, *Rinascimento e Barocco* (Torino, 1960), pp. 56 e passim; Rosario Assunto, *La critica d'arte nel pensiero medioevale* (Milano, 1961), pp. 294 e passim; Michael Baxandall, *Giotto and the Orators: Humanistic Observers of Painting in Italy and the Discovery of Pictorial Composition, 1350-1450* (Oxford, 1971). Il rapporto con l'amore francescano per la natura è stato finemente riesaminato da A. Cutler, "*Admirari alta montium:* Franciscan Elements in Petrarch's Christian Topography", in *The Classics and the Classical Tradition: Essays Presented to Robert E. Dengler,* eds. E. N. Borza e Robert W. Carrubba (University Park, Pa., 1973), pp. 51-62. L'esistenza di disegni del Petrarca stesso, come il paesaggio idealizzato di Valchiusa, venne divulgata, per cosí dire, da Pierre de Nolhac, *Pétrarque et l'humanisme* (Parigi, 1907), II, 69-83; 269-271, con una riproduzione per i tempi eccellente. L'unico studio specifico, la dissertazione di laurea di L. Chiovenda, *Die Zeichnungen Petrarcas,* discussa a Frankfurt sul Meno nel 1929, parzialmente pubblicata nell' *Archivum Romanicum,* XVI (1933), è ora completamente sostituito dalle schede di Degenhart-Schmitt nel *Corpus der italienischen Zeichnungen, 1300-1450* (Berlin, 1968), I. V. scheda 60.

lui imitati), dovette identificare, miticamente, il suo paesaggio poetico con luoghi reali, come Valchiusa, e quale conseguenza continua ad avere su di noi questa identificazione.

Si potrebbe, per la prima domanda, tagliar corto con un riferimento inoppugnabile alla teoria coeva della poesia, secondo cui il poeta deve riferirsi ad un episodio reale, se non vuol essere accusato di menzogna, ma di nuovo ciò significa solo spostare il problema: perché Valchiusa e non un altro posto? E in seguito, perché a Milano la casa presso S. Ambrogio, ecc., e a Padova, Arquà? In nessun caso si tratta di una scelta imposta, o non laboriosamente predisposta e giustificata. Per il secondo problema, che riguarda il nostro modo di fruire sia Valchiusa, che altri paesaggi privilegiati dal Petrarca di cui egli ci ha lasciato una o piú descrizioni, una soluzione risulta anche più difficile. Vedendo le illustrazioni date in xilografia durante il Cinquecento di Valchiusa, per quanto fantastiche risultino rispetto al sito reale non si può impedire che vengano alla memoria interpretazioni di foreste, montagne, rivi, nella pittura dello stesso periodo, precisamente ispirate alle poesie di Petrarca ed a imitazioni di esse, il che prova, perlomeno, un parallelo accordarsi, intuitivamente, dell'immagine ricavata dal pellegrinaggio sul posto, e di quella derivata dalla lettura. Ma Valchiusa attrae, in tutte le stagioni, migliaia e migliaia di visitatori, confermando quanto il Petrarca ebbe a dichiarare con orgoglio: di esser stato lui a rendere il luogo famoso. Esso, cioè, costituisce ancora per il nostro secolo un frammento privilegiato dello spettacolo naturale, allo stesso modo che lo è da millenni la grotta della Sainte-Baume, o dal Trecento la cima del Monte Ventoso (cui i turisti arrivano anche quando la strada è ghiacciata, e nonostante i cartelli che vietano l'accesso trattandosi di zona militare). Leggendo le lettere del Petrarca si constata, poi, facilmente ch'egli è stato il primo dei moderni a privilegiare altre famosissime zone topografiche, rendendole esteticamente significanti: come la costa ligure, da Genova a Porto Venere, quella a nord di Napoli, lungo i campi Flegrei, il lago

---

L'interesse per questo problema deriva dalle letture fatte per una conferenza dal titolo *"Natura Artificiosa* to *Natura Artificialis"*, tenuta a Dumbarton Oaks nel 1970, e pubblicata nel volume di atti di quel convegno sul giardino italiano. Come testi, mi sono servito, oltre che delle opere uscite nell'Edizione nazionale, e di quelle listate dal Wilkins, della traduzione del *De remediis* di fra Remigio Nannini, Venezia 1549 (ed. del 1589, posseduta dalla Pattee Library della Pennsylvania State University), dell'antologia a cura di Emilio Bigi (Milano, 1963) per la traduzione dei *Salmi Penitenziali* e le *Poesie Latine Minori*; per il *Bucolicum Carmen* dell'edizione di Tonino T. Mattucci (Pisa, 1970). Mi sono state, però, più volte indispensabili l'edizione del 1581, con l'opera completa, anch'essa posseduta dalla Pattee Library, senza ci cui questo lavoro sarebbe stato assai più difficile da imbastire, e le traduzioni del Fracassetti.

di Garda, i colli della Brianza, quelli Euganei e cosí via. In altre parole, ha ritagliato, dal flusso ininterrotto dell'esperienza di viaggio, delle impressioni, quasi come si trattasse di cartoline illustrate, rappresentative di una speciale condizione, quella che il Settecento ed Ottocento avrebbero definito pittoresca, e facendole divenire, o ridivenire, punti collettivi di riferimento e fruizione specializzata. L'arte concettuale di oggi ha cercato di fare qualche cosa di analogo, ma con maggior timidezza e padronanza geografica, meno ambizione e meno autorità. L'esempio di Petrarca dimostra come questi interventi ideali possano restare conseguenti e attivi anche a distanza di secoli, piú ancora e meglio di quelli operati praticamente sul paesaggio. Dimenticavo infatti di aggiungere, in proposito, che la biografia dello scrittore è anche caratterizzata da numerosi *horti* e *pomaria,* da lui accuratamente piantati, che comportarono considerevoli lavori anche architettonici: egli costruí un'isola artificiale nella Sorga, e ad Arquà dovette livellare il pendio, mediante terrazzamenti. che anticipano, su scala ovviamente ridotta, viste le limitate condizioni economiche, quelli fatti costruire, con meraviglia di tutti, da Cosimo il Vecchio per la sua villa a Fiesole e per la Badia.

Il Petrarca descrive un tipo di natura che potrebbe benissimo essere definita un giardino (tanto piú che questo termine include quello medievale e precedente al poeta, di *barco,* cioè di parco naturale nel senso piú attuale della parola, dove vegetazione e fauna erano mantenute ad una condizione il piú possibile vicina a quella primordiale, a costo di occupare anche un vastissimo territorio e circondarlo, quando era necessario, di mura o palizzate). Egli interviene su quella natura come un giardiniere, cioè ulteriormente estetizzandola, godendo del rapido crescere degli alberi piantati e preoccupandosi delle loro condizioni tanto da registrare, quasi giorno per giorno, i lavori compiuti, specialmente se le condizioni erano avverse, ed entrando cosí, con pieno diritto, nella storia della botanica e dell'agricoltura. Pubblicizza questi ed altri paesaggi, in modo da rendere la loro fruizione estensibile ai suoi lettori e prolungata, se non permanente nel tempo (quelli andati distrutti sono stati vittime di un disordinato sviluppo urbano, ma è almeno patetico rileggere, ancora in scrittori tardivi fino al Settecento, descrizioni di queste zone che riecheggiano la terminologia del Petrarca). E su tutta l'operazione compiuta egli fornisce, a chi voglia rifletterci sopra, una quantità di dati con cui, come vedremo, non è affatto inutile lavorare. Prima di entrare in tema, mi sia lecito indugiare ancora un momento sui problemi di metodo, e cioè appunto sui tipi di documenti che costituiscono, per cosí dire, gli strumenti usati dal Petrarca per divulgare tutta questa complessa operazione. Essi sono diversi e numerosi, allo stesso modo in cui l'abbondanza di citazioni d'ogni specie relative a Valchiusa assegna a questo luogo una dignità letteraria non inferiore a quella goduta da famose metropoli del tempo, e addirittura da celebri santuari religiosi. I documenti, specialmente su Valchiusa che costituisce, mi si scusi il gioco di parole, il più privilegiato dei luoghi da lui privilegiati, rientrano, pressapoco, in circa dieci categorie. Si tratta: 1) di descrizioni topografiche del luogo; 2) di descrizioni dei rapporti sociali con gli abitanti ed i servitori e del loro comportamento; 3) di commenti, anche in scritti morali, sul tipo di vita condotto a Valchiusa; 4) di citazioni di fonti antiche pertinenti alla località, e paragoni con ville classiche; 5) di un diario dei lavori fatti alla casa ed ai giardini; 6) di alcuni componimenti ispirati al motivo classico della ninfa della fonte; 7) di poesie, specialmente in volgare, dove il tema dell'acqua e della selva è talmente insistente da costringerci ad associarle con la Sorga e Valchiusa; 8) di componimenti allegorici in cui compare lo stesso tipo di natura descritta dalle lettere ed accennata dalle poesie volgari, per cui siamo nuovamente condotti a tale associazione; 9) di un disegno, allusivo, ma che costituisce, fra l'altro, forse il primo paesaggio autonomo della storia artistica occidentale; 10) di un madrigale coevo al disegno, scritto per musica, di cui ci resta la notazione dovuta a Jacopo da Bologna, il cui soggetto è ad un tempo mitologico (il bagno di Diana) e pastorale (la contadina che lava il suo velo alla fonte). Questi documenti non risalgono necessariamente ai soggiorni a Valchiusa: anzi il paesaggio disegnato sul margine del Plinio, ora alla Bibliothèque Nationale, ed il madrigale vennero composti nel 1350 in Italia, a Verona,[2] forse in un momento di nostalgia; l'ordine delle Rime e delle Lettere non è affatto rigidamente sistematico, e potrebbe anche darsi che la piú famosa composizione svolgente il motivo della fonte, "Chiare, fresche e dolci acque", sia stata composta anch'essa in Italia.

Le fonti che ispirano questi testi sono notevolmente diverse: lettere di scrittori antichi, le *Georgiche* e le *Bucoliche,* frammenti di poemi classici, elegie, i contrasti giullareschi, il calendimaggio, la poesia provenzale, i miti e le leggende popolari, gli scritti religiosi, e viceversa i trattati sull'agricoltura, le descrizioni topografiche, addirittura mappe tardo-antiche in originale o in copia. Il carattere delle fonti impronta in modo sostanziale le loro imitazioni o derivazioni, ma per il Petrarca l'elaborazione del paesaggio di Valchiusa compiuta con questi strumenti dovette, presumibilmente, apparire del tutto omogenea e co-

2. Jacopo da Bologna era al servizio della corte di Verona. Il Plinio venne acquistato a Mantova il 6 luglio 1350 e lasciato a Verona quando Petrarca ritornò in Francia nel giugno 1351.

erente, e certo non contradditoria con i giardini da lui costruiti praticamente, pur senza voler far divenire questi (che tali certo non erano) simbolici o moralizzati nel senso manieristico e settecentesco. Oggi, invece, leggendo e schedando i dati pervenutici, ricaviamo, paradossalmente, altrettanto diverse interpretazioni di quella esperienza naturale, e quando li riferiamo ad essa, cioè speriamo di trovare in tali fonti la spiegazione del perché, ad esempio, il Petrarca scelse come suo eremitaggio Valchiusa, esse ce ne suggeriscono livelli di lettura estremamente diversi. In parte questa disomogeneità dipende, presumibilmente, dal nostro diverso modo di recepire il messaggio: se ci serviamo, come termine di riscontro, del paesaggio reale, constatiamo che le descrizioni nettamente topografiche corrispondono alla lettera ed in spirito a ciò che noi immediatamente percepiamo, mentre gli altri *media,* comprese le poesie volgari e il disegno, riflettono una elaborazione mentale che s'inserisce, quasi originalmente autonoma, fra realtà e noi. L'ascoltare poi il madrigale cantato ci allontana totalmente da ogni riferimento cui siamo soliti.[3] Una spiegazioni potrebbe essere questa. Il linguaggio topografico, che Petrarca riintroduce in Europa in modo definitivo, con una competenza ed una scientificità che meriterebbero maggiore apprezzamento anche in sede letteraria, è basato su una lingua morta, il latino, riesumata ovviamente in modo personale, ma codificata e perciò abbastanza facile da reinterpretare, nei risvolti dubbi, mediante il riferimento ai passi o ai vocaboli antichi da cui deriva. L'italiano e gli stessi modi di rappresentare la realtà in disegno o in musica sono stati invece sottoposti ad infiniti mutamenti, per cui neppure con le massime avvertenze filologiche è possibile risalire al significato che originariamente la loro rettorica emotiva e linguisticamente alcune espressioni dovevano avere per gl'iniziali fruitori. Inoltre essi si riferiscono ad un assai più complesso sistema d'idee: la stessa mitologia, che qua e là riprende una corretta formulazione sia lessicale che d'immagine, doveva risuonare assai diversamente moderna ed esoterica all'inizio di questo recupero, e in epoca anche solo di uno o due secoli posteriore, allorchè Diana era già divenuta un riferimento talmente banale da trasformarsi in una moda galante. I rapporti ormai ben stabiliti fra il Petrarca e l'Ovidio Moralizzato potrebbero mettere meglio in luce la stessa ambiguità ed oscillazione fra significato classico e significato religioso che il tema stesso dell'eremitaggio assume coinvolgendo anche la tematica connessa di Laura. Ma poiché, presumibilmente, risulterebbe impossibile ripri-

3. Un'accessibile e buona esecuzione è in *The Seraphim Guide to Renaissance Music,* lato 3, banda 2, Will Kippersluys, Contralto e Marius van Altena, Tenore. Syntagma Musicum di Amsterdam.

stinare l'unità originaria di fondo dell'esperienza naturale del Petrarca, ci è almeno possibile isolare, nei vari *media,* gli specifici caratteri ch'essa costí assume, nella speranza di verificare almeno la complessità dell'intero processo e le sue possibili contraddizioni.

Già il paesaggio di Valchiusa è contrastante e complesso.[4] La gola vera e propria è breve, percorribile in circa un quarto d'ora di piacevole passeggiata. E chi, dall'attuale ponte, discenda per altri pochi minuti lungo il corso della Sorga, la vede trasformarsi in un sereno e maestoso fiume, che percorre campi uniformi ed aprichi. La casa del Petrarca sorgeva dove il corso d'acqua si era già regolarizzato, dopo alcune centinaia di metri di rapide, mantenendosi però trasparente e intensamente rumoroso. L'attrattiva dell'acqua era per lui fortissima, secondo le testimonianze scritte; imitando lo studio di Cicerone e forse il criptoportico della villa di Plinio a Laurentum Petrarca si costruí un riparo all'aperto, orientato verso la Sorga. Il rapporto acqua-poesia cosí stabilito è d'altronde codificato dal poeta e musicista Philippe de Vitry, suo amico, secondo cui l'etimologia di Musica, sul tipo di etimologie di Isidoro da Siviglia, deriverebbe da "moys, quod est aqua, et ycos, scientia, quia inventa fuit juxta aquas".[5] Il simbolismo dell'acqua, d'altra parte, è talmente multiforme da riuscire mal definibile. Un altro poeta della cerchia del Petrarca, Deschamps, nella Ballata MCXXII, canta il suo scorrere come simbolo del consumarsi inarrestabile della vita umana:

Flums naturelz, granz et petiz ruisseaulx,
De fontaines procedans des montaignes
Et des plains lieux, eaues a cours ysneaulx
Naissans de mer et par diverses vaines,
Tousjours courez par bas lieux et par plaines,
Sans remonter dont vous estes venues,
En retournant, se vous n'estes tenues
Par aucun art qui vostre force oppresse;
Ainsi courent noz aages soubz les nues:
Plourons, chetis, nostre fole jeunesse![6]

4. Su Valchiusa non conosco alcuno studio specifico che aggiunga qualcosa a quanto si trova nelle grandi opere biografiche del Prince d'Essling ed Eugène Müntz (Parigi, 1902), e P. De Nolhac, *Pétrarque et l'humanisme.* I dati vanno però verificati sull'accuratissime documentazioni raccolte da E. H. Wilkins.

5. *Philippi de Vitriaco Ars Nova et De Musica,* in *Scriptorum de Musica Medii Aevi,* a cura di E. de Coussemaler, vol. III (ried. Hildesheim, 1963), p. 17. V. anche p. 36: "quasi scientia aquatica vel composita juxta aquas".

6. Deschamps, *Oeuvres,* VI (Parigi, 1889); ma vedi anche vol. II, CXXXIII:
L'eaue descent tousjours et coule aval,

Il tema del fluire del tempo, peraltro, pur essendo analogamente espresso da Petrarca,[7] mi pare secondario, come motivazione dell'amore per l'acqua scorrente rispetto al clima poetico e sonoro da essa prodotto. La connessione ideale fra la Sorga e il mare (ideale in quanto non esperibile direttamente) è invece assai chiaramente testimoniata in una lettera in cui il Petrarca indica come pervenire, per via d'acqua, al suo rifugio montano dal Mediterraneo. Un'altra lettura possibile del luogo sarebbe in chiave religiosa, muovendo da una breve nota circa la sua intenzione di costruire una cappella alla Madonna in Valchiusa, probabilmente proprio là dove le acque scaturite dal bacino sorgivo incominciano a precipitare spumeggianti nella valle.[8] La simbologia mariana è assai ricca di analoghi riferimenti: in base al Cantico dei Cantici Maria è detta "fontana dei giardini, fonte di acqua viva", e in decine di inni dell'XI-XIII secoli questi attributi vennero per cosí dire popolarizzati. "Rivus mellifluus", "fons irriguus", "puritatis fons signatus", "fons hortorum et piscina aqua vitae irrorata" non trovano però riscontro nel lessico petrarchesco, per cui la simbologia propriamente religiosa dell'acqua va abbandonata, insieme alla tentazione di trovarvi Laura, riflessavi: "I' l'ho più volte (or chi fia che mel creda?) / Nell'acqua chiara . . . / veduta viva . . . ", solo per influenza d'una metafora di S. Ambrogio: "non lasciate che alcuno intorbidi l'acque del chiuso fonte, o che alcuno le turbi, cosicché tu possa vedere la tua immagine chiaramente riflessa nel suo specchio".[9]

Mais retourner ne puet naturelment;
Chascun jour naist et puis defflue ou val
De la grant mer. . . .

---

7. Nel *De vita solitaria*, Libro III, p. 368 ed. 1581, Petrarca si riferisce direttamente a Virgilio, considerando indispensabile ed immediata l'associazione fra l'osservare il corso rapido di un fiume e il fuggire del tempo, stabilita dai suoi versi

Flumina nulla quidem cursu leviore fluunt quam
Tempus abit vitae.

Questo simbolismo sembra talmente radicato, che nella *Fam.* 13 del libro XIX commenta come, paradossalmente, alla maturità della vita egli veda le sorgenti del Reno, di cui, in gioventú, aveva visto invece il medio corso.

8. Cosí è detto, infatti, in *De vita solitaria*, II, cap. ii, p. 287 della edizione del 1581: "Adest tibi tuus, Sorgia, rex fontium, ad cujus murmur haec tibi scribo. . . . (Aras) quas ego jampridem, Christum testor, si qua voto facultas affulserit, illic in hortulo meo, qui fontibus imminet ac rupibus subjacet, erigere meditor, non Nymphis, ut Seneca sentiebat, neque ullius fontium fluminumque numinibus, sed Mariae. . . ".

9. Citato in Yrjö Hirn, *The Sacred Shrine* (Boston, 1957), pp. 447-449. Ma v. *Antologia Palatina*, Libro VII: cito dalla trad. di G. Gualtieri (Firenze, 1973), in Paolo Silenziario:

La tua dolce immagine nel mare
la vedo e nelle chiare acque del fiume,
e nella coppa del mio vin m'appare.

Meno opportuno, invece, è cancellare totalmente dal contesto l'associazione fra acqua e Spirito Santo (che potrebbe essere degradata alla semplice relazione fra acqua ed ispirazione intellettuale sulla scia della fantasiosa etimologia di "muse" con cui abbiamo iniziato questa parte di esposizione). Essa è cosí proposta da Ugo di San Vittore, *De Sacramentis Fidei,* I, pars IX, c. 11: "Habet autem omnis aqua ex naturali qualitate similitudinem quamdam cum gratia Spiritus Sancti . . . et ex hac ingenita qualitate omnis aqua spiritualem gratiam representare habuit, priusquam etiam illam ex superaddita institutione significavit." (Migne, CLXXVI, col. 318.)

L'acqua della Sorga è peraltro soprattutto associata con il motivo dell'isolamento, anzi la fuga da Babilonia, la città del peccato (una definizione di Avignone che non è unicamente del Petrarca, anzi è assai meglio comprensibile se leggiamo ed ascoltiamo il *Romance de Fauvel*). Questo atteggiamento di protesta, peraltro, è del tutto sopraffatto dall'imitazione classica. Come la parte aggiunta della villa, cioè il portico esterno a volta, cosí il tipo di comportamento è del tutto modellato su esempi letterari d'insigne moralità. Date le sue responsabilità politiche Petrarca pensa addirittura al ritiro a Liternum di Scipione l'Africano: "Nihil audio quod audisse, nihil dico quod dixisse paeniteat; . . . nullis rumoribus inquietor: mecum tantum et cum libellis loquor . . .". In questo caso è Plinio che scrive a Minucius Fundanus (I, 9), ed egli anticipa un topos del Petrarca parlando del suo eremitaggio come Mouseion, cioè Elicona. La caccia era un tipico passatempo aristocratico del medioevo, ma è sempre Plinio scrivendo a Cornelio Tacito che dice di essersi appartato, con gli strumenti per scrivere, invece che con le freccie, nelle poste e negli agguati: "iam undique silvae et solitudo ipsumque illud silentium quod venationi datur, magna cogitationis incitamenta sunt". E cosí "experieris non Dianam magis montibus quam Minervam inerrare". La nostalgia per l'eremitaggio di Valchiusa, quando egli ne è lontano, ricorre nelle lettere e forse nelle poesie, ma non è dissimile dal rimpianto di Plinio, espresso a Caninus Rufus (II, 8), "studia altissimus iste secessus adfatim suggerunt". Un ricalco è avvertibile, anche, nella descrizione della Sorga che improvvisamente si trasforma da impetuosa sorgente in placido e navigabile corso d'acqua: "fons adhuc et iam amplissimum flumen". Il modello, in questo caso, sono le ben più arcadiche polle del Clitunno (VIII, 8), e di qui forse venne al Petrarca l'idea di costruire un tempietto là dove sgorga la Sorga e di usarlo come romitorio, o addirittura—si è detto sopra—trasformarlo in cappella. Egli avrebbe potuto benissimo incidere sulla porta della sua casa i famosi versi di Virgilio che avrebbero più tardi fatto mostra di sé sul ninfeo di una villa antiquaria, sul Quirinale, in pieno Cinquecento: "at secura quies et nescia fallere vita / dives opum variarum, at latis otia fundis / speluncae vivique lacus et frigida Tempe / mugitusque boum mollesque sub arbore somni / non absunt". Il suo eremitaggio, anzi, è unico al mondo, egli dice; la solitudine e l'isolamento sono—per un altro gioco etimologico, questa volta corretto—già impliciti nel nome e nell'inerente simbolismo della "chiusa valle"; la sua antichità è accertata, la sua frequentazione da parte degl'intellettuali già tale da renderla famosa, l'identificazione con l'Elicona spinta tanto avanti da trasformarla in una tappa obbligata del pellegrinaggio poetico.

Abbiamo parlato di fiume, foresta, montagne, e sono questi gl'ingredienti che effettivamente compaiono nella raffigurazione a disegno di Valchiusa, di mano del Petrarca stesso. Vi si vede, da una caverna, sgorgare la Sorga, senza alcuna casa o segno di vita attorno; apparentemente solo canne crescono sulla riva. La fonte è dominata, simbolicamente, da un monte sulla cui cima è una chiesa (che sarebbe un eremitaggio esistente oggi diruto); ma a leggere il disegno secondo la rettorica del Trecento, la chiesa corona il monte, invitando il riguardante ad una specie di ascensione religiosa. Accanto all'enigmatica figura di un trampoliere che mangia un pesce appena tolto dall'acqua, si legge: "Transalpina solitudo mea iocundissima". *Iocundus,* probabilmente, è un sinonimo di *amoenus*. Ma la nera caverna, l'aspro monte, viceversa, commenta un'altra definizione del luogo, sempre di Petrarca: "... plenus stimulis ardentibus, quibus piger licet animus in altissimas curas possit assurgere". Cioè, Valchiusa è un *locus asper*. Come vedremo, questi due caratteri sono congiunti nel duplice giardino, differentemente usato dal poeta, e la loro associazione rimarrà un tratto tipico del giardino rinascimentale italiano.

Gli elementi che abbiamo finora ricavato dai testi sono peraltro estremamente generici, allorché paragonati alla Valchiusa reale. Tale valle infatti poteva essere scelta solo da uno studioso di fenomeni geologici (come Petrarca effettivamente fu) e da un patito di terrori naturali, di panteismo, di leggende e di miti. Su questo secondo aspetto le informazioni che abbiamo sono indirette e non coprono, certamente, tutte le sollecitazioni possibili. Non c'è cenno, ad esempio, delle numerose grotte scavate dal vento nei monti che circondano a conca il villaggio di Valchiusa, e una descrizione meno affrettata avrebbe meritato il canale sotterraneo, oggi usato come strada, scavato forse in epoca romana.[10] Petrarca è taciturno sopra questi ed altri aspetti. Anzi, sembra differenziarsi dalla gente comune là dove si vanta di aver visitato la caverna

10. Il Petrarca attribuisce il tunnel a Saint Véran, il fondatore della chiesa.

della fonte, ed esservi entrato durante le magre, di notte, mentre essa incuteva terrore anche di giorno. C'è però nel secondo libro del *De otio religiosorum* un improvviso riferimento all'enorme picco a strapiombo che la domina (da cui egli vide calarsi, mediante corde, un contadino per distruggere il nido d'un'aquila che aggrediva gli armenti),[11] là dove, quasi alzando gli occhi dal manoscritto alla finestra, paragona, con un brusco passaggio, l'inabissarsi dell'anima nel peccato ad un cervo che dall'alto di quella cima si precipiti entro la sorgente senza fondo sottostante: "non si quis ex summo saxi hujus, quod haec scribenti imminet, quo neque altius visus frustratur extimatio, neque promptius ullum vidi, cervus in vivum Sorgiae fontem cadat". Una origine celtica, per questa immagine, è probabile, giacché estratta da tale mitologia si ritrova in un famosissimo testo teatrale, cioè Peer Gynt, dove il passaggio all'irrazionale ed al visionario è simboleggiato proprio dal precipitarsi del protagonista, a cavallo d'una renna, in un profondissimo fiordo.

L'altro aspetto, quello dell'interesse geologico stimolato dalla località anche negli odierni turisti, è chiaramente riconosciuto, sebbene tardivamente, da Petrarca stesso, che da buon topografo[12] lasciò delle precise indicazioni tecniche anche sull'orientamento di Valchiusa, specialmente rispetto all'Italia. Nei *Quattuor libri invectivarum contra quemdam medicum* (IV, I) egli annota che alla sua propensione per la solitudine "si è aggiunta anche la consuetudine, in gara con la natura; si è aggiunto anche lo studio e l'amore per i monti". La sorgente di Valchiusa, una delle meraviglie geologiche della Francia, è in realtà un fiume sotterraneo che ritorna alla superficie avendo attraversato un massiccio montano, ed il suo obliquo cunicolo è visibile in profondità, data l'eccezionale trasparenza delle acque. A seconda delle piogge o dello scioglimento delle nevi, la caverna può riempirsi completamente, rigurgitando all'esterno, dove crea un lago, oppure può vuotarsi, lasciando scendere il curioso fin quasi al limite del sotterraneo percorso. Il fenomeno, giustificato come se si trattasse d'un sifone, fu già analizzato

11. L'episodio della discesa dalla cima della roccia, mediante funi e ganci, è narrato nella *Fam.* III, 19.

12. Da un'approssimativa consultazione di testi sembrerebbe addirittura che il Petrarca per questi interessi (ch'egli lascia intendere ai suoi tempi rari) si ponga come unico anello importante fra Alberto Magno e Ruggero Bacone, da un lato, e Pierre d'Ailly, dall'altro. Va ricordato ch'egli non poté conoscere ancora la *Geografia* di Tolomeo, tradotta da Jacobus Angelus solo nel 1406-11. Cfr. Pierre M. Duhem, *Les Systèmes du monde de Platon à Copernic* (Parigi, 1913-1917); George H. T. Kimble, *Geography in the Middle Ages* (Londra, 1938); Boies Penrose, *Travel and Discovery in the Renaissance, 1420-1620* (Harvard, 1952; New York, 1962), dove Petrarca è totalmente ignorato.

dagli scrittori classici in altre località dove analogamente si manifesta. Cosí Plinio parla diffusamente della fonte intermittente a Torno sul Lago di Como (IV, 30) e del corso, per un tratto carsico, dell'emissario del lago di Bassano (VIII, 20). Nuovamente, il *background* erudito e letterario sembra determinare la scelta, o almeno l'interesse per un luogo corrispondente, se non identificabile con un topos classico (e Petrarca infatti si affretta a sottolineare, nel suo Plinio, una presunta allusione alla Sorga).

Ma anche la scienza ha un suo lessico e, per cosí dire, una sua iconografia. Questa, abbiamo detto, è relativamente piú comprensibile e recepibile forse per le limitate modifiche che il latino, lingua scientifica per eccellenza, ha subito. L'aderenza della descrizione petrarchesca ai luoghi è strettissima, e proprio per ciò affascinante. Difficile, ad esempio, descrivere altrimenti che con i versi latini giovanili l'interno, stillante purissima acqua, raccolta in bacini, dell'altrimenti inabitabile grotta della Sainte-Baume. Arduo, invece, comprendere, anzi individuare questo linguaggio quando è tradotto in italiano. Ci è voluta l'ingegnosità e l'erudizione di Alessandro Parronchi per ritradurre, negli originali termini di Vitellione, l'inizio della più famosa canzone associata a Valchiusa e, in particolare, alla sorgente della Sorga. Le "chiare, dolci, fresche acque" sono infatti caratterizzate da attributi che riguardano le loro proprietà di rifrazione e trasparenza secondo i trattati di ottica, e in particolare il libro X della *Perspectiva*. La condizione perfetta è proprio quella riscontrabile a Valchiusa, dove le acque scaturendo direttamente dalla montagna, filtrate e purificate da essa, sgorgano, ancor oggi, *frigidae, clarae, dulces*. La bellezza di Laura nuda era dunque pienamente rilevata agli occhi desiderosi del poeta, obbligandola, secondo un altro episodio delle rime, a gettargli acqua negli occhi, o a turbare l'immobilità del bacino per pudicizia. Altro passaggio di Vitellione è all'origine del processo metamorfico, che avviene quasi a livello di psicologia del profondo, in Petrarca, secondo cui a causa dei turbamenti della vista l'immagine di Laura può essere trasferita, in base a fugaci somiglianze, a forme naturali, o ivi scoperta, come nel già citato

> I' l'ho piú volte (or chi fia che mel creda?)
> Nell'acqua chiara, e sopra l'erba verde
> Veduta viva, e nel troncon d'un faggio;
> E 'n bianca nube. . . .

Al contrario la trasparenza cristallina dell'acqua si accompagna altre volte a quella atmosferica, cosicché "l'aere sacro, sereno" non interpone alcuno schermo alla contemplazione di Laura, mentre lascia cadere la veste che, allargandosi sul prato, copre i fiori, e prima di tentare l'acqua della sorgente si appoggia, per discendere verso essa, ad un albero che, con un richiamo preciso all'architettura primordiale descritta da Vitruvio, le fa da colonna. La delicatezza con cui la situazione erotica è mascherata, nel famoso componimento, sembra contrastare con questo contesto di perspicuità ottica, che dovrebbe togliere, in modo profano, ogni mistero, ma tale induzione sarebbe certamente erronea: infatti la visione precisa e in nessun modo turbata da schermi sensoriali è una caratteristica paradisiaca.[13]

È ora giunto il momento di verificare le fonti letterarie che influenzarono la scelta di Valchiusa (luogo, ripeto, già noto e visitato e per certe presenze archeologiche atto a venire ricalcato sul modello delle famose ville d'intellettuali antichi, inoltre non differente, come carattere, dagli eremitaggi originari benedettini), con gl'interventi giardinistici compiuti, non senza notevole impegno e spesa, dal Petrarca. L'idea originaria di chi scrive era infatti di partire proprio dalla loro descrizione e dai loro resti per chiarire il rapporto con la natura del poeta e dell'umanista, ma come sta ormai generalmente accadendo, la storia del giardino, invece di servire da scienza ausiliaria, appare talmente complessa e compenetrata di problemi interdisciplinari, da richiedere piú commenti e spiegazioni di quel che ne dà. Il concetto stesso di giardino è difficile da definire. Abbiamo già accennato come, durante il XII e XIII secolo, le riserve di caccia, come quella di Hesdin, oltre ad estendersi per miglia e miglia si proponessero esplicitamente un programma che oggi si direbbe ecologico, subentrando, con il merito in qualche caso di averci trasmesso frammenti di natura arcaica, al tipo di tutela esercitato dai santuari pagani dedicati a Diana o alle divinità delle sorgenti e dei boschi. È molto probabile che la gola di Valchiusa rientrasse in codesta categoria, il che spiega come mai paesisticamente si sia conservata pressoché intatta, nonostante la costruzione lungo il corso della Sorga, a sostituzione degli antichi mulini, di manifatture sette-ottocentesche, oggi in disuso e rovina. La necessità di ampliare il concetto di giardino a dimensioni territoriali è chiaramente documentata dalle parole di Petrarca stesso. E, come si vede, non siamo lontani dal

13. Questo concetto è espresso in trattati tardi, come Bartholomeus Rimbertinus, *De deliciis sensibilibus paradisi* (Venezia, 1498); Celsus Maffeus, *De sensibilibus deliciis paradisi* (Verona, 1504); ma è certamente più antico, e si rifà ai trattati d'ottica. Cfr. A. Parronchi, "Le fonti di Paolo Uccello, 'I filosofi'", in *Studi su la dolce prospettiva* (Milano, 1970), pp. 522-6 e Michael Baxandall, *Painting and Experience in Fifteenth Century Italy* (Oxford, 1972), pp. 103-104.

suo ritagliare, durante i viaggi, o anche solo percorrendo carte geografiche, larghe zone naturali da celebrare letterariamente, ed a cui imporre, cosí, una specie di culto. Viene invece meno la possibilità di un paragone, per altro tentante, con gli affreschi della Stanza della Guardaroba, nel Palazzo Papale di Avignone, o con quelli, posteriori, provenienti da Isle-sur–Sorgues, dove abbiamo la raffigurazione di verzieri che sembrano replicare affreschi romani ed un interesse per singole specie botaniche da *Tacuinum sanitatis*[14] che pare assente in Petrarca, in questo momento. Neppure nella sua poesia, d'altronde, troviamo qualcosa di analogo alla seguente elencazione tecnica, cioè da erbario, fatta da Deschamps:

XXVII (Balade contre la multiplicité des mauvaises herbes)
Je voy l'ortie et le chardon,
Le jone marin et la sicue,
La cauppe treppe et le tendon,
Et toute herbe qui point et tue.
. . . . . .
Je ne voy rose ne bouton,
Lavende, violette drue,
Marjolaine, basilicon,
Balme ne douce odeur en rue.[15]

Là dove è direttamente coltivato, il giardino a Valchiusa è esclusivamente un *pomarium,* con alberi da frutta. I fiori sono assenti sia dalla pratica che dalla poesia, e la indifferenza totale per il tipo di giardino islamico, caratterizzato ad esempio dalla commistione di rose e viti, contrasta con la sua divulgazione anche attraverso i poemi cavallereschi. Neppure a Napoli, famosa per giardini di questo tipo, Petrarca si sofferma su di essi. Il giardino petrarchesco, che come vedremo è altrettanto letterario e trasfigurato che il suo ambiente alpestre, non può essere semplicemente identificato con il *locus amoenus* di cui il Curtius ha tracciato la millenaria vicenda, benché alcune delle fonti siano identiche.[16] Il duplice aspetto del Petrarca stesso, cioè la sua apertura a

14. È accertata la presenza di erbari illustrati alla corte di Avignone. Cfr. per tutto questo complesso argomento, che poco per volta trova il suo preciso inquadramento storico, le eccellenti schede nel catalogo della mostra *Arte Lombarda dai Visconti agli Sforza* (Milano, 1958), specialmente schede 78-81.

15. Deschamps, *Oeuvres,* I (Parigi, 1878), pp. 107-109.

16. Non è il caso, tanto son celebri, di riassumere qui le dimostrazioni date da E. R. Curtius in *La littérature européenne et le moyen âge latin,* che cito dalla trad. francese di Jean Brejoux (Parigi, 1956), di come questo paesaggio ideale giunga al medioevo tramite la poesia e la retorica antica.

vivacissimi scambi umani, quindi alla civiltà nel suo progredire, e la sua chiusura in un ben difeso isolamento, a Valchiusa protetto da inaccessibili monti, si riflettono negli opposti caratteri degli appropriamenti da lui compiuti, del territorio a valle e a monte, da lui descritti come "ortulus cultior" e "ortulus asperior". La loro contrapposizione s'ispira ancora una volta alle descrizioni di ville antiche, con una fronte sul mare e l'altra sulla campagna, ma, come subito vedremo, il contrasto di carattere giunge addirittura al di là del pittoresco manieristico e settecentesco.

La casa del Petrarca doveva sorgere non distante da quella trasformata in museo, verso il 1920, dall'Università di Aix-en-Provence. L'interpretazione, basata su xilografie cinquecentesche, che si trovasse a mezza costa contraddice le informazioni della *Familiaris* XIII, 8, assai precisa in proposito. Il giardino costruito entro la Sorga, evidentemente per mancanza di spazio, trovandosi la casa sulla riva, è detto "proximus" ad essa, ed il luogo di studio, fatto ad imitazione di quello di Cicerone e costruito a volta, si trovava "ultima domus in parte", avendo come eccezionale caratteristica "praeterlabentem Sorgiam". Valicando un ponticello, quasi certamente di legno, si giungeva all'isola che tuttora sorge nel fiume e conserva al centro un gruppo simmetrico di alberi, antichi ma certamente non trecenteschi. Questo ramo della Sorga era probabilmente solo un canale, mantenuto a scopi d'irrigazione, che oggi sopravvive. La zona è stata sconvolta dall'industrializzazione ottocentesca che ha costruito dighe e condotte; solo uno studio approfondito degli antichi catasti ed una serie di saggi e scavi potrà chiarire definitivamente la sua storia. Un'altra isola artificiale è stata costruita piú a monte, piú lontano dall'abitato (che ai tempi di Petrarca doveva consistere di pochissime case); anche qui saggi sarebbero opportuni, benché la zona sembri esclusivamente moderna. Nell'isola artificiale cosí costruita Petrarca fece piantare, sotto la sua diretta sorveglianza, viti, peri, meli, peschi, fichi, mandorli e noci, rallegrandosi per la loro rapida crescita. La famosa miniatura di Simone Martini, certamente eseguita fra la primavera del 1342 e l'estate del 1343,[17] celebra l'attività di Pe-

17. Il periodo possibile d'incontri diretti fra il Petrarca e Simone Martini è assai ristretto, per cui le opere realizzate dal pittore per l'umanista sono facilmente databili. L'arrivo di Simone—nonostante il parere del Bacci—vien posto dopo il 24 ottobre 1340; egli morì nel luglio del 1344. Deriviamo questi dati, con relativa bibliografia, da *Simone Martini à Avignon,* numero speciale di *Les Monuments Historiques de la France* (1963, 3, luglio-settembre), in occasione del restauro degli affreschi nel portico di Notre-Dame-des-Doms d'Avignone. Il manoscritto di Virgilio, oggi alla Biblioteca Ambrosiana, fu ritrovato da lui solo nel 1340, in coincidenza quindi con il presunto arrivo di Simone. Il ritratto di Laura, perduto, presumibilmente allegorico, non è databile documentariamente.

trarca giardiniere oltre l'insegnamento di Virgilio, considerato un tecnico dell'agricoltura. Particolarmente significativa la figura in basso a sinistra, che si riferisce alle *Georgiche,* cioè alla coltivazione dei campi. L'operazione rappresentata è la potatura, sembra delle viti. Il contadino si rivolge a Virgilio, per averne dirette istruzioni.

Che un intellettuale si occupasse di giardinaggio e di lavori nell'orto non è un fatto eccezionale nella storia della cultura. Il famosissimo antico esempio di Ciro re di Persia[18] venne seguito, perlomeno, da Renato d'Angiò e Cosimo il Vecchio, che intesero cosí compiere un'azione anche morale.[19] La distanza fra poesia ed agricoltura, d'altronde, è

Ora, Petrarca lasciò Avignone per Napoli e Roma il 16 febbraio 1341; ci tornò solo all'inizio della primavera del 1342, restandoci fino al settembre del 1343, data di nuova missione in Italia che doveva concludersi dopo la morte del pittore. La primavera 1343-estate 1343 è l'unico periodo coincidente. Controprova è la stretta affinità stilistica fra la miniatura del Virgilio e la Sacra Famiglia della Walker Art Gallery di Liverpool, del 1342. A proposito di questa, estremamente importante da un punto di vista iconografico per la posizione centrale, di assoluto rilievo, data a San Giuseppe (che eccezionalmente fa addirittura da mediatore fra Cristo e la Madonna), vorrei ricordare che nella chiesa di St-Agricole, ad Avignone, una lapide forse ottocentesca ricorda l'istituzione, per opera di Gregorio XI, della festa di S. Giuseppe. Il dipinto di Simone dimostra che già vari decenni prima S. Giuseppe riceveva un culto particolare e specialissimo.

18. Così parafrasa Matteo Palmieri, *Della Vita Civile* (1438-9): "Ciro re dei Persi, d'ingegno e potenza prestante . . . tanta iocondità cavava da' campi bene culti che, spesso, spogliandosi le porpore e ornamenti regali, secondo il costume persico d'oro e di gemme splendidi e nobili, s'essercitava a cultivare i suoi orti". All'ambasciatore spartano Lisandro, "mostrandogli molte cose preziose e nobili, (poi) il menò in uno orto diligentemente composto, e copioso di frutti bene culti, e con ordine mirabile posti. Lisandro meravigliandosi della grandezza e rigoglioso vigore degli alberi, con diritta misura ordinati e inserti di dilettevole varietà di piacevoli pomi, e oltra questi, del cultivato e bene disposto terreno, e della ioconda suavità, di mille odori spirante di vari fiori, domandò chi con tanto ordine conducea tali orti, dicendo che la diligenza di tale lavoratore era meritamente laudabile. Ciro rispose: Tutto questo ordine è composto da me, e gran parte di questi frutti con le mie mani sono stati seminati, transpiantati, innestati e condotti". Uso l'edizione di C. Varese, in *Prosatori volgari del Quattrocento* (Milano–Napoli, 1955), pp. 385-6. La fonte è Senofonte, *Oikonomikos,* IV, 20-25.

19. Curiosamente, il tema del giardinaggio, o della coltivazione diretta di un piccolo campo, rimane associato a valori morali nella cultura contemporanea *underground.* Si veda la larghissima dotazione strumentale messa a disposizione di privati e comuni dallo *Whole Earth Catalog* (mi riferisco all'ultima edizione del 1971, edita dal Portola Institute), o articoli di mistica orientale e neoalchimistici come "Farming" di Chogyam Trungpa, in *Maitreya Three* (*Gardening*), edito da Shambala Publications Inc. (Berkeley, California). Anzi, credo che poche pagine come queste siano prossime all'atteggiamento del Petrarca, oscillante fra lo scientifico e lo psicologico: "The farmers' belief that he is cultivating a mystical farm is challenged because he is uncertain whether the growth

minima, concettualmente, allorché si consideri che una musa, Thalia, presiede alla coltivazione.

Accennando all'enfasi da lui posta sullo scorrere rumoroso della Sorga, eravamo rimasti dubbiosi se associare a tale preferenza un valore anche simbolico; ma ogni dubbio cade rispetto al valore morale, positivo o negativo, della coltivazione di quest'isola, difesa da Petrarca stesso contro le piene del fiume, mediante un largo impiego di manodopera. Nel *De otio religioso* l'itinerario spirituale ideale è paragonato ad un "praeclarum iter . . . per opacas valles et prata roscida, per frondosos et faciles colles, secus amoenas et floreas fluminum ripas". Lo stesso concetto, questa volta attribuito a Dio stesso, di "fons vitae", "gaudii fons limpidissimus", è associato ad un contesto vegetale, cioè all'*ubertas,* e paragonato al ristoro che danno all'affaticato viandante un "cespes herbosus" e specialmente l'ombra degli alberi. Come supremi piaceri sono elencati: terre apriche, rami fioriti, verdi prati, cesellati ori e perle indiane, vista dell'amata e colloquio con lei. Il verde, in particolare, diventa l'aggettivo di colore assolutamente predominante nel *Canzoniere* (con ben 66 comparse, di fronte alle 54 dell'intero corpus virgiliano).[20] Ora il verde è proprio l'effetto della benefica presenza di Talia, "ut et nomen indicat, a germinando veniens; idcirco arbusculas varias manibus gestet; vestis esto floribus foliisque distincta".[21]

---

of this farm is really due to his enrichment of the property or whether the crops and the orchard have just grown naturally. Yet there is some kind of magic as is said in the Heart Sutra. This is the greatest incantation that could turn the world upside down. It is the farming process of letting things grow. . . . The farmer has to yield to the organic process of nature. Having done that, he must come to believe that his watchful eye has no use" (p. 38).

20. Mi servo della *Concordance of the Rymes of Francesco Petrarca* compilata da Kenneth McKenzie (Oxford-New Haven, 1912), e dell'*Index verborum virgilianus* di Monroe Nichols Wetmore (New York-London-Oxford, 1911).

21. Il verde, inoltre, è un colore usato anche araldicamente, come insegna amorosa, in testi coevi. Confronta il *Virelay* di Eustache Deschamps in *Oeuvres complètes,* IV, 1884, DCCXXVIII:

> Plus vert que nulle verdure
> Est mon cuer qui tant endure
> De dolour
> Chascun jour
> Pour vous, douce creature;
>
> Mais parti d'autre coulour,
> En honnour,
> De loyauté fine et pure:
> C'est de bleu, et la verdour,
> Sans folour,
> Y sera tant que je dure

Dal *De remediis* si possono ricavare assai precise indicazioni sul valore non soltanto della contemplazione passiva della natura, ma di una sua trasformazione appunto mediante l'agricoltura. Intanto l'ideale "stato tranquillo" è raggiungibile solo allorché "hai edificata la casa, arato il campo, potata la vigna, rigati i prati, acconcia l'aja, annestati gli alberi, cavati i rivi, tessuta la siepe" (XC), Inoltre, per "gli huomini dati a gli studj", il giardino costituisce un'esperienza particolarmente positiva "perché l'ingegno è svegliato dal luogo, e spinge alcuni alla penitenza e altri alla lascivia". L'ambivalenza di carattere del giardino è un elemento da tener presente, piú tardi, quando discuteremo quanto di questa tematica entri nel *Canzoniere*. Tuttavia, il coltivare il giardino o il campo ha un'accezione prevalentemente positiva, tanto da divenire simbolo dell'azione morale: "e per dir meglio, il campo è l'animo, il colto l'intenzione, il seme il pensiero, la ricolta la fatica, e questa mieterai con grande abondanza" (LVII). A causa del peccato originale, la terra stessa "incolta produrrebbe lappole e triboli". "A fenderla col ferro, e con grande arte farla piacevole ne sforzò la mortal miseria. Et di qui hebbe principio l'agricoltura, già segno d'una santissima et innocentissima vita, hora colma della antica fatica et de nuovi vitii, poi che non essendo cosa inaccessibile alla invidia et alla avaritia, i civili sacrilegii entrarono nelle rustiche case". I contadini, tuttavia, secondo il Petrarca, che si vale di Virgilio come *auctoritas,* sarebbero stati gli ultimi degli uomini a incattivirsi.

Come si vede, l'elogio del coltivare sfiora il tono religioso e certo corrisponde all'amore costante di Petrarca, che dovunque si stabilí, con l'eccezione forse del palazzo a Venezia, piantò giardini. Nella psicomachia rappresentata dal *De remediis,* a differenza di altri casi, finisce cosí per mancare una opposizione realmente forte, magari appoggiata su Salomone cui il Deschamps, ad esempio, si rifà per criticare chi come lui "Fist maisons, sales et jardins . . . / Vignes planta, cedres et pins,/ Oliviers, cyprès et sapins", e, altrove, "il fist palais, jardins plains de verdure,/ il ot estancs, boys et quanqu'il vouloit, . . . / Et nonpourquant dist il en verité, / Qu'en ce monde n'a fors que Vanité."[22] Dopo una considerazione di carattere esclusivamente pratico sullo scarso

Pour servir sans mespresure
Vostre tresdouce figure
Que j'aour;
Car meillour
Ne fourma oncques Nature,
Plus vert que nulle verdure.

22. *Oeuvres complètes* di Eustache Deschamps, II, p. 279, 24 e CXIX.

reddito della coltivazione in proprio, Ragione non riesce che a commentare: "Quanto vorrei io piú tosto che coltivassi te stesso, ma essendo tu terreno animale ami la terra, e non ci passerà molto tempo che tu stesso ingrasserai la terra che tu lavori; coltiva quanti campi e quanti alberi tu vuoi, che finalmente non occuperai molti palmi di terra, né alcuno (come dice Horatio) di questi alberi ti seguirà fuor che l'odiato cipresso". Passo in cui peraltro si può leggere fra le righe un altro tema moralistico, quello del lavoro fatto per gli eredi, e non per sé, e l'identificazione dell'uomo, fatto di terra, con la terra, da cui è nato ed entro cui si dissolverà.

Ma abbandoniamo, ormai, l'isola-giardino di fronte alla casa, per risalire, sempre sulla riva destra, guardando verso la sorgente, il corso del fiume. Qui, ancora in larghissima parte intatto, è il secondo giardino del Petrarca, che occupava tutta la fascia in declivo piuttosto ripido fra la riva del fiume ed il castello. È piú che probabile che l'uso di questo terreno gli fosse concesso dall'amico Cardinale Philippe de Cabassole, vescovo di Cavaillon, e come tale proprietario del castello che domina il villaggio di Valchiusa. Poiché la fonte sgorga notevolmente in alto, un sentiero quasi pianeggiante conduce ad essa dal castello, oggi in rovina, mentre lungo il rio la salita è erta. La fonte, come si è detto, sgorga al centro di un anfiteatro montano, solo in basso coperto da un bosco, e praticamente inaccessibile se non agli uccelli ed agli animali selvaggi. Il senso di chiusura di questa parte è, invero, singolare, ed è completato, psicologicamente, dal rumore dell'acque, specialmente quando il fiume è in piena. Come l'incombente parete rocciosa verticale aveva rievocato, nella mente di Petrarca, una fiaba celtica, quella del cervo che si precipita dall'alto del monte nel sottostante, minuscolo specchio d'acqua, il fragore delle rapide bianche di schiuma gli ispira citazioni di spettacolosi ed a volte inesistenti paesaggi lontani, e sembra costituire una esperienza tanto permanente da rappresentare, per sempre, una cortina contro la mondanità. Cosí, nel *De remediis* a chi si lamenta: "Io ho grandemente in odio i romori della città, e le strida del volgo", la Ragione suggerisce: "Ama il silentio della villa, e delle selve, perché quelle cose che non si possono né scacciare, né sopportare, bisogna fuggirle. . . . Fingi ancora nell'animo tuo d'udire un romore di acque, che percuotano in un grande scoglio; persuaditi d'essere al fonte del fiume Sorga, d'onde l'acqua lucidissima esce da una caverna horribile, o dove l'Aniene mette in Tevere, cadendo da uno altissimo colle, o veramente dove il Nilo sbocca in mare a quel luogo che si chiama Cadidupla, o dove il Danubio cade nel mare maggiore, o finalmente dove nel mare di Sicilia, Scilla e Cariddi combat-tono; onde la consuetudine farà che tu ascolterai con dolcezza quello che hora tu odi con tedio".[23]

Questo paesaggio inquietante, che può piacere solo a chi sia accostumato ad un epico senso della natura ed abbia già in sé l'anima di un Friedrich (che ne sarebbe stato il pittore ideale), venne fruito dal Petrarca quotidianamente. Egli considera questo, anzi, il giardino principale, enunciandolo per primo: "Est enim alter umbrosus, solique studio aptus et nostro sacer Apollini; hic nascenti Sorgie impendet, ultra quem nichil est nisi rupes et avia prorsum nisi feris aut volucribus inaccessa". Il tempo di frequentazione è il pomeriggio, ma a volte anche la notte. E non basta.

Abbiamo detto che la Sorga sgorga da un sifone sotterraneo, che si vede sprofondare sotto il monte quando la caverna è piena d'acqua e costituisce un lago, o presso a cui si può accedere, quando è in magra. L'acqua, per dar luogo alla Sorga, deve superare la riva del lago, cioè un piccolo dosso, dal quale immediatemente incominciano le rapide, cioè un corso accelerato, in forte discesa, fra rocce. È su questo minimo dossale che Petrarca si costruí una specie di belvedere, "alta sub rupe ac mediis in undis", vincendo con l'artificio la natura, "augustus quidem sed plenus stimulis ardentibus, quibus piger licet animus in altissimas curas possit assurgere". C'è da rimpiangere che nessun illustratore romantico sia stato affascinato da questo tema: il gorgo ribollente, la drammatica conca rocciosa, il precipitarsi schiumoso della Sorga verso il mare, e Petrarca, in una *gloriette* da parco romantico, che scrive mosso da una carica emotiva artificiosamente creata mediante l'immersione nel sublime naturale.

Potremmo supplire a questa assente illustrazione, fingendolo astante in una delle altrettanto suggestive raffigurazioni di gole alpine, di ponti del diavolo, ecc., ma poiché Petrarca intende questo tipo d'orrido come "ortulus asperior", forse è meglio, scavalcando varie generazioni, introdurre un paragone apparentemente incongruo ma, come vedremo, abbastanza giustificato, con il giardino inglese vero e proprio. Fra i

23. E cosí, acusticamente, la vallata della Sorga s'identifica con quella solenne, per la presenza di vetusti dei fluviali, di Tempe:

Est nemus Haemoniae, praerupta quod undique claudit
Silva: vocant Tempe. Per quae Peneus ab imo
Effusus Pindo spumosis volvitur undis,
Deiectuque gravi tenues agitantia fumos
Nubila conducit, summisque aspergine silvis
Inpluit, et sonitu plus quam vicina fatigat.
Haec domus, haec sedes, haec sunt penetralia magni
Amnis. In his, residens facto de cautibus antro,
Undis iura dabat nymphisque colentibus undas.

vari riferimenti possibili, scelgo una splendida descrizione di Ippolito Pindemonte, che fornisce programmi e consigli. "L'arte . . . consiste nell' abbellir cosí un terreno assai vasto, che sembrar possa che la natura l'abbia in quella guisa abbellito ella stessa"; ora questa manipolazione è assente a Valchiusa, dove tutto restò, fedelmente, allo stato originario, né possiamo supporre che il ritiro, sulla sorgente, fosse stato addirittura costruito da Petrarca in stile rustico. Ma a volte, come qui, la natura procede come l'arte "intesa a far cosa piú squisita e compiuta, che far non le veggiamo comunemente, riunendo in un dato spazio molte bellezze che non suole riunir mai, e dando a quelle bellezze stesse una perfezione ed un finimento maggiore". Fra gl'ingredienti piú rari, e perciò piú necessari, sono "l'acque, senza le quali par cosa morta un giardino, o queste stagnino in forma di lago, o scorrano in quella di ruscello o di fiume, con ponti e con isolette, o precipitino d'alto in cascata, il che nondimeno è sí difficile ad eseguirsi, che molti hanno queste cascate con savia disperazione affatto sbandite. Dicasi il medesimo delle rupi: quegli che per sorte le ha, può bene con qualche modificazione farle al suo intento rispondere, ma folle e perduto tentativo sarebbe il voler crearsele; e cosí quanto alle fabbriche, fortunato chiameremo chi possedesse un vecchio castello . . .". Valchiusa ha tutto questo, come d'altronde diligentemente annota il Petrarca nelle sue lettere, e nelle sue evocazioni del luogo. "Che dirò poi degli animali, onde la terra e l'acqua son popolate, e avvivato è il tutto". La fauna di Valchiusa, nelle testimonianze dateci, era ricca di pesci, di selvaggina, di uccelli (fra cui un'aquila, una gru). "Finalmente osservisi che l'uomo inglese s'insignorisce, per dir cosí, e gode dell'intero paese che lo circonda, ordinando egli le cose tutte in maniera, che un monte, una torre, o altro oggetto importante, ch'è fuori del giardino suo, par collocato là a bella posta per contribuire ai piaceri di lui, creando un prospetto, o perfezionando, senza saperlo, una delle scene del suo giardino". Petrarca, nel suo vagabondaggio quotidiano, include colli, prati, al di là appunto del suo possesso.

Dobbiamo spiegare, ora, come sia possibile associare un comportamento trecentesco ad uno ottocentesco. Ma proprio la storia del giardino inglese ce ne dà la prova. Si credeva, un secolo fa, ch'esso fosse nato dalla impressione creata, appunto nei nobili inglesi, dalle pitture di Salvator Rosa rappresentanti luoghi selvaggi, foreste, scogliere, ecc. In realtà il giardino inglese non è che la continuazione di quello italiano, manieristico: le incisioni che illustrano la distrutta sistemazione di Pratolino fanno vedere padiglioni sospesi sugli alberi, e già prima si sono avute grotte artificiali, addirittura subacquee (nel giardino della Farnesina, a Roma, per opera del Peruzzi). Un caso impressionante è quella, destinata a costituire una specie di eremitaggio quasi religioso, che introduce, nel Castello di Gaillon, una replica, notevolmente grandiosa, della Grotta della Maddalena alla Sainte-Baume. Ma anche l'Appennino del Giambologna e del Buontalenti a Pratolino serviva da eremitaggio con le sue due stanze interne, e forse analogamente la grotta di Boboli. Una linea intima e persistente unisce, attraverso diverse strutturazioni stilistiche, il medioevo all'età moderna proprio lungo questo motivo del giardino pittoresco. Il Petrarca, con le sue impressionanti testimonianze, dovette contribuire non poco, d'altronde, alla creazione del giardino rinascimentale, quando, addirittura, i suoi interventi non costituiscano esempi direttamente e largamente imitati. Se Cosimo de Medici o Pio II hanno letto le sue pagine (o Alberti le lesse e commentò per loro), l'idea, ad esempio, di un *hortus citerior* e di un *hortus ulterior* (come sono definiti i giardini petrarcheschi di Parma, e come potrebbero benissimo essere definiti quelli di Arquà), poté sembrare una perfetta anticipazione del nuovo concetto di villa come luogo esteticamente qualificato. Rustico e civile, confrontati, danno però luogo, come ha osservato sagacemente Elisabeth MacDougall,[24] al contrasto fra un giardino geometrizzato, formale ed un bosco o una selva lasciati o finti in condizioni naturali. Di questo arrangiamento una delle testimonianze sicure piú antiche è la Montagnola artificiale costruita da Borso d'Este negli anni 1470-80 presso il palazzo di San Giorgio a Ferrara. Si giungeva ad essa dopo aver attraversato un giardino regolare, e in contrasto con questo, essa appariva "senz'ordine piantata", ad alberi e vigne, ed era anzi preceduta, a mo' di quinta, da un boschetto piuttosto folto. Fra i suoi arredi c'era una grotta artificiale. Un ricordo ce n'è dato da un arazzo dossesco. Ma è piú che probabile che essa abbia anche ispirato i poeti di Ferrara, nei loro racconti di avventure cavalleresche ed amorose. Curiosamente, un'altra villa ferrarese, quella di Belvedere, in costruzione nel 1516, sorse in un'isola in mezzo al Po, forse ispirandosi a Marziale (*Epigrammi,* XII, 50), o al *Sogno di Polifilo.* Ora, non è tanto importante rintracciare questi episodi, che anticipano il sublime paesistico, quanto constatare, insieme ad Elisabeth MacDougall, che essi corrispondono ad una diversa, opposta interpretazione del rapporto fra uomo e natura, da un lato attivo e razionale, dall'altro passivo e mirante a realizzare, attraverso l'integrazione (magari artificiosa) e la contemplazione, una più diretta osmosi. I due processi, pur essendo antitetici, son correlati

24. Mi riferisco al saggio incluso negli atti del convegno citato, sul giardino italiano, a Dumbarton Oaks.

reciprocamente, e quindi considerati entrambi indispensabili ed urgenti. Ora il Petrarca non ha certamente esplorato per primo gole montane, o coltivato pomarii, ma è certo che è stato il primo ad associare sistematicamente sia nella pratica come nei viaggi e nel suo stesso sistema di vita, le due esperienze (sebbene nella seconda metà della sua vicenda egli rinneghi, considerandolo legato anche a particolari umori della giovinezza, il modo tenuto a Valchiusa e da esso ispirato). Inoltre è il primo che di tali esperienze dia un resoconto letterario, cioè le compia con un continuo metodo di autocontrollo, nulla lasciando all'intuito.

Prima di abbandonare la Valchiusa reale, bisogna commentare un'ultima espressione, con cui Petrarca la definisce, nella fondamentale lettera che stiamo citando a frammenti. "Hunc Elicona nostrum transalpinum vocitare soleo". Elicona è il monte delle muse, e letteralmente Valchiusa sarebbe il luogo, al di là delle Alpi, dove Petrarca trovò, o meglio esercitò, la sua ispirazione poetica. Ma abbiamo dell'Elicona una curiosa rappresentazione, a disegno, in un codice quattrocentesco dell'*Ovide moralisé* (77840 Ms. fr. 871 della Bibliothèque Nationale) ed in una sua variante nel Ms. 472 della Bibliothèque Municipale di Lione.[25] Su una delle due cime del monte regna, con la sua cetra, Apollo; Pegaso, con una zampa, fa scaturire il sacro fonte dalla roccia, e dove questo si unisce con un altro rivo, formando un fiume o un lago, troviamo immerse nell'acque come ninfe, quasi una moltiplicazione di Laura, le nove muse, che si rivolgono verso la regale Pallas, anch'essa incoronata. Rivali delle muse, su alcuni alberi, stanno le nove piche. Benché siano per ora attestati rapporti solo letterari ed

25. L'ambito di storia delle arti meglio studiato è appunto quello di Petrarca come mitografo, per opera dei maestri dell'iconologia, come Panofsky, in *Studies in Iconology* (Oxford University Press, 1939); in un articolo su Holbein e Tiziano nel *Burlington Magazine,* XLIX (1926), 177-81, rielaborato e incluso poi in *Meaning in the Visual Arts* (Garden City, N.Y., 1955); e ancora, con importante documentazione da manoscritti, in *Renaissance and Renascences in Western Art* (Uppsala, 1960): e come Jean Seznec, *La Survivance des dieux antiques,* Studies of the Warburg Institute, XI (Londra, 1940) e Edgar Wind, *Pagan Mysteries in the Renaissance* (2a ed. New York, 1968).

Petrarca, come mitografo, si assimila a Petrarca che moralizza la mitologia antica, e si introduce quindi a pieno diritto nella dinastia degli scrittori di emblemi, come uno dei capostipiti. Cfr. in proposito Don Cameron Allen, *Mysteriously Meant: The Rediscovery of Pagan Symbolism and Allegorical Interpretation in the Renaissance* (Baltimore e Londra, 1970), specialmente pp. 140 e 170; dove troviamo indicato come questa essenziale funzione fosse già stata riconosciuta nel 1878 da Gustav Koerting. Un tramite essenziale fra il Petrarca e l'iconografia posteriore è certamente costituito dalla moralizzazione d'Ovidio, compiuta fra l'altro da Pierre Bersuire ad Avignone verso il 1340, e che si valse, come fonte, dell'*Africa.* Ma mi par lecito presupporre che i testi descrittivi del Petrarca stesso abbiano determinato un piuttosto largo influsso anche sulle posteriori illustrazioni.

eruditi fra Petrarca e l'*Ovidio moralizzato,* è abbastanza notevole il rapporto fra il disegno di Valchiusa fatto dal poeta e questa illustrazione. Il monte, analogamente schematizzato secondo uno stile di rappresentare che è ancora medievale, ma modificato in base ai modi di Giotto e delle scuole italiane trecentesche, è un simbolo di ascensione spirituale; una cappella, cioè un simbolo religioso sostituisce, in Petrarca, l'irradiazione forse neoplatonica di Apollo come sole. La sorgente scaturisce in modo analogamente magico, ma la grande caverna, affascinante e paurosa, è sottolineata nello schizzo di Valchiusa. Al posto delle muse, per una interpretazione nuovamente religiosa, in senso ampio, abbiamo un simbolo di solitudine; un trampoliere, forse riferibile, vagamente, al pellicano che secondo Rabano Mauro, *Allegoriae in Sacram Scripturam,* "est quilibet eremita, ut in Psalmis 'Similis factus sum pelicano' id est, in solitudine ad instar illius avis commoratus" *(P.L.,* col. 1026). In altre parole, gli elementi, schematizzati, sono analoghi, l'organizzazione è la medesima, il significato, intenzionalmente, è trasformato. Ma Valchiusa, come Elicona, sembra rientrare in una precisa immagine; non è, in altre parole, una vaga occasionale metafora. Nell'*Ovidio moralizzato* c'è un'altra illustrazione, abbastanza emblematica, che potrebbe chiarire sia la *gloriette,* sorgente là dove le acque del lago sorgivo si riversano in rapide, sia il giardino, costruito con dispendio in mezzo alla Sorga: Orfeo, che col suo canto affascina gli animali, è analogamente rappresentato in un mandala naturale, cioè in un magico cerchio tracciato da un rio (figg. 4 e 5).

L'interesse per Valchiusa, nei visitatori del Cinquecento e di oggi, è probabilmente determinato più dall'associazione del luogo con l'itinerario amoroso del *Canzoniere,* che con le descrizioni, specializzate, in latino. Che ci sia nelle poesie italiane e amorose un rapporto fra ambiente naturale, tematica e linguaggio, è probabile, ma a noi ormai appare estremamente tenue e generico. Ci sono due modi di spiegare questo rapporto. Il primo, piú tradizionale, è di analizzare cos'è che sostanzialmente capita, a Valchiusa, accettando in senso lato che le poesie siano anche un diario. Il secondo è di vedere, attraverso un'analisi del glossario, quali elementi dello specifico paesaggio intervengano.

La prima strada è notevolmente inconcludente. L'episodio dell'innamorarsi di una donna scorta in primavera in una foresta (il *lucus* che funge da *locus amoenus*) era già un topos prima del Petrarca, ed è infatti svolto in identica maniera da svariati testi, fra cui mi sembra utile citare, in particolare, le *Jeu de la Fueillée* di Adam de la Halle, trattandosi di un testo teatrale che, pur essendo indirizzato ad un gruppo di amici, cioè d'intellettuali, per il fatto di essere recitato in palcoscenico, e per la presenza di episodi certamente popolari come la venuta delle fate, o popolareschi come la scena di osteria, sembra riferirsi, sopratutto, a situazioni ben note, cioè proprio a luoghi comuni poetici e narrativi. Qui l'innamoramento di Adam è così descritto:

Sí, fui preso (d'amore) al primo ribollire, nel piano della verde stagione e nella foga della giovinezza. . . . Era un'estate bella e chiara, dolce e verde e limpida e gioiosa, i canti d'uccelli la rendevano meravigliosa in un bosco profondo, presso una piccola sorgente scorrente su una ghiaia adorna di molteplici colori. È allora che mi venne la visione di quella che mi è oggi moglie e che, ora, mi sembra pallida e gialla. Era allora bianca e vermiglia, sorridente, amorosa e snella; oggi la vedo grassa e deforme, triste e brontolona.[26]

Qualsiasi sfondo pastorale è atto a svolgere il motivo dell'innamoramento, addirittura meglio che l'alquanto cupa ed austera Valchiusa. Lo stesso dicasi per il motivo, altrettanto tradizionale, del capo d'anno e della festa della primavera e di quello, che compare in talune poesie estremamente serene del contrasto amoroso, fra pastore e pastorella, tipo Robin e Marion. Nulla di nuovo, neppure, nella tensione fra irraggiungibile amore e desiderio, o altre volte nel lamentare che al momentaneo e troppo corto appagamento segua uno stacco definitivo. Il glossario, riferibile a scenografie paesaggistiche, che accompagna tali avvenimenti, non comporta analogamente alcuna specificità descrittiva.

Una fondamentale conseguenza del tema dell'innamoramento primaverile è la idealizzazione di quasi tutti gli attributi dello spettacolo naturale secondo le formule di cortesia, abbellimento, stilizzazione cosí ben raccolte, nel suo celebre saggio sul medioevo gotico, da Georg Weise. L'erbetta è verde, i rivi sono lucidi, freschi e snelli, il colle è fresco, ombroso, fiorito, l'aura è gentile, la neve sui monti è tenera, la contrada è soave. Laura è facilmente identificabile, per i suoi attributi, con la primavera, e come l'aria, cui s'assimila, è dolce e serena. Dove cammina, quasi come nel famoso dipinto di Botticelli—che certamente è nato in un momento di *revival,* dovuto a Poliziano e a Lorenzo de Medici, della simbologia floreale petrarchesca—, "intorno i fiori apre e rinova", e il prodigio si compie per una "virtú . . . che de le tenere piante sue par ch'esca". La sua libera peregrinazione attraverso il territorio (assai singolare in una società che teneva le donne chiuse, come schiave, nei palazzi) ha un significato cosmologico, di rinnovamento della stagione, ed è per questo che, invece di appassire, come normal-

26. Ritraduco da *Théâtre comique du Moyen-Age,* a cura di Claude-Alain Chevalier (Parigi, 1973), p. 90. *Le Jeu de la Feuillée* è il primo testo teatrale in volgare finora ritrovato, e data al 1276.

mente farebbero, i fiori sono vivificati dal suo passaggio:

Lieti fiori et felici, e ben nate erbe
che Madonna pensando premer sole;
piaggia ch'ascolti sue dolci parole
et del bel piede alcun vestigio serbe. (CLXII)

La sua veste si compone anche d'un "ceruleo lembo sparso di rose", e i capelli sciolti, come l'Alberti più tardi chiederà che fossero dipinti,

ella spargea sí dolcemente
e raccoglieva con sí leggiadri modi
che, ripensando, ancor trema la mente. (CLXXXVI)

L'associazione Laura-l'aura, assai felicemente caratterizzata da questa ultima immagine, è dunque assai piú che un *senhal* di origine provenzale. Petrarca è del tutto giustificato, al di là della finzione biografica, nell'omaggiare cosí Flora o Talia:

Qualunque erba o fior colgo
credo che nel terreno
aggia radice, ov'ella ebbe in costume
gir fra le piagge e'l fiume,
e talor farsi un seggio
fresco, fiorito e verde. (CXXV)

Su questo livello, inizialmente senza alcun contrasto, anzi con intime e spontanee correlazioni, s'inserisce un processo ancor piú generico di mitologizzazione classicheggiante del paesaggio agreste. Il tema predominante, all'inizio (ma con efficaci comparse anche tardive) è quello della ninfa della fonte, che immediatamente si trasforma in Diana. La fanciulla dei calzari colorati, in *Nimpha Vallis Clause* (1338), che cantando coglie fiori, ha un facile *pendant* nel madrigale, forse composto a Verona:

Non al suo amante piú Diana piacque
quando, per tal ventura, tutta ignuda
la vide in mezo delle gelide acque,
ch'a me la pastorella alpestra e cruda
posta a bagnar un legiadretto velo. . . . (LII)

Il senso d'ingenuo naturalismo che si accompagna a queste rievocazioni mitologiche è lo stesso delle illustrazioni che qui abbiamo riprodotto dall'*Ovide moralisé*. Lo conferma un'altra leggiadra vignetta, quella delle muse attorno ad Apollo, in una barca:

Dodici donne onestamente lasse
anzi dodici stelle, e 'n mezzo un sole,
vidi in una barchetta allegre e sole,
qual non so s'altra mai onde solcasse. (CCXXV)

È facile immaginarle nude, come Laura nell'Elicona.

Essendo cosí idealizzati sia il motivo classico che il suo sfondo, tranne la coincidenza, certo non secondaria, della fonte, nulla lega questa serie d'immagini a Valchiusa. Che, fra l'altro, quando è esplicitamente citata nelle rime, assume un carattere psicologicamente opposto, prevalentemente negativo, alquanto inconsueto, che è il terzo di questo elenco, e si allontana di una misura pari a quella della stilizzazione gotica dalla Valchiusa classica e perfino dal ritiro privato celebrato, ad esempio nell'epigramma "Vallis Clausa", come il luogo piú grato e piú atto agli studi, caro al poeta già nell'infanzia, coincidente con la sua gioventú per la sua amena serenità.[27] La ritroviamo, nelle rime, trasformata in questo modo:

Non è sterpo, né sasso in questi monti,
non ramo o fronda verde in queste piagge,
non fiore in queste valli o foglia d'erba,
stilla d'acqua non ven di queste fonti,
né fiere àn questi boschi sí selvagge,
che non sappian quanto è mia pena acerba. (CCLXXXVIII)

I colli diventano aspri, faticosi, il sentiero si fa erto, l'acqua della fonte gusta amara, la selva suggerisce col suo silenzio un solitario orrore, la salita è alpestra e dura, l'ambiente, i campi, sono deserti, il girovagare è senza fine, senza conforto, non s'interrompe neppure di notte. È estremamente significativa anche l'inversione di segno, rispetto a Laura ed al suo mito. Essa è a questo punto decisamente assente da Valchiusa,

27. Il simbolismo, totalmente conscio, è spiegato in una lunga serie di metafore nella lettera 2 del XI libro delle *Seniles:* "Sembrami dunque la vita nostra essere . . . deserto orribile, fangosa palude, spinosa valle, precipitosa rupe, tenebrosa spelonca, tana di belve, terreno sterile, campo pietroso, spinoso bosco . . . fonte di affanni, fiume di lagrime . . .". La categorizzazione simbolica che stiamo delineando è già chiaramente proposta da Isidoro da Siviglia: "amoena loca Varrius Flaccus dicta ait, eo quod solum amorem praestent, et ad se amandum alliciant. Varro, quod sine munere sunt, nec quidquam in his officii, quasi *amunia,* hoc est, sine fructu, unde nullus fructus exsolvitur". Il passo spiega benissimo l'associazione fra tematica erotica, *locus amoenus* e conseguente senso di colpa, meccanismo tipico del *Canzoniere* e della psicologia letteraria del poeta. Altre due definizioni di paesaggio sembrano adatte, particolarmente, ad una interpretazione moralistica di esso: "lucus est locus densis arboribus septus, sub lucem detrahens"; "Devia sunt loca secreta, et abdita, quasi extra viam". Cito dal libro XIV, cap. 8, 30, 31, 32, secondo l'edizione *S. Isidori Hispalensis Episcopi . . . Opera Omnia denuo correcta et aucta recensente* Faustino Arevalo . . . , tomus IV (Roma, 1801).

anzi il luogo sembra scelto proprio in quanto mai essa ci ha messo piede:

> In una valle chiusa d'ogn'intorno
> ch'è refrigerio de' sospir' miei lassi,
> giunsi sol con Amor, pensoso e tardo;
> ivi non donne, ma fontane e sassi,
> e l'imagine trovo di quel giorno
> che'l pensier mio figura, ovunque io sguardo. (CXVI)

In questa accezione, Valchiusa s'identifica addirittura con la foresta delle Ardenne (CLXXVI):

> Per mezz'i boschi inospiti e selvaggi
> onde vanno a gran rischio uomini ed arme . . .
> l'ho negli occhi; e veder seco parme
> donne e donzelle, e sono abeti e faggi.
> Parme d'udirla, udendo i rami e l'ore
> e le frondi, e gli augei lagnarsi, e l'acque
> mormorando fuggir per l'erba verde. . . .

Il Wilkins ha suggerito, in modo del tutto convincente, che la fonte per questa nuova interpretazione della natura sia l'elegia di Properzio "Haec certe deserta loca", il cui verso iniziale è quasi tradotto letteralmente in "solo e pensoso i piú deserti campi".[28] Isolamento e solitudine, accompagnati da sconforto ed orrore, deserti di sassi, rauche sorgenti, antri e grotte, diventano una specie di spontanea espansione della psicologia, mi si lasci dire penitenziale, dello scrittore. E bisogna, indubbiamente, aggiungere frequenti riferimenti biblici. "Passer mai solitario in alcun tetto" (CCXXVI) deriva dal Salmo CI, 8, "sicut passer solitarius in tecto"; l'immagine dell'uccello solitario, inclusa nel disegno, diventa un autoritratto profondamente sofferto, ed i rapporti fra questo modo espressivo e quello dei Salmi scritti da Petrarca stesso sono insistenti: "Di mia volontà abbandonai il retto cammino; e fui tratto in lungo e in largo per luoghi senza vie. Penetrai in ogni luogo aspro e inaccessibile; e dovunque fatica e affanni" (I); "La mia stanza divenga il mio purgatorio, e il mio lettuccio conosca le mie lacrime" (II); "le mie notti trascorrono nell'afflizione, e mi agitano con innumeri terrori. . . . Il mio sonno è turbato da varie illusioni, e non mi arreca riposo ma affanno" (V). "Mi son guardato attorno nella nebbia, ho seguito nella vita vie sbagliate e tortuose; e mi attraevano per la mia rovina" (VII). La connessione fra l'allegoria, che possiamo ben dire religiosa, e il paesaggio di

28. E. H. Wilkins, *The Making of the* Canzoniere *and Other Petrarchan Studies* (Roma, 1951), pp. 295-8.

Valchiusa ci è d'altronde fornita, con spiegazioni minute, dal Petrarca stesso, in un commento a Virgilio e in certo senso a Dante (*Seniles,* IV, 5):

E che altro son esse le cupe grotte, entro le quali i venti si rintanano, se non le ascose e recondite cavità de' nostri petti ove, secondo la dottrina platonica, han loro albergo le passioni? La mole sovraimposta indica il capo, che Platone stesso assegnò come sede alla ragione. . . . Nella Selva vedi l'immagine di questa vita: piena è d'errori, di tenebre, di strade tortuose ed incerte, e popolata di fiere, che è quanto dire ingombra di difficoltà e di pericoli, sterile, inospitale, ma pur talvolta lusinghiera allo sguardo de' passeggeri e degli abitanti, che tratti sono in inganno, e per poco ancor dilettati dal verdeggiar delle foglie, dal canto degli augelli, dal mormorio delle fonti, figure ed immagini della caduca speranza e dei piacere fugaci ed ingannevoli. Ma come piú t'inoltri inestricabile ed orrida si fa la boscaglia, che al sopravvenir dell'inverno tutta deserta, fangosa, attraversata da tronchi caduti, ed irta di brutte e disfrondate piante ti si dimostra. La Venere che in sul bel mezzo ti si fa incontro è la voluttà, che quando appunto siam presso al mezzo del cammin della vita più ci tenta e ci assale, e sembianze e vesti ha di vergine. E succinta descrivesi a denotare come veloce ella fugga. . . . Di cacciatrice ha la veste perché va d'anime a caccia.

Regno di Venere, in nome di quel rinnovato interesse per la mitologia di cui il Petrarca è raro esponente poetico, insieme a Jean de la Mote, Philippe de Vitry, Jean Campion,[29] regno di Diana o delle ninfe; quindi regno della voluttà travestita, in una reminiscenza assai precisa della foresta in cui Dante si sperde a metà della vita; Arcadia, paesaggio classico che sopraffà il millefiori gotico; e un cupo senso tragico che cancella l'uno e l'altro. Eppure nessuno dei tre livelli di lettura aderisce completamente con Valchiusa, tanto che, cessando la collazione generale di questi rapporti, uno sarebbe tentato di rifugiarsi in quegli interstizi in cui qualche data di cronaca sfugge al controllo intellettualistico ed alla censura come nella Canzone LXVI, il rigido inverno, con i fiumi quasi completamente ghiacciati, la neve sui monti, la descrizione (C) dell'esposizione della casa con una parete a tramontana, l'altra a mezzodí, l'annotare il rapido mutarsi delle ombre, secondo le ore del giorno, sulle opposte coste montane (XXXVII).

Ma sarebbe una scappatoia irriguardosa visto il metodo stesso usato dal Petrarca.[30] Le due categorie con cui egli intende lavorare (a giudicare dall'Orazione declamata sul Campidoglio) sono il "velamen figmento-

29. Cfr. E. Pognon, "Ballades Mythologiques de Jean de la Mote, Philippe de Vitry, Jean Campion", *Bibliothèque d'Humanisme et Renaissance* (1938), 385-417.

30. Mi sto servendo ampiamente del fondamentale saggio di E. H. Wilkins, "The Coronation of Petrarch", incluso come capitolo 2 in *The Making of the* Canzoniere *and other Petrarchan Studies,* cit. Il valore allegorico della buona poesia è ribadito

rum" e la laboriosità interpretativa. La prima riguarda il poeta, che deve rappresentare il vero, per dirla con Lattanzio, "obliquis figurationibus cum decore aliquo". Valchiusa può venire modificata, trascritta, schematizzata, ma, come ha acutamente appuntato il Wilkins sempre in base a Lattanzio, l'esperienza reale o plausibile del vero non può venire soppressa, altrimenti egli sarebbe "ineptus et mendax". La seconda categoria poetica riguarda il lettore e l'interprete, il quale secondo una tesi che diventerà carissima ai cultori dell'arguzia e degli emblemi, riterrebbe che "eo tamen dulcior fit poesis quo laboriosius quesita veritas magis atque inventa dulcescit". Non c'è alcuna ragione di credere che le poesie volgari debbano essere composte diversamente, e lette non simbolicamente. Eccoci quindi costretti a sovrapporre all'impressione ed alle "obliquae figurationes cum decore aliquo" del paesaggio o della vicenda erotica narrata, un processo euristico che si serve di fonti, come quelle classiche allora ben note e quindi meglio riconoscibili che oggi, e di riferimenti, morali o religiosi, cui siamo ancor meno propensi, ma che dovevano essere di immediato intendimento anche per la loro monotonia.

Il Petrarca, in altre parole, si vale di diversi codici, a volte compresenti, a volte successivi. Uno è quello provenzale, l'altro quello classico, il terzo quello morale. Ogni codice deforma, a causa del proprio vocabolario d'immagini e delle clausole compositive, lo spunto iniziale, sia questo sentimentale o paesistico, o come quasi sempre accade, una combinazione dei due. Ma togliere a Laura le treccie d'oro e la veste fiorita, o a Diana la nudità e dignità, equivale a distruggere una parte della personalità poetica della donna petrarchesca, come accadrebbe escludendo i fiori ed il verde, o le chiare e fresche acque della sorgente cara alle ninfe, per mantenerne solo l'orrida caverna, le aspre roccie, le impenetrabili selve. Una polifonia di significati è necessaria.

Bisognerebbe, a questo punto, aprire un altro capitolo circa i rapporti di Petrarca e la natura, cioè schedare, analogamente, il *Bucolicum Carmen,* cosí ricco di annotazioni cosmografiche, e dove la storia dell'umanità è narrata attraverso una sequela di catastrofi fisiche, come uragani, grandinate, siccità, alluvioni, pestilenze. Bisognerebbe inserire meglio Valchiusa nel quadro delle esperienze di viaggio e cartografiche di Petrarca. Ma la frustrazione, di cui parlavo all'inizio, aumenterebbe,

---

nel *De remediis,* ed. cit., L. I, *f.* 92v: "Cercare il vero è una fatica sola, ma questa è doppia, cioè cercare, et adornare, e fingere per dilettar gli orecchi è cosa difficile, grande, e faticosa, e per questo rarissima. I veri poeti studiano d'haver l'una, e l'altra parte, ma i comuni dispreggiando la prima, si contentan de gli adornamenti."

invece di diminuire. Il grande umanista, con una pedante onestà esegetica, quasi da commentatore di se stesso, ha lasciato una poetica elencazione dei suoi ingredienti naturali:

> Fonti, fiumi, montagne, boschi e sassi . . .
> Selve, sassi, campagne, fiumi e poggi . . .
> Fior', frondi, erbe, ombre, antri, onde, aure soavi.

Ma ha lasciato a noi di capire che cosa significassero per lui, e come di tutto ciò egli si sia servito.

I. A View of Vaucluse

11. A View of Vaucluse, from *Il Petrarca con l'Espositione di Alessandro Vellutello* . . . (Venezia, 1528)

III. Petrarch's Drawing of Vaucluse. From folio 143v, MS. Lat. 6802, Bibliothèque Nationale of Paris (Pliny codex)

IV. Mount Helicon. From f. 116^{v}, MS. fr. 871, Bibliothèque Nationale of Paris (*Ovide moralisé*)

V. Orpheus and the animals. From f. 196ᵛ, MS. fr. 871, Bibliothèque Nationale of Paris (*Ovide moralisé*)

XVII

MOURNERS OF PETRARCH

by Benjamin G. Kohl
Vassar College

Fame came early to Francesco Petrarca. As a youthful poet and promising scholar he had been recognized and patronized by some of the great of Avignonese society; in 1341 he received the poet's laurel on the Capitoline in Rome; and in his prime he became the critic of and advisor to an emperor, several popes, prelates, and ruling lords. In short, Petrarch knew the praises and esteem of his own and earlier generations, but, more importantly, even as an old man, he continued to merit the friendship and win the respect of many younger colleagues and admirers. Hence, when he died the loss was felt acutely not only by survivors from his own generation, notably Giovanni Boccaccio, but by many younger scholars and authors as well.

These mourners of Petrarch who composed letters of consolation for friends or commemorative poems at the humanist's demise were typically men whom he had come to know during the last decade of his life as he had passed it in Venice, Padua, Pavia, and, for the final five years, in the village of Arquà in the Euganean Hills.[1] These authors of the consolations and poems had known the distinguished humanist in a variety of ways—as his physician, his scribe, his closest living friend, an admiring young acquaintance, and a young Tuscan who as a papal curialist had once been his correspondent. The recipients of the letters were often closer friends than were their authors; they included Petrarch's own son-in-law, another of his Paduan medical doctors, a colleague from his Venetian days, and a brief acquaintance from a stay in Milan a decade before. But even these persons were relatively recent friends who had come to know Petrarch during his own middle age and to appreciate his genius long after his status as Italy's leading scholar, poet and author had been secured. As might be expected with a man who had lived to be nearly seventy, Petrarch's death was to be observed and lamented by those who knew him not as a close, lifelong friend, but as a revered figure—distant, reproving, paternal.

1. See the Appendix, where are listed the letters and poems treated in this paper, together with the more accessible editions of them. I have excluded from consideration several lives, letters, and poems written soon after Petrarch's death, but which were not strictly consolatory in intention or tone.

Petrarch's death during the night of the 18th of July 1374 provoked, then, a release of emotion and grief from men who respected the humanist, but who (with the exception of Boccaccio and the secretary Giovanni Malpaghini) did not know him intimately. As a result, these letters and poems more often tried to place Petrarch in the context of his age and record his greatness than they attempted to assuage the grief of the mourning recipients. From the very beginning, Petrarch's reputation was to have a bookish, learned, academic quality often purged of liveliness and verisimilitude.[2]

The first letter of consolation—a report on Petrarch's death—written on the 19th of July was, however, a rather direct and personal document. It was from the Paduan physician and scientist, Giovanni Dondi dall'Orologio (1318-1389) to a fellow medical doctor, Giovanni dall'Aquila. Giovanni Dondi was perhaps the most distinguished member of a well-known Paduan academic dynasty, himself famed for the invention of a unique planetary clock, the astrarium, as well as an acquaintance of Petrarch's during the five years prior to his death.[3] In fact, in June 1370 Giovanni had felt familiar enough to write Petrarch reproving his ascetic habits and recommending a less arduous daily regimen. To these suggestions, Petrarch, admitting his poor health, acceded in part, but, at the same time, he persisted in some of his old habits, including fasting, the eating of fruit, and his preference for water to the exclusion of wine. A further exchange of letters left both lines of argument stalemated, though the pair's sincere affection is apparent from the tone of the letters. Later in the summer of 1371, the report of Petrarch's improved health prompted another letter from Giovanni praising Petrarch's wise discussion and telling of family matters. On Petrarch's not infrequent trips to Padua, the humanist and his physician doubtless had several conversations, but no record of these remains.[4]

2. These letters and poems have not, of course, been completely absent in discussions of Petrarch's reputation. Among the more useful studies are: W. Handschin, *Francesco Petrarca als Gestalt der Historiographie* (Basel, 1964), pp. 4-17; M. S. Korelin, *Rannii ital'ianski gumanizm i ego istoriografiia* [early Italian Humanism and Its Historiography] (4 vols., 2nd edn., St. Petersburg, 1914), IV, 115-120; O. Bacci, *La critica letteraria dall'Antichità classica al Rinascimento* (Milan, 1910), pp. 195-99, 218-22, 228-30; E. Bonora, "Francesco Petrarca," in W. Binni, ed., *I classici italiani nella storia della critica,* vol. I (2nd edn., Florence, 1970), pp. 103-106.

3. On Giovanni Dondi's life and works, see A. Gloria, *Monumenti dell'Università di Padova (1318-1405),* 2 vols. (Padua, 1888), I, 381-86, and S. A. Bedini and F. R. Maddison, *Mechanical Universe, The Astrarium of Giovanni de' Dondi,* Trans. American Philosophical Society, n.s., 56, pt. 5 (1966), 11-17.

4. On these exchanges, see E. H. Wilkins, *Petrarch's Later Years* (Cambridge, Mass., 1959), pp. 194-96, 206-210. The first exchange is the *Epistolae Seniles*

The letter to Giovanni dall'Aquila begins, appropriately, with a report on the manner of Petrarch's death: the humanist had succumbed after a few hours of suffering to the same illness that had troubled him so often in his declining years.[5] Next, Giovanni noted Petrarch's standing as one of the few great men of his age and remarked his special devotion to Italy; further, he predicted that Petrarch's fame would endure not just for the present age but for a thousand years. In consolation, Giovanni urged his colleague to dwell upon the lively discussions and rewarding encounters he had had with Petrarch; thus, through the remembrance of these former happier times he could soften his present and future grief. Giovanni's letter was mainly an antidote for a grief that was characteristic of a friend who admired Petrarch as a person, but who had not much concern for his achievements as an author, poet, or philosopher.

Five days after Giovanni Dondi penned this letter, the great and near-great of north-eastern Italy gathered at Arquà to lay Petrarch's remains to rest. This distinguished group was headed by the humanist's last patron, the *signore* of Padua Francesco il Vecchio da Carrara, and it included the bishops of Padua, Vicenza, Verona, and Treviso as well as a throng of friends and admirers.[6] Petrarch's body was borne in a stately cortege by sixteen doctors of law and the funeral oration was pronounced by one of the poet's closest Paduan friends, the Augustinian friar Bonaventura Badoer. This orator was a fitting choice since during Petrarch's first visits to Padua he had met and formed a friendship with Bonaventura and his brother Bonsembiante, likewise an Augustinian monk.[7] In a letter written in the summer of 1367 to Donato Albanzani, Petrarch had spoken gratefully of the brothers' friendship and support during his encounter with his Averroist critics,[8] and during one of the

XII.1, XII.2, and the second is XIII.15, XIII.16. For the "Senile Letters" I have used the text in vol. II of Petrarch's *Opera omnia* (1554, rept. Amsterdam, 1969), with the aid of G. Fracassetti's Italian translation and notes, *Lettere senili* (2 vols., Florence, 1892). Giovanni's second letter to Petrarch is published in A. Zardo, *Il Petrarca e i Carraresi* (Milan, 1887), pp. 279-81, with discussion on pp. 105 ff.

5. The text is in Zardo, pp. 282-85, with discussion on pp. 225-26.

6. See G. and B. Gatari, *Cronaca Carrarese*, ed. A. Medin and G. Tolomei, in *Rerum Italicarum Scriptores*, n.e. XVII, pt. 1 (Bologna, 1910-1933), p. 138, and the account in M. F. Jerrold, *Francesco Petrarca, Poet and Humanist* (London, 1909), pp. 242-43.

7. On the Badoer brothers and Petrarch, G. Cracco, "Badoer, Bonaventura," *Dizionario Biografico degli Italiani* V (Rome, 1963), 103-106; U. Mariani, *Il Petrarca e gli agostiniani* (2nd edn., Rome, 1959), pp. 79-85; and Wilkins, *Later Years*, pp. 7, 172, 195.

8. *Seniles* VIII.6.

humanist's illnesses two years later, Bonaventura had loyally and frequently visited the infirm Petrarch. After Bonsembiante unexpectedly died soon thereafter, Petrarch comforted the surviving brother with a lengthy and heart-felt letter of condolence.[9] Less than five years later it became Bonaventura's sad duty to commemorate the passing of his famous friend.

Taking as his text the verse of Psalm 38: "My heart is troubled within me," Bonaventura lamented his own grief at Petrarch's death, but spent most of the oration in cataloguing the humanist's holy and noble character.[10] He noted Petrarch's Florentine origins, Roman laurels, and long service to the Paduan church. Further, he emphasized his saintly life, his purity, and his penchant for vigils and midnight prayers; he asserted that Petrarch had functioned as a theologian, orator, historian and poet, and that he had taught everyone how to cope with both favorable and adverse fortune in his *De remediis utriusque fortunae* (the only of Petrarch's works mentioned by name). Amid a plethora of Biblical quotations the friar concluded by underlining Petrarch's personal qualities, his uprightness and his propriety. Compared at times in the sermon with St. Paul, David, and even Christ, Petrarch was presented as an ideal Christian scholar and gentleman.

Among the crowd of mourners who heard this sermon may have been Petrarch's neurotic erstwhile copyist, Giovanni Malpaghini (1346-1412). Born in Ravenna and educated there at least partially in Donato Albanzani's school, Giovanni was introduced to Petrarch by his former teacher early in 1364 and was promptly taken into the humanist's household for the specific task of making a final copy of the "Familiar Letters." This Giovanni did in his neat, elegant hand much to Petrarch's pleasure and, then, he undertook to copy as well a final version of the *Canzoniere*.[11] But this faithful and expert service lasted for only three years. In 1367, tired of the exacting task of copying, Giovanni quarrelled with a bewildered Petrarch and—furnished with letters of introduction from his former master—went off to seek his fortune. The next year found Giovanni in Rome, and, by 1370, he was part of Francesco Bruni's entourage at the papal court in Avignon.[12] But in 1371, Giovanni da

9. *Seniles* XI.14; cf. Zardo, p. 96.

10. I have used the text in A. Solerti, *Le vite di Dante, Petrarca e Boccaccio scritte fino al secolo decimosesto,* Storia letteraria d'Italia, vol. IV, Appendice (Milan, 1904), pp. 273-74, where other editions are listed.

11. On Giovanni Malpaghini, see R. Sabbadini, *Giovanni da Ravenna, insigne figura d'umanista* (Como, 1924), pp. 241-47, and A. Foresti, *Aneddoti della vita di Francesco Petrarca* (Brescia, 1928), pp. 425-57.

12. I follow, mainly, Wilkins, *Later Years,* pp. 106-124, 145-50, 197-98.

Ravenna may have been a student in Padua; hence, it is possible that he was still in the vicinity and witnessed Petrarch's funeral at Arquà in the summer of 1374, though he was probably back at Avignon.[13]

In any case, some time not long after Petrarch's death, Giovanni composed a brief letter entitled "Conquestus de morte Petrarce," addressed to an unknown correspondent.[14] The letter begins with Giovanni's description of his special relation with Petrarch who had befriended and helped him, and, as the need arose, encouraged or reproved him. As a result of such a close relationship, his grief was natural and inevitable. Yet, quoting Cicero, Giovanni went on to assert that his tears were not only useless but even inappropriate since Petrarch, by his life and works, had surely earned immortality. Indeed, Petrarch was seen as superior to all his contemporaries and even to several ancient authors, namely Catullus, Propertius, Sedulius, Dares Phrygius, and Cresconius Corippus; with his fine style and sure use of language, he had "equalled or perhaps surpassed the dignity of Cicero and the power of Statius."[15] Further, Petrarch's abilities were equal to many tasks; his works possessed "the dignity of the epic poet, the charm of the comedian, the pleasantness of the lyric poet, the truth of the historian, and the accomplished turn of the phrase of the orator."[16] Finally, to these qualities, Petrarch added the ability to proffer good advice, expertise in contemporary affairs as well as in ancient history, and a capacity for friendship and memory. He was, in short, the greatest of the men of his time.

Appropriately, the only known letter of consolation to members of Petrarch's immediate family, the son-in-law Francescuolo da Brossano and the daughter Francesca, came from his most ardent admirer and closest surviving friend, Giovanni Boccaccio (1313-1375). Their personal friendship (begun in 1350) had been anticipated by several

13. Giovanni's exact whereabouts during the five years after 1370 remain a mystery. Against Sabbadini, p. 245, B. L. Ullman, *Studies in the Italian Renaissance* (Rome, 1955), pp. 209-13, has argued that Giovanni was at the papal court in Avignon during these years. But there was a Giovanni da Ravenna enrolled at the Paduan *Studium* in January 1371 (see Gloria, *Monumenti,* vol. II, 86), who could not have been Giovanni di Conversino and might have been Malpaghini, but he might have been, of course, a third Ravennate named Giovanni.

14. I think that Ullman, p. 211, has shown conclusively that the correspondent was not Coluccio Salutati as Foresti, pp. 449 ff., imagined. I follow this text, ibid., pp. 446-48.

15. Foresti, 448: "ut Ciceronis gravitatem et Statiani ponderis fulmen aut equiparaverit aut superaverit."

16. Ibid.: "Quicquid habet heroicus arduum, comicus lepidum, lyricus iocosum, historicus verum, orator maturum, ille sacris suarum litterarum monimentis inseruit."

youthful works of Boccaccio's including a letter written in praise of Petrarch in 1339, and introductions to four of Petrarch's *epistolae metricae* recorded in Boccaccio's *Zibaldone*. But his most important Petrarchan piece of these early years was the *De vita et moribus . . . Francisci Petracchi* written in 1349 and containing notes on the humanist's appearance and works as well as a brief biography. This was to remain a major contemporary evaluation, useful to Petrarch himself (after Boccaccio had presented him with a copy as a gift) in his own literary self-portrait.[17]

All these early tributes came to fruition for Boccaccio in the autumn of 1350 when (after the exchange of several letters) Petrarch stopped on his way to Rome as a guest of his younger admirer in Florence.[18] There the humanist first met the maniple of Florentine admirers which included several future friends, and there the most renowned literary friendship of the Trecento was born.

During the next quarter-century, the two authors became the most intimate of friends, an intimacy fostered by frequent visits, mutual criticism of their literary works, and a copious correspondence.[19] On a trip to Venice in the spring of 1367, Boccaccio even came to know Petrarch's daughter Francesca and her husband. After a final visit by Boccaccio to Petrarch in Padua in 1368, the two maintained contact only through correspondence which lasted until the humanist's last days. In a letter to Petrarch (now lost) written in 1373, Boccaccio praised his correspondent unstintingly; he averred that Petrarch was the equal of Virgil in poetry and of Cicero in prose. But in the same letter, he felt familiar enough to voice complaints that Petrarch passed too much time in the service of governments and too little devoted to his studies. In a reply which served as a covering letter for his Latin version of Boccaccio's "Griselda," Petrarch denied both charges and asserted rather that his embassies took but a few months of his entire life.[20] Boccaccio was never to receive this letter; and when Petrarch heard that it had not arrived, he penned in the late spring of 1373 what was to be his last letter to Boccaccio—a complaint on the difficulties

17. See E. H. Wilkins, "Boccaccio's Early Tributes to Petrarch," *Speculum*, 38 (1963), 79-87.

18. For a full account of their relationship, see Giuseppe Billanovich, *Petrarca Letterato, I. Lo scrittoio del Petrarca* (Rome, 1947), passim, and E. H. Wilkins, *Life of Petrarch* (Chicago, 1961), passim.

19. A convenient guide to their correspondence is E. H. Wilkins, "A Survey of the Correspondence Between Petrarch and Boccaccio," *Italia Medioevale e Umanistica*, 6 (1963), 179-84.

20. *Seniles* XVII.2.

of correspondence and a criticism of the men who caused them.[21] A little more than a year later, Boccaccio had from Francescuolo da Brossano word of Petrarch's death.

In response to the news, Boccaccio, ill and bedridden at Certaldo, expressed in what was to be his last letter condolences to the bereaved daughter and her husband. He began by recording his own profound grief at the news of Petrarch's death, felt not because of any danger to the humanist, "who had doubtless soared up into the presence of the eternal Father," but because of the great loss to Petrarch's many friends, to himself, and most bitterly, to the surviving members of the family.[22] At this point, Boccaccio directed the husband to see to the comforting of Francesca. Moved by his typical Florentine patriotism, Boccaccio lamented that Petrarch was buried in Arquà and not in his native city, but, if Petrarch had to be buried in the Euganean village, he asked Francescuolo to provide a fitting monument for his remains (an injunction that was carried out with the erection of the porphyry tomb five years later). Boccaccio, next, expressed the desire that Petrarch's works, though unfinished, be preserved from destruction. He understood that the disposition of Petrarch's property was in the hands of a board of lawyers (often men of little literary taste); therefore, he feared that the *Africa* and *I trionfi* would not escape harm. Asserting his love for Petrarch whom, he claimed, he had known for more than forty years, Boccaccio made clear his acceptance of the bequest in Petrarch's testament. In conclusion, he asked for copies of the last letters from Petrarch, of which he knew from Luigi Marsili but which had never reached him. Bemoaning his own poor health, evidenced by the fact that it required three days to compose so brief a letter, Boccaccio ended his consolations.

About this same time, Boccaccio authored a sonnet addressed to Petrarch in heaven.[23] There Petrarch had gone to be with his Laura and his friend Fiammetta, and, there seated with other poets—Dante, Cino da Pistoia, and Sennuccio del Bene, Petrarch is to pull up Boccaccio so that he might be reunited with his own beloved. Less than a year after he composed these lines, Boccaccio died.

Petrarch's death prompted other poetic inventions from less talented authors. Franco Sacchetti, who had already written a sonnet to

21. *Seniles* XVII.4.

22. Text in *Opere latine minori,* ed. A. Massera (Bari, 1928), pp. 222-27, quotation on p. 223.

23. Most conveniently, in Boccaccio, *Le Rime, l'Amorosa Visione, la Caccia di Diana,* ed. V. Branca (Bari, 1939), p. 74, with other edns. listed on pp. 320-22.

Petrarch during one of his last illnesses, now attempted a *canzone* on the theme of Petrarch in heaven.[24] The poem begins by stressing the humanist's virtues: his eloquence, his knowledge of languages and of antiquity, as well as his upright personal life. It then describes Petrarch as compared with ancient leaders and the fate of his philosophical enemies the Epicureans and Averroes in Hell. Sacchetti also treats the theme of Arquà as Petrarch's resting place so far from Florence and, in closing, expresses fear for the worthiness of his poem for so great a person. Another somewhat longer poem, "La pietosa fonte," by a member of the Carrara court in Padua, Zenone da Pistoia, treats of Petrarch's close relations with his last patrons, the Carrara family, but offers little more than political propaganda dressed in mythical garb.[25]

Perhaps the most extravagant praise offered at Petrarch's death came from a then obscure Florentine notary, Coluccio Salutati (1333-1406), who alone of all those who had written letters or poems, had for certain never met his subject. But Salutati had early in his life read several of Petrarch's works and he soon developed a reverence and attachment to the great figure. In 1368 Salutati's employment as an assistant on the staff of the Florentine Francesco Bruni in the papal Curia finally permitted a way to bring about a correspondence with the revered master. In a letter to Bruni, Petrarch had casually sent his greetings to Salutati, whom he knew only by name. The notary immediately replied with fulsome praise and an elaborate argument designed to induce Petrarch to join the Curia in Rome.[26] Petrarch answered promptly rejecting Salutati's invitation, reproving his extravagant praise, and averring that he had little time for future correspondence.[27] (In fact, Petrarch never wrote another letter to Salutati.) But spurred on even by this short reply, as well as perhaps by the sincere desire of Pope Urban V to have Petrarch in Rome, Salutati wrote four letters to Petrarch during the next eight months.[28] In them, he treated such topics as the poor reaction of the French cardinals to Petrarch's criticism of them and the Avignonese papacy, the rebuilding of Rome be-

24. Franco Sacchetti, *Il libro delle rime,* ed. A. Chiari (Bari, 1936), p. 110 for the sonnet and pp. 179-83 for the *canzone.*

25. The text is available in an edn. by F. Zambrini, Scelta di curiosità letterarie (Bologna, 1874), and the poem is discussed in N. Sapegno, *Il Trecento,* 3rd edn. (Milan, 1949), p. 134.

26. Salutati, *Epistolario,* ed. F. Novati (4 vols., Rome, 1891-1911), I, 61-62.

27. See the letter ibid., IV, 276-77.

28. Published ibid., I, 72-76, 80-84, 95-99. This correspondence has been discussed in A. von Martin, *Coluccio Salutati und das humanistische Lebensideal* (Leipzig, 1916), pp. 17-21, and Wilkins, *Later Years,* pp. 153-56, 165-74.

ing carried out under Urban, the crowded celebrations in Rome during Holy Week, and his concerns for Petrarch's health. These topics reveal an intensely admiring Salutati—a younger man who was a little unsure of his relations with a revered author, but one already implacable in his hatred of the Visconti and dedicated to the cause of bringing Petrarch to Rome.

Leaving Rome after two years in papal service, Salutati continued to think of his great compatriot and sought news of his doings,[29] his health, and, eventually, of his death.[30] By the middle of August, certain that the rumors were only too true, Salutati essayed a letter of consolation of an acquaintance of Petrarch's, Roberto Guidi, Count of Battifolle, and an evaluation of the humanist's achievements. Beginning with a conventional disclaimer of his own abilities and a sincere profession of his own grief, Salutati soon proceeded to the letter's central theme—Petrarch's place in the history of world literature.[31] In this fashion, Salutati emphasized Petrarch's eloquence and his function as advisor through his writings on moral philosophy and his letters. He also claimed for Petrarch greatness in comparison with the ancients; more especially, Petrarch surpassed Virgil in poetry and Cicero in prose. Hence, he had raised the culture of his own age to the level of antiquity. In this argument, Salutati provided a list of Petrarch's writings and brief characterizations of many of them, thus beginning the critical evaluation of Petrarch's literary achievements. In a second letter on Petrarch's death, this one to Benvenuto da Imola, Salutati continued and elaborated these arguments.[32] He observed that Petrarch merited divine grace by spurring men on to great achievements and for the pleasure afforded to the survivors by his great works. This thought leads Salutati to hope that his friends in Padua will strive to preserve Petrarch's poems and treatises and not destroy them or contaminate them with emendations. Rather, it is hoped that "this famous man shall, as I suppose, survive for posterity and that he shall shine eternally with the thousand lights of his works."[33] Hence, it was crucial to prevent the destruction of the *Africa* at Padua, and he even promised a journey to that city after Easter (which was not taken) to secure its preserva-

29. Cf. *Epistolario,* I, 120, letter of 27 Feb. 1369 to Gaspare Squaro de' Broaspini.

30. At the end of his letter to Benvenuto da Imola, ibid., I, 172.

31. Ibid., pp. 176-186; for Petrarch's relations with Guidi, see E. H. Wilkins, "Petrarch and Roberto di Battifolle," *Romanic Review,* 50 (1959), 3-8.

32. *Epistolario,* I, 199-201.

33. Ibid., 200: "ille celeberrimus, ut arbitror, transibit in posteros et mille operum suorum luminibus perpetuo relucebit."

tion. But later that year, Salutati did send letters and a Latin poem to Lombardo della Seta designed to fulfill that object—the preservation of Petrarch's epic.

Another letter of condolence written in late summer was from Giovanni di Conversino (or Conversini) da Ravenna (1343-1408) to one of Petrarch's closest friends from his Venetian period, Donato Albanzani (ante 1328—post 1411).[34] Like Malpaghini, this Giovanni da Ravenna had been a pupil of Donato's at his grammar school in the Adriatic city, and likewise had been introduced to Petrarch in Venice in the spring of 1364. But instead of seeking employment in the humanist's household, this young Ravennate had followed the itinerant life of a Goliard and, later, of a schoolmaster for most of the decade after this first meeting. Eventually the young teacher sought employment in Venice hoping for the good offices of his uncle and guardian, the Franciscan prelate Tommaso da Frignano. Disappointed in these expectations, Giovanni travelled to Strà on the Brenta and to Padua late in 1373, paid a Christmas visit to Petrarch at Arquà, and early the next year took up residence at Belluno as master of the grammar school. Six months later after hearing of Petrarch's death, Giovanni wrote a letter of consolation to his former teacher, Donato Albanzani, to be read by his uncle and other friends in Venice before it was sent on to Ravenna.

Studded with classical allusions and scriptural quotations, this letter was (more than Salutati's) a sincere effort to assuage the grief of a friend and to discuss Petrarch as a person rather than as a literary figure. Giovanni included no canon of Petrarch's writings and made but few references to specific works or accomplishments. This letter was a portrait of the life and habits of a saintly, much admired figure whose worldly renown was not so important as his moral qualities, his capacity for friendship, and his ability to improve others through advice and example. Much of the letter is employed in genuine condolences, in showing that Petrarch really dwells in heaven, and in proving that their tears and lamentations were, therefore, useless and ultimately misguided. Largely a Christian-Stoic tract on the powerlessness of death for the righteous and on the moral goodness of Petrarch, Giovanni's letter, more than any other contemporary response, sought to console the mourner through appeals to universal theological and philosophic

34. For a text of the letter and background to its composition, see B. G. Kohl and J. Day, "Giovanni Conversini's *Consolatio ad Donatum* on the Death of Petrarch," *Studies in the Renaissance,* 21 (1974). In my discussion of its contents, I have made use of James Day's as yet unpublished translation of the *Consolatio.*

truths and to present a lifelike portrait of a great and respected man.

Limited by the conventions of the late-medieval Christian *consolatoria* and treating a single, well-defined figure, the works composed at Petrarch's death showed a remarkable similarity in topics treated and in qualities observed. Deriving from their genre, the letters shared a common progression of argument: the author usually began by expressing his own grief and averring the need for fortitude, then, he often dwelt on Petrarch's fine moral and intellectual qualities, and, finally, he sometimes sought to place the humanist in the history of western culture and literature.

This range of topics permitted each author to describe Petrarch's personal qualities and to compare him with other great literary figures. Those who knew Petrarch well or had recently observed him (such as Badoer, Boccaccio, Giovanni Dondi, and Giovanni Conversini) stressed his fine personal habits, his penchant for prayer and fasting, and the seriousness with which he took his Christian faith. In addition to these observations, most remarked Petrarch's capacity for friendship and his willingness to help others through giving freely advice either directly or in letters. Many noticed his great intellectual abilities—his capacity for study, his prodigious memory, and his accomplished Latin style and elegant diction. Most mourners observed that Petrarch was one of the leaders of Italian culture and humane letters. The Florentine writers, including Boccaccio and Sacchetti, claimed him as a brilliant son of the Arno city. Conversely, Zenone da Pistoia saw him as an outstanding example of Paduan culture. Most noticed that he had become a friend and advisor to the great of his age, including an emperor, popes, and political leaders. Those who especially valued Petrarch's literary accomplishments were concerned that his works escape any premature destruction or contamination by literary executors. Both Salutati and Boccaccio expressed worry over the fate of Petrarch's unfinished epic, the *Africa,* and the latter wanted word of the text of *I trionfi* on which he had worked with Petrarch years before.[35]

But the most significant similarity of all these works was the attempt to compare Petrarch with great historical figures. Almost all expressed the belief that he was one of the great men of his age. A few with a strong religious orientation, such as the friar Badoer, compared Petrarch with the great figures of the Christian tradition, such as St. Paul or the Church fathers. But most mourners inevitably looked back to classical antiquity in seeking figures for comparison. Several writers,

35. On the literary cooperation between Petrarch and Boccaccio, see V. Branca, *Boccaccio medievale* (2nd edn., Florence, 1970), pp. 278 ff.

including Salutati and Giovanni Malpaghini, explicitly claimed that Petrarch was at least the equal of the greatest authors of the Roman world, including Cicero, Virgil, and Statius. Most, however, were content to view Petrarch as a commanding figure in the history of Latin literature without making any comparisons to past greats. On one thing all agreed: because of his works in poetry, philosophy, and the liberal arts, Petrarch would be known and esteemed by posterity. Never again would the appraisal of Petrarch's stature be so unanimously acknowledged. Future generations of critics would see Petrarch's achievement more variously.[36] But for a moment, these mourners were virtually of one mind on the nature of Petrarch's fame.

Appendix: Works Written Concerning Petrarch on the Occasion of His Death

Date, Author, and Work	Edition(s)
1374, July 19 Giovanni Dondi dall'Orologio, letter to Giovanni dall'Aquila.	Antonio Zardo, *Il Petrarca e i Carraresi* (Milan, 1887), pp. 282-285.
1374, July 24 Bonaventura Badoer, "Habitus in exequiis domini Francisci Petrarcae," funeral oration spoken at Arquà.	Angelo Solerti, *Le Vite di Dante, Petrarca e Boccaccio scritte fino al secolo decimosesto* (Milan, 1904), pp. 273-274, with a list of other edns.
1374, late summer Giovanni Malpaghini da Ravenna, "Conquestus de morte Petrarce."	R. Sabbadini, *Giovanni da Ravenna* (Como, 1924), pp. 248-249; A. Foresti, *Aneddoti della vita di Francesco Petrarca* (Brescia, 1928), pp. 446-448, with Italian translation.
1374, early November Giovanni Boccaccio, letter to Francescuolo da Brossano.	*Opere latine minori,* ed. A. Massera (Bari, 1928), pp. 222-227; *Lettere edite ed inedite di Giovanni Boccaccio,* ed. F. Corazzini (Bologna, 1877), pp. 377-384, with Italian translation on pp. 369-377; M. F. Jerrold, *Francesco Petrarca, Poet and Humanist* (London, 1909), pp. 242-246, partial English translation, complete in E. Hutton, *G. Boccaccio,* A Biographical Study (London, 1910), pp. 282-288.

36. Salutati himself began the changed view toward Petrarch's greatness; see R. P. Oliver, "Salutati's Criticism of Petrarch," *Italica,* 16 (1939), 49-57, and, for a general treatment of Petrarch's reputation, the work of W. Handschin cited in fn. 2 above.

1374, late Giovanni Boccaccio, sonnet: "Or sei salito, caro signor mio."	*Le Rime, l'Amorosa Visione, la Caccia di Diana,* ed. V. Branca (Bari, 1939), p. 74 with many other edns. listed on pp. 320-322; English translation in Jerrold, op. cit., pp. 246-247.
1374, late Franco Sacchetti, canzone: "Festa ne fa il cielo, piange la terra."	*Il Libro delle rime,* ed. A. Chiari (Bari, 1936), pp. 179-183, with other edns. listed on p. 464.
1374, early autumn Zenone da Pistoia, poem: "La Pietosa Fonte," dedicated to Francesco il Vecchio da Carrara.	Ed. F. Zambrini, Scelta di curiosità letterarie, no. 137 (Bologna, 1874); for variant readings, cf. Zardo, op. cit., pp. 239-241.
1374, August 16 Coluccio Salutati, letter to Roberto Guidi, Count of Battifolle.	*Epistolario,* ed. F. Novati (4 Vols., Rome, 1891-1911), Vol. I, 176-187; English translation in D. Thompson and A. F. Nagel, *The Three Crowns of Florence* (New York, 1972), pp. 3-13.
1375, March 24 Coluccio Salutati, letter to Benvenuto da Imola.	*Epistolario,* Vol. I, 198-201.
1374, late summer Giovanni Conversini da Ravenna, letter to Donato Albanzani.	B. G. Kohl and J. Day, "Giovanni Conversini's *Consolatio ad Donatum* on the Death of Petrarch," *Studies in the Renaissance,* 21 (1974), 9-30.

XVIII

PETRARCA, POGGIO, AND BIONDO: HUMANISM'S FOREMOST INTERPRETERS OF ROMAN RUINS*

Angelo Mazzocco
Northern Illinois University (De Kalb)

Never during her long history did Rome suffer greater physical and moral degradation than in the fourteenth and early fifteenth centuries. Deprived of her papal court and torn by schismatic rivalries and popular uprisings, Rome became one of the most barbaric cities in Europe. The literature of the time is almost unanimous in conveying the deplorable state of the Eternal City. In the third novella of the fifth day, Boccaccio speaks of a "Roma, la quale come è oggi coda, così già fu capo del mondo."[1] The distinguished scholar and papal secretary Pier Paolo Vergerio the Elder, writes the following upon his first exposure to the Holy City in 1398:

> Roma che fu d'ogni virtude hospitio,
> Maestra de juste arme e sante lege,
> Del mal ladron ora è speloncha e rege,
> Non disciplina, non rason, ma vitio.[2]

* This article is a slightly revised version of a paper delivered at the Italian session on the Middle Ages and the Renaissance during the annual meeting of the Modern Language Association in December, 1973.

The works of Petrarca, Poggio, and Biondo dealing with the Roman ruins have been the object of some speculation among contemporary scholars. H. Jordan, *Topographie der Stadt Rom im Alterthum* (2 vols., Berlin, 1878-1885), I; R. Valentini and G. Zucchetti, *Codice topografico della città di Roma* (4 vols., Rome, 1940-1953), IV; E. Mandowsky and C. Mitchell, *Pirro Ligorio's Roman Antiquities* (London: The Warburg Institute of the University of London, 1963); and Roberto Weiss, *The Renaissance Discovery of Classical Antiquity* (Oxford, 1969) have dealt with the antiquarian studies of these three humanists. All of these scholars, however, have emphasized the archeological accuracy of Petrarca, Poggio, and Biondo. My major concern shall be their emotional reaction to the ruins and the method utilized in studying them.

1. Giovanni Boccaccio, *Decameron,* ed. Vittore Branca (2 vols., Florence, 1960), II, 31.

2. Leonardo Smith, *Epistolario di Pier Paolo Vergerio* (Rome, 1934), p. 205.

Likewise, the chronicler Stefano Infessura gives a gruesome account of early-fifteenth-century Rome. According to Infessura the city was tormented by intrigues, brigandage and killing; its strategic points forever bedeviled by the decaying human flesh of political saboteurs and criminals.[3] No less a clever observer of fifteenth-century Italy than Vespasiano da Bisticci describes Rome as a desolate, poverty-stricken community, which upon the return of Pope Eugene IV in 1443, looked more like a provincial town than the capital of Christendom. Vespasiano writes: "Era tornata Roma, per l'assenza del papa, come una terra di vaccai: perché si tenevano le pecore e le vacche in sino dove sono oggi i banchi de' mercatanti; e tutti erano in capperone e in istivali, per essere istati tanti anni sanza la corte, e per le guerre avute."[4]

However intense the destruction and the squalor of fourteenth- and early-fifteenth-century Rome, the city never completely lost the memory of her classical grandeur. The numerous temples transformed into churches, and especially the great masses of ancient buildings—triumphal arches, theaters, columns, palaces—which could be seen towering over the abandoned spaces or standing up among the modern structures, were vivid reminders of antiquity's most formidable civilization. It was through these ruins that the humanists, well versed in classical literature and endowed with more effective methods of investigation, sought to unravel the mystery of the ancient world. It was through these ruins that they sought to comprehend the golden, martial, cosmopolitan Rome described in the works of Cicero, Varro, Virgil, Livy. As they observed the miserable state of these colossal structures, they meditated, philosophized, but above all longed for a day when contemporary Rome would once again rise to her classical splendor.[5]

As for every other intellectual activity of Renaissance humanism, the first important account of Roman ruins was provided by Francesco Petrarca.[6] None before Petrarca and few after him have equaled his

3. Stefano Infessura, *Diario della città di Roma,* ed. Oreste Tommasini (Rome, 1890).

4. Vespasiano da Bisticci, *Vite di uomini illustri del secolo XV,* eds. P. D'Ancona and E. Aeschlimann (Milan, 1951), p. 20.

5. The following are some of the most useful works on the state of fourteenth- and fifteenth-century Rome: Arturo Graf, *Roma nella memoria e nelle immaginazioni del medioevo* (Torino, 1882-1898); Ferdinand Gregorovius, *History of the City of Rome in the Middle Ages,* trans. Mrs. Gustavus W. Hamilton (New York, 1967), VI, VII; R. Lanciani, *Ancient Rome in the Light of Recent Discoveries* (New York, 1898); Ludwig Pastor, *The History of the Popes,* ed. F. I. Antrobus (London, 1938), I.

6. Prior, perhaps, to Petrarca, impetus to the study of the ancient ruins came from Cola di Rienzo, who probed and exploited classical inscriptions and authors

enthusiasm for the remains of ancient Rome. As tangible evidence of a cultural heritage whose grandeur knew no match, the Roman ruins possessed a profoundly emotive and inspiring force for the poet. His friend, Cardinal Giovanni Colonna, feared that Petrarca's exposure to the battered ruins would dim his fervor for the ancient city. However, while in the midst of his first visit to Rome (1337), the poet writes to Colonna that, if anything, his direct contact with the ruins had enhanced his admiration for classical Rome. Indeed, such had been the impact of those imposing structures on his spirit that he was unable to reveal his impressions of them: "Ab urbe Roma quid expectet, qui tam multa de montibus acceperit? Putabas me grande aliquid scripturum, cum Romam pervenissem. Ingens mihi forsan in posterum scribendi materia oblata est; in praesens nihil est quod inchoare ausim miraculo rerum tantarum et stuporis mole obrutus."[7]

In 1341 Petrarca made a second visit to Rome, to be crowned poet laureate on the Capitol. A few months after the completion of this visit he wrote a letter (*De rebus familiaribus,* VI, 2) to Giovanni Colonna di San Vito, whom he had visited in Rome, where he recalls their wandering through the ruins.[8] This letter constitutes the first antiquarian document of humanism. The poet recounts how he and his friend used to stroll in and around the city, encountering at each step something that would excite their imagination.[9] After much wandering, they would come to rest among the ruins of the Baths of Diocletian, often climbing to the top of the structure, where the air was pure, the view unobstructed and the silence complete. As they gazed at the broken walls and at the numerous ruins lying around them, they would forget ordinary everyday matters and concentrate on history, moral philosophy and the origin of the arts.[10]

for political ends. However, he left no written account of ancient remains. "Deh come e quanto era veloce leitore!" writes Cola's anonymous biographer, "moito usava Tito Livio, Seneca, e Tullio, e Balerio Massimo; moito li dilettava le magnificentie de Julio Cesari raccontare. Tutta die se speculava nelli intagli de marmo che iaccio intorno a Roma. Non c'era aitri che esso che sapessi leijere li antichi pitaffij. Tutte scritture antiche vulgarizzava; queste fegure de marmo iustamente interpretava. Deh come spesso dicia: 'Dove sono questi buoni Romani? dove ene loro summa Justitia? Poterame trovare in tiempo che questi fussiro!'" Alberto M. Ghisalberti, ed., *La vita di Cola di Rienzo* (Rome, 1928), pp. 3-4.

7. *De rebus familiaribus,* II, 14 in Giuseppe Fracassetti, *Francisci Petrarcae epistolae de rebus familiaribus et variae* (3 vols., Florence, 1859-1863), I, 134. Hereafter referred to as Fracassetti.

8. For the dating of this letter see E. H. Wilkins, "On Petrarch's *Ep. Fam.* VI, 2," *Speculum,* XXXVIII (1963), 620-622.

9. *De rebus familiaribus,* VI, 2 in Fracassetti, I, 311.

10. Ibid., pp. 314-315.

Petrarca's letter does not even come close to a reconstruction of the topography of ancient Rome. He mentions many monuments, but he does not describe them, nor does he indicate their location. He is not interested in the ruin per se, but in its power to evoke the great events of classical history. Hence, his letter is a potpourri of toponyms and historical remembrances. But worse yet from an archeological point of view, Petrarca's letter accepts some of the misconceptions of the *Mirabilia urbis Romae,* the most popular work on Roman topography in the Middle Ages. It agrees with the *Mirabilia,* for example, that the ashes of Julius Caesar are enclosed in the top of the Vatican obelisk and that the Pantheon had been dedicated to the goddess Cybele.[11] The letter also accepts the traditional view that the pyramid of Cestius was the tomb of Remus, when the inscriptions on it clearly indicated otherwise.[12]

Petrarca's less than brilliant accomplishment in the field of archeology is due, it seems, to a lack of confidence in archeological remains vis-à-vis literary sources as a means of historical evidence. The Roman ruins which had survived the onslaught of time were too battered to afford a conclusive reconstruction of Rome's magnificent past. In one of the dialogues of *De remediis utriusque fortunae* he writes: "Quaere in libris, invenies nomina. Quaere urbem totam, aut nihil invenies, aut perexigua tantorum operum vestigia."[13]

Despite its numerous shortcomings, the letter still remains a remarkable document. The letter's merit lies in Petrarca's great admiration for the classical remains. In fact, his objective was not to reconstruct the origin and meaning of the classical monuments, but to awaken in his contemporary Romans, through these monuments, an interest for ancient Rome. The magnificence of Roman civilization had just about been forgotten. Nowhere was this ignorance more severe than in Rome herself: "Nusquam minus Roma cognoscitur, quam Romae."[14] Should the Romans rediscover their ancient heritage, they would most certainly reacquire the classical virtues: "Quis enim dubitare potest, quin illico surrectura sit, si coeperit se Roma cognoscere?"[15]

The belief that the ruins could serve as an inspirational force and that their presence in Rome gave the city dignity and veneration, however deplorable its state, recurs throughout most of the Petrarchian literature

11. Ibid., p. 313.
12. Ibid., p. 311.
13. Francisci Petrarcae *De remediis utriusque fortunae* (Bern, 1605), I, 118, p. 350.
14. *De rebus familiaribus,* VI, 2 in Fracassetti, I, 314.
15. Ibid.

dealing with the Eternal City. Thus in the letters written in an attempt to lure the papal court to return to Rome, Petrarca argues that the numerous classical antiquities together with the Christian relics made of Rome Christendom's capital par excellence.[16] In the eighth book of the *Africa* (862-951) the ancient remains spur the poet to a vivid, resplendent, though not necessarily historically accurate, portrayal of the classical metropolis. In the letters to Cola di Rienzo and the Roman people,[17] but especially in the canzone 53, the ruins are seen as a powerful force which will stimulate the leaders to restore the city to its classical magnificence. In canzone 53 the poets writes:

> L'antiche mura ch'ancor teme et ama
> e trema 'l mondo, quando si rimembra
> del tempo andato e 'n dietro si rivolve,
> e i sassi dove fur chiuse le membra
> di ta' che non saranno senza fama
> se l'universo pria non si dissolve,
> e tutto quel ch'una ruina involve,
> per te spera saldar ogni suo vizio.
> O grandi Scipioni, o fedel Bruto,
> quanto v'aggrada, s'egli è ancor venuto
> romor là giù del ben locato offizio!
> Come cre' che Fabrizio
> si faccia lieto udendo la novella!
> E dice:—Roma mia sarà ancor bella.—[18]

Petrarca's admiration for the classical ruins exercised an enormous influence on Italian scholars of the fourteenth and fifteenth centuries. Giovanni Cavallini, Pier Paolo Vergerio the Elder, and possibly Giovanni Dondi wrote accounts of ancient remains under the Petrarchian spell.[19] However, for a novel interpretation of classical ruins we must go to Poggio Bracciolini, himself a connoisseur of Petrarca's antiquarian activities.[20]

All of Poggio's views on the ancient remains are contained in

16. See, among others, *De rebus familiaribus,* IX, 13; XV, 8; *Epistolae de rebus senilibus,* IX, 1; and *Invectiva contra eum qui maledixit Italiae.*

17. *Epistolae variae,* 48; *Epistolae sine titulo,* 4.

18. *Il Canzoniere,* ed. Dino Provenzal (Milan: Rizzoli, 1954), pp. 78-79.

19. For the influence of Petrarca on the antiquarian works of the humanists see *Codice topografico della città di Roma,* I. See also Mandowsky and Mitchell, *Pirro Ligorio's Roman Antiquities,* p. 8.

20. Poggio reproaches Petrarca for having mistaken the pyramid of Cestius for the tomb of Remus. *De varietate Fortunae* in *Codice topografico della città di Roma,* IV, 233.

Ruinarum urbis Romae descriptio. Conceived around 1431, this study later became part of the *Historiae de varietate Fortunae.* It was as part of the *De varietate Fortunae* that the treatise on Roman ruins was first published in 1448.[21] Much like Petrarca's letter, Poggio's *Descriptio* was prompted by the author's exposure to the ancient ruins. In the introduction to the treatise, Poggio notes that, shortly after the death of Pope Martin V, he and his friend Antonio Loschi climbed to the top of the Capitol to observe the numerous ruins lying in the surrounding area. The spectacular view of the many colossal structures surrounding them caused Loschi to grieve over the destruction of the mistress of the world. Rome, mother of illustrious senators, generals, emperors; Rome, example of every virtue; Rome, seat of the greatest empire known to history had disappeared forever. So complete was her destruction, so deplorable her appearance that one could justifiably change the famous Virgilian verse: "Aurea nunc, olim silvestribus horrida dumis" to read: "Aurea quondam, nunc squalida, spinetis vepribusque referta."[22] The observations of Loschi stimulated Poggio to give a description of the Roman ruins lest their memory would die forever.

Poggio was indeed qualified for such an undertaking. Besides being an accomplished latinist, the illustrious humanist was also a connoisseur of archeological remains, having compiled a substantial collection of classical inscriptions.[23] Unlike Petrarca, therefore, who relied solely on written sources, Poggio made use of both literary and archeological information. Indeed, he was the first humanist to blend archeology with philology in his study of the Roman ruins. The result is an account more detailed and more historically accurate than those of his predecessors. To be sure Poggio makes several errors—among other things he mistakes the Basilica of Constantine for the Templum Pacis, the Temple of Venus and Rome for that of Castor and Pollux[24]—nevertheless, his treatise is free of the medieval misconceptions which prevail in the letter of Petrarca. Throughout the work there is a genuine effort to penetrate the legendary aura which had enveloped the ancient ruins in the Middle Ages and redefine their original features.

21. Riccardo Fubini estimates that the *Descriptio* was written during the period 1424-1431. See Poggius Bracciolini, *Opera Omnia,* ed. R. Fubini (Torino, 1966), II, 499-500.

22. *Codice topografico della città di Roma,* IV, 230.

23. For an account of the epigraphic activities of Poggio, see G. B. De Rossi, "Le prime raccolte d'antiche iscrizioni compilate in Roma," *Giornale arcadico di scienze, lettere ed arti,* CXXVII (1852).

24. *Codice topografico della città di Roma,* IV, 234.

Poggio shares Petrarca's emotive and elegiac value for the classical remains. Their presence often spurs his imagination to relive the splendid world of antiquity. Thus the colossal structures of the Temple of Venus and Rome, which he mistakes for one of the meeting places of the Roman senate, cause him to hear the elegant and powerful orations of Crassus, Hortentius, and Cicero.[25] The discrepancy between the real and the imagined, that is to say between contemporary and classical Rome, greatly disturbs Poggio. Speaking of the Capitol, for example, he argues that it is odious that this hill, once the nerve center of the Empire, the stronghold of the entire world, where victorious generals ascended triumphantly, and where the spoils from many nations enriched its temples, should now be reduced to a receptacle of animal and human excrements with vineyards covering that very area where once stood the marble chairs of the senate.[26] Equally enraging to Poggio is the destruction of the ancient monuments, which at his time threatened to extirpate every vestige of antiquity. Hence, while describing the theaters he remarks: "Ingens pulcherrimumque omnium fuisse dicunt, quod est media fere urbe, ex lapide Tiburtino, opus Divi Vespasiani, *Coliseum* vulgo appellatum, atque ob stultitiam Romanorum, maiori ex parte ad calcem deletum."[27]

However novel the approach and accurate the narration of Poggio's work, his *Descriptio* remains basically inconclusive as an account of the physical aspect of classical Rome. Poggio's objective was not to reconstruct systematically the whole topography of the ancient metropolis, but to describe those aspects of classical Rome of which there still was physical evidence. For a complete reconstruction of the physical appearance of the ancient city we must turn to Poggio's curial colleague Biondo Flavio.

Like Petrarca and Poggio, Biondo nourished a profound admiration for the ancient relics. In a letter to Leonello D'Este written on November 13, 1444, he relates that while observing the many remains encountered between Via Latina and Via Appia, he had marveled at the imposing ruins of the Roman aqueducts, a truly extraordinary and incredible work: "certe insanum opus et illis, qui non aspexerunt, incredibile."[28] He had also been fascinated with the remains of the statues,

25. Ibid.
26. Ibid., p. 241.
27. Ibid., p. 238.
28. Bartolomeo Nogara, *Scritti inediti e rari di Biondo Flavio* (Rome, 1927), p. 155.

villas, and palaces abounding in the same area. Such was the beauty and the grandeur of these structures that one would almost be inclined to consider them the product of superhumans: "ut supra humanam potentiam fuisse videatur talia extruxisse."[29] It is understandable, Biondo goes on to say, that some had made the ridiculous mistake of attributing them to Virgil's magic: "quod quidem minus ridiculum facit errorem asserentium eas vias a Virgilio magicarum artium incantationibus fabricatas."[30]

It was this type of enthusiasm for the ancient remains which caused Biondo to write the *Roma instaurata,* a study of the topography of classical Rome. Begun shortly after Pope Eugene IV's return to Rome in 1443, the work was completed in 1446. The account of the ancient ruins described in the *Roma instaurata* was later complemented by the *Roma triumphans* (1453-1459), a study of the public and private life of the classical metropolis with occasional descriptions of those ancient remains previously overlooked by Biondo.

Even though Biondo cites neither Petrarca nor Poggio in his antiquarian works, the two scholars undoubtedly exercised some influence on his antiquarianism. Biondo was very familiar with Petrarca, having cited him copiously in his *Decades*[31] and having acknowledged him as the father of the modern era in his *Italia illustrata.*[32] It can be assumed, therefore, that Biondo was aware of Petrarca's antiquarian studies. In fact, it is very likely that the poet's enormous enthusiasm for antiquity served as a stimulus for Biondo's antiquarianism. The nature and the extent of Poggio's influence on Biondo is also a matter of conjecture. Since Poggio's *Descriptio* was published only in 1448, almost two years after the completion of the *Roma instaurata,* the question arises: who influenced whom? Riccardo Fubini argues that Biondo influenced Poggio. He maintains that the Florentine borrowed factual information from the *Roma instaurata.*[33] Though not disputing the possibility that Poggio may have utilized some of Biondo's facts for the final version of his study, I would contend, nevertheless, that Poggio did influence Biondo. If nothing else, he provided him with new techniques of research and with an intellectual atmosphere conducive to

29. Ibid.

30. Ibid.

31. Petrarca is cited primarily in the tenth book of the third decade.

32. *Italia illustrata,* pp. 346-347. All references to Biondo's major works—*Roma instaurata, Decades, Italia illustrata, Roma triumphans*—are to the 1531 Basel edition by Froben.

33. For Fubini's remarks see *Biondo Flavio* (Rome: Istituto della Enciclopedia Italiana, 1968), p. 16. Also in *Dizionario biografico degli italiani.*

the investigation of ancient ruins. It is inconceivable that a scholar as inquisitive and as interested in classical antiquities as Biondo would have been unaware of the antiquarian activities of his curial colleague.

Biondo shared Petrarca's conviction that the ruins were the most formidable reminders of the classical grandeur of Rome. In the introduction to the *Roma instaurata* he notes that the memory of the classical metropolis lived primarily through her remains. Should this memory disappear because of the total destruction of the ruins, the cultural influence of ancient Rome on the world would be severely curtailed.[34] But whereas for Petrarca the ruins were objects of inspiration for the fertile imagination of the poet, for Biondo they were objects of emulation. Through his assiduous investigation of antiquity, certainly the most thorough in his time, Biondo had become convinced that classical Rome excelled contemporary civilization in every aspect of architecture. The rugged and practical roads, the colossal and efficient aqueducts, the imposing and harmonious temples, the spacious and elegant villas, indeed the whole architectural apparatus of ancient Rome were testimony to an engineering genius unequaled in the history of the human race. The architecture of antiquity, therefore, should serve as an ideal, which contemporary society should strive to attain. For this imitation to be effective, however, it was important that the classical metropolis be recreated in its total splendor. Unlike Petrarca, therefore, who had provided a fragmentary and incoherent account of the ancient relics, and unlike Poggio, who had given only brief descriptions of the existing monuments, Biondo undertakes a systematic reconstruction of the entire architectural apparatus of classical Rome. The result is a detailed account of all the architectural characteristics—gates, obelisks, temples, theaters, private residences, roads, etc.—of the various quarters of the ancient city and of her numerous suburbs. Occasionally, in order to render the description more plausible, he fills it with the bustling, hectic flow of classical daily life. In the tenth book of the *Roma triumphans,* for example, the majestic buildings of the *Via Triumphalis* are blended with the numerous contingents of the triumphal march—festive soldiers, colorful religious sects, enchained slaves, exotic animals—to give the whole account a vivid, almost pictorial quality.[35]

Like Poggio, Biondo is deeply saddened by the sharp contrast between the magnificence of the past and the squalor of the present. Thus upon completing the description of the Capitol, the Palatine, and the Aventine he laments that these three hills which were once the pride

34. *Roma instaurata,* p. 222.
35. *Roma triumphans,* pp. 211-215.

of Rome had now been reduced to pasture as at the fabled time of Evander.[36] Biondo also shares Poggio's indignation for the destruction of the ancient remains. At one point in the *Roma instaurata* he complains that the systematic destruction of the classical ruins by selfish Romans had rendered his residence in Rome unbearable.[37]

Biondo's success in the study of antiquities is due, to a large degree, to his refined method of research. Even while he follows Poggio's example in making use of both philological and archeological sources, his utilization of the sources is more sophisticated and extensive than that of Poggio. Nothing escapes his attention, be it engraved images of ancient coins,[38] the inscriptions of recently uncovered ruins,[39] or marble carved figures.[40] He even goes so far as to consider the value of the popular nomenclature of ancient edifices and to gauge the significance of their building materials. The archeological information is collated with dozens of literary sources.[41] Whenever unable to identify a ruin because of lack of information, he admits candidly that its identity must remain unknown. However, he hopes that future scholars will clarify whatever he has been forced to leave in obscurity.[42] Biondo's antiquarian works, therefore, are not only formidable renditions of classical civilization, but also monuments of humanist scholarship.[43] With Biondo the study of ancient remains comes of age. His *Roma instaurata,* although widely imitated, remained the undisputed manual on Roman ruins for over a hundred years.[44]

36. *Roma instaurata,* pp. 235-236.
37. Ibid., p. 262.
38. Ibid., p. 248.
39. Ibid., p. 258; *Roma triumphans,* p. 213.
40. *Roma triumphans,* p. 215.
41. The most recurrent classical author in Biondo's antiquarian works is Cicero. Other classical authors used extensively are Livy, Varro, Virgil, Ovid, *Scriptores Historiae Augustae,* Pliny the Elder, Pliny the Younger, Tacitus, Suetonius, Pompeius Festus, Aulus Gellius, Macrobius, and the *Digest.* Biondo also makes great use of Christian and medieval sources, such as St. Augustine, St. Jerome, Eusebius, Lactantius, St. Ambrose, Paulus Orosius, Paulus Diaconus, Gregory the Great, Cassiodorus, Bede, *Acta Martyrorum,* and the *Liber Pontificalis.*
42. See especially the conclusion of the *Roma instaurata,* pp. 270-271.
43. Speaking of the *Roma triumphans,* the distinguished student of Biondo, Bartolomeo Nogara observes: "A dare un'idea dell'immensità del lavoro compiuto dal B. basterebbe anche l'elenco degli autori e delle opere citate nel corso dell'opera, autori e opere che formerebbero pure uno *specimen* interessante della cultura storica e filologica dell'Italia verso la metà del Quattrocento," *Scritti inediti e rari di Biondo Flavio,* op. cit., p. clv.
44. The *Roma instaurata* remained unchallenged until the publication of the second edition of Marliani's handbook on Roman topography in 1544. Some of the most important imitations of the *Roma instaurata* are *De urbe Roma* (about

In Petrarca, Poggio, and Biondo, then, we have humanism's foremost interpreters of Roman ruins. Their works went on to become the primary sources on Roman antiquities in Italy and abroad, inspiring many a writer to veneration for the Roman relics and for the civilization which produced them. In a letter to Biondo written after reading the *Roma instaurata,* the distinguished Genoese historian Giacomo Bracelli notes that he had acquired such a vivid view of the various sectors and monuments of Rome that he would be able to discuss them with Roman citizens, even though he had never set foot in the region of Latium.[45] The poet Giovanni Vitali hails Biondo as the second founder of Rome, whose antiquarian works would perpetuate the city's glory and fame.[46]

Perhaps even more important than the influence exercised on the literary circles, is the impact which the antiquarian works of these three humanists had on the architecture of Renaissance Rome. As Petrarca had predicted, these works did indeed function as a major force in the revival of antiquity. Inspired by their descriptions, artists from all over Italy began to probe the forms, proportions and measurements of the classical monuments in order to capture their pristine beauty and aesthetic effect.[47] Their knowledge was utilized for the embellishment of the Eternal City, making it possible for Rome to embark on a second Augustan age. In the fourteenth century Petrarca had remarked: "Roma mia sarà ancor bella"; in the sixteenth century Rome would rise to a splendor which even such a daring visionary as Petrarca could not have anticipated.

1495) by Bernardo Rucellai, *Commentaria urbana* (1506) by Raffaele Maffei, and the *Antiquitates Urbis* (1527) by Andrea Fulvio.

45. C. Braggio, "Giacomo Bracelli e l'umanesimo dei liguri al suo tempo," in *Atti della Società ligure di Storia Patria,* XXIII (1890), 288-289.

46. Paolo Giovio, *Elogia veris clarorum virorum imaginibus apposita, quae in Museo Ioviano Comi spectantur* (Venice, 1546), p. 12.

47. The following are some of the most prominent scholars who probed the Roman ruins for artistic and aesthetic purposes: Leon Battista Alberti (*Descriptio urbis Romae*), Brunelleschi, Donatello, Raffaello, and Pirro Ligorio (*Le antichità di Roma*).

XIX

FRAUNCEYS PETRAK AND THE *LOGYK* OF CHAUCER'S CLERK

by Jerome Taylor
University of Wisconsin (Madison)

At first sight, it may strike one as odd that Chaucer should have chosen to make his Clerk of Oxenford, on the one hand, a long-time student of logic and devotee of Aristotle and his philosophy, and, on the other hand, a one-time student and devotee of Petrarch, who, from early till late in his life, was a consistent critic of scholastic logic, of self-styled Aristotelians, and, within limits, of Aristotle himself. Chaucer's Clerk, in the flush of his devotion to logic and to Aristotle's philosophy,[1] is presented not as one who has escaped from, or forgiven, Petrarch's outspoken criticisms of dialecticians and Aristotelians, but as one who remembers and praises the laureate poet's sweet rhetoric for having illumined all Italy no less than had the writings of Giovanni da Legnano, professor at the University of Bologna, in law, philosophy, and natural science.[2] It may seem a crowning inconsistency that Chaucer's

1. Chaucer describes him thus in the General Prologue to *The Canterbury Tales,* I(A), 285-308 (all citations of Chaucer's text taken from F. N. Robinson, ed., *The Works of Geoffrey Chaucer,* 2nd edition [Boston: Houghton Mifflin Company, 1957]):

> A CLERK ther was of Oxenford also,
> That unto logyk hadde longe ygo.
> . . . hym was levere have at his beddes heed
> Twenty bookes, clad in blak or reed,
> Of Aristotle and his philosophie,
> Than robes riche, or fithele, or gay sautrie.
> But al be that he was a philosophre,
> Yet hadde he but litel gold in cofre;
> But al that he myghte of his freendes hente,
> On bookes and on lernynge he it spente,
> And bisily gan for the soules preye
> Of hem that yaf hym wherwith to scoleye.
> Of studie took he moost cure and moost heede.
> Noght o word spak he moore than was neede,
> And that was seyd in forme and reverence,
> And short and quyk and ful of hy sentence;
> Sownynge in moral vertu was his speche,
> And gladly wolde he lerne and gladly teche.

2. *CT,* IV(E), 26-35. Says the Clerk:

> I wol yow telle a tale which that I

Clerk, this adept in logic, when confronted with the Wife of Bath's propositions about multiple marriage, the use of genitals, the advantages of lying and of aggressive volubility in marital disputes, her misapplied and misinterpreted Scriptural authorities, the kind of grace available at vigils and on pilgrimages and at miracle plays, the proper supine position of husbands under wives' purgative rods, the male chauvinism of clerks, and ways in which even old hags can put idealizations of poverty, low birth, and old age to good use, is made to select for his logician's rebuttal not one single touch of dialectical dispute or syllogistic reasoning, not even a rationalistic allegory, but only the tropological parable into which Petrarch had converted Boccaccio's hundredth tale of the *Decameron*—the tale of the patient Griselda.

To be sure, Petrarch's tale saves the Clerk from speechlessness before the Wife of Bath, but the tale patently contains no passages of abstract reasoning, is no vehicle for Aristotelian philosophy, not even Aristotelian ethics, and is generally considered a masterpiece of illogicality as fiction.[3] The obvious fact, as Severs has so well shown in his

---

Lerned at Padowe of a worthy clerk,
As preved by his wordes and his werk.
He is now deed and nayled in his cheste,
I prey to God so yeve his soule reste!
  Fraunceys Petrak, the lauriat poete,
Highte this clerk, whos rethorike sweete
Enlumyned al Ytaille of poetrie,
As Lynyan dide of philosophie,
Or lawe, or oother art particuler. . . .

On Giovanni da Legnano (or Lignaco) and his works, see Robinson, p. 700, n. 34. Chaucer's "art particuler" may refer to natural philosophy, or *physica,* which develops general laws from the concrete particulars of the natural world. Giovanni da Legnano, or "Lynyan," appears to have written on astronomy as well as on law, ethics, and theology.

3. See, for example, James Sledd, "The *Clerk's Tale:* The Monsters and the Critics," *Modern Philology,* LI (1953-54), 73-82; reprinted in Richard J. Schoeck and Jerome Taylor, eds., *Chaucer Criticism,* I: *The Canterbury Tales* (Notre Dame, Ind.: University of Notre Dame Press, 1960), 160-74. Professor Sledd reviews the efforts of Kittredge, D. D. Griffith, W. A. Cate, J. Burke Severs, and T. R. Lounsbury to deal with what they regard as the immorality and improbability of characters and action and who, by assuming "the standards of realistic fiction," find the story "peculiar, contradictory, and irrational." Sledd, attempting what he calls a "simple narrative analysis," is nonetheless led to say: "It is far from a perfect tale, as I would be the last to deny. . . . It has been suggested that Chaucer himself had some reservations about his story, and one might guess that his attitude toward it was somewhat mixed." Cf. William R. Crawford, *Bibliography of Chaucer: 1954-63* (Seattle: University of Washington Press, 1967), who, in his "Introduction: New Directions in Chaucer Criticism," p. xv, observes that if "realism" is taken as the hallmark of Chaucer's poetic

book-length study of the tale,[4] is that Chaucer's version is all but totally and completely Petrarch's; Chaucer adds or omits here and there, to be sure, partly relying on an anonymous French translation of Petrarch and partly guided by his own invention: but even his "improvements" prove Petrarchan in quality. As I hope to show, however, on closer inspection of Petrarch's views of logic and of Aristotle and his philosophy, Chaucer's Clerk, even in his "logyk," is as Petrarchan as his tale. Chaucer, then, through his Clerk, stands forth as the first great English poet who, as a younger contemporary of Petrarch, projects in his own art such

---

and forms the basis of criticism, one will be led to value his poetry "more highly for his 'observations' of human nature (his psychological insight into character) than for his ability to make character serve the interest of a larger narrative design. . . . When the critic is faced, as he is in the 'Clerk's Tale,' with a poem in which there is no observable connection between literary character and psychological reality, he is forced to condemn the story in which the characters appear as 'in no way consonant with the truth of life.'" The last phrase is cited from Lounsbury and also appears in Sledd's article. Recent attempts to deal with Chaucer's Clerk and his tale have argued that the tale shows the Clerk to be torn by "moral ambivalence," a man unable "to separate seed from chaff, good from evil," disturbed about "the discrepancy between the real and the ideal," one who "breathed an atmosphere charged with individualism and revolt" of which Oxford was a center, who "leaned toward nominalism," "was conducting a debate within himself," that "the message of Christian parable is by no means the full meaning of any of [Chaucer's] writing, certainly not of the tale of Griselda," that the tale contains "the roots of secularism," that the tale "is really less about marriage than the Clerk's own intellectual predicament," that the Clerk in his present state "has no chance of engaging in meaningful action that is both honest and assertive" but is infected with "moral paralysis of the will," that the tale represents "the characteristic professional sentimentality of the committed celibate, combined with the overwrought learnedness-without-penetration of a bright but unseasoned graduate student" and drains "the emotional reservoir left in the Clerk's own consciousness," that "Chaucer's modifications of the story are mainly directed toward making the Clerk formulate the 'monstrous' trial of Griselda in terms of the scholastic theory of motion," that the Clerk is saturated "with a clerkly ideolect which could only define psychological realities in logical or geometrical terms," and the like. Articles from which this pastiche is taken are: J. Mitchell Morse, "The Philosophy of the Clerk of Oxenford," *Modern Language Quarterly,* XIX (1958), 3-20; Patrick Morrow, "The Ambivalence of Truth: Chaucer's 'Clerkes Tale,'" *Bucknell Review,* XVI (1968), 74-90; Joseph E. Grennen, "Science and Sensibility in Chaucer's Clerk," *The Chaucer Review,* VI (1971), 81-93; Dolores Warwick Frese, "Chaucer's *Clerk's Tale:* The Monsters and the Critics Reconsidered," *The Chaucer Review,* VIII (1973), 133-45; and other articles cited in these. Misreadings of the Clerk's Tale as literal fiction continue. Better understanding of Petrarch and of Chaucer's closeness to him in thought and method, as this article seeks to explore these, may remove the source of such misreading.

4. J. Burke Severs, *The Literary Relationships of Chaucer's* Clerkes Tale (New Haven: Yale University Press, 1942).

views on philosophy, logic, poetry, and moral persuasion as Petrarch may be found to express directly.

Petrarch's detestation of dialecticians and his dislike of self-styled Aristotelians were expressed early in his life, continued throughout it, became notorious by the end of it, and can hardly have been soon forgotten after he was "deed and nayled in his cheste,"[5] as Chaucer has his Clerk ruefully report him to be. As early as 1335, in a letter to Tommaso Caloria, who had studied with him at Bologna a decade before, Petrarch expresses his contempt for what he calls "dialectical cavilers" or quibblers: "Who does not laugh at the insignificant little conclusions in which these highly educated people fatigue themselves and others," he asks. "They waste their whole lives in such conclusions, since they are not good for anything else and especially destructive in this particular case." He cites Cicero and Seneca against dialectical syllogisms and gives an example of a false syllogism which a "quarrelsome dialectic debater" uses to attack Diogenes: " 'What I am you are not,' [the contentious debater] began. When Diogenes admitted this statement, he went on: 'But I am a man.' When Diogenes did not deny this either, the caviler smuggled in the conclusion: 'Thus you are not a man.' It was then that Diogenes replied: 'This is a wrong conclusion, and if you want it to become right, you must [reverse the subject of the first proposition and] start with me.' "[6]

In the same letter Petrarch warns against spending much time on the study of dialectic:

> I know that [dialectic] is one of the liberal arts and a stepping-stone for those who want to rise to higher grades. It is not a useless weapon in the hands of those who try to find a way through the thickets of philosophy. It sharpens the intellect, marks off the path toward truth, and teaches how to avoid fallacies. If it does not achieve anything else, it certainly gives a man a ready wit and makes him most resourceful. All this I do not deny. But where we pass with honor, we do not stay with praise. A wayfarer who forgets the goal he has set to himself because the road is so pleasant is not of sound mind. . . . Occupation with dialectic may cover part of this road; it ought never to be the goal.[7]

5. *CT*, IV(E), 29; quoted above, fn. 2. Further quotations from Chaucer's *Canterbury Tales* will be accompanied by citations from fragment number and line number only, and these will appear in the text, directly after the quotation.

6. Quoted from the translation by Hans Nachod in Ernst Cassirer, Paul Oskar Kristeller, and John Herman Randall, Jr., eds., *The Renaissance Philosophy of Man* (Chicago: The University of Chicago Press, 1948), pp. 136-37; bracketed phrase added. Original in V. Rossi, ed., *Le Familiari,* I (Florence: Sansoni, 1933), 35-38.

7. Ibid., pp. 137-38.

We would make a singular error of interpretation if we were to suppose that Chaucer's Clerk, who "unto logyk hadde longe ygo," was such a malingering wayfarer, or that he had wasted his life in "insignificant little conclusions," or that he had failed to acquire a ready and resourceful wit, as quick as Diogenes in recognizing and responding to sophistry. Neither can we confidently equate him with that host of dialectical quibblers who, as Petrarch learned from Tommaso, were then swarming over England and of whom he wrote:

I did not know that a new kind of monster had arrived there, armed with double-edged enthymemes, a gang more insolent than the wild breakers on the shore of Taormina. One thing I had not noticed before you brought it to my attention: They shield their sect with the splendid name of Aristotelians and pretend that Aristotle was wont to discuss in their manner. It is a kind of excuse to stick to the footsteps of famous leaders. . . . But they are mistaken: Aristotle, who was a man of fervent spirits, discussed problems of the highest order and wrote about them. . . . No greater contrast can be imagined than that between this great philosopher and a man who does not write anything, understands but little, and shouts much and without consequence.[8]

That Chaucer's Clerk is not to be equated with these English "monsters," nor his "logyk" with their insolence, may be determined in part from the comprehensive extension assigned to the Latin term *logica* throughout the Middle Ages, thanks to the Platonic and the Aristotelian divisions of philosophy reported by Augustine and Boethius respectively, and to interpretations and conflations of these by medieval commentators and philosophers. In *The City of God,* VIII, 4, and XI, 25, Augustine describes Plato's tripartite division of philosophy into *physica* or the study of the natures of things, *ethica* or the moral sciences, and *logica* or all sciences of word and reason, the *artes sermocinales* or *eloquentia,* which the Greek word *logos* properly comprehends. Boethius, in his second Commentary on Porphyry's Introduction to Aristotle's Categories,[9] delivers Aristotle's bipartite division of philosophy into the theoretical and the practical sciences—the former including metaphysics or theology, mathematics, and natural philosophy, and the latter including politics, domestic economy, and personal ethics; but to this bipartite division

8. Ibid., pp. 135-36.

9. *Commentaria in Porphyrium a se translatum,* in J. P. Migne, ed., *Patrologiae cursus completus; series latina,* XLIV, 71-158; see esp. 73B-75A; also in *Corpus scriptorum ecclesiasticorum latinorum,* XLVIII, 138-43. For succinct but detailed summary of the Platonic and Aristotelian divisions of philosophy from Augustine and Boethius on, see Jerome Taylor, *The Didascalicon of Hugh of St. Victor: A Medieval Guide to the Arts* (New York: Columbia University Press, 1961), pp. 3-19, and pp. 161-62, fn. 21.

Boethius here adds logic, which he identifies both as an instrument of all the other sciences, including ethics, and as itself a part of philosophy.[10]

Scholarly discussion of the medieval divisions of philosophy in relation to medieval poetry has been accumulating in recent years,[11] but one twelfth-century figure, Domingo González, or Gundissalinus, the Toledo translator, deserves fuller attention than he has received in such discussions, and such attention is appropriate here. Six points from his *De divisione philosophiae*[12] will provide historical perspective for what will subsequently be quoted from Petrarch regarding the kind of "demonstration" necessary for effective moral instruction, and said of the demonstrative "logyk" of Chaucer's Clerk. The following points are partly translated, partly summarized:

(1) Since knowledge of whatever exists is alone insufficient for attaining future felicity unless it be followed by knowledge of doing what is good, theoretical science must be accompanied by practical science, which is of three kinds: The first is knowledge of how to conduct one's relations with all men. Necessary for this are grammar, poetics, rhetoric, and knowledge of secular laws, in which resides knowledge of how cities are ruled and what the obligations of citizens are. These constitute political science, or what Tully calls the *civilis ratio*. The second is knowledge of how to manage one's own home and family, or how a man should live with his wife and children and domestics, and this is called *ordinacio familiaris*. The third is knowledge through which a person recognizes how to arrange and order his conduct according to what is fit for his soul, that is, how to remain incorrupt and useful in his behavior . . . so that all may be well with him and in no way at variance with himself.[13]

10. See texts cited in fn. 9, above.

11. See, e.g., Richard McKeon, "Poetry and Philosophy in the Twelfth Century: The Renaissance of Rhetoric," in R. S. Crane, ed., *Critics and Criticism: Ancient and Modern* (Chicago: The University of Chicago Press, 1952), pp. 297-318, and, for a recent book-length study, Winthrop Wetherbee, *Platonism and Poetry in the Twelfth Century* (Princeton: Princeton University Press, 1972).

12. Ludwig Baur, ed., *Dominicus Gundissalinus: De divisione philosophiae*, in Clemens Baeumker and Georg Freih. von Hertling, eds., *Beiträge zur Geschichte der Philosophie des Mittelalters,* Band IV, Heft 2-3 (Münster, 1903). Text on pp. 1-142; for extended history of the divisions of philosophy see the accompanying study, ch. 3: *Die philosophische Einleitungsliteratur bis zum Ende der Scholastik,* pp. 316-97.

13. Ibid., p. 16: ". . . quia ad consequendam futuram felicitatem non sufficit sola sciencia intelligendi quicquid est, nisi sequatur eciam sciencia agendi quod bonum est: ideo post theoricam sequitur practica, que similiter dividitur in tres partes. Quarum una est sciencia disponendi conversacionem suam cum omnibus hominibus. Cui necessaria est grammatica, poetica, rhetorica et sciencia legum secularium, in quibus est sciencia regendi civitates et sciencia cognoscendi iura civium, et hec dicitur politica sciencia et a Tullio 'civilis racio' vocatur. Secunda

(2) Poetics is the science of composing poems metrically. It forms a part of civil or political science, which in turn forms a part of eloquence. For what delights or edifies in matters of knowledge and morals has no small effect in the social or civic order.[14]

(3) Rhetoric deals with hypotheses. A hypothesis is a case or cause inviting question or controversy surrounding an incontrovertible fact, for example: Did Orestes do right in killing his mother? That he killed her is incontrovertible; that he did right in doing so is controversial. The incontrovertible fact is surrounded by determining circumstances, such as: the persons involved, the things they did, their reasons and aims, the places and times, the manner in which they proceeded, their alternative recourses and resources (*facultates*), and the like. Such controversies are called *demonstrative causes* if they are *de honesto,* that is, if they deal with integrity or virtue, and are laid before people gathered together in an assembly.[15]

(4) There are eight parts of logic, and the sciences treated in each are named by each of the eight books Aristotle devotes to them: the Categories, On Interpretation, the Prior Analytics, the Posterior Analytics, the Topics, On Sophistical Refutations, the Rhetoric, and the Poetics. The fourth of these, the Posterior Analytics, on scientific demonstration, is the principal goal and intention of all logic, and the first three parts or books are preparation and introduction thereto. The last four parts or books, however —namely, Topics, On Sophistical Refutations, Rhetoric, and Poetics—are a quasi-instrument of the fourth—a departure (*profectio*) from it, yet a support and aid to it in order that persons who do not know how to be swayed by the inevitable necessity of demonstration (*qui inevitabili necessitate demonstracionis nesciunt flecti*) may little by little become more probably and more persuasively amenable to being moved (*probabilius*

---

est sciencia disponendi domum et familiam propriam; per quam cognoscitur qualiter vivendum sit homini cum uxore et filiis et servis et cum omnibus domesticis suis et hec sciencia vocatur ordinacio familiaris. Tercia est sciencia, qua cognoscit homo ordinare modum proprium sui ipsius secundum honestatem anime sue, scilicet ut sit incorruptus et utilis in suis moribus . . . ut sibi bene conveniat et in nullo a se dissideat" ("u" changed to "v" and capitals added at beginning of sentences).

14. Ibid., p. 54: "Poetica est sciencia componendi carmina metrice. . . . Genus huius artis est, quod ipsa est pars civilis sciencie, que est pars eloquencie. Non enim parum operatur in civilibus, quod delectat vel edificat in sciencia vel in moribus."

15. Ibid., p. 65: "Materia autem artis rethorice est hypothesis, que a latinis causa dicitur. . . . Hypothesis vero sive causa est res, que habet in se controversiam in dicendo positam de certo facto vel dicto alicuius certe persone ut hec controversia: an Horestes iure occiderit matrem suam . . . ut cum argumentis probabilibus ostenditur an Horestes iure matrem suam occiderit. . . . Hypothesis vero, i.e. suppositum dicitur, quoniam sub thesi continetur. Dicitur eadem questio, implicata circumstanciis, i.e. certis determinacionibus personarum, factorum, causarum, locorum, temporum, modorum, facultatum. . . . Civiles autem controversie . . . de honesto apud populum in concionibus . . . demonstrative dicuntur."

vel persuasibilius paulatim assuescant moveri).[16]

(5) The term "logic" derives from the Greek *logos* and has three meanings, for the Greek word is translatable into the Latin *sermo* (speech) and *ratio* (reason). Exterior *ratio* is reason voiced, as when through language we interpret what is in the mind. On the other hand, there is that reason which is fixed in the mind, the mental conception which speech signifies. Thus, logic includes both the signifying process and that which is signified (*significans et significata*). Thirdly, however, logic is that virtue, created in man, by which he discerns between good and evil and by which he apprehends the sciences and arts. All men have this virtue or power, but in infants and certain adults it is weak and unable to perform its function, just as the infant's foot is too infirm to walk well, and just as a small flame is too weak to burn a great stack of wood: such is logic in the demented and the intoxicated.[17]

(6) The function of poetry is to address those who are led by their imaginations to neglect what they properly know and think. By its words, poetry causes something to be imagined as beautiful or repulsive which is not so, in order that the hearer may believe it and sometimes abhor or desire it. For although we are certain that the thing is not so in truth, nevertheless our minds are drawn to abhor or desire what is imagined for us. Imagination at times works more powerfully in man than knowledge or thought; indeed, often a man's knowledge or thought are contrary to what he imagines, yet he acts by what he imagines, not by knowledge or thought, or, as the saying has it: *mel videtur esse stercus hominis,* man's excrement seems honey to his eyes.[18]

16. Ibid., p. 71: "Secundum Alfarabium octo sunt partes logice: cathegorie, perihermenias, analetica priora, analetica posteriora, thopica, sophistica, rethorica, poetica. Nomina autem librorum ponuntur pro nominibus scienciarum, que continentur in illis. . . . Set quia pars quarta vehemencioris probacionis est, ideo omnibus antecellit sublimitate et dignitate. Nam per totam logicam principaliter non intenditur nisi pars quarta. Relique vero partes non sunt invente nisi per quartam. Unde tres partes, que antecedunt eam ordine doctrine, non sunt nisi preparaciones, introductiones ad illam. Relique vero quattuor, que eam secuntur, duabus de causis invente sunt: una est, quod quia unaqueque est quasi instrumentum quarte parti, profectio, sustentamentum et adiutorium est aliquod ad illam videlicet ut probabilius vel persuasibilius paulatim assuescant moveri, qui inevitabile necessitate demonstracionis nesciunt flecti, licet quorundam adiutorium sit maius et quorundam minus."

17. Ibid., p. 77: "Logica dicta est a 'logos' secundum tres intenciones. 'Logos' enim grece, sermo vel racio dicitur latine. Set racio alia est exterior cum voce, que per linguam interpretatur id quod est in mente; et alia est racio fixa in anima que dicitur mentis concepcio, quam dictiones significant. Unde illa est significans et hec significata. Tercia est virtus creata in homine, qua discernit inter bonum et malum et qua apprehendit sciencias et artes: et hec est in omni homine. Set in infantibus et in quibusdam adultis infirma est, non valens suas perficere actiones, sicut pes infantis infirmus est ad ambulandum et parvus ignis ad grossa ligna comburendum, qualis est eciam in demoniacis et ebriis."

18. Ibid., p. 74: "Proprium est poetice sermonibus suis facere ymaginari aliquid pulchrum vel fedum, quod non est, ita, ut auditor credat et aliquando

Whatever quarrel Petrarch may have had with dialecticians, clearly it was no quarrel with logic in the broad and representative sense given it by Gundissalinus and numerous other writers, Christian and Muslim, who, however they may vary in detail, write in the same tradition. Any conception of logic which includes rhetoric and poetry, which recognizes a civic and moral responsibility, which is not merely a tool of analytic science but an adaptable support in controversial cases *de honesto,* is consistent with the spirit and practice of Petrarch. The humanist requires, even of analytic science, that it look to its humanizing effect upon humanity.

In 1368, some thirty-three years after his letter to Tommaso Caloria, Petrarch found himself attacked by four young Venetians of quality who were circulating the charge that Petrarch, though a good old man, was no proper scholar because he was ignorant of Aristotle's works and the commentaries on them by Averroes the Arab philosopher. Petrarch's reply, his invective *De sui ipsius et multorum ignorantia,*[19] reveals not only the extent to which he had read Aristotle but the lack of humanizing effect he had found in Aristotle's *Nicomachean Ethics* in particular:

> I have read all Aristotle's moral books if I am not mistaken. Some of them I have also heard commented on. I seemed to understand something of them before this huge ignorance [of mine] was detected. Sometimes I have perhaps become more learned through them when I went home, but not better, not so good as I ought to be; and I often complained to myself, occasionally to others too, that by no facts was the promise fulfilled which the philosopher makes at the beginning of the first book of his *Ethics,* namely, that "we learn this part of philosophy not with the purpose of gaining knowledge but of becoming better" [cf. *Eth. Nic.* i. III. 1095a 4]. I see virtue, and all that is peculiar to vice as well as to virtue, egregiously defined and distinguished by him and treated with penetrating insight. When I learn all this, I know a little bit more than I knew before, but mind and will remain the same as they were, and I myself remain the same. It is one thing to know, another to love; one thing to understand, another to will. He teaches what virtue is, I do not deny that; but his lesson lacks the words that

---

abhorreat vel appetat: quamvis enim certi sumus, quod non est ita in veritate, tamen eriguntur animi nostri ad abhorrendum vel appetendum quod ymaginatur nobis. Ymaginacio enim quandoque plus operatur in homine quam sciencia vel cogitacio; sepe etenim sciencia vel cogitacio hominis contraria est eius ymaginacioni et tunc operatur homo secundum quod ymaginatur, non secundum quod scit vel cogitat, sicut per hoc quod dicitur: mel videtur esse stercus hominis."

19. Trans. Hans Nachod, in op. cit. above, n. 6, pp. 47-133. Original in *Opera* (Basel, 1554), pp. 1123-68; (1581), pp. 1035-59; L. M. Capelli, *Pétrarque: Le traité De sui ipsius et multorum ignorantia* (Paris, 1906); and P. Rajna, "Il codice Hamiltoniano 493 della R. Biblioteca di Berlino," *Rendiconti dell'Accademia dei Lincei,* XVIII (5a ser., 1909), 479-508.

sting and set afire and urge toward love of virtue and hatred of vice, or, at any rate does not have enough of such power. . . . Therefore, the true moral philosophers and useful teachers of the virtues are those whose first and last intention is to make hearer and reader good, those who do not merely teach what virtue and vice are and hammer into our ears the brilliant name of the one and the grim name of the other but sow into our hearts love of the best and eager desire for it and at the same time hatred of the worst and how to flee it.[20]

It is hardly surprising that for so "symbolist" a mind as Petrarch's the logic of Aristotle's demonstration in the *Ethics* should seem deficient because it lacks the power of poetry's logic, the stinging and converting power of the right fable in the right circumstances, the rhetoric of fiction, which has its own mode of demonstration. M.-D. Chenu, in his brilliant essay on "The Symbolist Mentality" of the Middle Ages, calls attention to the essential difference between dialectical and symbolist demonstration and notes that the ambiguity of the term, like that of "logic" itself, must not trap one into confusing the two modes of thought or into preferring one to another:

While historians of rationalist orientation—even historians of theology—have noted and value the rise of dialectic under Abelard's influence, they have shown some contempt for those areas of literature which used symbolism as a method of inquiry and formulation. This adverse judgment, which even the worst excesses of allegorism do not justify, cannot in any case conceal that vast literature with its extraordinary diversity of product, from mirrors of the cosmos to biblical typologies. In the whole range of its culture, the medieval period was an era of the symbol as much as, indeed more than, an era of dialectic. . . . 'A symbol,' said Hugh of Saint-Victor, 'is a juxtaposition, that is, a coaptation of visible forms brought forth to demonstrate some invisible matter.' The play of this sort of reasoning did not constitute proof. Hugh's 'demonstration' was hardly that of Aristotle, and it ought rather to be rendered as 'display'; to think the opposite would be seriously to confuse two distinct modes of thought to the detriment of both. To bring symbolism into play was not to extend or supplement a previous act of the reason; it was to give primary expression to a reality which reason could not attain and which reason, even afterwards, could not conceptualize.[21]

20. Ibid., pp. 103-05.

21. Quoted from M.-D. Chenu, *Nature, Man, and Society in the Twelfth Century: Essays on New Theological Perspectives in the Latin West,* trans. Jerome Taylor and Lester K. Little (Chicago: University of Chicago Press, 1968), pp. 102-03. Nothing so strikingly reveals Petrarch's symbolist view of reality as his letter to Fra Dionigi di Borgo San Sepolcro (*Fam.,* IV. 1) on his ascent of Mont Ventoux with his brother Gherardo; Petrarch would have one believe that he instantly saw the whole experience as a figure of his spiritual state, a historic event converted into a parable for him by the poetic hand of

Finally, not only had Aristotle, unlike his master Plato, failed to make use of the power of symbolic demonstration, but his conception of happiness was likewise deficient for Petrarch, for it did not rest upon the full revelation of God's sanctifying and cleansing relationship to man's spiritual life, a revelation which gives even the simplest believing Christian—Griselda, say—a recognition of happiness which Aristotle was unhappily prevented from attaining:

Of happiness [Aristotle] has indeed said a good deal in the beginning and at the end of his *Ethics*. However, I will dare to say—and my censors may shout as loud as they please—he knew so absolutely nothing of true happiness that any pious old woman, any faithful fisherman, shepherd or peasant is—I will not say more subtle but happier in recognizing it.[22]

To this point an effort has been made to clarify, in broad terms, the kind of "logyk" which Chaucer's Clerk, like Petrarch, espoused; the kinds of qualifications that would attend any spiritually oriented medieval man's admiration of Aristotle, as they attended Petrarch's; and the kind of converting demonstration which the Clerk's Tale may be expected to perform vis-à-vis the Wife of Bath's case, especially since it is told by a narrator whose every word, Chaucer says, is "quyk and ful of hy sentence" and of whom it is said that "sownynge in moral vertu was his speche." "Gladly wolde he lerne," to be sure, but it remains to examine the mode by which he would also "gladly teche."

Turning, then, to the specific mode in which Chaucer had his Clerk

God, which guided him to the revealing page of Augustine's *Confessions* at the mountaintop. The late Morris Bishop observes that Petrarch's planning of the ascent "for April 26, 1336, exactly ten years from the day he and Gherardo had left Bologna" was probably "by design, for Petrarch had a great sense of anniversaries" (*Petrarch and His World* [Bloomington: Indiana University Press, 1963], p. 104), though he disagrees with Professor Giuseppe Billanovich, who proposes "that Petrarch wrote this letter in 1352 or 1353, as a sort of allegorical fairy tale, to provide after the event a forecast of Gherardo's conversion" (ibid., p. 381; see G. Billanovich, *Lo scrittoio del Petrarca* [Rome, 1947], p. 194). Professor Billanovich's view is supported, however, by Petrarch's remarks, in the Coronation Oration, on "the nature of the profession of poetry," especially by his citation from Lactantius: ". . . the office of the poet consists in this, that he should take things that have really come to pass and transform them by means of subtle figures into things of a different sort"; see the translation of the Coronation Oration by Ernest H. Wilkins, *Studies in the Life and Works of Petrarch* (Cambridge, Mass.: The Mediaeval Academy of America, 1955), p. 306. Petrarch's immediate interest in, and reformulation in Latin, of Boccaccio's tale of Griselda must be understood in terms of its personal moral significance for him.

22. Nachod (cited above, n. 6), p. 74.

respond to the case presented by the Wife of Bath, one must consider not only the case or thesis regarding woman's sovereignty in marriage for which she contends in her prologue and tale, but also her personal case or condition. The latter will be considered first.

This widow—a perpetual wife of a sort, if her wish were fulfilled—is probably passing fifty, for she was forty when she married the twenty-year old Jankyn (III, 600-601), her fifth husband, and he must have lasted at least a decade, or one suspects that Chaucer would have provided her with a complaint of his early demise. Married since age twelve, she had chosen her first three husbands, all "goode men, and riche, and olde," for "hir lond and hir tresor" (III, 197, 204). Like January in the Merchant's Tale, they could hardly discharge their marriage debt, and like May, January's young wife, Alisoun of Bath "tolde no deyntee of hir love" (III, 198-200, 208). In consequence, through false allegations and false witnesses, she charged her husbands with infidelity and with mental cruelty to her in their drunkenness, and, in exchange for her forgiveness for wrongs they could never have committed, she obtained their permission to gad about in search of the very promiscuity with which she had falsely charged, and flattered, them: the old men, she tells us, were all but impotent and "ful gilteless," where she herself "was in the gilt" and forstalled inquiries by chiding her husbands first (III, 379-92).

Her "freedom" made possible her "visitaciouns" to vigils, preachings, processions, and miracle plays in her "gaye scarlet gytes," not to mention her pilgrimages abroad—to shrines at Cologne, Boulogne, Compostela, Rome, and thrice to Jerusalem (I, 463-67): she never knew where her "grace / Were shapen for to be, or in what place" (III, 551-59). Her "grace" was opportunity to satisfy an irresistible appetite for which she blamed the stars, a peculiar constellation of Venus, Mars, and Taurus the Bull:

> I folwed ay myn inclinacioun
> By vertu of my constellacioun;
> That made me I koude noght withdrawe
> My chambre of Venus from a good Felawe. . . .
> I ne loved never by no discrecioun,
> But evere folwed myn appetit,
> Al were he short, or long, or blak, or whit;
> I took no kep, so that he liked me. . . .
> (III, 615-25)

Her fourth and fifth marriages were to young men who could bring pleasure from road to home ground, but her fourth husband, like her, was unfaithful, and her jealousy aroused, she was reduced, as she says, to making him fry in his own grease—in fact, to taking another pilgrimage to Jerusalem, after which he died (III, 453-54, 481-95).

Her fifth husband was the twenty-year old Jankyn, a "som tyme . . . clerk of Oxenford" who "hadde left scole," gone to board with her gossip, and, it appears, become a golden-haired apprentice in her husband's weaving establishment (III, 303-04, 527-29). She gave him her heart "for love and no richesse" (III, 526) when she gazed upon his "paire / Of legges and of feet so clene and faire" as he walked behind her fourth husband's bier (III, 596-601); perhaps she chose him also for his "cheste" and "nether purs," features by which she "pyked out the beste" among men, she says (III, 44a-f). This drop-out clerk-husband of Oxenford was nothing like the Clerk who is to tell Griselda's story. He was hardly a moral "philosophre" or logician, though he could wheedle temptingly and had other virtues relative to a certain level of love:

> . . . in oure bed he was so fresh and gay,
> And therwithal so wel koude he me glose,
> Whan that he wolde han my *bele chose,*
> That thogh he hadde me bete on every bon,
> He koude wynne agayn my love anon.
> (III, 508-12)

He was hardly a collector of Aristotle's works: his sole book, so far as we are told, was Jankyn's famous "book of wikked wyves" (III, 685), in parts a vitriolic, gossipy, and selectively pornographic collection (despite its august origins), containing among its choicer morsels (to cite only two) the story of how Xantippe, wife of Socrates, "caste pisse upon his heed" (III, 729) and how Queen Pasiphae of Crete fashioned a brazen cow into which she crept to accommodate the bull she lusted for, and so brought forth the minotaur: "For shrewednesse, hym thoughte the tale sweete" (III, 734), the Wife tartly observes of Jankyn's taste for Pasiphae. Jankyn found it appealing to read endlessly to her from this book, but if he thought that his reading would have a corrective influence upon her, he was certainly wrong, for as she declares:

> . . . I sette noght an hawe
> Of his proverbes n'of his olde sawe,
> Ne I wolde nat of hym corrected be.
> I hate hym that my vices telleth me,
> And so doo mo, God wot, of us than I.
> (III, 659-63)

No clerk, she claims, is capable of praising any woman, but only of sermonizing about how "wommen kan nat kepe hir mariage" (III, 710).

Far from complete, this sketch suffices to limn her "new morality" —her view that it cannot matter how many men light their candles at her lantern, to use her metaphor (III, 333-36), or that she "koude walke as fresh as is a rose" if she would sell her "belle chose" (III, 447-48), and that in the sexual relationship, "Wynne whoso may, for al is for to selle" (III, 414). Not considered here is the style of her presentation: her spirited humor about it all, her arresting and (for some) engaging frankness about herself, and, to come to another most significant aspect of her situation, a certain recognition on her part that her conduct does not quite suit the traditional spiritual morality of her religious heritage. "Allas! allas!" she is made to say, "that evere love was synne" (III, 614). Before regaling the pilgrims with her experience of the "wo that is in mariage" (III, 3), she digresses for 153 lines in order to apply defensively to herself a sophistical revision of authorities on marriage, virginity, counsel, precept, and intercourse, hunting the letter but not searching the spirit from passages of Sacred Scripture, and touching only her preferred points of functional anatomy (III, 9-162). Finally, she is tickled at heart, she confesses, for having had her world in her bygone time, for age, which poisons all, has bereft her of beauty and pith; the flour is gone and she must now sell the bran as best she can, while vowing to remain "right myrie" as she tries (III, 469-79).

Of this personal situation, her tale astonishingly emerges as an objective correlative. In it, just such a "lusty bacheler" as she prefers, has displayed his virtue through forcing a young virgin surprised alone near a river, and, to save his neck from the authorities—Queen Guinevere and all her ladies, no less—he answers their riddling question, "What do women most desire?", by taking saving counsel from an Old Hag at the price of marrying her. And from her he learns, while writhing impotently in their marriage bed on their wedding night, that submission to the Old Hag's "maistrie" will make even her aged foulness beautiful, will make wealth strangely irrelevant, and (startling to hear it from Alisoun's lips) will show him that God's grace and virtuous living are the true sources of gentility.

By the time that Harry Bailly calls upon the pilgrim Clerk of Oxford to speak his first word in all that day, Alison of Bath has, it is true, already been spoken to, or of, by three men officially devoted to exercise of the Church's pastoral care—the Pardoner, the Friar, and the Summoner—, yet none of the three has shown any awareness of her sophistry or of her spiritual situation. The Pardoner, whose official task is to solicit charity in exchange for pardons from spiritual purgatory after death, has attended only to the Wife's salacious instruction on marriage, which he pretends to be contemplating but could never consummate, for it is evident that "he were a geldynge or a mare" (I, 691). The Friar, whose official task is to preach, to hear confessions and absolve, and to exemplify by his own poverty, chastity and obedience the spiritual orientation which man's life should have, is himself a lecher, an avaricious money-maker, "the beste beggere in his hous," who would exercise his faculties only "ther as profit sholde arise" (I, 240-52); he merely laughed at the Wife's long confessional prologue and advised her to leave to the clergy such preaching as he fails to offer her (III, 829-31, 1265-77). The Summoner, who has already made known that he delivers summonses for church-trials to those who commit adultery and fornication, is himself a fornicator and is too embroiled in hate and wrath against the Friar to pay official attention to the Wife's overt declarations of her covert delinquencies, in any case.

What, then, at this point in the evolving situation, is Chaucer artistically committed to having the Clerk of Oxenford do and say, and how is his artistic resolution of that commitment reflective of both Aristotle and Petrarch? To recapitulate: As a devotee of logic in its broadest medieval sense, the Clerk cannot be presented as a dialectical quibbler, nor made to launch insolent attacks against the Wife's reasoning, repeating the Friar's and Summoner's insolence to each other. As one who is personally as well as professionally dedicated to "moral vertu" he cannot be expected to ignore the Wife's sophistry or spiritual situation, yet he must also be expected to know that a scientific disquisition on ethics will lack words that sting and will set no one afire with love for virtue and flight from vice, but that the right rhetoric, the right story for the right circumstances, may have its own converting effect by the power and "logic" of its demonstration. Further, he has the reputation of another clerk of Oxford, now a dead husband, to live down and correct, and he has heard that the Wife of Bath, like all men, hates those who tell her directly of her vices, and that any faulty representation of a woman will be credited to clerical prejudice. In this setting, Petrarch's tale of Griselda provided for Chaucer a poetic *tour de force,* for, while providing another set of antagonists than the Wife of Bath and her husbands, the tale sets up a series of contraries to her positions, at first strikingly sympathetic to her allegations against men, then strikingly averse to her claim for female sovereignty, and finally, through moralization, strikingly applicable to her violations of *civilis ratio, ordinacio familiaris,* and such arrangement and ordering of her conduct as would preserve her incorrupt and useful and in no way at variance with herself.[23]

It is unnecessary to re-do here the meticulous work of Severs by detailing the deft additions which Chaucer made to Petrarch's tale and the ways in which these make the tale more directly applicable to characteristics of the Wife. One may limit the inquiry to ways in which Chaucer's placement of the tale at this juncture in the Canterbury collection and in the mouth of such a narrator as the Clerk, adds to Petrarch's tale a striking use of certain of Aristotle's instructions in the *De sophisticis elenchis* on how to refute sophistical refutations of truth.

When the Wife, and then the insolent Friar and Summoner, have finished their speeches and tales, Chaucer first has Harry Bailly turn to the Clerk and accuse him of having remained as "coy and still" as a virginal bride newly espoused and blushing at her bridal banquet, and indeed to look like one (IV, 1-4). The simile is potentially allusive, though its potentialities are not fully developed; if the unblemished espousal were to suggest more clearly the spiritual marriage of soul and God at the heavenly banquet, it would prepare the way for the final moralization of the tale to come. Harry Bailly next accuses the Clerk of musing about some sophism, that is, some speciously good but intrinsically fallacious argument which uses ingenious deceit to score a point. He is told that there is "no tyme for to studien heere" but that he must tell "som myrie tale" and so enter properly into the "pley" to which he is committed (IV, 5-14).

We have heard not one but a string of sophisms from the Wife of Bath. According to Aristotle, there are four classes of sophistical arguments in dialogue form, and the fourth he calls contentious dialogues, which, he says, "reason or appear to reason to a conclusion from premisses that appear to be generally accepted but are not so."[24] Just such are the contentious dialogues which the Wife of Bath has been made to dramatize as she recalls her disputes with her husbands. For an example of one of her sophistical refutations of husbandly correction in which she misreasons from premisses that appear to be generally accepted but are not so, one may examine the following:

> Oon of us two moste bowen, doutelees;
> And sith a man is moore resonable
> Than womman is, ye moste been suffrable.
>
> (III, 440-42)

23. See above p. 369; for Gundissalinus' statements about philosophy, moral science, logic, rhetoric, poetic, and the orientation of these to human needs.

24. *De sophisticis elenchis,* 2, 154a 35—165b 20, in Richard McKeon, *The Basic Works of Aristotle* (New York: Random House, 1941), pp. 209-10.

If, like the Clerk, one muses upon this sophism, one finds it restatable in a form much like that of the syllogism which the dialectical quibbler addressed to Diogenes as Petrarch reports it in his letter to Tommaso Caloria. So restated, it reads thus:

> Of two disputing persons, the one more reasonable is more capable of accommodation than the other.
>
> Man is more reasonable than woman.
>
> Therefore, in disputes between man and woman, man is more capable of accommodation than woman.

The trouble with the Wife's use of this argument is that, in the first premiss, "accommodation" is not generally understood to mean capitulation to unjustifiable demands, charges, and shrewish domination. Moreover, it is not generally accepted, even by clerks, that man is more reasonable than woman—instance: Andreas Capellanus, a cleric, has women win in the contentious dialogues of his *De amore*.[25] Lastly, even if it were true that man is more capable of accommodation than woman, and even if accommodation meant what the Wife makes it mean, it still would not follow that man should exercise this capability regardless of "determining circumstances."[26] That he should do so remains a controversial hypothesis, a "demonstrative cause *de honesto*." The Wife's conclusion that her husbands "*moste* been suffrable" has not been demonstrated.

Were the Clerk to have behaved like such a scholastic dialectician as Petrarch detested, he would have distinguished the terms, negated the premisses, and denied the conclusions of all the Wife's sophistical syllogisms in the manner just illustrated. In some sense he would have "won" the argument. However, he is more interested in winning the Wife of Bath to moral reflection than he is in winning an argument by scoring technical victory. The tale he tells is a strategic refutation directed to this end.

The Wife's argument for "maistrie," for "liberty" or the libertine life, abstractly stated, had run like this:

> Woman, more expert than man in deceit and specious reasoning (III, 227-28, 400-02; the Wife restates the point more than once), deserves to extract from man whatever she pleases.
>
> I am a woman just so expert in deceit and specious reasoning.
>
> I therefore deserve to have extracted from five husbands all that I can boast of having done, and "Welcome the sixte, when that ever he shal" (III, 45).

25. See *The Art of Courtly Love by Andreas Capellanus*, trans. John Jay Parry (New York: Columbia University Press, 1941), pp. 36-141.

26. See Gundissalinus, third point, p. 370 above.

The argument is so point-blank a reversal or refutation of what is commonly thought true and proper in an ideal wife that it is as laughable as the quibbler's proof that Diogenes was no man. Diogenes exploded the sophistry of the quibbler's proof by proposing a reversal of subject in the first proposition and thus proving that the quibbler was not a man—an equally absurd and laughable conclusion. In fact, the Clerk of Oxford's use of the Griselda story does the same to the Wife's sophistical argument. Abstractly stated, the story's reverse argument goes like this:

> Man, more expert than woman in deceit and specious reasoning, deserves to subject woman to whatever he pleases.
>
> The Marquis Walter was just so expert in deceit and specious reasoning.
>
> He therefore deserved to have extracted from Griselda such an accumulation of "accommodating" suffering as the tale tells us he has.

In the tale, "specious reasoning" is transformed into unaccountable irrationality, and Chaucer makes the Clerk say so in passages Chaucer adds to Petrarch's version. He charges Walter's behavior with being "nedelees, God wot" (IV, 455) and thus having the Clerk, in deft maneuver of apparent agreement with the Wife's attack against husbands, accuse "wedded men" of knowing "no mesure / Whan that they fynde a pacient creature" (IV, 622-23).

The tale, then, is careful to present Walter as, first, attractive and corrigible, then irrational and unjustifiable. As told by the Clerk, the Tale of Griselda has become an *argumentum e contrario*—a rejoinder by the substitution of a contrary in the Wife's major premiss. She had contended that sovereignty is inescapable in marriage and should belong to woman. Momentarily accepting the proposition that sovereignty is inescapable in marriage, the Clerk's Tale is used to show what it looks like when sovereignty belongs to a man as monstrous in his extractions as the Wife has been in hers. If "maistrye" seems monstrous in a man otherwise as charming and reformable as Walter is—and the Wife and all other hearers or readers are expected to see it as such—then it follows *a fortiori* that it will be even more montrous in a woman otherwise as charming and reformable as the Wife of Bath, who, in thought if not in practice, knows that through virtuous living comes true "gentilesse," that material wealth is irrelevant to spiritual integrity, and that true beauty may be clouded but is not destroyed by the outward appearances of old age. This is the *logos* or logic of the Clerk's Tale, and if one does not see the tale as a refutational argument cast in the form of a fabulous demonstration, if one worries about its literal verisimilitude and probability in character and situation, then one approaches it with considerations irrelevant to the stratagem of its art.

Petrarch's moralization of the tale of Griselda fits perfectly with what has been called his "symbolist mentality."[27] The moralization, moreover, adds yet another dimension to the Clerk's response to the Wife of Bath, so that Chaucer carefully retains it. If there is any personal relationship in which sovereignty and submission are appropriate, it is the relationship between the sovereign God and the human soul, in which "greet skile is, he preeve that he wroghte" (IV, 1152). It is God's "skile," his reason or logic, "to preeve," to prove or improve, what he has wrought. Griselda-like acceptance and constancy before such perfective probation is "for oure beste." Petrarch had his own reasons for being moved by this tropological interpretation of the story; the Wife of Bath had need of being moved in the same manner, if it were possible.

Did Chaucer expect that his Clerk could or should move the Wife of Bath by the stratagems thus far discussed? Is one to think of her as having been moved? If Chaucer considered this question, he has left no evidence that he had determined upon an answer. In very few instances has he worked out how particular pilgrims, particularly those to whom or on whom tales were told, responded, though in the cases of the Reeve and the Summoner the responses are clear. After the Clerk's Tale, it is the Merchant, not the Wife, who instantly picks up the verbal thread, though hardly the inner meaning, and excitedly but with predictable imperceptiveness, responds. Still, in the Envoy to the Clerk's Tale, uniquely added by Chaucer, one is given some sign that the Clerk doubts the efficacy of his efforts and so attempts one final method of refuting a sophistical argument.

In his *De sophisticis elenchis,* Aristotle considers "the number of aims entertained by those who argue as competitors" and says they are five: to refute one's opponent directly, to trap one's opponent in fallacy, paradox, or solecism, or to reduce one's opponent to "babbling —i.e. to constrain him to repeat himself a number of times."[28] Explicitly and literally, the Envoy is a broadside invitation to the Wife of Bath, and all "noble wyves" like her, to babble and perform in contentious self-defensiveness without cease. In brief, the exhortations are these:

> Let *no* humility nail your tongues.
> Let *no* clerks have occasion to write such marvels
>   of you as they have of Griselda.
> *Do* counterattack like Echo.
> *Don't* be caught innocent and hoodwinked.
> *Do* defend yourselves physically, like strong camels.

27. See above p. 373, esp. fn. 21.
28. 165b 12ff.; op. cit., p. 210.

> *Do* let the arrows of your crabbed eloquence pierce
> your husbands' armor and wound them.
> *Do* make your husbands jealous and reduce them to
> quivering like quails.
> *Do* show off in appearance and clothes.
> *Do* spend freely.
> *Do* get your own men and women friends.
> And *do* make your husbands miserable with care and weeping
> and wringing of their hands and wailing.

If the exhortation were to be accepted literally and acted upon by the Wife of Bath and women like her, she and "al hir secte" (IV, 1171) would indeed have defeated themselves by self-reduction to incessant babbling and contention. Read ironically, with every injunction taken as the inverse statement of its contradictory, the exhortation is transmuted into a dehortation of inept behavior and an oblique invitation to humility, restraint of tongue, turning of the other cheek, innocence, modesty of dress, in short, counsels of perfection all. For the Clerk thus ironically to "defeat" a sophistical and contentious opponent through inviting her to find her own spiritual perfection outlined in her bad habits "turned up-so-doun" is both to follow Aristotle on sophistical refutations and to go him one better. It is to spiritualize, indeed Christianize Aristotle in a way Petrarch would have understood and approved.

The "logyk" of Chaucer's Clerk, then, as it is displayed in the performance which Chaucer invented for him, relates to a larger conception of logic than dialectic or scientific demonstration. His performance as a "logician" in this larger sense avoids the inanities of which Petrarch accuses dialectical quibblers and self-styled Aristotelians. His tale, Petrarch's tale, as a response to the Wife of Bath's case, overcomes a deficiency which Petrarch found in Aristotle's moral philosophy. In short, Chaucer's Clerk of Oxenford is given the best of two only apparently conflicting worlds: the best of the world of Aristotle and "logic" as the Middle Ages and Petrarch would interpret these, and the best of the fabulous poetic world of Petrarch, who used the demonstrations of rhetoric and poetry to induce a better world of better men.

XX

PETRARCHISM AND THE END OF THE RENAISSANCE

by Donald L. Guss
University of California at Santa Barbara

In the seventeenth century, when France replaced Italy as the center of European letters, the learning and imitativeness of Renaissance verse was repudiated and a new aesthetic was formed. French critics then praised logic, politeness and modernity; they denounced studied conceits, affected sentiments and pedantic imitation; they particularly rejected Petrarchism. Discussing Petrarch in the late sixteenth century, Italian critics developed principles very like those of their French successors. For just a moment Italian poetry might have turned towards Malherbe. It did not do so; in new forms, Petrarchism continued to be the main stream of Italian verse. Yet the momentary crisis is fascinating in itself; and it reveals much about the decline of humanism and the rise of seventeenth-century styles.

Renaissance humanists were educators and rhetoricians. In classical poetry they discovered rules of conduct and grammar, arts of rhetoric, all the science which cultivated citizens needed to know. Making a literary canon the core of a liberal education, they treated poetry as an authoritative epitome of culture.[1] But the new taste of seventeenth-century France found humanists ridiculous. Critics scorned "les fleurs de Rhétorique, la broderie du stile figuré, l'ostentation et la pompe de l'Ecole." They looked with contempt upon the humanist's "mauvais air du Cicéron," and congratulated themselves upon living in a time when "les Poètes sont reglés par le goût de la Cour plûtot que la Cour par le goût des Poètes." As Spingarn says, "the control of criticism was passing from *savants* to *beaux-esprits*." Ready like Descartes to reject whatever they could not understand, beaux-esprits wanted easy, natural verse—"un ordre secret et naturel qui ne sente ni l'art ni l'étude:

1. See for example Foster Watson, *English Grammar Schools to 1660* (Cambridge, 1908); Jean Seznec, *La survivance des dieux antiques* (London, 1940); Henri-Irénée Marrou, *St. Augustin et la fin de la culture antique* (Paris, 1949); and, on the similar treatment of Petrarch, Bernard Weinberg, "The *Sposizione* of Petrarch in the Early Cinquecento," *RP,* XIII (1959-60), 347-86, and D. L. Guss, "Renaissance Practical Criticism: A Polemical Survey," *Papers of the Michigan Academy,* LII (1967), 337-44.

une netteté de pensées et d'expression"; "politesse sans affectation et une élégance sans fard."[2] Humanists then were mocked as pedants and "rhetoric" became a term of contempt; Ronsard and Virgil himself were reproached for an air of the schoolroom.[3] The poet was no longer a sage artificer addressing posterity; he was a sensible man writing politely to *gens du monde*. Critics desired verisimilitude, ease and logical clarity—"nature" and "sense." They exalted *bon esprit* over scholarship, "reason" over authority, and modernism over the classical revival.

In the earlier sixteenth century, Petrarchism was part of the classical revival; it was humanism in the vernacular. As Sperone Speroni said "In morte del Card. Pietro Bembo" (*Orationi,* Venice, 1596), Bembo showed that a great literature might be produced if Petrarch were studied and imitated in Italian just as the classics were in Latin. After Bembo, works such as the *Annotationi brevissime sovra le Rime di M. F. Petrarca* (Padua, 1566) and Orazio Toscanella's *Discorsi* (Venice, 1575) presented Petrarch as a model of wisdom and eloquence like Cicero and Virgil. The *Canzoniere* had become a classic. Humanists used to teach schoolboys how to think, feel and write by analyzing the classics; now, addressing a wider audience, they made Petrarch's verse a text through which men might achieve a liberal education. Giovanni Andrea Gesualdo declared that Petrarch's commentators should teach proper feelings, philosophic maxims, and the vocabulary, grammar, ornaments and rhetoric of Italian (*Petrarcha,* Venice, 1533); the *Annotationi brevissime* said that from the *Canzoniere* as from the classics, readers might learn doctrine and ornament. Petrarch had become a means of teaching the age what the age needed to know.

By the mid-century, however, the humanist's conception of Petrarch was widely challenged. From different points of view, courtiers, anti-

2. The quotations in this passage are respectively from Balzac, cited in E. B. O. Borgerhoff, *The Freedom of French Classicism* (Princeton, 1950), pp. 18-9; de Méré, in Borgerhoff, pp. 93-4; Chapelain, in Borgerhoff, p. 41; Joel E. Spingarn, *Critical Essays of the Seventeenth Century,* I (Oxford, 1908), p. xxv; de Méré, in Borgerhoff, p. 99; Boissimon, cited by Arnaldo Pizzorusso, *La poetica di Fénelon* (Milan, 1959), pp. 21-2. Of Descartes, Preserved Smith rightly says that philosopher's greatness consisted in a "popular education which taught the choicer spirits among the cultivated classes to admit only what they could understand": *History of Modern Culture,* I (N.Y., 1930), 201.

3. Jean Chapelain, *Opuscules critiques,* ed. A. C. Hunter (Paris, 1936), pp. 421-3 reproaches Ronsard; de Méré does the same to Virgil (cited in Joel E. Spingarn, *Critical Essays of the Seventeenth Century,* III, Oxford, 1909, 298, n. 2). The pre-neoclassicism to which I refer is not that of genres and rules; it is the related desire for mathematical sense and polite manners. See Spingarn, I; Arnaldo Pizzorusso, *Teorie letterarie in Francia* (Pisa, 1968); E. B. O. Borgerhoff, *The Freedom of French Classicism* (Princeton, 1950); and Hubert Gillot, *La querelle des anciens et des modernes* (Geneva, 1968).

Petrarchists and Aristotelians denied that the *Canzoniere* is a cultural repository; in reading it, they put common sense above learning. A century later in France, critics condemned the grammarians for finding in the classics more than is there; they said that Homer, for example, is made only of song and story, and that readers should be contented with the literal sense.[4] Similarly, in sixteenth-century Italy Petrarch's readers began to free him from philologists. Through ideas of verisimilitude, good sense and good manners, they gradually developed a conception of poetry which marked the end of humanism and beginning of the Age of Reason.

Manners

In the late Middle Ages, the collected verse of a Provençal poet was usually preceded by a speculative biography, a narrative frame for the poems. The *Canzoniere* seems autobiographical, and Petrarch insisted that it is. Thus it was natural for Petrarch's editors to indulge themselves in biographical glosses; and they did. They were partly gossips interested in an old love story and partly philologists engaged in historical reconstruction. They were also interested in the manners of men—that is, in cultivated behavior and eternal human passions.

In deriving biographical information from the *Canzoniere,* early commentators were often literal-minded. Francesco Filelfo (1478, 1488, 1492, 1493) worried over such questions as what stream Petrarch wept into, and how many years he spent sighing. When Filelfo explained the occasion of a sonnet, he was extremely and even foolishly exact. For example, "Benedetto sia 'l giorno" is a hymn of joy; Filelfo explained that the poet was happy because Laura had invited him to dinner. "Io temo sí de' begli occhi" expresses awe at the sight of Laura; Filelfo explained that Petrarch turned his back on Laura and then, upon hearing of her resentment, wrote the sonnet to apologize. In making moral points Filelfo was similarly heavy-handed. In "Sennuccio, i' vo' che sappi," Petrarch professes to brood over Laura's every mood; noting the variety of her moods, Filelfo drew the lesson that women are inconstant. In "Amor, natura e la bell'alma umíle" Petrarch fears that Laura's noble soul is too delicate for her to remain alive long; Filelfo observed that Laura was noble, though humbly born, because she refused to fulfill Petrarch's lascivious desires. Early commentators were often interested less in a sonnet's general purpose than in those incidental elements which might support a biographical explanation or moral lesson.

4. See Balzac, quoted by Borgerhoff, p. 17.

During the course of the sixteenth century, interpretations like Filelfo's went out of fashion. For one thing, critics like Toscanella (ff. Fl^{r}-F4^{r}) thought the poet's biography less significant than his artistry. For another, as historical methods improved unsubstantiated biographical speculation came to seem merely silly. For example, the old commentators explained that in "Non fûr ma' Giove" Laura weeps for her mother's death; in 1609 Tassoni noted that for all anyone knew it was the cat which had died. Given a more critical assessment of historical evidence, biographical interpretation became—as Dolce suggested (*Osservationi,* Venice, 1566, pp. 181-3)—a study of the manners of men. Critics paid less attention to identifying Petrarch's streams, and more to such general questions as whether his love was sensual.[5] As humanism purged itself of philological speculations, the *Canzoniere* became a picture of universal and eternal motives—of youthful love, mature repentance, and the eternal conflict between sense and reason.

Courtiers shared with humanists an interest in the *Canzoniere* as a manual of polite behavior. Like Bernardo di Giunta, *Sonetti e Canzoni di diversi antichi autori toscani* (Florence, 1527), most humanists thought of Petrarch as one who had refined the customs of a barbarous age. Ladies and gentlemen, meanwhile, carried copies of the *Canzoniere* as a useful guide to politeness, a manual of delicate sentiments and refined phrases for fashionable use. Indeed, in handbooks of polite letter-writing and fashionable phrases—like Aldo Mannuccio's *Eleganze* (Venice, 1580) and Paolo Filippi della Briga's *I complimenti* (Turin, 1619)—the *Canzoniere* provided a pattern of social conduct.

It was precisely affected elegance that offended the "anti-Petrarchisti," those few but much-read satirical and jocose authors who burlesqued Petrarchan manners, revealing crude events beneath delicate Petrarchan phrases and interspersing gross vulgarities among Petrarchan refinements. Singing the love of a peasant for a fishwife or a beggar for a slut, often in dialect, many of their efforts remain amusing. One might note such collections as *Delle Rime piacevoli . . . del Berni, Casa,* etc. (Venice, 1603); . . . *del Berni, Copetta,* etc. (Venice, 1603); . . . *del Bor-*

5. The general view was that Petrarch's love was in fact sensual, though distinctly more modest than that of the classics. See for example *Il Petrarca . . . con un nuovo discorso sopra la qualità del suo amore* (Venice, 1607), b6^{r}-b12^{r}; Giovan Battista Gelli, "Lettione seconda," *Tutte le lettioni* (Florence, 1551), dl^{r}-f8^{r}; Giovanni Cervoni da Colle, *Sopra il sonetto del Petrarca, "Amor, fortuna, e la mia mente schiva"* (Florence, 1560); Hieronimo Malipiero Venetiano, *Il Petrarca spirituale* (Venice, 1567), a2^{r}-b4^{r}; and Francesco Patrizio, "Discorso," in *Le rime di M. Luca Contile* (Venice, 1565), C7^{r-v}.

As an example of biographical simplification, cf. Filelfo and Castelvetro, *Petrarca* (Basel, 1582) which also stresses the battle between reason and appetite.

gogna, Ruscelli, etc. (Venice, 1603); and in Venetian dialect, Andrea Calmo's delightful *Bizzarie faconde* (Venice, 1583). These early burlesques share with their seventeenth-century successors vigorous common sense, artistic sophistication and a pleasant raillery of affectation.

Like the Petrarchan lover the Petrarchan commentator was burlesqued by anti-Petrarchists,[6] who pretended to be solemn, stupid commentators discovering through conscientious research that Laura's hair was not so golden nor her eyes so radiant as Petrarch had claimed. In *Il Petrarchista* (Venice, 1541), Nicolò Franco made ridiculous the commentator's erudite search for fact and the theory that Petrarch's sonnets are an epitome of language, learning and philosophy—which, Franco amusingly insisted, everyone should rob, line by line. In Andrea Calmo's *Opere diverse* (Trivigi, 1600), some burlesque Petrarchan verses (ff. e7^r-f8^r) were accompanied by mock-commentaries wherein the commentator learnedly explained, for example, how it is that the poet's sock, though good, yet developed a hole. And in *Rime del Burchiello comentate dal Doni,* revised (Venice, 1566), the nonsense of Burchiello was discussed with a host of learned references, in a panegyric mode. Analyzing the first sonnet, for example, the commentator explained that the verses of Burchiello fall into five kinds; some can be understood only by the addressee, some only by Burchiello, some not even by Burchiello, some only by God, and some not by Him. The first sonnet, the commentator eulogized, is a perfect example of high art, combining verses in each kind. Such burlesques mocked irrelevant erudition, misplaced solemnity and blind enthusiasm. They scorned the premises of humanists, and treated humanists themselves as pedants. In seventeenth-century France, scorn of pedantry was an essential element of *bon ton*;[7] anti-Petrarchists foreshadowed the French desire for good sense and unaffected manners.

Doctrine

The idea that poetry contains scientific and philosophic information goes back to classical times. Perhaps its most discussed form is the notion that beneath an allegorical veil poets present secret truths—whence erudite interpretations of pagan divinities, and moral readings of Ovid. Another, equally ancient mode of instructive reading was that which

6. Serious poets viewed commentators with suspicion. In his *Rime spirituali* (Venice, n.d.), Gabriel Fiamma provided expositions of his own poems because, he said, expositors are often far from the intentions of the poet they gloss (A5^r-A7^r).

7. See Gillot, espec. pp. 374 ff.; also pp. 325-69 for the transformation of classical learning, the heart of Renaissance culture, to a polite acquirement.

attached elaborate botanical glosses to Ovid's mentions of vegetation, or long geographical notes to Homer's catalogue of ships. Finally, when ethics seemed as "hard" a science as physics, moral lessons were drawn from the behavior of poetic characters. Thus, by various means commentators found in poetry occasions to teach "doctrine."

Early commentators inclined to read an enormous amount of miscellaneous erudition into the *Canzoniere*. For example, where Petrarch says that he cannot find Laura's image in others ("Movesi il vecchierel"), Fausto da Longiano (*Il Petrarcha,* Venice, 1532) explained that internal forms are invisible. In "Quando giunge per gl'occhi" Fausto found a little treatise on epistemology, as knowledge comes through the eyes to the visual power, then to the imaginative virtue, and then to the soul. And of "Se mai foco" he said that the opening refers to the philosophic truth that like grows by like; that "un'alma in duo corpi" repeats an Aristotelian dictum; and that "il desio, che seco non s'accorda" unlooses the knot formed by the fact that philosophy says that the will desires good, while theology says that it may desire evil. The importance such learning had is suggested by Hieronymo Centone's *Petrarcha* (1492), where Filelfo's commentary is accompanied by an index of learned subjects. Those who used the index found Petrarch a guide to classical literature, philosophy and all the sciences.

In seeking doctrine, the first commentators overread the parts of sonnets, and took metaphors as scientific dicta. Filelfo, for example, understood Petrarch's heats and colds as medical facts, and elaborately described the laws which governed their causes and effects; he treated "Piovommi amare lagrime" as a little treatise on the physical effects of passion. Fausto da Longiano, though more sensitive to Petrarch's intentions, was still emphatically erudite. Discussing "Quando 'l pianeta," he used astronomy to determine the time of year; he explained why "pianeta" is feminine; and he showed that Petrarch's description of the sun is astronomically accurate. In discussing "Io mi rivolgo indietro" he considered the relation between body and soul, the way love changes that relation, and other sonnets in which the problem is discussed. In such readings Fausto found many occasions to cite the opinions of philosophers and to elucidate scientific theories.

Commentators of the High Renaissance generally had a more rhetorical emphasis. Bernardo Daniello da Lucca (*Petrarcha,* Venice, 1541), for example, meant primarily to compare Petrarch with his literary sources. And Giovanni Andrea Gesualdo (*Il Petrarcha,* Venice, 1533) paid most attention to arts of expression and general moral notions. Such commentators as Daniello, Gesualdo and Alessandro Vellutello (*Il Petrarcha,* Venice, 1528) used scientific knowledge when Petrarch's lines seemed absolutely to require it, but they no longer saw the *Canzoniere* as an encyclopedia of erudition. Indeed, Toscanella (1575) argued that Petrarch's commentators should be less interested in philosophy than in "art." Such statements suggest that humanism had changed its direction; rhetoric and literature had become more important than philosophy.

Early commentators sought learning and wisdom where the poet claimed to burn and freeze or to die and be reborn. For them such statements were literal and scientific. But later Benedetto Varchi insisted that in such passages Petrarch speaks not as a doctor or natural philosopher, but as a poet.[8] Lucio Oradini (*Due Lezzioni,* Florence, 1550) said that Petrarch is not everywhere scientific, that he often speaks to ordinary men. And, in annotating the *Sonetti* of Bernardino Rota (Naples, 1560), Pompeo de Paladini treated Petrarchan commonplaces as mere hyperboles. In short, criticism had become more "sensible." The poet no longer seemed a master of all wisdom whose every word deserved infinite study. He was a man speaking to men in a generally comprehensible language. By the mid-century, Giovan Battista Gelli (*Sopra un sonetto,* Florence, 1549, ff. a3^v-a5^v; *Tutte le lettioni,* Florence, 1551, ff. P1^v-V4^r, ZZ^v-CC4^r) found it necessary to defend the very notion that there is doctrine in Petrarch; and even Gelli claimed a serious intellectual content only for the verse of Petrarch's maturity, conceding that his early sonnets were purely amorous.

In part humanism itself diminished critics' interest in Petrarch's doctrine; for, as rhetoricians, humanists were less concerned with science than with those moral principles and moving phrases which stir men to action. In part, however, the change marked the end of humanism and the beginning of an age of skeptical common sense. Courtiers felt that poetry and doctrine are inimical (as recognized by Bernardino Tomitano, *Quattro libri,* Padua, 1570, f. L2^v). Philosophers like Varchi, meanwhile, said that Petrarch teaches not science, as commentators had argued, but common sense.[9] Here one sees that influence of courtly taste and common sense which was to characterize the next age. Particularly interesting are the remarks of two poets. In his *Lezzione* on a sonnet by Della Casa (in *Delle Rime, et Prose,* Venice, 1583), Torquato Tasso rejected the search for detailed learning in poetry. He said that poets seek to delight a wide audience; that they can imitate only the superfices of science; and that their ideas must be essentially common-

8. Benedetto Varchi, "Lezioni sul Petrarca," in *Opere* (Trieste, 1859), II, 444.
9. Cited by Ezio Raimondi, *Rinascimento inquieto* (Palermo, 1965), pp. 81-2.

place. According to Tasso, poets talk about great things not to teach but to awaken a wondering contemplation, and so evoke delight and marvel. Later, in his *Considerazioni sopra le Rime del Petrarca* (Modena, 1609), Alessandro Tassoni mocked those who found erudition in the *Canzoniere,* and expressed his own preference for Petrarch's simplest sonnets. Tasso's emphasis upon marvel anticipated secentismo, where Tassoni's desire for simplicity suggests Malherbe. Both removed poetry from the schoolroom and prepared it for its entrance into the salon.

Though critics generally were abandoning the notion that the *Canzoniere* is a great work of science and philosophy, Platonists like Sebastiano Erizzo (*Espositione,* Venice, 1561) and Giovambattista da Castiglione (*I luoghi difficili de Petrarcha,* Venice, 1532) continued to attribute a technical precision to Petrarch's language and a scientific consistency to his thought. Where the poet speaks of seeing his beloved, they discussed the role of vision in knowledge; where he speaks of dying for love, they referred to Platonic theories of death and resurrection. By collating such passages with others of a similar stamp, they suggested that the *Canzoniere* is consistently and rigorously Neoplatonic. There were many causes for such readings, both in Petrarch and in the temper of the Renaissance. But perhaps the chief cause was the premise that a great poet must teach great truths; for Neoplatonism gave a philosophic dimension to Petrarch's subject, love, which might otherwise seem trivial.

To religious men at least, Petrarch's subject did indeed seem poor. Thus in his *Rime spirituali* (Venice, n.d.) Gabriel Fiamma said that though mature men might find Platonism in the *Canzoniere,* young readers found nothing but secular love; and so he set out to rival Petrarch in a collection of religious verses. In *Il Petrarcha spirituale* (Venice, 1567), Frate Hieronimo Malipiero told how Petrarch's ghost had said that his love was concupiscent, as any sensible reader could see from his sonnets of repentance. Malipiero then revised the *Canzoniere,* turning it to Christian love—for example, changing "S'Amor non è, che dunque è quel ch' io sento" to "S'Amor sol Dio è di vita, et io nol sento."

Though motivated in part by the Counter-Reformation, the religious reaction to Petrarchism also reflected a triumph of good sense over philology. Rhetoricians too had come to ignore Petrarch's subject, and stress the learning with which he treated it;[10] Girolamo Ruscelli said that Petrarch's subject is thin (*Del modo,* 1594, f. B3^{r}). Such remarks sig-

10. *Annotationi brevissime* (1566) has it that Petrarch's subject is merely love, though with classical precedents; but that his poems become valuable by his method of treatment ("Ai lettori").

nalled a broad philosophic change. In his *Rimario* (Naples, 1535), Benedetto del Falco said that critics should prefer Aristotle to Plato because where Plato needs a rapt reader, anyone can understand Aristotle (ff. h5^{v}-i4^{v}).

In the academies the *Canzoniere* continued to provide occasions for philosophic statement; but Petrarch himself no longer seemed a philosopher. In his Platonic analysis of "Poi che voi et io" (*Cinque lezzioni,* Florence, 1575), Lionardo Salviati did not insist upon Petrarch's philosophic accuracy; instead, he said that where the poet departs from Platonic theory, he indulges in hyperbole. In *Sopra il sonetto del Petrarca "Amor, fortuna"* (Florence, 1560), Cervoni da Colle used Petrarch's perturbation as the subject of a lecture on Aristotelian and Stoic doctrines, but he did not insist that those doctrines could be found in the *Canzoniere* itself. And in his *Nuova spositione* (Florence, 1554) of "In nobil sangue vita umile e queta," Simone de la Barba da Pescia similarly used the *Canzoniere* as an occasion to discuss nobility. In short, academicians still used Petrarch as their text; but they no longer saw him as an all-knowing teacher, nor did they read his poems as profound truths beneath an esoteric veil. As philosophy became more Aristotelian, critics limited the meaning of Petrarch's sonnets to the things he clearly said. At the same time, courtiers rejected erudite readings and religious men wanted Christian truths to be stated directly. Thus a new, rationalistic attitude towards poetic doctrine developed. Poetry was no longer a repository in which erudite men might find all truth. It had become more what the ordinary reader might find it, an artful expression of common feelings and ideas.

Art

Several writers urged commentators to pay less attention to doctrine, and more heed to art. They recognized that a metaphor need not be scientifically precise, and that a hyperbole need not express a philosophic theory. In this they seem modern and humane. But often they were insistently pedantic. Sometimes they wrote grammars, illustrating their points from Petrarch and incidentally correcting misinterpretations based upon grammatical misconstruction. For example, there is Francesco Fortunio's *Regole grammaticali* (Venice, 1545) and Alberto Acharisio da Cento's *Vocabolario, grammatica, et orthographia de la lingua volgare . . . con ispositioni di molti luoghi di Dante, del Petrarca, et del Boccaccio* (Cento, 1543). Sometimes they wrote basic rhetoric texts illustrated from the *Canzoniere,* like Simone de la Barba da Pescia's *La Topica di Cicerone, . . . esempi di tutti i luoghi cavati da Dante, dal*

Petrarca, e dal Boccaccio (Venice, 1556). Love sonnets were fashionable, and courtiers wanted to know how to write them. Moreover, poetic composition was the prime fruit of a humanistic education. When the commentator discussed Petrarch's "art," therefore, he generally meant to instruct aspiring poets in their trade.

It is in this context that the *Annotationi brevissime* (Padua, 1566) presented Petrarch as an Italian Virgil full of doctrine and ornaments—a source of places taken from Scripture, dialectics, philosophy, the sciences and Latin authors; a mine of information about rivers, trees, fountains, birds and planets; a handbook of figures, arguments, maxims and metaphors. Under various headings, the *Annotationi* provided a handy encyclopedia of "Ornamenti Artificiosi del Petrarca"—lists of arguments from fables and history, lists of circumlocutions, comparisons, metaphors, and other figures of speech. The idea was to make Petrarch a textbook from which a reader might learn the Italian language, and from which he might derive ideas and ornaments for his own writing. Among editions of the poet, Dolce's *Il Petrarcha* (Venice, 1557) included a list of Petrarch's rime words, alphabetized according to rhyme sounds; a concordance of his words, with their definitions; a table of nouns with the epithets Petrarch applied to them; a table of beautiful Petrarchan figures of speech; and similar tables of ideas, comparisons and similes.

Pietro Biadi's *Il Petrarcha* (Venice, 1535), ff. C4^{r}-D4^{v} and Dolce's *Osservationi,* 4th ed. (Venice, 1556), ff. A4^{r}ff. suggest that such tables were primarily intended for the young and unlearned. In any event they are a primary reason that sixteenth-century Italian verse is as it is; and they are a sign of what Petrarch had become—a model for poetic novices. Among works like Dolce's might be mentioned Nicolò Liburnio's *Le tre fontane . . . sopra la grammatica, et eloquenza di Dante, Petrarcha et Boccaccio* (Venice, 1526); Pellegrino Moreto Mantovano's *Rimario de tutte le cadentie di Dante, et Petrarca* (Venice, 1529)—a work in which (f. A2^{v}) Moreto promised a later volume defining the obscure words of those poets in alphabetical order; Sebastiano Fausto da Longiano's *Il Petrarcha . . . con rimario et epiteti in ordine d'alphabeto,* reprint (Venice, 1532); Francesco Alunno da Ferrara's *Le osservationi sopra il Petrarca . . . con tutte le sue autoritá, et dechiarationi delle voci ai luoghi loro per ordine di alphabeto collocate* (Venice, 1550); and Girolamo Ruscelli's *Il Petrarca . . .* [*con*] *un pieno vocabolario del medesimo, sopra tutte le voci, che nel libro si contengono, bisognose di dichiaratione, d'avvertimento, e di regola, et con uno utilissimo rimario . . . et un raccolto de tutti gli epiteti usati dall'autore* (Venice, 1554). When boys were taught to compose in Latin by compiling pastiches from classical authors, the *Canzoniere* seemed a collection of rhetorical figures, grammatical illustrations and fine phrases.

Such a conception of Petrarch tended to produce imitations which were strings of ornate expressions.[11] Within humanism itself there was a corrective force. In his posthumous *De' commentarii della lingua italiana* (Venice, 1581), for example, Girolamo Ruscelli continued to admire ornateness; but (especially in Books IV and VI) he proposed as well ideals he considered equally important, namely clarity, grammatical correctness and logical accuracy, an avoidance of affectation, and a governing suitability.[12] Similar ideas were expressed by Toscanella, who blamed the commentators for doing little more than naming rhetorical figures, and said that each figure must be understood as it works in its place (ff. Fl[r-v]). In discussing Petrarch, Toscanella approved ornaments but noted the necessity for a strong, clear logic—for ligatures, verbal accuracy, exact antitheses and sensible statements. He also cautioned against "bischizzi" like "De me medesmo meco mi vergogno." And in a "Discorso" prefaced to *Le rime di Luca Contile* (Venice, 1565), Francesco Patrizi attacked rhetoricians and asserted against them the importance of the central idea in each poem. Though not novel, such judgments anticipated the anti-rhetorical tone of the seventeenth century. They signalled a movement away from individual ornaments, towards an appreciation of a clear, general outline and lucid statement.

As Francesco Berni's *Dialogo contra i poeti* suggests, anti-Petrarchists mocked the motion of poetry as a supreme wisdom and art. Yet they denounced Petrarch's followers for writing words, where he himself wrote things. For an emphasis upon clear, substantial statement was a feature of the time. Perhaps there were two alternative ideals of rhetoric, both distinct from that of the early humanists. For Castelvetro and Muzio—to some degree for Ruscelli and Toscanella—poetry had to be "proper,"[13] lucid and accurate, governed by a

11. Imitation also led to fine and original poetry. Rewarding studies are Luigi Baldacci, *Il petrarchismo italiano nel Cinquecento* (Milan, 1957); W. Theodor Elwert, "Il Bembo imitatore," *Studi di letteratura veneziana* (Venice, 1958), pp. 111-45; and Ferruccio Ulivi, *L'imitazione nella poetica del Rinascimento* (Milan, 1959).

12. Perhaps particularly pre-classical is Ruscelli's great admiration for a sequence of two or three substantives, each different, each with its proper epithet, and for one noun with two or three epithets, each proper (Bk. VII, Ch. 5, ff. NN3[v]-NN5[v]).

13. The emphasis upon "propriety"—that is, words in their most exact senses—conforms to the ideal which Jean-Antoine du Cerceau, for example, expressed

rational decorum, a logical syntax and neat antitheses. To others, like Tasso[14] and to some extent Toscanella, it had above all to create an emotional effect. In short, the collection of beauties had become old-fashioned. Critics sought a governing logic or a governing emotion—approaching the poetics, respectively, of France and Italy in the seventeenth century.

Language

A central motive for Petrarchism was the desire for a vernacular literature, a desire which sixteenth-century literary men across Europe shared. In Italy the situation was especially difficult, for the peninsula was not a country but a collection of city states, papal states and French, Spanish and Austrian territories; the problem was to form a national language and literature before there was a nation. What Bembo attempted, and in large part achieved, was to create Italian much as the humanists had created Neo-Latin. As they had repudiated the contemporary Latin of the church, law and diplomacy, so he repudiated contemporary Italian; as they had turned for their models to Virgil and Cicero, so he turned to Petrarch and Boccaccio.

For what Bembo achieved, his contemporaries were rightly grateful. But there was much to be lost in remoulding a living language upon the practice of authors long dead, who had never attempted to write upon every subject or for every occasion. Bemboism, therefore, evoked a great debate, whose general outlines are clear in Claudio Tolomei's *Il Cesano* (Venice, 1555). Other significant tracts are Dolce, *Le osservationi,* 4th ed., Venice, 1556, a practical application, meant to benefit the unlearned, of Bembo's *Prose della volgar lingua*; Giovan Giorgio Trissino, *Il Castellano,* Venice, 1529; Benedetto Varchi, *L'Hercolano,* Florence, 1570; Lodovico Castelvetro, *Correttione,* Basel, 1572; Hieronimo Mutio Giustinopolitano, *Battaglie . . . Varchina,* Venice, 1582; and the sensible if less famous Orazio Lombardelli, *I fonti toscani,* Florence, 1598.

The debate about the language involved many philological issues, such as the relation of Italian to written Latin, spoken Latin, Provençal, and various dialects. Often (as Tolomei's *Il Cesano* made especially clear) the motives of the disputants were impure; academicians thought

---

when he said that in the Renaissance eloquence belonged to the savant, but in the seventeenth-century the spirit of geometry recalled taste to clarity and regularity (summarized by Pizzorusso, pp. 403-4).

14. See his *Lettione,* and also his *Del poema eroico,* Libro quarto.

that Italian should be academic and courtiers that it should be courtly, Tuscans thought it should be Tuscanized and non-Tuscans thought not. The chief issue, however, was whether Italian should be based upon the practice of old authors or upon contemporary speech, especially the speech of courtiers. In short, the argument was a form of the ancient-modern controversy. Some held that the language was complete and perfect in Petrarch; others insisted upon contemporaneity and courtly taste.

Seventeenth-century French verse reflected the triumph of "moderns" over "ancients";[15] in Italy, the modernists were Bembo's opponents. In a preface to the *Rime di Lodovico Paterno* (Venice, 1560), Mario degli Andini for example denied that one must limit himself to the words Petrarch had used (ff. a8^{r-v}); so did the preface to *Le rime di Luca Contile* (Venice, 1565). In the later volume, Francesco Patrizi's "Discorso" denied that old poets knew everything about love and eloquence; it asserted that as Petrarch had improved upon his antecedents, so moderns might improve upon him. And in his *Correttione* (1572), Castelvetro like Malherbe insisted upon the current language, declaring that only the people, finally, can judge the vernacular. By the seventeenth century, the "moderns" had triumphed. Latinisms were rejected as turgid and difficult, and a current, polite language was the ideal—as one can see in *L'Anticrusca . . . nel qual si mostra chiaramente che l'antica* [*lingua*] *sia inculta e rozza: e la moderna regolata e gentile* (Padova, 1613). Here one finds the ideal of regularity and politeness ("regolata e gentile") which was proclaimed by critics in seventeenth-century France.

Bembo had assumed that, like Latin, Italian could become artful only when moderns imitated its classics. Under the impetus of modernism his premise lost its strength. The practice of Petrarch (or of any poet) was not long accepted as a final authority on the capabilities of the language. By the third quarter of the century many, perhaps most, writers on the subject proposed a sensible eclecticism. They said that speech should imitate speech, prose prose, and verse verse; in verse they offered different models for different effects—for example, Della Casa for grandeur and Guarino for delightfulness.

The eclecticism of such writers as Varchi and Orazio, however, revealed that authority alone no longer sufficed; implicitly, principles (and not merely authoritative practice) had come to govern the lan-

15. An interpretation convincingly argued by Gillot. See also Spingarn and R. F. Jones, *Ancients and Moderns* (Seattle, 1936). Tasso's *Apologia* is an interesting document in the context of the ancient-modern controversy.

guage. Especially important among such principles were those which appeared in the debate about Caro's "Venite a l'ombra de' gran gigli d'oro." For, foreshadowing secentismo, Caro sacrificed lucidity to evoke wonder. In his *Correttione* (Basel, 1572) and *Ragione* (Parma, 1573), Castelvetro attacked Caro, demanding clarity. Now, clarity had been recognized as an important principle by Ruscelli and Tolomei (*Delle lettere,* Venice, 1572, ff. $B3^v$-$B5^v$); indeed, as early as 1519 Baldassare Tacone said that a modern poet as genteel, ornate and vigorous as Petrarch could do better than he by being open rather than dark (preface to *Sonetti* [*di*] *Antonio Lornazano Placentino,* Milan, 1519). But Castelvetro's demand for clarity was enormously exacting and detailed; he demanded a logical justification of each word and phrase. (Tasso's *Lettere* suggest that some decades later such a demand was widespread.) In response such books as the *Apologia de gli Academici Bianchi* (Parma, 1573) said that poetry is not mathematics; that delight and wonder, not clarity, are the highest ends of verse. Thus two principles were set in conflict—on the one hand an ideal of lucid rationality which anticipated French neoclassicism; on the other an ideal of the marvellous which foreshadowed the seicento.

Petrarch was soon involved in the debate. When he attacked Caro, Castelvetro held up Petrarch as a model of clarity; but in commenting upon the *Canzoniere* (*Le rime del Petrarca,* Basel, 1582), he noted redundancies, obscurities, false grammar, senseless phrases and factual inaccuracies. In support of Castelvetro, Muzio Giustinopolitano devoted his *Bellissime annotationi* (Venice, 1582) to Petrarch's sins against grammar, logic, clarity and decorum. He objected that "Voi" in "Voi ch'ascoltate" is tied to nothing. Since a neck has no manners and light no hardness, he noted the impropriety in calling a "collo" "gentile" or "lume" "piano." He considered "il fior . . . luce sparte" ("In quella parte") wrong, since flowers spread odors, not light. He demanded logical accuracy. Moreover he objected to imperfect antitheses, such as that between "vissi" and "struggo"; he noted that in the line "Al dolce aere sereno al fosco e greve" ("Pommi ove"), "greve" does not respond precisely to "dolce." Further, Muzio had a strict sense of decorum; he thought it hideous to place reins and spurs in Laura's face in "O passi sparsi." Muzio's demand for logical accuracy was so severe that he failed to appreciate Petrarch's achievement and sometimes misunderstood Petrarch's meaning. Yet the critiques of Castelvetro and Muzio were rightly recognized to be enormously important. They represented the forces of modernism and "reason." Attacking a revered master, they insisted upon lucidity and common sense.

In France Petrarch went out of favor during the seventeenth century; his reputation revived only with Romanticism.[16] In Italy too his richly artful meditations were sometimes felt to lack clarity, but here his merit was not really in question. Varchi defended both Petrarch and Bembo, and Varchi was followed by many others, among them Hieronimo Zoppio in his *Ragionamenti* (Bologna, 1583). What was in question was the nature of poetic authority. There was a demand for originality,[17] especially for the new and marvellous; equally there was an insistence upon lucidity. It had become impossible to accept Petrarch as an absolute model who had established what is good once and for all. Even Zoppio accepted the notion that clarity and good sense are more important than Petrarch's practice; he only argued that Petrarch had not violated such principles. In short, Petrarch had become what the classics soon became for the French—an enduring influence, but not a definitive example of all that poetry might achieve.

When Alessandro Tassoni published his *Considerazioni* in 1609, the new critical spirit prevailed. Tassoni's irreverent clarity and vulgar good sense recall the anti-Petrarchisti and anticipate those seventeenth-century burlesques his *Secchia rapita* did much to inspire. His conception of manners also suggests the Age of Reason. For example, he considered Petrarch's reference to a child and rod, low and unsuitable in "Io temo sì." In "Se la mia vita" he found unnatural the desire that Laura become ugly. He objected that "Io mi rivolgo," though a sonnet of parting, evokes the image of an hydroptic asking charity. Of "Sì traviato" he said that the conceit of gathering bitter fruit from a lady would have been more appropriate if Petrarch had caught the French disease from a prostitute. He considered that unless Petrarch was answering one who had commented upon it, the poet could be blamed for noting Laura's loss of beauty in "Erano i capei d'oro." In "Quand'io movo" he thought offensive the reference to the "stato real" of a poor village girl, and considered it ridiculous to call amorous sighing an "alta impresa" worthy of Hercules. Further, he considered that "Se voi poteste" violates decorum by making Laura act out of

16. A small but revealing incident is discussed by Claude Pichois, "Autour de Pétrarque; un épisode de la bataille romantique en France (1822)," *Petrarca e il petrarchismo: Atti del Terzo Congresso dell'Associazione Internazionale per gli Studi di Lingua e Letteratura Italiana* (Bologna, 1961), pp. 265-76.

17. Many of the repudiations of Petrarch's authority come in defense of more modern poets; Falco's *Rimario* (Naples, 1535), for example, is largely a defense of the Neapolitan style, which, though it violated Bemboist tastes, was yet to become dominant with the publication of *Rime di diversi . . . Libro quinto* (Venice, 1552). Patrizi and Tacone, cited above, also wrote in defense of contemporary poets whose verses a strict Bemboist would challenge.

character, since she is humble. In short he had a neoclassical conception of decorum, sharply distinguishing between "high" and "low," demanding consistency, and judging poems as he would the politeness of one who spoke similar sentiments in contemporary society.

In language, Tassoni demanded elegance and absolute clarity. In "Voi ch'ascoltate" he objected to "giovenile errore" on the ground that Petrarch remained in error well into maturity; he suggested that "Favola fui" is a poor phrase, since fables give pleasure and Petrarch means that his behavior was shameful; and he considered "Quand'era in parte altr'uom da quel ch'i' sono" neither prose nor verse, artless and unnatural, without choice phrases, graceful words or conceits. Finally, he faulted Petrarch for saying that his "vaneggiar" led him to know life's vanity—for, Tassoni said, "vaneggiar" destroys knowledge. In "Quand'io movo" Tassoni attacked the play on names, saying that the ancients knew better; he found a senseless contradiction in Petrarch's resolution to praise and be silent; and he considered inappropriate the association of Apollo with praise, reverence and silence. Elsewhere he objected to such phrases as "farsi men duro il riso" ("Di tempo in tempo"), since smiles are neither hard nor soft. In "Amor piangeva" he thought "dritto camin" ambiguous, and said that clarity would have been preferable whatever the phrase means. Insisting upon absolute clarity, he wanted even metaphors to be almost literal. In "È questo 'l nido" Petrarch says that Laura put on plumes; Tassoni remarked that the figure is proper to birds, which are born naked and grow feathers, but that Laura grew nothing but teeth and hair. In short, Tassoni desired that thin, lucid, stylized language of love which became fashionable in France in the seventeenth century.

As to doctrine, Tassoni was glad to note Petrarch's ignorance—like Castelvetro and Muzio, he saw a confusion about astronomical matters in "Era il giorno" and an error about wet rope in "Passa la nave mia." But in general he was interested only in common sense; he neither expected nor found science in Petrarch. In the hands of the commentators "Quando giunge per gli occhi" had become a treatise on amorous philosophy like Cavalcanti's "Donna me prega"; Tassoni thought it senseless. Contradictions between Petrarch's fire and ice, hopes and fears, etc. had given rise to much philosophic speculation; Tassoni explained them simply by saying that the poet spoke differently as his feelings changed (see his comment upon "Voi ch'ascoltate," vv. 5-6). Tassoni called Platonic love a subtle hyprocrisy of Petrarch's time ("Amor, che nel pensier mio"); he said that the idea that it is good to die loving, is a doctrine the poet himself invented ("Perché quel, che mi trasse").

Nor did he share the humanist's love of moral maxims; he mocked the vacuity of Petrarch's declaration that no man can be called blessed until he dies ("Se co'l cieco desir"). In part such remarks were directed against the humanists, who found more meaning in the *Canzoniere* than Petrarch had put there. But in part Tassoni's comments reflected the new assumption that poetry is not a supreme form of wisdom—that it is nothing but polite, clear conversation which everyone can understand.

As to art, Tassoni desired "natural" poetry. He said that "Per fare una leggiadra" lacks that vivacity which should pertain to young love; and that "Quand'io son tutto volto" is very artificial, costing much and worth little. He thought "Voi ch'ascoltate" mediocre; as he said in annotating "Erano i capei," he preferred Petrarch's facile sonnets. In short, like P. Lemoyne in the next century he wanted a verse purged of "la doctrine et la teinture du collège," "la sécheresse des dogmes et [les] duretés de l'école"; like de Méré he admired "un air galant," a "je ne sais quoi de naif, et principalement pour ce qui regarde les moeurs et la vie; une façon adroite et délicate," "une netteté de pensée et d'expression qui ne laisse rien d'embarrassé."[18]

Like the *Aeneid* and *Paradise Lost,* the *Canzoniere* is a conscious classic everywhere sensitive to its literary inheritance; it epitomized the culture of its past and remained a model for posterity. Such works bear continuous reinterpretation, and in the history of Petrarchan criticism the Renaissance did not do badly. Bembo's sensitivity to Petrarch's sweet, grave phrases is as valid as the Romantics' sense of his love of nature, or the more modern concern with his Augustinianism; and Daniello (1541) at least—perhaps Vellutello (1538) too—remains a model of sensitive appreciation. Nor can the various shifts of taste truly be reprehended; for example, in preferring the Petrarchism of Della Casa, Tasso misled few readers, and prepared the way for his own heroic style and Milton's.[19] The issue here, then, is not one of a loss of perception, a narrowing appreciation of a great master; it is instead a great cultural change reflected in the small sphere of Petrarchan criticism.

At the beginning of the sixteenth century, the *Canzoniere* seemed a repository of wisdom and learning, a perfect model of syntax and diction, and a compendium of poetic and rhetorical devices. For critics then saw poetry as a means of bringing culture to their contemporaries. By the end of the century new principles of criticism prevailed. Petrarch's

18. Lemoyne is cited by Gillot, p. 258; de Méré by Borgerhoff, p. 99.

19. See F. T. Prince, *The Italian Elements in Milton's Verse* (Oxford, 1954).

sonnets no longer seemed immensely erudite and philosophic, and their details became less important. Poets who imitated them part-by-part were then considered mere pedants without poetry or politeness (see Benedetto del Falco, ff. $h5^v$-$i4^v$). In short, the *Canzoniere* had been taken out of the humanists' schoolroom. The way had been prepared for the novel elaborations and contortions of secentismo.[20] But secentismo and neoclassicism—if one likes, the Italian and French baroque—have much in common, and Petrarch's critics showed a new interest in generally comprehensible ideas, a clear, modern style and neat antitheses. Petrarch and poetry had been freed from their more solemn commentators. The Renaissance had passed; across the Alps at least, the age of rationalism was soon to begin.

20. See Aldo Scaglione, "Cinquecento Mannerism and the Uses of Petrarch," in O. B. Hardison, ed., *Medieval and Renaissance Studies,* V (Chapel Hill: U.N.C. Press, 1971), 122-155.

XXI

UN MS. DELLE *RIME* DI GALEAZZO DI TARSIA

by Paolo Cherchi
University of Chicago

Galeazzo di Tarsia "scrisse poco e per sé":[1] così suona un vecchio giudizio in cui si rende conto della scarsa sua produzione coll'addurne il carattere privato e originale nell'ambito del movimento del petrarchismo. È noto infatti che le *Rime* di Galeazzo di Tarsia (m. 1553) furono pubblicate per la prima volta da G. B. Basile nel 1617 a Napoli presso il Vitali e presso il Roncagliolo: due edizioni che differiscono per alcune notevoli varianti, e delle quali è difficile stabilire la priorità dell'una rispetto all'altra.[2] Questa prima versione del canzoniere tarsiano contiene trentaquattro sonetti, una canzone e un madrigale. L'edizione del Basile (quella Vitali) fu ristampata varie volte durante il '600 e i primi del '700. Nel 1738 apparve l'ed. Seghezzi che, su basi congetturali, correggeva i molti errori dell'ed. Basile. Vent'anni più tardi il marchese Salvatore Spiriti procurava una nuova e più ampia edizione delle *Rime:* basandosi su un autorevole codice (il Cavalcanti, oggi perduto), non solo offriva rispetto alla versione Basile un testo migliore e in molti casi diverso, ma poteva aggiungere ben dodici sonetti, una canzone e una sestina. Sull'ed. Spiriti son condotte quella del Bartelli (1888), non priva d'errori; e quella del Ponchiroli (1951),[3] certamente la migliore, benché non esente da qualche difetto e comunque lontana dall'ideale di una vera edizione critica.[4] Per avvicinarsi a quest'ideale si dovrebbe forse ridimensionare l'indiscussa autorità attribuita al ms. Cavalcanti; considerare che l'ed. Spiriti—sospetta per alcune difficoltà testuali—presenta

1. U. Foscolo, *Vestigi della storia del sonetto italiano,* in *Opere,* ed. naz. (Firenze, 1933), vol. VIII, p. 136 (cit. da L. Baldacci, *Lirici del Cinquecento,* Firenze, 1957, p. 639).

2. Dell'ed. stampata dal Roncagliolo dà una succinta notizia, in un poscritto, L. Baldacci, "Sul testo di G. di T.", in *Convivium,* VI (1952), 935 ss.; ma già M. Parenti, *Prime edizioni* (Milano, 1948^2), dava quella del Roncagliolo come prima edizione.

3. Parigi, 1951, con un'introduzione di G. Contini. La storia della vicenda delle *Rime* si può vedere qui nella "Nota al testo". A questa storia s'è aggiunta recentemente una nuova ed. delle *Rime* a c. di Gabriele Turchi (Cosenza, 1971): opera divulgativa anche se non senza pretese circa i problemi dell'ordinamento del canzoniere e delle attribuzioni.

4. Cfr. L. Baldacci, "Sul testo", cit.

in molti casi delle varianti che possono considerarsi d'autore; includere nella collazione anche l'edizione Basile-Roncagliolo che dipende certamente da una redazione diversa; e, infine, tener conto di un manoscritto—l'unico esistente[5]—che vogliamo qui segnalare.[6]

Si tratta di un ms. di provenienza strozziana, recentemente acquistato dalla Newberry Library di Chicago. È un ms. miscellaneo della seconda metà del '500/prima metà del '600, cartaceo (ma due fogli di pergamena), con copertina originale di cartone (mm. 175 x 250). Contiene 479 carte numerate, oltre ai fogli di guardia, con al dorso la scritta *Canzonette e Miscelane Diverse*. Le cc. 61r. - 84r. costituiscono un quadernetto vergato da una sola mano. Alla ca. 61r. (che segue le cc. 58-60 bianche) si legge un frontespizio "Canzone" il cui testo vien dato nelle cc. seguenti (62r.-69v.). La ca. 70r. contiene un sonetto ("Ben veggio ahi lasso e non m'inganna amore"); la ca. 70v. è bianca e le cc. 71r.-84r. contengono ventuno dei sonetti noti del Tarsia e la canzone "A qual pietra somiglia". Il testo di questi sonetti e della canzone presenta delle *lectiones singulares* rispetto alle altre edizioni, ed esse ascendono senz'altro ad una redazione diversa da quelle cui attingono gli altri editori. Ma prima di passare al rilievo di queste varianti, trascriviamo la canzone che precede i testi noti, modernizzandone in parte la grafia (eliminando l'*h* etimologica, ponendo gli accenti, riducendo a minuscole le innecessarie maiuscole) e l'interpunzione. Accanto al testo, nel luogo indicato, si trascrivono le poche glosse vergate dalla stessa mano.

A piè d'un verde faggio,
Del bel Meandro a la sinistra riva,
Endimion s'udiva
Chiamar l'amato e fuggitivo raggio
De la cerva del cielo,
Vaga sorella del signor di Delo.

Era in su l'ora apunto
Che 'l celeste bifolco il carro guida
Ver l'orsa che s'annida;
E la notte il suo manto avea trapunto
Di que' beati lumi
Che fan quaggiù correr di latte i fiumi

5. Ibid., p. 935: "l'edizione del Tarsia, del quale purtroppo non possediamo né autografi né manoscritti . . ." .

6. In realtà, di questo ms. abbiamo dato notizia in "Nuovi appunti sulle *Rime* del Coppetta", *G. S. L. I.*, CXLVII (1970), 534 ss. La segnatura del ms.—allora non ancora data—è *Case Ms. 6A 11*.

Quando il giovin dolente,
Bramoso di mirar la vaga luce
Ch'a morte lo conduce,
Con fredda lingua e con affetto ardente
Cose dicea sì nove
Ch'a pietà mosse Radamanto e Giove.

Allor fra selve e boschi
Mille ninfe s'udir, mille pastori
I mal graditi amori
Pianger di quest'amante, e i neri e i foschi
Giorni de la sua vita
Ch'aspettan sol da la sua morte aita.

E perché fosse noto
L'eterno suo martir, l'eterno foco,
E inteso in ogni loco,
Quinci Euro e Coro e quindi Borea e Noto
Ciascun per la sua parte
Lo sparse in mille lingue, in mille carte.

—Apri il balcon celeste—
Dicea—di novi lumi adorna e cinta,
Da tanti prieghi vinta;
E 'n quel petto di smalto alfin si deste,
O mia gelata face,
Qualch'ombra di pietà che mi dia pace.

Scopri serena al mondo
Quel più tranquillo e più sereno aspetto
Che suol produrre effetto
In terra più felice e più giocondo;
E con più tardo giro
Frena il tuo corso, mentr'io piango e miro.

Ecco il Silenzio e 'l Sonno,
Prodotti a un parto della Notte usciti,
Più dell'usato uniti,
Dalle Cimmerie grotte a[7] quanto ponno
Fan con licor di Lete
Per l'oriente le campagne quete.

A queste piaghe mie
Pietoso il Sol, con novo stile, in fretta,
A chi di là l'aspetta
N'ha rimenato assai cortese il die;
Né corse quel sentiero
Ch'è di questa stagion il camin vero.

Ecco ch'ad una ad una
Espero chiama le dorate stelle
Vie più lucenti e belle,
Per coronarne l'argentata Luna:
Elle per torte strade
Vengon ratte a 'nchinar l'alma beltade.

LA CORONA D'ARIADNA

La stellata corona
De la schernita giovane di Creta,
Più luminosa e lieta
Veggio un che reverente a' piè ti dona,
E tutto umil t'inchina,
Qual de le stelle in cielo alta regina.

IL TRIANGOLO DI SICILIA

Or lampeggia la stampa
De l'Isola ove ancor la terra bagna
La tua fedel compagna
Là ov'Alfeo corre e fra l'onde avvampa,
Ove fu l'alto acquisto
Che il regno alluma tenebroso e tristo.

Ecco di nove fiamme

IL GRANCHIO

Adorno l'animal che Garamante
Tenne all'acceso amante
Di Bagrade fra l'onde; e par ch'infiamme
La parte ov'egli gira,
E di tanto indugiar seco s'adira.

7. Il ms. dà *e*. Nei vv. successivi si è corretto anche *Lete* e *quete* per *Leti* e *queti* del ms.

Quel tempestoso figlio
ORIONE Mira di Ereo, che festi in mezo il fiume,
Privo di vita e lume,
E fu poi segno in ciel per tuo consiglio,
Ch'or lieto e disarmato
Stanca il petto chiamando il raggio amato.

Il vecchio che soggiorna
L'ATLANTIADE Converso in selce 'n su'l gran lito moro
Vede le figlie al Toro
Fregiar la bocca e l'infiammate corna,
E se ne gode tanto
Ch'appaga il duol del variato manto.

E quella che mai sempre
ELETTRA L'inevitabil fato, il caso reo
Ond'arse Ilio e Sigeo
Pianse là sotto il polo in nove tempre,
E con l'inculto crine
Prediceva a' mortai doglioso fine,

Or già de le più vaghe
DA SOFOCLE E luminose stelle a paragone,
Non più segno o cagione
Di mal ch'il mondo orribilmente impiaghe,
Fora de'[8] propri calli
Mena con l'altre lascivetti balli.

Dolente a' dolor miei
Ne vien la bella Astrea con quella prole
Cui par non vide il sole:
Io dico del gran figlio di colei
Ch'in forma d'aureo nembo
Il fallace amator raccolse in grembo.

O che lucente schiera
ANDROMEDA Seco mena costui[9] ch'in riva al mare
Trovò luci sì care!
Ecco Cassiopea sdegnosa e altera;

8. Ms.: *di*.

9. Se l'allusione ad Andromeda è precisa, bisognerebbe correggere in *costei*. Ma tanto Andromeda quanto il suo salvatore Perseo furono trasformati, dopo la morte, in costellazioni (cfr. Ovidio, *Met.* IV, 609 ss.); per cui *costui* potrebbe riferirsi a Perseo, e la glossa alluderebbe genericamente ai due amanti.

Ecco Cefeo appresso,
Smarrito ancora per l'orribil messo:

E perché novi onori
DA SOFOCLE
Ti porge il ciel, questa superba volto
Ha nel suo loco il volto,
Perché qual duce al tuo apparir t'adori,
Rotto il fatal destino
Di girar sempre il mondo a capo chino.

E tu, invida Notte,
Che spronando i destrier foschi e alati
M'hai tolto i raggi amati
E l'ore del piacer spesso interrotte,
Pietosa a tanto affanno
Gira quel cerchio c'hai maggior nell'anno:

Di te più lieto giorno
Dal gran seno del tempo unqua non venne,
Se ben talor'avvenne
Ch'un sol dì fosse di più soli adorno,
S'or gira in terra il guardo
Colei per cui tant'anni agghiaccio e ardo.

Dunque, o mio lume eterno,
O giel che m'ardi il core ott'anni interi,
O cagion di sinceri
Pianti ch'intenerir potrian l'Inferno,
Deh! mostra omai, cortese,
Quel ch'indarno fin qui la mente attese.

Io dissi: Un raggio solo,
Un picciol segno di pietà che faccia
Fede che non ti piaccia
Viver de la mia morte e del mio duolo,
Ché basteria sol questo
Il mio stato addolcir penoso e mesto.

Io so ch'altro non volsi
Da te già mai, e tu saper lo puoi,
Ch'il sol de gli occhi tuoi;
Né ad altro fin questa mia voce sciolsi
Se non perché ti chiami
Con la mia lingua il mondo, e adori e ami.

Bramai che tanti doni,
Tante doti celesti onde vai carca,
Non tronche man di Parca,
Ma l'alto tuo valor tanto risoni
Che vinca la memoria
D'ogni età, d'ogni tempo e d'ogni istoria.

E se sperar dovea,
Per languir e servir con tanta fede,
Qualche giusta mercede
Un cor ch'adori in terra immortal dea,
Con gli spirti sì accensi,
Qual a Dio sol per debito conviensi,

Dillo nel tuo secreto
A te stessa, o d'Amor fiera nimica,
Saggia, santa, pudica
Face del mondo per divin decreto,
Scala al sommo bene,
D'una in altra sembianza ergi la spene.

Ma che può far Medusa
Altro che transformarmi in freddo sasso
Che spiri e mova il passo,
E tra speme e timor sempre confusa
Tenga la mente, e stille
Lagrime il volto e mandi il cor faville?—

Mentre piagato e arso
Così bramando Endimion si strugge,
E pur s'asconde e fugge
Quel raggio che talor benigno è apparso,
Ecco venir dall'onde
Voce ch'ogni suo ben turba e confonde:

—Non ir più desiando,
O travagliato amante arso dal ghiaccio,
D'aver la Luna in braccio;
Ma, il tuo frale terren stato mirando,
Frena il superbo ardire
Ché non è da mortal tanto desire.

Ritorna[10] al sonno antico:

10. Nel ms. si ha *Risona,* sottolineato e corretto dalla stessa mano in *Ritorna*; nel verso successivo *Teco* è cancellato e sostituito da *Ivi.*

Ivi la lunga fe', l'acceso core
Pasci d'ombre e d'errore
Con quel vano sperar che t'è sì amico.
Forse sognando avrai
Quel che non mai sperar desto potrai—. 192

Chi è l'autore di questa lunga canzone? Non mi risulta che sia mai stata stampata; ma sarebbe rischioso escludere tale possibilità: la lussureggiante produzione di canzonieri fra il '500 e il '600, e la difficile accessibilità di molti di essi, rende pressoché impossibile una verifica esaustiva in tal senso. Pertanto, in attesta che qualche specialista provi il contrario, si può qui, col manoscritto, ascriverne cautamente la paternità a Galeazzo di Tarsia. Certo non si vuol dare un valore definitivo al fatto che una sola mano abbia apprestato questo quadernetto di versi; ma è interessante notare che il copista puntava ad organizzare in forma di canzoniere (e cioè, secondo una ordinata ricostruzione psicologica di una storia d'amore) i componimenti del Tarsia. Alcune indicazioni potrebbero provarlo: il sonetto che segue la canzone dovrebbe andare alla fine; i due sonetti "S'affaticano invan, donna reale" e "Te lacrimosa pianta sembra Amore" dovrebbero essere invertiti nella successione di componimenti, come si può dedurre dalle lettere *b* e *a* poste in testa alle rispettive pagine; l'ordine dei vari componimenti differisce da quello delle edizioni a stampa; infine, alcune correzioni di errori ovvi e altre con caratteri di varianti (entrambe della stessa mano) fanno pensare all'allestimento del ms. per la stampa, o almeno ad una riproduzione da un testo a penna, ordinato secondo nuovi criteri.

Se questi dati vanno così interpretati, non stupirà vedere preposto a questo canzoniere un poemetto-canzone che ha per tema il mito d'Endimione, un mito caro ai lirici del '500, che diede il titolo alla raccolta del Cariteo, e che lo stesso Tarsia ricordò nel sonetto "Vide vil pastorel". Non stupirà perché in quel poemetto-canzone sembra cagliarsi emblematicamente il senso della poesia tarsiana, con quella sua tendenza a risolversi più che in recupero della "memoria", in un corposo e irsuto discorso di immagini e simboli: personificazioni icastiche in cui si brucia, oggettivandosi, una tensione metafisica che ha il suo lievito nel paradosso dell'amore. Tale tendenza rinviene qui il suo esito più naturale, ché il mito di Endimione è da leggere come una perfetta trascrizione della vicenda amorosa del Tarsia, tanto che il poeta non ritiene necessario rendere esplicito il paragone.

Quanto al genere, questa canzone si può ascrivere a quel tipo di poemetti favolosi che dall'Alemanni arrivano fino agli *idilli favolosi* raccolti nella *Sampogna* del Marino (che pensava di comporne uno su Endimione). Ma l'impasto umanistico delle favole dell'Alemanni o l'estenuata freschezza degli idilli del Marino o la malinconica vena degli idilli del Tansillo non hanno niente in comune con la nostra canzone. Essa sembra trovare dei paralleli al suo tono in certo alessandrinismo di Bernardo Tasso o di Lelio Capilupi, ma senza nessuna concessione alla tonalità madrigalesca di questi ultimi. Ancora una volta dunque il Tarsia avrebbe scritto "come uomo che non sa e non vuole imitare".[11]

Tema della canzone è l'ultima preghiera che Endimone rivolge alla Luna. Il pastore frigio è "arso dal ghiaccio", cioè dalla sorella d'Apollo, e "spera dalla morte aita". Alla sua preghiera si unisce quella delle varie costellazioni che, quasi in un balletto, entrano ad una ad una nella scena del firmamento per preparare e propiziare l'apparizione dell' "argentata Luna". Ma la preghiera non sarà esaudita ché "non è da mortal tanto desire", benché altre volte la Luna sia scesa fra le braccia dell'amante. La situazione di Endimione è sostanzialmente paradossale e pertanto la sua preghiera è infarcita di *oxymora,* la sua linea melodica è inceppata da frequenti inarcature o perseguita con delle facili zeppe; il terso disegno delle costellazioni, invocate a pregare la Luna, sottolinea di fatto la fissità e l'aseità del cielo precluso al mortale amante; la sentenza finale, col ricordare che solo in sogno il pastore potrà realizzare il suo amore, raccoglie il senso della paradossalità della situazione di Endimione. Insomma, in questa canzone la propensità tarsiana al "gioco scoperto dell'antitesi e del paradosso"[12] compie una delle sue prove più alte, cifrando nella perpetuità del mito l'esagitata e frustrata ansia di assoluto che ispira il resto del suo canzoniere.

11. Sempre a giudizio del Foscolo (cfr. n.1).

12. L. Baldacci, "Sulla poesia del T.", *Inventario* (1953), 86. Sulla lirica del T., oltre ai cappelli nelle antologie di L. Baldacci, *Lirici,* cit., pp. 636 ss., e di D. Ponchiroli, *Lirici del Cinquecento* (Torino, 1958), pp. 569 ss., sono da vedere: la citata introduzione del Contini; le pagine che B. Croce dedica al Nostro nel saggio "La lirica cinquecentesca", raccolto in *Poesia popolare e poesia d'arte* (Bari, 1933), pp. 339 ss. (al T. 385 ss.); il cap. di E. Bonora in *Storia della lett. ital.* diretta da Cecchi-Sapegno, vol. IV, *Il Cinquecento* (Milano, 1966), pp. 234 ss.; il saggio di G. Petrocchi, "Il lessico sentimentale di G. di T.", in *Miscellanea .... Trombatore,* e ora in *I fantasmi di Tancredi* (Caltanisetta-Roma, 1972), pp. 353 ss., e infine le pagine di E. Raimondi in "Il Petrarchismo nell'Italia meridionale", negli *Atti del convegno intern. sul tema "premarinismo e pregongorismo", 1971* (Roma: Acc. Naz. dei Lincei, 1973), 95 ss. Del T. si discorre in molte storie della letteratura italiana che sarebbe superfluo citare qui, mentre impossibile sarebbe ricordare i numerosi riferimenti che al T. fanno quanti si sono occupati del petrarchismo (una fitta bibliografia sull'argomento si può vedere in A. Scaglione, "Cinquecento Mannerism and the Uses of Petrarch," in O. B. Hardison, ed., *Medieval and Renaissance Studies,* V [Chapel Hill: U.N.C. Press, 1971], 122 ss.).

Alla canzone fa seguito il sonetto "Ben veggio ahi lasso", anch'esso inedito. In testa alla pagina si legge "Fine", ed è probabile, come già s'è detto, che sia un'indicazione del posto che il sonetto dovrebbe avere nel canzoniere, non essendo verosimile che si tratti di un titolo o che valga a ricordare che la canzone della pagina a fronte sia terminata. Ecco il testo:

Ben veggio, ahi lasso, e non m'inganna Amore,
Che l'audace pensier trapassa il segno,
Ma che poss'io se non ha legge il regno
Del tiranno crudel c'ha in preda il core?

Ben riconobbi dal mio primo ardore
Che sì alto, sì ricco e sì gran pegno
Del cielo al ciel si serba ed è sol degno
Del santo grembo del divin Fattore.

Ma vago a forza di mia tristi pianti
Con fallace sperar pasco la sete
Dell'ostinata voglia ognor più accesa,

Tal che s'io mi morrò quindi vedrete,
O ben nate alme e voi cortesi amanti,
Che raro è senza duol tropp'alta impresa.

Il sonetto sembra raccogliere le meste considerazioni che ad Endimione ispira la "voce ch'ogni suo ben turba e confonde". E se davvero il sonetto è da porre alla fine della raccolta (e non proprio da appendere alla canzone stessa, creando così un caso di componimento polimetrico di cui sarà maestro il Marino), verrebbe a chiudere ancora emblematicamente la vicenda del poeta, e a definire i poli entro cui si colloca il suo spazio lirico: aspirazione all'assoluto, votata al diniego.

Raccogliamo qui di seguito le varianti significative[13] che gli altri componimenti presentano rispetto all'ed. Basile–Vitali (=B), Basile–Roncagliolo (=R: nel caso che i due testi coincidano si darà solo B), e Spiriti (=S). Per agevolare i riscontri diamo tra parentesi il numero rispettivo dell'ed. Ponchiroli. Nessuna proposta sulla preferibilità o meno

13. Si son trascurate per lo più le varianti ortografiche, come per es. *altieri* per *alteri, scopre* per *scuopre*.
Le varianti del Basile-Vitali le abbiamo ricavate dall'apparato dell'ed. Ponchiroli, dell'ed. Bartelli, nonché dell'ed. Spiriti: purtroppo questa prima ed. napoletana ci è inaccessibile, nonostante le intense ricerche fatte in Italia e altri paesi.

delle lezioni verrà avanzata: in questo senso deciderà un futuro editore. A lui spetterà anche decidere se la lezione del nostro ms. sia in qualche caso chiaramente erronea, e se il metodo da seguire nello stabilire il testo non possa essere che quello della *selectio*.

1) Son. *Dura impresa* (II); ca. 71r.
   v. 5: "Or sì vaga prigion" con B, contro "Or sì dolce prigion" di S.
   v. 6: "Ch'io non cerco più schermo a ricovrarmi" con B, contro "Non cerco altro schermo a ricovrarmi" di S.
   v. 11: "L'una vil voglia e l'altra Amor governa" con B, contro "L'una vil voglia e l'altra onor governa" di S.
2) Son. *Quello, ond'io vissi nell'età fiorita* (XV); ca. 71v.
   v. 1: "Quello, ond'io vissi" con R e S, contro "quello onde vissi" di B.
   v. 8: "son d'entrar vago a la pensosa vita" con R, contro B ed S: "son d'entrar vago all'amorosa vita".
3) Son. *Donna che di beltà vivo oriente* (XLVII); ca. 72r.
   v. 2: "Fusti et al fianco mio" contro "foste" di R e "fosti" di B ed S.
   v. 3: "incontro al mondo" rispetto a "incontro il mondo" di R e "in contra il mondo" di B ed S.
   v. 6: "Risguarda in questo calle oscuro et ermo" con R contro "colle oscuro ed ermo" di B ed S.
   v. 11: "via più" contro "vie più" di B ed S.
   v. 13: "Altra Aurora, altro Sole" con R e con S, contro "Altro sol, altr' Aurora" di B.
4) Son. *Non così lieve piuma aer sereno* (XL IV); ca. 72v.
   v. 2: "spalmato legno quest'onda marina" contro "spalmato legno queta onda marina" di B ed S.
   v. 9: "Ma se va dietro al ver ch'a destro (=opportunamente) sorge" contro "al ver ch'a destra sorge" di B ed S.
   v. 10: "quasi augel senza piume" con B, contro "senza piuma" di S.
5) Son. *Bellezza è un raggio che dal primo bene* (XIV); ca. 73r.
   v. 10: "oro, perle, rubin, smeraldo et ostro" contro "smeraldi" di B ed S.
6) Son. *Vidde vil pastorel pietosa e leve* (XII); ca. 73v.
   v. 3: "un pudico garzon" con B, contro "un selvaggio garzon" di S.
   v. 4: "questa nembo di fior, quella di neve" contro "questa cinta di fior" di B ed S.
   v. 8: "un freddo marmo intenerirn'in breve" contro "intenerirsi in breve" di B ed S.

7) Son. *Se restasse di voi sembianza intera* (XXXVI); ca. 74r.
v. 2: "nelle carte o ne' marmi o ne' colori" contro "nelle carte, ne' marmi o ne' colori" di B, e "nelle carte, ne' marmi e ne' colori" di S.
v. 5: "L'alta che pinge e cria bellezza vera" contro "L'altra che pinge" di B ed S.
v. 6: "Oro, stella, onda" contro "oro, stelle, onda" di B ed S.
v. 8: "che l'arte invano d'agguagliarla spera" con R contro "indarno l'arte" di S, e "in vano l'arte" di B.
v. 14: "chi può dir come invola e tende l'arco" con B, contro "invola o tende l'arco" di S.

8) Son. *S'affaticano invan Donna reale* (XXXVII); ca. 74v.
v. 2: "mille alme penne e mille puri inchiostri" con R ed S e con la *Raccolta,*[14] contro "chiari inchiostri" di B.
v. 4: "che mal simiglia il sole opra mortale" contro "al sole opra mortale" della *Raccolta* e contro "il sol cosa mortale" di B ed S.
v. 5: "il ciel vi fece" con B ed S e contro la *Raccolta* "il ciel v'ha fatto".
v. 10: "che 'l vostro nome" con B e la *Raccolta,* contro "che il nome vostro" di S.
v. 13: "andrete nuova sposa al sommo bene" con B e la *Raccolta,* contro "vostro bene" di S.
v. 14: "Nei vostri parti ove dipinta sete" con B, contro "nel vostro parto ove dipinta sete" della *Raccolta,* e "nei vostri parti che dipinta siete" di S.

9) Son. *Te lagrimosa pianta sembra amore* (XVII); ca. 75r.
v. 9: "Ei da la speme onde si nutre e nasce" con R ed S, contro B: "si nutre e pasce".
v. 11: "E spiega mille poi freschi desiri" con B, contro "Ma spiega mille ognor freschi desiri" di S.
v. 13: "onda, terra, pratello, orto non pasce" contro B ed S: "onda, rena, pratello".

10) Son. *Prospero questa che ti onora e piange* (XLIX); ca. 75v.
v. 4: "Nei volti scritto" con B, contro "nei volti impresso" di S.
v. 5: "Mira Basento, e il suo fratel che piange" contro B ed S: "il suo fratel che frange".
v. 11: "Marmo l'intaglio" con B, contro "marmo l'incido" di S.
v. 14: "sepolti insieme" con B ed S, contro R "sepolte insieme".

14. Così indichiamo una raccolta di *Rime in lode di Giovanna Castriota Caraffa*... (Vico Equense, 1585) in cui compaiono, *editio princeps,* due sonetti del Tarsia, ristampati ora in appendice all'ed. di G. Turchi, cit.

11) Son. *Amore è una virtù che né per onda* (VIII); ca. 76r.
v. 2: "Pesce guizza né crudo aspe in sentero" contro "né cruda aspe è in sentero" di B; contro "né crudo aspe è in sentero" di R; contro "né crudo angue è in sentero" di S.
v. 4: "Né cresce erbetta in rivo o in ramo fronda" contro "erbetta in riva" di B ed S.
v. 5: "Né vento questa o quella aggira e sfronda" con B, contro "agita e sfronda" di S.
v. 9: "Che non scaldi, addolcisca, prenda a volo" con S, contro "prenda volo" di B. Nel ms. si legge, sotto una cancellatura, la parola "sdegno", cioè "prende a sdegno". La correzione è della stessa mano.
v. 10: "Nutra, rinverda" contro "rinverda, nutra" di B ed S.

12) Son. *Già corsi l'Alpi gelide e canute* (XLI); ca. 76v.
v. 1: "Già corsi l'Alpi" (B: "l'Alpe") è sottolineato e la stessa mano soprascrive: "Corso ho già".
v. 9: "O felice colui ch'un breve e colto" contro "ch'in breve e colto" di B (non capisco come il Bartelli gli attribuisca "ch'un breve") e di S (accettato dal Bartelli e corretto in "ch'un breve" dal Ponchiroli; ma già la correzione era nel Seghezzi).

13) Son. *Donna che viva già portavi i giorni* (XLVI); ca. 77r.
v. 3: "Non sono spenti i tuoi splendori e morti" con B, contro "i tuoi splendori o smorti" di S.
v. 7: "Sembrano i lumi tuoi di freddi e smorti" contro "da freddi e smorti" di B, e contro "da freddi e morti" di S.

14) Son. *Ove più ricovrar Amor poss'io* (XIII); ca. 77v.
v. 3: "Qual più selvaggia parte ov'io m'involi" con B, contro "qual più riposta parte" di S.
v. 5: "Stavami in questo scoglio alpestre e rio" contro B ed S: "alpestro e rio".
v. 6: "Co' miei pensieri scompagnati e soli" con B, contro "pensieri accompagnati e soli" di S.
v. 9: "Che renduto a me stesso" contro "Così reso a me stesso" di B ed S.
v. 10: "quasi servo fedel" con B, contro "come servo fedel" di S.

15) Son. *Queste fiorite e dilettose sponde* (XXXI); ca. 78r.
v. 4: "Ove eran l'aure ai miei desir feconde" con B, contro "a' miei sospir" di S.
v. 8: "Lasciato han l'herbe" con R, contro "Lasciate han l'erbe" di B ed S.
v. 14: "Se ti fur care e le mie chiome e 'l viso" con R, contro "Se ti

fur care le mie chiome e il viso" di B ed S.

16) Son. *Come in limpido vetro o in onda pura* (XVI); ca. 78v.
v. 4: "Debil vista a mirar non s'assicura" contro "debil vista mirar" di B ed S.
v. 8: "Ch'occhio non sano a gran fulgor non dura" contro "a gran splendor" di B ed S.
v. 10: "Riceve il balenar del vostro viso" contro "il folgorar del vostro viso" di B, e contro "il folgorar del vago viso" di S.
v. 13: "Se il veggio meno assai qualhor l'affiso" contro "Se il veggio assai via men se in lui m'affiso" di R ed S, e contro "Se il veggio assai via men se in voi m'affiso" di B.

17) Son. *"Che cerchi più da Donna alma reale"* (XVIII); ca. 79r.
v. 1: "Che cerchi più da Donna alma reale" contro "Che cerchi più la donna alma reale" di B ed S (che pongono la virgola dopo "donna", mentre R la pone dopo "alma").
v. 5: "Ella è tutta voler dolce mortale" contro "tutta venen" di B ed S.
v. 7: "Dunque debbio [debb'io] morir" contro "Dunque debbo morir" di B e "deggio morir" di S.
v. 11: "Si, ma chieder più innanzi a te non lice" contro B "chieder inanzi" ed S "chieder innanzi".
v. 14: "E vivrò poi? Vivrai forte e felice" contro "vivrai forse e felice" di B ed S.

18) Son. *Da l'orto il sole, e dall'occaso aperse* (IV); ca. 79v.
v. 2: "La mia donna le luci, e il nuovo giorno" con R, contro "le luci al nuovo giorno" di B ed S.
v. 3: "Questa d'Amor, quegli de raggi adorno", contro B ed S: "quegli di raggi adorno".
v. 5: "Egli la terra, ella il mio core aperse" con B, contro "core asperse" di S.
v. 14: "E vostra o Donna la Vittoria sia" dove Vittoria è con maiuscola con B, contro R ed S.

19) Canzone *A qual Pietra somiglia* (XIX); cc. 80r—82v.
v. 4: "Una è ch'avaro peregrin n'adduce" con R, contro "una ch'avaro peregrino adduce" di B ed S.
v. 13: "Ai molli lidi in seno" con R, contro B "A' molli Lidi", e contro "A' colli Lidi" di S.
v. 17: "E di mortali avari" con B, contro "e de' mortali avari" di S.
v. 18: "E i difetti del'or toccando scuopre" con B (= del or), contro R (= de l'or) ed S (= dell'or); il Seghezzi aveva emendato "del cor".

v. 31: "Così del pianto che m'è cibo e gioco" con R, contro "dal pianto" di B ed S.
v. 32: "Move con strano errore" contro "con novo (B,R—"nuovo" in S.) errore" di B ed S.
v. 35: "Così mi cuoce il core" contro "sì che mi coce il core" di B ed S.
v. 36: "Con l'onda che dovria spenger l'ardore" contro "dovrà [R = devria] spegner l'ardore" di B ed S.
v. 42: "Memoria d'un rapace e falso toro" contro "d'un fallace e falso toro" di B ed S.
v. 48: "Mille scorgo d'Amor più chiare stelle" con B, contro "più vaghe stelle" di S.
v. 52: "Sfavilla e manda fuor favilla nuova" contro "facella nova" di B ed S.
v. 56: "Cotal convien ch'allume" con B, contro "Con tal convien nel lume" di S.
v. 58: "Selce d'honor, la mia stagion più verde" con R, contro "in mia stagion più verde" di B ed S.
v. 60: "Né pavente d'Amor fuoco né lume" contro "Né paventi d'amor foco né lume" di B ed S.
v. 64: "Ma divelto da scogli" con B, contro "divelto da' sassi" di S.
v. 70: "Mentre rio fato la mi chiuda e vieta" contro "Mentre rio fato la m'invola e vieta" di B, e "Mentre il rio fato la m'invola e vieta" di S.
v. 73: "S'alta pietà" con B ed S, contro "S'altra pietà" di R.
v. 79: "Temo cangiarmi in scoglio" con B, contro "Bramo cangiarmi" di S.

20) Son. *Fiamma gentil ch'in cielo, in mare in terra* (VII); ca. 83r.
v. 1: con S, contro "ch'in cielo, in mare e in terra" di B.
v. 2: "E ne lo abisso" con R, contro "E negli abissi" di B ed S.
v. 10: "Al santo tempio" con R, contro "Al sacro tempio" di B ed S.
v. 12: "In se stessa raccolta le divine" con B ed S, contro "In se stessa raccolte" di R.

21) Son. *A voi de' fondi suoi muscosi amari* (IX); ca. 83v.
v. 3: "E l'Indo e 'l Tago i lor riposti honori" con R ed S, contro "i più riposti" di B.
v. 8: "Et v'alzi Roma et mille et mille altari" con R, contro "Roma mille e mille altari" di B ed S.
v. 10: "E di neve e di giel l'estade impliche" contro B ("l'estate")

e contro S ("la state").

22) Son. *Tempestose, sonanti e torbid'onde* (VI); ca. 84r.
v. 8: "Queste luci e quest'hore egre e 'nquiete" contre "egre inquiete" di B e S.
v. 9: "Lasso verrà ben tempo" con B, contro "Lasso! e' verrà tempo" di S.
v. 14: "Non fia che pace un'hora unqua m'apporte" contro "non fia che il mio tiranno unqua m'apporte" di B e S.

XXII

PETRARCH: THE GERMAN CONNECTION

by Frank L. Borchardt
Duke University

Petrarch, alive and dead, has had no more ardent suitor than Germany. From the fervent appeals to settle in the court of the German Emperor to the extravagant affection heaped upon him by modern German scholars, Petrarch, his influence, and his reputation have had a consistent and enthusiastic welcome in the barbaric north. The suit seems, however, to have been largely one-sided, and in recent times its ardor has raised more than one scholarly eyebrow.

In a broader perspective the affair is but a single episode in the long history of German infatuation with the south. The hidden roots of that history lie deep in the Great Migrations and the visible fruits were consistently spectacular, like Theodoric's brilliant court at Ravenna, Charlemagne's Roman coronation, and Otto III's attempt at world government in a restored *Roma aurea.* That the fruits were spectacular does not mean that they were consistently sweet, that they necessarily represented the happiest developments of Italian or German history. However that may be, German and Italian history were tied together by an especially close bond for well over a thousand years. The focus of the relationship was, from the first Germanic kingdom in Italy to the expulsion of Austria after World War I, the monarchy. Translated into the terms of the Middle Ages that means, the Empire. And it is the Empire that lies at the focal point of Petrarch's German connection in his lifetime.

Even Petrarch's early visit to *Germania dura*[1] (in the spring and summer of 1333), well before his correspondence with the emperor and his court, reveals an imperial aspect. The possibility of finding Roman antiquities drew him to Cologne and Aachen.[2] At Cologne he was told stories of the deeds of Marcus Agrippa and Drusus Germanicus, at

1. As he regularly called Germany: Domenico Rossetti, ed., *Francisci Petrarchae Poemata Minora,* 3 vols. (Milan, 1829-1834), III, 78 [henceforth "Rossetti"].

2. Paul Piur and Konrad Burdach, eds., *Petrarcas Briefwechsel mit deutschen Zeitgenossen,* Vom Mittelalter zur Reformation, V (Berlin, 1933), pp. 168-9 [henceforth PBW].

Aachen marvelous stories about Charlemagne. The symbolic identity of ancient Roman and medieval German empire was, of course, taken for granted in Petrarch's day. One of the Charlemagne stories deals with the emperor's strange attachment to a dead beloved. She had, it turns out, concealed a magic ring under her tongue. The emperor's counselor, the Archbishop of Cologne, discovered it and discarded it in a nearby eddy. Charlemagne was thereupon revolted at the corpse, but loved no place on earth dearer than the spot at which the ring had been cast into the waters. There indeed he built his palace and church, there he lies buried, and there he ordered his successors to be crowned "as long as the German hand guides the reins of the *Imperium Romanum*" (PBW, pp. 162-64).[3]

This story, curiously enough, entered German literary tradition not in the native telling—for example, of Jansen Enikel (fl. 1276), some version of which Petrarch probably heard at Aachen—but in Petrarch's version. So great was his authority in Germany. Even in 1333, long before he reached the height of his fame, he was known and respected in Cologne (PBW, p. xxiii). His reports about that city too left a mark on German literary tradition. At the Rhine he had observed women conjuring the river with herbs in what he recognized to be a most ancient popular ritual (PBW, p. 169). Knowledge of it in Germany comes from no other source but Petrarch. The learned had every opportunity to verify his descriptions, but, as it seems, they never bothered. They were content to note that Petrarch had observed it, and hence it must be so.[4] Elsewhere Petrarch writes that he had heard of a woman in Lower Germany who concluded thirty years of life without ever having taken any food at all. He admits that it is a bit beyond belief.[5] All of this seems to represent the scattered beginnings of a project—like many of those of Petrarch, unfinished—meant to describe and interpret for civilized Italy the customs of the peoples of the barbaric north.[6]

The contrast between barbaric and Italian was as characteristic of the relations between Germany and Italy as the discussion of imperial prerogatives. When Petrarch had good words for Germany they

3. Cf. Gaston Paris, *Histoire poétique de Charlemagne,* 2nd ed. (Paris, 1905), pp. 382ff.

4. Hartmann Schedel, *Buch der Croniken* (1493; facs. rpt. Munich, 1965), fol. XCI^r.

5. Francesco Petrarca, *Rerum Memorandarum Libri,* ed. Giuseppe Billanovich (Florence, n.d. [1943]), p. 271.

6. Konrad Burdach et al., *Aus Petrarcas ältestem deutschen Schülerkreis,* Vom Mittelalter zur Reformation, IV (Berlin, 1929), p. 66.

were generally not for German ears. In the same letter which described the ancient popular ritual, Petrarch wrote his friend, Giovanni Cardinal Colonna, of his own surprise at the culture, the beauty of the city, the seriousness of the men, the elegance of the matrons (PBW, p. 168f.):

> Mirum in terra barbarica quanta civilitas, que urbis species, que virorum gravitas, que munditie matronarum . . . .

And the sight of the women conjuring the Rhine moved him to exclaim:

> Dii boni! que forma! quis habitus!

In his dejection at Italian anarchy Petrarch even went so far once as to cite Lucan (*Pharsalia,* VII, 432f.) to the effect that Freedom had abandoned Italy and retreated beyond the Rhine to be enjoyed by Germans.[7] In general, however, his words about Germany were as harsh as he considered its climate to be.[8] To be sure, a summer heat-wave as he left Cologne, 30 July 1333, made him wonder what happened to all those miserable "alpinas nives ac frigora Rheni" (PBW, p. 170) Virgil talked about in the *Eclogues* (X, 47). His experience notwithstanding, Germany was and remained the "fera Theutoniae tellus," the home of the "tedesco furor," the "tedesca rabbia."[9] Barbaric is the most recurrent attribute attached to things German. It is much to Petrarch's credit that he refused to transfer his animosity to his German correspondents.

The unhappy political condition of his beloved Italy moved Petrarch to initiate a correspondence with the emperor. With the failure of Cola di Rienzo's Roman revolution yet another possibility for order and unity had collapsed, and Petrarch's hopes for Italy had once more been disappointed. Early in 1350 or 1351 Petrarch wrote to Prague urging Charles IV to turn his attentions to Italy (PBW, pp. 1, 7-8). It was actually an open letter, a political broadside, and the emperor had no real need to answer it. Furthermore, the pacification of Italy was the last project on which the emperor intended to squander his resources. He was far too astute to be lured by that can of worms but was flattered by the attentions of the most famous man of learning in Europe. And so he responded in an elegant letter, citing Livy and Terence and declining Petrarch's proposals (PBW, pp. 12-16). One manuscript tradition and internal stylistic evidence sug-

7. Ibid., p. 146.
8. Rossetti, II, 72.
9. Ibid., p. 68; Petrarch, *Sonnets and Songs,* trans. Anna Maria Armi (New York, 1968), pp. 40 and 204.

gest that the letter was written—one assumes, reluctantly—by Cola di Rienzo, at the time an honored prisoner and guest at the imperial court. Petrarch wrote again, not in response to this letter which took three years to reach him, but on the occasion of a shift in political sentiment in Italy, which Petrarch deemed favorable to imperial intervention (PBW, pp. 17-20). The letter is filled with high pathos. Petrarch prays, begs, implores the emperor to undertake actions "for the honor of the Empire, for the salvation of Italy, for the consolation of the city of Rome, thy utterly abandoned bride," etc. We know nothing of a response on the part of Charles. Only one further letter to Petrarch survives over Charles' signature, and it is a decade later (1361/2), being a third invitation to Petrarch to sojourn in Prague. It opens: "Honorabilis vir, deuote karissime" (PBW, pp. 134-6).

Charles IV was one of the first modern northern monarchs to discern the political advantage of intellectual and artistic patronage. His court at Prague was by far the most splendid in the north after Avignon. The paintings of the Bohemian School, the architecture and sculpture of the Parler brothers, and the miniatures of Johannes von Neumarkt's Prayer Book alone indicate a modest but noteworthy concentration of genius in the Prague of Charles IV. Add to that the scholars called to the new university and the artists and artisans summoned with the Parler brothers to the construction of the new cathedral, and the era in Prague deserves to be called a "renaissance" with or without Italian connections. But Italian connections there were, with Cola in Prague after the failure of the Roman coup (1350-52) and Petrarch there a few years later (1356).[10] Charles earnestly tried to bring Petrarch to Prague permanently as the crowning jewel, presenting him with a golden goblet by way of persuasion (PBW, pp. 129-31). Petrarch appears to have been moved by the offer and certainly contemplated another visit to Prague but, finally, was not to be persuaded. He met with the emperor at Udine and Padua in 1368, and thereafter all traces of contact between Petrarch and Prague vanish. Perhaps the poet despaired of the restoration of Roman grandeur at the hands of the German "Realpolitiker."

But in the time between the first and last contact, a cordial relationship had been established between Petrarch and Prague. A correspondence of some thirty-six letters survives including letters to or from the emperor's chancellor Johannes von Neumarkt, Empress Anna, and

10. Paul Piur, *Cola di Rienzo: Darstellung seines Lebens und seines Geistes* (Vienna, 1931), p. 160; Ernest Hatch Wilkins, *Life of Petrarch* (Chicago and London, 1963), pp. 152f. [henceforth "Wilkins"].

Ernst, the Archbishop of Prague. The tenor of the correspondence, especially between Petrarch and Johannes von Neumarkt is particularly pleasant and revealing. Von Neumarkt approaches Petrarch humbly, Petrarch responds magnanimously (PBW, pp. 21-25). Thereafter von Neumarkt took particular pleasure in designating himself "a pupil of Petrarch" (PBW, p. lxiv). And Petrarch returned the favor by praising Neumarkt's pen as an eloquent witness to "transalpine fertility" (PBW, pp. 94-97). The loyal pupil asked the master for his best known works, once for *De viris illustribus*. A few years later (1361) the poet sent his friend a presentation copy of the *Bucolicum Carmen*. The chancellor was delighted and, scholar that he was, asked Petrarch for a commentary (PBW, pp. 145-6). On the occasion of another invitation to court he asked Petrarch to bring along a copy of his in fact not yet finished *Remedia utriusque fortunae* (PBW, pp. 137-9). These letters Johannes incorporated into the formulary of the imperial chancery.

The young empress, Anna von Schweidnitz, had, as it seems, written Petrarch personally to inform him of the birth of a daughter. Petrarch responded on 23 May 1358 with a splendid letter congratulating the empress and consoling her for the birth of a daughter with a catalogue of famous women: Minerva, mistress of the arts among the ancient Romans; Isis who first gave the Egyptians letters; Sappho. "I pass over the Sibyls, those divine women who knew the future and were complicit in the divine wisdom." And so on through the great queens of history, Orithia of the Amazons, Penthesilea, Semiramis of the Assyrians, Thamiris of the Scythians, Cleopatra, Zenobia, and up to "our own times" ("apud nos") Countess Mathilda, who controlled a great part of Italy (PBW, pp. 75-86). The letter must have provided great comfort to the disappointment Anna must have been made to feel for failing to provide an heir.[11]

The year before (1357) Petrarch had been made Count Palatine by the emperor. The document must have been impressive, it covers three pages of print in a modern edition and had a great gold seal attached to it (PBW, pp. 221-4). Petrarch accepted the title but at first declined to accept the gold seal, returning it to the chancellor as a sign of his esteem. In the letter covering the return, he described the seal in some detail, revealing his clear, if reluctant understanding that Charles was King of Bohemia as well as Roman Emperor. However, he took genuine satisfaction in the seal's motto, *Aurea Roma*. Eventually, however, he accepted the gold seal as well (PBW, pp. 59-62, 72-4). The designation as Count Palatine was largely honorific, but it did carry the au-

11. Wilkins, p. 160.

thority to name certain judges and to confer legitimacy to bastards. He once made use of the second power and the beneficiary won a court case on the basis of Petrarch's action.[12]

In other legal matter Petrarch was called upon for an opinion on the authenticity of the privileges purportedly granted by Julius Caesar and Nero to Austria (PBW, pp. 114-123). Nothing reveals more clearly the abyss between north and south in Petrarch's time and the bridge that Charles and his court provided. The privileges were, of course, forgeries, but Petrarch recognized them to be recent forgeries. Modern documentary study confirms his findings. The forgers were living in the Middle Ages and were wholly without the historical perspective to notice that Julius Caesar was not likely to employ "Augustus" as an honorific. Petrarch naturally had that perspective. The court at Prague had enough sense to consult Petrarch on the matter. It could not have been expected to explode the forgeries itself, for it governed lands in which anachronism was a way of life, and forgeries supported countless legal structures. Petrarch's opinion is not an unequivocal indication that he himself had made recognition of anachronism a principle of his historical understanding; after all, he clearly considered Charles IV a successor of Augustus (PBW, p. 185). But it does indicate that he was en route to the principle which would separate Italian humanistic historiography from its medieval precursor and its popular competitors at home and abroad.

It was, no doubt, Petrarch's veneration for Roman Antiquity that led him to reject the forgery with quite as much annoyance as his affidavit reveals. And the same veneration underlies the genuine affection he felt for the imperial chancellor. He clearly regarded Neumarkt's concern for style and respect for learning as good omens for the cult of Roman antiquity in the north. He explicitly congratulates Neumarkt for his linguistic purifications in the imperial registry (PBW, p. 91). This activity of Neumarkt is one considered to have had the widest possible ramifications. The chancellor compiled two formularies which contained letters out of the Petrarch correspondence. These were meant as models for the conduct of the epistolary business of the empire. It was during his tenure that the chancery began to turn attention to the vernacular in at least a portion of its transactions. The authority of the imperial chancery would, of course, make its practice the criterion of correct style in other German chanceries as well, for example, in the Saxon and Thuringian chanceries, on the language of which Luther

12. Ibid., p. 240.

would, one hundred and fifty years later, base the standard German of his Bible translation.

This conjecture has been the subject of enormous controversy.[13] There are indeed several missing links between the Prague formularies of the 1360's and the usage of the Saxon chanceries in the 1520's. But not many. And there are striking similarities in phonology. Johannes von Neumarkt and his pupils were clearly writing Early New High German at a time when older forms of the language were still in wide use. The one significant document written directly in the tradition of the linguistic reforms of the chancery was the *Ackermann aus Böhmen* (*The Ploughman from Bohemia*) by Johannes von Tepl, a pupil of von Neumarkt's. Explicit humanistic content was detected in this work, and Petrarch received credit for the new spirit.[14] This conjecture became the subject of even greater controversy and the howls of the medievalists have often seemed to drown out rational discourse on the question of the German reception of the Italian Renaissance.[15]

Before turning to that chapter of the history of Petrarch in Germany, let us look to the evidence of his presence in Germany where there can be no dispute. Manuscripts of Petrarch's works—more the Latin than the Italian—found their way in considerable numbers into the libraries of the southern and eastern territories of the Empire even in the poet's lifetime and not long thereafter.[16] One hears tell of a "cult of Petrarch," and intimate connections between the court of Jost of Moravia (1375-1411) and the first generation of Petrarch's students.[17] The last fine medieval poet of Germany and its first modern composer, Oswald von Wolkenstein (1377-1445), cites Petrarch by name and in an offhand fashion that transparently reveals the Italian poet's unquestioned authority.[18] Oswald clearly knew Petrarch's work and ex-

13. Adolf Bach, *Geschichte der deutschen Sprache,* 7th ed. (Heidelberg, 1961), pp. 195-8.

14. Karl Otto Brogsitter, *Das hohe Geistergespräch* (Diss. Bonn, 1957), p. 208.

15. Cf. the bibliographical survey in James E. Engel, *Renaissance, Humanismus, Reformation,* Handbuch der deutschen Literaturgeschichte, 2. Abt. Bibliographien, IV (Bern and Munich, 1969), pp. 32-34.

16. Konrad Burdach, *Vorspiel* I, 2, Deutsche Vierteljahrschrift für Literaturwissenschaft und Geistesgeschichte, Buchreihe, II (Halle, 1925), pp. 57f. [henceforth "Vorspiel"].

17. Idem, "Zur Kenntnis altdeutscher Handschriften und zur Geschichte altdeutscher Literatur und Kunst," *Centralblatt für Bibliothekswesen,* VIII (1891), 477-80.

18. Karl Kurt Klein, ed., *Die Lieder Oswalds von Wolkenstein,* Altdeutsche Textbibliothek, No. 55 (Tübingen, 1962), p. 27.

pected of his readers and listeners both the recognition and respect due to an *auctor*. At the Council of Constance (1414-1417), which Oswald attended in the court of Emperor Sigismund, Petrarch's name and works were repeatedly on the lips of the Germans.[19] The most important German propagandist at the Council, Dietrich von Niem (1340/45-1418) is in conscious and profound debt to Petrarch. He competed with Bruni and Poggio for advancement in curial service, and knew the Italian scene intimately. To be sure, his was not a humanistic and literary interest, but rather a political one. Nonetheless since he was a popular and widely read journalist he provided a large conduit for the fame of Petrarch among the Germans.[20] As early as 1432 Petrarch's telling of the Griselda story appeared in a German version by one Erhart Gross. The adaptation was quite popular, as was Gross who wrote edifying works for the consumption of the pious citizens of Nürnberg.[21]

At the court of the Countess Palatine of the Rhine, Mechthild (1418/9-1482), literary endeavors of all kinds were encouraged, predominantly the revival of the great literature of the Middle High German flowering, but also of the New Learning.[22] Nicolas von Wyle's pioneering *Translatzen* contains a German rendering of two dialogues from Petrarch's *Remedia utriusque fortunae* dedicated to Mechthild (1469).[23] And he was apparently only one of several translators patronized by the countess for the purpose of making the new Italian literature available to the readers of the German vernacular. A translator of Boccaccio, Heinrich Steinhöwel also turned his hand to the Griselda fable, and his version saw print at least three times in the fifteenth century (1473 and 1482).[24] Albrecht von Eyb further ad-

19. Heinrich Finke et al., eds., *Acta Concilii Constanciensis,* 4 vols. (Münster, 1896-1928), II, 277f.

20. Hermann Heimpel, *Dietrich von Niem,* Veröffentlichungen der historischen Kommission des Provinzialinstituts für Westf. Landes- und Volkskunde, Westfälische Biographien, II (Münster, 1932), pp. 30, 159, 171-1-4; Alfons Lhotsky and Karl Pivec, eds., *Dietrich von Nieheim: Viridarium Imperatorum et Regum Romanorum,* MGH, Staatsschriften des späten Mittelalters, V, 1 (Stuttgart, 1956), pp. xiv and 8.

21. Hans Rupprich, *Die deutsche Literatur vom späten Mittelalter bis zum Barock,* 2 vols., Geschichte der deutschen Literatur von den Anfängen bis zur Gegenwart, eds. Helmut de Boor and Richard Newald, IV (Munich, 1970-73), I, 570.

22. *Vorspiel,* pp. 80-83.

23. Adalbert von Keller, ed., *Translationen von Niclas von Wyle,* Bibliothek des literarischen Vereins in Stuttgart, LVII (1861; rpt. Hildesheim, 1967), pp. 314-324.

24. Frederick R. Goff, *Incunabula in American Libraries: A third Census* (New York, 1964), p. 478, nos. P-403-5.

vanced the fame of Petrarch with German translations of his views on marriage in the *Ehebüchlein* (printed 1472) and numerous extracts from Petrarch in an extremely convenient handbook on rhetoric, the *Margarita poetica* (fifteen editions between 1472 and 1503).[25]

When humanism struck permanent roots in Germany, around the middle of the fifteenth century, the spirit of Petrarch was, as one might expect, on the scene. The first generation of German humanists studied in Italy among the second generation of Petrarch's pupils. Sigismund Gossenbrot (1417-1493), a patrician of Augsburg, regularly cited Petrarch in his correspondence as though he were a classical authority.[26] In fact, Petrarch had become so in Germany. Gossenbrot's sons bragged back and forth in their correspondence on the availability of Petrarch's works in such centers of enlightenment as Augsburg. Although far more modern, gracious, and witty models were available to them—Aeneas Sylvius Piccolomini and Poggio Bracciolini —they kept Petrarch as their master: "Der eigentliche Meister dieser Schüler ist Petrarcha."[27] The important libraries, at first personal collections of humanistically inclined Germans, naturally contain a representative sampling of the works of Petrarch. Hieronymus Münzer (1437-1508) bound his copies of Petrarch's *Epistolae familiares* and the *Remedia* with works of Reuchlin, Valla, Sabellico, Baptista Mantuanus, and Ficino to make a splendid humanistic miscellany.[28] The incredibly industrious copiers and collectors, Hermann and Hartmann Schedel of Nürnberg, gathered or themselves transcribed no fewer than ten Petrarch manuscripts. And Hermann went to the trouble of compiling an index for an early print of Petrarch's *Rerum memorandarum liber*.[29] By the end of the fifteenth century, perfectly conventional histories list the death of Petrarch as an event fully as noteworthy as any political catastrophe.[30] Perhaps the simplest and clearest indication of Petrarch's patronage over German humanism is Rudolph Agricola

25. Joseph Anthony Hiller, *Albrecht von Eyb: Medieval Moralist,* The Catholic University of America Studies in German, XIII (Washington, 1939), pp. 69-73; 133-4.

26. Hartmut Boockmann, *Laurentius Blumenau,* Göttinger Bausteine zur Geschichtswissenschaft, XXXVII (Göttingen, Berlin, and Frankfurt, 1965), p. 228.

27. Paul Joachimsohn [sic], *Die humanistische Geschichtschreibung in Deutschland, Die Anfänge: Sigismund Meisterlin* (Bonn, 1895), pp. 18f.

28. E. P. Goldschmidt, *Hieronymus Münzer und seine Bibliothek,* Studies of the Warburg Institute, IV (London, 1938), p. 145.

29. Richard Stauber, *Die Schedelsche Bibliothek,* Studien und Darstellungen aus dem Gebiete der Geschichte, VI, 2/3 (1908; rpt. Niewkoop, 1969), pp. 111-116, 199.

30. Johannes Pistorius, ed., *Illustrium veterum scriptorum . . . Tomus unus,* (Frankfurt, 1583), p. 842.

(1443-86). On the hundredth anniversary of his death Agricola wrote the first biography of Petrarch not by the pen of an Italian. Its unifying motif: nothing can be considered more appropriate of man than to know man.[31]

The fifteenth century laid such a firm foundation for the veneration of Petrarch that not even the Reformation could shake his towering authority. For his secret attack on the curia he was numbered among the "witnesses to the truth" by the uncompromising reformer, Mathias Illyricus Flacius.[32] In the seventeenth century, Petrarch was held up for imitation by the most influential of Baroque literary theorists in Germany, Martin Opitz.[33] Thereafter his name was attached, for better or worse, to the fate of "Petrarchism," until what appears to have been his final rescue by Jacob Burckhardt.

By far the most important manifestation of Germany's affection for Italy in the last century or so is the simultaneous discovery in 1860 by Jacob Burckhardt and Georg Voigt of the golden age of Italian cultural history, the Renaissance. Their discovery inaugurated an epoch in the German courtship of Italy. Scholarship provided the setting; the Renaissance dispute provided the excuse.

One trend in the revisions of Burckhardt—these, after all, constitute the Renaissance dispute—expressed profound distress at the secular-pagan facets of Burckhardt's insight. The scholars representing this trend, Heinrich Thode among the earliest, cast about for alternatives. They eventually threw the origins of the Renaissance back to the religious upheavals of the early thirteenth century and connected the Renaissance with the rise of the burgher class for which the medieval social universe had no room. Francis of Assisi became the patron saint of the competing theory, followed hard upon by Joachim of Fiore. The Spirituals contributed the ideological evidence with their doctrines of renewal and rebirth; the Observants contributed the sociological evidence with their settlements in the cities. This theory of the Renaissance was and is the occasion of intense partisanship. In Germany, the adherents rallied around Konrad Burdach, about whose scholarly head a storm of controversy has ever since raged.

In general, Burdach's perspective conformed with Thode's. They

31. Heinz Otto Burger, *Renaissance, Humanismus, Reformation: Deutsche Literatur im europäischen Kontext,* Frankfurter Beiträge zur Germanistik, VII (Bad Homburg, 1969), pp. 191f.

32. Paul Piur, *Petrarcas "Buch ohne Namen" und die päpstliche Kurie,* Deutsche Vierteljahrschrift für Literaturwissenschaft und Geistesgeschichte, Buchreihe, VI (Halle, 1925), p. [xl].

33. Gerhart Hoffmeister, *Petrarkistische Lyrik* (Stuttgart, 1973), pp. 65ff.

both saw the Renaissance as a broad intellectual and artistic revolution with sources in the spiritual life of the High Middle Ages, particularly of heretics and religious radicals. Burdach's researches and those of his pupil, Paul Piur, concentrated for years on the person of Cola di Rienzo, resulting in the monumental publication of the correspondence and an important biography by Piur. Burdach and Piur detected in Cola a combination of Spiritualist and antiquarian sentiments that seemed to them quintessentially characteristic of the Renaissance. It was by way of Cola that Burdach and Piur came to Petrarch, whose Renaissance credentials they never for a moment doubted.

Their studies of Cola and Petrarch eventually turned to the defense of one argument: that the early Italian Renaissance received immediate and enthusiastic welcome at the imperial court at Prague and thereupon exerted profound influence on adjacent lands, particularly on the development of the Early New High German literary language. As to the truth of the first part of the argument there can be no doubt. The emperor, the empress, the chancellor, and the archbishop all fell under the spell of the new style or at least of the men who proclaimed it. It is even defensible to maintain that in the case of Charles the influence went deeper than style alone. Petrarch's views on the position of history with rhetoric and poetry in humane letters clearly moved Charles to assign the composition of a history of his kingdom to a renowned Italian traveller, Johannes of Marignola, and perhaps also moved him to compose his own biography.[34] The fact that both works bear more the stamp of the Middle Ages than of the Renaissance is witness only to the transitional character of the Prague flowering.

The influence of Petrarch beyond Prague also cannot be doubted. In a few cases, such as the court of Jost of Moravia, the influence may even have been humanistic. But this is the weak point in the Burdach-Piur thesis and fundamentally contradicts their own broad view of the Renaissance. Implicit in the argument is the attempt to identify Petrarch wholly with humanism, and humanism wholly with the Renaissance. Petrarch was indeed influential in the north beyond Prague. But both in Prague and beyond one aspect of his influence was not humanistic but moralistic. It was felt that he conformed with the sentiments of late medieval morality and in truth he did. The reception of Petrarch in these circumstances implies nothing in the way of a

34. Paul Joachimsen, *Geschichtsauffassung und Geschichtschreibung in Deutschland unter dem Einfluss des Humanismus,* Beiträge zur Kulturgeschichte des Mittelalters und der Renaissance, VI (Berlin and Leipzig, 1910), pp. 15-18.

reception of humanism. If the impact of Petrarch on Prague had been exclusively humanistic, one would expect the flight of Prague's German scholars to Leipzig to have meant a great infusion of humanism into Saxony. There is no evidence whatsoever to this effect. In fact, later in the fifteenth century, Leipzig was notorious for its hostility to humanism. To be sure, when and where the north was ready for humanism, the orthodox moralism of Petrarch did nothing to hinder its acceptance and may have encouraged it. But the two aspects of Petrarch's reception must not be confused.

Even the acceptance of humanistic views on history need not imply an infusion of humanism. The Bohemian history of Johannes of Marignola and Charles' autobiography are cases in point. Dietrich von Niem—a thoroughly unreconstructed medieval Latinist—depended heavily on Petrarch (and Boccaccio, incidentally) for his view of history and historical argument. This view is radically new in Germany, has analogues in only one or two Latin and vernacular chroniclers of the time, and anticipates in detail the nationalistic history of the German humanists of the later fifteenth and early sixteenth century.[35] In this case, the reception of Petrarch is not humanistic, at least not in style, but very clearly innovative and a sign of Renaissance activity in the broad sense of Burdach and Piur.

The third point, Petrarch's impact on the development of the Early New High German literary language requires a great deal more proof than Burdach, Piur, and the other disciples were able to supply. What they did prove beyond doubt was the possibility of such influence. The close comparative study of the German prose of Neumarkt and his successors and the Latin and Italian texts of the early humanists available to him and his school has never been undertaken to anyone's satisfaction. This failure has led some scholars to deny Prague any important place at all in the development of Early New High German.[36] This position, however, represents an excess far more unreasonable than any ever committed by the school of Burdach whose *prima facie* case has never been overturned. Early New High German is, generally speaking, easily accessible to anyone who commands the modern language. Neumarkt's German prose and that of his successors is clearly Early New High German. Far later texts—Oswald von Wolkenstein, for example, but actually the bulk of fifteenth-century German literature—require linguistic training in Middle High German. The Prague circle may simply

35. Frank L. Borchardt, *German Antiquity in Renaissance Myth* (Baltimore and London, 1971), pp. 288-92 and esp. 297.

36. Cf. fn. 13 above.

have anticipated developments in the language without influencing them. Although possible, this hardly seems likely and the burden of proof clearly lies with those who would defend the likelihood.

For some reason I do not fully understand, Burdach's position tends to disturb the scholarly equanimity of his critics. The reactions have ranged between rage, not altogether dignified dismissal, and a haughty condescension that indicates an inability to approach the man's work free of bias. Karl Brandi created a straw man superficially resembling Burdach's Rienzo and proceeded to tear him to shreds.[37] The genuinely fine historian Paul Joachimsen actually called upon Burdach to stop publishing texts and instead to compose a comprehensive theory[38]—as though humane letters had too many texts and too few comprehensive theories. Wallace K. Ferguson's treatment of the Burdach thesis in his essential historiography of the Renaissance dispute is inexplicably one-sided and tends toward innuendo.[39] He ignores Burdach's herculean efforts at balance and restraint, and most mysteriously, passes over in absolute silence Burdach's resolution to the Renaissance dispute: "Denn das Mittelalter war viel humanistischer, die Renaissance viel mittelalterlicher, als das allgemeine gelehrte Bewusstsein annimmt."[40] It is, after all, much the same conclusion Ferguson reached twenty years later.[41]

Whether or not one concurs with the Burdach thesis, whether or not one sympathizes with his critics, his life's work guaranteed Petrarch and his friends a permanent place in the discussion of German intellectual life at the end of the Middle Ages. It is now only by sleight-of-hand that one can avoid the Italians. The reception and naturalization of high culture from abroad is one of the oldest and noblest characteristics of German history. Germans do not always think so, and their neighbors do not always (or even often) believe it. But from Boniface to grand opera it has been so. In this context the wooing of Petrarch is

37. Karl Brandi, "Renaissance und Reformation: Wertungen und Unwertungen," *Preussische Jahrbücher,* CC (1925), 120-135; rpt. under the title *Renaissance: Zwei Beiträge,* Reihe Libelli, CLXXVI (Darmstadt, 1967), pp. 34f., which I consulted.

38. Paul Joachimsen, "Vom Mittelalter zur Reformation," *Historische Vierteljahrschrift,* XX (1920/21), 426-70; rpt. Reihe Libelli, L (Darmstadt, 1959), pp. 61f.

39. *The Renaissance in Historical Thought: Five Centuries of Interpretation* (Cambridge, 1948), pp. 306-311.

40. Konrad Burdach, *Rienzo und die geistige Wandlung seiner Zeit,* Briefwechsel des Cola di Rienzo, I, Vom Mittelalter zur Reformation, II, 1 (Berlin, 1913-1928), pp. viiif.

41. Op. cit., p. 397.

actually nothing extraordinary. Whether Petrarch wooed meant Petrarch won is beside the point. To the point is the very fact of the authority of the poet in Germany and the attempt of the Germans to come to terms with it.

Petrarch thought Italy well provided that the Alps stood between it and the German fury. They were, however, not high enough to keep either Petrarch or his works from crossing over, there to be greeted not by fury but by a great embrace.

XXIII

PETRARCH IN GERMANY DURING THE THIRTY YEARS' WAR

by Gerhard Dünnhaupt
University of Washington

The savage conquest and wanton destruction of Magdeburg by the army of General Tilly in May 1631 was a cataclysmic event that stirred the minds and hearts of Central Europe. Hundreds of pamphlets and broadsheets were published in several languages to commemorate the burning of the city in poetry or prose.[1] Among them was a "mourning song" by the German poet Diederich von dem Werder "upon the lamentable destruction of the famous and ancient city of Magdeburg," which he appended to his translation of the penitential psalms of David.[2] The slender volume also includes the first German version of Petrarch's three Avignonese sonnets, a fact that appears to have eluded most compilers of such information,[3] no doubt on account of the extreme rarity of the little book, of which only eleven copies are known to exist.[4]

It may be safely assumed that these three poems, which had been created by Petrarch under entirely different historical circumstances, appealed to the Calvinist German poet mainly on account of their antipapal invectives which complement his own polemics about the destruc-

1. Cf. the extensive bibliography of W. Lahne, *Magdeburgs Zerstörung in der zeitgenössischen Publizistik* (Magdeburg: Magdeburgischer Geschichtsverein, 1931), pp. 214-259.

2. *Die Busz Psalmen/ in Poesie gesetzt. Sampt angehengtem TrawerLied vber die klägliche Zerstörung der Löblichen vnd Vhralten Stadt Magdeburg* (Leipzig: Rehefeld, 1632). Case Memorial Library, Hartford, Conn. possesses the only copy recorded in the U.S.A.

3. The existence of the 3 German sonnets is noted only by G. Witkowski, *D. v. d. Werder* (Leipzig, 1887), pp. 40 and 125; B. Geiger, *F. Petrarca: Das lyrische Werk* (Neuwied, 1958), p. 820. They are not recorded in any of the following studies of German Petrarca translations: H. Welti, *Geschichte des Sonetts* (Leipzig, 1884); H. Souvageol, *Petrarca in der deutschen Lyrik des 17. Jahrhunderts* (Ansbach, 1911); E. Kanduth, *Der Petrarkismus in der Lyrik des deutschen Frühbarock* (Diss. Wien, 1953); J.-U. Fechner, *Das deutsche Sonett* (München, 1969); G. Hoffmeister, *Petrarkistische Lyrik* (Stuttgart, 1973). The Fischart translation (cf. note 15) also remains generally unrecorded.

4. For locations see the bibliography in Werder's Tasso translation *Gottfried von Bulljon (1626),* ed. G. Dünnhaupt (Tübingen: Niemeyer, 1974), no. I.4; also reprinted in *Philobiblon,* 18 (1974), 26-38.

tion of Magdeburg by the imperial catholic troops. Werder solely translated the sonnets "Fiamma dal ciel su le tue treccie piova" (CXXXVI), "L'avara Babilonia à colmo il sacco" (CXXXVII), and "Fontana di dolore, albergo d'ira" (CXXXVIII),[5] in which Petrarch chastised the excesses of the papal court. The once debated question whether these sonnets refer to Avignon[6] was of no concern to the translator, for within the context of his Calvinist polemics only Rome, as the current seat of the Curia, could possibly be meant:

I. ES müss auff deinen Kopff dess Himmelsflamme krachen/
Mit Wasser wurdest du vnd Eicheln erst ernehrt/
Nun bist du gross vnd reich/ weil andre seyn verheert/
Vnd dir das Vbelthun ist lauter Frewd vnd Lachen.

Nest der Verrähterey; drinn alle lose Sachen/
Die auff der Erden seyn/ gehalten werden wehrt/
Bist eine Magdt dess Weyns/ mit Speiss' vnd Lust beschwert/
Da jhre letzte Prob' all' Vppigkeiten machen.

Jn deinen Kammern jung' vnd alte Buhlen sehr/
Beelzebub ist selbst auch mitten drunter hehr/
Vnd sich mit Spiegeln Fewr/ vnd Blasebälgen zeiget.

Bey Schatten in dem Bett' du erst nicht bist geborn/
Besondern bloss im Wind'/ vnd Barfuss vnter Dorn/
Lebst so nun: dass zu Gott hin dein Gestanck auffsteiget.[7]

To a German protestant reader during the Thirty Years' War these verses must have sounded as if expressly written against Roman corruption, for many contemporary writers employed similar invectives.[8] The "Him-

5. All references to Petrarch's Italian text are based on the following edition: *Le rime di Francesco Petrarca,* a cura di Nicola Zingarelli (Bologna: Zanichelli, 1964), pp. 802-812.

6. Zingarelli, pp. 802 f., argues convincingly in favor of Avignon. An introduction to various alternate readings is offered by G. Carducci in *Francesco Petrarca: Le Rime* (Firenze: Sansoni, 1960), p. 217.

7. Werder, *Busz Psalmen,* fol. [D iij]v.

8. In 1635, a mere three years after Werder, the Venetian senator Giovanni Francesco Loredano criticized Rome even more severely:

> La crudeltà ivi tiene la residenza, non conoscendo amore coloro, che non sanno se non distruggere la natura. L'oro diviene merito per i più vili, e per i più ignoranti. La santità, l'innocenza, e la bontà, professata nelle voci, e nell'habito, è affatto conculcata dall'opere. . . . L'hippocrisia occupa una gran parte di coloro, che bramano ingannar' i semplici. Tentano l'oppressione della verità, e la prohibiscono alle penne, ed a i pennelli. Vietano a gli altri quelle cose, che vogliono goder soli, e castigano con maggior severità queglı errorı, ne i quali essi peccano. In somma i vitij più esecrabili, detestati dalle leggi della natura, e dal mondo, sono connaturali in questa corte.

melsflamme" of divine justice is called upon to strike that sinful city which has grown from humble, pure beginnings (I,2) to its present state of splendor, power, and corruption, while the cities of others fell subject to destruction (I,3). Werder's contemporaries must have interpreted the words "weil andre seyn verheert" as direct hint at the recent burning of Magdeburg. Petrarch's original makes no mention of "verheert"; his verse merely states "Per l'altrui *impoverir* se' ricca e grande." Through this slight textual alteration the inhabitants' delight in "Vbelthun" (I,4) assumes the far more sinister aspect of sheer malice. In the two adjoining verses Werder follows the Italian text "Nido di tradimenti . . ." almost verbatim, except that he renders the word "cova" in I,6—probably for rhyme's sake—with "gehalten . . . wehrt," so that part of the nest metaphor is lost. The "letzte Prob' " in I,8 with its meaning of "last stand" corresponds exactly to Petrarch's "ultima prova." In I,9 "jung' vnd alte" must be understood as nouns but "Buhlen" as verb, for German spelling and capitalization rules were still rather vague and depended largely on the preferences of individual printers. For the same reason, the word "hehr" in I,10 has to be read as "her." With I,12 the poet returns to the topic of the city's original poverty and purity, which enables him to reintroduce the subject of its present corruption antithetically in the final verse.

The second sonnet (*Canzoniere* CXXXVII) sharpens the polemics by introducing the "Babylon" simile which had up to now only been implied by the enumeration of the city's sins:

II. Du geitzigs Babylon! hast deinen Sack so voll
Von Gottes schwerem Zorn/ von Lastern/ Angst vnd Wehen/
Daß er bald bersten wirdt; hast deine Götter stehen/
Nicht Pallas/ Jupiter/ besondern Venus wol

Sampt Bacchus; vnd ich werd' auss Vngedult schier toll/
Dein newer Soldan wirdt mit Macht herein baldt gehen/
Auf dass er mach auss dir (nicht dass ichs werde sehen)
Nur einen Sitz; vnd dich hin nach Baldacko hol'.

Jhr stoltzen Thürm'/ als Feind' dess Himmels/ sollet werden
Mit allen Götzen rab geworffen zu der Erden/
Auss- vnd inwendig auch die Zinnen abgebrandt/

La Dianea, 1st ed. 1635; cited from *Opere del Loredano,* I.3 (Venetia, 1653), pp. 263-264. Again it was Werder who translated this work: *Dianea oder Rähtselgedicht* (Nürnberg, 1644); reprint, ed. G. Dünnhaupt (Bern: Lang, in preparation).

Die schönen Seelen dann/ als die Liebhaberinnen
Der Tugendt/ werden wol zu bringen recht beginnen
Die Welt in güldne Zeit/ vnd dich in alten Standt.[9]

Terrifying will be the fury of the Lord when it finally wipes out this nest of iniquity (II,1-2) where false idols like Venus and Bacchus (II,4-5) are venerated and little homage is paid to wisdom ("Pallas") and justice ("Jupiter"). Here Petrarch prophetically announces the coming of a new pontiff who will return the papal seat from Avignon to its rightful place in Rome, even though the poet himself harbors little hope that he will witness this event during his own lifetime (II,6-7). At first glance, "Baldacko" seems to indicate Bagdad as capital of the infidels. However, since the new pope is referred to as "Soldan" in II,6, the poet could even have Rome in mind.[10] Be this as it may, for Werder's audience there can only be one possible interpretation: a change must come to purge the corruption and restore law, order, and moral fortitude. Although the "stoltzen Thürm'" in II,9 obviously refer to the palace of Avignon in Petrarch's original, a seventeenth-century German reader could just as easily have visualized Rome in these verses. The false idols ("Götzen") that must be toppled (II,10) are of course Venus and Bacchus again. While Petrarch's final tercet calls for a renewal of the power and glory of Roman antiquity, Werder's audience probably interpreted the last three verses merely as an appeal for the eventual restoration of virtue and justice "in den alten Standt."

In the third and final sonnet (*Canzoniere* CXXXVIII) Werder pulls all stops of his powerful baroque language with a force that reminds us of Gryphius' famed "Zentnerworte." With thundering might he hurls his biting invectives against this den of iniquity:

III. Ein Herberg' Hasses/ Zorns/ vnd aller Qualen Quelle/
Dess Jrrthumbs hohe Schuel/ ein Ketzerischer Thron/
Vor warstu Rom/ vnd nun das falsche Babylon/
Vmb die man schmertzlich seufftzt/ auch weint/ vnd schreyet helle/

O Amboss dess Betrugs! O finstre Kercker-stelle/
Da gutes stirbt/ vnd lebt das böss' in Ehr' vnd Wonn'/
Ein lebendiges Grab; O wunder! wann dein Lohn
Nicht seyn wirdt Christi Zorn/ vnd endtlich gar die Helle.

9. Werder, *Busz Psalmen,* fol. [D iij]^{v} to [D iv].

10. Witkowski, p. 125, argues that Werder misunderstood this verse. However, his translation does correspond to one of several possible interpretations offered by P. Piur, *Petrarcas 'Buch ohne Namen' und die päpstliche Kurie* (Halle, 1925), p. 43, with reff. to further literature; cf. also Carducci, pp. 219-221 and Zingarelli, pp. 807-808.

Mit armer Demut erst gelegt auff keuschen Grundt/
Jetzt deinen Stifftern selbst dein Zorn zu trotze wetzest/
Du Schandthur! Ey wo steht dein' Hoffnung hin jetzundt/

Dein schlim erworbnes Gut du nur allein hoch schätzest/
Vnd dein Ehbrecherey: nun bleib auss Constantin/
Der/ der die böse Welt erhelt/ sie reisse hin.[11]

Like Petrarch, the German poet pours out a flood of fiery accusations over the pontifical seat. While the first sonnet had already yielded such colorful attributes as "Nest der Verrähterey" (I,5) and "Magdt dess Weyns" (I,7), it is only now that Werder gains an opportunity to show off the full extent of his word power which has much in common with the language of those thundering fire-and-brimstone sermons that were hurled from the baroque pulpits of his day by men like Abraham à Sancta Clara. With his invectives "Herberg' [des] Hasses" (III,1), "Dess Jrrthumbs hohe Schuel/ ein ketzerischer Thron" (III,2), and "Amboss dess Betrugs" (III, 5) he follows Petrarch almost to the letter. We note especially the brilliant alliteration "aller Qualen Quelle" he invents to render "Fontana di dolore." Verse III,3 reads "*Già* Roma, *or* Babilonia falsa e ria" in the original. Such a juxtaposition of the two papal seats of Rome and Avignon would of course have run counter to Werder's anti-Roman polemics. He therefore translates: "Vor [= zuvor] *warstu* Rom/ vnd nun das falsche Babylon," thus eliminating the reference to Avignon altogether. The word "Helle" in III,8 is to be read as "Hölle." The preceding threats of divine ire and infernal punishment are followed in III,9 by a return to the original antithesis of "then" and "now" (cf. I,2-3 and I,12-14 above). Once again the immaculate purity of the past (III,9) is contrasted to the present-day corruption (III,10 ff.). Under such circumstances, even Emperor Constantine would probably have retracted his generous donation (III,13),[12] for the downfall of the false Babylon appears to be imminent.

On account of their subject matter the three Avignonese sonnets were not translated as early as the poetry about Laura. In fact, they were even omitted from many early Italian editions.[13] According to Geiger,[14] Diederich von dem Werder was the first to translate these sonnets into

11. Werder, *Busz Psalmen,* fol. [D iv].
12. To Petrarch, the Donation of Constantine was still historical fact. Despite Lorenzo Valla's widely publicized proof that it was a forgery, Werder adheres strictly to the original text.
13. Cf. Carducci, p. 223.
14. Geiger, p. 820.

German. Though accurate, this statement needs to be somewhat qualified. True enough, Werder was first to reproduce them in strict sonnet form, but in the preceding century Johann Fischart had already translated the last one in fifteen irregular tetrameters.[15] In Werder's rendering, these three sonnets demonstrate the translator's astonishing facility in adapting pre-existing poetry that was created in a totally different historical context. A few years later Werder succeeded in a similar undertaking on a much larger scale, namely his *Friedensrede,* a skilful "imitatio" of the *Querela pacis* by Erasmus of Rotterdam. In this magnificent pacifist oration, he frequently departs so far from the Neo-Latin original that his use of the earlier work went unrecognized until recently.[16] By contrast, the three poems we have discussed here follow Petrarch quite closely, and depart from the original solely where the German poet requires a change to suit his specific purposes. Diederich von dem Werder does not come from the ranks of the German Petrarchists. If he nevertheless follows in the footsteps of the great master on this one occasion, it can only be because the topic of these three sonnets happened to fit his own wartime polemics.

15. "Alles Kummers ein rechte Quell," in *Bienenkorb Dess Heil. Röm. Jmmenschwarms . . . Durch Jesuwald Pickhart* [i.e. Johannes Fischart], Christlingen, n.d. [i.e. Strassburg, 1588], fol. 255^{v}. First ed. publ. 1579. Fischart also reproduces the 4 verses I,5-8 in 3 rhymed couplets, ibid.

16. Cf. G. Dünnhaupt, "Die 'Friedensrede' Diederichs von dem Werder und ihr Verhältnis zur 'Querela Pacis' des Erasmus von Rotterdam," in *Europäische Tradition und deutscher Literaturbarock,* ed. G. Hoffmeister (Bern: Francke, 1973), pp. 371-390.

XXIV

THE SNOW-WHITE MISTRESS: A PETRARCHIST TOPOS IN GERMAN BAROQUE LYRICS

by Gerhart Hoffmeister
Wayne State University

Since time immemorial, man has shown a desire to put a woman on a pedestal to let her rule over his heart. This supremacy of woman over man in the realm of love and letters has invariably been expressed by the color white, which adorned Helena and Dido, Kriemhilde and Isolde. The association of the color white with a beloved lady has also penetrated folklore. Some examples for this are, of course, "Schneeweisschen" and "Schneewittchen"—the snow-whites known to all readers of Grimm's *Fairy Tales*. Though the ideal of beauty differs from country to country and from generation to generation, white as a *summum pulchritudinis* has suffered little from the patina of time—perhaps with the notable exception of Shakespeare's "Dark Lady" and the modern slogan "black is beautiful," which moves outside the domain of literature.

Simple white, however, has not been considered to be enough; as a consequence very early in the history of love poetry similes were sought going beyond the common ground like "white as milk" and "white as a lily," but above all "white as snow." This last comparison stands out from all others. So much so that as early as the Italian Cinquecento, Nicolò Franco was prompted to parody the hackneyed use of snow-white to praise a lady.[1] In the following pages we will observe how this topos was given new life in the italianate lyrics of the German Baroque, because there around 1600 the case was completely different. Hardly any secular, and very little love poetry, was written in the vernacular.

The Reformation had forced many humanists into their ivory tower where they produced Neolatin verse, among them the most famous of them all, Johannes Secundus, who utilized the conceits of the Italian Renaissance in his sensual lyrics written in the manner of Catullus. He had learned from both traditions,[2] whereas the vernacular German

1. *Il Petrarchista* (Venice, 1539); repr. in J. Hösle, *Texte zum Antipetrarkismus*, Romanische Übungstexte, 55 (Tübingen, 1970), No. 8.

2. See L. W. Forster, *The Icy Fire: Five Studies in European Petrarchism* (London, 1969), p. 44: "My Lydia hit me with a ball of snow / And straight my heart with fire began to glow. . . ."

poets had lost touch with their own lyrical heritage and were yearning for new topics and motifs, which they suddenly discovered in Italy and attempted to convey to their audience as best they could in music (*Gesellschaftslied*) and poetry.

Among the earliest German poets to take upon themselves the formidable task of transforming the medieval misogynistic tradition to catch up belatedly with the European mainstream, we find Schallenberg and Kuffstein, both apparently still influenced by the folksong when they wrote such lines as the following:

Cupido mit sein pfeilen
mich nit so hart vergifft
als mein hertzliebstes freulein
wan sie mit schnee mich trifft.[3]

or: Ach Stella meine Göttin vnd Frewdt /
Viel weisser dann der Schnee:
Vnd röther als zur Sommerszeit /
Die Rösslein an einem See. . . .[4]

About the same time Weckherlin, who was exposed to Renaissance lyrics on his tours through Europe, completely mastered their conceits, as his poems addressed to his beloved's white hands[5] and breasts (No. 212) reveal. Here we find the conventional antithesis of snow and flame, which expresses at once the frightening cold beauty of the lady and her devastating effect on the lover.[6] Opitz was so well aware of the success of the new vogue and so sure of his own mastery that he translated both petrarchist and antipetrarchist lyrics into his native tongue, praising women and ridiculing them on the same page.[7] With Opitz' efforts at adapting the German poetical language to the achievements of foreign literatures, the petrarchist description of beauty is taken up with a snow–balling effect in all the leading cultural centers, like Nuremberg, Hamburg, Leipzig, and Königsberg.

Typical for the successful diffusion of the snow-image is a song by Gottfried Finckelthaus, a minor student poet in Leipzig:

3. H. Hurch, ed., *Chr. von Schallenberg* (Tübingen, 1910), "Das XX. lied" (BLVS 252).

4. Hans L. von Kuffstein, *Diana* (Linz, 1619), part II, p. 337; repr. in G. Hoffmeister, *Die spanische Diana in Deutschland* (Berlin, 1972), p. 161.

5. H. Fischer, ed., *G. R. Weckherlins Gedichte* (Tübingen, 1907), I, No. 67, 220, 226 (BLVS 199 f.).

6. Cf. No. 212: "Solt ich nicht klüger gedacht haben, / Daβ under solche schnee ein hertz von eyβ sein must."

7. See "An eine Jungfrau": "Da gegen ihnen [hands] Schnee zu gleichen sey der Dinten"; Hösle No. 29.

Vber die Hand der Astree

Du schöne Hand: Was / Hand! ja Ketten / denn sie bindt.
Was Ketten? Wollen mehr/ weil sie so weich zu drücken.
Was / Wollen? Fewer mehr / denn sie das Hertz entzündt.
Was / Fewer? Mehr als Schnee / die Weisse muß sie schmücken.
Doch keines: Ketten nicht: ich bin ja frey zu nennen.
Nicht Wollen / die sonst bald verwehen kan der Wind.
Nicht Fewer: siehstu denn die Gluth so helle brennen?
Nicht Schnee / weil sich in der die rechte Wärme findt.
Jedennoch siehet dich des Volckes blinder Wahn
Aus Liebe vor Schnee / Fewr / Wollen / Ketten an.[8]

Though in keeping with the conventions of his age only one feature is singled out as representative of the lady's charms, its effects are as sweeping and disconcerting as if the whole person of his mistress had been described. With all due respect to the poet, and considering the early stage in the development of the German lyrical language, we regard this poem as a conventional exercise in the Opitzian school.[9] In a witty fashion, the white hand[10] is first characterized by a sequence of similes which are rejected in turn as insufficient, until, through rhetorical augmentation, a climax is achieved with the metaphor snow-white, but then—after the first *volta* ("Doch keines")—all of these metaphors are discarded once more on account of their one-sidedness, since all of them do include their opposites. Thus the gradation of metaphors in the first four lines is followed by four lines of antithetical statements arranged in the same order ("Ketten, Wollen, Fewer, Schnee"), which repeat the climactic build-up, before the second *volta* ("Jedennoch") turns the negative arguments around and affirms the original definitions in an inverted order—this time, however, from the naive people's point of view. In conclusion, it appears that the poet's technique reflects quite aptly the beholder's and the lover's dilemma when exposed to the lady's puzzling beauty: her hand seems hot like fire and white like snow, which are mutually exclusive effects and yet epitomize love's essence. Thus Finckelthaus—in spite of his obvious shortcomings as a totally rational poet—manages to get something across to his audience about the irrational nature of love.

Finckelthaus is not the only one to be intrigued by love. His rival

8. Text: Chr. Wagenknecht, ed., *Epochen der deutschen Lyrik*, vol. 4 (München, 1969), p. 88—dtv. 4018.

9. Cf. Opitz, "Sonnet über die augen der Astree," p. 67, and Zesen, "Klünggetichte auf das Härz seiner Träuen," pp. 158 f.

10. See M. B. Ogle, "The White Hand as a Literary Conceit," *Sewanee Review*, 20 (1912), 459-69.

poets in the Leipzig region depict the overwhelming effect of love in a similar vein. For Caspar Stieler love increases like a rolling snowball;[11] David Schirmer is enthralled by the tender snow of white breasts which he calls "Ballen von Liebesschnee gefallen."[12] Like Petrarch before him he feels completely helpless against his mistress: he melts *come al sol neve* (Petrarch, *Canz.*, 133) in the spring sun.[13]

About the same time that the petrarchist topos conquers secular erotic poetry, it is transferred to the mystical realm as well. Laurentius von Schnüffis (= Johann Martin) appears to be outstanding among the poets who apply the snow metaphor mainly to express the vanity of life on earth.[14] Like Spee before him,[15] he describes Jesus in erotic terms as if he were his lady. "My lover red and white wounded my heart . . . he is much whiter than the snow which fell fresh in the winter. . . . White he is by virtue of his innocence . . . red signifies his love."[16]

Toward the close of the century the metaphor had been so widely adopted that it was in danger of becoming hopelessly stereotyped, an impression which is quite deceptive, as the following observations will show. From the rise of Petrarchism, there existed hardly any cleavage between poetry and prose: though the ideal was achieved by the congruence of theme and lyrical form, structural devices and motifs quickly gained ground in narrative poetry and prose as well.[17] Thus it is not surprising to come across descriptions of beautiful and ugly ladies in the petrarchist tradition in German prose works as early as Zesen and Harsdörffer.[18] Grimmelshausen devotes an entire chapter to the sarcastic praise of a beauty queen (*Simplicissimus* II, 9), and in Zigler von Kliphausen's *Asiatische Banise* (1689) the concept of the cold-hearted and

11. "Liebe vergrößert sich wie ein gewältzer Schneeball." Text in F. Martini, ed., *Gedichte des deutschen Barock* (Stuttgart, 1948), p. 78 (Parthenon Bücher).

12. *Rosengepüsche,* 1657, p. 328.

13. Sonett XXX "Er ist der Liebe Spiel": "Wie wann der kühle Schnee nach Thal vnd Auen rinnt, vnd das zu feige Wachs im Sommer muß vergehen. . . ."

14. Cf. Balde: "quae polito / Frons ebori nivibusque certat," J. Balde, *Dichtungen,* ed. M. Wehrli (Köln—Olten, 1963), p. 66; and his "Decident olim virides capilli / In nivem cana subeunte Bruma," p. 48; cf. A. Gryphius, "Vber die Gebaine der außgegrabenen Philosetten": "O Häßlich' Anblick! ach! wo sind die güldnen Haar! Wo ist der Stirnen Schnee?", A. Gryphius, *Dichtungen,* ed. C. O. Conrady (Reinbek, 1968), p. 26—RK 500/01.

15. "O Arm vnd Hände Jesv weiß / Ihr Schwesterlein der Schwanen," *Epochen der dt. Lyrik,* p. 175.

16. "Clorinda die Schönheit ihres himmlischen Bräutigams Betrachtende," *Epochen,* pp. 304 f.

17. Cf. G. Hoffmeister, *Petrarkistische Lyrik* (Stuttgart, 1973), p. 87 (Sammlung Metzler 119).

18. See Zesen, *Assenat* (Amsterdam, 1670, new edition Tübingen, 1967), p. 132, the description of Sefira; Harsdörffer, *Frauenzimmer Gesprechspiele,* 1641,

the ugly beauty determines part of the plot. He likens breasts to burning vivid snow[19] and mentions the snowhills of an icy lady where the flames are missing (p. 281).

In his zeal for moral guidance the Augustinian monk Abraham à Sancta Clara exploits the tradition and the German and Latin languages alike when he makes this pun: "Die Jungfrauen seynd *Nix* wehrt." The snow of purity lasts longer when it avoids the hot sun of sin and the warm winds of lust.[20]

Before we take a closer look at Hofmannswaldau as the paragon of the "second Silesian school," it may be appropriate to halt our chronological approach for a moment to place our findings into the proper perspective. Almost any feature of the beloved can be described in terms of immaculate snow: her forehead, teeth, neckline, shoulders, breasts, hands, and calves—but the meaning of whiteness depends on the context. It may very often express her purity, virtue, and her faithfulness; but in other instances its connotation tends to vary from her bitter coldness and her unfaithful behavior (like melting snow) to old age (her light hair covered with white snow), which in turn may open the way to invective or ridicule of the former beauty who failed to take time by the forelock (*carpe diem*). Without the contrasting red glow of flames the snow image does not seem to be complete, because the lady's beauty has to be ravaging like fire. Starting from here, the snow metaphor is often transferred to the lover who is exposed to this kind of bitter-sweet or icy-hot love. Set in a lovely valley with snow-covered slopes, little love stories may flow from this situation.[21] In a nutshell, the overpowering effect of love as a cosmic force is symbolized through whiteness which stuns the poet-lover and wounds his heart, because the inherent correlation of snow and fire causes fear in it as well as admiration and complete surrender. If unrequited, however, the lover may quickly change his worship to cursing.[22]

These summarizing remarks may serve as a backdrop for the following observations about Hofmannswaldau's poetry. We choose him not only because he is the most accomplished *virtuoso* among German erotic

---

vol. I, No. 18; cf. also Longus, *Daphnis and Chloe,* transl. G. Thornley, 1657, ed. G. Saintsbury (London, s.a.), p. 115: "We will go as soon as the snow melts. But it lies very deep, Chloe, and I fear I shall melt first. Courage man, the Sun burns hot. I would it burnt like that fire which now burns my very heart."

19. *A. Banise,* ed. W. Pfeiffer-Belli (Darmstadt, 1968), p. 277.

20. *Wohlangefüllter Weinkeller* (Würzburg, 1710), pp. 329 f.; cf. W. F. Scherer, "Abraham A Sancta Clara's Frauenspiegel," *The Univ. of Dayton Review,* 7 (1971), No. 3, pp. 16 f.

21. See, for example, Schallenberg or Joh. Secundus, Elegy II, 4 in his *Basia.*

22. Cf. footnote 7.

poets, but also because the snow-topos recurs in his verse more frequently than in his contemporaries', and for that matter with all its possible varieties and transformations—quite often even stretched beyond the boundaries of accepted standards of taste. His ingenious play with the snow metaphor places him at the receiving end of a long tradition, which we will attempt to throw into relief later. When Hofmannswaldau's reader encounters "synthetic representations"[23] of the lady, the poet's heightened awareness of the possibilities inherent in the lyrical language is conveyed, particularly if we compare it with the naive employment of the topos at the beginning of the century. As an example I quote the first four lines from his poem "Sie nähete ein weisses Tuch":

Es führte Lesbia in ihrer weissen hand
    Ein wunderschönes tuch / dem kreide nicht zu gleichen /
    So nur alleine will dem schnee der hände weichen /
Weil dieser es beschützt vor ihrer augen brand. . . .[24]

With some elegant strokes of his pen Hofmannswaldau establishes a contrast between the snow of her hands and her fiery eyes and then exploits this antithesis by taking the metaphor literally—a device which is quite frequent in his work and usually leads to surprising results, as can be seen in these lines addressed to Sylvien:

Was fluchst du, Sylvia, wenn meine schwarze Hand
    Um deinen Busen spielet?
Sie war so weiß als du, eh' sie der Liebe Brand
    Und deine Macht gefühlet.
Flößt du das Feuer nun in meine Glieder ein,
So kann ja meine Hand nicht Schnee und Marmor sein.[25]

Taking the metaphor of the flames of love literally, or "renaturalizing" it,[26] results in the transformation of a snow-white hand into a charred one. Another cherished target of the poet's pen is her bosom, second only to her lap ("Die brüste sind mein zweck"[27]). He likens breasts to snow mountains in which sparks glimmer, causing even the hardest steel to melt, yet unable to melt themselves.[28] The underlying oxymoron of

23. A. H. Schutz, "Ronsard's *Amours* XXXII and the Tradition of the Synthetic Lady," *Romance Philology,* 1 (1947-48), 127.

24. Text in: Chr. Hofmann von Hofmannswaldau, *Gedichte,* ed. H. Heißenbüttel (Frankfurt, 1968), p. 81 (Fischer 874).

25. Text in Martini, see note 11, p. 77.

26. B. Bauer-Formiconi, *Die Strambotti des Serafino dall'Aquila* (Freiburg. 1967), p. 75.

27. Heißenbüttel 47.

28. Heißenbüttel 46.

fiery snow undergoes but little variation in his lengthy poem on the competition among black eyes, red lips, and white breasts.[29] In his ingenious treatment of metaphors Hofmannswaldau prefers to build up fake contrasts among them which stem from the mixing of two or more layers of meaning, the literal and the figurative. He achieves quite astounding results, which he so intended from the outset. This procedure of a true concettist can be observed more in detail by taking a closer look at two of his poems. The first one is called "Auff ihre schultern":[30]

Ist dieses schnee? nein / nein / schnee kan nicht flammen führen.
 Ist dieses helffenbein? bein weiß nicht weis zu seyn.
 Ist hier ein glatter schwan? mehr als der schwanen schein /
Ist weiche woll allhier? wie kan sich wolle rühren?
Ist alabaster hie? er wächst nicht bey saphiren /
 Ist hier ein liljen–feld? der acker ist zu rein.
 Was bist du endlich doch? weil schnee und helffenbein /
Weil alabaster / schwan / und liljen sich verlieren.
 Du schaust nun / Lesbie / wie mein geringer mund
Vor deine schultern weiß kein rechtes wort zu finden /
Doch daß ich nicht zu sehr darf häufen meine sünden /
 So macht ein kurtzer reim dir mein gemüthe kund:
Muß Atlas und sein hals sich vor dem himmel biegen /
So müssen götter nur auf deinen schultern liegen.

We are immediately reminded of Finckelthaus' poem: but there are—apart from the more "advanced" choice of the lady's shoulders instead of her hands as an object of encomium—quite significant differences. While the earlier poet needed ten lines in an as yet unpolished style to arrive at the general conclusion that no single simile is able to express beauty and its effects, the latter uses eight lines to produce a similar stalemate, then he sets out anew, slowly building the climax first in a prose-like statement, then in a pointed couplet which conceals and betrays his sinful thoughts ("meine sünden"). He turns the Atlas myth upside down implying that she would make him a god if she would carry him on her white shoulders.

Though not expressly stated, the final idea behind this embellished love declaration is the *piccola morte* of a sensual sex encounter. His exploitation of the image, however, is so ingenious that the carnal desire in the reader's eyes gives way to the artistic achievement. And yet Hofmannswaldau's poetry is not merely a call for "living it up;" first of all

29. Ibid., 53 ff.
30. Heißenbüttel 80.

one should bear in mind that he wanted to write modish verse equal to Italian and French patterns; so it seems that many of his lines stem from his desire to contribute to the formation of a gallant society for the upper middle class, as it existed for instance in France. Secondly, his *bel esprit* induced him to reject love and to parody erotic poetry often as strongly as he praises them.[31] With all his contemporaries, but particularly with Gryphius, he shares a fundamentally pessimistic world view, which is aptly expressed by his recurrent phrase of the snowy hair,[32] a striking reminder of the vanity of mortal beauty. This is also the theme of one of his most famous and probably most often analyzed poems: "Vergänglichkeit der schönheit."[33] Let us therefore devote our attention to one single line: "Der schultern warmer schnee wird werden kalter sand." This verse may well be considered the key line of the poem, summarizing the decay from beauty to death in the *memento mori* tradition.

The shoulders are obviously white, but sheer whiteness is not white enough for the baroque poet. It is too prosaic and for this reason he enhances its impression by the hyperbole of the snow. By an unusual syntactical manoeuvre he removes the logical subject "shoulders" to a genitive position, thus subordinating it to "snow" and raising the embellishing means to an imposing end in itself, while at the same time diminishing the role of the original concrete object. And yet another step is taken when Hofmannswaldau adds the adjective "warm" to snow. "Warm snow" amounts to a union of two contradictory terms in an oxymoron which has several functions: first to reveal the artificiality of the snow metaphor, then to connotate the standard hot-cold essence of love, and third to anticipate the ephemeral character of all beauty which has to turn into cold sand.

This exquisite metaphor "der schultern warmer schnee" deserves more than passing attention. Let us therefore conclude our remarks with a short attempt to track down its origin in order to provide us with some better understanding of Hofmannswaldau's achievement. He seems to be quite fond of this image, though—to our knowledge—he never again applies it to a lady's shoulder. In his erotic poems he refers once to her calves ("die waden / mit warmem schnee bedeckt"),[34] but more frequently to her breasts: "Du warmer Schnee, darauf Granaten blühen"[35] or: "Ich schau auff warmem schnee die rothen beeren stehen / Die ohne

31. Cf. "Entwurff der liebe," Heißenbüttel 40 and 41.

32. Heißenbüttel 52, 101; *Epochen* 327.

33. Heißenbüttel 68.

34. Ibid., 71.

35. *Teutsche Übersetzungen und Getichte* (Breslau, 1679), "Poetische Geschicht Reden," 20.

zucker auch dem zucker ähnlich seyn."[36] In this instance Hofmannswaldau gives further evidence of his abilities as a superb concettist who strives for the *concetto arguto* or the ingenious metaphor.[37] His Silesian friend Lohenstein tries to equal him, when he has a lover embrace "den nackten schnee der warmen brust,"[38] but falls short of the former's stylistic *finesse.*[39]

Bodmer called Hofmannswaldau "the Silesian Marino;" and this label leads us to the strongest literary influence on his poetry. In Marino's lyrics we find frequent allusions to snow; as a matter of fact, he often strikes a *fuoco d'artificio* unequalled by the more rationalistic Hofmannswaldau. He coins "di viva neve le membra,"[40] "di quelle membra l'animate nevi" (p. 245). That he has in mind warm or even fiery snow becomes apparent when exquisite extended metaphors grow from this: "l'animate nevi esca aggiungendo a scelerati ardori" (p. 245); or the "singing snow"—much fiercer than Hofmannswaldau's tame "warm snow"—gives rise to the paradoxical poem "Al seno della sua donna,"[41] in which the lover is caught between the flaming eyes and the unmelting snow of her breasts, using them for protection and being even more attracted, because Amor shoots his glowing arrows from her ivory Alpine hills; for the lover it snows and burns at the same time.[42]

Thus it seems that Hofmannswaldau follows in Marino's footsteps as far as the use of oxymoron, *concetto arguto,* and the renaturalized metaphor is concerned—but in a more subdued fashion. Marino has his predecessors as well as followers in Europe—and among the latter we could mention Gracián, who provided a theoretical analysis of manneristic art in his *Agudeza y arte de ingenio* (1648) and some examples on how to find surprising correspondences between ideas which exclude one another.[43] Looking from Marino into the past we discover the snow-

36. Heißenbüttel 50, cf. Hofmannswaldau, *Heldenbriefe* 73 and M. Windfuhr, *Die Barocke Bildlichkeit und ihre Kritiker* (Stuttgart, 1966), p. 278.

37. Windfuhr, p. 278: "Scharfsinnige Metapher."

38. "Venus," line 909; text in: B. Neukirch, *Herrn v. Hofmannswaldau und anderer Deutschen auserlesene . . . Gedichte,* ed. de Capua and Philippson (Tübingen, 1961), part I.

39. Cf. "Venus," line 333: "die krausen locken hiengen / Um ihrer schultern schnee" and the sexual deterioration of the snow metaphor among the so-called "Galante Dichtung" around 1700; see, for ex., Celander, "Als er ihre Brüste küßte" and Chr. Eltester, "Die liebe steigt nicht über sich, sondern unter sich," texts in C. Wiedemann, ed., *Der galante Stil* (Tübingen, 1969), Nos. 59 and 70.

40. Marino, *Poesie Varie,* ed. B. Croce (Bari, 1913), p. 46.

41. Ibid., 76.

42. Cf. H. Friedrich, *Epochen der italienischen Lyrik,* 1964, pp. 637 f.

43. See "Oh, nix flamma mea," text edited in Buenos Aires, 1945, p. 16, and Góngora's "nieve roja," *Polifemo y Galatea* in *Obras completas,* ed. Milé y Jiménez (Madrid, 1951). Cf. G. R. Hocke, *Manierismus in der Literatur* (Reinbek, 1959), ch. "Roter Schnee," pp. 80 f.

motif quite often among the representatives of "il terzo Petrarchismo" like Luigi Groto and Torquato Tasso. Tasso made twofold use of it by either expressing the onslaught of old age,[44] or employing it as a love metaphor (Sonnet 3). Once he comes strikingly close to Hofmannswaldau's oxymoron with his "calda e bianca neve" (di petto),[45] but even earlier Tebaldeo achieved quite a feat in his Latin and vernacular poems when his icy lady burns her lover[46] or when he, engulfed in passionate flames, melts the snow around him.[47]

All of these poets and many more were trained in the petrarchist tradition by imitating one another and, above all, "master Petrarch" himself, who is to be considered the main source of the Renaissance and Baroque language of love in Europe, though his work might more aptly be described as a prism for the classical and medieval tradition, which he revived and invigorated. In his *Canzoniere* we find a spectrum of snow metaphors which could be largely divided into two groups: those referring to the poet-lover and those characterizing Laura. Whereas the former describe the impact of her beauty ("com'al sol neve," 133, cf. canzoni 4,7,28, etc.) and her death ("et facto 'l cor tepida neve," 328), those concerning Laura apply to her hands and her face.[48] When, for example, Petrarch praises her face, "et calda neve il volto" (157), we are very close to Hofmannswaldau, though the context is different.[49]

Though Petrarch learned many a rhetorical device from the classical poets, the troubadours and the poets of the Stilnuovo,[50] it seems that the diffusion of the oxymoron "calda neve" leads essentially back to him; from him it started to conquer the poets' minds in Southern and Western Europe before it reached Germany after 1600. Hofmannswaldau writes clearly in this petrarchist tradition; with his frivolous sexual overtones he seems to be the last great poet who develops the manneristic late petrarchist style to its full potential; compared to his Italian predecessors, however, he lacks Petrarch's introspection and serious involvement as well as Marino's imagination.

44. Cf. his "Rime per Lucrezia Bendidio," *Opere,* a cura di E. Mazzali, (Napoli, 1970²), vol. 2, Sonnets 12 and 14.

45. Edition Solerti, Sonnet 18: "Loda la gola de la sua donna."

46. G. Ellinger, *Geschichte der neulateinischen Literatur Deutschlands im 16. Jahrhundert* (Berlin, 1929 f.), vol. I, 227.

47. "Cinto da le montagne alte e superbe," in: *Soneti & Capitoli di Misser A. Thebaldeo* (Modena, 1500).

48. No. 131: "Le rose vermiglie infra la neve."

49. No. 146: "O fiamma, o rose sparse in dolce falda / Di viva neve." Cf. this conceit with Marino's and Hofmannswaldau's technique.

50. "Viso di neve colorato in grana," in: *Rimatori del dolce stil novo,* ed. D. Benedetto (Bari, 1939), p. 16.

NORTH CAROLINA STUDIES IN THE ROMANCE LANGUAGES AND LITERATURES

I.S.B.N. Prefix 0-88438

Recent Titles

THE OLD PORTUGUESE "VIDA DE SAM BERNARDO," EDITED FROM ALCOBAÇA MANUSCRIPT ccxci/200, WITH INTRODUCTION, LINGUISTIC STUDY, NOTES, TABLE OF PROPER NAMES, AND GLOSSARY, by Lawrence A. Sharpe. 1971. (No. 103). *-903-0.*

A CRITICAL AND ANNOTATED EDITION OF LOPE DE VEGA'S "LAS ALMENAS DE TORO," by Thomas E. Case. 1971. (No. 104). *-904-9.*

LOPE DE VEGA'S "LO QUE PASA EN UNA TARDE," A CRITICAL, ANNOTATED EDITION OF THE AUTOGRAPH MANUSCRIPT, by Richard Angelo Picerno. 1971. (No. 105). *-905-7.*

OBJECTIVE METHODS FOR TESTING AUTHENTICITY AND THE STUDY OF TEN DOUBTFUL "COMEDIAS" ATTRIBUTED TO LOPE DE VEGA, by Fred M. Clark. 1971. (No. 106). *-906-5.*

THE ITALIAN VERB. A MORPHOLOGICAL STUDY, by Frede Jensen. 1971. (No. 107). *-907-3.*

A CRITICAL EDITION OF THE OLD PROVENÇAL EPIC "DAUREL ET BETON," WITH NOTES AND PROLEGOMENA, by Arthur S. Kimmel. 1971. (No. 108). *-908-1.*

FRANCISCO RODRIGUES LOBO: DIALOGUE AND COURTLY LORE IN RENAISSANCE PORTUGAL, by Richard A. Preto-Rodas, 1971. (No. 109). *-909-X.*

RAIMON VIDAL: POETRY AND PROSE, edited by W. H. W. Field. 1971. (No. 110). *-910-3.*

RELIGIOUS ELEMENTS IN THE SECULAR LYRICS OF THE TROUBADOURS, by Raymond Gay-Crosier. 1971. (No. 111). *-911-1.*

THE SIGNIFICANCE OF DIDEROT'S "ESSAI SUR LE MERITE ET LA VERTU," by Gordon B. Walters. 1971. (No. 112). *-912-X.*

PROPER NAMES IN THE LYRICS OF THE TROUBADOURS, by Frank M. Chambers. 1971. (No. 113). *-913-8.*

STUDIES IN HONOR OF MARIO A. PEI, edited by John Fisher and Paul A. Gaeng. 1971. (No. 114). *-914-6.*

DON MANUEL CAÑETE, CRONISTA LITERARIO DEL ROMANTICISMO Y DEL POSROMANTICISMO EN ESPAÑA, por Donald Allen Randolph. 1972. (No. 115). *-915-4.*

THE TEACHINGS OF SAINT LOUIS. A CRITICAL TEXT, by David O'Connell. 1972. (No. 116). *-916-2.*

HIGHER, HIDDEN ORDER: DESIGN AND MEANING IN THE ODES OF MALHERBE, by David Lee Rubin. 1972. (No. 117). *-917-0.*

JEAN DE LE MOTE "LE PARFAIT DU PAON," édition critique par Richard J. Carey. 1972. (No. 118). *-918-9.*

CAMUS' HELLENIC SOURCES, by Paul Archambault. 1972. (No. 119). *-919-7.*

FROM VULGAR LATIN TO OLD PROVENÇAL, by Frede Jensen. 1972 (No. 120). *-920-0.*

GOLDEN AGE DRAMA IN SPAIN: GENERAL CONSIDERATION AND UNUSUAL FEATURES, by Sturgis E. Leavitt. 1972. (No. 121). *-921-9.*

THE LEGEND OF THE "SIETE INFANTES DE LARA" (*Refundición toledana de la crónica de 1344* versión), study and edition by Thomas A. Lathrop. 1972. (No. 122). *-922-7.*

STRUCTURE AND IDEOLOGY IN BOIARDO'S "ORLANDO INNAMORATO", by Andrea di Tommaso. 1972. (No. 123). *-923-5.*

STUDIES IN HONOR OF ALFRED G. ENGSTROM, edited by Robert T. Cargo and Emanuel J. Mickel, Jr. 1972. (No. 124). *-924-3.*

NORTH CAROLINA STUDIES IN THE ROMANCE LANGUAGES AND LITERATURES

I.S.B.N. Prefix 0-88438

Recent Titles

A CRITICAL EDITION WITH INTRODUCTION AND NOTES OF GIL VICENTE'S "FLORESTA DE ENGAÑOS", by Constantine Christopher Stathatos. 1972. (No. 125). *-925-1.*

LI ROMANS DE WITASSE LE MOINE. *Roman du treizième siècle.* Édité d'après le manuscrit, fonds français 1553, de la Bibliothèque Nationale, Paris, par Denis Joseph Conlon. 1972. (No. 126). *-926-X.*

EL CRONISTA PEDRO DE ESCAVIAS. UNA VIDA DEL SIGLO XV, by Juan Bautista Avalle-Arce. 1972. (No. 127). *-927-8.*

AN EDITION OF THE FIRST ITALIAN TRANSLATION OF THE CELESTINA, by Kathleen Kish. 1973. (No. 128). *-928-6.*

MOLIERE MOCKED: THREE CONTEMPORARY HOSTILE COMEDIES, by Frederick W. Vogler. 1973. (No. 129). *-929-4.*

INDEX ANALYTIQUE DE "CHATEAUBRIAND ET SON GROUPE LITTERAIRE SOUS L'EMPIRE" DE SAINTE-BEUVE, by Lorin A. Uffenbeck. 1973. (No. 130). *-930-8.*

THE ORIGINS OF THE BAROQUE CONCEPT OF PEREGRINATIO, by Juergen S. Hahn. 1973. (No. 131). *-931-6.*

THE "AUTO SACRAMENTAL" AND THE PARABLE IN THE SIXTEENTH AND SEVENTEENTH CENTURIES, by Donald T. Dietz. 1973. (No. 132). *-932-4.*

FRANCISCO DE OSUNA AND THE SPIRIT OF THE LETTER, by Laura Calvert. 1973. (No. 133). *-933-2.*

ITINERARIO DI AMORE: DIALETTICA DI AMORE E MORTE NELLA VITA NUOVA, by Margherita de Bonfils Templer. 1973. (No. 134). *-934-0.*

L'IMAGINATION POETIQUE CHEZ DU BARTAS, ELEMENTS DE SENSIBILITE BAROQUE DANS LA "CREATION DU MONDE," by Bruno Braunrot. 1973. (No. 135). *-935-9.*

ARTUS DÉSIRÉ, PRIEST AND PAMPHLETEER OF THE SIXTEENTH CENTURY, by Frank Giese 1973. (No. 136). *-936-7.*

JARDIN DE NOBLES DONZELLAS BY FRAY MARTÍN DE CÓRDOBA, by Harriet Goldberg. 1974. (No. 137). *-937-5.*

MOLIERE: TRADITIONS IN CRITICISM, by Laurence Romero. 1974 (Essays, No. 1). *-001-7.*

STUDIES IN TIRSO, I, by Ruth Lee Kennedy. 1974. (Essays, No. 3). *-003-3.*

LAS MEMORIAS DE GONZALO FERNÁNDEZ DE OVIEDO, Vols. I and II, by Juan Bautista Avalle-Arce. 1974. (Texts, Textual Studies, and Translations, Nos. 1 and 2). *-401-2; 402-0.*

ESTUDIOS DE LITERATURA HISPANOAMERICANA EN HONOR A JOSÉ J. ARROM, edited by Andrew P. Debicki and Enrique Pupo-Walker. 1975. (Symposia, No. 2). *952-9.*

When ordering please cite the *ISBN Prefix* plus the last four digits for each title.

Send orders to:

International Scholarly Book Service, Inc.
P.O. Box 4347
Portland, Oregon 97208
U.S.A.